THE UNCOMMERCIAL TRAVELLER
AND OTHER PAPERS
1859–70

THE DENT UNIFORM EDITION OF DICKENS' JOURNALISM, Vol. I
Sketches by Boz and Other Early Papers 1833–39 (1994)

THE DENT UNIFORM EDITION OF DICKENS' JOURNALISM, Vol. II
'The Amusements of the People' and Other Papers 1834–51 (1996)

THE DENT UNIFORM EDITION OF DICKENS' JOURNALISM, Vol. III
'Gone Astray' and Other Papers from Household Words *1851–59* (1998)

THE DENT UNIFORM EDITION OF

DICKENS'
JOURNALISM
Volume 4

THE UNCOMMERCIAL TRAVELLER AND OTHER PAPERS
1859–70

EDITED BY MICHAEL SLATER
AND JOHN DREW

Ohio State University Press
Columbus

The Uncommercial Traveller *and Other Papers 1859–70*
First published in Great Britain by J. M. Dent in 2000

Published in the United States by the
Ohio State University Press in 2000

Introduction, preliminary material, headnotes and index
© J. M. Dent 2000

Chronology from *The Dickens Index* by Nicolas Bentley,
Michael Slater and Nina Burgis (1988);
Reprinted by kind permission of Oxford University Press

Library of Congress Cataloging-in-Publication data
available from Ohio State University Press

ISBN 0-8142-0875-4

Typeset by Selwood Systems, Midsomer Norton
Printed by Butler & Tanner Ltd, Frome and London

The paper used in this publication meets the minimum
requirements of the American National Standard
for Information Sciences—Permanence of Paper for
Printed Library Materials. ANSI Z39.48–1992.

9   8   7   6   5   4   3   2   1

CONTENTS

ABBREVIATIONS

ATYR	*All The Year Round* (1859–95)
Forster	John Forster, *The Life of Charles Dickens*, ed. J. W. T. Ley (1928)
Hill	T. W. Hill, unpublished notes to *The Uncommercial Traveller* (The Staples Bequest, Dickens House Museum, London [1948])
Household Words	*Household Words* (1850–59)
MP	*Miscellaneous Papers*, ed. B. W. Matz, vols 35 and 36 of the National Edition of *The Works of Charles Dickens* (1908)
Nonesuch	*The Letters of Charles Dickens* (The Nonesuch Edition), ed. Walter Dexter, 3 vols. (1938)
Oppenlander	*Dickens' All the Year Round: Descriptive Index and Contributor List*, comp. Ella Ann Oppenlander (1984)
Pilgrim	*The Letters of Charles Dickens* (The Pilgrim Edition), eds M. House, G. Storey, K. Tillotson et al., 11 vols (1965–in progress)
Speeches	*The Speeches of Charles Dickens*, ed. K. J. Fielding (1960)
Stone	*The Uncollected Writings of Charles Dickens: Household Words 1850–59*, ed. Harry Stone, 2 vols (1969)
Stonehouse	*Reprints of the Catalogues of the Libraries of Charles Dickens and W. M. Thackeray Etc.*, ed. J. H. Stonehouse (1935)
UT1	*The Uncommercial Traveller* (The Charles Dickens Edition), (Chapman & Hall, 1868)
UT2	*The Uncommercial Traveller* (Library Edition, illustrated), (Chapman & Hall, 1874)
UT3	*The Uncommercial Traveller* (The Gadshill Edition), ed. & intro. Andrew Lang (Chapman & Hall, 1898)
UT4	*The Uncommercial Traveller*, ed. & intro. Charles Dickens Jnr (Macmillan, 1925)

PREFACE

This, the fourth and last volume of *The Dent Uniform Edition of Dickens' Journalism*, presents, in chronological order of publication, all but three of the eleven miscellaneous articles that Dickens is definitely known to have written as sole author for his weekly journal *All The Year Round* between 1859 and his death in 1870, together with all of the thirty-six papers he wrote as 'The Uncommercial Traveller'. The eleven non-'Uncommercial' articles were first collected, together with other stray papers, poems and dramatic pieces, by B. W. Matz, the first editor of *The Dickensian*, in 1908 as part of the National Edition of Dickens's work (vols 34–6). The 'Uncommercial' papers were collected by Dickens himself under the title *The Uncommercial Traveller* in 1860 and again in 1865 (reprinted in the Charles Dickens Edition in 1868), with further 'round-up' collections being published after his death (see p. vii). The present volume also includes Dickens's 'In Memoriam' notice of Thackeray written for *The Cornhill*, and a plug for the actor Charles Fechter written for the *Atlantic Monthly*; both of these items were first collected by Matz.

Appended to this volume will be found: (1) *The Great International Walking-Match*, a lively parody of sporting journalism written by Dickens for private circulation; and (2) all examples of another form of occasional writing practised by Dickens, i.e. Prefaces or Forewords to books written by people having a special claim on him. These, too, were gathered up by Matz in Vol. 34 of the National Edition, apart from the Preface, surely written by Dickens, to Catherine Dickens's cookery book. Matz also included the 'Introductory Chapter' Dickens wrote in 1838 for his edition of *The Memoirs of Joseph Grimaldi* – not, however, the 'Concluding Chapter' that Dickens also wrote for this work – but this item has been excluded here as not properly belonging with a collection of journalism and occasional writings.

As in previous volumes in this Edition, headnotes preceding each item supply relevant background historical and biographical information and seek to identify as many as possible of Dickens's numerous literary allusions. The headnotes to all the *Uncommercial Traveller* pieces are by John Drew, the remainder are by Michael Slater. As in previous volumes, these headnotes are supplemented with an Index at the end of the volume that functions also as a Glossary and a Biographical Dictionary.

M. S., J. D.

INTRODUCTION

Dickens's peremptory termination of his weekly magazine *Household Words* in May 1859, after launching, five weeks earlier, a look-alike replacement called *All The Year Round*, has been described in the Introduction to the previous volume of this edition. His actions followed a quarrel with Bradbury and Evans, his publishers and co-owners with him of *Household Words*. They had, sensibly enough, refused to publish in *Punch* Dickens's personal statement about the end of his marriage (see previous volume, pp. 488–90). In an announcement at the front of the last number of *Household Words* (28 May 1859), in which he refers readers to *All The Year Round* for the future, Dickens says that he is transferring his 'strongest energies' to the new publication and continues:

> I have the happiness of taking with me the staff of writers with whom I have laboured, and all the literary and business co-operation that can make my work a pleasure. In some important respects, I am now free greatly to advance on past arrangements. Those I leave to testify for themselves in due course.

The last two sentences refer to the fact that he was in virtually complete control of the new journal. No publisher had any longer the right to interfere with his editorial freedom because he owned three-quarters of the shares in *All The Year Round*, the remaining quarter being owned by W. H. Wills, who had been his sub-editor on *Household Words* and whom he had appointed to the same position on *All The Year Round*. (Dickens had the greatest admiration for Wills as a man of business and believed that he had another use, too, as a sounding-board, being 'in literary matters, sufficiently commonplace to represent a very large portion of our readers'.') *All The Year Round*'s publishers, Chapman and Hall, acted simply as distribution agents. As to the title and the goodwill, those items, Dickens made emphatically clear to Wills (*Pilgrim*, Vol. IX, p. 98), belonged to him alone. The title had taken some finding. Dickens was keen to continue with one derived from Shakespeare ('Household Words' came from Henry V's speech before Agincourt) and was with difficulty dissuaded by Forster from settling on *Household Harmony* (3 Henry VI, Act 4, Sc. 6), which would inevitably have exposed him to mockery given the recent dramatic upheaval in his own domestic life. He tried out a number of other titles, among them *The Hearth*, *The Anvil of the Time*, *Charles Dickens's Own*, *Home-Music* and *Good Humour*, before hitting upon some lines in *Othello* (Act 1, Sc. 3), 'The story of my life/ From year to year', which inspired him to create what he deemed 'really an admirable' title, *All The Year Round* (Forster, p. 672). Percy Fitzgerald, one of Dickens's young literary protégés, who was a regular on both *Household Words* and *All The Year Round*, thought, however, that this title 'had a *pragmatical* flavour and was uninteresting', also that the new magazine was 'never so heartily relished' as its predecessor.[2] The fact is, nevertheless, that the new journal, 'heartily relished' or not, certainly outsold its predecessor. At 100,000 copies per week, the steady circulation figure for *All The Year Round* more than doubled that for *Household Words* (36/40,000) and it could on occasion even triple that figure when it came to the special extra Christmas Numbers published between 1859 and 1868 (later collected with their *Household Words* predecessors under the title *Christmas Stories*).

Although identical to its predecessor in appearance (twenty-four double-columned pages, unillustrated), *All The Year Round* was, in fact, very different – most notably in the much greater emphasis placed on fiction. Pride of place in each number went to the current instalment of a long-running serial, while shorter-run serials and short stories appeared additionally in most numbers (but Dickens drew the line at running more than two serials simultaneously: 'the public', he wrote to Sheridan Le Fanu, 'have a natural tendency, having more than two serial stories to bear in mind at once, to jumble them all together, and do justice to none of them'[3]). He himself inaugurated the sequence of long serials with *A Tale of Two Cities* (30 April–26 November 1859) and later responded, with great success, to a worrying fall in the circulation figures by serialising *Great Expectations* (1 December 1860–3 August 1861).[4] At the conclusion of *A Tale of Two Cities* and just before the beginning of its successor, Wilkie Collins's *The Woman in White*, there appeared an editorial announcement that 'the first place in these pages' would always be reserved for 'a continuous original work of fiction' in the hope that such serials might include 'some sustained works of imagination that may become a part of English Literature'.[5]

Fiction apart, the great achievement of *All The Year Round* was, according to Dickens looking back in 1866 (as quoted by Percy Fitzgerald), to have provided

> a collection of miscellaneous articles interesting to the widest range of readers, consisting of Suggestive, Descriptive and Critical Dissertations on the most prominent topics, British and foreign, that form the social history of the past eight years.[6]

There were many more antiquarian articles (e.g., George Thornbury's series, 'Old Stories Re-told') and articles about foreign countries than there had been in *Household Words*. In a bitter attack on *All The Year Round* for its hostility to Roman Catholicism and especially the Papacy (the journal strongly supported the Italian Risorgimento), Cardinal Wiseman, writing in the *Dublin Review,* commented: 'Opening at hazard volumes of "All The Year Round", we are struck by the number of articles which relate to foreign countries, their manners and customs – French, German, Russian, Austrian, Italian' – morosely adding, 'None of these are remarkable for ability, and few appear characterised by candour.'[7] One reason for this more international scope of the new journal was no doubt the necessity for it to appeal to American readers as well as English ones. Dickens and Wills made a succession of profitable arrangements with American publishers for the transmission of stereotype plates and early proofs of each number to the United States so as to facilitate simultaneous publication of the journal in both countries.[8] This did, however, mean that each number had to be put to bed at least two weeks ahead of publication date, which rather limited the opportunities for the kind of highly topical, up-to-the minute article, satirical or otherwise, that had featured so often and so effectively in *Household Words*.[9] 'The perpetual sliding away of temporary subjects at which I could dash with effect, is a *great* loss,' Dickens lamented to Wills in a letter of 29 January 1863.[10] The second article in this volume, 'Five New Points of Criminal Law', is the only one that has quite the urgent, angry topicality that was characteristic of so many of Dickens's *Household Words* articles.

As his surviving correspondence shows, Dickens continued for the rest of his life to be just as energetically and indefatigably involved editorially with *All The Year Round* as he had been with *Household Words*, and this despite the distractions of his arduous Public Readings tours. Letters to Wills, and to potential or actual contributors, deal with the make-up of particular numbers, with ideas for contributions, and with the pruning, correction and revising (sometimes quite drastic revision) of contributors' work, both fictional and non-fictional. In December 1862, for example, he tells Wills that, in order to produce a satisfactory mix for the next number, he has been obliged to cut heavily an article by Eliza Lynn Linton, an established contributor, 'for it is not only a poor article full of repetitions, but a disagreeable one – written in a bad humour ... and looking at life out of disagreeable and unnecessary windows. Which is not our A.Y.R. Vocation.'[11] (We may be reminded here of Dickens's ideal recipe for a journal propounded many years before in which he specified 'cheerful views' and 'jolly good temper';[12] clearly, some such general notion still attached to *All The Year Round*.)

When it came to articles written by himself, however, Dickens was a good deal less prolific than he had been in *Household Words*. During the first six months of *All The Year Round*'s existence, he is, of course, busy writing *A Tale of Two Cities* and contributes only non-fictional pieces, one of which, as already noted, is in the old *Household Words* vein and another (article 3 in this volume) is the response that he really has to make (and that otherwise might have been done through a letter to *The Times*) to renewed criticism of his use of Leigh Hunt in depicting the parasitic Skimpole in *Bleak House*. An amusing parody of provincial journalism, 'The Tattlesnivel Bleater' (article 4 in this volume), appears in the last number for 1859 but thereafter – apart from his intermittent 'Uncommercial Traveller' series, to be discussed in a moment, the special Christmas Numbers and, of course, *Great Expectations* – Dickens writes very little for his journal as sole author. After the outbreak of the American Civil War, he indulges in some self-congratulatory crowing about how his criticisms of American social and political life, much condemned at the time, seem in the event to have been justified ('The Young Man from the Country', *All The Year Round*, 1 March 1862 – not reprinted here since the piece consists mainly of quotations from *American Notes*). And, a year later, having found himself once more involved in controversy about Spiritualism, he uses some pages of his journal to ridicule books by two leading Spiritualists (see article 22, pp. 202–9).[13] It is probable that he wrote much for the journal 'invisibly', i.e. either as co-author by arrangement or by such extensive revision of contributors' work as to justify our regarding him as joint author, but we do not have the evidence for this that we have so abundantly in the case of *Household Words*, thanks to the survival of that journal's Office Book.[14]

With the early success of Collins's highly sensational *The Woman in White* (26 November–25 August 1860), *All The Year Round* enjoyed an excellent start to the new year in 1860, but Dickens was doubtless aware of the threat posed by the launch in December 1859 of the *Cornhill* magazine, a well-financed and luxuriously produced monthly, with illustrations, to be edited by his great rival Thackeray. The first number, seen by an estimated half-a-million readers,[15] not only opened with the first instalment of a six-part tale by Thackeray, 'Lovel the Widower', but closed with a familiar essay by him called 'On a Lazy Idle Boy', printed under the heading 'Roundabout Papers. No. 1'. In it, the narrator-as-editor confides in his readers that 'We are fellow travellers and shall make acquaintance as the voyage proceeds' (p. 357). This was a clear indication of Thackeray's intention to create a personalised relationship with his public through such editorial interventions, and is likely to have stimulated Dickens to consider how he himself might establish such a relationship with readers of *All The Year Round*. This was, after all, the kind of bond he had always striven to encourage in his fiction issued in monthly numbers. He refers to it openly in the prefaces to various volume editions, and it runs through most of his manuscript proposals for founding periodical magazines.[16] Percy Fitzgerald later recalled Dickens's decision in January 1860 to announce a series of personal contributions to *All The Year Round*, as 'one of his happiest conceptions, though, I fancy, rather suggested by the success of Thackeray's "Roundabout Papers" '.[17]

By 7 January, however, Dickens still had not hit upon an appropriate manner of address, writing to Wilkie Collins that he planned 'coming in to back you up [in *All The Year Round*], if I can get an idea for my series of gossiping papers'.[18] One rather sombre paper – an account of a trip to the Welsh coast where hundreds had drowned in a shipwreck – was already written and set up for print (see headnote to article 5), but to precede it Dickens needed an appropriate introduction for his new editorial persona. Two further notions current in Dickens's mind seem to have influenced the invention during the next few days of the persona known as 'The Uncommercial Traveller', first introduced to readers in the four paragraphs leading into the account of the shipwreck. Under this guise he was to publish, over the next nine years, thirty-six essays and reports which contain some of his very finest journalism.[19]

The first of these notions concerned the rising importance and status of commercial travellers (formerly known merely as 'bagmen'), and the parallels that could be drawn between them, at a local level, and the great travellers and explorers of the globe. Dickens had recently enlarged on these ideas in his rousing speech to supporters of the Commercial Travellers' Schools, given at the London Tavern on 22 December.[20] However, in his coining of '*un*commercial' as an epithet for his travelling persona,[21] and in his opening self-portrait, Dickens takes pains to distance himself from the negative notions attaching to commerce – something vividly brought before the public in January 1860 with the signing of a notorious Commercial Treaty with France by Richard Cobden MP, the leading light of the so-called 'Manchester School' of political economy, which Dickens disparaged.[22] The Treaty – discussion of which dominated debates in both Houses of Parliament until late March – was intended to prevent all possibility of war between Britain and France, but was held by its critics to demonstrate the extent to which mercenary, economic motives, rather than ethical considerations, were now the mainspring of foreign policy. A similar critique of the dehumanising effect of 'wholesale' values on national life runs continually through the Uncommercial Traveller's reports.[23]

Yet despite being clearly influenced both by contemporary events and events in Dickens's public life, the concept of the 'Uncommercial Traveller' as introduced and subsequently developed in *All The Year Round*, owes much to a great tradition in British essay-writing and travel-writing, reaching back through Romantic essayists to the periodical essayists of the eighteenth century whom Dickens had loved since childhood.[24] In projecting the 'Uncommercial' as a single gentleman residing in the heart of the city, Dickens pays tribute to Addison and Steele's 'Spectator', and to Henry Mackenzie's 'Lounger'; in depicting his whimsical, self-deprecatory response to human encounters, Dickens recalls Lamb's 'Elia' and Irving's 'Geoffrey Crayon'. Thus, although many of the papers contain elements of journalistic exposé, encouraging Dickens to adopt the Carlylean rhetoric common in his papers for *Household Words* (see Volumes 2 and 3 of this edition, *passim*), one of the most striking qualities of the 'Uncommercial' pieces is their relaxed, non-combative air. A writer for the *Saturday Review* (probably Sir James Fitzjames Stephen) noted this in an unusually complimentary review of the first volume edition, contrasting the style with that of *The Pickwick Papers*:

> The *Uncommercial Traveller* is much quieter, for men cannot preserve high spirits for a quarter of a century; but it is in Mr Dickens's good manner. It is pleasant, witty, shrewd and unhackneyed. It treats of things we like to read about....[25]

One of the things that later readers have most liked to read about in the 'Uncommercial Traveller' papers, however, has been detail of Dickens's own life. Dickens's first biographer, John Forster, draws frequently on them in his *Life*, remarking how they 'have supplied traits, chiefly of [Dickens's] younger days to portions of this memoir; ... parts of his later life receive illustration from others ... hardly any is without its personal interest or illustration' (Book 8, Ch. 5). Perhaps significantly, Forster does not apply the term 'autobiographical' to the collection, and credits them with a degree of creative licence that later biographers and critics have not always allowed. Indeed, the aim of several of the headnotes to the 'Uncommercial' articles has been to indicate their divergence from what might be expected of a strictly autobiographical or historiographical account, as much as to bring out the myriad correlations between what is set down about the Uncommercial's activities and experiences, and what is known, from external evidence, of Dickens's (see, for example, headnotes to articles 15, 18 and 25).

The narrator's mention in article 5, for example, and in nine subsequent papers, of his 'rooms in Covent-garden, London' is a sly half-truth on Dickens's part. Some magazine readers would have known that both the old *Household Words* and the new *All The Year Round* offices were in that part of the city, and some would also have known that Dickens had furnished a set of rooms above the *Household Words* offices at No. 16 Wellington Street, where he frequently stayed. However, since the abandonment of these premises in Spring 1859, Dickens had, in fact, been without this particular convenience, and not until the autumn of 1860 was an apartment fitted up above the new *All The Year Round* offices at No. 11 (re-numbered 76). The five rooms were what he called his 'temporary Town Tent', and were, as he wrote to his daughter Mamie on 23 September 1860, 'really a success. As comfortable, cheerful and private as anything of the kind can possibly be.'[26] Dickens's location of the 'Uncommercial Traveller' in Covent Garden thus related the character to aspects of his own public image, while neatly maintaining the traditional essayical persona of the peripatetic bachelor residing in the heart of a city. The fact that Dickens had been living apart from his wife Catherine since 1858, and perhaps now thought of himself as single, adds a further dimension to the masquerade.

As the 1860s progressed, Dickens made use of the 'Uncommercial Traveller' persona as a flexible alter-ego through which he could keep himself in the public eye, in the pages of *All The Year Round*, during those periods when he was not publishing serial fiction or physically before his audience, as a public reader. After collecting and re-publishing the 'First Series' of sixteen papers as a single volume in 1861, he even contemplated combining the two roles when, in June 1862, he received the offer of £10,000 for an eight-month public reading tour of Australia. On 22 October he wrote to Forster that while in Australia he 'would do, for *All the Year Round* while I was away, The Uncommercial Traveller Upside Down'.[27] The project got no further than this, but a new series of 'Uncommercial' papers was clearly on Dickens's mind at the time. On 17 October 1862 he had written to Wills from northern France that in between reading engagements he had 'leisure for adventure' and was 'now going to have a look at Dunquerque – in the Uncommercial interest'.[28] In fact, the Second Series of 'Uncommercial Traveller' papers did not commence publication until May 1863 – rather a long gestation period for Dickens's journal articles – and there are other, curious disjunctures between Dickens's references in his letters to 'uncommercial' research trips and the eventual topics of 'Uncommercial Traveller' papers published in *All The Year Round*. Notes to Thomas Mitton and Georgina Hogarth in late August 1860, for example, had mentioned an 'Uncommercial Journey' out of London, planned for the week of 20–24 August,[29] yet none of the 'Uncommercial Traveller' papers published between these dates and the end of the First Series (13 October 1860) incorporated this kind of material. The alternative phrasing used in one of two letters to Georgina about the arrangements ('I THINK I shall run away tomorrow, until Saturday') leads to the suspicion that references to 'uncommercial' journeys in letters to confidantes function on occasions as a coded periphrasis for visits of a more private nature – perhaps to Ellen Ternan (then installed by Dickens, as some biographers have inferred, in a chalet near

Boulogne).[30] Letters to Wilkie Collins and Frederic Ouvry in August 1863 further support the conclusion that, for Dickens, the mention of an 'uncommercial' trip could be akin to Algy's use of Bunbury in *The Importance of Being Earnest*.

Thus, although the 'Uncommercial Traveller' never caught on as earlier nick-names (such as 'Boz' or the 'Inimitable') had done, Dickens himself came to feel it was particularly well suited to his lifestyle in the 1860s, referring to himself in letters to his great Boston friend James T. Fields as 'the Uncommercial' and as 'The Great British Wanderer' (*Nonesuch*, Vol. III, pp. 718, 605). On at least one occasion, the popular press picked up on the aptness of the title, as evidenced in the following newspaper account of Dickens's ministrations to the victims of the Staplehurst railway disaster of 9 June 1865:

> ... 'the Uncommercial Traveller' endeavoured at first to procure some brandy; but none being produced in answer to his energetic calls, he filled his hat with water, and ran round with the refreshing liquid to his helpless fellow-passengers, assuaging their pangs with a genial word of good cheer as well.[31]

When a third series of 'Uncommercial' papers was planned for December 1868, to coincide with the introduction of a 'New Series' of *All The Year Round*,[32] Dickens chose to write a paper relating openly to his return from a much-publicised Reading Tour in America (see article 38, 'Aboard Ship'). The beginning of the article, while re-establishing the fanciful character of the 'Uncommercial', contained jokey messages intended for James T. Fields and his wife Annie, which must have been lost on the wider readership of *All The Year Round*, indicating how Dickens wished to exploit the persona simultaneously as a mask and as a mode of personal communication (see headnote). Yet the most striking example of Dickens's equivocal use of his journalistic persona to make the public aware of his private feelings came at a time when his incessant travels for the highly commercial purpose of public reading led to a serious breakdown in his health and the consequent arrival of much unsolicited mail. While the characteristic nuances of Dickensian irony are not lacking in the paper, Dickens himself seems unaware of the irony involved in using his 'uncommercial' persona to voice them (see article 43 and headnote).

In stressing the complexities of the autobiographical matrix in the 'Uncommercial Traveller' papers, their breadth of objective interest in an astonishing range of contemporary issues must not be overlooked. Homelessness, violence on the streets of London, workhouse conditions, Mormon emigration, police inefficiency, the life of the merchant sailor and the tramp, new initiatives in education, mass-market catering and childcare, unemployment and the depopulation of the urban centre, the safe manufacture of white-lead, shipbuilding: these are just some of the issues tackled in the polished weighty prose typical of Dickens's artistic maturity. In all these essays, Dickens the journalist presents his reports with 'scrupulous exactness': 'my predispositions and prejudices', he declares, 'must not affect me as an honest citizen' (see article 27, pp. 259–60). In his introductory remarks to Dent's 1911 edition of *The Uncommercial Traveller*, G. K. Chesterton singled out this impression of objectivity as characteristic of the collection: 'Critics have talked of an artist with his eye on the object. Dickens as an essayist always had his eye on an object before he had the faintest notion of a subject.'[33]

In the majority of papers, in fact, Dickens-as-'Uncommercial' has fixed objects in view, with only the faintest notion of himself as subject, however much psycho-biography we care to read into his texts. As he insists at the outset of one such account, 'the character I myself sustained was so very subordinate, that I may relate its story without any fear of being suspected of self-display' (see article 20, p. 191). Perhaps the closest Dickens comes to describing the fascinating alloy of familiar intimacy and engaging digression with focused analysis and determined pursuit of journalistic targets which characterises the 'Uncommercial Traveller' papers, is when he sets out to describe – using the trope of travelling-as-writing that is skilfully developed elsewhere in the collection – his two main styles of walking: 'My walking is of two kinds; one, straight on end to a definite goal at a round pace; one, objectless, loitering, and purely vagabond' (see article 13, p. 119). The appeal of Dickens's finest journalism – delightfully evidenced throughout the 'Uncommercial Traveller' papers – is surely its ability to accommodate, under the flâneur's cape, a rich diversity of social and artistic purpose.

Dickens had returned home from his American Reading Tour in May 1868 to find Wills suffering from the after-effects of concussion of the brain (the result of a hunting accident) with all the 'business and money details' of *All The Year Round* consequently devolving on himself.[34] Although Wills struggled on for a while as sub-editor, he never fully recovered and Dickens increasingly relied on his eldest son Charley to help him with the running of the journal. In July 1869 he wrote to Macready that Charley showed 'considerable aptitude in sub-editing work',[35] and shortly before his death, he officially appointed his son as sub-editor. He also bequeathed to Charley in his will all of his own share and interest in *All The Year Round*. Charley became sole proprietor in 1871 after buying Wills out, and continued to edit the journal ('respectably', according to Fitzgerald's patronising assessment) until 1895. Although the vast bulk of serialised fiction published under his editorship was undistinguished, it did include no less than three novels by Anthony Trollope, *Is He Popenjoy?*, *The Duke's Children* and *Mr Scarborough's Family*, so that Charley may be said to have done his part towards realising his father's ambition that some at least of the novels serialised in *All The Year Round* might 'become a part of English Literature'.

This volume is the final one of *The Dent Uniform Edition of Dickens' Journalism* and includes, in the 'Uncommercial Traveller' essays, some of his very finest work in this genre, rightly seen by Grahame Smith as 'the climax of Dickens's career as a periodical essayist'.[36] The energetic young *Morning Chronicle* reporter with his keen eye (and ear) for the ludicrous and the outrageous in human behaviour, 'Boz' the vivid sketcher of 'everyday' London street life, London neighbourhoods and London characters, and the hard-hitting polemical journalist of the late 1840s making his anonymous contributions to *The Examiner*, had all played their part in forming the Dickens who, in the 1850s, poured out, in his own crusading journal *Household Words*, a rich stream of scathing and highly topical satire, mocking *jeux d'esprit* and superb specimens of investigative reporting. At the same time, he was showing himself, in such pieces as 'Where We Stopped Growing' and 'Gone Astray', to be a master of the genre of the familiar essay developed by some of the greatest literary favourites of his boyhood, Goldsmith, Charles Lamb and Leigh Hunt.

Following the tremendous upheaval in his personal life of 1857–9 and the establishment of his new journal came, as we have seen, Dickens's invention of the persona or mask of 'The Uncommercial Traveller'. This enabled him to write the series of papers featured in this volume, a series in which all his powers as satirist, as investigative reporter and as familiar essayist are at full stretch but in which, because of the slight detachment resulting from the use of the persona, he is also able to observe and reflect on *himself* and on his reactions to experiences both past and present, giving full play to something in his make-up of which he was very much aware (see his comment in 'A Fly-Leaf in a Life' [below, p. 388]: 'Being accustomed to observe myself as curiously as if I were another man ...'). It is this, in the end, that makes the 'Uncommercial Traveller' essays his greatest journalistic achievement.

M. S., J. D.

NOTES

1. *Pilgrim*, Vol. IX, p. 415 (to Bulwer Lytton, 15 May 1861).
2. *Memories of Charles Dickens* (1913), p. 196.
3. *Nonesuch*, Vol. III, p. 752 (24 November 1869).
4. For the fullest (as well as the most entertaining) account of the crisis that resulted in the serialisation of *Great Expectations* in *ATYR*, see Edgar Rosenberg's Norton Edition of the novel (1999).

5. For an interesting discussion of Dickens as a publisher of fiction in *ATYR*, see John Sutherland's *Victorian Novelists and Publishers* (1976), Ch. 8. Sutherland points out that as *ATYR* did not carry advertisements its revenue depended almost entirely on high sales, which in turn depended primarily on the popularity of the current serial. For an illuminating placing of *Great Expectations* in the context of other fiction published in *ATYR*, see D. Wynne, ' "We were unhealthy and unsafe": Dickens' *Great Expectations* and *All The Round*'s Anxiety Stories', *Journal of Victorian Culture*, Vol. 5 (Spring 2000), pp. 45–59.

6. Fitzgerald, *Memories*, p. 240. For a full discussion of the journal, its main contributors, Dickens's editorial policies, etc., see the Introduction to Oppenlander.

7. See 'Modern Periodical Literature', *The Dublin Review*, May 1862 (Vol. 51, pp. 275–308).

8. For details of Dickens's and Wills's arrangements with American publishers, see Robert L. Patten, *Dickens and His Publishers* (1978), p. 276; also Gerald Grubb in *Papers of the Bibliographical Society of America*, Vol. 47 (1953), pp. 301–4. In another article, Grubb estimates the American circulation at over three million readers, quoting J. M. Emerson (of Emerson & Co., the principal American publisher of *ATYR*), who described it as 'the largest circulation of any similar publication in the world ('Editorial Policies of Charles Dickens', *PMLA*, Vol. 58 [1943], p. 1110 & n.).

9. See headnote to article 11, 'The Great Tasmania's Cargo', for an example of the difficulties resulting from the time-lag imposed by the arrangements with American publishers. Headnotes to articles 9 ('Refreshments for Travellers') and 37 ('The Ruffian') illustrate how CD's response in *ATYR* to news stories in the daily papers could be three or four weeks in arrears.

10. *Pilgrim*, Vol. x, p. 202.

11. *Pilgrim*, Vol. x, p. 181 (26 December 1862).

12. *Pilgrim*, Vol. iv, p. 328 & n. (to Forster, [?early July 1845]).

13. Dickens also used *ATYR* for the English publication of various items written for American journals: two long short stories – 'Hunted Down' (4 and 11 August 1860) and 'George Silverman's Explanation' (1, 15 and 29 February 1868) – and his children's stories, collectively titled 'Holiday Romance' (25 January, 8 February, 14 March and 4 April 1868). Dickens's authorship of all these items was publicised in the journal.

14. See Anne Lohrli, *Household Words: A Weekly Journal 1850–1859 Conducted by Charles Dickens. Table of Contents, List of Contributors and Their Contributions Based on the HOUSEHOLD WORDS Office Book in Princeton University Library* (1973), and Stone. The Office Book for *ATYR* has not survived, though a certain amount of evidence for attribution exists in a letter-book containing press copies of business letters, mainly for the early years of the journal. See

description in Oppenlander and Philip Collins, 'The *All The Year Round* Letter Book', *Victorian Periodicals Newsletter*, Vol. 10 (1970), pp. 23–9. Evidence can also be found in Dickens's surviving correspondence. See, for example, Philip Collins's article 'Dickens on Keeley the comedian. An Uncollected Piece', *The Dickensian*, Vol. 60 (1964), pp. 5–10, which shows how Dickens wrote most of an article on the actor Robert Keeley.

15. Gordon N. Ray, *Thackeray*, Vol. II, 'The Age of Wisdom' (1958), p. 293.
16. E.g. prefaces to the 1st eds of *Nicholas Nickleby* (1839) and *David Copperfield* (1850), plus: CD's 'Rough notes of proposals for the New Work' [July 1839], *Pilgrim*, Vol. I, pp. 563–5 & n.; letter to Forster in which the concept of 'The Cricket' is outlined (see note 12 above); letter to Forster of [22 and 23rd] November 1846 (*Pilgrim*, Vol. IV, p. 660); letter to Forster of [7 October] 1849, in which the persona of 'The Shadow' is outlined (*Pilgrim*, Vol. V, pp. 621–3 & n.).
17. *Memories of Charles Dickens, with an Account of* Household Words *and* All the Year Round *and of the Contributors thereto* (1913), p. 236.
18. *Pilgrim*, Vol. IX, p. 195 & n.
19. For convenience, these are often divided into three series: 'First Series' (sixteen papers published in 1860); 'Second Series' (twelve papers published in 1863); 'New Uncommercial Samples' (seven papers published 1868–9). A one-off paper, published in response to public events just before the commencement of the 'New Uncommercial Samples', brings the total to thirty-six (see article 37, 'The Ruffian').
20. *Speeches*, pp. 288–93.
21. Dickens may have come across one of the first recorded usages of 'uncommercial' in Henry Hunter's standard translation of Bernadin de St Pierre's *Paul et Virginie* (*Studies in Nature* [1796], Vol. V, p. 65), a book which Dickens refers to as early as October 1834 (see Vol. I of this edition, p. 381; also *Little Dorrit*, Book I, Ch. 13), and later owned in editions of 1839 and 1848 (*Pilgrim*, Vol. IV, p. 724; Stonehouse).
22. See CD's letter to W. H. Wills, *Pilgrim*, Vol. X, p. 166 & n.; also 'State and Prospects of Cotton', *All The Year Round*, Vol. VIII, p. 322.
23. For discussion of this and other aspects of the genesis of the 'Uncommercial' persona, see John M. L. Drew's 'The Nineteenth-Century Commercial Traveller and Dickens's "Uncommercial" Philosophy', Part I, *Dickens Quarterly*, Vol. 15 (1998), pp. 50–61.
24. For a discussion of CD's knowledge of eighteenth-century periodicals and *récits de voyage*, and its influence on *UT*, see John M. L. Drew's 'Voyages Extraordinaires: Dickens's "Travelling Essays" and *The Uncommercial Traveller*', *Dickens Quarterly*, Vol. 13 (1996), pp. 76–96, 127–50.
25. Vol. XI [23 February 1861], p. 195.
26. *Pilgrim*, Vol. IX, pp. 289, 315.
27. *Pilgrim*, Vol. X, p. 148.

28. *Pilgrim*, Vol. x, p. 147.

29. *Pilgrim*, Vol. ix, pp. 289, 292.

30. See Janine Watrin's careful sifting of the evidence in *De Boulogne à Condette, Une histoire d'Amitié* (1992), pp. 75–86.

31. 'Gossiper', *The Penny Illustrated News* (London), 9 June 1865, p. 54.

32. The 'New Series' differed from the old in offering the public an improved typeface and an illustrated masthead showing (in imitation of *The Cornhill*) fruits and flowers representative of the four seasons.

33. Introduction, *The Uncommercial Traveller* (J. M. Dent, London, 1911), p. vii.

34. *Nonesuch*, Vol. iii, p. 654.

35. *Nonesuch*, Vol. iii, p. 731.

36. G. Smith, *Charles Dickens: A Literary Life* (1996), p. 82.

ACKNOWLEDGEMENTS

We would like to express our great gratitude to the following people for much valuable advice and assistance during the course of our work on this volume: Susan Brady, Assistant Head of Public Services, Beinecke Rare Books and Manuscripts Library at Yale University; Paul Cannon, Assistant Curator of the Newbury District Museum; Professor Andrew Sanders (particularly for the generous long-term loan of his copy of Ella Oppenlander's *Dickens'* ALL THE YEAR ROUND: *Descriptive Index and Contributor List*); Andrew Xavier and Martha Hawting, Curator and Assistant Curator of the Dickens House Museum; Professor Duane DeVries; John Grigg; and Dr Paul Schlicke. Dr David Atkinson has once more shown himself to be splendidly resourceful, thoughtful and efficient in the compilation of the Index and Glossary. Mr Mark Dickens has kindly allowed us to quote from the manuscripts of 'City of London Churches' and 'On an Amateur Beat' (pp. 107 and 379–80). We gratefully acknowledge a Faculty Research Grant from the Faculty of Arts, Birkbeck College, which has materially assisted in bringing this volume to completion.

M.S., J.D.

As this volume is the last one of *The Dent Uniform Edition of Dickens' Journalism* and as the previous three were edited by me alone, I should like to record here my deepest thanks to Linda Osband for having been throughout the whole project not only a quite superlative copy-editor but also for having been always so supportive and encouraging. I would like to record here also the tremendous debt that I owe to the University of London Library and to express my great gratitude to the Librarian, Emma Robinson, and her always most helpful staff, especially Steve Crews, Charlotte McDonough and Michael Mulcay. The Library's magnificent holdings, particularly in the field of Victorian studies, made it possible to carry out most of the research for this edition there.

M.S.

NOTE ON THE TEXT AND ILLUSTRATIONS

The text of each article in this volume is the text as first published in the relevant magazine, newspaper, book or privately circulated publication, with any obvious misprints silently corrected and the original spelling and punctuation, italicisations, etc., preserved with four exceptions: in accordance with standard modern usage, single quotation marks are used before double ones; the full stop has been omitted after Mr, Mrs, Dr, etc.; words like 'today', 'downstairs', 'anybody', 'juxtaposition', that were printed as two words in the nineteenth century, or else hyphenated, are here printed as single words; and the opening words of various paragraphs printed with an ornate capital followed by plain capitals in the originals have been converted to lower case with a preceding capital letter. The location of any manuscript and/or corrected proof version of an article is recorded in the relevant headnote and any interesting variants noted. Significant alterations made when Dickens himself (rather than subsequent editors) re-published one of the *ATYR* essays in editions of *The Uncommercial Traveller* are also recorded, though these are rare. A collation of texts between *UT1* and the original *ATYR* texts for the First and Second Series of 'Uncommercial Traveller' papers shows that, apart from the addition of a separate title for each article, and the addition or suppression of semantically insignificant commas, alterations were mainly confined to occasional adjustments required by taking the article out of its original context in a particular issue of a weekly periodical and publishing it in a book. Thus, the reference made to 'a volume of this publication' in *ATYR* in the paper here republished as article 11 ('The Great Tasmania's Cargo') becomes shortened to 'this volume' in editions of *The Uncommercial Traveller.*

The illustrations in this volume include the frontispiece and three further woodcuts by G. J. Pinwell published in *UT1*, plus the four designs by the unidentified artist 'W. M.' which appeared in *UT2*. A single sketch by 'Phiz' intended to accompany article 9 has also been reproduced, as have an illustration of Thackeray's study from *The Cornhill* (article 35) and a cartoon inspired by Dickens's puff for Fechter's acting in the *Atlantic Monthly* (article 46).

SELECT BIBLIOGRAPHY

Note: Not included here are books or articles primarily relevant only to one particular article. These will be found cited in the appropriate headnote. The place of publication, unless otherwise stated, is London.

ACKROYD, Peter, *Dickens*, Sinclair-Stevenson, 1990. The best modern biography (though difficult to use for reference purposes) – an astonishing combination of exhaustive research and insight into the workings of Dickens's imagination.

COLLINS, Philip, *Dickens and Crime*, Macmillan, 1962 (reprinted in paperback, 1995). Comprehensive and authoritative survey of the subject, which pays great attention to its central place in Dickens's social journalism.

DREW, John M. L., 'Voyages Extraordinaires: Dickens's "Travelling Essays" and *The Uncommercial Traveller*', *Dickens Quarterly*, Vol. 13 (1996), pp. 76–96, 127–50. Documents Dickens's twin interests in the periodical essay and in travel literature, relating them to the style and substance of his journalism in *UT*.

DREW, John M. L., 'The Nineteenth-Century Commercial Traveller and Dickens's "Uncommercial" Philosophy', *Dickens Quarterly*, Vol. 15 (1998), pp. 50–61, 83–110. Explores the significance of the 'uncommercial epithet' in *UT*, and examines the way Dickens sets out his objections to commercialism in *UT*.

DREW, Philip, 'Dickens and the Real World: A Reading of *The Uncommercial Traveller*', *Essays and Studies*, Vol. 38 (1985), pp. 66–82. Draws attention to the virtues of Dickens as a writer of non-fictional prose, arguing eloquently that the twentieth century's neglect of *UT* has been unjustified.

DVORAK, Wilfred P., 'Dickens' Ambivalence as a Social Critic in the 1860s: Attitudes to Money in *All the Year Round* and *The Uncommercial Traveller*', *The Dickensian*, Vol. 80 (1984), pp. 89–104. Focuses on change of editorial policy evident between *HW* and *ATYR*, noting the marked increase in the latter in articles about money, finance, speculation and commercial practice; considers Dickens's writing in *UT* in this context.

FIELDING, K. J. (ed.), *The Speeches of Charles Dickens*, Oxford: Clarendon Press, 1960; new edn, 1988. Essential companion volume to any collection of Dickens's writings on public affairs.

FORSTER, John, *The Life of Charles Dickens*, ed. J. W. T. Ley, Samuel Palmer, 1928. Useful, annotated edition of the indispensable Dickens biography by his lifelong friend (first published 1872–4).

HOLLINGTON, Michael, 'Dickens the Flâneur', *The Dickensian*, Vol. 77 (1981), pp. 71–87. Illuminating article relating Dickens's lifelong passion for walking to narrative tendencies in his novels and journalism, and to the cultural concept of 'flânerie' (strolling, promenading).

HOUSE, Humphry, *The Dickens World*, Oxford: Oxford University Press, 1942 (Oxford Paperback, 1960). The first study of Dickens to pay detailed attention to his social journalism and the connections between it and his fiction. Still very important.

HOUSE, M., STOREY, G., TILLOTSON, K., *et al.* (eds), *The Letters of Charles Dickens* (The Pilgrim Edition), Vols 1–11 (1820–67); Oxford: Oxford University Press, 1965–2000.

OPPENLANDER, Ella Ann, comp., *Dickens' All the Year Round: Descriptive Index and Contributor List*, New York: Whitston Publishing, 1984. Invaluable work of reference covering the period of Dickens's editorship, although well over half of the articles remain unattributed; opens with a succinct overview of the journal's aims, audience and business practices; contains a subject and keyword index.

PASCOE, David (ed. & intro.), *Charles Dickens: Selected Journalism 1850–1870*, Harmondsworth: Penguin Classics, 1997. Annotated selection of Dickens's journalism from *Household Words* and *All The Year Round*.

SCHLICKE, Paul (ed.), *Oxford Reader's Companion to Dickens*, Oxford: Oxford University Press, 1999. Draws together a huge diversity of information on Dickens's life, work, reputation, contemporaries and cultural context; contains detailed entries on Dickens as a journalist and on his journals.

SCHWARZBACH, Frederic, '*A Tale of Two Cities, The Uncommercial Traveller* and *Great Expectations*: Paradise Revisited', in *Dickens and the City*, Athlone Press, University of London, 1979, pp. 178–84. Valuable part-chapter offering a psycho-biographical interpretation of the themes and implications of the 'First Series' of *UT* essays (1860).

SMITH, Grahame, *Charles Dickens: A Literary Life*, Basingstoke: Macmillan, 1996. Contains an important chapter on 'Periodicals, Journalism and the Literary Essay'.

DICKENS'S
LIFE AND TIMES 1859–70

CD's personal life	*Writing Career*	*Historical and Literary*
1859 Second provincial Reading Tour (10–27 Oct.).	First number of CD's new weekly journal *All The Year Round* containing the opening instalment of *A Tale of Two Cities* appears (30 Apr.). Last number of *Household Words* (28 May). 'Hunted Down' published in *All The Year Round* (Aug.). Serialisation of *A Tale of Two Cities* concluded (26 Nov.).	Gounod's *Faust* performed. Deaths of Leigh Hunt and Washington Irving. Darwin's *On the Origin of Species*, George Eliot's *Adam Bede*, Meredith's *Ordeal of Richard Feverel*, Smiles's *Self-Help* and Tennyson's *Idylls of the King* published.
1860 Katey Dickens marries Charles Collins. CD settles permanently at Gad's Hill.	'The Uncommercial Traveller' series begins appearing in *All The Year Round* (28 Jan.). First instalment of *Great Expectations* in *All The Year Round* (1 Dec.).	Commercial Treaty signed between Britain and France. Garibaldi captures Naples and Sicily. Wilkie Collins's *The Woman in White* and George Eliot's *The Mill on the Floss* published.
1861 Readings in London (Mar./Apr.). Third provincial Reading Tour (Oct.–Jan. 1862). Charles Dickens Jr marries.	*Great Expectations* published in 3 volumes (Aug.).	Death of Prince Albert. Outbreak of American Civil War (Lincoln President). Mrs Beeton's *Book of Household Management*, Turgenev's *Fathers and Sons*, Dostoevsky's *The House of the Dead* and George Eliot's *Silas Marner* published.
1862 Readings in London (Mar./June).		Bismarck Prime Minister of Prussia. Début of Sarah Bernhardt at the

			Comédie Française, Paris. Hugo's *Les Misérables*, Christina Rossetti's *Goblin Market*, George Eliot's *Romola*, Flaubert's *Salammbô* and Ruskin's *Unto this Last* published.
1863	Charity readings at the British Embassy in Paris (Jan.). Readings in London (June). Deaths of Elizabeth Dickens and CD's fourth child, Walter (in India).	Second Series of 'Uncommercial' papers begins in *All The Year Round* (May–Oct.).	Death of Thackeray. Lincoln's Gettysburg Address. Opening of London's first Underground Railway. Manet paints *Le Déjeuner sur l'herbe*. Kingsley's *The Water Babies* published.
1864		*Our Mutual Friend* begins serialisation in 20 monthly numbers (1 May).	First Trades Union Conference. Tennyson's *Enoch Arden* and Newman's *Apologia pro Vita Sua* published. Tolstoy's *War and Peace* begins publication.
1865	CD and Ellen Ternan involved in serious railway accident at Staplehurst, Kent (9 June).	*Our Mutual Friend* published in 2 volumes (Nov.).	Assassination of Lincoln. Death of Mrs Gaskell. Wagner's *Tristan and Isolde* performed. Matthew Arnold's *Essays in Criticism*, Lewis Carroll's *Alice in Wonderland* and Swinburne's *Atalanta in Calydon* published.
1866	Reading Tour in London and the provinces (Apr./June).		Dr Barnardo opens home for destitute children in East London. Dostoevsky's *Crime and Punishment*, George Eliot's *Felix Holt* and Verlaine's *Poèmes saturniens* published.
1867	Reading Tour in England and Ireland	Last Christmas Story (*No Thoroughfare*, written jointly with Wilkie	Death of Clarkson Stanfield. Fenian rising in Ireland. Garibaldi

(Jan./May). Arrives in Boston for American Reading Tour (Nov.).

Collins) published in *All The Year Round*.

invades Papal States. Zola's *Thérèse Raquin*, Vol. 1 of Marx's *Das Kapital* and Ibsen's *Peer Gynt* published.

1868 Leaves New York for England (22 Apr.). Farewell Reading Tour begins (Oct.).

Wills retires as sub-editor of *All The Year Round*. 'George Silverman's Explanation' published in *All The Year Round* (Feb.). 'A Holiday Romance' published in *All The Year Round* (Jan./Feb./Mar./Apr.). Charles Dickens Edition of *The Uncommercial Traveller* published. 'New Uncommercial Samples' series begins in *All The Year Round*.

Browning's *The Ring and The Book*, Wilkie Collins's *The Moonstone*, Louisa May Alcott's *Little Women* and Dostoevsky's *The Idiot* published.

1869 First public Reading of 'Sikes and Nancy' (5 Jan.). Reading Tour broken off because of CD's serious illness (22 Apr.).

Last 'Uncommercial' article in *All The Year Round* (5 June); CD's last journal article, published in *The Atlantic Monthly* (Aug.).

Girton College for Women at Cambridge founded. Opening of Suez Canal. Arnold's *Culture and Anarchy*, Blackmore's *Lorna Doone*, W. S. Gilbert's *Bab Ballads*, Mill's *On the Subjection of Women*, Twain's *Innocents Abroad* and Flaubert's *L'Education sentimentale* published.

1870 Twelve Farewell Readings in London (Jan.). CD received by Queen Victoria (9 Mar.). Dies of cerebral haemorrhage at Gad's Hill (9 June); buried in Westminster Abbey (14 June).

Charles Dickens Jr appointed as sub-editor of *All The Year Round*. First monthly number of *The Mystery of Edwin Drood* appears (1 Apr.): only 6 of the intended 12 numbers completed when CD died.

Franco–Prussian War. End of Second Empire in France, establishment of Third Republic. First Elementary Education Act for England and Wales.

ILLUSTRATIONS

THE UNCOMMERCIAL TRAVELLER AND OTHER PAPERS

The Poor Man and His Beer

All The Year Round, 30 April 1859

During the nineteenth century many associations such as the one described here were formed to provide rural workers with an 'allotment' of land on which they could cultivate fruit and vegetables for themselves. The 'Friar Bacon' of the following article was John Bennet Lawes, chemist and agriculturist, who had in 1845 established an agricultural experiment station on his family estate at Rothamsted near St Albans in Hertfordshire with its 'picturesque Tudor mansion', here 'faithfully depicted' by Dickens according to F. G. Kitton (*Minor Writings of Charles Dickens* [1900], p.144). Forster gets Lawes's initials wrong and mistakenly describes him as a clergyman, but provides useful background for this article. Lawes, he says,

> had been associated upon a sanitary commission with Mr Henry Austin, Dickens's brother-in-law ... and this connection led to Dickens's knowledge of a club that Mr Lawes had established at Rothamsted, which he became eager to recommend as an example to other country neighbourhoods. The club had been set on foot to enable the agricultural labourers of the parish to have their beer and pipes independent of the public-house. [Forster, p. 673]

For a biography of Lawes, see George Vaughan Dyke's *John Lawes of Rothamsted* (1993).

Austin was a civil engineer and keen sanitary reformer who had served as Secretary to the Metropolitan Commission of Sewers and subsequently as an active unpaid member of the Sewage Commission (see *Pilgrim*, Vol. IX, pp. 569–70), hence Dickens's name for him here, 'Philosewers'. Just before going down to Rothamsted, Dickens had told Wills that, if he found there 'any good notion', he would 'come down to the Office early tomorrow morning [12 April], and write another short paper' for the first number of *ATYR* 'to strengthen it' (*Pilgrim*, Vol. IX, p. 50). In the event, he wrote the paper during the 25-mile return journey from Rothamsted to London, having refused Lawes's offer of overnight hospitality (Forster, p. 673). He returned to the subject of working men's clubs five years later in a long article co-authored with Edmund Ollier ('Working Men's Clubs', *ATYR*, Vol. 11 [26 March 1864], pp. 149–54; see headnote to article 30), but does not include any mention of the Rothamsted one. According to the 'Country Notes' columnist writing in *The Glasgow Herald* (21 January 1961), the club visited by Dickens was still being used at that date by locals in preference to crowded public houses taken over by newcomers from the city. It finally ceased operating following the demolition of the clubhouse (1962–3).

In the paragraph about the pig as 'the poor man's friend' (a cliché phrase of the day which Dickens had already had sport with in *The Chimes* [1844]), Dickens mocks Parliamentary jargon ('comes down to this house', etc.).

Literary allusions (below) 'an old ditty': *unidentified*; (p.5) 'Romeo … father Lawrence … Juliet': Shakespeare, *Romeo and Juliet*; (p.6) 'Old Cousin Feenix, ambling along St James's Street': alludes to a character in Dickens's *Dombey and Son* (1848); (p.11) 'the Indian Drum': *unidentified*; (p.11) 'the Village Blacksmith': musical setting of Longfellow's popular poem (1839); (p.11) *'Ah! non giunge'*: aria from Bellini's opera *La Sonnambula* (1831), Act 3, Sc. 2; (p.11) *'Mi manca la voce'*: quartet from Rossini's opera *Mosè in Egitto* (1818), Act 2.

My friend Philosewers and I, contemplating a farm-labourer the other day, who was drinking his mug of beer on a settle at a road-side alehouse door, we fell to humming the fag-end of an old ditty, of which the poor man and his beer, and the sin of parting them, form the doleful burden. Philosewers then mentioned to me that a friend of his in an agricultural county – say a Hertfordshire friend – had, for two years last past, endeavoured to reconcile the poor man and his beer to public morality, by making it a point of honour between himself and the poor man that the latter should use his beer and not abuse it. Interested in an effort of so unobtrusive and unspeechifying a nature, 'O Philosewers,' said I, after the manner of the dreary sages in Eastern apologues, 'Show me, I pray, the man who deems that temperance can be attained without a medal, an oration, a banner, and a denunciation of half the world, and who has at once the head and heart to set about it!'

Philosewers expressing, in reply, his willingness to gratify the dreary sage, an appointment was made for the purpose. And on the day fixed, I, the Dreary one, accompanied by Philosewers, went down Nor'-West per railway, in search of temperate temperance. It was a thunderous day; and the clouds were so immoderately watery, and so very much disposed to sour all the beer in Hertfordshire, that they seemed to have taken the pledge.

But, the sun burst forth gaily in the afternoon, and gilded the old gables, and old mullioned windows, and old weathercock and old clock-face, of the quaint old house which is the dwelling of the man we sought. How shall I describe him? As one of the most famous practical chemists of the age? That designation will do as well as another – better, perhaps, than most others. And his name? Friar Bacon.

'Though, take notice, Philosewers,' said I, behind my hand, 'that the first Friar Bacon had not that handsome lady-wife beside him. Wherein, O Philosewers, he was a chemist, wretched and forlorn, compared with his successor. Young Romeo bade the holy father Lawrence hang up philosophy, unless philosophy could make a Juliet. Chemistry would infallibly be hanged if its life were staked on making anything half so pleasant as this Juliet.' The gentle Philosewers smiled assent.

The foregoing whisper from myself, the Dreary one, tickled the ear of Philosewers, as we walked on the trim garden terrace before dinner, among the early leaves and blossoms; two peacocks, apparently in very tight new boots, occasionally crossing the gravel at a distance. The sun, shining through the old house-windows, now and then flashed out some brilliant piece of colour from bright hangings within, or upon the old oak panelling; similarly, Friar Bacon, as we paced to and fro, revealed little glimpses of his good work.

'It is not much,' said he. 'It is no wonderful thing. There used to be a great deal of drunkenness here, and I wanted to make it better if I could. The people are very ignorant, and have been much neglected, and I wanted to make *that* better if I could. My utmost object was, to help them to a little self-government and a little homely pleasure. I only show the way to better things, and advise them. I never act for them; I never interfere; above all, I never patronise.'

I had said to Philosewers as we came along Nor'-West that patronage was one of the curses of England. I appeared to rise in the estimation of Philosewers when thus confirmed.

'And so,' said Friar Bacon, 'I established my Allotment-club, and my pig-clubs, and those little Concerts by the ladies of my own family, of which we have the last of the season this evening. They are a great success, for the people here are amazingly fond of music. But there is the early dinner-bell, and I have no need to talk of my endeavours when you will soon see them in their working dress.'

Dinner done, behold the Friar, Philosewers, and myself the Dreary one, walking, at six o'clock, across the fields, to the 'Club-house.'

As we swung open the last field-gate and entered the Allotment-grounds, many members were already on their way to the Club, which stands in the midst of the allotments. Who could help thinking of the wonderful contrast between these club-men and the club-men of St James's-street, or Pall-mall, in London! Look at yonder prematurely old man, doubled up with work, and leaning on a rude stick more crooked than himself, slowly trudging to the club-house, in a shapeless hat like an Italian harlequin's, or an old brown-paper bag, leathern leggings, and dull green smock-frock, looking as though duck-weed had accumulated on it – the result of its stagnant life – or as if it were a vegetable production, originally meant to blow into something better, but stopped somehow. Compare him with Old Cousin Feenix, ambling along St James's-street, got up in the style of a couple of generations ago, and with a head of hair, a complexion, and a set of teeth, profoundly impossible to be believed in by the widest stretch of human credulity. Can they both be men and brothers? Verily they are. And although Cousin Feenix has lived so fast that he will die at Baden-Baden, and although this club-man in the frock has lived, ever since he came to man's estate, on nine shillings a week, and is sure to die in the Union if he die in bed, yet he brought as much into the world as Cousin Feenix, and will take as much out – more, for more of him is real.

A pretty, simple building, the club-house with a rustic colonnade outside, under which the members can sit on wet evenings, looking at the patches of ground they cultivate for themselves; within, a well-ventilated room, large and lofty, cheerful pavement of coloured tiles, a bar for serving out the beer, good supply of forms and chairs, and a brave big chimney-corner, where the fire burns cheerfully. Adjoining this room, another:

'Built for a reading-room,' said Friar Bacon; 'but not much used – yet.'

The dreary sage, looking in through the window, perceiving a fixed reading-desk within, and inquiring its use:

'I have Service there,' said Friar Bacon. 'They never went anywhere to hear prayers, and of course it would be hopeless to help them to be happier and better, if they had no religious feeling at all.'

'The whole place is very pretty.' Thus the sage.

'I am glad you think so. I built it for the holders of the Allotment-grounds, and gave it them: only requiring them to manage it by a committee of their own appointing, and never to get drunk there. They never have got drunk there.'

'Yet they have their beer freely.'

'O yes. As much as they choose to buy. The club gets its beer direct from the brewer, by the barrel. So they get it good; at once much cheaper, and much better, than at the public-house. The members take it in turns to be steward, and serve out the beer: if a man should decline to serve when his turn came, he would pay a fine of twopence. The steward lasts, as long as the barrel lasts. When there is a new barrel, there is a new steward.'

'What a noble fire is roaring up that chimney!'

'Yes, a capital fire. Every member pays a halfpenny a week.'

'Every member must be the holder of an Allotment-garden?'

'Yes; for which he pays five shillings a year. The Allotments you see about us, occupy some sixteen or eighteen acres, and each garden is as large as experience shows one man to be able to manage. You see how admirably they are tilled, and how much they get off them. They are always working in them in their spare hours; and when a man wants a mug of beer, instead of going off to the village and the public-house, he puts down his spade or his hoe, comes to the club-house and gets it, and goes back to his work. When he has done work, he likes to have his beer at the club, still, and to sit and look at his little crops as they thrive.'

'They seem to manage the club very well.'

'Perfectly well. Here are their own rules. They made them. I never interfere with them, except to advise them when they ask me.'

RULES AND REGULATIONS
MADE BY THE COMMITTEE
From the 21st September, 1857
One half-penny per week to be paid to the club by each member.

1.—Each member to draw the beer in order, according to the number of his allotment; on failing, a forfeit of twopence to be paid to the club.

2.—The member that draws the beer to pay for the same, and bring his ticket up receipted when the subscriptions are paid; on failing to do so, a penalty of sixpence to be forfeited and paid to the club.

3.—The subscriptions and forfeits to be paid at the club-room on the last Saturday night of each month.

4.—The subscriptions and forfeits to be cleared up every quarter; if not, a penalty of sixpence to be paid to the club.

5.—The member that draws the beer to be at the club-room by six o'clock every evening, and stay till ten; but in the event of no member being there, he may leave at nine; on failing so to attend, a penalty of sixpence to be paid to the club.

6.—Any member giving beer to a stranger in this club-room, excepting to his wife or family, shall be liable to the penalty of one shilling.

7.—Any member lifting his hand to strike another in this club-room shall be liable to the penalty of sixpence.

8.—Any member swearing in this club-room shall be liable to a penalty of twopence each time.

9.—Any member selling beer shall be expelled from the club.

10.—Any member wishing to give up his allotment, may apply to the committee, and they shall value the crop and the condition of the ground. The amount of the valuation shall be paid by the succeeding tenant, who shall be allowed to enter on any part of the allotment which is uncropped at the time of notice of the leaving tenant.

11.—Any member not keeping his allotment-garden clear from seed-weeds, or otherwise injuring his neighbours, may be turned out of his garden by the votes of two-thirds of the committee, one month's notice being given to him.

12.—Any member carelessly breaking a mug, is to pay the cost of replacing the same.

I was soliciting the attention of Philosewers to some old old bonnets hanging in the Allotment-gardens to frighten the birds, and the fashion of which I should think would terrify a French bird to death at any distance, when Philosewers solicited my attention to the scrapers at the club-house door. The amount of the soil of England which every member brought there on his feet, was indeed surprising; and even I, who am professedly a salad-eater, could have grown a salad for my dinner, in the earth on any member's frock or hat.

'Now,' said Friar Bacon, looking at his watch, 'for the Pig-clubs!'

The dreary Sage entreated explanation.

'Why, a pig is so very valuable to a poor labouring man, and it is so very difficult for him at this time of the year to get money enough to buy one, that I lend him a pound for the purpose. But, I do it in this way. I leave such of the club members as choose and desire it, to form themselves into parties of five. To every man in each company of five, I lend a pound, to buy a pig. But, each man of the five becomes bound for every other man, as to the repayment of his money. Consequently, they look after one another, and pick out their partners with care; selecting men in whom they have confidence.'

'They repay the money, I suppose, when the pig is fattened, killed, and sold?'

'Yes. Then they repay the money. And they do repay it. I had one man, last year, who was a little tardy (he was in the habit of going to the public-house); but even he did pay. It is an immense advantage to one of these poor fellows to have a pig. The pig consumes the refuse from the man's cottage and Allotment-garden, and the pig's refuse enriches the man's garden besides. The pig is the poor man's friend. Come into the club-house again.'

The poor man's friend. Yes. I have often wondered who really was the poor man's friend among a great number of competitors, and I now clearly perceive him to be the pig. *He* never makes any flourishes about the poor man. *He* never gammons the poor man – except to his manifest advantage in the article of bacon. *He* never comes down to this house, or goes down to his constituents. He openly declares to the poor man, 'I want my sty because I am a Pig; I desire to have as much to eat as you can by any means stuff me with, because I am a Pig.' *He* never gives the poor man a sovereign for bringing up a family. *He* never grunts the poor man's name in vain. And when he dies in the odour of Porkity, he cuts up, a highly useful creature and a blessing to the poor man, from the ring in his snout to the curl in his tail. Which of the poor man's other friends can say as much? Where is the MP who means Mere Pork?

The dreary Sage had glided into these reflections, when he found himself sitting by the clubhouse fire, surrounded by green smock-frocks and shapeless hats: with Friar Bacon lively, busy, and expert, at a little table near him.

'Now, then, come. The first five!' said Friar Bacon. 'Where are you?'

'Order!' cried a merry-faced little man, who had brought his young daughter with him to see life, and who always modestly hid his face in his beer-mug after he had thus assisted the business.

'John Nightingale, William Thrush, Joseph Blackbird, Cecil Robin, and Thomas Linnet!' cried Friar Bacon.

'Here, sir!' and 'Here, sir!' And Linnet, Robin, Blackbird, Thrush, and Nightingale, stood confessed.

We, the undersigned, declare, in effect, by this written paper, that each of us is responsible for the repayment of this pig-money by each of the other. 'Sure you understand, Nightingale?'

'Ees, sur.'

'Can you write your name, Nightingale?'

'Na, sur.'

Nightingale's eye upon his name, as Friar Bacon wrote it, was a sight to consider in after years. Rather incredulous was Nightingale, with a hand at the corner of his mouth, and his head on one side, as to those drawings really meaning him. Doubtful was Nightingale whether any virtue had gone out of him in that committal to paper. Meditative was Nightingale as to what would come of young Nightingale's growing up to the acquisition of that art. Suspended was the interest of Nightingale, when his name was done – as if he thought the letters were only sown, to come up presently in some other form. Prodigious, and wrong-handed was the cross made by Nightingale on much encouragement – the strokes directed from him instead of towards him; and most patient and sweet-humoured was the smile of Nightingale as he stepped back into a general laugh.

'OR—der!' cried the little man. Immediately disappearing into his mug.

'Ralph Mangel, Roger Wurzel, Edward Vetches, Matthew Carrot, and Charles Taters!' said Friar Bacon.

'All here, sir.'

'You understand it, Mangel?'

'Iss, sir, I unnerstaans it.'

'Can you write your name, Mangel?'

'Iss, sir.'

Breathless interest. A dense background of smock-frocks accumulated behind Mangel, and many eyes in it looked doubtfully at Friar Bacon, as who should say, 'Can he really though?' Mangel put down his hat, retired a little to get a good look at the paper, wetted his right hand thoroughly by drawing it slowly across his mouth, approached the paper with great determination, flattened it, sat down at it, and got well to his work. Circuitous and sea-serpent-like, were the movements of the tongue of Mangel while he formed the letters; elevated were the eyebrows of Mangel and sidelong the eyes, as, with his left whisker reposing on his left arm, they followed his performance; many were the misgivings of Mangel, and slow was his retrospective meditation touching the junction of the letter p with h; something too active was the big forefinger of Mangel in its propensity to rub out without proved cause. At last, long and deep was the breath drawn by Mangel when he laid down the pen; long and deep the wondering breath drawn by the back ground – as if they had watched his walking across the rapids of Niagara, on stilts, and now cried, 'He has done it!'

But, Mangel was an honest man, if ever honest man lived. 'T'owt to be a hell, sir,' said he, contemplating his work, 'and I ha' made a t on't.'

The over-fraught bosoms of the background found relief in a roar of laughter.

'Or—DER!' cried the little man. 'CHEER!' And after that second word, came forth from his mug no more.

Several other clubs signed, and received their money. Very few could write their names; all who could not, pleaded that they could not, more or less sorrowfully, and always with a shake of the head, and in a lower voice than their natural speaking voice. Crosses could be made standing; signatures must be sat down to. There was no exception to this rule. Meantime, the various club-members smoked, drank their beer, and talked together quite unrestrained. They all wore their hats, except when they went up to Friar Bacon's table. The merry-faced little man offered his beer, with a natural good-fellowship, both to the Dreary one and Philosewers. Both partook of it with thanks.

'Seven o'clock!' said Friar Bacon. 'And now we had better get across to the concert, men, for the music will be beginning.'

The concert was in Friar Bacon's laboratory; a large building near at hand, in an open field. The bettermost people of the village and neighbourhood were in a gallery on one side, and, in a gallery opposite the orchestra. The whole space below was filled with the labouring people and their families, to the number of five or six hundred. We had been obliged to turn away two hundred tonight, Friar Bacon said, for want of room – and that, not counting the boys, of whom we had taken in only a few picked ones, by reason of the boys, as a class, being given to too fervent a custom of applauding with their boot-heels.

The performers were the ladies of Friar Bacon's family, and two gentlemen; one of them, who presided, a Doctor of Music. A piano was the only instrument. Among the vocal pieces, we had a negro melody (rapturously encored), the Indian Drum, and the Village Blacksmith; neither did we want for fashionable Italian, having *Ah! non giunge*, and *Mi manca la voce*. Our success was splendid; our good-humoured, unaffected, and modest bearing, a pattern. As to the audience, they were far more polite and far more pleased than at the Opera; they were faultless. Thus for barely an hour the concert lasted, with thousands of great bottles looking on from the walls, containing the results of Friar Bacon's Million and one experiments in agricultural chemistry; and containing too, no doubt, a variety of materials with which the Friar could have blown us all through the roof at five minutes' notice.

God save the Queen being done, the good Friar stepped forward and said a few words, more particularly concerning two points; firstly, that Saturday half-holiday, which it would be kind in farmers to grant; secondly, the additional Allotment-grounds we were going to establish, in consequence of the happy success of the system, but which we could not guarantee should entitle the holders to be members of the club, because the present members must consider and settle that question for themselves: a bargain between man and man being always a bargain, and we having made over the club to them as the original Allotment-men. This was loudly applauded, and so, with contented and affectionate cheering, it was all over.

As Philosewers, and I the Dreary, posted back to London, looking up at the moon and discussing it as a world preparing for the inhabitation of responsible creatures, we expatiated on the honour due to men in this world of ours who try to prepare it for a higher course, and to leave the race who live and die upon it better than they found them.

Five New Points of Criminal Law

All The Year Round, 24 September 1859

The following piece more closely resembles, in its intense topicality and its fiercely sarcastic tone, the kind of article Dickens sometimes dashed off for *HW* rather than the kind of thing he wrote for his new journal, nor does it have any successors in the same vein in *ATYR*. Any hint of murderers, especially poisoners, being treated with leniency, or even escaping justice altogether, would arouse Dickens to fury. The case that provoked this particular outburst was that of Thomas Smethurst, a former surgeon, who was tried before the Chief Baron of the Exchequer, Sir J. B. Pollock, for poisoning a woman he had married bigamously. He made a speech of nearly half an hour protesting his innocence, but was convicted and sentenced to death on 20 August. Writers of letters to *The Times* cast doubt on the reliability of the medical evidence, however, and in September Smethurst was reprieved by the Home Secretary (the 'political gentleman' of the following piece). Later he was pardoned of the murder but sentenced to twelve months' hard labour for bigamy. On 25 August Dickens wrote to Forster about the case, praising 'our brave and excellent friend the Chief Baron' and adding:

> Of course I saw the beast of a prisoner (with my mind's eye) delivering his cut-and-dried speech, and read in every word of it that no one but a murderer could have delivered or conceived it. Of course I have been driving the girls out of their wits here, by incessantly proclaiming that there needed no medical evidence either way, and that the case was plain without it. Lastly, of course ... I would hang any Home Secretary (Whig, Tory, Radical, or otherwise) who should step in between that black scoundrel and the gallows. [*Pilgrim*, Vol. IX, p. 112]

In his 'The Critical Autonomy of *Great Expectations*' (*Review of English Literature*, Vol. 2 [1961], p. 27), K. J. Fielding speculates that Dickens's response to the Smethurst case 'may have a reference to the treatment of Orlick and Mrs Joe', but does not pursue the idea (*Great Expectations* began publication in December 1860).

The existing Criminal Law has been found in trials for Murder, to be so exceedingly hasty, unfair, and oppressive – in a word, to be so very objectionable to the amiable persons accused of that thoughtless act – that it is, we understand, the intention of the Government to bring in a Bill for its amendment. We have been favoured with an outline of its probable provisions.

It will be grounded on the profound principle that the real offender is the Murdered Person; but for whose obstinate persistency in being murdered, the interesting fellow-creature to be tried could not have got into trouble.

Its leading enactments may be expected to resolve themselves under the following heads:

1. There shall be no Judge. Strong representations have been made by highly popular culprits that the presence of this obtrusive character is prejudicial to their best interests. The Court will be composed of a political gentleman, sitting in a secluded room commanding a view of St James's Park, who has already more to do than any human creature can, by any stretch of the human imagination, be supposed capable of doing.

2. The Jury to consist of Five Thousand Five Hundred and Fifty-five Volunteers.

3. The Jury to be strictly prohibited from seeing either the accused or the witnesses. They are not to be sworn. They are on no account to hear the evidence. They are to receive it, or such representations of it, as may happen to fall in their way; and they will constantly write letters about it to all the Papers.

4. Supposing the trial to be a trial for Murder by poisoning, and supposing the hypothetical case, or the evidence, for the prosecution to charge the administration of two poisons, say Arsenic and Antimony; and supposing the taint of Arsenic in the body to be possible but not probable, and the presence of Antimony in the body, to be an absolute certainty; it will then become the duty of the Jury to confine their attention solely to the Arsenic, and entirely to dismiss the Antimony from their minds.

5. The symptoms preceding the death of the real offender (or Murdered Person) being described in evidence by medical practitioners who saw them, other medical practitioners who never saw them shall be required to state whether they are inconsistent with certain known diseases – *but, they shall never be asked whether they are not exactly consistent with the administration of Poison.* To illustrate this enactment in the proposed Bill by a case: – A raging mad dog is seen to run into the house where Z lives alone, foaming at the mouth. Z and the mad dog are for some time left together in that house under proved circumstances, irresistibly leading to the conclusion that Z has been bitten by the dog. Z is afterwards found lying on his bed in a state of hydrophobia, and with the marks of the dog's teeth. Now, the symptoms of that disease being identical with those of

another disease called Tetanus, which might supervene on Z's running a rusty nail into a certain part of his foot, medical practitioners who never saw Z, shall bear testimony to that abstract fact, and it shall then be incumbent on the Registrar-General to certify that Z died of a rusty nail.

It is hoped that these alterations in the present mode of procedure will not only be quite satisfactory to the accused person (which is the first great consideration), but will also tend, in a tolerable degree, to the welfare and safety of Society. For it is not sought in this moderate and prudent measure to be wholly denied that it is an inconvenience to Society to be poisoned overmuch.

3

Leigh Hunt. A Remonstrance.

All The Year Round, 24 December 1859

Dickens had always expressed great admiration and affection for the journalist, poet and essayist, James Henry Leigh Hunt, co-founder of *The Examiner* and a hero of radicalism, for having been, in 1813, imprisoned for libelling the Prince Regent in its pages. During 1847–8, indeed, Dickens had devoted tremendous energy to the organisation of elaborate amateur theatrical performances in order to raise money for Hunt, who was notoriously improvident and feckless in financial matters. Yet as soon as the odiously parasitic and cunningly careless Harold Skimpole made his appearance in the pages of *Bleak House* in 1852, he was widely recognised as a savage portrayal of Hunt, a portrayal described by John Stores Smith, one of Hunt's former associates, as an 'exact moral photograph of him, drawn to a nicety by a master's hand'. Smith's comments appear in his 'Personal Reminiscences' published in a Manchester journal, *Freelance*, in 1868 (quoted by K. J. Fielding in his 'Skimpole and Leigh Hunt Again', *Notes and Queries*, Vol. 200 [April 1955], p.175). Smith considered Dickens's claims in the 'Remonstrance' printed below, that Skimpole was his own invention though 'he might have unconsciously taken a few hints from Hunt', as 'one of the most astonishing pieces of self-deception, or one of the coolest instances of effrontery, in the records of literary history'. Hunt himself, having been made aware of the connection that was being made between himself and Dickens's character, was deeply hurt by what he saw as an incomprehensible attack made on him by an old friend whose work was read by everyone, and he was only partly mollified by Dickens's attempted reassurances that the character was not meant for him (see Forster, p. 550). We can see how far this was from being the case from a letter Dickens wrote earlier to his much-loved friend the Hon. Mrs Watson, evidently responding to some enquiry she had made about the character:

> ... I suppose he is the most exact portrait that ever was painted in words! ...
> The likeness is astonishing. I don't think he could possibly be more like himself.
> ... There is not an atom of exaggeration or suppression. It is an absolute
> reproduction of a real man. Of course I have been careful to keep the outward
> figure away from the fact; but in all else it is the Life itself. [*Pilgrim*, Vol. VII,
> p. 132]

The republication, following Hunt's death in 1859, of his 1850 *Autobiography* with an introduction by his son Thornton stirred up gossip about Skimpole again, and Dickens felt obliged to publish the following 'Remonstrance', a proof of which was shown to Thornton Hunt. According to the *Athenaeum*, which quoted in extenso what it called Dickens's 'explanation' of a 'silly but widely-circulated bit of slander' (24 December 1859, pp. 853–4), Hunt found it 'perfectly satisfactory'.

The 'two intimate literary friends' of Hunt whom Dickens consulted about the extent of his use of Hunt to create Skimpole were Forster and Bryan Procter ('Barry Cornwall'). According to Forster (p. 550), both considered the likeness too obvious, whereupon Dickens made 'considerable' alterations, changing the character's first name from Leonard to Harold and so on. Nevertheless, Forster comments, 'the radical wrong remained'.

For a persuasive account of what might have caused Dickens to caricature Hunt so mercilessly in the early 1850s, see K. J. Fielding's 'Leigh Hunt and Skimpole' in *The Dickensian*, Vol. 64 (1968), pp. 5–9 (Fielding also notes that Dickens, significantly, calls his piece a 'Remonstrance' rather than an 'Apology'); for an illuminating discussion of the possible artistic process involved, see Peter Ackroyd, *Dickens* (1990), pp. 652–3; and for a skilful defence of Dickens's good faith in his 'Remonstrance', see Adam Roberts, 'Skimpole, Leigh Hunt and Dickens's "Remonstrance"', *The Dickensian*, Vol. 92 (1996), pp. 177–86.

Literary allusions (p.16) 'man that is born of woman ... live': from the Burial Service in *The Book of Common Prayer*; (p.18) 'Not only we, the latest seed of time ...': Tennyson, 'Godiva' (1842), ll. 5–8; (p. 18) 'Desdemona and Othello ... Iago's leg in the picture': paintings of scenes from Shakespeare's plays (in this case, *Othello*) were a staple ingredient at Royal Academy Exhibitions – see R. D. Altick, *Paintings from Books* (1985); Dickens may here refer particularly to a painting of Othello and Iago by Solomon

Hart exhibited in 1855 and unfavourably reviewed, for making Iago look far too obviously villainous, in *Fraser*'s (review quoted by Altick, pp. 307–8).

'The sense of beauty and gentleness, of moral beauty and faithful gentleness, grew upon him as the clear evening closed in. When he went to visit his relative at Putney, he still carried with him his work, and the books he more immediately wanted. Although his bodily powers had been giving way, his most conspicuous qualities, his memory for books, and his affection remained; and when his hair was white, when his ample chest had grown slender, when the very proportion of his height had visibly lessened, his step was still ready, and his dark eyes brightened at every happy expression, and at every thought of kindness. His death was simply exhaustion: he broke off his work to lie down and repose. So gentle was the final approach, that he scarcely recognised it till the very last, and then it came without terrors. His physical suffering had not been severe; at the latest hour he said that his only uneasiness was failing breath. And that failing breath was used to express his sense of the inexhaustible kindness he had received from the family who had been so unexpectedly made his nurses, – to draw from one of his sons, by minute, eager, and searching questions, all that he could learn about the latest vicissitudes and growing hopes of Italy, – to ask the friends and children around him for news of those whom he loved, – and to send love and messages to the absent who loved him.'

Thus, with a manly simplicity and filial affection, writes the eldest son of Leigh Hunt in recording his father's death. These are the closing words of a new edition of 'The Autobiography of Leigh Hunt,' published by Messrs Smith and Elder, of Cornhill, revised by that son, and enriched with an introductory chapter of remarkable beauty and tenderness. The son's first presentation of his father to the reader, 'rather tall, straight as an arrow, looking slenderer than he really was; his hair black and shining, and slightly inclined to wave; his head high, his forehead straight and white, his eyes black and sparkling, his general complexion dark; in his whole carriage and manner an extraordinary degree of life,' completes the picture. It is the picture of the flourishing and fading away of man that is born of a woman and hath but a short time to live.

In his presentation of his father's moral nature and intellectual qualities, Mr Hunt is no less faithful and no less touching. Those who knew Leigh Hunt, will see the bright face and hear the musical voice again, when he is recalled to them in this passage: 'Even at seasons of the greatest depression in his fortunes, he always attracted many visitors, but still not so much for any repute that attended him as for his personal qualities.

Few men were more attractive, in society, whether in a large company or over the fireside. His manners were peculiarly animated; his conversation, varied, ranging over a great field of subjects, was moved and called forth by the response of his companion, be that companion philosopher or student, sage or boy, man or woman; and he was equally ready for the most lively topics or for the gravest reflections – his expression easily adapting itself to the tone of his companion's mind. With much freedom of manners, he combined a spontaneous courtesy that never failed, and a considerateness derived from a ceaseless kindness of heart that invariably fascinated even strangers.' Or in this: 'His animation, his sympathy with what was gay and pleasurable; his avowed doctrine of cultivating cheerfulness, were manifest on the surface, and could be appreciated by those who knew him in society, most probably even exaggerated as salient traits, on which he himself insisted *with a sort of gay and ostentatious wilfulness.*'

The last words describe one of the most captivating peculiarities of a most original and engaging man, better than any other words could. The reader is besought to observe them, for a reason that shall presently be given. Lastly: 'The anxiety to recognise the right of others, the tendency to "refine," which was noted by an early school companion, and the propensity to elaborate every thought, made him, along with the direct argument by which he sustained his own conviction, recognise and almost admit all that might be said on the opposite side.' For these reasons, and for others suggested with equal felicity, and with equal fidelity, the son writes of the father, 'It is most desirable that his qualities should be known as they were; for such deficiencies as he had are the honest explanation of his mistakes; while, as the reader may see from his writing and his conduct, they are not, as the faults of which he was accused would be, incompatible with the noblest faculties both of head and heart. To know Leigh Hunt as he was, was to hold him in reverence and love.'

These quotations are made here, with a special object. It is not, that the personal testimony of one who knew Leigh Hunt well, may be borne to their truthfulness. It is not, that it may be recorded in these pages, as in his son's introductory chapter, that his life was of the most amiable and domestic kind, that his wants were few, that his way of life was frugal, that he was a man of small expenses, no ostentations, a diligent labourer, and a secluded man of letters. It is not, that the inconsiderate and forgetful may be reminded of his wrongs and sufferings in the days of the Regency, and of the national disgrace of his imprisonment. It is not, that their forbearance may be entreated for his grave, in right of his graceful fancy or his political labours and endurances, though

> Not only we, the latest seed of Time,
> New men, that in the flying of a wheel
> Cry down the past, not only we, that prate
> Of rights and wrongs, have loved the people well.

It is, that a duty may be done in the most direct way possible. An act of plain, clear duty.

Four or five years ago, the writer of these lines was much pained by accidentally encountering a printed statement, 'that Mr Leigh Hunt was the original of Harold Skimpole in Bleak House.' The writer of these lines, is the author of that book. The statement came from America. It is no disrespect to that country, in which the writer has, perhaps, as many friends and as true an interest as any man that lives, good-humouredly to state the fact, that he has, now and then, been the subject of paragraphs in Transatlantic newspapers, more surprisingly destitute of all foundation in truth than the wildest delusions of the wildest lunatics. For reasons born of this experience, he let the thing go by.

But, since Mr Leigh Hunt's death, the statement has been revived in England. The delicacy and generosity evinced in its revival, are for the rather late consideration of its revivers. The fact, is this:

Exactly those graces and charms of manner which are remembered in the words we have quoted, were remembered by the author of the work of fiction in question, when he drew the character in question. Above all other things, that 'sort of gay and ostentatious wilfulness' in the humouring of a subject, which had many a time delighted him and impressed him as being unspeakably whimsical and attractive, was the airy quality he wanted for the man he invented. Partly for this reason, and partly (he has since often grieved to think) for the pleasure it afforded him to find that delightful manner reproducing itself under his hand, he yielded to the temptation of too often making the character *speak* like his old friend. He no more thought, God forgive him! that the admired original would ever be charged with the imaginary vices of the fictitious creature, than he has himself ever thought of charging the blood of Desdemona and Othello, on the innocent Academy model who sat for Iago's leg in the picture. Even as to the mere occasional manner, he meant to be so cautious and conscientious, that he privately referred the proof sheets of the first number of that book to two intimate literary friends of Leigh Hunt (both still living), and altered the whole of that part of the text on their discovering too strong a resemblance to his 'way'.

He cannot see the son lay this wreath on the father's tomb, and leave him to the possibility of ever thinking that the present words might have righted the father's memory and were left unwritten. He cannot know that his own son may have to explain his father when folly or malice can wound his heart no more, and leave this task undone.

4

The Tattlesnivel Bleater

All The Year Round, 31 December 1859

Dickens suffered, like all celebrities in his own day and in ours, from irresponsible newspaper gossip about both his professional and personal life. The particular spur that led to his writing the following hilarious parody of self-important and meretricious provincial journalism may possibly have been the lucubrations of the London correspondent of the *Bath Chronicle* in the 15 October 1859 issue of that paper. In addition to alluding to revived metropolitan gossip about the caricaturing of Leigh Hunt as Skimpole (see headnote to previous article), the author of the *Chronicle*'s 'Our London Letter' also made knowing reference to certain opinions expressed by Dickens in a 'new book' of his. Writing to Forster on 24 October, Dickens says:

> As to the London Correspondent of the Bath paper, he really seems to me too absurd to be thought of. For instance, the 'new book' of mine he has seen extracts from, 'to be published in America', is a story of a few pages written for a New York Journal [i.e. 'Hunted Down']; and the conclusion to which *I* have come on the subject of physiognomy (I have not the least doubt, by the way, that I could read Donkey in his) and which the Idiot sets out as if I had delivered it in a speech, is the remark of a Life-Office Actuary who relates the story! [*Pilgrim*, Vol. IX, p. 141]

Lord John Russell, contemplating retirement from Cabinet politics, had refused office under Palmerston in 1855, but in June 1859 accepted the Foreign Secretaryship under him, following the fall of Lord Derby's ministry.

Literary allusions (p. 23) 'Moses going to the Fair': refers to Ch. 12 of Goldsmith's *The Vicar of Wakefield* (1766) – for the immense popularity of Goldsmith's novel as a source of subjects for Royal Academy painters, see Vol. 2 of this edition, p. 258; (p. 24) 'By their fruits they shall be known': Matthew 7:20; (p.26) 'birthright ... a mess of potage': Genesis 25:34.

The pen is taken in hand on the present occasion, by a private individual (not wholly unaccustomed to literary composition), for the exposure of a conspiracy of a most frightful nature; a conspiracy which, like the deadly Upas-tree of Java, on which the individual produced a poem in his earlier youth (not wholly devoid of length), which was so flatteringly received (in circles not wholly unaccustomed to form critical opinions), that he was recommended to publish it, and would certainly have carried out the suggestion, but for private considerations (not wholly unconnected with expense.)

The individual who undertakes the exposure of the gigantic conspiracy now to be laid bare in all its hideous deformity, is an inhabitant of the town of Tattlesnivel – a lowly inhabitant, it may be, but one who, as an Englishman and a man, will n'er abase his eye before the gaudy and the mocking throng.

Tattlesnivel stoops to demand no championship from her sons. On an occasion in History, our bluff British monarch, our Eighth Royal Harry, almost went there. And long ere the periodical in which this exposure will appear, had sprung into being, Tattlesnivel had unfurled that standard which yet waves upon her battlements. The standard alluded to, is THE TATTLESNIVEL BLEATER, containing the latest intelligence, and state of markets, down to the hour of going to press, and presenting a favourable local medium for advertisers, on a graduated scale of charges, considerably diminishing in proportion to the guaranteed number of insertions.

It were bootless to expatiate on the host of talent engaged in formidable phalanx to do fealty to the Bleater. Suffice it to select, for present purposes, one of the most gifted and (but for the wide and deep ramifications of an unEnglish conspiracy), most rising, of the men who are bold Albion's pride. It were needless, after this preamble, to point the finger more directly at the LONDON CORRESPONDENT OF THE TATTLESNIVEL BLEATER.

On the weekly letters of that Correspondent, on the flexibility of their English, on the boldness of their grammar, on the originality of their quotations (never to be found as they are printed, in any book existing), on the priority of their information, on their intimate acquaintance with the secret thoughts and unexecuted intentions of men, it would ill become the humble Tattlesnivellian who traces these words, to dwell. They are graven in the memory; they are on the Bleater's file. Let them be referred to.

But, from the infamous, the dark, the subtle conspiracy which spreads its baleful roots throughout the land, and of which the Bleater's London Correspondent is the one sole subject, it IS the purpose of the lowly Tattlesnivellian who undertakes this revelation, to tear the veil. Nor will he shrink from his self-imposed labour, Herculean though it be.

The conspiracy begins in the very Palace of the Sovereign Lady of our Ocean Isle. Leal and loyal as it is the proud vaunt of the Bleater's readers, one and all, to be, the inhabitant who pens this exposure does not personally impeach, either her Majesty the Queen, or the illustrious Prince Consort. But, some silken-clad smoothers, some purple parasites, some fawners in frippery, some greedy and begartered ones in gorgeous garments, he does impeach – ay, and wrathfully! Is it asked on what grounds! They shall be stated.

The Bleater's London Correspondent, in the prosecution of his import-ant inquiries, goes down to Windsor, sends in his card, has a confidential interview with her Majesty and the illustrious Prince Consort. For a time, the restraints of Royalty are thrown aside in the cheerful conversation of the Bleater's London Correspondent, in his fund of information, in his flow of anecdote, in the atmosphere of his genius; Her Majesty brightens, the illustrious Prince Consort thaws, the cares of State and the conflicts of Party are forgotten, lunch is proposed. Over that unassuming and domestic table, Her Majesty communicates to the Bleater's London Correspondent that it is her intention to send his Royal Highness the Prince of Wales to inspect the top of the Great Pyramid – thinking it likely to improve his acquaintance with the views of the people. Her Majesty further communicates that she has made up her royal mind (and that the Prince Consort has made up his illustrious mind) to the bestowal of the vacant Garter, let us say on Mr Roebuck. The younger Royal children having been introduced at the request of the Bleater's London Correspondent, and having been by him closely observed to present the usual external indications of good health, the happy knot is severed, with a sigh the Royal bow is once more strung to its full tension, the Bleater's London Correspondent returns to London, writes his letter, and tells the Tattlesnivel Bleater what he knows. All Tattlesnivel reads it, and knows that he knows it. But, *does* his Royal Highness the Prince of Wales ultimately go to the top of the Great Pyramid? *Does* Mr Roebuck ultimately get the Garter? No. Are the younger Royal children even ultimately found to be well? On the contrary, they have – and on that very day had – the measles. Why is this? *Because the conspirators against the Bleater's London Correspondent have stepped in with their dark machinations.* Because Her Majesty and the Prince Consort are artfully induced to change their minds, from north to south, from east to west, immediately after it is known to the conspirators that they have put themselves in com-munication with the Bleater's London Correspondent. It is now indig-nantly demanded, by whom are they so tampered with? It is now indignantly demanded, who took the responsibility of concealing the indisposition of those Royal children from their Royal and Illustrious parents, and of bringing them down from their beds, disguised, expressly to confound the London Correspondent of the Tattlesnivel Bleater? Who are those persons, it is again asked? Let not rank and favour protect them. Let the traitors be exhibited in the face of day!

Lord John Russell is in this conspiracy. Tell us not that his Lordship is a man of too much spirit and honour. Denunciation is hurled against him. The proof? The proof is here.

The Time is panting for an answer to the question, Will Lord John Russell consent to take office under Lord Palmerston? Good. The London Correspondent of the Tattlesnivel Bleater is in the act of writing his weekly letter, finds himself rather at a loss to settle this question finally, leaves off, puts his hat on, goes down to the lobby of the House of Commons, sends in for Lord John Russell, and has him out. He draws his arm through his Lordship's, takes him aside, and says, 'John, will you ever accept office under Palmerston?' His Lordship replies, 'I will not.' The Bleater's London Correspondent retorts, with the caution such a man is bound to use, 'John, think again; say nothing to me rashly; is there any temper here?' His Lordship replies, calmly, 'None whatever.' After giving him time for reflection, the Bleater's London Correspondent says, 'Once more, John, let me put a question to you. Will you ever accept office under Palmerston?' His Lordship answers (note the exact expressions), 'Nothing shall induce me, ever to accept a seat in a Cabinet of which Palmerston is the Chief.' They part, the London Correspondent of the Tattlesnivel Bleater finishes his letter, and – always being withheld by motives of delicacy, from plainly divulging his means of getting accurate information on every subject, at first hand – puts in it, this passage: 'Lord John Russell is spoken of, by blunderers, for Foreign Affairs; but I have the best reasons for assuring your readers, that' (giving prominence to the exact expressions, it will be observed) ' "NOTHING WILL EVER INDUCE HIM, TO ACCEPT A SEAT IN A CABINET OF WHICH PALMERSTON IS THE CHIEF." On this you may implicitly rely.' What happens? On the very day of the publication of that number of the Bleater – the malignity of the conspirators being even manifested in the selection of the day – Lord John Russell takes the Foreign Office! Comment were superfluous.

The people of Tattlesnivel will be told, have been told, that Lord John Russell is a man of his word. He may be, on some occasions; but, when overshadowed by this dark and enormous growth of conspiracy, Tattlesnivel knows him to be otherwise. 'I happen to be certain, deriving my information from a source which cannot be doubted to be authentic,' wrote the London Correspondent of the Bleater, within the last year, 'that Lord John Russell bitterly regrets having made that explicit speech of last Monday.' These are not roundabout phrases; these are plain words. What does Lord John Russell (apparently by accident), within eight-and-forty hours after their diffusion over the civilised globe? Rises in his place in Parliament, and unblushingly declares that if the occasion could arise five hundred times, for his making that very speech, he would make it five hundred times! Is there no conspiracy here? And is this combination against one who would be always right if he were not proved always wrong, to be endured in a country that boasts of its freedom and its fairness?

But, the Tattlesnivellian who now raises his voice against intolerable oppression, may be told that, after all, this is a political conspiracy. He may be told, forsooth, that Mr Disraeli's being in it, that Lord Derby's being in it, that Mr Bright's being in it, that every Home, Foreign, and Colonial Secretary's being in it, that every ministry's and every opposition's being in it, are but proofs that men will do in politics what they would do in nothing else. Is this the plea? If so, the rejoinder is, that the mighty conspiracy includes the whole circle of Artists of all kinds, and comprehends all degrees of men, down to the worst criminal and the hangman who ends his career. For, all these are intimately known to the London Correspondent of the Tattlesnivel Bleater, and all these deceive him.

Sir, put it to the proof. There is the Bleater on the file – documentary evidence. Weeks, months, before the Exhibition of the Royal Academy, the Bleater's London Correspondent knows the subjects of all the leading pictures, knows what the painters first meant to do, knows what they afterwards substituted for what they first meant to do, knows what they ought to do and won't do, knows what they ought not to do and will do, knows to a letter from whom they have commissions, knows to a shilling how much they are to be paid. Now, no sooner is each studio clear of the remarkable man to whom each studio-occupant has revealed himself as he does not reveal himself to his nearest and dearest bosom friend, than conspiracy and fraud begin. Alfred the Great becomes the Fairy Queen; Moses viewing the Promised Land, turns out to be Moses going to the Fair; Portrait of His Grace the Archbishop of Canterbury, is transformed, as if by irreverent enchantment of the dissenting interest, into A Favourite Terrier, or Cattle Grazing; and the most extraordinary work of art in the list described by the Bleater, is coolly sponged out altogether, and asserted never to have had existence at all, even in the most shadowy thoughts of its executant! This is vile enough, but this is not all. Picture-buyers then come forth from their secret positions, and creep into their places in the assassin-multitude of conspirators. Mr Baring, after expressly telling the Bleater's London Correspondent that he had bought No. 39 for one thousand guineas, gives it up to somebody unknown for a couple of hundred pounds; The Marquis of

LANSDOWNE pretends to have no knowledge whatever of the commissions to which the London Correspondent of the Bleater swore him, but allows a Railway Contractor to cut him out for half the money. Similar examples might be multiplied. Shame, shame, on these men! Is this England?

Sir, look again at Literature. The Bleater's London Correspondent is not merely acquainted with all the eminent writers, but is in possession of the secrets of their souls. He is versed in their hidden meanings and references, sees their manuscripts before publication, and knows the subjects and titles of their books when they are not begun. How dare those writers turn upon the eminent man and depart from every intention they have confided to him? How do they justify themselves in entirely altering their manuscripts, changing their titles, and abandoning their subjects? Will they deny, in the face of Tattlesnivel, that they do so? If they have such hardihood, let the file of the Bleater strike them dumb. By their fruits they shall be known. Let their works be compared with the anticipatory letters of the Bleater's London Correspondent, and their falsehood and deceit will become manifest as the sun; it will be seen that they do nothing which they stand pledged to the Bleater's London Correspondent to do; it will be seen that they are among the blackest parties in this black and base conspiracy. This will become apparent, sir, not only as to their public proceedings but as to their private affairs. The outraged Tattlesnivellian who now drags this infamous combination into the face of day, charges those literary persons with making away with their property, imposing on the Income Tax Commissioners, keeping false books, and entering into sham contracts. He accuses them on the unimpeachable faith of the London Correspondent of the Tattlesnivel Bleater. With whose evidence they will find it impossible to reconcile their own account of any transaction of their lives.

The national character is degenerating under the influence of the ramifications of this tremendous conspiracy. Forgery is committed, constantly. A person of note – any sort of person of note – dies. The Bleater's London Correspondent knows what his circumstances are, what his savings are (if any), who his creditors are, all about his children and relations, and (in general, before his body is cold) describes his will. Is that will ever proved? Never! Some other will is substituted; the real instrument, destroyed. And this (as has been before observed), is England!

Who are the workmen and artificers, enrolled upon the books of this treacherous league? From what funds are they paid, and with what ceremonies are they sworn to secrecy? Are there none such? Observe what follows. A little time ago the Bleater's London Correspondent had this passage: 'Boddleboy is pianoforte playing at St Januarius's Gallery, with pretty tolerable success! He clears three hundred pounds per night. Not bad this!!' The builder of St Januarius's Gallery (plunged to the throat in the conspiracy) met with this piece of news, and observed, with characteristic coarseness, 'that the Bleater's London Correspondent was a Blind Ass.' Being pressed by a man of spirit to give his reasons for this extraordinary statement, he declared that the Gallery, crammed to suffocation, would not hold two hundred pounds, and that its expenses were, probably, at least half what it did hold. The man of spirit (himself a Tattlesnivellian) had the Gallery measured within a week from that hour, and it would *not* hold two hundred pounds! Now, can the poorest capacity doubt that it had been altered in the mean time?

And so the conspiracy extends, through every grade of society, down to the condemned criminal in prison, the hangman, and the Ordinary. Every famous murderer within the last ten years has desecrated his last moments by falsifying his confidences imparted specially to the London Correspondent of the Tattlesnivel Bleater; on every such occasion, Mr Calcraft has followed the degrading example; and the reverend Ordinary, forgetful of his cloth, and mindful only (it would seem, alas!) of the conspiracy, has committed himself to some account or other of the criminal's demeanour and conversation, which has been diametrically opposed to the exclusive information of the London Correspondent of the Bleater. And this (as has been before observed) is Merry England!

A man of true genius, however, is not easily defeated. The Bleater's London Correspondent, probably beginning to suspect the existence of a plot against him, has recently fallen on a new style, which, as being very difficult to countermine, may necessitate the organisation of a new conspiracy. One of his masterly letters, lately, disclosed the adoption of this style – which was remarked with profound sensation throughout Tattlesnivel – in the following passage: 'Mentioning literary small talk, I may tell you that some new and extraordinary rumours are afloat concerning the conversations I have previously mentioned, alleged to have taken place in the first floor front (situated over the street door), of Mr X. Ameter (the poet so well known to your readers), in which, X. Ameter's great uncle, his second son, his butcher, and a corpulent gentleman with one eye universally respected at Kensington, are said not to have been on the most friendly footing; I forbear, however, to pursue the subject further, this week, my informant not being able to supply me with exact particulars.'

But, enough, sir. The inhabitant of Tattlesnivel who has taken pen in hand to expose this odious association of unprincipled men against a shining (local) character, turns from it with disgust and contempt. Let him in few words strip the remaining flimsy covering from the nude object of the conspirators, and his loathsome task is ended.

Sir, that object, he contends, is evidently twofold. First, to exhibit the London Correspondent of the Tattlesnivel Bleater in the light of a mischievous Blockhead who, by hiring himself out to tell what he cannot possibly know, is as great a public nuisance as a Blockhead in a corner can be. Second, to suggest to the men of Tattlesnivel that it does not improve their town to have so much Dry Rubbish shot there.

Now, sir, on both these points Tattlesnivel demands in accents of Thunder, Where is the Attorney-General? Why doesn't THE TIMES take it up? (Is the latter in the conspiracy? It never adopts his views, or quotes him, and incessantly contradicts him.) Tattlesnivel, sir, remembering that our forefathers contended with the Norman at Hastings, and bled at a variety of other places that will readily occur to you, demands that its birthright shall not be bartered away for a mess of potage. Have a care, sir, have a care! Or Tattlesnivel (its idle Rifles piled in its scouted streets) may be seen ere long, advancing with its Bleater to the foot of the Throne, and demanding redress for this conspiracy, from the orbed and sceptred hands of Majesty itself!

5

The Uncommercial Traveller

All The Year Round, 28 January 1860 (*UT1* as 'His General Line of Business' and 'The Shipwreck')

On 29 December 1859 Dickens travelled to the village of Llanallgo in Anglesey to inspect the site of the wreck of the *Royal Charter*, a full-rigged iron liner en route to Liverpool from Melbourne with 498 passengers on board and £800,000 in gold specie and bullion. After a good passage as far as Holyhead, the ship met fearsome gales and was driven off course, and sank on the night of 26 October 1859, holed by rocks in Muffa Redwharf Bay. Only thirty-nine of those on board survived. Later reports have suggested that the Captain's judgement was impaired by heavy drinking on the leg from Queenstown to Holyhead (see Jack Shaw, 'The Wreck of the "Royal Charter", 1859', *The Dickensian*, Vol. 3 [1907], pp. 185–6). By the time of Dickens's visit, numerous factual accounts had already appeared in the newspapers, along with graphic depictions of the disaster (e.g. in the *Illustrated London News*, 29 October 1859, p. 413; 5 November 1859, pp. 447–8). As in Dickens's account here, there was some dwelling on the practical difficulties which the local Church of Wales clergyman, the Rev. Stephen Roose Hughes, found in burying 145 corpses in a small parish churchyard. After the publication of the first volume edition of *The Uncommercial Traveller* in December 1860, opinion was mixed as to the propriety of Dickens's praise of the priest; the *Saturday Review* considered it 'questionable taste' to have 'thus placarded ... the virtues of a Welsh clergyman ... for helping the sufferers' (23 February 1861, p. 195), while the *Morning Chronicle* asserted that 'so long as our language endures will this marvellous narrative of the wreck be read, and the good deeds of the Rev. Stephen Roose Hughes ... be remembered' (10 January 1861, p. 2, col. b).

The almost morbid interest in the burial process revealed by Dickens's narrator here may be partly explained by the fact that four of his relations by marriage had been drowned in the shipwreck. These were Robert and Peter Hogarth, the latter's wife, Georgina, and young son Robert: all cousins of Catherine Dickens, but also, of course, cousins of Georgina and the late Mary Hogarth, whose memory Dickens cherished with such extravagant tenderness. He had doubtless heard pleasant reports of Robert and Peter from Mary, who had spent part of her seventeen years at their family home at 'dear happy Scremerston' in Northumbria (see *Pilgrim*, Vol. I, pp. 689–90). The body of Robert Hogarth Jr was never recovered, but those of the three older cousins had been buried by Mr Hughes.

Dickens's reference to the possibility of 'superstitious avoidance of the drowned' among the peasantry is illuminated by Walter Scott's note to Chapter 8 of *The Pirate* (1821) concerning an 'inhuman superstition' common among the 'lower orders' that 'to save a drowning man was to run the risk of future injury from him'. This had sometimes led to local people refusing their aid when a ship was wrecked on their shores, but the practice, while 'almost general' in the early eighteenth century, had by 1800 been 'weeded out by the sedulous instructions of the clergy and the rigorous injunctions' of landowners.

Dickens seems to have spent the night of 30 December 1859 at the Rectory in Llanallgo (see letter from D. W. Irons, 'A Letter from Wales', *The Dickensian*, Vol. 80 [1984], p. 177) and to have drafted the paper fairly soon after his return to London. By 10 January, he was able to send a printer's proof to Mr Hughes for the correction of details, and to return, by the same post, grateful letters to Hughes from relatives of the victims, which Dickens had excerpted liberally in his article. He remarks in his covering letter that 'I have written [the essay] out of the honest convictions of my heart.... It says for me, all that I should otherwise have attempted to say to you in this note, and merely strives to express what any visitor to you must surely feel' (*Pilgrim*, Vol. IX, pp. 196–7).

Literary allusions (p. 32) 'flourishing of trumpets': Matthew 6:2 ('do not sound a trumpet before thee'); (p.32) 'weeping and wailing': Jeremiah 9:10;

(p. 38) 'not left off your kindness to the living and the dead': Ruth 2:20.

Textual note As with all the papers published in the first two series of 'The Uncommercial Traveller' papers in 1860 and 1863, this item appeared untitled under that heading in *ATYR* (Vol. 2, pp. 321–6), and was later given titles by Dickens for the volume edition. Back-page advertisements in *ATYR* at the time announced 'The Uncommercial Traveller / a Series of Occasional Journeys / By Charles Dickens', this being the first time Dickens had given advance notice of authorship of any of his journalism. In all volume editions, including *UT1*, the first four paragraphs of this item were printed as a separate introductory chapter called 'His General Line of Business', omitting the final sentence of paragraph four, and the remaining paragraphs were printed as a second chapter, titled 'The Shipwreck'.

Allow me to introduce myself – first, negatively.

No landlord is my friend and brother, no chambermaid loves me, no waiter worships me, no boots admires and envies me. No round of beef or tongue or ham is expressly cooked for me, no pigeon-pie is especially made for me, no hotel-advertisement is personally addressed to me, no hotel-room tapestried with greatcoats and railway-wrappers is set apart for me, no house of public entertainment in the United Kingdom greatly cares for my opinion of its brandy or its sherry. When I go upon my journeys, I am not usually rated at a low figure in the bill; when I come home from my journeys, I never get any commission. I know nothing about prices, and should have no idea, if I were put to it, how to wheedle a man into ordering something he doesn't want. As a town traveller, I am never to be seen driving a vehicle externally like a young and volatile pianoforte van, and internally like an oven in which a number of flat boxes are baking in layers. As a country traveller, I am rarely to be found in a gig, and am never to be encountered by a pleasure train, waiting on the platform of a branch station, quite a Druid in the midst of a light Stonehenge of samples.

And yet – proceeding now, to introduce myself positively – I am both a town traveller and a country traveller, and am always on the road. Figuratively speaking, I travel for the great house of Human Interest Brothers, and have rather a large connexion in the fancy goods way. Literally speaking, I am always wandering here and there from my rooms in Covent-garden, London – now about the City streets: now about the country bye-roads – seeing many little things, and some great things, which, because they interest me, I think may interest others.

These are my brief credentials as the Uncommercial Traveller. Business is business, and I start.

Never had I seen a year going out, or going on, under quieter circumstances. Eighteen hundred and fifty-nine had but another day to live, and truly its end was Peace on that sea-shore that morning. So settled and orderly was everything seaward, in the bright light of the sun and under the transparent shadows of the clouds, that it was hard to imagine the bay otherwise, for years past or to come, than it was that very day. The Tug-steamer lying a little off the shore, the Lighter lying still nearer to the shore, the boat alongside the Lighter, the regularly turning windlass aboard the Lighter, the methodical figures at work, all slowly and regularly heaving up and down with the breathing of the sea, all seemed as much a part of the nature of the place as the tide itself. The tide was on the flow, and had been for some two hours and a half; there was a slight obstruction in the sea within a few yards of my feet: as if the stump of a tree, with earth enough about it to keep it from lying horizontally on the water, had slipped a little from the land – and as I stood upon the beach, and observed it dimpling the light swell that was coming in, I cast a stone over it.

So orderly, so quiet, so regular – the rising and falling of the Tug-steamer, the Lighter, and the boat – the turning of the windlass – the coming in of the tide – that I myself seemed, to my own thinking, anything but new to the spot. Yet, I had never seen it in my life, a minute before, and had traversed two hundred miles to get at it. That very morning I had come bowling down, and struggling up, hill-country roads; looking back at snowy summits; meeting courteous peasants, well to do, driving fat pigs and cattle to market; noting the neat and thrifty dwellings, with their unusual quantity of clean white linen, drying on the bushes; having windy weather suggested by every cotter's little rick, with its thatch straw-ridged and extra straw-ridged into overhanging compartments, like the back of a rhinoceros. Had I not given a lift of fourteen miles to the Coast-Guardsman (kit and all), who was coming to his spell of duty there, and had we not just now parted company? So it was; but the journey seemed to glide down into the placid sea, with other chafe and trouble, and for the moment nothing was so calmly and monotonously real under the sunlight as the gentle rising and falling of the water with its freight, the regular turning of the windlass aboard the Lighter, and the slight obstruction so very near my feet.

O reader, haply turning this page by the fireside at Home and hearing the night wind rumble in the chimney, that slight obstruction was the uppermost fragment of the Wreck of the Royal Charter, Australian trader and passenger ship, Homeward bound, that struck here on the terrible morning of the twenty-sixth of last October, broke into three parts, went down with her treasure of at least five hundred human lives, and has never stirred since!

From which point, or from which, she drove ashore, stern foremost; on which side, or on which, she passed the little Island in the bay, for ages henceforth to be aground certain yards outside her; these are rendered bootless questions by the darkness of that night and the darkness of death. Here she went down.

Even as I stood on the beach with the words 'Here she went down!' in my ears, a diver in his grotesque dress, dipped heavily over the side of the boat alongside the Lighter, and dropped to the bottom. On the shore by the water's edge, was a rough tent, made of fragments of wreck, where other divers and workmen sheltered themselves, and where they had kept Christmas-day with rum and roast beef, to the destruction of their frail chimney. Cast up among the stones and boulders of the beach were great spars of the lost vessel, and masses of iron twisted by the fury of the sea into the strangest forms. The timber was already bleached, and iron rusted; and even these objects did no violence to the prevailing air the whole scene wore, of having been exactly the same for years and years.

Yet, only two short months had gone, since a man, living on the nearest hill-top overlooking the sea, being blown out of bed at about day-break by the wind that had begun to strip his roof off, and getting upon a ladder with his nearest neighbour to construct some temporary device for keeping his house over his head, saw, from the ladder's elevation as he looked down by chance towards the shore, some dark troubled object close in with the land. And he and the other, descending to the beach, and finding the sea mercilessly beating over a great broken ship, had clambered up the stony ways like staircases without stairs, on which the wild village hangs in little clusters, as fruit hangs on boughs, and had given the alarm. And so, over the hill-slopes, and past the waterfall, and down the gullies where the land drains off into the ocean, the scattered quarrymen and fishermen inhabiting that part of Wales had come running to the dismal sight – their clergyman among them. And as they stood in the leaden morning, stricken with pity, leaning hard against the wind, their breath and vision often failing as the sleet and spray rushed at them from the ever forming and dissolving mountains of sea, and as the wool which was a part of the vessel's cargo blew in with the salt foam and remained upon the land when the foam melted, they saw the ship's life-boat put off from one of the heaps of wreck; and first, there were three men in her, and in a moment she capsized, and there were but two; and again, she was struck by a vast mass of water, and there was but one; and again, she was thrown bottom upward, and that one, with his arm struck through the broken planks and waving as if for the help that could never reach him, went down into the deep.

It was the clergyman himself from whom I heard this, while I stood on the shore, looking in his kind wholesome face as it turned to the spot where the boat had been. The divers were down then, and busy. They were 'lifting' today the gold found yesterday – some five-and-twenty thousand pounds. Of three hundred and fifty thousand pounds worth of gold, three hundred thousand pounds worth, in round numbers, was at that time recovered. The great bulk of the remainder was surely and steadily coming up. Some loss of sovereigns there would be, of course; indeed, at first sovereigns had drifted in with the sand, and been scattered far and wide over the beach, like sea-shells; but most other golden treasure would be found. As it was brought up, it went aboard the Tug-steamer, where good account was taken of it. So tremendous had the force of the sea been when it broke the ship, that it had beaten one great ingot of gold deep into a strong and heavy piece of her solid iron-work: in which, also, several loose sovereigns, that the ingot had swept in before it, had been found, as firmly embedded as though the iron had been liquid when they were forced there. It had been remarked of such bodies come ashore, too, as had been seen by scientific men, that they had been stunned to death, and not suffocated. Observation, both of the internal change that had been wrought in them, and of their external expression, showed death to have been thus merciful and easy. The report was brought, while I was holding such discourse on the beach, that no more bodies had come ashore since last night. It began to be very doubtful whether many more would be thrown up until the north-east winds of the early spring set in. Moreover, a great number of the passengers, and particularly the second-class women-passengers, were known to have been in the middle of the ship when she parted, and thus the collapsing wreck would have fallen upon them after yawning open, and would keep them down. A diver made known, even then, that he had come upon the body of a man, and had sought to release it from a great super-incumbent weight; but that, finding he could not do so without mutilating the remains, he had left it where it was.

It was the kind and wholesome face I have made mention of as being then beside me, that I had purposed to myself to see, when I left home for Wales. I had heard of that clergyman, as having buried many scores of the shipwrecked people; of his having opened his house and heart to their agonised friends; of his having used a most sweet and patient diligence for weeks and weeks, in the performance of the forlornest offices that Man can render to his kind; of his having most tenderly and thoroughly devoted himself to the dead, and to those who were sorrowing for the dead. I had said to myself, 'In the Christmas season of the year,

I should like to see that man!' And he had swung the gate of his little garden in coming out to meet me, not half an hour ago.

So cheerful of spirit and guiltless of affectation, as true practical Christianity ever is! I read more of the New Testament in the fresh frank face going up the village beside me, in five minutes, than I have read in anathematising discourses (albeit put to press with enormous flourishing of trumpets), in all my life. I heard more of the Sacred Book in the cordial voice that had nothing to say about its owner, than in all the would-be celestial pairs of bellows that have ever blown conceit at me.

We climbed towards the little church, at a cheery pace, among the loose stones, the deep mud, the wet coarse grass, the outlying water, and other obstructions from which frost and snow had lately thawed. It was a mistake (my friend was glad to tell me, on the way) to suppose that the peasantry had shown any superstitious avoidance of the drowned; on the whole, they had done very well, and had assisted readily. Ten shillings had been paid for the bringing of each body up to the church, but the way was steep, and a horse and cart (in which it was wrapped in a sheet) were necessary, and three or four men, and, all things considered, it was not a great price. The people were none the richer for the wreck, for it was the season of the herring-shoal – and who could cast nets for fish, and find dead men and women in the draught?

He had the church keys in his hand, and opened the churchyard gate, and opened the church door; and we went in.

It is a little church of great antiquity; there is reason to believe that some church has occupied the spot, these thousand years or more. The pulpit was gone, and other things usually belonging to the church were gone, owing to its living congregation having deserted it for the neighbouring schoolroom, and yielded it up to the dead. The very Commandments had been shouldered out of their places, in the bringing in of the dead; the black wooden tables on which they were painted were askew, and on the stone pavement below them, and on the stone pavement all over the church, were the marks and stains where the drowned had been laid down. The eye, with little or no aid from the imagination, could yet see how the bodies had been turned, and where the head had been and where the feet. Some faded traces of the wreck of the Australian ship may be discernible on the stone pavement of this little church, hundreds of years hence, when the digging for gold in Australia shall have long and long ceased out of the land.

Forty-four shipwrecked men and women lay here at one time, awaiting burial. Here, with weeping and wailing in every room of his house, my companion worked alone for hours, solemnly surrounded by eyes that could not see him, and by lips that could not speak to him, patiently examining the tattered clothing, cutting off buttons, hair, marks from linen, anything that might lead to subsequent identification, studying faces, looking for a scar, a bent finger, a crooked toe, comparing letters sent to him with the ruin about him. 'My dearest brother had bright grey eyes and a pleasant smile,' one sister wrote. O poor sister! well for you to be far from here, and keep that as your last remembrance of him!

The ladies of the clergyman's family, his wife and two sisters-in-law, came in among the bodies often. It grew to be the business of their lives to do so. Any new arrival of a bereaved woman would stimulate their pity to compare the description brought, with the dead realities. Sometimes, they would go back, able to say, 'I have found him,' or, 'I think she lies there.' Perhaps the mourner, unable to bear the sight of all that lay in the church, would be led in blindfold. Conducted to the spot with many compassionate words, and encouraged to look, she would say, with a piercing cry, 'This is my boy!' and drop insensible on the insensible figure.

He soon observed that in some cases of women, the identification of persons, though complete, was quite at variance with the marks upon the linen; this led him to notice that even the marks upon the linen were sometimes inconsistent with one another; and thus he came to understand that they had dressed in great haste and agitation, and that their clothes had become mixed together. The identification of men by their dress, was rendered extremely difficult, in consequence of a large proportion of them being dressed alike – in clothes of one kind, that is to say supplied by slopsellers and outfitters, and not made by single garments, but by hundreds. Many of the men were bringing over parrots, and had receipts upon them for the price of the birds; others had bills of exchange in their pockets, or in belts. Some of these documents, carefully unwrinkled and dried, were little less fresh in appearance that day, than the present page will be under ordinary circumstances, after having been opened three or four times.

In that lonely place, it had not been easy to obtain even such common commodities in towns, as ordinary disinfectants. Pitch had been burnt in the church, as the readiest thing at hand, and the frying-pan in which it had bubbled over a brazier of coals was still there, with its ashes. Hard by the Communion-Table, were some boots that had been taken off the drowned and preserved – a gold-digger's boot, cut down the leg for its removal – a trodden down man's ankle-boot with a buff cloth top – and others – soaked and sandy, weedy and salt.

From the church, we passed out into the churchyard. Here, there lay, at that time, one hundred and forty-five bodies, that had come ashore from the wreck. He had buried them, when not identified, in graves containing four each. He had numbered each body in a register describing it, and had placed a corresponding number on each coffin, and over

each grave. Identified bodies he had buried singly, in private graves, in
another part of the churchyard. Several bodies had been exhumed from
the graves of four, as relatives had come from a distance and seen his
register; and, when recognised, these had been reburied in private graves,
so that the mourners might erect separate headstones over the remains.
In all such cases he had performed the funeral service a second time,
and the ladies of his house had attended. There had been no offence in
the poor ashes when they were brought again to the light of day; the
beneficent Earth had already absorbed it. The drowned were buried in
their clothes. To supply the great sudden demand for coffins, he had got
all the neighbouring people handy at tools, to work the livelong day, and
Sunday likewise. The coffins were neatly formed; — I had seen two,
waiting for occupants, under the lee of the ruined walls of a stone hut
on the beach, within call of the tent where the Christmas Feast was held.
Similarly, one of the graves for four was lying open and ready, here, in
the churchyard. So much of the scanty space was already devoted to the
wrecked people, that the villagers had begun to express uneasy doubts
whether they themselves could lie in their own ground, with their
forefathers and descendants, by-and-by. The churchyard being but a step
from the clergyman's dwelling-house, we crossed to the latter; the white
surplice was hanging up near the door, ready to be put on at any time,
for a funeral service.

The cheerful earnestness of this good Christian minister was as
consolatory, as the circumstances out of which it shone were sad. I never
have seen anything more delightfully genuine than the calm dismissal by
himself and his household of all they had undergone, as a simple duty
that was quietly done and ended. In speaking of it, they spoke of it with
great compassion for the bereaved; but laid no stress upon their own
hard share in those weary weeks, except as it had attached many people
to them as friends, and elicited many touching expressions of gratitude.
This clergyman's brother — himself the Clergyman of two adjoining
parishes, who had buried thirty-four of the bodies in his own churchyard,
and who had done to them all that his brother had done as to the larger
number — must be understood as included in the family. He was there,
with his neatly arranged papers, and made no more account of his
trouble than anybody else did. Down to yesterday's post outward, my
clergyman alone had written one thousand and seventy-five letters to
relatives and friends of the lost people. In the absence of all self-assertion,
it was only through my now and then delicately putting a question as
the occasion arose, that I became informed of these things. It was only
when I had remarked again and again, in the church, on the awful
nature of the scene of death he had been required so closely to familiarise
himself with for the soothing of the living, that he had casually said,

without the least abatement of his cheerfulness, 'indeed, it had rendered him unable for a time to eat or drink more than a little coffee now and then, and a piece of bread.'

In this noble modesty, in this beautiful simplicity, in this serene avoidance of the least attempt to 'improve' an occasion which might be supposed to have sunk of its own weight into my heart, I seemed to have happily come, in a few steps, from the churchyard with its open grave, which was the type of Death, to the Christian dwelling side by side with it, which was the type of Resurrection. I never shall think of the former, without the latter. The two will always rest side by side in my memory. If I had lost anyone dear to me in this unfortunate ship, if I had made a voyage from Australia to look at the grave in the churchyard, I should go away thankful to GOD that that house was so close to it, and that its shadow by day and its domestic lights by night fell upon the earth in which its Master had so tenderly laid my dear one's head.

The references that naturally rose out of our conversation, to the descriptions sent down of shipwrecked persons, and to the gratitude of relations and friends, made me very anxious to see some of those letters. I was presently seated before a shipwreck of papers, all bordered with black, and from them I made the following few extracts.

A mother writes:

REVEREND SIR. Amongst the many who perished on your shore was numbered my beloved son. I was only just recovering from a severe illness, and this fearful affliction has caused a relapse, so that I am unable at present to go to identify the remains of the loved and lost. My darling son would have been sixteen on Christmas-day next. He was a most amiable and obedient child, early taught the way of salvation. We fondly hoped that as a British seaman he might be an ornament to his profession, but, 'it is well;' I feel assured my dear boy is now with the redeemed. Oh, he did not wish to go this last voyage! On the fifteenth of October I received a letter from him from Melbourne, date August twelfth; he wrote in high spirits, and in conclusion he says: 'Pray for a fair breeze, mamma, and I'll not forget to whistle for it! and, God permitting, I shall see you and all my little pets again. Good-by, dear mother – good-by, dearest parents. Good-by, dear brother.' Oh, it was indeed an eternal farewell. I do not apologise for thus writing you, for oh, my heart is very sorrowful.

A husband writes:

MY DEAR KIND SIR. Will you kindly inform me whether there are any initials upon the ring and guard you have in possession, found, as the Standard says, last Tuesday? Believe me, my dear sir, when I say that I cannot express my deep gratitude in words sufficiently for your kindness to me on that fearful and appalling day. Will you tell me what I can do for you, and will you write me a consoling letter to prevent my mind from going astray?

A widow writes:

Left in such a state as I am, my friends and I thought it best that my dear husband should be buried where he lies, and, much as I should have liked to have had it otherwise, I must submit. I feel, from all I have heard of you, that you will see it done decently and in order. Little does it signify to us, when the soul has departed, where this poor body lies, but we who are left behind would do all we can to show how we loved them. This is denied me, but it is God's hand that afflicts us, and I try to submit. Some day I may be able to visit the spot, and see where he lies, and erect a simple stone to his memory. Oh! it will be long, long before I forget that dreadful night. Is there such a thing in the vicinity, or any shop in Bangor, to which I could send for a small picture of Moelfra or Llanallgo Church, a spot now sacred to me?

Another widow writes:

I have received your letter this morning, and do thank you most kindly for the interest you have taken about my dear husband, as well for the sentiments yours contains, evincing the spirit of a Christian who can sympathise with those who, like myself, are broken down with grief.

    May God bless and sustain you, and all in connexion with you, in this great trial. Time may roll on, and bear all its sons away, but your name as a disinterested person will stand in history, and, as successive years pass, many a widow will think of your noble conduct, and the tears of gratitude flow down many a cheek, the tribute of a thankful heart, when other things are forgotten for ever.

A father writes:

I am at a loss to find words to sufficiently express my gratitude to you for your kindness to my son Richard, upon the melancholy occasion of his visit to his dear brother's body, and also for your ready attention in pronouncing our beautiful burial service over my poor unfortunate son's remains. God grant that your prayers over him may reach the Mercy

Seat, and that his soul may be received (through Christ's intercession) into heaven!

His dear mother begs me to convey to you her heartfelt thanks.

Those who were received at the clergyman's house, write thus, after leaving it:

DEAR AND NEVER-TO-BE-FORGOTTEN FRIENDS. I arrived here yesterday morning without accident, and am about to proceed to my home by railway.

I am overpowered when I think of you and your hospitable home. No words could speak language suited to my heart. I refrain. God reward you with the same measure you have meted with!

I enumerate no names, but embrace you all.

MY BELOVED FRIENDS. This is the first day that I have been able to leave my bedroom since I returned, which will explain the reason of my not writing sooner.

If I could only have had my last melancholy hope realised in recovering the body of my beloved and lamented son, I should have returned home somewhat comforted, and I think I could then have been comparatively resigned.

I fear now there is but little prospect, and I mourn as one without hope.

The only consolation to my distressed mind is in having been so feelingly allowed by you to leave the matter in your hands, by whom I well know that everything will be done that can be, according to arrangements made before I left the scene of the awful catastrophe, both as to the identification of my dear son, and also his interment.

I feel most anxious to hear whether anything fresh has transpired since I left you; will you add another to the many deep obligations I am under to you by writing to me? And, should the body of my dear and unfortunate son be identified, let me hear from you immediately, and I will come again.

Words cannot express the gratitude I feel I owe to you all for your benevolent aid, your kindness, and your sympathy.

MY DEARLY BELOVED FRIENDS. I arrived in safety at my house yesterday, and a night's rest has restored and tranquillised me. I must again repeat that language has no words by which I can express my sense of obligation to you. You are enshrined in my heart of hearts.

I have seen him! and can now realise my misfortune more than I have hitherto been able to do. Oh, the bitterness of the cup I drink! But I bow submissive. God *must* have done right. I do not want to feel less, but to acquiesce more simply.

There were some Jewish passengers on board the Royal Charter, and the gratitude of the Jewish people is feelingly expressed in the following letter, bearing date from 'the office of the Chief Rabbi:'

REVEREND SIR. I cannot refrain from expressing to you my heartfelt thanks on behalf of those of my flock whose relatives have unfortunately been among those who perished at the late wreck of the Royal Charter. You have indeed, like Boaz, 'not left off your kindness to the living and the dead.'

You have not alone acted kindly towards the living by receiving them hospitably at your house, and energetically assisting them in their mournful duty, but also towards the dead, by exerting yourself to have our co-religionists buried in our ground, and according to our rites. May our heavenly Father reward you for your acts of humanity and true philanthropy!

The 'Old Hebrew congregation of Liverpool' thus express themselves through their secretary:

REVEREND SIR. The wardens of this congregation have learned with great pleasure that, in addition to those indefatigable exertions, at the scene of the late disaster to the Royal Charter, which have received universal recognition, you have very benevolently employed your valuable efforts to assist such members of our faith as have sought the bodies of lost friends to give them burial in our consecrated grounds, with the observances and rites prescribed by the ordinances of our religion.

The wardens desire me to take the earliest available opportunity to offer to you, on behalf of our community, the expression of their warm acknowledgments and grateful thanks, and their sincere wishes for your continued welfare and prosperity.

A Jewish gentleman writes:

REVEREND AND DEAR SIR. I take the opportunity of thanking you right earnestly for the promptness you displayed in answering my note with full particulars concerning my much-lamented brother, and I also herein beg to express my sincere regard for the willingness you displayed and for the facility you afforded for getting the remains of my poor brother exhumed. It has been to us a most sorrowful and painful event, but when we meet with such friends as yourself, it in a measure, somehow or other, abates that mental anguish, and makes the suffering so much easier to be borne. Considering the circumstances connected with my poor brother's fate, it does, indeed, appear a hard one. He had been away in all seven years; he returned four years ago to see his family. He was then engaged to a very amiable young lady. He had been very successful abroad, and was now returning to fulfil his sacred vow; he brought all his property with him in gold uninsured. We heard from him when the ship stopped at Queenstown, when he was in the highest of hope, and in a few short hours afterwards all was washed away.

Mournful in the deepest degree, but too sacred for quotation here, were the numerous references to those miniatures of women, worn round the necks of rough men (and found there after death), those locks of hair, those scraps of letters, those many many slight memorials of hidden tenderness. One man cast up by the sea bore about him, printed on a perforated lace card, the following singular (and unavailing) charm:

A BLESSING

May the blessing of God await thee. May the sun of glory shine around thy bed; and may the gates of plenty, honour, and happiness be ever open to thee. May no sorrow distress thy days; may no grief disturb thy nights. May the pillow of peace kiss thy cheek, and the pleasures of imagination attend thy dreams; and when length of years makes thee tired of earthly joys, and the curtain of death gently closes around thy last sleep of human existence, may the Angel of God attend thy bed, and take care that the expiring lamp of life shall not receive one rude blast to hasten on its extinction.

A sailor had these devices on his right arm. 'Our Saviour on the Cross, the forehead of the Crucifix and the vesture stained red; on the lower part of the arm, a man and woman; on one side of the Cross, the appearance of a half moon, with a face; on the other side, the sun; on the top of the Cross, the letters I.H.S.; on the left arm, a man and woman dancing, with an effort to delineate the female's dress, under which, initials.' Another seaman 'had, on the lower part of the right arm, the device of a sailor and a female; the man holding the Union Jack with a streamer, the folds of which waved over her head, and the end of it was held in her hand. On the upper part of the arm, a device of Our Lord on the Cross, with stars surrounding the head of the Cross, and one large star on the side in Indian ink. On the left arm, a flag, a true lovers' knot, a face, and initials.' This tattooing was found still plain, below the discoloured outer surface of a mutilated arm, when such surface was carefully scraped away with a knife. It is not improbable that the perpetuation of this marking custom among seamen, may be referred back to their desire to be identified, if drowned and flung ashore.

It was some time before I could sever myself from the many interesting papers on the table, and then I broke bread and drank wine with the kind family before I left them. As I brought the Coast-guard down, so I took the Postman back, with his leathern wallet, walking-stick, bugle, and terrier dog. Many a heart-broken letter had he brought to the Rectory House within two months; many a benignantly painstaking answer had he carried back.

As I rode along, I thought of the many people, inhabitants of this mother country, who would make pilgrimages to the little churchyard in the years to come; I thought of the many people in Australia, who would have an interest in such a shipwreck, and would find their way here when they visit the Old World; I thought of the writers of all the wreck of letters I had left upon the table; and I resolved to place this little record where it stands. Convocations, Conferences, Diocesan Epistles, and the like, will do a great deal for Religion, I dare say, and Heaven send they may! but I doubt if they will ever do their Master's service half so well, in all the time they last, as the Heavens have seen it done in this bleak spot upon the rugged coast of Wales.

Had I lost the friend of my life, in the wreck of the Royal Charter; had I lost my betrothed, the more than friend of my life; had I lost my maiden daughter, had I lost my hopeful boy, had I lost my little child; I would kiss the hands that worked so busily and gently in the church, and say, 'None better could have touched the form, though it had lain at home.' I could be sure of it, I could be thankful for it: I could be content to leave the grave near the house the good family pass in and out of every day, undisturbed, in the little churchyard where so many are so strangely brought together.

Without the name of the clergyman to whom − I hope, not without carrying comfort to some heart at some time − I have referred, my reference would be as nothing. He is the Reverend Stephen Roose Hughes, of Llanallgo, near Moelfra, Anglesey. His brother is the Reverend Hugh Robert Hughes, of Penrhos Alligwy.

6

The Uncommercial Traveller

All The Year Round, 18 February 1860 (*UT1* as 'Wapping Workhouse')

'My knowledge of the general conditions of the sick poor in workhouses is not of yesterday,' Dickens wrote in 1866 to the Secretary of the newly formed Association for the Improvement of the Infirmaries of London Workhouses, 'nor are my efforts in my vocation to call merciful attention to it. Few anomalies in England are so horrible to me as the unchecked existence of many shameful sick wards for paupers side by side with the constantly increasing expansion of conventional wonder that the poor should creep into corners and die rather than fester and rot in such places' (*Pilgrim*, Vol. XI [late February 1866], pp. 164–5). Dickens's 'efforts' included the commissioning and publishing of dozens of articles in *HW* and *ATYR* on workhouse conditions, and also the writing of such powerful papers as 'A Walk in a Workhouse' (see Vol. 2 of this edition, article 46), 'A Nightly Scene in London' (see Vol. 3, article 45), and the present article.

In *The Times* of 23 January 1860, a Thames Police Court Magistrate (Henry Selfe) was reported to have said during a case that 'a most disgraceful and painful state of things existed' in the Wapping Workhouse for female paupers, that the place was 'a perfect bear-garden', that 'it was a great shame', and that 'the Guardians of the Stepney Union should look to [it]' (p. 10, cols a, b). Acting on this account, Dickens visited the workhouse sometime before the end of the month, but found its management excellent under the circumstances, as described in the present article. According to *The Times* of 30 January, 'persons in authority had visited the Wapping poorhouse in the course of last week ... and on leaving said the Guardians were a very much ill-used body' (p. 9, cols e, f), which may be a veiled reference to a visit by Dickens and others prior to the writing of the present paper. On 28 January, meanwhile, the Guardians of the Union sent a deputation to the magistrate to defend their arrangements, but Selfe repeated his erroneous accusations that there was no classification among inmates at the Workhouse and no separate ward for Refractories. The deputation pointedly suggested that Selfe should visit the Workhouse himself, which in due course he did, causing Dickens to comment on 10 February that 'it would have been as well if the magistrate ... had so timed *his* visit as to have given it the precedence of his remarks' (*Pilgrim*, Vol. IX, pp. 204–5 & n., 212 & n.). The two Refractories described, who confess to having been 'taken before the magistrate', may be identified from the *Times'* reports as Elizabeth Francis and Elizabeth Regan, two able-bodied paupers.

The reference to 'the fancy-dressing and pantomime-posturing at St George's in [the East]', and, later in the article, to 'these unfortunate dissensions', alludes to another news story of the time. For some months, the Rev. Bryan King, Anglican incumbent of St George's-in-the-East (Cannon Street Road, E1), had been at the centre of disturbances over allegedly 'Romish' innovations in his conduct of divine services and in his own dress. Since the previous autumn, violent anti-Catholic protests reminiscent of the so-called 'Gordon' riots of the 1780s had been proceeding unchecked during services, as neither police commissioners nor the Bishop of London were certain how to proceed (see accounts by Charles Collins, 'Our Eye Witness at Church', *ATYR* I [1 October 1859], pp. 537–40, and in *The Examiner*, 4 February 1860, p. 81, cols a, b); problems continued until 25 July 1860, when Mr King resigned *pro tem.*

The bridge dubbed 'Mr Baker's Trap' has been identified as the swingbridge which formerly carried Old Gravel Lane across the lock connecting two of the London Dock basins. For its popularity with suicides, it was known to locals as 'The Bridge of Sighs' (*The Dickensian*, Vol. 2 [1906], pp. 42–3). Dickens's reference to levels of provision 'at Boston in the state of Massachusetts' shows him recalling an inspection of the Boston House of Industry made on his first Amercian trip and recorded in *American Notes*, Ch. 3. The demand for equalisation of the Poor Rates with which Dickens forcibly concludes his account of the workhouse for women was not to be met until 1894 with the bringing in of the Equalisation of Rates Act and the establishment of Parish Councils. The St George's-in-the-East Workhouse for Women was situated near Cable Street, E1, and was finally demolished in 1868.

Literary allusions (p. 43) 'the constancy of the young woman ... 'baccer-box marked with his name': paraphrases the ballad 'Wapping Old Stairs' set to music by John Perry (d. 1797); the relevant stanza runs:

> Your Molly has never been false she declares,
> Since the last time we parted at Wapping Old Stairs;
> When I said that I still would continue the same
> And gave you the bacco box marked with my name
> When I pass'd a whole fortnight between decks with you,
> Did I e'er give a kiss, Tom, to one of your crew?

(p. 43) 'wisest men of the East': 'wise men from the east', Matthew 2:1; (p.46) 'my honourable friend Mrs Gamp': drunken old nurse and midwife in Dickens's *Martin Chuzzlewit* (1844), Ch. 19 et seq.; (p. 47) 'poetical commission to the baker's man': paraphrase of the nursery rhyme beginning

'Pat-a-cake, pat-a-cake, Baker's man'; (p. 47) 'marshalled me the way that I was going': Shakespeare, *Macbeth*, Act 2, Sc. 2; (p. 49) 'this vault to brag of': Shakespeare, *Macbeth*, Act 2, Sc. 3; (p. 50) 'When Britain first, at Heaven's command ...': from James Thomson's *Alfred, A Masque* (1740), Act 2, Scene the Last, lines later popularised as 'Rule, Britannia'; (p. 51) 'when they had sung an hymn': Mark 14:26.

My day's no-business beckoning me to the East end of London, I had turned my face to that point of the metropolitan compass on leaving Covent Garden, and had got past the India House, thinking in my idle manner of Tippoo-Sahib and Charles Lamb, and had got past my little wooden midshipman, after affectionately patting him on one leg of his knee-shorts for old acquaintance' sake, and had got past Aldgate Pump, and had got past the Saracen's Head (with an ignominious rash of posting-bills disfiguring his swarthy countenance), and had strolled up the empty yard of his ancient neighbour the Black or Blue Boar, or Bull, who departed this life I don't know when, and whose coaches are all gone I don't know where; and I had come out again into the age of railways, and I had got past Whitechapel Church, and was – rather inappropriately for an Uncommercial Traveller – in the Commercial Road. Pleasantly wallowing in the abundant mud of that thoroughfare, and greatly enjoying the huge piles of building belonging to the sugar refiners, the little masts and vanes in small back gardens in back streets, the neighbouring canals and docks, the India-vans lumbering along their stone tramway, and the pawnbrokers' shops where hard-up Mates had pawned so many sextants and quadrants, that I should have bought a few cheap if I had the least notion how to use them, I at last began to file off to the right, towards Wapping.

Not that I intended to take boat at Wapping Old Stairs, or that I was going to look at the locality, because I believe (for I don't) in the constancy of the young woman who told her seagoing lover, to such a beautiful old tune, that she had ever continued the same since she gave him the 'baccer-box marked with his name; I am afraid he usually got the worst of those transactions, and was frightfully taken in. No, I was going to Wapping, because an Eastern police magistrate had said, through the morning papers, that there was no classification at the Wapping workhouse for women, and that it was a disgrace and a shame and divers other hard names, and because I wished to see how the fact really stood. For, that Eastern police magistrates are not always the wisest men of the East, may be inferred from their course of procedure respecting the fancy-dressing and pantomime-posturing at St George's in that quarter: which is usually, to discuss the matter at issue, in a state of mind

betokening the weakest perplexity, with all parties concerned and uncon-
cerned, and, for a final expedient, to consult the complainant as to what
he thinks ought to be done with the defendant, and take the defendant's
opinion as to what he would recommend to be done with himself.

Long before I reached Wapping I gave myself up as having lost my
way, and, abandoning myself to the narrow streets in a Turkish frame
of mind, relied on predestination to bring me somehow or other to the
place I wanted if I were ever to get there. When I had ceased for an
hour or so to take any trouble about the matter, I found myself on a
swing-bridge, looking down at some dark locks in some dirty water. Over
against me, stood a creature remotely in the likeness of a young man,
with a puffed sallow face, and a figure all dirty and shiny and slimy, who
may have been the youngest son of his filthy old father, Thames, or the
drowned man about whom there was a placard on the granite post like
a large thimble, that stood between us.

I asked this apparition what it called the place? Unto which, it replied,
with a ghastly grin and a sound like gurgling water in its throat:

'Mister Baker's trap.'

As it is a point of great sensitiveness with me on such occasions to be
equal to the intellectual pressure of the conversation, I deeply considered
the meaning of this speech, while I eyed the apparition – then engaged
in hugging and sucking a horizontal iron bar at the top of the locks.
Inspiration suggested to me that Mr Baker was the acting Coroner of
that neighbourhood.

'A common place for suicide,' said I, looking down at the locks.

'Sue?' returned the ghost, with a stare. 'Yes! And Poll. Likewise Emily.
And Nancy. And Jane;' he sucked the iron between each name; 'and all the
bileing. Ketches off their bonnets or shorls, takes a run, and headers down
here, they doos. Always a headerin' down here, they is. Like one o'clock.'

'And at about that hour of the morning, I suppose?'

'Ah!' said the apparition. '*They* an't partickler. Two 'ull do for *them*.
Three. All times o' night. On'y mind you!' Here the apparition rested
its profile on the bar, and gurgled in a sarcastic manner. 'There must be
somebody comin'. They don't go a headerin' down here, wen there an't
no Bobby nor gen'ral Cove, fur to hear the splash.'

According to my interpretation of these words, I was myself a General
Cove, or member of the miscellaneous public. In which modest character,
I remarked:

'They are often taken out, are they, and restored?'

'I dunno about restored,' said the apparition, who, for some occult
reason, very much objected to that word; 'they're carried into the werkiss
and put into a 'ot bath, and brought round. But I dunno about restored,'
said the apparition; 'blow *that!*' – and vanished.

As it had shown a desire to become offensive, I was not sorry to find myself alone, especially as the 'werkiss' it had indicated with a twist of its matted head, was close at hand. So I left Mr Baker's terrible trap (baited with a scum that was like the soapy rinsing of sooty chimneys), and made bold to ring at the workhouse gate, where I was wholly unexpected and quite unknown.

A very bright and nimble little matron, with a bunch of keys in her hand, responded to my request to see the House. I began to doubt whether the police magistrate was quite right in his facts, when I noticed her quick active little figure and her intelligent eyes.

The Traveller (the matron intimated) should see the worst first. He was welcome to see everything. Such as it was, there it all was.

This was the only preparation for our entering 'the Foul wards.' They were in an old building squeezed away in a corner of a paved yard, quite detached from the more modern and spacious main body of the workhouse. They were in a building most monstrously behind the time – a mere series of garrets or lofts, with every inconvenient and objectionable circumstance in their construction, and only accessible by steep and narrow staircases, infamously ill adapted for the passage upstairs of the sick, or downstairs of the dead.

A-bed in these miserable rooms, here on bedsteads, there (for a change, as I understood it) on the floor, were women in every stage of distress and disease. None but those who have attentively observed such scenes can conceive the extraordinary variety of expression still latent under the general monotony and uniformity of colour, attitude, and condition. The form a little coiled up and turned away, as though it had turned its back on this world for ever; the uninterested face, at once lead-coloured and yellow, looking passively upward from the pillow; the haggard mouth a little dropped, the hand outside the coverlet, so dull and indifferent, so light and yet so heavy; these were on every pallet; but, when I stopped beside a bed, and said ever so slight a word to the figure lying there, the ghost of the old character came into the face, and made the Foul ward as various as the fair world. No one appeared to care to live, but no one complained; all who could speak, said that as much was done for them as could be done there, that the attendance was kind and patient, that their suffering was very heavy, but they had nothing to ask for. The wretched rooms were as clean and sweet as it is possible for such rooms to be; they would become a pest-house in a single week, if they were ill-kept.

I accompanied the brisk matron up another barbarous staircase, into a better kind of loft devoted to the idiotic and imbecile. There was at least Light in it, whereas the windows in the former wards had been like sides of school-boys' birdcages. There was a strong grating over the fire here, and, holding a kind of state on either side of the hearth, separated by the breadth of this grating, were two old ladies in a condition of feeble dignity, which was surely the very last and lowest reduction of self-complacency, to be found in this wonderful humanity of ours. They were evidently jealous of each other, and passed their whole time (as some people do, whose fires are not grated) in mentally disparaging each other, and contemptuously watching their neighbours. One of these parodies on provincial gentlewomen was extremely talkative, and expressed a strong desire to attend the service on Sundays, from which she represented herself to have derived the greatest interest and consolation when allowed that privilege. She gossiped so well, and looked altogether so cheery and harmless, that I began to think this a case for the Eastern magistrate, until I found that, on the last occasion of her attending chapel, she had secreted a small stick, and had caused some confusion in the responses by suddenly producing it and belabouring the congregation.

So, these two old ladies, separated by the breadth of the grating – otherwise they would fly at one another's caps – sat all day long, suspecting one another, and contemplating a world of fits. For everybody else in the room had fits, except the wardswoman: an elderly, able-bodied pauperess, with a large upper lip, and an air of repressing and saving her strength, as she stood with her hands folded before her, and her eyes slowly rolling, biding her time for catching or holding somebody. This civil personage (in whom I regretted to identify a reduced member of my honourable friend Mrs Gamp's family) said, 'They has 'em continiwal, sir. They drops without no more notice than if they was coach-horses dropped from the moon, sir. And, when one drops, another drops, and sometimes there'll be as many as four or five on 'em at once, dear me, a rollin' and a tearin', bless you! – this young woman, now, has 'em dreadful bad.'

She turned up this young woman's face with her hand as she said it. This young woman was seated on the floor, pondering, in the foreground of the afflicted. There was nothing repellant either in her face or head. Many, apparently worse, varieties of epilepsy and hysteria were about her, but she was said to be the worst there. When I had spoken to her a little, she still sat with her face turned up, pondering, and a gleam of the mid-day sun shone in upon her.

—Whether this young woman, and the rest of these so sorely troubled, as they sit or lie pondering in their confused dull way, ever get mental glimpses among the motes in the sun-light, of healthy people and healthy things? Whether this young woman, brooding like this in the summer season, ever thinks that somewhere there are trees and flowers, even mountains and the great sea? Whether, not to go so far, this young woman ever has any dim revelation of that young woman – that young woman who is not here and never will come here, who is courted, and caressed, and loved, and has a husband, and bears children, and lives in a home, and who never knows what it is to have this lashing and tearing coming upon her? And whether this young woman, God help her, gives herself up then, and drops like a coach-horse from the moon?

I hardly knew whether the voices of infant children, penetrating into so hopeless a place, made a sound that was pleasant or painful to me. It was something to be reminded that the weary world was not all weary, and was ever renewing itself; but, this young woman was a child not long ago, and a child not long hence might be such as she. Howbeit, the active step and eye of the vigilant matron conducted me past the two provincial gentlewomen (whose dignity was ruffled by the children), and into the adjacent nursery.

There were many babies here, and more than one handsome young mother. There were ugly young mothers also, and sullen young mothers, and callous young mothers. But, the babies had not appropriated to themselves any bad expression yet, and might have been, for anything that appeared to the contrary in their soft faces, Princes Imperial and Princesses Royal. I had the pleasure of giving a poetical commission to the baker's man to make a cake with all despatch, and toss it into the oven for one red-headed young pauper and myself, and felt much the better for it. Without that refreshment, I doubt if I should have been in a condition for 'the Refractories,' towards whom my quick little matron – for whose adaptation to her office I had by this time conceived a genuine respect – drew me next, and marshalled me the way that I was going.

The Refractories were picking oakum, in a small room giving on a yard. They sat in line on a form, with their backs to a window; before them, a table, and their work. The oldest Refractory was, say twenty; youngest Refractory, say sixteen. I have never yet ascertained, in the course of my uncommercial travels, why a Refractory habit should affect the tonsils and uvula; but, I have always observed that Refractories of both sexes and every grade, between a Ragged School and the Old Bailey, have one voice, in which the tonsils and uvula gain a diseased ascendancy.

'Five pound, indeed! I hain't a going fur to pick five pound,' said the Chief of the Refractories, keeping time to herself with her head and chin. 'More than enough to pick what we picks now, in sitch a place as this, and on wot we gets here!'

(This was in acknowledgment of a delicate intimation that the amount of work was likely to be increased. It certainly was not heavy then, for one Refractory had already done her day's task – it was barely two o'clock – and was sitting behind it, with a head exactly matching it.)

'A pretty Ouse this is, matron, ain't it?' said Refractory Two, 'where a pleeseman's called in, if a gal says a word!'

'And wen you're sent to prison for nothink or less!' said the Chief, tugging at her oakum, as if it were the matron's hair. 'But any place is better than this; that's one thing, and be thankful!'

A laugh of Refractories, led by Oakum Head with folded arms – who originated nothing, but who was in command of the skirmishers outside the conversation.

'If any place is better than this,' said my brisk guide, in the calmest manner, 'it is a pity you left a good place when you had one.'

'Ho, no, I didn't, matron,' returned the Chief, with another pull at her oakum, and a very expressive look at the enemy's forehead. 'Don't say that, matron, 'cos it's lies!'

Oakum Head brought up the skirmishers again, skirmished, and retired.

'And *I* warn't a going,' exclaimed Refractory Two, 'though I was in one place for as long as four year – *I* warn't a going fur to stop in a place that warn't fit for me – there! And where the fam'ly warn't 'spectable characters – there! And where I fort'nately or hunfort'nately found that the people warn't what they pretended to make theirselves out to be – there! And where it wasn't their faults, by chalks, if I warn't made bad and ruinated – Hah!'

During this speech, Oakum Head had again made a diversion with the skirmishers, and had again withdrawn.

The Uncommercial Traveller ventured to remark that he supposed Chief Refractory and Number Two, to be the two young women who had been taken before the magistrate?

'Yes!' said the Chief, 'we har! and the wonder is, that a pleeseman an't 'ad in now, and we took off agen. You can't open your lips here, without a pleeseman.'

Number Two laughed (very uvularly), and the skirmishers followed suit.

'I'm sure I'd be thankful,' protested the Chief, looking sideways at the Uncommercial, 'if I could be got into a place, or got abroad. I'm sick and tired of this precious Ouse, I am, with reason.'

So would be, and so was, Number Two. So would be, and so was, Oakum Head. So would be, and so were, Skirmishers.

The Uncommercial took the liberty of hinting that he hardly thought it probable that any lady or gentleman in want of a likely young domestic of retiring manners, would be tempted into the engagement of either of the two leading Refractories, on her presentation of herself as per sample.

'It ain't no good being nothink else here,' said the Chief.

The Uncommercial thought it might be worth trying.

'Oh no it ain't,' said the Chief.

'Not a bit of good,' said Number Two.

'And I'm sure I'd be very thankful to be got into a place, or got abroad,' said the Chief.

'And so should I,' said Number Two. 'Truly thankful, I should.'

Oakum Head then rose, and announced as an entirely new idea, the mention of which profound novelty might be naturally expected to startle her unprepared hearers, that she would be very thankful to be got into a place, or got abroad. And, as if she had then said, 'Chorus, ladies!' all the Skirmishers struck up to the same purpose. We left them, thereupon, and began a long long walk among the women who were simply old and infirm; but whenever, in the course of this same walk, I looked out of any high window that commanded the yard, I saw Oakum Head with all the other Refractories looking out at their low window for me, and never failing to catch me, the moment I showed my head.

In ten minutes I had ceased to believe in such fables of a golden time as youth, the prime of life, or a hale old age. In ten minutes, all the lights of womankind seemed to have been blown out, and nothing in that way to be left this vault to brag of, but the flickering and expiring snuffs.

And what was very curious, was, that these dim old women had one company notion which was the fashion of the place. Every old woman who became aware of a visitor, and was not in bed, hobbled over a form into her accustomed seat, and became one of a line of dim old women confronting another line of dim old women across a narrow table. There was no obligation whatever upon them to range themselves in this way; it was their manner of 'receiving.' As a rule, they made no attempt to talk to one another, or to look at the visitor, or to look at anything, but sat silently working their mouths, like a sort of poor old Cows. In some of these wards, it was good to see a few green plants; in others, an isolated Refractory acting as nurse, who did well enough in that capacity when separated from her compeers; every one of these wards, day room, night room, or both combined, was scrupulously clean and fresh. I have seen as many such places as most travellers in my line, and I never saw one such, better kept.

Among the bedridden there was great patience, great reliance on the books under the pillow, great faith in GOD. All cared for sympathy, but none much cared to be encouraged with hope of recovery; on the whole, I should say, it was considered rather a distinction to have a complication of disorders, and to be in a worse way than the rest. From some of the windows the river could be seen, with all its life and movement; the day was bright, but I came upon no one who was looking out.

In one large ward, sitting by the fire in armchairs of distinction, like the President and Vice of the good company, were two old women, upwards of ninety years of age. The younger of the two, just turned ninety, was deaf, but not very, and could easily be made to hear. In her early time she had nursed a child, who was now another old woman, more infirm than herself, inhabiting the very same chamber. She perfectly understood this when the matron told it, and, with sundry nods and motions of her forefinger, pointed out the woman in question. The elder of this pair, ninety-three, seated before an illustrated newspaper (but not reading it), was a bright-eyed old soul, really not deaf, wonderfully preserved, and amazingly conversational. She had not long lost her husband, and had been in that place little more than a year. At Boston, in the State of Massachusetts, this poor creature would have been individually addressed, would have been tended in her own room, and would have had her life gently assimilated to a comfortable life out of doors. Would that be much to do in England for a woman who has kept herself out of a workhouse more than ninety rough long years? When Britain first, at Heaven's command, arose, with a great deal of allegorical confusion, from out the azure main, did her guardian angels positively forbid it in the Charter which has been so much be-sung?

The object of my journey was accomplished when the nimble matron had no more to show me. As I shook hands with her at the gate, I told her that I thought Justice had not used her very well, and that the wise men of the East were not infallible.

Now, I reasoned with myself, as I made my journey home again, concerning those Foul wards. They ought not to exist; no person of common decency and humanity can see them and doubt it. But what is this Union to do? The necessary alteration would cost several thousands of pounds; it has already to support three workhouses; its inhabitants work hard for their bare lives, and are already rated for the relief of the Poor to the utmost extent of reasonable endurance. One poor parish in this very Union is rated to the amount of FIVE AND SIXPENCE in the pound, at the very same time when the rich parish of Saint George's, Hanover-square, is rated at about SEVENPENCE in the pound, Paddington at about FOURPENCE, Saint James's, Westminster, at about TENPENCE! It is only through the equalisation of Poor Rates that what is left undone in this wise can be done. Much more is left undone, or is ill-done, than I have space to suggest in these notes of a single uncommercial journey; but, the wise men of the East, before they can reasonably hold forth about it, must look to the North and South and West; let them also, any morning before taking the seat of Solomon, look into the shops and dwellings all around the Temple, and first ask themselves 'How much more can these poor people – many of whom keep themselves with difficulty enough out of the workhouse – bear?'

I had yet other matter for reflection, as I journeyed home, inasmuch as, before I altogether departed from the neighbourhood of Mr Baker's trap, I had knocked at the gate of the workhouse of St George's-in-the-East, and had found it to be an establishment highly creditable to those parts, and thoroughly well administered by a most intelligent master. I remarked in it, an instance of the collateral harm that obstinate vanity and folly can do. 'This was the Hall where those old paupers, male and female, whom I had just seen, met for the Church service, was it?' – 'Yes.' – 'Did they sing the Psalms to any instrument?' – 'They would like to very much; they would have an extraordinary interest in doing so.' – 'And could none be got?' – 'Well, a piano could even have been got for nothing, but these unfortunate dissensions –' Ah! better, far better, my Christian friend in the beautiful garment, to have left the singing boys alone, and left the multitude to sing for themselves! You should know better than I, but I think I have read that they did so, once upon a time, and that 'when they had sung an hymn,' Some one (not in a beautiful garment) went up unto the Mount of Olives.

It made my heart ache to think of this miserable trifling, in the streets of a city where every stone seemed to call to me, as I walked along, 'Turn this way, man, and see what waits to be done!' So I decoyed myself into another train of thought to ease my heart. But, I don't know that I did it, for I was so full of paupers, that it was, after all, only a change to a single pauper, who took possession of my remembrance instead of a thousand.

'I beg your pardon, sir,' he had said, in a confidential manner, on another occasion, taking me aside; 'but I have seen better days.'

'I am very sorry to hear it.'

'Sir, I have a complaint to make against the master.'

'I have no power here, I assure you. And if I had—'

'But allow me, sir, to mention it, as between yourself and a man who has seen better days, sir. The master and myself are both masons, sir, and I make him the sign continually; but, because I am in this unfortunate position, sir, he won't give me the countersign!'

7

The Uncommercial Traveller

All The Year Round, 25 February 1860 (*UT1* as 'Two Views of a Cheap Theatre')

The 'cheap theatre' in question was the Britannia Theatre on Old St, Hoxton, which had been entirely rebuilt by its owner Samuel Lane in 1858. On its former incarnation, the 'Britannia Saloon', Dickens had already reported in 1850 (see Vol. 2 of this edition, article 42). For a comprehensive history of the theatre's construction and management, see Jim Davis's *The Britannia Diaries, 1863–75* (1992). According to Dickens's former *HW* colleague John Hollingshead, the theatre became 'familiar to most theatrical people and to many others' through the publication of this essay (*My Lifetime* [1895]; Vol. I, p. 33).

The 'two views' offered are of the audience and bill of fare at a Saturday night pantomime ('Needles and Pins. The Spirit of Liberty') and melodrama ('The Mysterious Unknown; or, The Maid and the Mirror'), and of the audience the following Sunday evening, when a sermon was preached. Dickens's correspondence shows him planning to make these expeditions on 28 and 29 January 1860, in the company of Wilkie Collins and Edmund Yates on the Saturday, and of Collins alone on the Sunday. An instructive parallel to Dickens's paper can be found in Yates's bland essay 'Preaching in Playhouses', clearly based on the same experience, reprinted in the volume *After Office Hours* (1861, pp. 193–9). In his letter to Collins, Dickens asks him to '... Observe. I have said nothing to Y. of the reason of the visit, or of the Sunday notion. Nor shall I mention the latter, even to Mr Lane the proprietor' (*Pilgrim*, Vol. IX, p. 201). Dickens's caution is perhaps because of the politically sensitive nature of his publishing an account of the Sunday service. Only a few weeks earlier, the newly formed United Commission for Special Services (whose committee included Lord Shaftesbury and members of the London City Mission) had opened five London theatres for 'special services' in the hope of spreading the basic Gospel message beyond the confines of conventional church congregations. In Parliament, the event had not gone unnoticed, and only the day before Dickens's account was published, Viscount Dungannon had condemned the scheme in the House of Lords, stressing the danger to orthodox religion posed by dubious theatrical mores (*Hansard*, 3rd Series, 24 February 1860, Vol. CLVI, p. 1663). When Dickens's narrator speaks out against the 'slangs and twangs of the conventicle', and in favour of the preacher's 'renunciation of all priestly authority', he is on the one hand, as Norris Pope observes, 'aligning himself with the United Committee' and (unusually) supporting a missionary enterprise, but, on the other hand 'attacking an old foe: the social irresponsibility and conservatism of the Church of England' (see *Dickens and Charity* [1978], pp. 143–51).

According to the ultra-evangelical Low Church journal *The Record*, which reported Dickens's presence at the Britannia on 29 January and his 'commendable attention' to the service, the preacher that evening was the Reverend Newman Hall, Sabbatarian incumbent at Surrey Chapel ([London], 30 January 1860, p. 3).

Literary allusions (p. 54) 'like guilty things upon a fearful summons': Shakespeare, *Hamlet*, Act 1, Sc. 1; (p. 54) 'the Death's head pipes were like a theatrical memento mori': echoes *Henry IV* Part I, Act 3, Sc. 3 ('a death's-head or a memento mori'); (p. 59) 'I am the son of a Prince! My father is the King of Kings ...': Revelation 17:14; (p. 60) 'work out their own salvation': Philippians 2:12; (p. 62) 'you have the widow's son to tell me about, the ruler's daughter, the other figure at the door when the brother of the two sisters was dead': Luke 7:12, 8:49; John 11:28.

As I shut the door of my lodging behind me, and came out into the streets at six on a drizzling Saturday evening in the last past month of January, all that neighbourhood of Covent-garden looked very desolate. It is so essentially a neighbourhood which has seen better days, that bad weather affects it sooner than another place which has not come down in the world. In its present reduced condition, it bears a thaw almost worse than any place I know. It gets so dreadfully low-spirited, when damp breaks forth. Those wonderful houses about Drury-lane Theatre, which in the palmy days of theatres were prosperous and long-settled places of business, and which now change hands every week, but never change their character of being divided and subdivided on the ground floor into mouldy dens of shops where an orange and half a dozen nuts, or a pomatum-pot, one cake of fancy soap, and a cigar-box, are offered for sale and never sold, were most ruefully contemplated that evening, by the statue of Shakespeare, with the rain-drops coursing one another down its innocent nose. Those inscrutable pigeon-hole offices, with nothing in them (not so much as an ink-stand) but a model of a theatre before the curtain, where, in the Italian Opera season, tickets at reduced prices are kept on sale by nomadic gentlemen in smeary hats too tall for them, whom one occasionally seems to have seen on race-courses, not wholly unconnected with strips of cloth of various colours and a rolling ball – those Bedouin establishments, deserted by the tribe, and tenantless except when sheltering in one corner an irregular row of ginger-beer-bottles which would have made one shudder on such a night, but for its being plain that they had nothing in them, shrunk from the shrill cries of the newsboys at their Exchange in the kennel of Catherine-street, like guilty things upon a fearful summons. At the pipe-shop, in Great Russell-street, the Death's-head pipes were like a theatrical memento mori, admonishing beholders of the decline of the playhouse as an Institution. I walked up Bow-street, disposed to be angry with the shops there, that were letting out theatrical secrets by exhibiting to work-a-day humanity, the stuff of which diadems and robes of kings are made. I noticed that some shops which had once been in the dramatic line, and had struggled out of it, were not getting on prosperously − like some actors I have known, who took to business and failed to make it answer. In a word, those streets looked so dull, and, considered as theatrical streets, so broken and bankrupt, that the FOUND DEAD on the black board at the police station might have announced the decease of the Drama, and the pools of water outside the fire-engine maker's at the corner of Long-acre might have been occasioned by his having brought out the whole of his stock to play upon its last smouldering ashes.

And yet, on such a night in so degenerate a time, the object of my journey was theatrical. And yet within half an hour I was in an immense theatre, capable of holding nearly five thousand people.

What Theatre? Her Majesty's? Far better. Royal Italian Opera? Far better. Infinitely superior to the latter for hearing in; infinitely superior to both, for seeing in. To every part of this Theatre spacious fireproof ways of ingress and egress. For every part of it, convenient places of refreshment and retiring rooms. Everything to eat and drink carefully supervised as to quality, and sold at an appointed price; respectable female attendants ready for the commonest women in the audience; a general air of consideration, decorum, and supervision, most commendable; an unquestionably humanising influence in all the social arrangements of the place.

Surely a dear Theatre, then? Because there were in London (not very long ago) Theatres with entrance-prices up to half a guinea a head, whose arrangements were not half so civilised. Surely, therefore, a dear Theatre? Not very dear. A gallery at threepence, another gallery at fourpence, a pit at sixpence, boxes and pit-stalls at a shilling, and six private boxes at half-a-crown.

My uncommercial curiosity induced me to go into every nook of this great place, and among every class of the audience assembled in it − amounting that evening, as I calculated, to about two thousand and odd hundreds. Magnificently lighted by a firmament of sparkling chandeliers, the building was ventilated to perfection. My sense of smell, without being particularly delicate, has been so offended in some of the commoner places of public resort, that I have often been obliged to leave them when I have made an uncommercial journey expressly to look on. The air of this Theatre was fresh, cool, and wholesome. To help towards this end, very sensible precautions had been used, ingeniously combining the experience of hospitals and railway stations. Asphalte pavements substituted for wooden floors, honest bare walls of glazed brick and tile – even at the back of the boxes – for plaster and paper, no benches stuffed, and no carpeting or baize used: a cool material, with a light glazed surface, being the covering of the seats.

These various contrivances are as well considered in the place in question as if it were a Fever Hospital; the result is, that it is sweet and healthful. It has been constructed from the ground to the roof, with a careful reference to sight and sound in every corner; the result is, that its form is beautiful, and that the appearance of the audience, as seen from the proscenium – with every face in it commanding the stage, and the whole so admirably raked and turned to that centre, that a hand can scarcely move in the great assemblage without the movement being seen from thence – is highly remarkable in its union of vastness with compactness. The stage itself, and all its appurtenances of machinery, cellarage, height, and breadth, are on a scale more like the Scala at Milan, or the San Carlo at Naples, or the Grand Opera at Paris, than any notion a stranger would be likely to form of the Britannia Theatre at Hoxton, a mile north of Saint Luke's Hospital in the Old-street-road, London. The Forty Thieves might be played here, and every thief ride his real horse, and the disguised captain bring in his oil jars on a train of real camels, and nobody be put out of the way. This really extraordinary place is the achievement of one man's enterprise, and was erected on the ruins of an inconvenient old building in less than five months, at a round cost of five-and-twenty thousand pounds. To dismiss this part of my subject, and still to render to the proprietor the credit that is strictly his due, I must add that his sense of the responsibility upon him to make the best of his audience, and to do his best for them, is a highly agreeable sign of these times.

As the spectators at this Theatre, for a reason I will presently show, were the object of my journey, I entered on the play of the night as one of the two thousand and odd hundreds, by looking about me at my neighbours. We were a motley assemblage of people, and we had a good many boys and young men among us; we had also many girls and young women. To represent, however, that we did not include a very great number, and a very fair proportion, of family groups, would be to make a gross mis-statement. Such groups were to be seen in all parts of the house; in the boxes and stalls particularly, they were composed of persons

A Cheap Theatre − Saturday Night

of very decent appearance, who had many children with them. Among our dresses there were most kinds of shabby and greasy wear, and much fustian and corduroy that was neither sound nor fragrant. The caps of our young men were mostly of a limp character, and we who wore them, slouched, high-shouldered, into our places with our hands in our pockets, and occasionally twisted our cravats about our necks like eels, and occasionally tied them down our breasts like links of sausages, and occasionally had a screw in our hair over each cheek-bone with a slight Thief-flavour in it. Besides prowlers and idlers, we were mechanics, dock-labourers, costermongers, petty tradesmen, small clerks, milliners, stay-makers, shoe-binders, slop workers, poor workers in a hundred highways and bye-ways. Many of us − on the whole, the majority − were not at all clean, and not at all choice in our lives or conversation. But we had all come together in a place where our convenience was well consulted, and where we were well looked after, to enjoy an evening's entertainment in common. We were not going to lose any part of what we had paid for, through anybody's caprice, and as a community we had a character to lose. So we were closely attentive, and kept excellent order; and let the man or boy who did otherwise instantly get out from this place, or we would put him out with the greatest expedition.

We began at half-past six with a pantomime − with a pantomime so long, that, before it was over, I felt as if I had been travelling for six weeks − going to India, say, by the Overland Mail. The Spirit of Liberty was the principal personage in the Introduction, and the Four Quarters of the World came out of the globe, glittering, and discoursed with the Spirit, who sang charmingly. We were delighted to understand that there was no Liberty anywhere but among ourselves, and we highly applauded the agreeable fact. In an allegorical way, which did as well as any other way, we and the Spirit of Liberty got into a kingdom of Needles and Pins, and found them at war with a potentate who called in to his aid their old arch-enemy Rust, and who would have got the better of them if the Spirit of Liberty had not in the nick of time transformed the leaders into Clown, Pantaloon, Harlequin, Columbine, Harlequina, and a whole family of Sprites, consisting of a remarkably stout father and three spineless sons. We all knew what was coming, when the Spirit of Liberty addressed the king with the big face, and His Majesty backed to the side-scenes and began untying himself behind, with his big face all on one side. Our excitement at that crisis was great, and our delight unbounded. After this era in our existence, we went through all the incidents of a pantomime; it was not by any means a savage pantomime in the way of burning or boiling people, or throwing them out of window, or cutting them up; was often very droll, was always liberally got up, and cleverly presented. I noticed that the people who kept the shops, and who represented the passengers in the thoroughfares and so forth, had no conventionality in them, but were unusually like the real thing – from which I infer that you may take that audience in (if you wish to) concerning Knights and Ladies, Fairies, Angels, or such like, but they are not to be done as to anything in the streets. I noticed, also, that when two young men, dressed in exact imitation of the eel-and-sausage-cravated portion of the audience, were chased by policemen, and, finding themselves in danger of being caught, dropped so suddenly as to oblige the policemen to tumble over them, there was great rejoicing among the caps – as though it were a delicate reference to something they had heard of before.

The Pantomime was succeeded by a Melo-Drama. Throughout the evening, I was pleased to observe Virtue quite as triumphant as she usually is out of doors, and indeed I thought rather more so. We all agreed (for the time) that honesty was the best policy, and we were as hard as iron upon Vice, and we wouldn't hear of Villany getting on in the world – no, not upon any consideration whatever.

Between the pieces, we almost all of us went out and refreshed. Many of us went the length of drinking beer at the bar of the neighbouring public-house, some of us drank spirits, crowds of us had sandwiches and ginger-beer at the refreshment-bars established for us in the Theatre. The sandwich – as substantial as was consistent with portability, and as cheap as possible – we hailed as one of our greatest institutions. It forced its way among us at all stages of the entertainment, and we were always delighted to see it; its adaptability to the varying moods of our nature was surprising; we could never weep so comfortably as when our tears fell on our sandwich; we could never laugh so heartily as when we choked with sandwich; Virtue never looked so beautiful, or Vice so deformed as when we paused, sandwich in hand, to consider what would come of that resolution of Wickedness in boots, to sever Innocence in flowered chintz from Honest Industry in striped stockings. When the curtain fell for the night, we still fell back upon sandwich, to help us through the rain and mire, and home to bed.

This, as I have mentioned, was Saturday night. Being Saturday night, I had accomplished but the half of my uncommercial journey; for its object was to compare the play on Saturday evening, with the preaching in the same Theatre on Sunday evening.

Therefore, at the same hour of half-past six on the similarly damp and muddy Sunday evening, I returned to this Theatre. I drove up to the entrance (fearful of being late, or I should have come on foot), and found myself in a large crowd of people who, I am happy to state, were put into excellent spirits by my arrival. Having nothing to look at but the mud and the closed doors, they looked at me, and highly enjoyed the comic spectacle. My modesty inducing me to draw off, some hundreds of yards, into a dark corner, they at once forgot me, and applied themselves to their former occupation of looking at the mud and looking in at the closed doors: which, being of grated iron-work, allowed the lighted passage within to be seen. They were chiefly people of respectable appearance, odd and impulsive as most crowds are, and making a joke of being there as most crowds do.

In the dark corner I might have sat a long while, but that a very obliging passer-by informed me that the Theatre was already full, and that the people whom I saw in the street were all shut out for want of room. After that, I lost no time in worming myself into the building, and creeping to a place in a Proscenium box that had been kept for me.

There must have been full four thousand people present. Carefully estimating the pit alone, I could bring it out as holding little less than fourteen hundred. Every part of the house was well filled, and I had not found it easy to make my way along the back of the boxes to where I sat. The chandeliers in the ceiling were lighted; there was no light on the stage; the orchestra was empty. The green curtain was down, and packed pretty closely on chairs on the small space of stage before it were some thirty gentlemen, and two or three ladies. In the centre of these, in a desk or pulpit covered with red baize, was the presiding minister. The kind of rostrum he occupied, will be very well understood, if I liken it to a boarded-up fireplace turned towards the audience, with a gentleman in a black surtout standing in the stove and leaning forward over the mantelpiece.

A portion of Scripture was being read when I went in. It was followed by a discourse, to which the congregation listened with most exemplary attention and uninterrupted silence and decorum. My own attention comprehended both the auditory and the speaker, and shall turn to both in this recalling of the scene, exactly as it did at the time.

'A very difficult thing,' I thought, when the discourse began, 'to speak appropriately to so large an audience, and to speak with tact. Without it, better not to speak at all. Infinitely better to read the New Testament well, and to let *that* speak. In this congregation there is indubitably one pulse; but I doubt if any power short of genius can touch it as one, and make it answer as one.'

I could not possibly say to myself as the discourse proceeded, that the minister was a good speaker. I could not possibly say to myself that he expressed an understanding of the general mind and character of his audience. There was a supposititious working-man introduced into the homily to make supposititious objections to our Christian religion and be reasoned down, who was not only a very disagreeable person, but remarkably unlike life – very much more unlike it than anything I had seen in the pantomime. The native independence of character this artisan was supposed to possess, was represented by a suggestion of a dialect that I certainly never heard in my uncommercial travels, and with a coarse swing of voice and manner anything but agreeable to his feelings I should conceive, considered in the light of a portrait, and as far away from the fact as a Chinese Tartar. There was a model pauper introduced in like manner, who appeared to me to be the most intolerably arrogant pauper ever relieved, and to show himself in absolute want and dire necessity of a course of Stone Yard. For, how did this pauper testify to his having received the gospel of humility? A gentleman met him in the workhouse, and said (which I myself really thought good-natured of him), 'Ah, John? I am sorry to see you here. I am sorry to see you so poor.' 'Poor, sir!' replied that man, drawing himself up, 'I am the son of a Prince! *My* father is the King of Kings. *My* father is the Lord of Lords. *My* father is the ruler of all the Princes of the Earth!' &c. And this was what all the preacher's fellow-sinners might come to, if they would embrace this blessed book – which I must say it did some violence to my own feelings of reverence, to see held out at arm's length at frequent intervals and soundingly slapped, like a slow lot at a sale. Now, could I help asking myself the question, whether the mechanic before me who must detect the preacher as being wrong about the visible manner of himself and the like of himself, and about such a noisy lip-server as that pauper, might not, most unhappily for the usefulness of the occasion, doubt that preacher's being right about things not visible to human senses?

Again. Is it necessary or advisable to address such an audience continually, as 'fellow-sinners'? Is it not enough to be fellow-creatures, born yesterday, suffering and striving today, dying tomorrow? By our common humanity, my brothers and sisters, by our common capacities for pain and pleasure, by our common laughter and our common tears, by our common aspiration to reach something better than ourselves, by our common tendency to believe in something good, and to invest whatever we love or whatever we lose with some qualities that are superior to our own failings and weaknesses as we know them in our own poor hearts – by these, Hear me! – Surely, it is enough to be fellow-creatures. Surely, it includes the other designation and some touching meanings over and above.

Again. There was a personage introduced into the discourse (not an absolute novelty, to the best of my remembrance of my reading), who had been personally known to the preacher, and had been quite a Crichton in all the ways of philosophy, but had been an infidel. Many a time had the preacher talked with him on that subject, and many a time had he failed to convince that intelligent man. But he fell ill, and died, and before he died he recorded his conversion – in words which the preacher had taken down, my fellow-sinners, and would read to you from this piece of paper. I must confess that to me, as one of an uninstructed audience, they did not appear particularly edifying. I thought their tone extremely selfish, and I thought they had a spiritual vanity in them which was of the before-mentioned refractory pauper's family.

All slangs and twangs are objectionable everywhere, but the slang and twang of the conventicle – as bad in its way as that of the House of Commons, and nothing worse can be said of it – should be studiously avoided under such circumstances as I describe. The avoidance was not complete on this occasion. Nor was it quite agreeable to see the preacher addressing his pet 'points' to his backers on the stage, as if appealing to those disciples to shore him up, and testify to the multitude that each of those points was a clincher.

But, in respect of the large Christianity of his general tone; of his renunciation of all priestly authority; of his earnest and reiterated assurance to the people that the commonest among them could work out their own salvation if they would, by simply, lovingly, and dutifully following Our Saviour, and that they needed the mediation of no erring man; in these particulars, this gentleman deserved all praise. Nothing could be better than the spirit, or the plain emphatic words of his discourse in these respects. And it was a most significant and encouraging circumstance that whenever he struck that chord, or whenever he described anything which Christ himself had done, the array of faces before him was very much more earnest, and very much more expressive of emotion, than at any other time.

And now, I am brought to the fact, that the lowest part of the audience of the previous night, *was not there.* There is no doubt about it. There was no such thing in that building, that Sunday evening. I have been told since, that the lowest part of the audience of the Victoria Theatre has been attracted to its Sunday services. I have been very glad to hear it, but on this occasion of which I write, the lowest part of the usual audience of the Britannia Theatre, decidedly and unquestionably stayed away. When I first took my seat and looked at the house, my surprise at the change in its occupants was as great as my disappointment. To the most respectable class of the previous evening, was added a great number of respectable strangers attracted by curiosity, and drafts from the regular congregations of various chapels. It was impossible to fail in identifying the character of these last, and they were very numerous. I came out in a strong, slow tide of them setting from the boxes. Indeed, while the discourse was in progress, the respectable character of the auditory was so manifest in their appearance, that when the minister addressed a supposititious 'outcast,' one really felt a little impatient of it, as a figure of speech not justified by anything the eye could discover.

The time appointed for the conclusion of the proceedings was eight o'clock. The address having lasted until full that time, and it being the custom to conclude with a hymn, the preacher intimated in a few sensible words that the clock had struck the hour, and that those who desired to go before the hymn was sung, could go now, without giving offence. No one stirred. The hymn was then sung, in good time and tune and unison, and its effect was very striking. A comprehensive benevolent prayer dismissed the throng, and in seven or eight minutes there was nothing left in the Theatre but a light cloud of dust.

That these Sunday meetings in Theatres are good things, I do not doubt. Nor do I doubt that they will work lower and lower down in the social scale, if those who preside over them will be very careful on two heads: firstly, not to disparage the places in which they speak, or the intelligence of their hearers; secondly, not to set themselves in antagonism to the natural inborn desire of the mass of mankind to recreate themselves and to be amused.

There is a third head, taking precedence of all others, to which my remarks on the discourse I heard, have tended. In the New Testament there is the most beautiful and affecting history conceivable by man, and there are the terse models for all prayer and for all preaching. As to the models, imitate them, Sunday preachers – else why are they there, consider? As to the history, tell it. Some people cannot read, some people will not read, many people (this especially holds among the young and ignorant) find it hard to pursue the verse-form in which the book is presented to them, and imagine that those breaks imply gaps and want of continuity. Help them over that first stumbling-block, by setting forth the history in narrative, with no fear of exhausting it. You will never preach so well, you will never move them so profoundly, you will never send them away with half so much to think of. Which is the better interest: Christ's choice of twelve poor men to help in those merciful wonders among the poor and rejected; or the pious bullying of a whole Union-full of paupers? What is your changed philosopher to wretched me, peeping in at the door out of the mud of the streets and of my life, when you have the widow's son to tell me about, the ruler's daughter, the other figure at the door when the brother of the two sisters was dead, and one of the two ran to the mourner, crying, 'The Master is come, and calleth for thee'? – Let the preacher who will thoroughly forget himself and remember no individuality but one, and no eloquence but one, stand up before four thousand men and women at the Britannia Theatre any Sunday night, recounting that narrative to them as fellow-creatures, and he shall see a sight!

8

The Uncommercial Traveller

All The Year Round, 10 March 1860 (*UT1* as 'Poor Mercantile Jack')

As Basil Lubbock has noted, 'legislation in the days of sail gave absolute power into the hands of the sea-captain' ('The Mercantile Marine, 1830–65', in *Early Victorian England*, ed. G. M. Young [1935], Vol. 1, pp. 387–8). The Merchant Shipping Act of 1854 tightened rather than eased the procedures by which an ordinary merchant sailor might formally complain of mistreatment by senior officers, to discourage the lodging of unfounded complaints. While the same Act devoted a small number of its sections to steps for the 'Protection of Seamen from Imposition' (17 & 18 Vict. Cap. 104, Sections 233–8), these applied only while seamen returning to the United Kingdom remained aboard their vessels, and the only penalties were small fines (£5 to £20).

Dickens's description of the 'Uncommercial Traveller''s enrolment in the

Liverpool Police Force to 'look after Jack' on a wintry Friday cannot be positively identified with any similar experience on the author's part. The last occasions on which he is known to have been in Liverpool on a Friday were on 20 August and 15 October 1858, during successful public reading engagements at the Philharmonic. No visits are recorded in early 1860, notwithstanding the internal evidence of both this article and article 11 (see headnote, p. 97). The narrative is cast as a kind of nightmarish descent into the underworld, hence the attribution of supernatural powers to 'Mr Superintendent' and his talented officers, whose names are adapted from the Grimm fairytale of 'Fortunio'. The Dickens family had staged a pantomime version called 'Fortunio and his Seven Gifted Servants' at Tavistock House on 6 January 1855 (see Forster, Book 7, Ch. 2). Hence also imaginative referents such as the picture of the 'Norwood Gypsy' which Dickens recalls from a chapbook (see Harry Stone, 'Dark Corners of the Mind: Dickens' Childhood Reading', *Horn Book Magazine*, June 1963, p. 313), an illustration from Cervantes's *Don Quixote*, and the three witches from *Macbeth* (pp. 72–3 below). Dickens's use of a 'fairytale' motif allows him to avoid explicitly naming the kinds of vice encountered on this underworld expedition; these included both male and female prostitution, and, in the penultimate scene described, child prostitution. The euphemistic tendency partly explains Dickens's attitude towards 'Dark Jack', by whom he intends African American sailors plying the trade route between Liverpool and the cotton-growing Southern states of America. The Negro master of ceremonies – counterpart to the modern 'MC' – issues the dance instructions in what seems to be a mixture of English and French (balloon say = 'balancez', lemonade = 'promenade' [?]), appropriate as the dance is a quadrille, typical of the ''Cadien' music of the American South, imported by refugees from French Canada during the Seven Years' War. That 'Dark Jack' was an important and often underestimated feature of the Atlantic economy, and, when not at sea, indulged in musical recreations such as those described here by Dickens, is attested in W. Jeffrey Bolster's pioneering study, *Black Jacks: African American Seamen in the Age of Sail* (1997).

Dickens's doubt, voiced in the conclusion to this paper, that his own 'comfortable thoughts of Seaman's Homes' would ever become a reality, was to be ironically justified by subsequent events, as the Liverpool Sailors' Home was burnt down in a suspected arson attack on 29 April, shortly after the publication of the article (*Illustrated London News*, 5 May 1860, p. 423, col. b).

Literary allusions (p. 64) The nickname Dickens invents for sailors of the merchant navy, 'Poor Mercantile Jack,' and the reference to 'the sweet little cherub who sits smiling aloft', parodies Charles Dibdin's popular ballad 'Poor Jack'; the relevant line runs: 'There's a sweet little cherub sits smiling aloft ...'; (p. 64) 'the multitudinous seas incarnadine': Shakespeare, *Macbeth*, Act 2, Sc. 1; (p. 66) 'Jack's Delight, his (un)lovely Nan': adapts another Dibdin lyric, 'Lovely Nan', which contains the refrain 'But, oh! much sweeter than all these,/ Is Jack's delight, his lovely Nan'; (p. 70) 'a leaf out of Don Quixote': Cervantes, *Don Quixote* (1605, 1615); (p. 73) to 'die in an odour of devilry': reverses the dictum of the Roman Catholic Church, that the good die 'in the odour of sanctity'.

Is the sweet little cherub who sits smiling aloft and keeps watch on the life of Poor Jack, commissioned to take charge of Mercantile Jack, as well as Jack of the national navy? If not, who is? What is the cherub about, and what are we all about, when Poor Mercantile Jack is having his brains slowly knocked out by pennyweights, aboard the brig Beelzebub, or the bark Bowie-knife – when he looks his last at that infernal craft, with the first officer's iron boot-heel in his remaining eye, or with his dying body towed overboard in the ship's wake, while the cruel wounds in it do 'the multitudinous seas incarnadine'?

Is it unreasonable to entertain a belief that if, aboard the brig Beelzebub or the bark Bowie-knife, the first officer did half the damage to cotton that he does to men, there would presently arise from both sides of the Atlantic so vociferous an invocation of the sweet little cherub who sits calculating aloft, keeping watch on the markets that pay, that such vigilant cherub would, with a winged sword, have that gallant officer's organ of destructiveness out of his head in the space of a flash of lightning?

If it be unreasonable, then am I the most unreasonable of men, for I believe it with all my soul.

This was my thought as I walked the dock-quays at Liverpool, keeping watch on poor Mercantile Jack. Alas for me! I have long outgrown the state of sweet little cherub; but there I was, and there Mercantile Jack was, and very busy he was, and very cold he was; the snow yet lying in the frozen furrows of the land, and the north-east winds snipping off the tops of the little waves in the Mersey, and rolling them into hailstones to pelt him with. Mercantile Jack was hard at it, in the hard weather, as he mostly is in all weathers, poor Jack. He was girded to ships' masts and funnels of steamers, like a forester to a great oak, scraping and painting; he was lying out on yards, furling sails that tried to beat him off; he was dimly discernible up in a world of giant cobwebs, reefing and splicing; he was faintly audible down in holds, stowing and unshipping cargo; he was winding round and round at capstans, melodious, monotonous, and drunk; he was of a diabolical aspect, with coaling for the Antipodes; he was washing decks barefoot, with the breast of his red shirt open to the blast, though it was sharper than the knife in his leathern girdle; he was looking over bulwarks, all eyes and hair; he was standing by at the shoot of the Cunard steamer, off tomorrow, as the stocks in trade of several butchers, poulterers, and fishmongers, poured down into the ice-house; he was coming aboard of other vessels, with his kit in a tarpaulin bag, attended by plunderers to the very last moment of his shore-going existence. As though his senses when released from the uproar of the elements were under obligation to be confused by other turmoil, there was a rattling of wheels, a clattering of hoofs, a clashing of iron, a jolting of cotton and hides and casks and timber, an incessant deafening disturbance, on the quays, that was the very madness of sound. And as, in the midst of it, he stood swaying about, with his hair blown all manner of wild ways, rather crazedly taking leave of his plunderers, all the rigging in the docks was shrill in the wind, and every little steamer coming and going across the Mersey was sharp in its blowing off, and every buoy in the river bobbed spitefully up and down, as if there was a general taunting chorus of 'Come along, Mercantile Jack! Ill-lodged, ill-fed, ill-used, hocussed, entrapped, anticipated, cleaned out. Come along, Poor Mercantile Jack, and be tempest-tossed till you are drowned!'

The uncommercial transaction which had brought me and Jack together was this; – I had entered the Liverpool police-force, that I might have a look at the various unlawful traps which are every night set for Jack. As my term of service in that distinguished corps was short, and as my personal bias in the capacity of one of its members has ceased, no suspicion will attach to my evidence that it is an admirable force. Besides that it is composed, without favour, of the best men that can be picked, it is directed by an unusual intelligence. Its organisation against Fires, I take to be much better than the metropolitan system, and in all respects it tempers its remarkable vigilance with a still more remarkable discretion.

Jack had knocked off work in the docks some hours, and I had taken, for purposes of identification, a photograph-likeness of a thief, in the portrait-room at our head police-office (on the whole, he seemed rather complimented by the proceeding), and I had been on police-parade, and the small hand of the clock was moving on to ten, when I took up my lantern to follow Mr Superintendent to the traps that were set for Jack. In Mr Superintendent I saw, as anybody might, a tall, well-looking, well set-up man of a soldierly bearing, with a cavalry air, a good chest, and a resolute but not by any means ungentle face. He carried in his hand a plain black walking-stick of hard wood; and whenever and wherever, at any after-time of the night, he struck it on the pavement with a ringing sound, it instantly produced a whistle out of the darkness, and a policeman. To this remarkable stick I refer an air of mystery and magic which pervaded the whole of my perquisition among the traps that were set for Jack.

We began by diving into the obscurest streets and lanes of the port. Suddenly pausing in a flow of cheerful discourse, before a dead wall, apparently some ten miles long, Mr Superintendent struck upon the ground, and the wall opened and shot out, with military salute of hand to temple, two policemen – not in the least surprised themselves, not in the least surprising Mr Superintendent.

'All right, Sharpeye?'

'All right, sir.'

'All right, Trampfoot?'

'All right, sir.'

'Is Quickear there?'

'Here am I, sir.'

'Come with us.'

'Yes, sir.'

So, Sharpeye went before, and Mr Superintendent and I went next, and Trampfoot and Quickear marched as rear-guard. Sharpeye, I soon had occasion to remark, had a skilful and quite professional way of opening doors – touched latches delicately, as if they were keys of musical instruments – opened every door he touched, as if he were perfectly confident that there was stolen property behind it – instantly insinuated himself, to prevent its being shut.

Sharpeye opened several doors of traps that were set for Jack, but Jack did not happen to be in any of them. They were all such miserable places that really, Jack, if I were you, I would give them a wider berth. In every trap, somebody was sitting over a fire waiting for Jack. Now, it was a crouching old woman, like the picture of the Norwood Gipsy in the old sixpenny dream-books; now, it was a crimp of the male sex in a checked shirt and without a coat, reading a newspaper; now, it was a man crimp and a woman crimp, who always introduced themselves as united in holy matrimony; now, it was Jack's delight, his (un)lovely Nan; but they were all waiting for Jack, and were all frightfully disappointed to see us.

'Who have you got upstairs here?' says Sharpeye, generally. (In the Move-on tone.)

'Nobody, surr; sure not a blessed sowl!' (Irish feminine reply.)

'What do you mean by nobody? Didn't I hear a woman's step go upstairs when my hand was on the latch?'

'Ah! sure thin you're rhight, surr, I forgot her! 'Tis on'y Betsy White, surr. Ah! you know Betsy, surr. Come down, Betsy darlin', and say the gintlemin.'

Generally, Betsy looks over the banisters (the steep staircase is in the room) with a forcible expression in her protesting face, of an intention to compensate herself for the present trial by grinding Jack finer than usual when he does come. Generally, Sharpeye turns to Mr Superintendent, and says, as if the subject of his remarks were wax-work:

'One of the worst, sir, this house is. This woman has been indicted three times. This man's a regular bad one likewise. His real name is Pegg. Gives himself out as Waterhouse.'

'Never had sitch a name as Pegg near me back, thin, since I was in this house, bee the good Lard!' says the woman.

Generally, the man says nothing at all, but becomes exceedingly round-shouldered, and pretends to read his paper with rapt attention. Generally, Sharpeye directs our observation with a look, to the prints and pictures that are invariably numerous on the walls. Always, Trampfoot and Quickear are taking notice on the door-step. In default of Sharpeye being acquainted with the exact individuality of any gentleman encountered, one of these two is sure to proclaim from the outer air, like a gruff spectre, that Jackson is not Jackson, but knows himself to be Fogle; or that Canlon is Walker's brother, against whom there was not sufficient evidence; or that the man who says he never was at sea since he was a boy, came ashore from a voyage last Thursday, or sails tomorrow morning. 'And that is a bad class of man, you see,' says Mr Superintendent, when he got out into the dark again, 'and very difficult to deal with, who, when he has made this place too hot to hold him, enters himself for a voyage as steward or cook, and is out of knowledge for months, and then turns up again worse than ever.'

When we had gone into many such houses, and had come out (always leaving everybody relapsing into waiting for Jack), we started off to a singing-house where Jack was expected to muster strong.

The vocalisation was taking place in a long low room upstairs; at one end, an orchestra of two performers, and a small platform; across the room, a series of open pews for Jack, with an aisle down the middle; at the other end, a larger pew than the rest, entitled SNUG, and reserved for mates and similar good company. About the room, some amazing coffee-coloured pictures varnished an inch deep, and some stuffed creatures in cases; dotted among the audience, in Snug and out of Snug, the 'Professionals;' among them, the celebrated comic favourite Mr Banjo Bones, looking very hideous with his blackened face and limp sugar-loaf hat; beside him, sipping rum-and-water, Mrs Banjo Bones, in her natural colours – a little heightened.

It was a Friday night, and Friday night was considered not a good night for Jack. At any rate, Jack did not show in very great force even here, though the house was one to which he much resorts, and where a good deal of money is taken. There was British Jack, a little maudlin and sleepy, lolling over his empty glass, as if he were trying to read his fortune at the bottom; there was Loafing Jack of the Stars and Stripes, rather an unpromising customer, with his long nose, lank cheek, high cheekbones, and nothing soft about him but his cabbage-leaf hat; there was Spanish Jack, with curls of black hair, rings in his ears, and a knife not far from his hand, if you got into trouble with him; there were Maltese Jack, and Jack of Sweden, and Jack the Finn, looming through the smoke of their pipes, and turning faces that looked as if they were carved out of dark wood, towards the young lady dancing the hornpipe, who found the platform so exceedingly small for it, that I had a nervous expectation of seeing her, in the backward steps, disappear through the window. Still, if all hands had been got together, they would not have more than half filled the room. Observe, however, said Mr Licensed Victualler, the host, that it was Friday night, and, besides, it was getting on for twelve, and Jack had gone aboard. A sharp and watchful man, Mr Licensed Victualler, the host, with tight lips, and a complete edition of Cocker's arithmetic in each eye. Attended to his business himself, he said. Always on the spot. When he heard of talent, trusted nobody's account of it, but went off by rail to see it. If true talent, engaged it. Pounds a week for talent – four pound – five pound. Banjo Bones was undoubted talent. Hear this instrument that was going to play – it was real talent! In truth it was very good; a kind of piano-accordion, played by a young girl of a delicate prettiness of face, figure, and dress, that made the audience look coarser. She sang to the instrument, too; first, a song about village bells, and how they chimed; then a song about how I went to sea; winding up with an imitation of the bagpipes, which Mercantile Jack seemed to understand much the best. A good girl, said Mr Licensed Victualler. Kept herself select. Sat in Snug, not listening to the blandishments of Mates. Lived with mother. Father dead. Once, a merchant well to do, but over speculated himself. On delicate inquiry as to salary paid for item of talent under consideration, Mr Victualler's pounds dropped suddenly to shillings – still, it was a very comfortable thing for a young person like that, you know; she only went on, six times a night, and was only required to be there from six at night to twelve. What was more conclusive was, Mr Victualler's assurance that he 'never allowed any language, and never suffered any disturbance.' Sharpeye confirmed the statement, and the order that prevailed was the best proof of it that could have been cited. So, I came to the conclusion that poor Mercantile Jack might do (as I am afraid he does) much worse than trust himself to Mr Victualler, and pass his evenings here.

But we had not yet looked, Mr Superintendent – said Trampfoot, receiving us in the street again with military salute – for Dark Jack. True, Trampfoot. Ring the wonderful stick, rub the wonderful lantern, and cause the spirits of the stick and lantern to convey us to the Darkies.

There was no disappointment in the matter of Dark Jack; *he* was producible. The Genii set us down in the little first-floor of a little public-house, and there, in a stiflingly close atmosphere, were Dark Jack and Dark Jack's Delight, his *white* unlovely Nan, sitting against the wall all round the room. More than that: Dark Jack's Delight was the least unlovely Nan, both morally and physically, that I saw that night.

As a fiddle and tambourine band were sitting among the company, Quickear suggested, why not strike up? 'Ah, la'ads!' said a negro sitting by the door, 'gib the jebblem a darnse. Tak' yah pardlers, jebblem, for 'um QUAD-rill.'

This was the landlord, in a Greek cap, and a dress half Greek and half English. As master of the ceremonies, he called all the figures, and occasionally addressed himself parenthetically – after this manner. When he was very loud, I use capitals.

'Now den! Hoy! ONE. Right and left. (Put a steam on, gib 'um powder.) LA-dies' chail. BAL-loon say. Lemonade! TWO. AD-warnse and go back (gib 'ell a breakdown, shake it out o' yerselbs, keep a movil). SWING-corners, BAL-loon say, and Lemonade! (Hoy!) THREE. GENT come for'ard with a lady and go back, hoppersite come for'ard with a lady and go back, ALL four come for'ard and do what yer can. (Aeiohoy!) BAL-loon say, and leetle lemonade (Dat hair nigger by 'um fireplace 'hind a' time, shake it out o' yerselbs, gib 'ell a breakdown). Now den! Hoy! FOUR! Lemonade. BAL-loon say, and swing. FOUR ladies meets in 'um middle, FOUR gents goes round 'um ladies, FOUR gents passes out under 'um ladies' arms, SWING – and Lemonade till 'a moosic can't play no more! (Hoy, Hoy!)'

The male dancers were all blacks, and one was an unusually powerful man of six feet three or four. The sound of their flat feet on the floor was as unlike the sound of white feet as their faces were unlike white faces. They toed and heeled, shuffled, double-shuffled, double-double-shuffled, covered the buckle, and beat the time out, rarely, dancing with a great show of teeth, and with a childish, good-humoured enjoyment that was very prepossessing. They generally kept together, these poor fellows, said Mr Superintendent, because they were at a disadvantage singly, and liable to slights in the neighbouring streets. But, if I were Light Jack, I should be very slow to interfere oppressively with Dark Jack, for, whenever I have had to do with him I have found him a simple and gentle fellow. Bearing this in mind I asked his friendly permission to leave him restoration of beer, in wishing him good night, and thus it fell out that the last words I heard him say, as I blundered down the worn stairs, were, 'Jebblem's elth! Ladies drinks fust!'

The night was now well on into the morning, but, for miles and hours we explored a strange world, where nobody ever goes to bed, but everybody is eternally sitting up, waiting for Jack. This exploration was among a labyrinth of dismal courts and blind alleys, called Entries, kept in wonderful order by the police, and in much better order than by the corporation: the want of gaslight in the most dangerous and infamous of these places being quite unworthy of so spirited a town. I need describe but two or three of the houses in which Jack was waited for, as specimens of the rest. Many we attained by noisome passages so profoundly dark that we felt our way with our hands. Not one of the whole number we visited, was without its show of prints and ornamental crockery; the quantity of the latter set forth on little shelves and in little cases, in otherwise wretched rooms, indicating that Mercantile Jack must have an extraordinary fondness for crockery, to necessitate so much of that bait in his traps.

Among such garniture, in one front parlour in the dead of the night, four women were sitting by a fire. One of them had a male child in her arms. On the stool among them was a swarthy youth with a guitar, who had evidently stopped playing when our footsteps were heard.

'Well! how do *you* do?' says Mr Superintendent, looking about him.

'Pretty well, sir, and hope you gentlemen are going to treat us ladies, now you have come to see us.'

'Order there!' says Sharpeye.

'None of that!' says Quickear.

Trampfoot, outside, is heard to confide to himself, 'Meggisson's lot, this is. And a bad 'un!'

'Well!' says Mr Superintendent, laying his hand on the shoulder of the swarthy youth, 'and who's this?'

'Antonio, sir.'

'And what does he do here?'

'Come to give us a bit of music. No harm in that, I suppose?'

'A young foreign sailor?'

'Yes. He's a Spaniard. You're a Spaniard, aint you, Antonio?'

'Me Spanish.'

'And he don't know a word you say, not he, not if you was to talk to him till doomsday.' (Triumphantly, as if it redounded to the credit of the house.)

'Will he play something?'

'Oh, yes, if you like. Play something, Antonio. *You* ain't ashamed to play something; are you?'

The cracked guitar raises the feeblest ghost of a tune, and three of the women keep time to it with their heads, and the fourth with the child. If Antonio has brought any money in with him, I am afraid he will never take it out, and it even strikes me that his jacket and guitar may be in a bad way. But, the look of the young man and the tinkling of the instrument so change the place in a moment to a leaf out of Don

Quixote, that I wonder where his mule is stabled, until he leaves off.

I am bound to acknowledge (as it tends rather to my uncommercial confusion), that I occasioned a difficulty in this establishment, by having taken the child in my arms. For, on my offering to restore it to a ferocious joker not unstimulated by rum, who claimed to be its mother, that unnatural parent put her hands behind her, and declined to accept it; backing into the fireplace, and very shrilly declaring, regardless of remonstrance from her friends, that she knowed it to be Law, that whoever took a child from its mother of his own will, was bound to stick to it. The uncommercial sense of being in a rather ridiculous position with the poor little child beginning to be frightened, was relieved by my worthy friend and fellow constable, Trampfoot; who, laying hands on the article as if it were a Bottle, passed it on to the nearest woman, and bade her 'take hold of that.' As we came out, the Bottle was passed to the ferocious joker, and they all sat down as before, including Antonio and the guitar. It was clear that there was no such thing as a nightcap to this baby's head, and that even he never went to bed, but was always kept up – and would grow up, kept up – waiting for Jack.

Later still in the night, we came (by the court 'where the man was murdered,' and by the other court across the street, into which his body was dragged) to another parlour in another Entry, where several people were sitting round a fire in just the same way. It was a dirty and offensive place, with some ragged clothes drying in it; but there was a high shelf over the entrance-door (to be out of the reach of marauding hands, possibly), with two large white loaves on it, and a great piece of Cheshire cheese.

'Well!' says Mr Superintendent, with a comprehensive look all round. 'How do *you* do?'

'Not much to boast of, sir.' From the curtseying woman of the house. 'This is my good man, sir.'

'You are not registered as a common Lodging House?'

'No, sir.'

Sharpeye (in the Move-on tone) puts in the pertinent inquiry, 'Then why ain't you?'

'Ain't got no one here, Mr Sharpeye,' rejoins the woman and my good man together, 'but our own family.'

'How many are you in family?'

The woman takes time to count, under the pretence of coughing, and adds, as one scant of breath, 'Seven, sir.'

But she has missed one, so Sharpeye, who knows all about it, says:

'Here's a young man here makes eight, who ain't of your family?'

'No, Mr Sharpeye, he's a weekly lodger.'

'What does he do for a living?'

The young man here, takes the reply upon himself, and shortly answers, 'Ain't got nothing to do.'

The young man here, is modestly brooding behind a damp apron pendent from a clothes-line. As I glance at him I become – but I don't know why – vaguely reminded of Woolwich, Chatham, Portsmouth, and Dover. When we get out, my respected fellow-constable Sharpeye addressing Mr Superintendent, says:

'You noticed that young man, sir, in at Darby's?'

'Yes. What is he?'

'Deserter, sir.'

Mr Sharpeye further intimates that when we have done with his services, he will step back and take that young man. Which in course of time he does: feeling at perfect ease about finding him, and knowing for a moral certainty that nobody in that region will be gone to bed.

Later still in the night, we came to another parlour up a step or two from the street, which was very cleanly, neatly, even tastefully, kept, and in which, set forth on a draped chest of drawers masking the staircase, was such a profusion of ornamental crockery, that it would have furnished forth a handsome sale-booth at a fair. It backed up a stout old lady – HOGARTH drew her exact likeness more than once – and a boy who was carefully writing a copy in a copy-book.

'Well, ma'am, how do *you* do?'

Sweetly, she can assure the dear gentlemen, sweetly. Charmingly, charmingly. And overjoyed to see us.

'Why, this is a strange time for this boy to be writing his copy. In the middle of the night!'

'So it is, dear gentlemen, Heaven bless your welcome faces, and send ye prosperous, but he has been to the Play with a young friend for his diversion, and he combinates his improvement with entertainment by doing his school-writing afterwards, God be good to ye!'

The copy admonished human nature, to subjugate the fire of every fierce desire. One might have thought it recommended stirring the fire, the old lady so approved it. There she sat, rosily beaming at the copy-book and the boy, and invoking showers of blessings on our heads, when we left her in the middle of the night, waiting for Jack.

Later still in the night, we came to a nauseous room with an earth floor, into which the refuse scum of an alley trickled. The stench of this habitation was abominable; the seeming poverty of it, diseased and dire. Yet, here again, was visitor or lodger – a man sitting before the fire, like the rest of them elsewhere, and apparently not distasteful to the mistress's niece, who was also before the fire. The mistress herself had the misfortune of being in jail.

Three weird old women of transcendant ghastliness, were at needlework at a table in this room. Says Trampfoot to First Witch, 'What are you making?' Says she, 'Money-bags.'

'*What* are you making?' retorts Trampfoot, a little off his balance.

'Bags to hold your money,' says the witch shaking her head, and setting her teeth; 'you as has got it.'

She holds up a common cash-bag, and on the table is a heap of such bags. Witch Two laughs at us. Witch Three scowls at us. Witch sisterhood all, stitch, stitch. First Witch has a red circle round each eye. I fancy it like the beginning of the development of a perverted diabolical halo, and that when it spreads all round her head, she will die in the odour of devilry.

Trampfoot wishes to be informed what First Witch has got behind the table, down by the side of her, there? Witches Two and Three croak angrily, 'Show him the child!'

She drags out a skinny little arm from a brown dust-heap on the ground. Adjured not to disturb the child, she lets it drop again. Thus we find at last that there is one child in the world of Entries who goes to bed – if this be bed.

Mr Superintendent asks how long are they going to work at those bags?

How long? First Witch repeats. Going to have supper presently. See the cups and saucers, and the plates.

Mr Superintendent opines, it is rather late for supper, surely?

'Late? Ay! But we has to 'arn our supper afore we eats it!' Both the other witches repeat this after First Witch, and take the Uncommercial measurement with their eyes, as for a charmed winding-sheet. Some grim discourse ensues, referring to the mistress of the cave, who will be released from jail tomorrow. Witches pronounce Trampfoot 'right there,' when he deems it a trying distance for the old lady to walk; she shall be fetched by niece in a spring-cart.

As I took a parting look at First Witch in turning away, the red marks round her eyes seemed to have already grown larger, and she hungrily and thirstily looked out beyond me into the dark doorway, to see if Jack were there. For, Jack came even here, and the mistress had got into jail through deluding Jack.

When I at last ended this night of travel and got to bed, I failed to keep my mind on comfortable thoughts of Seaman's Homes (not overdone with strictness), and improved dock regulations giving Jack greater benefit of fire and candle aboard ship, through my mind's wandering among the vermin I had seen. Afterwards the same vermin ran all over my sleep. Evermore, when on a breezy day I see Poor Mercantile Jack running into port with a fair wind under all sail, I shall think of the unsleeping host of devourers who never go to bed, and are always in their set traps waiting for him.

9

The Uncommercial Traveller

All The Year Round, 24 March 1860 (*UT1* as 'Refreshments for Travellers')

The French idea of a 'restaurant' to refresh and restore travellers of both sexes during a journey was still foreign to British cities in 1860, but the end of March saw the second reading of Gladstone's 'Refreshment Houses and Wine Licensing Bill', which proposed: to let small retailers take out licences (at the discretion of the issuing magistrate) for the sale of wine to be consumed off the premises, to let eating-house keepers take out licences for the sale of wine to be consumed on the premises, and to place all eating houses under the control of the police; the Bill became law on 1 July 1860 (Refreshment Houses and Wine Licenses Act, 23 Vict. cap. 27). Dickens's paper is in one sense highly topical, anticipating a leader in *The Times* of 28 March, which repeats the main complaint in Dickens's essay: '[o]ne of the most grievous discomforts to which all visitors to London are exposed is the difficulty of finding in it either a dinner or a luncheon, more especially if ladies are of the party.... The want is in the deficiency of small Refreshment houses where people of moderate or even humble means may procure dinner and other necessary refreshments at a [small] cost' (p. 9, cols 4–5). Dickens may also have been encouraged to handle the subject following the enthusiastic response to his comments about railway hotels and travellers' fare, in his speeches to the Commercial Travellers' Schools in 1854 and 1859. The first of these had concluded with a description of 'that grope [in the dark] to the new Railway Hotel, which will be an excellent house when the customers come, but which at present has nothing to offer but a liberal allowance of damp mortar and new lime. [*Continued laughter*.]' (*Speeches*, p. 173). The joke about the railway pork-pie is still going strong (see also Vol. 3 of this edition, article 62).

The 'late high winds' mentioned by the 'Uncommercial Traveller' were a notable feature of the early spring 1860. An article in *The Times* of 29 February, headed 'Terrific Gale', noted how two men, thought to be dock labourers, had been blown off the towpath into the Surrey Canal 'at an early hour in the morning'; their bodies were never recovered. The same piece contained reports of falling masonry in Sydenham, Dulwich and Peckham, and of collapsed buildings and roofs at no fewer than five locations on or near the Walworth Road (p. 12, cols a, b). On 9 March Dickens wrote to Lever from Gad's Hill, 'We have fallen upon a second winter here, and are spinning like tops, in a vortex of east wind and snow' (*Pilgrim*, Vol. IX, p. 219). The 'Uncommercial Traveller' is not so reliable as a mere mask for Dickens himself, however, when he recalls 'breaking up' from boarding school (p. 77 below). While Dickens may have been content for his readers to imagine him to have received such a thoroughly middle-class education, he of course did not (see Michael Slater, 'How Many Nurses had Charles Dickens', *Prose Studies* 10 [1987], pp. 250–8). Then again, the reference to an 'oblong box of stale ... pastry' on display in a baker's window (p. 78) recalls a genuinely autobiographical recollection of Dickens's from the 'fragment' passed to Forster in 1847, about how he 'could not resist the stale pastry put out at half price on trays at the confectioners' doors on Tottenham Court Road' as he wandered to and fro from Warren's Blacking Factory (Forster, Book 1, Ch. 2).

The paper was considered as 'the most entertaining ... in the Uncommercial Traveller ... with the greatest accuracy and point', by the *Saturday Review* critic, Sir James Fitzjames Stephen (see Introduction, p. xvi), and excerpted at length in *The Examiner*, which called for an end to 'the sort of pastry-cook's shop so truthfully and graphically described in *All The Year Round*' (31 March 1860, p. 194, cols a, b).

Literary allusions (p. 76) 'saddling Surrey for the field': 'saddle white Surrey for the field', Shakespeare, *King Richard III*, Act 5, Sc. 3; (p. 76) 'I am aware that I never will be a slave': adapting 'Britons never, never, never will be slaves', lines from James Thomson's *Alfred, A Masque* (1740), Act 2, Scene the Last (later popularised as 'Rule, Britannia').

Illustration The preliminary sketch by 'Phiz' showing the arrival of the famous cutlet is something of an anomaly. According to D. Croal Thomson (*Life and Labours of Hablot Knight Browne, 'Phiz'* [1884], p. 147), Browne 'did no more work for Dickens after ... 1859', but Browne did have separate contracts with Chapman & Hall to illustrate reprints of Dickens's work such as the illustrated reissue of the 'Library Edition' (1861–85), under which he may have drawn the sketch. No plate was made from it, however, and it has never been used in volume editions of *UT*.

In the late high winds I was blown to a great many places – and indeed, wind or no wind, I generally have extensive transactions on hand in the article of Air – but I have not been blown to any English place lately, and I very seldom have been blown to any English place in my life, where I could get anything good to eat and drink in five minutes, or where, if I sought it, I was received with a welcome.

This is a curious thing to consider. But before (stimulated by my own experiences and the representations of many fellow-travellers of every uncommercial and commercial degree) I consider it further, I must utter a passing word of wonder concerning high winds.

I wonder why metropolitan gales always blow so hard at Walworth. I cannot imagine what Walworth has done to bring such windy punishment upon itself, as I never fail to find recorded in the newspapers when the wind has blown at all hard. Brixton seems to have something on its conscience; Peckham suffers more than a virtuous Peckham might be supposed to deserve; the howling neighbourhood of Deptford figures largely in the accounts of the ingenious gentlemen who are out in every wind that blows, and to whom it is an ill high wind that blows no good; but, there can hardly be any Walworth left by this time. It must surely be blown away. I have read of more chimney-stacks and house-copings coming down with terrific smashes at Walworth, and of more sacred edifices being nearly (not quite) blown out to sea from the same accursed locality, than I have read of practised thieves with the appearance and manners of gentlemen – a popular phenomenon which never existed on earth out of fiction and a police report. Again: I wonder why people are always blown into the Surrey Canal, and into no other piece of water? Why do people get up early and go out in groups, to be blown into the Surrey Canal? Do they say to one another, 'Welcome Death, so that we get into the newspapers'? Even that would be an insufficient explanation, because even then they might sometimes put themselves in the way of being blown into the Regent's Canal, instead of always saddling Surrey for the field. Some nameless policeman, too, is constantly, on the slightest provocation, getting himself blown into this same Surrey Canal. Will Sir Richard Mayne see to it, and restrain that weak-minded and feeble-bodied constable?

To resume the consideration of the curious question of Refreshment. I am a Briton, and, as such, I am aware that I never will be a slave – and yet I have a latent suspicion that there must be some slavery of wrong custom in this matter.

I travel by railroad. I start from home at seven or eight in the morning, after breakfasting hurriedly. What with skimming over the open landscape, what with mining in the damp bowels of the earth, what with banging, booming and shrieking the scores of miles away, I am hungry when I arrive at the 'Refreshment' station where I am expected. Please to observe, expected. I have said, I am hungry; perhaps I might say, with greater point and force, that I am to some extent exhausted, and that I need – in the expressive French sense of the word – to be restored. What is provided for my restoration? The apartment that is to restore me is a wind-trap, cunningly set to inveigle all the draughts in that country-side, and to communicate a special intensity and velocity to them as they rotate in two hurricanes: one, about my wretched head: one, about my wretched legs. The training of the young ladies behind the counter who are to restore me, has been from their infancy directed to the assumption of a defiant dramatic show that I am *not* expected. It is in vain for me to represent to them by my humble and conciliatory manners, that I wish to be liberal. It is in vain for me to represent to myself, for the encouragement of my sinking soul, that the young ladies have a pecuniary interest in my arrival. Neither my reason nor my feelings can make head against the cold glazed glare of eye with which I am assured that I am not expected, and not wanted. The solitary man among the bottles would sometimes take pity on me, if he dared, but he is powerless against the rights and mights of Woman. (Of the page I make no account, for, he is a boy, and therefore the natural enemy of Creation.) Chilling fast, in the deadly tornadoes to which my upper and lower extremities are exposed, and subdued by the moral disadvantage at which I stand, I turn my disconsolate eyes on the refreshments that are to restore me. I find that I must either scald my throat by insanely ladling into it, against time and for no wager, brown hot water stiffened with flour; or, I must make myself flaky and sick with Banbury cake; or, I must stuff into my delicate organisation a currant pincushion which I know will swell into immeasurable dimensions when it has got there; or, I must extort from an iron-bound quarry, with a fork, as if I were farming an inhospitable soil, some glutinous lumps of gristle and grease, called pork-pie. While thus forlornly occupied, I find that the depressing banquet on the table is, in every phase of its profoundly unsatisfactory character, so like the banquet at the meanest and shabbiest of evening parties, that I begin to think I must have 'brought down' to supper, the old lady unknown, blue with cold, who is setting her teeth on edge with a cool orange, at my elbow – that the pastrycook who has compounded for the company on the lowest terms per head, is a fraudulent bankrupt, redeeming his contract with the stale stock from his window – that, for some unexplained reason, the family giving the party have become my mortal foes, and have given it on purpose to affront me. Or, I fancy that I am 'breaking up' again at the evening conversazione at school, charged two-and-sixpence in the half-year's bill; or breaking down again at that celebrated evening party given at Mrs Bogles's boarding-house when I was a boarder there, on which occasion Mrs Bogles was taken in execution by a branch of the legal profession who got in as the harp, and was removed (with the keys and subscribed capital) to a place of durance, half an hour prior to the commencement of the festivities.

Take another case.

Mr Grazinglands, of the Midland Counties, came to London by railroad one morning last week, accompanied by the amiable and fascinating Mrs Grazinglands. Mr G. is a gentleman of a comfortable property, and had a little business to transact at the Bank of England, which required the concurrence and signature of Mrs G. Their business disposed of, Mr and Mrs Grazinglands viewed the Royal Exchange, and the exterior of St Paul's Cathedral. The spirits of Mrs Grazinglands then gradually beginning to flag, Mr Grazinglands (who is the tenderest of husbands) remarked with sympathy, 'Arabella, my dear, I fear you are faint.' Mrs Grazinglands replied, 'Alexander, I am rather faint; but don't mind me, I shall be better presently.' Touched by the feminine meekness of this answer, Mr Grazinglands looked in at a pastrycook's window, hesitating as to the expediency of lunching at that establishment. He beheld nothing to eat, but butter in various forms, slightly charged with jam, and languidly frizzling over tepid water. Two ancient turtle-shells, on which was inscribed the legend 'SOUPS,' decorated a glass partition within, enclosing a stuffy alcove, from which a ghastly mockery of a marriage-breakfast spread on a rickety table, warned the terrified traveller. An oblong box of stale and broken pastry at reduced prices, mounted on a stool, ornamented the doorway; and two high chairs, that looked as if they were performing on stilts, embellished the counter. Over the whole, a young lady presided, whose gloomy haughtiness as she surveyed the street, announced a deep-seated grievance against society, and an implacable determination to be avenged. From a beetle-haunted kitchen below this institution, fumes arose, suggestive of a class of soup which Mr Grazinglands knew, from painful experience, enfeebles the mind, distends the stomach, forces itself into the complexion, and tries to ooze out at the eyes. As he decided against entering, and turned away, Mrs Grazinglands, becoming perceptibly weaker, repeated, 'I am rather faint, Alexander, but don't mind me.' Urged to new efforts by these words of resignation, Mr Grazinglands looked in at a cold and floury baker's shop, where utilitarian buns unrelieved by a currant consorted with hard biscuits, a stone filter of cold water, a hard pale clock, and a hard little old woman with flaxen hair, of an undeveloped-farinaceous aspect, as if she had been fed upon seeds. He might have entered even here, but for the timely remembrance coming upon him that Jairing's was but round the corner.

Now, Jairing's being an hotel for families and gentlemen, in high repute among the midland counties, Mr Grazinglands plucked up a great spirit when he told Mrs Grazinglands she should have a chop there. That lady, likewise, felt that she was going to see Life. Arriving on that gay and festive scene, they found the second waiter, in a flabby undress, cleaning the windows of the empty coffee-room, and the first waiter, denuded of his white tie, making up his cruets behind the Post-office Directory. The latter (who took them in hand) was greatly put out by their patronage, and showed his mind to be troubled by a sense of the pressing necessity of instantly smuggling Mrs Grazinglands into the obscurest corner of the building. This slighted lady (who is the pride of her division of the county) was immediately conveyed, by several dark passages, and up and down several steps, into a penitential apartment at the back of the house, where five invalided old plate-warmers leaned up against one another under a discarded old melancholy sideboard, and where the wintry leaves of all the dining-tables in the house lay thick. Also, a sofa, of incomprehensible form regarded from any sofane point of view, murmured, 'Bed;' while an air of mingled fluffiness and heeltaps, added, 'Second Waiter's.' Secreted in this dismal hold, objects of a mysterious distrust and suspicion, Mr Grazinglands and his charming partner waited twenty minutes for the smoke (for it never came to a fire), twenty-five minutes for the sherry, half an hour for the table-cloth, forty minutes for the knives and forks, three-quarters of an hour for the chops, and an hour for the potatoes. On settling the little bill – which was not much more than the day's pay of a Lieutenant in the navy – Mr Grazinglands took heart to remonstrate against the general quality and cost of his reception. To whom the waiter replied, substantially, that Jairing's made it a merit to have accepted him on any terms; 'for,' added the waiter (unmistakably coughing at Mrs Grazinglands, the pride of her division of the county), 'when individuals is not staying in the 'Ouse, their favours is not as a rule looked upon as making it worth Mr Jairing's while; nor is it, indeed, a style of business Mr Jairing wishes.' Finally, Mr and Mrs Grazinglands passed out of Jairing's Hotel for Families and Gentlemen, in a state of the greatest depression, scorned by the bar; and did not recover their self-respect for several days.

Or take another case. Take your own case.

You are going off by railway, from any Terminus. You have twenty minutes for dinner, before you go. You want your dinner, and, like Doctor Johnson, sir, you like to dine. You present to your mind a picture of the refreshment-table at that terminus. The conventional shabby evening party supper – accepted as the model for all termini and all refreshment stations, because it is the last repast known to this state of existence of which any human creature would partake, but in the direst extremity – sickens your contemplation, and your words are these: 'I cannot dine on stale sponge-cakes that turn to sand in the mouth. I cannot dine on shining brown patties, composed of unknown animals within, and offering to my view the device of an indigestible star-fish in leaden pie-crust without. I cannot dine on a sandwich that has long been pining under an exhausted receiver. I cannot dine on barley-sugar. I cannot dine on Toffee.' You repair to the nearest hotel, and arrive, agitated, in the coffee-room.

It is a most astonishing fact that the waiter is very cold to you. Account for it how you may, smooth it over how you will, you cannot deny that he is cold to you. He is not glad to see you, he does not want you, he would much rather you hadn't come. He opposes to your flushed condition, an immovable composure. As if this were not enough, another waiter, born, as it would seem, expressly to look at you in this passage of your life, stands at a little distance, with his napkin under his arm and his hands folded, looking at you with all his might. You impress on your waiter that you have ten minutes for dinner, and he proposes that you shall begin with a bit of fish which will be ready in twenty. That proposal declined, he suggests – as a neat originality – 'a weal or mutton cutlet.' You close with either cutlet, any cutlet, anything. He goes, leisurely, behind a door and calls down some unseen shaft. A ventriloquial dialogue ensues, tending finally to the effect that weal only, is available on the spur of the moment. You anxiously call out, 'Veal then!' Your waiter, having settled that point, returns to array your tablecloth, with a table napkin folded cocked-hat-wise (slowly, for something out of window engages his eye), a white wine-glass, a green wine-glass, a blue finger-glass, a tumbler, and a powerful field battery of fourteen castors with nothing in them; or at all events – which is enough for your purpose – with nothing in them that will come out. All this time, the other waiter looks at you – with an air of mental comparison and curiosity, now, as if it had occurred to him that you are rather like his brother. Half your time gone, and nothing come but the jug of ale and the bread, you implore your waiter to 'see after that cutlet, waiter; pray do!' He cannot go at once, for he is carrying in seventeen pounds of American cheese for you to finish with, and a small Landed Estate of celery and watercress. The other waiter changes his leg, and takes a new view of you – doubtfully, now, as if he had rejected the resemblance to his brother, and had begun to think you more like his aunt or his grandmother. Again you beseech your waiter with pathetic indignation, to 'see after that cutlet!' He steps out to see after it, and by-and-by, when you are going away without it, comes back with it. Even then, he will not take the sham silver-cover off, without a pause for a flourish, and a look at the musty cutlet as if he were surprised to see it – which cannot possibly be the case, he must have seen it so often before. A sort of fur has been produced upon its surface by the cook's art, and, in a sham silver vessel staggering on two feet instead of three, is a cutaneous kind of sauce, of brown pimples and pickled cucumber. You order the bill, but your waiter cannot bring your bill yet, because he is bringing, instead, three flinty-hearted potatoes and two grim heads of broccoli, like the occasional ornaments on area railings, badly boiled. You know that you will never come to this pass, any more than to the cheese and celery, and you

Unpublished sketch by 'Phiz' intended to accompany 'Refreshments for Travellers'

imperatively demand your bill; but it takes time to get, even when gone for, because your waiter has to communicate with a lady who lives behind a sash-window in a corner, and who appears to have to refer to several Ledgers before she can make it out – as if you had been staying there a year. You become distracted to get away, and the other waiter, once more changing his leg, still looks at you – but suspiciously, now, as if you had begun to remind him of the party who took the great-coats last winter. Your bill at last brought and paid, at the rate of sixpence a mouthful, your waiter reproachfully reminds you that 'attendance is not charged for a single meal,' and you have to search in all your pockets for sixpence more. He has a worse opinion of you than ever, when you have given it to him, and lets you out into the street with the air of one saying to himself, as you cannot doubt he is, 'I hope we shall never see *you* here again!'

Or, take any other of the numerous travelling instances in which, with more time at your disposal, you are, have been, or may be, equally ill served. Take the old-established Bull's Head, with its old-established knife-boxes on its old-established sideboards, its old-established flue under its old-established four-post bedsteads in its old-established airless rooms, its old-established frouziness upstairs and downstairs, its old-established cookery, and its old-established principles of plunder. Count up your injuries, in its side-dishes of ailing sweetbreads in white poultices, of apothecaries' powders in rice for curry, of pale stewed bits of calf ineffectually relying for an adventitious interest on forcemeat balls. You have had experience of the old-established Bull's Head stringy fowls, with lower extremities like wooden legs, sticking up out of the dish; of its cannibalic boiled mutton, gushing horribly among its capers, when carved; of its little dishes of pastry – roofs of spermaceti ointment, erected over half an apple or four gooseberries. Well for you if you have yet forgotten the old-established Bull's Head fruity port: whose reputation was gained solely by the old-established price the Bull's Head put upon it, and by the old-established air with which the Bull's Head set the glasses and D'Oyleys on, and held that Liquid Gout to the three-and-sixpenny wax-candle, as if its old-established colour hadn't come from the dyer's.

Or lastly, take to finish with, two cases that we all know, every day.

We all know the new hotel near the station, where it is always gusty, going up the lane which is always muddy, where we are sure to arrive at night, and where we make the gas start awfully when we open the front door. We all know the flooring of the passages and staircases that is too new, and the walls that are too new, and the house that is haunted by the ghost of mortar. We all know the doors that have cracked, and the cracked shutters through which we get a glimpse of the disconsolate moon. We all know the new people who have come to keep the new hotel, and who wish they had never come, and who (inevitable result) wish *we* had never come. We all know how much too scant and smooth and bright the new furniture is, and how it has never settled down, and cannot fit itself into right places, and will get into wrong places. We all know how the gas, being lighted, shows maps of Damp upon the walls. We all know how the ghost of mortar passes into our sandwich, stirs our negus, goes up to bed with us, ascends the pale bedroom chimney, and prevents the smoke from following. We all know how a leg of our chair comes off, at breakfast in the morning, and how the dejected waiter attributes the accident to a general greenness pervading the establishment, and informs us, in reply to a local inquiry, that he is thankful to say he is an entire stranger in that part of the country, and is going back to his own connexion on Saturday.

We all know, on the other hand, the great station hotel belonging to the company of proprietors, which has suddenly sprung up in the back outskirts of any place we like to name, and where we look out of our palatial windows, at little back yards and gardens, old summer-houses, fowl-houses, pigeon-traps, and pigsties. We all know this hotel in which we can get anything we want, after its kind, for money; but where nobody is glad to see us, or sorry to see us, or minds (our bill paid) whether we come, or go, or how, or when, or why, or cares about us. We all know this hotel, where we have no individuality, but put ourselves into the general post, as it were, and are sorted and disposed of according to our division. We all know that we can get on very well indeed at such a place, but still not perfectly well; and this may be, because the place is largely wholesale, and there is a lingering personal retail interest within us that asks to be satisfied.

To sum up. My uncommercial travelling has not yet brought me to the conclusion that we are close to perfection in these matters. And just as I do not believe that the end of the world will ever be near at hand, so long as any of the very tiresome and arrogant people who constantly predict that catastrophe are left in it, so, I shall have small faith in the Hotel Millennium, while any of the uncomfortable superstitions I have glanced at, remain in existence.

IO

The Uncommercial Traveller

All The Year Round, 7 April 1860 (*UT1* as 'Travelling Abroad')

The 'German chariot' which conveys the narrator on his dreamy journey is modelled on the coach in which Dickens and his household made their trips to Italy (1844–5), Switzerland and France (1846–7). In (May) 1844 Dickens related to Forster how he hoped to find 'some good old shabby devil of a coach – one of those vast phantoms that hide themselves in a corner of the Pantechnicon' and how he had bought such a one for £45. 'As for comfort ...', he continued, 'it is about the size of your library; with night-lamps and day-lamps and pockets and imperials and leathern cellars, and the most extraordinary contrivances'; sitting inside it, he felt 'a perfect Sentimental Traveller' (*Pilgrim*, Vol. IV, p. 127 & n.). In *Pictures from Italy* this same carriage is described as 'an English travelling carriage of considerable proportions, fresh from the shady halls of the Pantechnicon' (1846; 'Going through France'). As in the travel book, Dickens here displays a tendency to give comically literal translations of common French expressions ('ordinary wine', 'It is well', p. 87); 'the British Boaxe' (p. 90) appears to be an imitation of how the concept of boxing might be rendered in a French accent.

According to Charles Dickens Jr, the narrator's description of meeting with 'a very queer small boy' on the high road between Gravesend and Rochester 'has been more extensively quoted, it may be fairly assumed, than anything [Dickens] ever wrote' (*UT4*, p. xviii). The description transforms an anecdote which Dickens liked to tell concerning his acquisition of Gad's Hill Place. Although he did not set up house there permanently until October 1860, he had bought it in 1856, and known of it since his time as a child in Chatham. Writing to M. de Cerjat in January 1857, Dickens relates (with embellishments) how, in 1855, he had walked past it with W. H. Wills and said to him,

> [the house] has always had a curious interest for me, because, when I was a small boy down in these parts, I thought it the most beautiful house ... ever seen. And my poor father used to bring me to look at it, and used to say that if I ever grew up to be a clever man, perhaps I might own that house, or such another house. In remembrance of which, I have always in passing, looked to see if it was to be sold or let; and it has never been to me like any other house, and it has never changed at all. [*Pilgrim*, Vol. VIII, pp. 265–6 & n.]

Later that day, the anecdote continues, Wills dined by chance with the owner's daughter, from whom he discovered that the house was for sale, and lost no time in informing Dickens. In fact, Dickens's letter to Wills of 9 February 1855 suggests a different sequence of events (see Alan S. Watts, *Dickens at Gad's Hill* [1989], p. 20). Nevertheless, Dickens clearly felt that a section of his readers would be familiar enough with some version of the anecdote to make his allusion to it in the present paper intelligible.

Forster comments that on arrival in Paris in the winter of 1846, Dickens 'went at first rather frequently to the Morgue, until shocked by something so repulsive that he had not courage for a long time to go back' (*Forster*, Book 5, Ch. 7). This experience may lie behind Dickens's account here of a 'haunting', while the remarks concerning the susceptibility of children to nightmares seem to echo opinions in one of Charles Lamb's *Essays of Elia*, a work which Dickens knew well ('Witches and Other Night-Fears'; see *Pilgrim*, Vol. II, p. 139 & n.). More certainly, the mention of an 'old grey man lying all alone' seen in the Morgue 'one Christmas Day' (p. 88 below) relates to the 'old man with a grey head' seen by Dickens there on 31 December 1846; 'he lay there, all alone, like an impersonation of the wintry eighteen hundred and forty-six', Dickens wrote later to Forster (*Pilgrim*, Vol. V, p. 3). Other visits to the Morgue are recounted in article 24 below, and articles 13 and 49 of Vol. 3 of this edition. Harry Stone considers in depth the nature of Dickens's continuing interest, in *The Night Side of Dickens* (1994), pp. 86–100, 564–6.

Literary allusions (p. 86) 'Where Falstaff went out to rob those travellers, and ran away': Shakespeare, *I Henry IV*, Act 2, Sc. 2; (p. 86) 'Blow, blow, thou winter wind': Amiens's song, Shakespeare, *As You Like It*, Act 2, Sc. 7; (p. 87) 'Sterne's Maria': the crazed country girl sentimentally described both in *The Life and Opinions of Tristram Shandy*, Vol. 9 (1767), Ch. 24, and in *A Sentimental Journey through France and Italy* (1768), sequence titled 'Maria – Moulines' et. seq.; (p. 87) 'France stood where I had left it': paraphrase of 'Stands Scotland where it did?', Shakespeare, *Macbeth*, Act 4, Sc. 3; (p. 94) 'the nursery rhyme about Banbury Cross': traditional rhyme beginning 'Ride a cock horse to Banbury Cross', collected in J. G. Rusher's *Banbury List and Directory* (1812 etc.); (p. 94) 'Don Quixote on the back of the wooden horse': Cervantes's *Don Quixote* Part II (1615), Ch. 41.

I got into the travelling chariot – it was of German make, roomy, heavy, and unvarnished – I got into the travelling chariot, pulled up the steps after me, shut myself in with a smart bang of the door, and gave the word 'Go on!'

Immediately, all that W. and S.W. division of London began to slide away at a pace so lively, that I was over the river, and past the Old Kent-road, and out on Blackheath, and even ascending Shooter's Hill, before I had had time to look about me in the carriage, like a collected traveller.

I had two ample Imperials on the roof, other fitted storage for luggage in front, and other up behind; I had a net for books overhead, great pockets to all the windows, a leathern pouch or two hung up for odds and ends, and a reading-lamp fixed in the back of the chariot, in case I should be benighted. I was amply provided in all respects, and had no idea where I was going (which was delightful), except that I was going abroad.

So smooth was the old high road, and so fresh were the horses, and so fast went I, that it was midway between Gravesend and Rochester, and the widening river was bearing the ships, white-sailed or black-smoked, out to sea, when I noticed by the wayside a very queer small boy.

'Halloa!' said I, to the very queer small boy, 'where do you live?'

'At Chatham,' says he.

'What do you do there?' says I.

'I go to school,' says he.

I took him up in a moment, and we went on. Presently, the very queer small boy says, 'This is Gadshill we are coming to, where Falstaff went out to rob those travellers, and ran away.'

'You know something about Falstaff, eh?' said I.

'All about him,' said the very queer small boy. 'I am old (I am nine), and I read all sorts of books. But *do* let us stop at the top of the hill, and look at the house there, if you please!'

'You admire that house?' said I.

'Bless you, sir,' said the very queer small boy, 'when I was not more than half as old as nine, it used to be a treat for me to be brought to look at it. And now, I am nine, I come by myself to look at it. And ever since I can recollect, my father, seeing me so fond of it, has often said to me, "If you were to be very persevering and were to work hard, you might some day come to live in it." Though that's impossible!' said the very queer small boy, drawing a low breath, and now staring at the house out of window with all his might.

I was rather amazed to be told this by the very queer small boy; for that house happens to be *my* house, and I have reason to believe that what he said was true.

Well! I made no halt there, and I soon dropped the very queer small boy and went on. Over the road where the old Romans used to march, over the road where the old Canterbury pilgrims used to go, over the road where the travelling trains of the old imperious priests and princes used to jingle on horseback between the continent and this Island through the mud and water, over the road where Shakespeare hummed to himself, 'Blow, blow, thou winter wind,' as he sat in the saddle at the gate of the inn yard noticing the carriers; all among the cherry orchards, apple orchards, cornfields, and hop gardens; so went I, by Canterbury to Dover. There, the sea was tumbling in, with deep sounds, after dark, and the revolving French light on Cape Grinez was seen regularly bursting out and becoming obscured, as if the head of a gigantic light-keeper in an anxious state of mind were interposed every half minute, to look how it was burning.

Early in the morning I was on the deck of the steam-packet, and we were aiming at the bar in the usual intolerable manner, and the bar was aiming at us in the usual intolerable manner, and the bar got by far the best of it, and we got by far the worst – all in the usual intolerable manner.

But, when I was clear of the Custom House on the other side, and when I began to make the dust fly on the thirsty French roads, and when the twigsome trees by the wayside (which, I suppose, never will grow leafy, for they never did) guarded here and there a dusty soldier, or field labourer, baking on a heap of broken stones, sound asleep in a fiction of shade, I began to recover my travelling spirits. Coming upon the breaker of the broken stones, in a hard, hot, shining hat, on which the sun played at a distance as on a burning-glass, I felt that now, indeed, I was in the dear old France of my affections. I should have known it, without the well-remembered bottle of rough ordinary wine, the cold roast fowl, the loaf, and the pinch of salt, on which I lunched with unspeakable satisfaction, from one of the stuffed pockets of the chariot.

I must have fallen asleep after lunch, for when a bright face looked in at the window, I started, and said:

'Good God, Louis, I dreamed you were dead!'

My cheerful servant laughed, and answered:

'Me? Not at all, sir.'

'How glad I am to wake! What are we doing, Louis?'

'We go to take relay of horses. Will you walk up the hill?'

'Certainly.'

Welcome the old French hill, with the old French lunatic (not in the most distant degree related to Sterne's Maria) living in a thatched dog-kennel half way up, and flying out with his crutch and his big head and extended nightcap, to be beforehand with the old men and women exhibiting crippled children, and with the children exhibiting old men and women, ugly and blind, who always seemed by resurrectionary process to be recalled out of the elements for the sudden peopling of the solitude!

'It is well,' said I, scattering among them what small coin I had; 'here comes Louis, and I am quite roused from my nap.'

We journeyed on again, and I welcomed every new assurance that France stood where I had left it. There were the posting-houses, with their archways, dirty stable-yards, and clean post-masters' wives, bright women of business, looking on at the putting-to of the horses; there were the postilions counting what money they got, into their hats, and never making enough of it; there were the standard population of grey horses of Flanders descent, invariably biting one another when they got a chance; there were the fleecy sheepskins, looped on over their uniforms by the postilions, like bibbed aprons, when it blew and rained; there were their jack-boots, and their cracking whips; there were the cathedrals that I got out to see, as under some cruel bondage, in no wise desiring to see them; there were the little towns that appeared to have no reason for being towns, since most of their houses were to let and nobody could be induced to look at them, except the people who couldn't let them and had nothing else to do but look at them all day. I lay a night upon the road and enjoyed delectable cookery of potatoes, and some other sensible things, adoption of which at home would inevitably be shown to be fraught with ruin, somehow or other, to that rickety national blessing, the British farmer; and at last I was rattled, like a single pill in a box, over leagues of stones, until – madly cracking, plunging, and flourishing two grey tails about – I made my triumphal entry into Paris.

At Paris, I took an upper apartment for a few days in one of the hotels of the Rue de Rivoli: my front windows looking into the garden of the Tuileries (where the principal difference between the nursemaids and the flowers seemed to be that the former were locomotive, and the latter not): my back windows looking at all the other back windows in the hotel, and deep down into a paved yard, where my German chariot had retired under a tight-fitting archway, to all appearance, for life, and where bells rang all day without anybody's minding them but certain chamberlains with feather brooms and green baize caps, who here and there leaned out of some high window placidly looking down, and where neat waiters with trays on their left shoulders passed and repassed from morning to night.

Whenever I am at Paris, I am dragged by invisible force into the Morgue. I never want to go there, but am always pulled there. One Christmas Day, when I would rather have been anywhere else, I was attracted in, to see an old grey man lying all alone on his cold bed, with a tap of water turned on over his grey hair, and running drip, drip, drip, down his wretched face until it got to the corner of his mouth, where it took a turn and made him look sly. One New Year's Morning (by the same token, the sun was shining outside, and there was a mountebank balancing a feather on his nose, within a yard of the gate), I was pulled in again to look at a flaxen-haired boy of eighteen with a heart hanging on his breast – 'from his mother,' was engraven on it – who had come into the net across the river, with a bullet-wound in his fair forehead and his hands cut with a knife, but whence or how was a blank mystery. This time, I was forced into the same dread place, to see a large dark man whose disfigurement by water was in a frightful manner, comic, and whose expression was that of a prize-fighter who had closed his eyelids under a heavy blow, but was going immediately to open them, shake his head, and 'come up smiling.' O what this large dark man cost me in that bright city!

It was very hot weather, and he was none the better for that, and I

Leaving the Morgue

was much the worse. Indeed, a very neat and pleasant little woman, with the key of her lodging on her forefinger, who had been showing him to her little girl while she and the child ate sweetmeats, observed monsieur looking poorly as we came out together, and asked monsieur, with her wondering little eyebrows prettily raised, if there were anything the matter? Faintly replying in the negative, monsieur crossed the road to a wineshop, got some brandy, and resolved to freshen himself with a dip in the great floating bath on the river.

The bath was crowded in the usual airy manner, by a male population in striped drawers of various gay colours, who walked up and down arm in arm, drank coffee, smoked cigars, sat at little tables, conversed politely with the damsels who dispensed the towels, and every now and then pitched themselves into the river head foremost, and came out again to repeat this social routine. I made haste to participate in the water part of the entertainments, and was in the full enjoyment of a delightful bath, when all in a moment I was seized with an unreasonable idea that the large dark body was floating straight at me.

I was out of the river, and dressing instantly. In the shock I had taken some water into my mouth, and it turned me sick, for I fancied that the contamination of the creature was in it. I had got back to my cool darkened room in the hotel, and was lying on a sofa there, before I began to reason with myself.

Of course, I knew perfectly well that the large dark creature was stone dead, and that I should no more come upon him out of the place where I had seen him dead, than I should come upon the cathedral of Notre-Dame in an entirely new situation. What troubled me was the picture of the creature; and that had so curiously and strongly painted itself upon my brain, that I could not get rid of it until it was worn out.

I noticed the peculiarities of this possession, while it was a real discomfort to me. That very day, at dinner, some morsel on my plate looked like a piece of him, and I was glad to get up and go out. Later in the evening, I was walking along the Rue St Honoré, when I saw a bill at a public room there, announcing small-sword exercise, broad-sword exercise, wrestling, and other such feats. I went in, and, some of the sword play being very skilful, remained. A specimen of our own national sport, The British Boaxe, was announced to be given at the close of the evening. In an evil hour, I determined to wait for this Boaxe, as became a Briton. It was a clumsy specimen (executed by two English grooms out of place), but, one of the combatants, receiving a straight right-hander with the glove between his eyes, did exactly what the large dark creature in the Morgue had seemed going to do – and finished me for that night.

There was a rather sickly smell (not at all an unusual fragrance in Paris) in the little ante-room of my apartment at the hotel. The large dark creature in the Morgue was by no direct experience associated with my sense of smell, because, when I came to the knowledge of him, he lay behind a wall of thick plate-glass, as good as a wall of steel or marble for that matter. Yet the whiff of the room never failed to reproduce him. What was more curious was the capriciousness with which his portrait seemed to light itself up in my mind, elsewhere; I might be walking in the Palais Royal, lazily enjoying the shop windows, and might be regaling myself with one of the ready-made clothes shops that are set out there. My eyes, wandering over impossible-waisted dressing-gowns and luminous waistcoats, would fall upon the master, or the shopman, or even the very dummy at the door, and would suggest to me, 'Something like him!' – and instantly I was sickened again.

This would happen at the theatre, in the same manner. Often, it would happen in the street, when I certainly was not looking for the likeness, and when probably there was no likeness there. It was not because the creature was dead that I was so haunted, because I know that I might have been (and I know it because I have been) equally attended by the image of a living aversion. This lasted about a week. The picture did not fade by degrees, in the sense that it became a whit less forcible and distinct, but in the sense that it obtruded itself less and less frequently. The experience may be worth considering by some who have the care of children. It would be difficult to overstate the intensity and accuracy of an intelligent child's observation. At that impressible time of life, it must sometimes produce a fixed impression. If the fixed impression be of an object terrible to the child, it will be (for want of reasoning upon) inseparable from great fear. Force the child at such a time, be Spartan with it, send it into the dark against its will, leave it in a lonely bedroom against its will, and you had better murder it.

On a bright morning I rattled away from Paris in the German chariot, and left the large dark creature behind me for good. I ought to confess, though, that I had been drawn back to the Morgue, after he was put under ground, to look at his clothes, and that I found them frightfully like him – particularly his boots. However, I rattled away for Switzerland, looking forward and not backward, and so we parted company.

Welcome again, the long long spell of France, with the queer country inns, full of vases of flowers and clocks, in the dull little towns, and with the little population not at all dull on the little Boulevard in the evening, under the little trees! Welcome Monsieur the Curé walking alone in the early morning a short way out of the town, reading that eternal Breviary of yours, which surely might be almost read, without book, by this time? Welcome Monsieur the Curé, later in the day, jolting through the highway dust (as if you had already ascended to the cloudy region), in a very big-headed cabriolet, with the dried mud of a dozen winters on it. Welcome again Monsieur the Curé, as we exchange salutations: you, straightening your back to look at the German chariot, while picking in your little village garden a vegetable or two for the day's soup; I, looking out of the German chariot window in that delicious traveller's-trance which knows no cares, no yesterdays, no tomorrows, nothing but the passing objects and the passing scents and sounds! And so I came, in due course of delight, to Strasbourg, where I passed a wet Sunday evening at a window, while an idle trifle of a vaudeville was played for me at the opposite house.

How such a large house came to have only three people living in it, was its own affair. There were at least a score of windows in its high roof alone; how many in its grotesque front, I soon gave up counting. The owner was a shopkeeper, by name Straudenheim; by trade − I couldn't make out what by trade, for he had forborne to write that up, and his shop was shut.

At first, as I looked at Straudenheim's through the steadily falling rain, I set him up in business in the goose-liver line. But, inspection of Straudenheim, who became visible at a window on the second floor, convinced me that there was something more precious than liver in the case. He wore a black velvet skull-cap, and looked usurious and rich. A large-lipped, pear-nosed old man, with white hair, and keen eyes, though near-sighted. He was writing at a desk, was Straudenheim, and ever and again left off writing, put his pen in his mouth, and went through actions with his right hand, like a man steadying piles of cash. Five-franc pieces, Straudenheim, or golden Napoleons? A jeweller, Straudenheim, a dealer in money, a diamond merchant, or what?

Below Straudenheim, at a window on the first floor, sat his house-keeper − far from young, but of a comely presence, suggestive of a well-matured foot and ankle. She was cheerily dressed, had a fan in her hand, and wore large gold earrings and a large gold cross. She would have been out holiday-making (as I settled it) but for the pestilent rain. Strasbourg had given up holiday-making for that once, as a bad job, because the rain was jerking in gushes out of the old roof-spouts, and running in a brook down the middle of the street. The housekeeper, her arms folded on her bosom and her fan tapping her chin, was bright and smiling at her open window, but otherwise Straudenheim's house front was very dreary. The housekeeper's was the only open window in it; Straudenheim kept himself close, though it was a sultry evening when air is pleasant, and though the rain had brought into the town that vague refreshing smell of grass which rain does bring in the summer-time.

The dim appearance of a man at Straudenheim's shoulder, inspired me with a misgiving that somebody had come to murder that flourishing merchant for the wealth with which I had handsomely endowed him: the rather, as it was an excited man, lean and long of figure, and evidently stealthy of foot. But, he conferred with Straudenheim instead of doing him a mortal injury, and then they both softly opened the other window of that room − which was immediately over the housekeeper's − and tried to see her by looking down. And my opinion of Straudenheim was much lowered when I saw that eminent citizen spit out of window, clearly with the hope of spitting on the housekeeper.

The unconscious housekeeper fanned herself, tossed her head, and laughed. Though unconscious of Straudenheim, she was conscious of somebody else – of me? – there was nobody else.

After leaning so far out of window, that I confidently expected to see their heels tilt up, Straudenheim and the lean man drew their heads in and shut the window. Presently, the house door secretly opened, and they slowly and spitefully crept forth into the pouring rain. They were coming over to me (I thought) to demand satisfaction for my looking at the housekeeper, when they plunged into a recess in the architecture under my window, and dragged out the puniest of little soldiers begirt with the most innocent of little swords. The tall glazed head-dress of this warrior, Straudenheim instantly knocked off, and out of it fell two sugar-sticks, and three or four large lumps of sugar.

The warrior made no effort to recover his property or to pick up his shako, but looked with an expression of attention at Straudenheim when he kicked him five times, and also at the lean man when *he* kicked him five times, and again at Straudenheim when he tore the breast of his (the warrior's) little coat open, and shook all his ten fingers in his face, as if they were ten thousand. When these outrages had been committed, Straudenheim and his man went into the house again and barred the door. A wonderful circumstance was, that the housekeeper who saw it all (and who could have taken six such warriors to her buxom bosom at once), only fanned herself and laughed as she had laughed before, and seemed to have no opinion about it, one way or other.

But, the chief effect of the drama was the remarkable vengeance taken by the little warrior. Left alone in the rain, he picked up his shako; put it on, all wet and dirty as it was; retired into a court, of which Straudenheim's house formed the corner; wheeled about; and bringing his two forefingers close to the top of his nose, rubbed them over one another, crosswise, in derision, defiance, and contempt of Straudenheim. Although Straudenheim could not possibly be supposed to be conscious of this strange proceeding, it so inflated and comforted the little warrior's soul, that twice he went away, and twice came back into the court to repeat it, as though it must goad his enemy to madness. Not only that, but he afterwards came back with two other small warriors, and they all three did it together. Not only that – as I live to tell the tale! – but just as it was falling quite dark, the three came back, bringing with them a huge, bearded Sapper, whom they moved, by recital of the original wrong, to go through the same performance, with the same complete absence of all possible knowledge of it on the part of Straudenheim. And then they all went away, arm in arm, singing.

I went away, too, in the German chariot at sunrise, and rattled on, day after day, like one in a sweet dream; with so many clear little bells on the harness of the horses, that the nursery rhyme about Banbury Cross, and the venerable lady who rode in state there, was always in my ears. And now I came into the land of wooden houses, innocent cakes, thin butter soup, and spotless little inn bedrooms with a family likeness to Dairies. And now the Swiss marksmen were for ever rifle-shooting at marks across gorges, so exceedingly near my ear, that I felt like a new Gesler in a Canton of Tells, and went in highly-deserved danger of my tyrannical life. The prizes at these shootings, were watches, smart handkerchiefs, hats, spoons, and (above all) tea-trays; and at these contests I came upon a more than usually accomplished and amiable countryman of my own, who had shot himself deaf in whole years of competition, and had won so many tea-trays that he went about the country with his carriage full of them, like a glorified Cheap-Jack.

In the mountain country into which I had now travelled, a yoke of oxen were sometimes hooked on before the post-horses, and I went lumbering up, up, up, through mist and rain, with the roar of falling water for change of music. Of a sudden, mist and rain would clear away, and I would come down into picturesque little towns with gleaming spires and odd towers; and would stroll afoot into market-places in steep winding streets, where a hundred women in bodices, sold eggs and honey, butter and fruit, and suckled their children as they sat by their clean baskets, and had such enormous goitres (or glandular swellings in the throat) that it became a science to know where the nurse ended and the child began. About this time, I deserted my German chariot for the back of a mule (in colour and consistency so very like a dusty old hair trunk I once had at school, that I half expected to see my initials in brass-headed nails on his backbone), and went up a thousand rugged ways, and looked down at a thousand woods of fir and pine, and would on the whole have preferred my mule's keeping a little nearer to the inside, and not usually travelling with a hoof or two over the precipice, though much consoled by explanation that this was to be attributed to his great sagacity, by reason of his carrying broad loads of wood at other times, and not being clear but that I myself belonged to that station of life, and required as much room as they. He brought me safely, in his own wise way, among the passes of the Alps, and here I enjoyed a dozen climates a day; being now (like Don Quixote on the back of the wooden horse) in the region of wind, now in the region of fire, now in the region of unmelting ice and snow. Here, I passed over trembling domes of ice, beneath which the cataract was roaring; and here was received under arches of icicles, of unspeakable beauty; and here the sweet air was so bracing and so light, that at halting-times I rolled in the snow when I saw my mule do it, thinking that he must know best. At this part of the journey we would come, at mid-day, into half an hour's thaw: when the rough mountain inn would be found on an island of deep mud in a sea of snow, while the baiting strings of mules, and the carts full of casks and bales, which had been in an Arctic condition a mile off, would steam again. By such ways and means, I would come to the cluster of châlets where I had to turn out of the track to see the waterfall; and then, uttering a howl like a young giant, on espying a traveller – in other words, something to eat – coming up the steep, the idiot lying on the wood-pile who sunned himself and nursed his goitre, would rouse the woman-guide within the hut, who would stream out hastily, throwing her child over one of her shoulders and her goitre over the other, as she came along. I slept at religious houses, and bleak refuges of many kinds, on this journey, and by the stove at night heard stories of travellers who had perished within call, in wreaths and drifts of snow. One night the stove within, and the cold outside, awakened childish associations long forgotten, and I dreamed I was in Russia – the identical serf out of a picture-book I had, before I could read it for myself – and that I was going to be knouted by a noble personage in a fur cap, boots, and earrings, who, I think, must have come out of some melodrama.

Commend me to the beautiful waters among these mountains! Though I was not of their mind: they, being inveterately bent on getting down into the level country, and I ardently desiring to linger where I was. What desperate leaps they took, what dark abysses they plunged into, what rocks they wore away, what echoes they invoked! In one part where I went, they were pressed into the service of carrying wood down, to be burnt next winter, as costly fuel, in Italy. But, their fierce savage nature was not to be easily constrained, and they fought with every limb of the wood; whirling it round and round, stripping its bark away, dashing it against pointed corners, driving it out of the course, and roaring and flying at the peasants who steered it back again from the bank with long stout poles. Alas! concurrent streams of time and water carried *me* down fast, and I came, on an exquisitely clear day, to the Lausanne shore of the Lake of Geneva, where I stood looking at the bright blue water, the flushed white mountains opposite, and the boats at my feet with their furled Mediterranean sails, showing like enormous magnifications of this goose-quill pen that is now in my hand.

The sky became overcast without any notice; a wind very like the March east wind of England, blew across me; and a voice said, 'How do you like it? Will it do?'

I had merely shut myself, for half a minute, in a German travelling chariot that stood for sale in the Carriage Department of the London Pantechnicon. I had a commission to buy it, for a friend who was going abroad; and the look and manner of the chariot, as I tried the cushions and the springs, brought all these hints of travelling remembrance before me.

'It will do very well,' said I, rather sorrowfully, as I got out at the other door, and shut the carriage up.

I I

The Uncommercial Traveller

All The Year Round, 21 April 1860 (*UT1* as 'The Great Tasmania's Cargo')

The London, Chatham & Dover railway, formed in 1859, had its terminus at London Bridge; there were barracks at Chatham. Dickens used this line frequently in the 1860s, boarding at Higham for journeys from Gad's Hill to both London and the south-east coast. Between 19 and 22 March 1860, an inquest was held at the Crown Court, St George's Hall, Liverpool, into the deaths of British soldiers discharged from active service in India, who had fallen ill on the transport ship *Great Tasmania* during the voyage home. The majority were soldiers who, 'refusing to be transferred from the service of the East India company to that of Her Majesty, without receiving the usual bounty given to recruits, were discharged and ordered to be sent home' (*The Times*, 20 March, p. 12, col. b). The ship had set out from Calcutta in November 1859 and had reached anchorage in the Mersey on the morning of 15 March, with doctors reporting 'two deaths and about 60 bad cases of scurvy' (*The Times, ibid.*), but, according to India Office records (The British Library) signed by Captain Alexander Pond, by the 23rd of the month, there had been no less than sixty-two casualties (L/MIL/10/320, p. 39). During the intervening period, the sick had been removed to the Liverpool Workhouse and given every medical attention. Over one in thirteen of the 971 passengers who made the journey thus failed to survive it.

Articles in the *Manchester Guardian* and *The Times* (21–23 March) reproduced the Coroner's Report and recorded much of the evidence taken during the Inquest. Gunner John Worth of the Bengal Horse Artillery had testified, for example, that of the ship's stores, '[t]he beef was very bad, and when boiled "stunk so horribly" that it had to be thrown overboard. ... The limejuice was weak and not fit to drink. The biscuits were hard, musty, mouldy and maggotty until they reached St Helena. The water was black and sometimes rusty. The suet "stunk" ...' (*Manchester Guardian*, 21 March 1860, p. 3, col. c). Other versions of events, however, stressed the excesses and intemperance of the men in the depot at Chinsurah, near Calcutta, prior to embarkation, as the major factor in their physical deterioration. A lieutenant in the 3rd Bengal recorded that 'there was one continued scene of drunkenness. On several occasions the men were so drunk that they were not able to parade, and sold their clothes and all they could possibly lay hold of to buy liquor' (*The Times*, 20 March 1860, p. 12, col. c). The jury's eventual verdict was that the officers who had signed the general inspection report were culpable 'so far as the quality of the stores was concerned', but considered it 'an imperative to urge upon the Government the necessity of ... a change in the system of military inspection ... before soldiers leave India, or any other foreign country' (*Manchester Guardian*, 23 March 1860, p. 3, col. c).

From such reports, a journalist of Dickens's calibre could easily have worked up the detailed descriptions included in the essay. Indeed, no explicit reference to the *Great Tasmania* scandal or to travelling to Liverpool at this period is to be found in Dickens's correspondence (see headnote to article 8). However, a letter states that on 15 March he is 'positively obliged to go out of town' on ' "All The Year Round" business', which 'cannot be postponed, and must be done'. Subsequent letters written from London show that he was 'expressly engaged out of town' on 17 March, while on 30 March he reports himself to 'have been much engaged away from home'. Dickens could thus well have been in Liverpool on one or more occasions during the last fortnight of March, to visit the Workhouse and/or to attend the inquest of which he writes so passionately. Writing to Wills on Wednesday, 28 March, Dickens states that a family problem arising 'when I got home last night' means that 'there is not a hope of my doing the Uncommercial, in time for Saturday's American Mail.... Can we make up the No. without it, for America, and afterwards re-make it up, with it, for this country?' (see *Pilgrim*, Vol. IX, pp. 225–7 & n.). The *Pilgrim* editors suggest that Dickens is referring here and in his letter to Charles Knight of 14 March (p. 225n.) to the writing of article 10, whereas both the print schedule of *ATYR*, and the substance of the present article, make it the more likely candidate. Consultation of the American edition of *ATYR*, published by Emerson & Co. (see Introduction, p. xiii), shows that, in the event, no 'Uncommercial' papers of around this time were published out of step with their counterparts in the British edition.

Literary allusions (p. 98) 'Circumlocutional': refers to the Circumlocution Office, Dickens's satirical creation in *Little Dorrit*; (p. 98) 'those who are put in authority over us': 'all that are put in authority under her' (i.e.

The Queen), 'A Catechism', *The Book of Common Prayer* (1662); (p. 98 et seq.) 'Pangloss': the name and character of 'Pangloss' are borrowed from those of the casuistical tutor satirised in Voltaire's *Candide* (1759), who believes that 'all is for the best in the best of all possible worlds'.

Textual note (p. 105) copy-text has 'I burn and blush to remember it': *UT1* has 'I blush to remember it'.

I travel constantly, up and down a certain line of railway that has a terminus in London. It is the railway for a large military depôt, and for other large barracks. To the best of my serious belief, I have never been on that railway by daylight, without seeing some handcuffed deserters in the train.

It is in the nature of things that such an institution as our English army should have many bad and troublesome characters in it. But, this is a reason for, and not against, its being made as acceptable as possible to well-disposed men of decent behaviour. Such men are assuredly not tempted into the ranks, by the beastly inversion of natural laws, and the compulsion to live in worse than swinish foulness. Accordingly, when any such Circumlocutional embellishments of the soldier's condition have of late been brought to notice, we civilians, seated in outer darkness cheerfully meditating on an Income Tax, have considered the matter as being our business, and have shown a tendency to declare that we would rather not have it misregulated, if such declaration may, without violence to the Church Catechism, be hinted to those who are put in authority over us.

Any animated description of a modern battle, any private soldier's letter published in the newspapers, any page of the records of the Victoria Cross, will show that in the ranks of the army, there exists under all disadvantages as fine a sense of duty as is to be found in any station on earth. Who doubts that, if we all did our duty as faithfully as the soldier does his, this world would be a better place? There may be greater difficulties in our way than in the soldier's. Not disputed. But, let us at least do our duty towards *him*.

I had got back again to that rich and beautiful port where I had looked after Mercantile Jack, and I was walking up a hill there, on a wild March morning. My conversation with my official friend Pangloss, by whom I was accidentally accompanied, took this direction as we took the up-hill direction, because the object of my uncommercial journey was to see some discharged soldiers who had recently come home from India. There were men of HAVELOCK's among them; there were men who had been in many of the great battles of the great Indian campaign, among them; and I was curious to note what our discharged soldiers looked like, when they were done with.

I was not the less interested (as I mentioned to my official friend Pangloss) because these men had claimed to be discharged, when their right to be discharged was not admitted. They had behaved with unblemished fidelity and bravery; but a change of circumstances had arisen, which, as they considered, put an end to their compact and entitled them to enter on a new one. Their demand had been blunderingly resisted by the authorities in India; but, it is to be presumed that the men were not far wrong, inasmuch as the bungle had ended in their being sent home discharged, in pursuance of orders from home. (There was an immense waste of money, of course.)

Under these circumstances – thought I, as I walked up the hill, on which I accidentally encountered my official friend – under these circumstances of the men having successfully opposed themselves to the Pagoda Department of that great Circumlocution Office, on which the sun never sets and the light of reason never rises, the Pagoda Department will have been particularly careful of the national honour. It will have shown these men, in the scrupulous good faith, not to say the generosity, of its dealing with them, that great national authorities can have no small retaliations and revenges. It will have made every provision for their health on the passage home, and will have landed them, restored from their campaigning fatigues by a sea-voyage, pure air, sound food, and good medicines. And I pleased myself with dwelling beforehand, on the great accounts of their personal treatment which these men would carry into their various towns and villages, and on the increasing popularity of the service that would insensibly follow. I almost began to hope that the hitherto-never-failing deserters on my railroad, would by-and-by become a phenomenon.

In this agreeable frame of mind I entered the workhouse of Liverpool. – For the cultivation of laurels in a sandy soil had brought the soldiers in question to *that* abode of Glory.

Before going into their wards to visit them, I inquired how they had made their triumphant entry there? They had been brought through the rain in carts, it seemed, from the landing-place to the gate, and had then been carried upstairs on the backs of paupers. Their groans and pains during the performance of this glorious pageant, had been so distressing, as to bring tears into the eyes of spectators but too well accustomed to scenes of suffering. They were so dreadfully cold, that those who could get near the fires were hard to be restrained from thrusting their feet in among the blazing coals. They were so horribly reduced, that they were awful to look upon. Racked with dysentery and blackened with scurvy, one hundred and forty wretched men had been revived with brandy and laid in bed.

My official friend Pangloss is lineally descended from a learned doctor of that name, who was once tutor to Candide, an ingenuous young gentleman of some celebrity. In his personal character, he is as humane and worthy a gentleman as any I know; in his official capacity, he unfortunately preaches the doctrines of his renowned ancestor, by demonstrating on all occasions that we live in the best of all possible official worlds.

'In the name of Humanity,' said I, 'how did the men fall into this deplorable state? Was the ship well found in stores?'

'I am not here to asseverate that I know the fact, of my own knowledge,' answered Pangloss, 'but I have grounds for asserting that the stores were the best of all possible stores.'

A medical officer laid before us, a handful of rotten biscuit, and a handful of split peas. The biscuit was a honey-combed heap of maggots, and the excrement of maggots. The peas were even harder than this filth. A similar handful had been experimentally boiled, six hours, and had shown no signs of softening. These were the stores on which the soldiers had been fed.

'The beef –' I began, when Pangloss cut me short.

'Was the best of all possible beef,' said he.

But, behold, there was laid before us certain evidence given at the Coroner's Inquest, holden on some of the men (who had obstinately died of their treatment), and from that evidence it appeared that the beef was the worst of all possible beef!

'Then I lay my hand upon my heart, and take my stand,' said Pangloss, 'by the pork, which was the best of all possible pork.'

'But, look at this food before our eyes, if one may so misuse the word,' said I. 'Would any Inspector who did his duty, pass such abomination?'

'It ought not to have been passed,' Pangloss admitted.

'Then the authorities out there –' I began, when Pangloss cut me short again.

'There would certainly seem to have been something wrong somewhere,' said he; 'but I am prepared to prove that the authorities out there, are the best of all possible authorities.'

I never heard of an impeached public authority in my life, who was not the best public authority in existence.

'We are told of these unfortunate men being laid low by scurvy,' said I. 'Since lime-juice has been regularly stored and served out in our navy, surely that disease, which used to devastate it, has almost disappeared? Was there lime-juice aboard this transport?'

My official friend was beginning 'the best of all possible –' when an inconvenient medical forefinger pointed out another passage in the evidence, from which it appeared that the lime-juice had been bad too.

Not to mention that the vinegar had been bad too, the vegetables bad too, the cooking accommodation insufficient (if there had been anything worth mentioning to cook), the water supply exceedingly inadequate, and the beer sour.

'Then, the men,' said Pangloss, a little irritated, 'were the worst of all possible men.'

'In what respect?' I asked.

'Oh! Habitual drunkards,' said Pangloss.

But, again the same incorrigible medical forefinger pointed out another passage in the evidence, showing that the dead men had been examined after death, and that they, at least, could not possibly have been habitual drunkards, because the organs within them which must have shown traces of that habit, were perfectly sound.

'And besides,' said the three doctors present, one and all, 'habitual drunkards brought as low as these men have been, could not recover under care and food, as the great majority of these men are recovering. They would not have strength of constitution to do it.'

'Reckless and improvident dogs, then,' said Pangloss. 'Always are — nine times out of ten.'

I turned to the master of the workhouse, and asked him whether the men had any money?

'Money?' said he. 'I have in my iron safe, nearly four hundred pounds of theirs; the agents have nearly a hundred pounds more; and many of them have left money in Indian banks besides.'

'Hah!' said I to myself, as we went upstairs, 'this is not the best of all possible stories, I doubt!'

We went into a large ward, containing some twenty or five-and-twenty beds. We went into several such wards, one after another. I find it very difficult to indicate what a shocking sight I saw in them, without frightening the reader from the perusal of these lines, and defeating my object of making it known.

O the sunken eyes that turned to me as I walked between the rows of beds, or — worse still — that glazedly looked at the white ceiling, and saw nothing and cared for nothing! Here, lay the skeleton of a man, so lightly covered with a thin unwholesome skin, that not a bone in the anatomy was clothed, and I could clasp the arm above the elbow, in my finger and thumb. Here, lay a man with the black scurvy eating his legs away, his gums gone, and his teeth all gaunt and bare. This bed was empty, because gangrene had set in, and the patient had died but yesterday. That bed was a hopeless one, because its occupant was sinking fast, and could only be roused to turn the poor pinched mask of face upon the pillow, with a feeble moan. The awful thinness of the fallen cheeks, the awful brightness of the deep-set eyes, the lips of lead, the hands of ivory, the recumbent human images lying in the shadow of death with a kind of solemn twilight on them, like the sixty who had died aboard the ship, and were lying at the bottom of the sea, O Pangloss, GOD forgive you!

In one bed, lay a man whose life had been saved (as it was hoped) by deep incisions in the feet and legs. While I was speaking to him, a nurse came up to change the poultices which this operation had rendered necessary, and I had an instinctive feeling that it was not well to turn away, merely to spare myself. He was sorely wasted and keenly susceptible, but the efforts he made to subdue any expression of impatience or suffering, were quite heroic. It was easy to see, in the shrinking of the figure, and the drawing of the bed-clothes over the head, how acute the endurance was, and it made me shrink too, as if *I* were in pain; but, when the new bandages were on, and the poor feet were composed again, he made an apology for himself (though he had not uttered a word), and said plaintively, 'I am so tender and weak, you see, sir!' Neither from him nor from any one sufferer of the whole ghastly number, did I hear a complaint. Of thankfulness for present solicitude and care, I heard much; of complaint, not a word.

I think I could have recognised, in the dismalest skeleton there, the ghost of a soldier. Something of the old air was still latent in the palest shadow of life that I talked to. One emaciated creature, in the strictest literality worn to the bone, lay stretched on his back, looking so like death that I asked one of the doctors if he were not dying, or dead? A few kind words from the doctor, in his ear, and he opened his eyes, and smiled – looked, in a moment, as if he would have made a salute, if he could. 'We shall pull him through, please God,' said the Doctor. 'Plase God, surr, and thankye,' said the patient. 'You are much better today; are you not?' said the Doctor. 'Plase God, surr; 'tis the slape I want, surr; 'tis my breathin' makes the nights so long.' 'He is a careful fellow this, you must know,' said the Doctor cheerfully; 'it was raining hard when they put him in the open cart to bring him here, and he had the presence of mind to ask to have a sovereign taken out of his pocket that he had there, and a cab engaged. Probably it saved his life.' The patient rattled out the skeleton of a laugh, and said, proud of the story, ' 'Deed, surr, an open cairt was a comical means o' bringin' a dyin' man here, and a clever way to kill him.' You might have sworn to him for a soldier when he said it.

One thing had perplexed me very much in going from bed to bed. A very significant and cruel thing. I could find no young man, but one. He had attracted my notice, by having got up and dressed himself in his soldier's jacket and trousers, with the intention of sitting by the fire; but he had found himself too weak, and had crept back to his bed and laid himself down on the outside of it. I could have pronounced him, alone, to be a young man aged by famine and sickness. As we were standing by the Irish soldier's bed, I mentioned my perplexity to the Doctor. He took a board with an inscription on it from the head of the Irishman's bed, and asked me what age I supposed that man to be? I had observed him with attention while talking to him, and answered, confidently, 'Fifty.' The doctor, with a pitying glance at the patient, who had dropped into a stupor again, put the board back, and said, 'Twenty-Four.'

All the arrangements of the wards were excellent. They could not have been more humane, sympathising, gentle, attentive, or wholesome. The owners of the ship, too, had done all they could, liberally. There were bright fires in every room, and the convalescent men were sitting round them, reading various papers and periodicals. I took the liberty of inviting my official friend Pangloss to look at those convalescent men, and to tell me whether their faces and bearing were or were not, generally, the faces and bearing of steady, respectable soldiers? The master of the workhouse, overhearing me, said that he had had a pretty large experience of troops, and that better conducted men than these he had never had to do with. They were always (he added) as we saw them. And of us visitors (I add) they knew nothing whatever, except that we were there.

It was audacious in me, but I took another liberty with Pangloss. Prefacing it with the observation that, of course, I knew beforehand that there was not the faintest desire, anywhere, to hush up any part of this dreadful business, and that the Inquest was the fairest of all possible Inquests, I besought four things of Pangloss. Firstly, to observe that the Inquest *was not held in that place*, but at some distance off. Secondly, to look round upon those helpless spectres in their beds. Thirdly, to remember that the witnesses produced from among them before that Inquest, could not have been selected because they were the men who had the most to tell it, but because they happened to be in a state admitting of their safe removal. Fourthly, to say whether the Coroner and Jury could have come there, to those pillows, and taken a little evidence? My official friend declined to commit himself to a reply.

There was a sergeant, reading, in one of the fireside groups; as he was a man of a very intelligent countenance, and as I have a great respect for non-commissioned officers as a class, I sat down on the nearest bed, to have some talk with him. (It was the bed of one of the grisliest of the poor skeletons, and he died soon afterwards.)

'I was glad to see, in the evidence of an officer at the Inquest, sergeant, that he never saw men behave better on board ship than these men.'

'They did behave very well, sir.'

'I was glad to see, too, that every man had a hammock.'

The sergeant gravely shook his head. 'There must be some mistake, sir. The men of my own mess had no hammocks. There were not hammocks enough on board, and the men of the two next messes laid hold of hammocks for themselves as soon as they got on board, and squeezed my men out, as I may say.'

'Had the squeezed-out men none then?'

'None, sir. As men died, their hammocks were used by other men who wanted hammocks; but many men had none at all.'

'Then you don't agree with the evidence on that point?'

'Certainly not, sir. A man can't, when he knows to the contrary.'

'Did any of the men sell their bedding for drink?'

'There is some mistake on that point too, sir. Men were under the impression – I knew it for a fact at the time – that it was not allowed to take blankets or bedding on board, and so men who had things of that sort came to sell them purposely.'

'Did any of the men sell their clothes for drink?'

'They did, sir.' (I believe there never was a more truthful witness than the sergeant. He had no inclination to make out a case.)

'Many?'

'Some, sir' (considering the question). 'Soldier-like. There had been long marching in the rainy season, by bad roads – no roads at all, in short – and when they got to Calcutta, men turned to and drank before taking a last look at it. Soldier-like.'

'Do you see any men in this ward, for example, who sold clothes for drink at that time?'

The sergeant's wan eye, happily just beginning to rekindle with health, travelled round the place, and came back to me. 'Certainly, sir.'

'The marching to Calcutta in the rainy season must have been severe?'

'It was very severe, sir.'

'Yet what with the rest and the sea air, I should have thought that the men (even the men who got drunk) would have soon begun to recover on board ship?'

'So they might; but the bad food told upon them, and when we got into a cold latitude, it began to tell more, and the men dropped.'

'The sick had a general disinclination for food, I am told, sergeant?'

'Have you seen the food, sir?'

'Some of it.'

'Have you seen the state of their mouths, sir?'

If the sergeant, who was a man of a few orderly words, had spoken the amount of a volume of this publication, he could not have settled that question better. I believe the sick could as soon have eaten the ship, as the ship's provisions.

I took the additional liberty with my friend Pangloss, when I had left the sergeant with good wishes, of asking Pangloss whether he had ever heard of biscuit getting drunk and bartering its nutritious qualities for putrefaction and vermin; of peas becoming hardened in liquor; of hammocks drinking themselves off the face of the earth; of lime-juice, vegetables, vinegar, cooking accommodation, water supply, and beer, all taking to drinking together, and going to ruin? 'If not (I asked him), what did he say in defence of the officers condemned by the Coroner's Jury, who, by signing the General Inspection report relative to the ship Great Tasmania chartered for these troops, had deliberately asserted all that bad and poisonous dunghill refuse, to be good and wholesome food? My official friend replied that it was a remarkable fact, that whereas some officers were only positively good, and other officers only comparatively better, those particular officers were superlatively the very best of all possible officers.

My hand and my heart fail me, in writing my record of this journey. The spectacle of the soldiers in the hospital-beds of that Liverpool workhouse (a very good workhouse, indeed, be it understood), was so shocking and so shameful, that as an Englishman I burn and blush to remember it. It would have been simply unbearable at the time, but for the consideration and pity with which they were soothed in their sufferings.

No punishment that our inefficient laws provide, is worthy of the name when set against the guilt of this transaction. But, if the memory of it die out unavenged, and if it do not result in the inexorable dismissal and disgrace of those who are responsible for it, their escape will be infamous to the Government (no matter of what party) that so neglects its duty, and infamous to the nation that tamely suffers such intolerable wrong to be done in its name.

12

The Uncommercial Traveller

All The Year Round, 5 May 1860 (*UT1* as 'City of London Churches')

In his notes to *UT4* (written in 1895) Charles Dickens Jr records having 'vivid recollections of some of the churches described in this paper, having on more than one occasion accompanied my father, when I was a boy, on Sunday expeditions from Devonshire Terrace into the City' (p. xx). As the Dickens household left their house at 1 Devonshire Terrace in November

1851, at least some of the 'expeditions' on which Dickens bases this paper clearly belong to the late 1840s or early 1850s. The sketch given in *Dombey and Son* of the church where Walter Gay and Florence Dombey marry (No. 18 [February 1848]; Ch. 56) is clearly a forerunner of the paper.

Although an impressionistic sketch, and despite the narrator's disparagement of putting names to individual churches, 'originals' for many of those described can be identified. Thus the first church drawn in detail (p. 109) corresponds to St James Garlickhythe, on Garlick Hill. The small church from 'the date of Queen Anne' (p. 111) is likely to be based on St Michael Paternoster Royal, on College Hill – a foundation with long-standing connections to the wine trade – although the church was in fact constructed in 1686–94 and the steeple in 1713–17, either side of the reign of Queen Anne. 'My own village church' (p. 111) almost certainly refers to Dickens's local church at Gadshill: St Mary's, on Church Street, Lower Higham, where the family attended services in the 1860s. If the 'Angelica' mentioned (p. 112) offers a faint recollection of Maria Beadnell, object of Dickens's unrequited love in the early 1830s (see Michael Slater, *Dickens and Women* [1983], Ch. 4), then the church 'in Huggin Lane' where they plighted their troth is likely to be St Michael Queenhithe, which stood on what is now Huggin Hill. This is close to Lombard Street, where the Beadnells lived. The 'City personage' and his child (pp. 112–15) appear to frequent All Hallows London Wall, which still possesses the inconvenience noted by the narrator. The churches noted for their smells (p. 115) are not positively identifiable, though E. Beresford Chancellor in *The London of Charles Dickens* (1924, p. 267) and Gwen Major, in a series of well-researched articles in *The Dickensian* (Vol. 37 [1941], pp. 125–47; Vol. 44 [1948], pp. 71 & 130f.; Vol. 64 [1968], pp. 28–33), offer suggestions.

As G. J. Worth has suggested (*The Dickensian*, Vol. 83 [1987], pp. 19–20), Dickens probably borrowed the name of 'Comport' (p. 110) from the surname on the ten small graves of children in Cooling Churchyard, Kent. The same graves re-emerge shortly afterwards as the 'five little stone lozenges' marking the tombs of Pip's brothers and sisters in the opening instalment of *Great Expectations* (*ATYR*, 1 December 1860), underlining the fact that the novel itself grew out of ideas Dickens was working with in his composition of this first series of 'Uncommercial Traveller' papers (see pp. 138, 149 and 158; *Pilgrim*, Vol. IX, p. 310 & n.). In 1863 Dickens wrote a companion piece to the present article, on disused city churchyards, for the second series of 'Uncommercial Traveller' papers in *ATYR* (see article 28 below).

Literary allusions (p. 108) 'whether of wrath or grace': 'children of wrath ... of grace', 'A Catechism', *The Book of Common Prayer*; (p. 115) 'the exact counterpart of the church in the Rake's Progress ...': alludes to one of Hogarth's famous series of paintings on 'modern moral subjects', *The Rake's Progress* (1733–5); the church Hogarth painted was old Mary-le-bone Church, while its City 'counterpart' was probably St Mildred's Bread Street (destroyed in the Second World War), located near the headquarters of the hide-trading Hudson Bay Company.

MS and textual note in the Houghton Library, Harvard University. MS Eng. 58. Dickens had the MS bound and sent to his close American friend James T. Fields, who, it would appear, had requested the original as a keepsake (see *Pilgrim*, Vol. IX, p. 255 & n.). The MS text is headed 'The Uncommercial Traveller', showing it to have been written during 1860 (most probably in April). From his familiarity with Dickens's handwriting, it is to be supposed that Fields could decipher the MS, which is a mass of corrections, deletions, additions and emendations. The second slip contains a paragraph of seven lines cancelled by two horizontal and four vertical slashes, omitted from the published version, originally running between the words 'he brought to me!' and 'Now, I have heard many preachers since ...' (p. 108). It can be tentatively restored as follows:

> Only once since have our ways lain together. Not long ago, within a year or two, I chanced on my uncommercial travels to [be in a?] place where there was a Fancy Sale in his behalf. It was not the place of my early days, but there was something in the look of the Posting Bills about the Sale, that took me back to it, and seemed to shrink me to the old smaller size.

'The place of my early days' is a reference to Chatham and the Medway towns where Dickens spent part of his childhood (see headnote to article 15 below); (below) copy-text has 'they will be satisfied (I hope)': whereas MS has 'they will be appeased (I hope)'; (p. 108) copy-text has 'journeys of curiosity': whereas MS has 'pilgrimages of curiosity'; (p. 109) copy-text has 'I jostle the clergyman, who is entering': whereas *UT1* has 'I jostle the clergyman in his canonicals, who is entering ...'.

If the confession that I have often travelled from this Covent Garden lodging of mine on Sundays, should give offence to those who never travel on Sundays, they will be satisfied (I hope) by my adding that the journeys in question were made to churches.

Not that I have any curiosity to hear powerful preachers. Time was, when I was dragged by the hair of my head, as one may say, to hear too many. On summer evenings, when every flower, and tree, and bird, might have better addressed my soft young heart, I have in my day been caught in the palm of a female hand by the crown, have been violently scrubbed from the neck to the roots of the hair as a purification for the

Temple, and have then been carried off, highly charged with saponaceous electricity, to be steamed like a potato in the unventilated breath of the powerful Boanerges Boiler and his congregation, until what small mind I had was quite steamed out of me. In which pitiable plight I have been hauled out of the place of meeting, at the conclusion of the exercises, and catechised respecting Boanerges Boiler, his fifthly, his sixthly, and his seventhly, until I have regarded that reverend person in the light of a most dismal and oppressive Charade. Time was, when I was carried off to platform assemblages at which no human child, whether of wrath or grace, could possibly keep its eyes open, and when I felt the fatal sleep stealing, stealing over me, and when I gradually heard the orator in possession, spinning and humming like a great top, until he rolled, collapsed, and tumbled over, and I discovered, to my burning shame and fear, that as to that last stage it was not he, but I. I have sat under Boanerges when he has specifically addressed himself to us – us, the infants – and at this present writing I hear his lumbering jocularity (which never amused us, though we basely pretended that it did), and I behold his big round face, and I look up the inside of his outstretched coat-sleeve as if it were a telescope with the stopper on, and I hate him with an unwholesome hatred for two hours. Through such means did it come to pass that I knew the powerful preacher from beginning to end, all over and all through, while I was very young, and that I left him behind at an early period of life. Peace be with him! More peace than he brought to me!

Now, I have heard many preachers since that time – not powerful; merely Christian, unaffected, and reverential – and I have had many such preachers on my roll of friends. But, it was not to hear these, any more than the powerful class, that I made my Sunday journeys. They were journeys of curiosity to the numerous churches in the City of London. It came into my head one day, here had I been cultivating a familiarity with all the churches of Rome, and I knew nothing of the insides of the old churches of London! This befell on a Sunday morning. I began my expeditions that very same day, and they lasted me a year.

I never wanted to know the names of the churches to which I went, and to this hour I am profoundly ignorant in that particular of at least nine-tenths of them. Indeed, saving that I know the church of old Gower's tomb (he lies in effigy with his head upon his books) to be the church of Saint Saviour's, Southwark, and the church of Milton's tomb to be the church of Cripplegate, and the church on Cornhill with the great golden keys to be the church of Saint Peter, I doubt if I could pass a competitive examination in any of the names. No question did I ever ask of living creature concerning these churches, and no answer to any antiquarian question on the subject that I ever put to books, shall harass the reader's soul. A full half of my pleasure in them, arose out of their mystery; mysterious I found them; mysterious they shall remain for me.

Where shall I begin my round of hidden and forgotten old churches in the City of London?

It is twenty minutes short of eleven on a Sunday morning, when I stroll down one of the many narrow hilly streets in the City that tend due south to the Thames. It is my first experiment, and I have come to the region of Whittington in an omnibus, and we have put down a fierce-eyed spare old woman, whose slate-coloured gown smells of herbs, and who walked up Aldersgate-street to some chapel where she comforts herself with brimstone doctrine, I warrant. We have also put down a stouter and sweeter old lady, with a pretty large prayerbook in an unfolded pocket-handkerchief, who got out at a corner of a court near Stationers' Hall, and who I think must go to church there, because she is the widow of some deceased Old Company's Beadle. The rest of our freight were mere chance pleasure-seekers and rural walkers, and went on to the Blackwall railway. So many bells are ringing, when I stand undecided at a street corner, that every sheep in the ecclesiastical fold might be a bell-wether. The discordance is fearful. My state of indecision is referable to, and about equally divisible among, four great churches, which are all within sight and sound, all within the space of a few square yards. As I stand at the street corner, I don't see as many as four people at once going to church, though I see as many as four churches with their steeples clamouring for people. I choose my church, and go up the flight of steps to the great entrance in the tower. A mouldy tower within, and like a neglected washhouse. A rope comes through the beamed roof, and a man in a corner pulls it and clashes the bell; a whity-brown man, whose clothes were once black; a man with flue on him, and cobweb. He stares at me, wondering how I come there, and I stare at him, wondering how he comes there. Through a screen of wood and glass, I peep into the dim church. About twenty people are discernible, waiting to begin. Christening would seem to have faded out of this church long ago, for the font has the dust of desuetude thick upon it, and its wooden cover (shaped like an old-fashioned tureen cover) looks as if it wouldn't come off, upon requirement. I perceive the altar to be rickety, and the Commandments damp. Entering after this survey, I jostle the clergyman, who is entering too from a dark lane behind a pew of state with curtains, where nobody sits. The pew is ornamented with four blue wands, once carried by four somebodys, I suppose, before somebody else, but which there is nobody now to hold or receive honour from. I open the door of a family pew, and shut myself in; if I could occupy twenty family pews at once, I might have them. The clerk, a brisk young man (how does *he* come here?), glances at me knowingly, as who should say, 'You have done it now; you must stop.' Organ plays. Organ-loft is in a small gallery across the church; gallery congregation, two girls. I wonder within myself what will happen when we are required to sing.

There is a pale heap of books in the corner of my pew, and while the organ, which is hoarse and sleepy, plays in such fashion that I can hear more of the rusty working of the stops than of any music, I look at the books, which are mostly bound in faded baize and stuff. They belonged, in 1754, to the Dowgate family; and who were they? Jane Comport must have married Young Dowgate, and come into the family that way; Young Dowgate was courting Jane Comport when he gave her her prayer-book, and recorded the presentation in the fly-leaf; if Jane were fond of Young Dowgate, why did she die and leave the book here? Perhaps at the rickety altar, and before the damp Commandments, she, Comport, had taken him, Dowgate, in a flush of youthful hope and joy, and perhaps it had not turned out in the long run as great a success as was expected?

The opening of the service recals my wandering thoughts. I then find, to my astonishment, that I have been, and still am, taking a strong kind of invisible snuff, up my nose, into my eyes, and down my throat. I wink, sneeze, and cough. The clerk sneezes; the clergyman winks; the unseen organist sneezes and coughs (and probably winks); all our little party wink, sneeze, and cough. The snuff seems to be made of the decay of matting, wood, cloth, stone, iron, earth, and something else. Is the something else, the decay of dead citizens in the vaults below? As sure as Death it is! Not only in the cold damp February day, do we cough and sneeze dead citizens all through the service, but dead citizens have got into the very bellows of the organ, and half choked the same. We stamp our feet, to warm them, and dead citizens arise in heavy clouds. Dead citizens stick upon the walls, and lie pulverised on the sounding-board over the clergyman's head, and, when a gust of air comes, tumble down upon him.

In this first experience I was so nauseated by too much snuff, made of the Dowgate family, the Comport branch, and other families and branches, that I gave but little heed to our dull manner of ambling through the service; to the brisk clerk's manner of encouraging us to try a note or two at psalm time; to the gallery-congregation's manner of enjoying a shrill duet, without a notion of time or tune; to the whity-brown man's manner of shutting the minister into the pulpit, and being very particular with the lock of the door, as if he were a dangerous animal. But, I tried again next Sunday, and soon accustomed myself to the dead citizens when I found that I could not possibly get on without them among the City churches.

Another Sunday. After being again rung for by conflicting bells, like a leg of mutton or a laced hat a hundred years ago, I make selection of a church oddly put away in a corner among a number of lanes – a smaller church than the last, and an ugly: of about the date of Queen Anne. As a congregation, we are fourteen strong; not counting an exhausted charity school in a gallery, which has dwindled away to four boys, and two girls. In the porch, is a benefaction of loaves of bread, which there would seem to be nobody left in the exhausted congregation to claim, and which I saw an exhausted beadle, long faded out of uniform, eating with his eyes for self and family when I passed in. There is also an exhausted clerk in a brown wig, and two or three exhausted doors and windows have been bricked up, and the service books are musty, and the pulpit cushions are threadbare, and the whole of the church furniture is in a very advanced stage of exhaustion. We are three old women (habitual), two young lovers (accidental), two tradesmen, one with a wife and one alone, an aunt and nephew, again two girls (these two girls dressed out for church with everything about them limp that should be stiff, and *vice versa*, are an invariable experience), and three sniggering boys. The clergyman is, perhaps, the chaplain of a civic company; he has the moist and vinous look, and eke the bulbous boots, of one acquainted with 'Twenty port and comet vintages.

We are so quiet in our dulness, that the three sniggering boys, who have got away into a corner by the altar-railing, give us a start, like crackers, whenever they laugh. And this reminds me of my own village church where, during sermon-time on bright Sundays when the birds are very musical indeed, farmers' boys patter out over the stone pavement, and the clerk steps out from his desk after them, and is distinctly heard in the summer repose to pursue and punch them in the churchyard, and is seen to return with a meditative countenance, making believe that nothing of the sort has happened. The aunt and nephew in this City church are much disturbed by the sniggering boys. The nephew is himself a boy, and the sniggerers tempt him to secular thoughts of marbles and string, by secretly offering such commodities to his distant contemplation. This young Saint Anthony for a while resists, but presently becomes a backslider, and in dumb show defies the sniggerers to 'heave' a marble or two in his direction. Herein he is detected by the aunt (a rigorous reduced gentlewoman who has the charge of offices), and I perceive that worthy relative to poke him in the side with the corrugated hooked handle of an ancient umbrella. The nephew revenges himself for this by holding his breath and terrifying his kinswoman with the dread belief that he has made up his mind to burst. Regardless of whispers and shakes, he swells and becomes discoloured, and yet again swells and becomes discoloured, until the aunt can bear it no longer, but leads him out, with no visible neck, and with his eyes going before him like a prawn's. This causes the sniggerers to regard flight as an eligible move, and I know which of them will go out first, because of the over-devout attention that he suddenly concentrates on the clergyman. In a little while, this hypocrite, with an elaborate demonstration of hushing his footsteps, and with a face generally expressive of having until now forgotten a religious appointment elsewhere, is gone. Number two gets out in the same way, but rather quicker. Number three, getting safely to the door, there turns reckless, and banging it open, flies forth with a Whoop! that vibrates to the top of the tower above us.

The clergyman, who is of a prandial presence and a muffled voice, may be scant of hearing as well as of breath, but he only glances up, as having an idea that somebody has said Amen in a wrong place, and continues his steady jog-trot, like a farmer's wife going to market. He does all he has to do, in the same easy way, and gives us a concise sermon, still like the jog-trot of the farmer's wife on a level road. Its drowsy cadence soon lulls the three old women asleep, and the unmarried tradesman sits looking out at window, and the married tradesman sits looking at his wife's bonnet, and the lovers sit looking at one another, so superlatively happy, that I mind when I, turned of eighteen, went with my Angelica to a City church on account of a shower (by this special coincidence that it was in Huggin-lane), and when I said to my Angelica, 'Let the blessed event, Angelica, occur at no altar but this!' and when my Angelica consented that it should occur at no other – which it certainly never did, for it never occurred anywhere. And O, Angelica, what has become of you, this present Sunday morning when I can't attend to the sermon; and, more difficult question than that, what has become of Me as I was when I sat by your side!

But we receive the signal to make that unanimous dive which surely is a little conventional – like the strange rustlings and settlings and clearings of throats and noses, which are never dispensed with, at certain points of the Church service, and are never held to be necessary under any other circumstances. In a minute more it is all over, and the organ expresses itself to be as glad of it as it can be of anything in its rheumatic state, and in another minute we are all of us out of the church, and Whity-brown has locked it up. Another minute or little more, and, in the neighbouring churchyard – not the yard of that church, but of another – a churchyard like a great shabby old mignionette-box with two trees in it, and one tomb – I meet Whity-brown, in his private capacity, fetching a pint of beer for his dinner from the public-house in the corner, where the keys of the rotting fire-ladders are kept, and were never asked for, and where there is a ragged, white-seamed, out-at-elbowed bagatelle board on the first floor.

In one of these City churches, and only in one, I found an individual who might have been claimed as expressly a City personage. I remember

The City Personage

the church, by the feature that the clergyman couldn't get to his own desk without going through the clerk's, or couldn't get to the pulpit without going through the reading-desk – I forget which, and it's no matter – and by the presence of this personage among the exceedingly sparse congregation. I doubt if we were a dozen, and we had no exhausted charity school to help us out. The personage was dressed in black of square cut, and was stricken in years, and wore a black velvet cap, and cloth shoes. He was of a staid, wealthy, and dissatisfied aspect. In his hand, he conducted to church a mysterious child: a child of the feminine gender. The child had a beaver hat, with a stiff drab plume that surely never belonged to any bird of the air. The child was further attired in a nankeen frock and spencer, brown boxing-gloves, and a veil. It had a blemish, in the nature of currant jelly, on its chin; and was a thirsty child. Insomuch that the personage carried in his pocket a green bottle, from which, when the first psalm was given out, the child was openly refreshed. At all other times throughout the service it was motionless, and stood on the seat of the large pew, closely fitted into the corner, like a rainwater pipe.

The personage never opened his book, and never looked at the clergyman. *He* never sat down either, but stood with his arms leaning on the top of the pew, and his forehead sometimes shaded with his right hand, always looking at the church door. It was a long church for a church of its size, and he was at the upper end, but he always looked at the door. That he was an old bookkeeper, or an old trader who had kept his own books, and that he might be seen at the Bank of England about Dividend times, no doubt. That he had lived in the City all his life and was disdainful of other localities, no doubt. Why he looked at the door I never absolutely proved, but it is my belief that he lived in expectation of the time when the citizens would come back to live in the City, and its ancient glories would be renewed. He appeared to expect that this would occur on a Sunday, and that the wanderers would first appear in the deserted churches, penitent and humbled. Hence, he looked at the door which they never darkened. Whose child the child was, whether the child of a disinherited daughter, or some parish orphan whom the personage had adopted, there was nothing to lead up to. It never played, or skipped, or smiled. Once, the idea occurred to me that it was an automaton, and that the personage had made it; but, following the strange couple out one Sunday, I heard the personage say to it, 'Thirteen thousand pounds;' to which it added, in a weak human voice, 'Seventeen and fourpence.' Four Sundays I followed them out, and this is all I ever heard or saw them say. One Sunday, I followed them home. They lived behind a pump, and the personage opened their abode with an exceeding large key. The one solitary inscription on their house related to a fire-plug. The house was partly undermined by a deserted and closed gateway; its windows were blind with dirt; and it stood with its face disconsolately turned to a wall. Five great churches and two small ones rang their Sunday bells between this house and the church the couple frequented, so they must have had some special reason for going a quarter of a mile to it. The last time I saw them, was on this wise. I had been to explore another church at a distance, and happened to pass the church they frequented, at about two of the afternoon when that edifice was closed. But, a little side-door, which I had never observed before, stood open, and disclosed certain cellarous steps. Methought, 'They are airing the vaults today,' when the personage and the child silently arrived at the steps, and silently descended. Of course, I came to the conclusion that the personage had at last despaired of the looked-for return of the penitent citizens, and that he and the child went down to get themselves buried.

In the course of my pilgrimages I came upon one obscure church which had broken out in the melodramatic style, and was got up with various tawdry decorations, much after the manner of the extinct London maypoles. These attractions had induced several young priests or deacons in black bibs for waistcoats, and several young ladies interested in that noble order (the proportion being, as I estimated, seventeen young ladies to a deacon), to come into the City as a new and odd excitement. It was wonderful to see how these young people played out their little play in the heart of the City, all among themselves, without the deserted City's knowing anything about it. It was as if you should take an empty counting-house on a Sunday, and act one of the old Mysteries there. They had impressed a small school (from what neighbourhood I don't know) to assist in the performances, and it was pleasant to notice frantic garlands of inscription on the walls, especially addressing those poor innocents in characters impossible for them to decipher. There was a remarkably agreeable smell of pomatum in this congregation.

But, in other cases, rot and mildew and dead citizens formed the uppermost scent, while, infused into it in a dreamy way not at all displeasing, was the staple character of the neighbourhood. In the churches about Mark-lane, for example, there was a dry whiff of wheat; and I accidentally struck an airy sample of barley out of an aged hassock in one of them. From Rood-lane to Tower-street, and thereabouts, there was often a subtle flavour of wine: sometimes, of tea. One church near Mincing-lane smelt like a druggist's drawer. Behind the Monument, the service had a flavour of damaged oranges, which, a little further down towards the river, tempered into herrings, and gradually toned into a cosmopolitan blast of fish. In one church, the exact counterpart of the church in the Rake's Progress where the hero is being married to the horrible old lady, there was no speciality of atmosphere, until the organ shook a perfume of hides all over us from some adjacent warehouse.

Be the scent what it would, however, there was no speciality in the people. There were never enough of them to represent any calling or neighbourhood. They had all gone elsewhere overnight, and the few stragglers in the many churches languished there inexpressively.

Among the uncommercial travels in which I have engaged, this year of Sunday travel occupies its own place, apart from all the rest. Whether I think of the church where the sails of the oyster-boats in the river almost flapped against the windows, or of the church where the railroad made the bells hum as the train rushed by above the roof, I recal a curious experience. On summer Sundays, in the gentle rain or the bright sunshine – either, deepening the idleness of the idle City – I have sat, in that singular silence which belongs to resting-places usually astir, in scores of buildings at the heart of the world's metropolis, unknown to far greater numbers of people speaking the English tongue, than the ancient edifices of the Eternal City, or the Pyramids of Egypt. The dark vestries and registries into which I have peeped, and the little hemmed-in churchyards that have echoed to my feet, have left impressions on my memory as distinct and quaint as any it has in that way received. In all those dusty registers that the worms are eating, there is not a line but made some hearts leap, or some tears flow, in their day. Still and dry now, still and dry! and the old tree at the window, with no room for its branches, has seen them all out. So with the tomb of the old Master of the old Company, on which it drips. His son restored it and died, his daughter restored it and died, and then he had been remembered long enough, and the tree took possession of him, and his name cracked out.

There are few more striking indications of the changes of manners and customs that two or three hundred years have brought about, than these deserted Churches. Many of them are handsome and costly structures, several of them were designed by WREN, many of them arose from the ashes of the great fire, others of them outlived the plague and the fire too, to die a slow death in these later days. No one can be sure of the coming time; but it is not too much to say of it that it has no sign in its outsetting tides, of the reflux to these churches of their congregations and uses. They remain, like the tombs of the old citizens who lie beneath them and around them, Monuments of another age. They are worth a Sunday-exploration now and then, for they yet echo, not unharmoniously, to the time when the City of London really was London; when the 'Prentices and Trained Bands were of mark in the state; when even the Lord Mayor himself was a Reality – not a Fiction conventionally be-puffed on one day in the year by illustrious friends, who no less conventionally laugh at him on the remaining three hundred and sixty-four days.

13

The Uncommercial Traveller

All The Year Round, 26 May 1860 (*UT1* as 'Shy Neighbourhoods')

With the opening sentence of the following paper, compare Dickens's reporting of 'The Great International Walking-Match' (see Appendix A, p. 410). Even during his lifetime, Dickens's passion for walking (although common among Victorian men of letters) was perceived as something of an obsession. Forster speaks of 'excesses in walking' encouraged by country life (Book 11, Ch. 3), while John Hollingshead recalls that 'when Dickens lived at Tavistock House [1851–60] he developed a mania for walking long distances which almost assumed the form of a disease. He suffered from Lumbago, and I have always thought that this was brought on by monotonous pedestrianism.' The same source affirms that in the late 1850s Dickens 'would frequently' walk from the *HW* office to Gadshill: a journey of some thirty miles (*My Lifetime* [1895], Book I, pp. 101–2). As well as country walking, Dickens's ubiquity as a 'flâneur' of the London streets remained undiminished in the 1860s. The language 'once pretty familiar to me' which the Uncommercial Traveller speaks while sleep-walking is probably Italian.

Mention of 'Mr Thomas Sayers' and 'Mr John Heenan' (alias 'The Benicia Boy') picks up a topical sporting story, in which Dickens took a keen interest. The English champion boxer and his American challenger had taken part in the so-called Great Fight, the biggest held in Britain for decades, on 17 April 1860, despite such fights being banned under the new Police Act. Dickens had considered attending, but in the end sent Hollingshead to cover the event for *ATYR* (see *Pilgrim*, Vol. IX, pp. 234–5& n., and 'The Great Pugilistic Revival', *ATYR*, 19 May 1860).

Forster asserts that he is himself 'in a position to vouch ... [f]or the truth of the personal adventure' recounted in the paper about the buying of a goldfinch that refused to drink (pp. 119–20). 'Walking by a dirty court in Spitalfields one day, the quick little busy intelligence of a goldfinch ... so attracted him that he bought the bird, which had other accomplishments; but not one of them would the little creature show off in his new abode in Doughty-street' (*Forster*, Book 8, Ch. 5). The incident may be dated to the late 1830s. This present paper seems to have been a personal favourite of Forster's; he quotes more extensively from it than from any of the other 'Uncommercials' (*ibid.*). Dickens's concluding remarks on the fowls of shy neighbourhoods appear to have been informed by a prosaic chapter on

'Classification of Fowls' and their origins in the Rev. Edmund Dixon's *Ornamental and Domestic Poultry* (1848), a copy of which was presented to Dickens by the author in June 1849, and which Dickens kept in his library (Stonehouse).

Literary allusions (p. 119) 'in the manner of Izaak Walton': the pastoral and contemplative style of Walton's popular guide to freshwater fishing, *The Compleat Angler* (1653); (p. 124) 'a man and a brother': adaptation of the famous anti-slavery slogan 'Am I not a man and a brother?' given wide currency by Josiah Wedgwood in 1787, when he used it on a jasper medallion depicting a black slave kneeling in chains.

Textual note (p. 119) copy-text has 'when leisure and inclination serve': *UT1* has 'when leisure and opportunity ...'; (p. 123) copy-text has 'hauling the blind man away': *UT1* has 'haling...'.

So much of my travelling is done on foot, that if I cherished betting propensities, I should probably be found registered in sporting newspapers under some such title as the Elastic Novice, challenging all eleven-stone mankind to competition in walking. My last special feat was turning out of bed at two, after a hard day, pedestrian and otherwise, and walking thirty miles into the country to breakfast. The road was so lonely in the night, that I fell asleep to the monotonous sound of my own feet, doing their regular four miles an hour. Mile after mile I walked, without the slightest sense of exertion, dozing heavily and dreaming constantly. It was only when I made a stumble like a drunken man, or struck out into the road to avoid a horseman close upon me on the path – who had no existence – that I came to myself and looked about. The day broke mistily (it was autumn time), and I could not disembarrass myself of the idea that I had to climb those heights and banks of clouds, and that there was an Alpine Convent somewhere behind the sun, where I was going to breakfast. This sleepy notion was so much stronger than such substantial objects as villages and haystacks, that, after the sun was up and bright, and when I was sufficiently awake to have a sense of pleasure in the prospect, I still occasionally caught myself looking about for wooden arms to point the right track up the mountain, and wondering there was no snow yet. It is a curiosity of broken sleep, that I made immense quantities of verses on that pedestrian occasion (of course I never make any when I am in my right senses), and that I spoke a certain language once pretty familiar to me, but which I have nearly forgotten from disuse, with fluency. Of both these phenomena I have such frequent experience in the state between sleeping and waking, that

I sometimes argue with myself that I know I cannot be awake, for, if I were, I should not be half so ready. The readiness is not imaginary, because I can often recal long strings of the verses, and many turns of the fluent speech, after I am broad awake.

My walking is of two kinds; one, straight on end to a definite goal at a round pace; one, objectless, loitering, and purely vagabond. In the latter state, no gipsy on earth is a greater vagabond than myself; it is so natural to me and strong with me, that I think I must be the descendant, at no great distance, of some irreclaimable tramp.

One of the pleasantest things I have lately met with, in a vagabond course of shy metropolitan neighbourhoods and small shops, is the fancy of a humble artist as exemplified in two portraits representing Mr Thomas Sayers, of Great Britain, and Mr John Heenan, of the United States of America. These illustrious men are highly coloured, in fighting trim, and fighting attitude. To suggest the pastoral and meditative nature of their peaceful calling, Mr Heenan is represented on emerald sward, with primroses and other modest flowers springing up under the heels of his half-boots; while Mr Sayers is impelled to the administration of his favourite blow, the Auctioneer, by the silent eloquence of a village church. The humble homes of England, with their domestic virtues and honeysuckle porches, urge both heroes to go in and win; and the lark and other singing birds are observable in the upper air, ecstatically carolling their thanks to Heaven for a fight. On the whole, the associations entwined with the pugilistic art by this artist are much in the manner of Izaak Walton.

But, it is with the lower animals of back streets and by-ways that my present purpose rests. For human notes, we may return to such neighbourhoods when leisure and inclination serve.

Nothing in shy neighbourhoods perplexes my mind more, than the bad company birds keep. Foreign birds often get into good society, but British birds are inseparable from low associates. There is a whole street of them in Saint Giles's; and I always find them in poor and immoral neighbourhoods, convenient to the public-house and the pawnbroker's. They seem to lead people into drinking, and even the man who makes their cages usually gets into a chronic state of black eye. Why is this? Also, they will do things for people in short-skirted velveteen coats with bone buttons, or in sleeved waistcoats and fur caps, which they cannot be persuaded by the respectable orders of society to undertake. In a dirty court in Spitalfields, once, I found a goldfinch drawing his own water, and drawing as much of it as if he were in a consuming fever. That goldfinch lived at a bird-shop, and offered, in writing, to barter himself against old clothes, empty bottles, or even kitchen-stuff. Surely a low thing and a depraved taste in any finch! I bought that goldfinch for money. He was sent home, and hung upon a nail over against my table. He lived outside a counterfeit dwelling-house, supposed (as I argued) to be a dyer's; otherwise it would have been impossible to account for his perch sticking out of the garret window. From the time of his appearance in my room, either he left off being thirsty – which was not in the bond – or he could not make up his mind to hear his little bucket drop back into his well when he let it go: a shock which in the best of times had made him tremble. He drew no water but by stealth, and under the cloak of night. After an interval of futile and at length hopeless expectation, the merchant who had educated him was appealed to. The merchant was a bow-legged character, with a flat and cushiony nose, like the last new strawberry. He wore a fur cap, and shorts, and was of the velveteen race, velveteeny. He sent word that he would 'look round.' He looked round, appeared in the doorway of the room, and slightly cocked up his evil eye at the goldfinch. Instantly, a raging thirst beset that bird; when it was appeased, he still drew several unnecessary buckets of water; and finally, leaped about his perch and sharpened his bill, as if he had been to the nearest wine vaults and got drunk.

Donkeys again. I know shy neighbourhoods where the Donkey goes in at the street door, and appears to live upstairs, for I have examined the back yard from over the palings, and have been unable to make him out. Gentility, nobility, Royalty, would appeal to that donkey in vain to do what he does for a costermonger. Feed him with oats at the highest price, put an infant prince and princess in a pair of panniers on his back, adjust his delicate trappings to a nicety, take him to the softest slopes at Windsor, and try what pace you can get out of him. Then, starve him, harness him anyhow to a truck with a flat tray on it, and see him bowl from Whitechapel to Bayswater. There appears to be no particular private understanding between birds and donkeys, in a state of nature; but in the shy neighbourhood state you shall see them always in the same hands, and always developing their very best energies for the very worst company. I have known a donkey – by sight; we were not on speaking terms – who lived over on the Surrey side of London-bridge, among the fastnesses of Jacob's Island and Dockhead. It was the habit of that animal, when his services were not in immediate requisition, to go out alone, idling. I have met him, a mile from his place of residence, loitering about the streets; and the expression of his countenance at such times was most degraded. He was attached to the establishment of an elderly lady who sold periwinkles, and he used to stand on Saturday nights with a cartful of those delicacies outside a gin-shop, pricking up his ears when a customer came to the cart, and too evidently deriving satisfaction from the knowledge that they got bad measure. His mistress was sometimes overtaken by inebriety. The last time I ever saw him (about five years ago) he was in circumstances of difficulty, caused by this failing. Having been left alone with the cart of periwinkles, and forgotten, he went off idling. He prowled among his usual low haunts for some time, gratifying his depraved taste, until, not taking the cart into his calculations, he endeavoured to turn up a narrow alley, and became greatly involved. He was taken into custody by the police, and the Green Yard of the district being near at hand, was backed into that place of durance. At that crisis, I encountered him; the stubborn sense he evinced of being – not to compromise the expression – a blackguard, I never saw exceeded in the human subject. A flaring candle in a paper shade, stuck in among his periwinkles, showed him, with his ragged harness broken and his cart extensively shattered, twitching his mouth and shaking his hanging head, a picture of disgrace and obduracy. I have seen boys being taken to station-houses, who were as like him as his own brother.

The dogs of shy neighbourhoods, I observe to avoid play, and to be conscious of poverty. They avoid work too, if they can, of course; that is in the nature of all animals. I have the pleasure to know a dog in a back street in the neighbourhood of Walworth, who has greatly distinguished himself in the minor drama, and who takes his portrait with him when he makes an engagement, for the illustration of the play-bill. His portrait (which is not at all like him) represents him in the act of dragging to the earth a recreant Indian, who is supposed to have tomahawked, or essayed to tomahawk, a British officer. The design is pure poetry, for there is no such Indian in the piece, and no such incident. He is a dog of the Newfoundland breed, for whose honesty I would be bail to any amount; but whose intellectual qualities in association with dramatic fiction, I cannot rate high. Indeed, he is too honest for the profession he has entered. Being at a town in Yorkshire last summer, and seeing him posted in the bill of the night, I attended the performance. His first scene was eminently successful; but, as it occupied a second in its representation (and five lines in the bill), it scarcely afforded ground for a cool and deliberate judgment of his powers. He had merely to bark, run on, and jump through an inn window after a comic fugitive. The next scene of importance to the fable was a little marred in its interest by his over-anxiety: forasmuch as while his master (a belated soldier in a den of robbers on a tempestuous night) was feelingly lamenting the absence of his faithful dog, and laying great stress on the fact that he was thirty leagues away, the faithful dog was barking furiously in the prompter's box, and clearly choking himself against his collar. But it was in his greatest scene of all, that his honesty got the better of him. He had to enter a dense and trackless forest, on the trail of the murderer, and there to fly at the murderer when he found him resting at the foot of a tree, with his victim bound ready for slaughter. It was a hot night, and he came into the forest from an altogether unexpected direction, in the sweetest temper, at a very deliberate trot, not in the least excited; trotted to the footlights with his tongue out; and there sat down, panting, and amiably surveying the audience, with his tail beating on the boards like a Dutch clock. Meanwhile the murderer, impatient to receive his doom, was audibly calling to him 'Co-o-ome here!' while the victim, struggling with his bonds, assailed him with the most injurious expressions. It happened through these means, that when he was in course of time persuaded to trot up and rend the murderer limb from limb, he made it (for dramatic purposes) a little too obvious that he worked out that awful retribution by licking butter off his blood-stained hands.

In a shy street behind Long-acre, two honest dogs live, who perform in Punch's shows. I may venture to say that I am on terms of intimacy with both, and that I never saw either guilty of the falsehood of failing to look down at the man inside the show, during the whole performance. The difficulty other dogs have in satisfying their minds about these dogs, appears to be never overcome by time. The same dogs must encounter them over and over again, as they trudge along in their off-minutes behind the legs of the show and beside the drum; but all dogs seem to suspect their frills and jackets, and to sniff at them as if they thought those articles of personal adornment an eruption – a something in the nature of mange, perhaps. From this Covent-garden window of mine I noticed a country dog, only the other day, who had come up to Covent-garden Market under a cart, and had broken his cord, an end of which he still trailed along with him. He loitered about the corners of the four streets commanded by my window; and bad London dogs came up, and told him lies that he didn't believe; and worse London dogs came up, and made proposals to him to go and steal in the market, which his principles rejected; and the ways of the town confused him, and he crept aside and lay down in a doorway. He had scarcely got a wink of sleep, when up comes Punch with Toby. He was darting to Toby for consolation and advice, when he saw the frill, and stopped in the middle of the street, appalled. The show was pitched, Toby retired behind the drapery, the audience formed, the drum and pipes struck up. My country dog remained immovable, intently staring at these strange appearances, until Toby opened the drama by appearing on his ledge, and to him entered Punch, who put a tobacco-pipe into Toby's mouth. At this spectacle, the country dog threw up his head, gave one terrible howl, and fled due west.

We talk of men keeping dogs, but we might often talk more expressively of dogs keeping men. I know a bulldog in a shy corner of Hammersmith who keeps a man. He keeps him up a yard, and makes him go to public-houses and lay wagers on him, and obliges him to lean against posts and look at him, and forces him to neglect work for him, and keeps him under rigid coercion. I once knew a fancy terrier that kept a gentleman – a gentleman who had been brought up at Oxford, too. The dog kept the gentleman entirely for his glorification, and the gentleman never talked about anything but the terrier. This, however, was not in a shy neighbourhood, and is a digression consequently.

There are a great many dogs in shy neighbourhoods, who keep boys. I have my eye on a mongrel in Somers-town who keeps three boys. He feigns that he can bring down sparrows, and unburrow rats (he can do neither), and he takes the boys out on sporting pretences into all sorts of suburban fields. He has likewise made them believe that he possesses some mysterious knowledge of the art of fishing, and they consider themselves incompletely equipped for the Hampstead ponds, with a pickle-jar and a wide-mouthed bottle, unless he is with them and barking tremendously. There is a dog residing in the Borough of Southwark who keeps a blind man. He may be seen, most days, in Oxford-street, hauling the blind man away on expeditions wholly uncontemplated by, and unintelligible to, the man: wholly of the dog's conception and execution. Contrariwise, when the man has projects, the dog will sit down in a crowded thoroughfare and meditate. I saw him yesterday, wearing the money-tray like an easy collar instead of offering it to the public, taking the man against his will, on the invitation of a disreputable cur, apparently to visit a dog at Harrow – he was so intent on that direction. The north wall of Burlington House Gardens, between the Arcade and the Albany, offers a shy spot for appointments among blind men at about two or three o'clock in the afternoon. They sit (very uncomfortably) on a sloping stone there, and compare notes. Their dogs may always be observed at the same time, openly disparaging the men they keep, to one another, and settling where they shall respectively take their men when they begin to move again. At a small butcher's, in a shy neighbourhood (there is no reason for suppressing the name; it is by Notting-hill, and gives upon the district called the Potteries), I know a shaggy black and white dog who keeps a drover. He is a dog of an easy disposition, and too frequently allows this drover to get drunk. On these occasions, it is the dog's custom to sit outside the public-house, keeping his eye on a few sheep, and thinking. I have seen him with six sheep, plainly casting up in his mind how many he began with when he left the market, and at what places he has left the rest. I have seen him perplexed by not being able to account to himself for certain particular sheep. A light has gradually broken on him, he has remembered at what butcher's he left them, and in a burst of grave satisfaction has caught a fly off his nose, and shown himself much relieved. If I could at any time have doubted the fact that it was he who kept the drover, and not the drover who kept him, it would have been abundantly proved by his way of taking undivided charge of the six sheep, when the drover came out besmeared with red ochre and beer, and gave him wrong directions, which he calmly disregarded. He has taken the sheep entirely into his own hands, has merely remarked with respectful firmness, 'That instruction would place them under an omnibus; you had better confine your attention to yourself – you will want it all;' and has driven his charge away, with an intelligence of ears and tail, and a knowledge of business, that has left his lout of a man very, very far behind.

As the dogs of shy neighbourhoods usually betray a slinking consciousness of being in poor circumstances – for the most part manifested in an aspect of anxiety, an awkwardness in their play, and a misgiving that somebody is going to harness them to something, to pick up a living – so the cats of shy neighbourhoods exhibit a strong tendency to relapse into barbarism. Not only are they made selfishly ferocious by ruminating on the surplus population around them, and on the densely crowded state of all the avenues to cat's-meat; not only is there a moral and politico-economical haggardness in them, traceable to these reflections; but they evince a physical deterioration. Their linen is not clean, and is wretchedly got up; their black turns rusty, like old mourning; they wear very indifferent fur; and take to the shabbiest cotton velvet, instead of silk velvet. I am on terms of recognition with several small streets of cats, about the Obelisk in Saint George's Fields, and also in the vicinity of Clerkenwell-green, and also in the back settlements of Drury-lane. In appearance, they are very like the women among whom they live. They seem to turn out of their unwholesome beds into the street, without any preparation. They leave their young families to stagger about the gutters, unassisted, while they frouzily quarrel and swear and scratch and spit, at street corners. In particular, I remark that when they are about to increase their families (an event of frequent occurrence) the resemblance is strongly expressed in a certain dusty dowdiness, down-at-heel self-neglect, and general giving up of things. I cannot honestly report that I have ever seen a feline matron of this class washing her face when in an interesting condition.

Not to prolong these notes of uncommercial travel among the lower animals of shy neighbourhoods, by dwelling at length upon the exasperated moodiness of the tom-cats, and their resemblance in many respects to a man and a brother, I will come to a close with a word on the fowls of the same localities.

That anything born of an egg and invested with wings, should have got to the pass that it hops contentedly down a ladder into a cellar, and calls *that* going home, is a circumstance so amazing as to leave one

nothing more in this connexion to wonder at. Otherwise I might wonder
at the completeness with which these fowls have become separated from
all the birds of the air − have taken to grovelling in bricks and mortar
and mud − have forgotten all about live trees, and make roosting-places
of shop-boards, barrows, oyster-tubs, bulk-heads, and door-scrapers. I
wonder at nothing concerning them, and take them as they are. I accept
as products of Nature and things of course a reduced Bantam family of
my acquaintance in the Hackney-road, who are incessantly at the
pawnbroker's. I cannot say that they enjoy themselves, for they are of a
melancholy temperament; but what enjoyment they are capable of, they
derive from crowding together in the pawnbroker's side-entry. Here, they
are always to be found in a feeble flutter, as if they were newly come
down in the world, and were afraid of being identified. I know a low
fellow, originally of a good family from Dorking, who takes his whole
establishment of wives, in single file, in at the door of the Jug Department
of a disorderly tavern near the Haymarket, manoeuvres them among the
company's legs, emerges with them at the Bottle Entrance, and so passes
his life: seldom, in the season, going to bed before two in the morning.
Over Waterloo-bridge, there is a shabby old speckled couple (they belong
to the wooden French-bedstead, washing-stand, and towel-horse-making
trade), who are always trying to get in at the door of a chapel. Whether
the old lady, under a delusion reminding one of Mrs Southcott, has an
idea of entrusting an egg to that particular denomination, or merely
understands that she has no business in the building, and is consequently
frantic to enter it, I cannot determine; but she is constantly endeavouring
to undermine the principal door: while her partner, who is infirm upon
his legs, walks up and down, encouraging her and defying the Universe.
But the family I have been best acquainted with, since the removal from
this trying sphere of a Chinese circle at Brentford, reside in the densest
part of Bethnal-green. Their abstraction from the objects among which
they live, or rather their conviction that those objects have all come into
existence in express subservience to fowls, has so enchanted me, that I
have made them the subject of many journeys at divers hours. After
careful observation of the two lords and the ten ladies of whom this
family consists, I have come to the conclusion that their opinions are
represented by the leading lord and leading lady: the latter, as I judge,
an aged personage, afflicted with a paucity of feather and visibility of
quill, that gives her the appearance of a bundle of office pens. When a
railway goods-van that would crush an elephant comes round the corner,
tearing over these fowls, they emerge unharmed from under the horses,
perfectly satisfied that the whole rush was a passing property in the air,
which may have left something to eat behind it. They look upon old
shoes, wrecks of kettles and saucepans, and fragments of bonnets, as a

kind of meteoric discharge for fowls to peck at. Pegtops and hoops they account, I think, as a sort of hail; shuttlecocks, as rain, or dew. Gaslight comes quite as natural to them as any other light; and I have more than a suspicion that, in the minds of the two lords, the early public-house at the corner has superseded the sun. I have established it as a certain fact, that they always begin to crow when the public-house shutters begin to be taken down, and that they salute the potboy, the instant he appears to perform that duty, as if he were Phoebus in person.

14

The Uncommercial Traveller

All The Year Round, 16 June 1860 (*UT1* as 'Tramps')

Dickens had strong feelings on the subject of begging and mendicity (see Vol. 2 of this edition, article 45 and headnote), and while openly describing in the present article some of his favourite Kent haunts and scenery, also reveals knowledge of the ploys used by tramps and beggars to extract donations from other pedestrians. In *David Copperfield* (1850), Dickens had described how the young David is robbed on the road to Dover by a young tinker who beats his female companion. 'The trampers', David recalls, '... inspired me with a dread that is yet quite fresh in my mind' (Ch. 13).

Charles Dickens Jr states that '[t]he old hall here described [on pp. 134–5] is Cobham Hall', which it resembles in many particulars; the hall was the seat of the Earl of Darnley, and Dickens had used it as a setting as early as 1836, in the fourth number of *Pickwick Papers* (*UT4*, p. xxiv). The 'ancient sign of the Crispin and Crispianus' still hangs outside a public house of that name at the bottom of Strood Hill, close to Gadshill, and is said to date from the fourteenth century. The anecdote of the six workmen required 'for a certain spell of work in a pleasant part of the country' (p. 135) finds a parallel in Dickens's attempts during the summer and early autumn of 1857 to have a water pump installed at Gads' Hill. His letter of 27–28 September (*Pilgrim* Editors unsure which date) states drily that 'five men have been looking attentively at the pump for a week, and ... may begin to fit it in the course of October'. Earlier in the same letter he comments to Forster that 'the seven miles between Maidstone and Rochester is one of the most beautiful walks in England'. This walk appears to inspire the lyrical description on pp. 136–7 (*Pilgrim*, Vol. VIII, p. 455). Likewise the mention of the prevalent belief that the smell of fresh hops was a 'sovereign remedy' for illness (p. 137) is anticipated in another letter of the same period: 'Hop-picking is going on, and people sleep in the garden, and breathe in at the keyhole of the house door. . . . I find it is a superstition that the dust of the newly-picked hop . . . is a cure for consumption' (*Pilgrim*, Vol. VIII, p. 435).

The speech of the 'well-spoken young man', from the words 'He says in a flowing confidential voice' (p. 130) to 'a long expectoration, as you leave him behind' (p. 131), Dickens later incorporated into an unperformed and unpublished comic duologue, probably composed, as Philip Collins surmises, 'for private performance at some house party' (see Collins, 'Some Unpublished Comic Duologues of Dickens', *Nineteenth-Century Fiction*, Vol. 31 [1977], pp. 440–9). Dickens's directions for the sketch describe a pedestrian, A, who is followed by a 'reduced young man', B: 'whenever A stops or looks round impatiently, B drops his voice to a still lower tone, and speaks more respectably and deferentially'. The banter of Negro singers, mock auctioneers and participants in a Public Meeting also features in the MS fragment, and shows Dickens's fondness for recreating comic patter.

Literary allusions (p. 131) 'John Anderson, . . . "pow" ': in Robert Burns's version of the traditional lyric 'John Anderson, my Jo' (*The Scots Musical Museum*, 1790), the worthy rustic John Anderson's wife blesses his 'frosty pow' (white-haired head); (p. 132) 'do as we wold be done by': Lord Chesterfield, *Letters to his Son* (1774), 16 October 1747, 'Do as you would be done by is the surest method that I know of pleasing'; (p. 132) '*fruges consumere nati*' [lit. 'those born to consume the earth's produce', i.e. countryfolk]: Horace, *Epistles*, Book 1, no. 2, l. 27.

The chance use of the word 'Tramp' in my last paper, brought that numerous fraternity so vividly before my mind's eye, that I had no sooner laid down my pen than a compulsion was upon me to take it up again, and make notes of the Tramps whom I perceived on all the summer roads in all directions.

Whenever a tramp sits down to rest by the wayside, he sits with his legs in a dry ditch; and whenever he goes to sleep (which is very often indeed), he goes to sleep on his back. Yonder, by the high road, glaring white in the bright sunshine, lies, on the dusty bit of turf under the bramble-bush that fences the coppice from the highway, the tramp of the order savage, fast asleep. He lies on the broad of his back, with his face turned up to the sky, and one of his ragged arms loosely thrown across his face. His bundle (what can be the contents of that mysterious bundle, to make it worth his while to carry it about?) is thrown down beside him, and the waking woman with him sits with her legs in the ditch, and her back to the road. She wears her bonnet rakishly perched on the front of her head, to shade her face from the sun in walking, and she ties her skirts round her in conventionally tight tramp-fashion with a sort of apron. You can seldom catch sight of her, resting thus, without seeing her in a despondently defiant manner doing something to her hair or her bonnet, and glancing at you between her fingers. She does not often go to sleep herself in the daytime, but will sit for any length of time beside the man. And his slumberous propensities would not seem to be referable to the fatigue of carrying the bundle, for she carries it much oftener and further than he. When they are afoot, you will mostly find him slouching on ahead, in a gruff temper, while she lags heavily behind with the burden. He is given to personally correcting her, too – which phase of his character develops itself oftenest, on benches outside alehouse doors – and she appears to become strongly attached to him for these reasons; it may usually be noticed that, when the poor creature has a bruised face, she is the most affectionate. He has no occupation whatever, this order of tramp, and has no object whatever in going anywhere. He will sometimes call himself a brickmaker, or a sawyer, but only when he takes an imaginative flight. He generally represents himself, in a vague way, as looking out for a job of work; but he never did work, he never does, and he never never will. It is a favourite fiction with him, however (as if he were the most industrious character on earth), that *you* never work; and as he goes past your garden and sees you looking at your flowers, you will overhear him growl, with a strong sense of contrast, '*You* are a lucky hidle devil, *you* are!'

The slinking tramp is of the same hopeless order, and has the same injured conviction on him that you were born to whatever you possess, and never did anything to get it; but he is of a less audacious disposition. He will stop before your gate, and say to his female companion with an air of constitutional humility and propitiation – to edify anyone who may be within hearing behind a blind or a bush – 'This is a sweet spot, ain't it? A lovely spot! And I wonder if they'd give two poor footsore travellers like me and you, a drop of fresh water out of such a pretty gen-teel crib? We'd take it wery koind on 'em, wouldn't us? Wery koind, upon my word, us would!' He has a quick sense of a dog in the vicinity, and will extend his modestly-injured propitiation to the dog chained up in your yard: remarking, as he slinks at the yard gate, 'Ah! You are a foine breed o' dog, too, and *you* ain't kep for nothink! I'd take it wery koind o' your master if he'd elp a traveller and his woife as envies no gentlefolk their good fortun, wi' a bit o' your broken wittles. He'd never

'*This is a Sweet spot, Ain't It? A Lovelly Spot*' *(frontispiece by G. J. Pinwell for UT1)*

know the want of it, nor more would you. Don't bark like that at poor persons as never done you no arm; the poor is down-trodden and broke enough without that; O DON'T!' He generally heaves a prodigious sigh in moving away, and always looks up the lane and down the lane, and up the road and down the road, before going on.

Both of these orders of tramp are of a very robust habit; let the hard-working labourer at whose cottage door they prowl and beg, have the ague never so badly, these tramps are sure to be in good health.

There is another kind of tramp, whom you encounter this bright summer day – say, on a road with the sea-breeze making its dust lively, and sails of ships in the blue distance beyond the slope of Down. As you walk enjoyingly on, you descry in the perspective at the bottom of a steep hill up which your way lies, a figure that appears to be sitting airily on a gate, whistling in a cheerful and disengaged manner. As you approach nearer to it, you observe the figure to slide down from the gate, to desist from whistling, to uncock its hat, to become tender of foot, to depress its head and elevate its shoulders, and to present all the characteristics of profound despondency. Arriving at the bottom of the hill, and coming close to the figure, you observe it to be the figure of a shabby young man. He is moving painfully forward, in the direction in which you are going, and his mind is so preoccupied with his misfortunes that he is not aware of your approach until you are close upon him at the hill-foot. When he is aware of you, you discover him to be a remarkably well-behaved young man, and a remarkably well-spoken young man. You know him to be well-behaved, by his respectful manner of touching his hat; you know him to be well-spoken by his smooth manner of expressing himself. He says in a flowing confidential voice, and without punctuation, 'I ask your pardon sir but if you would excuse the liberty of being so addressed upon the public Iway by one who is almost reduced to rags though it as not always been so and by no fault of his own but through ill elth in his family and many unmerited sufferings it would be a great obligation sir to know the time.' You give the well-spoken young man, the time. The well-spoken young man, keeping well up with you, resumes: 'I am aware sir that it is a liberty to intrude a further question on a gentleman walking for his entertainment but might I make so bold as ask the favour of the way to Dover sir and about the distance?' You inform the well-spoken young man that the way to Dover is straight on, and the distance some eighteen miles. The well-spoken young man becomes greatly agitated. 'In the condition to which I am reduced,' says he, 'I could not ope to reach Dover before dark even if my shoes were in a state to take me there or my feet were in a state to old out over the flinty road and were not on the bare ground of which any gentleman has the means to satisfy himself by looking Sir may I take the liberty of speaking to you?' As the well-spoken young man keeps so well up with you that you can't prevent his taking the liberty of speaking to you, he goes on, with fluency: 'Sir it is not begging that is my intention for I was brought up by the best of mothers and begging is not my trade I should not know sir how to follow it as a trade if such were my shameful wishes for the best of mothers long taught otherwise and in the best of omes though now reduced to take the present liberty on the Iway Sir my business was the law-stationering and I was favourably known to the Solicitor-General the Attorney-General the majority of the judges and the ole of the legal profession but through ill elth in my family and the treachery of a friend for whom I became security and he no other than my own wife's brother the brother of my own wife I was cast forth with my tender partner and three young children not to beg for I will sooner die of deprivation but to make my way to the seaport town of Dover where I have a relative i in respect not only that will assist me but that would trust me with untold gold Sir in appier times and hare this calamity fell upon me I made for my amusement when I little thought that I should ever need it excepting for my air this' – here the well-spoken young man puts his hand into his breast – 'this comb! Sir I implore you in the name of charity to purchase a tortoise-shell comb which is a genuine article at any price that your humanity may put upon it and may the blessings of a ouseless family awaiting with beating arts the return of a husband and a father from Dover upon the cold stone seats of London Bridge ever attend you Sir may I take the liberty of speaking to you I implore you to buy this comb!' By this time, being a reasonably good walker, you will have been too much for the well-spoken young man, who will stop short and express his disgust and his want of breath, in a long expectoration, as you leave him behind.

Towards the end of the same walk, on the same bright summer day, at the corner of the next little town or village, you may find another kind of tramp, embodied in the persons of a most exemplary couple whose only improvidence appears to have been, that they spent the last of their little All on soap. They are a man and woman, spotless to behold – John Anderson, with the frost on his short smock-frock instead of his 'pow,' attended by Mrs Anderson. John is over ostentatious of the frost upon his raiment, and wears a curious and, you would say, an almost unnecessary demonstration of girdle of white linen wound about his waist – a girdle, snowy as Mrs Anderson's apron. This cleanliness was the expiring effort of the respectable couple, and nothing then remained to Mr Anderson but to get chalked upon his spade, in snow-white copy-book characters, HUNGRY! and to sit down here. Yes; one thing more remained to Mr Anderson – his character; Monarchs could not deprive him of his hard-earned character. Accordingly, as you come up with this spectacle of virtue in distress, Mrs Anderson rises, and with a decent curtsey presents for your consideration a certificate from a Doctor of Divinity, the reverend the Vicar of Upper Dodgington, who informs his Christian friends and all whom it may concern that the bearers, John Anderson and lawful wife, are persons to whom you cannot be too liberal. This benevolent pastor omitted no work of his hands to fit the good couple out, for with half an eye you can recognise his autograph on the spade.

Another class of tramp is a man, the most valuable part of whose stock-in-trade is a highly perplexed demeanour. He is got up like a countryman, and you will often come upon the poor fellow, while he is endeavouring to decipher the inscription on a milestone – quite a fruitless endeavour, for he cannot read. He asks your pardon, he truly does (he is very slow of speech, this tramp, and he looks in a bewildered way all round the prospect while he talks to you), but all of us shold do as we wold be done by, and he'll take it kind if you'll put a power man in the right road fur to jine his eldest son as has broke his leg bad in the masoning, and is in this heere Orspit'l as is wrote down by Squire Pouncerby's own hand as wold not tell a lie fur no man. He then produces from under his dark frock (being always very slow and perplexed) a neat but worn old leathern purse, from which he takes a scrap of paper. On this scrap of paper is written, by Squire Pouncerby, of The Grove, 'Please to direct the Bearer, a poor but very worthy man, to the Sussex County Hospital, near Brighton' – a matter of some difficulty at the moment, seeing that the request comes suddenly upon you in the depths of Hertfordshire. The more you endeavour to indicate where Brighton is – when you have with the greatest difficulty remembered – the less the devoted father can be made to comprehend, and the more obtusely he stares at the prospect; whereby, being reduced to extremity, you recommend the faithful parent to begin by going to Saint Albans, and present him with half-a-crown. It does him good, no doubt, but scarcely helps him forward, since you find him lying drunk that same evening in the wheelwright's sawpit under the shed where the felled trees are, opposite the sign of the Three Jolly Hedgers.

But the most vicious, by far, of all the idle tramps, is the tramp who pretends to have been a gentleman. 'Educated,' he writes from the village beer-shop in pale ink of a ferruginous complexion; 'educated at Trin. Coll. Cam. – nursed in the lap of affluence – once in my small way the pattron of the Muses,' &c. &c. &c. – surely a sympathetic mind will not withhold a trifle to help him on to the market-town where he thinks of giving a Lecture to the *fruges consumere nati*, on things in general? This shameful creature lolling about hedge taprooms in his ragged clothes, now so far from being black that they look as if they never can have been black, is more selfish and insolent than even the savage tramp. He would sponge on the poorest boy for a farthing, and spurn him when he had got it; he would interpose (if he could get anything by it) between the baby and the mother's breast. So much lower than the company he keeps, for his maudlin assumption of being higher, this pitiless rascal blights the summer roads as he maunders on between the luxuriant hedges: where (to my thinking) even the wild convolvulus and rose and sweetbriar, are the worse for his going by, and need time to recover from the taint of him in the air.

The young fellows who trudge along barefoot, five or six together, their boots slung over their shoulders, their shabby bundles under their arms, their sticks newly cut from some roadside wood, are not eminently prepossessing, but are much less objectionable. There is a tramp-fellowship among them. They pick one another up at resting stations, and go on in companies. They always go at a fast swing – though they generally limp too – and there is invariably one of the company who has much ado to keep up with the rest. They generally talk about horses, and any other means of locomotion than walking: or, one of the company relates some recent experiences of the road – which are always disputes and difficulties. As for example. 'So, as I'm a standing at the pump in the market, blest if there don't come up a Beadle, and he ses, "Mustn't stand here," he ses. "Why not?" I ses. "No beggars allowed in this town," he ses. "Who's a beggar?" I ses. "You are," he ses. "Whoever see me beg? Did you?" I ses. "Then you're a tramp," he ses. "I'd rather be that, than a Beadle," I ses.' (The company express great approval.) ' "Would you?" he ses to me. "Yes I would," I ses to him. "Well," he ses, "anyhow, get out of this town." "Why, blow your little town!" I ses, "who wants to be in it? Wot does your dirty little town mean by comin' and stickin' itself in the road to anywhere? Why don't you get a shovel and a barrer, and clear your town out o' people's way?" ' (The company expressing the highest approval, and laughing aloud, they all go down the hill.)

Then, there are the tramp handicraft men. Are they not all over England, in this Midsummer time? Where does the lark sing, the corn grow, the mill turn, the river run, and they are not among the lights and shadows, tinkering, chair-mending, umbrella-mending, clock-mending, knife-grinding? Surely, a pleasant thing, if we were in that condition of life, to grind our way through Kent, Sussex, and Surrey. For the first six weeks or so, we should see the sparks we ground off, fiery bright against a background of green wheat and green leaves. A little later, and the ripe harvest would pale our sparks from red to yellow, until we got the dark newly-turned land for a background again, and they were red once more. By that time, we should have ground our way to the sea cliffs, and the whirr of our wheel would be lost in the breaking of the waves. Our next variety in sparks would be derived from contrast with the gorgeous medley of colours in the autumn woods, and, by the time we had ground our way round to the heathy lands between Reigate and Croydon, doing a prosperous stroke of business all along, we should show like a little firework in the light frosty air, and be the next best thing to the blacksmith's forge. Very agreeable, too, to go on a chair-mending tour. What judges we should be of rushes, and how knowingly (with a sheaf and a bottomless chair at our back) we should lounge on bridges, looking over at osier-beds. Among all the innumerable occupations that cannot possibly be transacted without the assistance of lookers-on, chair-mending may take a station in the first rank. When we sat down with our backs against the barn or the public-house, and began to mend, what a sense of popularity would grow upon us. When all the children came to look at us, and the tailor, and the general dealer, and the farmer who had been giving a small order at the little saddler's, and the groom from the great house, and the publican, and even the two skittle-players (and here note that, howsoever busy all the rest of village humankind may be, there will always be two people with leisure to play at skittles, wherever village skittles are), what encouragement would be on us to plait and weave! No one looks at us while we plait and weave these words. Clock-mending, again. Except for the slight inconvenience of carrying a clock under our arm, and the monotony of making the bell go, whenever we came to a human habitation, what a pleasant privilege to give a voice to the dumb cottage-clock, and set it talking to the cottage family again. Likewise we foresee great interest in going round by the park plantations, under the overhanging boughs (hares, rabbits, partridges, and pheasants, scudding like mad across and across the chequered ground before us), and so over the park ladder, and through the wood, until we came to the Keeper's lodge. Then would the Keeper be discoverable at his door, in a deep nest of leaves, smoking his pipe. Then, on our accosting him in the way of our trade, would he call to Mrs Keeper, respecting 't'ould clock' in the kitchen. Then would Mrs Keeper ask us into the lodge, and on due examination, we should offer to make a good job of it for eighteenpence: which offer, being accepted, would set us tinkling and clinking among the chubby awe-struck little Keepers for an hour and more. So completely to the family's satisfaction should we achieve our work, that the Keeper would mention how that there was something wrong with the bell of the turret stable-clock up at the Hall, and that if we thought good of going up to the housekeeper on the chance of that job too, why he would take us. Then, should we go, among the branching oaks and the deep fern, by silent ways of mystery known to the Keeper, seeing the herd glancing here and there as we went along, until we came to the old Hall, solemn and grand. Under the Terrace Flower Garden, and round by the stables, would the Keeper take us in, and as we passed we should observe how spacious and stately the stables, and how fine the painting of the horses' names over their stalls, and how solitary all: the family being in London. Then, should we find ourselves presented to the housekeeper, sitting, in hushed state, at needlework, in a bay-window looking out upon a mighty grim red-brick quadrangle, guarded by stone lions disrespectfully throwing somersaults over the escutcheons of the noble family. Then, our services accepted and we insinuated with a candle into the stable turret, we should find it to be a mere question of pendulum, but one that would hold us until dark. Then, should we fall to work, with a general impression of Ghosts being about, and of pictures indoors that of a certainty came out of their frames and 'walked,' if the family would only own it. Then should we work and work, until the day gradually turned to dusk, and even until the dusk gradually turned to dark. Our task at length accomplished, we should be taken into an enormous servants' hall, and there regaled with beef and bread, and powerful ale. Then, paid freely, we should be at liberty to go, and should be told by a pointing helper to keep round over yinder by the blasted ash, and so straight through the woods, till we should see the town-lights right afore us. Then, feeling lonesome, should we desire upon the whole, that the ash had not been blasted, or that the helper had had the manners not to mention it. However, we should keep on, all right, till suddenly the stable bell would strike ten in the dolefullest way, quite chilling our blood, though we had so lately taught him how to acquit himself. Then, as we went on, should we recal old stories, and dimly consider what it would be most advisable to do, in the event of a tall figure, all in white, with saucer eyes, coming up and saying, 'I want you to come to a churchyard and mend a church clock. Follow me!' Then, should we make a burst to get clear of the trees, and should soon find ourselves in the open, with the town-lights bright ahead of us. So should we lie that night at the ancient sign of the Crispin and Crispanus, and rise early next morning to be betimes on tramp again.

Bricklayers often tramp, in twos and threes, lying by night at their 'lodges' which are scattered all over the country. Bricklaying is another of the occupations that can by no means be transacted in rural parts, without the assistance of spectators – of as many as can be convened. In thinly-peopled spots, I have known bricklayers on tramp, coming up with bricklayers at work, to be so sensible of the indispensability of lookers-on, that they themselves have set up in that capacity, and have been unable to subside into the acceptance of a proffered share in the job, for two or three days together. Sometimes the 'navvy,' on tramp, with an extra pair of half-boots over his shoulder, a bag, a bottle, and a can, will take a similar part in a job of excavation, and will look at it, without engaging in it, until all his money is gone. The current of my uncommercial pursuits caused me only last summer to want a little body of workmen for a certain spell of work in a pleasant part of the country; and I was at one time honoured with the attendance of as many as seven-and-twenty, who were looking at six.

Who can be familiar with any rustic highway in summer-time, without storing up knowledge of the many tramps who go from one oasis of town or village to another, to sell a stock in trade, apparently not worth a shilling when sold? Shrimps are a favourite commodity for this kind of speculation, and so are cakes of a soft and spongy character, coupled with Spanish nuts and brandy balls. The stock is carried on the head in a basket, and, between the head and the basket, are the trestles on which the stock is displayed at trading times. Fleet of foot, but a careworn class of tramp this, mostly; with a certain stiffness of neck, occasioned by much anxious balancing of baskets; and also with a long Chinese sort of eye, which an overweighted forehead would seem to have squeezed into that form.

On the hot dusty roads near seaport towns and great rivers, behold the tramping Soldier. And if you should happen never to have asked yourself whether his uniform is suited to his work, perhaps the poor fellow's appearance, as he comes distressfully towards you, with his absurdly tight jacket unbuttoned, his neck-gear in his hand, and his legs well chafed by his trousers of baize, may suggest the personal inquiry, how you think *you* would like it. Much better the tramping Sailor, although his cloth is somewhat too thick for land service. But why the tramping merchant-mate should put on a black velvet waistcoat, for a chalky country in the dog-days, is one of the great secrets of nature that will never be discovered.

I have my eye upon a piece of Kentish road, bordered on either side by a wood, and having on one hand, between the road-dust and the trees, a skirting patch of grass. Wild flowers grow in abundance on this spot, and it lies high and airy, with the distant river stealing steadily away to the ocean, like a man's life. To gain the milestone here, which the moss, primroses, violets, blue-bells, and wild roses, would soon render illegible but for peering travellers pushing them aside with their sticks, you must come up a steep hill, come which way you may. So, all the tramps with carts or caravans – the Gipsy-tramp, the Show-tramp, the Cheap Jack – find it impossible to resist the temptations of the place, and all turn the horse loose when they come to it, and boil the pot. Bless the place, I love the ashes of the vagabond fires that have scorched its grass! What tramp children do I see here, attired in a handful of rags, making a gymnasium of the shafts of the cart, making a feather-bed of the flints and brambles, making a toy of the hobbled old horse who is not much more like a horse than any cheap toy would be! Here, do I encounter the cart of mats and brooms and baskets – with all thoughts of business given to the evening wind – with the stew made and being served out – with Cheap Jack and Dear Jill striking soft music out of the plates that are rattled like warlike cymbals when put up for auction at fairs and markets – their minds so influenced (no doubt) by the melody of the nightingales, as they begin to sing in the woods behind them, that if I were to propose to deal, they would sell me anything at cost price. On this hallowed ground has it been my happy privilege (let me whisper it), to behold the White-haired Lady with the pink eyes eating meat-pie with the Giant: while, by the hedge-side, on the box of blankets which I knew contained the snakes, were set forth the cups and saucers and the teapot. It was on an evening in August, that I chanced upon this ravishing spectacle, and I noticed that, whereas the Giant reclined half concealed beneath the overhanging boughs and seemed indifferent to Nature, the white hair of the gracious Lady streamed free in the breath of evening, and her pink eyes found pleasure in the landscape. I heard only a single sentence of her uttering, yet it bespoke a talent for modest repartee. The ill-mannered Giant – accursed be his evil race! – had interrupted the Lady in some remark, and, as I passed that enchanted corner of the wood, she gently reproved him with the words, 'Now, Cobby;' – Cobby! so short a name! – 'ain't one fool enough to talk at a time?'

Within appropriate distance of this magic ground, though not so near it as that the song trolled from tap or bench at door, can invade its woodland silence, is a little hostelry which no man possessed of a penny was ever known to pass in warm weather. Before its entrance, are certain pleasant trimmed limes: likewise, a cool well, with so musical a bucket-handle that its fall upon the bucket rim will make a horse prick up his ears and neigh, upon the droughty road half a mile off. This is a house of great resort for haymaking tramps and harvest tramps, insomuch that as they sit within, drinking their mugs of beer, their relinquished scythes and reaping-hooks glare out of the open windows, as if the whole establishment were a family war-coach of Ancient Britons. Later in the season, the whole countryside, for miles and miles, will swarm with hopping tramps. They come in families, men, women, and children, every family provided with a bundle of bedding, an iron pot, a number of babies, and too often with some poor sick creature quite unfit for the rough life, for whom they suppose the smell of the fresh hop to be a sovereign remedy. Many of these hoppers are Irish, but many come from London. They crowd all the roads, and camp under all the hedges and on all the scraps of common-land, and live among and upon the hops until they are all picked, and the hop-gardens, so beautiful through the summer, look as if they had been laid waste by an invading army. Then, there is a vast exodus of tramps out of the county; and if you ride or drive round any turn of any road at more than a foot pace, you will be bewildered to find that you have charged into the bosom of fifty families, and that there are splashing up all around you, in the utmost prodigality of confusion, bundles of bedding, babies, iron pots, and a good-humoured multitude of both sexes and all ages, equally divided between perspiration and intoxication.

15

The Uncommercial Traveller

All The Year Round, 30 June 1860 (*UT1* as 'Dullborough Town')

In the index of Vol. III of *ATYR*, the present article appears, along with article 18, under the title 'Childhood Associations', and the two are clearly linked by their presentation of what appear to be interesting recollections of Dickens's very early childhood. Accordingly, scholars and biographers since Forster have not hesitated to make use of both essays to supplement otherwise scanty evidence about his early life (see *Forster*, Book 1, Ch. 3, Book 8, Ch. 5; Edgar Johnson, *Charles Dickens, His Tragedy and His Triumph* [1952], Vol. 1, pp. 11–26 *passim*). The memory of arriving in London for the first time at the Cross Keys, Wood-street, Cheapside, in a coach smelling of straw (p. 140), is one Dickens later assigns to Pip in the thirteenth instalment of *Great Expectations* (*ATYR*, 23 February 1861).

'Dullborough' is a composite portrait of the Medway towns of Chatham, Strood and Rochester, which Dickens pretends not to have revisited since childhood. He had already described Rochester as it appeared to him in the 1850s, in a *HW* essay jointly composed with Henry Morley, 'One Man in a Dockyard' (Vol. III, 6 September 1851; repr. in Stone, Vol. 1, pp. 331–42). Topographical details of the three towns seem deliberately confused. For example, if the 'playing-field' referred to (p. 140) was that adjacent to the school of the Rev. William Giles in Clover-lane, Chatham, which Dickens attended (see *Forster*, Book 1, Ch. 1), then it could not have been 'swallowed up' by the South Eastern Railway station as the 'Uncommercial Traveller' claims. Until 1891 SER only reached as far as Strood, and in 1860, it was the London, Chatham and Dover Railway which had a station under construction in Chatham (see B. Matthews, *History of Strood District Council* [1971], p. 72). Likewise, while both the 'Miss Green' and the doctor 'Joe Specks' have been tentatively identified as actual childhood friends of Dickens – the former as Lucy Stroughill of Ordnance Terrace, Chatham; the latter as John Dan Brown (see Michael Slater, *Dickens and Women* [1983], pp. 40–1, and H. Smetham in *The Dickensian*, Vol. 33 [1937], pp. 52–3) – the 'originals' were never married to each other (see Gordon Spence, *Charles Dickens as a Familiar Essayist* [1978], pp. 123–4 & n.). The coach proprietor Timpson, said to have had an office 'up-street' (p. 140), seems likely to be based on the historical coach proprietor, Simpson, who operated a coach called 'The Blue-Eyed Maid', but from Brompton rather than from Rochester or Chatham (see W. Dexter, *The Dickensian*, Vol. 18 [1922],

p. 21f.). Similarly, in the description of the 'High-street' of what seems initially to be Rochester, Dickens blurs his details: the public clock in Rochester belonged to the Old Corn Exchange, not to the Town Hall; nor was the Town Hall of Rochester ever a venue for public entertainments (see R. Marsh, *Rochester: The Evolution of A City* [1974], p. 50f.). Finally, as Philip Collins has argued, the deprecatory sketch of the 'Dullborough' Mechanics Institution and its activities is strikingly at odds with what is known of Dickens's private efforts as 'the most notable literary supporter' of the Chatham, Rochester, Strood & Brompton Mechanics Institution (Collins, *Dickens and Education* [1963], pp. 91–2 & n.). He was its President until his death in 1870 and raised some £400 for its funds through public readings, such as that of 18 December 1860, when he expressed his hope 'that a time would come when a few mechanics would be found in a Mechanics' Institute' (*Speeches*, p. 298).

A critical study of the paper, and the means by which Dickens's retrospective portrait of the Medway towns 'broadens in a quite unforced way into a critique of cultural change', is to be found in Malcolm Andrews's *Dickens and the Grown-up Child* (1994), pp. 41–56.

Literary allusions (p. 143) 'Genie of the Lamp built the palace for Aladdin': the story of 'Aladdin and the Wonderful Lamp' from the *Arabian Nights*; (p. 143) 'Richard the Third … struggling for life against the virtuous Richmond': Shakespeare, *Richard III*, Act 5 Sc. 4; (p. 143) 'the good King Duncan couldn't rest in his grave': recalls 'Duncan is in his grave/After life's fitful fever he sleeps well', Shakespeare, *Macbeth*, Act 3, Sc. 2; (p. 145) 'Comin' through the Rye': title of Robert Burns's lyric 'Comin thro' the rye' (1796); (p. 146) 'Roderick Random … Narcissa … Strap': principal characters in Smollett's *The Adventures of Roderick Random* (1748); (pp. 147–8) 'Lieutenant Hatchway … Pickle': principal characters in Smollett's *The Adventures of Peregrine Pickle* (1751).

Textual note (p. 147) copy-text has 'it quite touched my heart': *UT1* has 'it quite touched my foolish heart'.

It lately happened that I found myself rambling about the scenes among which my earliest days were passed; scenes from which I departed when I was a child, and which I did not revisit until I was a man. This is no uncommon chance, but one that befals some of us any day; perhaps it may not be quite uninteresting to compare notes with the reader respecting an experience so familiar and a journey so uncommercial.

I will call my boyhood's home (and I feel like a Tenor in an English Opera when I mention it) Dullborough. Most of us come from

Dullborough who come from a country town.

As I left Dullborough in the days when there were no railroads in the land, I left it in a stage-coach. Through all the years that have since passed, have I ever lost the smell of the damp straw in which I was packed – like game – and forwarded, carriage paid, to the Cross Keys, Wood-street, Cheapside, London? There was no other inside passenger, and I consumed my sandwiches in solitude and dreariness, and it rained hard all the way, and I thought life sloppier than I had expected to find it.

With this tender remembrance upon me, I was cavalierly shunted back into Dullborough the other day, by train. My ticket had been previously collected, like my taxes, and my shining new portmanteau had had a great plaster stuck upon it, and I had been defied by Act of Parliament to offer an objection to anything that was done to it, or me, under a penalty of not less than forty shillings or more than five pounds, compoundable for a term of imprisonment. When I had sent my disfigured property on to the hotel, I began to look about me; and the first discovery I made, was, that the Station had swallowed up the playing-field.

It was gone. The two beautiful hawthorn-trees, the hedge, the turf, and all those buttercups and daisies, had given place to the stoniest of jolting roads; while, beyond the Station, an ugly dark monster of a tunnel kept its jaws open, as if it had swallowed them and were ravenous for more destruction. The coach that had carried me away, was melodiously called Timpson's Blue-Eyed Maid, and belonged to Timpson, at the coach-office up-street; the locomotive engine that had brought me back was called severely No. 97, and belonged to S.E.R., and was spitting ashes and hot-water over the blighted ground.

When I had been let out at the platform-door, like a prisoner whom his turnkey grudgingly released, I looked in again over the low wall, at the scene of departed glories. Here, in the haymaking time, had I been delivered from the dungeons of Seringapatam, an immense pile (of haycock), by my countrymen, the victorious British (boy next door and his two cousins), and had been recognised with ecstasy by my affianced one (Miss Green), who had come all the way from England (second house in the terrace) to ransom me, and marry me. Here had I first heard in confidence, from one whose father was greatly connected, being under Government, of the existence of a terrible banditti, called 'The Radicals,' whose principles were, that the Prince Regent wore stays, and that nobody had a right to any salary, and that the army and navy ought to be put down – horrors at which I trembled in my bed, after supplicating that the Radicals might be speedily taken and hanged. Here, too, had we, the small boys of Boles's, had that cricket match against the small boys of Coles's, when Boles and Coles had actually met upon the ground, and when, instead of instantly hitting out at one another with the utmost fury, as we had all hoped and expected, those sneaks had said respectively, 'I hope Mrs Boles is well,' and 'I hope Mrs Coles and the baby are doing charmingly.' Could it be that, after all this, and much more, the Playing-field was a Station, and No. 97 expectorated boiling-water and red-hot cinders on it, and the whole belonged by Act of Parliament to S.E.R.?

As it could be, and was, I left the place with a heavy heart for a walk all over the town. And first of Timpson's, up-street. When I departed from Dullborough in the strawy arms of Timpson's Blue-Eyed Maid, Timpson's was a moderate-sized coach-office (in fact, a little coach-office), with an oval transparency in the window, which looked beautiful by night, representing one of Timpson's coaches in the act of passing a milestone on the London road with great velocity, completely full inside and out, and all the passengers dressed in the first style of fashion, and enjoying themselves tremendously. I found no such place as Timpson's now – no such bricks and rafters, not to mention the name – no such edifice on the teeming earth. Pickford had come and knocked Timpson's down. Pickford had not only knocked Timpson's down, but had knocked two or three houses down on each side of Timpson's, and then had knocked the whole into one great establishment, with a pair of big gates, in and out of which his (Pickford's) waggons are, in these days, always rattling, with their drivers sitting up so high, that they look in at the second floor windows of the old fashioned houses in the High-street as they shake the town. I have not the honour of Pickford's acquaintance, but I felt that he had done me an injury, not to say committed an act of boyslaughter, in running over my childhood in this rough manner; and if ever I meet Pickford driving one of his own monsters, and smoking a pipe the while (which is the custom of his men), he shall know by the expression of my eye, if it catches his, that there is something wrong between us.

Moreover, I felt that Pickford had no right to come rushing into Dullborough and deprive the town of a public picture. He is not Napoleon Bonaparte. When he took down the transparent stage-coach, he ought to have given the town a transparent van. With a gloomy conviction that Pickford is wholly utilitarian and unimaginative, I proceeded on my way.

It is a mercy I have not a red and green lamp and a night-bell at my door, for in my very young days I was taken to so many lyings-in that I wonder I escaped becoming a professional martyr to them in after-life. I suppose I had a very sympathetic nurse, with a large circle of married acquaintance. However that was, as I continued my walk through Dullborough, I found many houses to be solely associated in my mind with this particular interest. At one little greengrocer's shop, down certain steps from the street, I remembered to have waited on a lady who had had four children (I am afraid to write five, though I fully believe it was five) at a birth. This meritorious woman held quite a Reception in her room on the morning when I was introduced there, and the sight of the house brought vividly to my mind how the four (five) deceased young people lay, side by side, on a clean cloth on a chest of drawers: reminding me by a homely association, which I suspect their complexion to have assisted, of pigs' feet as they are usually displayed at a neat tripe-shop. Hot caudle was handed round on the occasion, and I further remembered as I stood contemplating the greengrocer's, that a subscription was entered into among the company, which became extremely alarming to my consciousness of having pocket-money on my person. This fact being known to my conductress, whoever she was, I was earnestly exhorted to contribute, but resolutely declined: therein disgusting the company, who gave me to understand that I must dismiss all expectations of going to Heaven.

How does it happen that when all else is change wherever one goes, there yet seem, in every place, to be some few people who never alter? As the sight of the greengrocer's house recalled these trivial incidents of long ago, the identical greengrocer appeared on the steps, with his hands in his pockets, and leaning his shoulder against the door-post, as my childish eyes had seen him many a time; indeed, there was his old mark on the door-post yet, as if his shadow had become a fixture there. It was he himself; he might formally have been an old-looking young man, or he might now be a young-looking old man, but there he was. In walking along the street, I had as yet looked in vain for a familiar face, or even a transmitted face; here was the very greengrocer who had been weighing and handling baskets on the morning of the reception. As he brought with him a dawning remembrance that he had had no proprietary interest in those babies, I crossed the road, and accosted him on the subject. He was not in the least excited or gratified or in anyway roused, by the accuracy of my recollection, but said, Yes, summut out of the common − he didn't remember how many it was (as if half a dozen babes either way made no difference) − had happened to a Mrs What's-her-name, as once lodged there − but he didn't call it to mind, particular. Nettled by this phlegmatic conduct, I informed him that I had left the town when I was a child. He slowly returned, quite unsoftened, and not without a sarcastic kind of complacency, *Had* I? Ah! And did I find it had got on tolerable well without me? Such is the difference (I thought, when I had left him a few hundred yards behind, and was by so much in a better temper) between going away from a place and remaining in it. I had no right, I reflected, to be angry with the greengrocer for his want of interest. I was nothing to him: whereas he was the town, the cathedral, the bridge, the river, my childhood, and a large slice of my life, to me.

Of course the town had shrunk fearfully, since I was a child there. I had entertained the impression that the High-street was at least as wide as Regent-street, London, or the Italian Boulevard at Paris. I found it little better than a lane. There was a public clock in it, which I had supposed to be the finest clock in the world; whereas it now turned out to be as inexpressive, moon-faced, and weak a clock as ever I saw. It belonged to a Town Hall, where I had seen an Indian (who I now suppose wasn't an Indian) swallow a sword (which I now suppose he didn't). This edifice had appeared to me in those days so glorious a structure, that I had set it up in my mind as the model on which the Genie of the Lamp built the palace for Aladdin. A mean little brick heap, like a demented chapel, with a few yawning persons in leather gaiters, and in the last extremity for something to do, lounging at the door with their hands in their pockets, and calling themselves a Corn Exchange!

The Theatre was in existence, I found, on asking the fishmonger, who had a compact show of stock in his window, consisting of a sole and a quart of shrimps – and I resolved to comfort my mind by going to look at it. Richard the Third, in a very uncomfortable cloak, had first appeared to me there, and had made my heart leap with terror by backing up against the stage-box in which I was posted, while struggling for life against the virtuous Richmond. It was within those walls that I had learnt, as from a page of English history, how that wicked King slept in war-time on a sofa much too short for him, and how fearfully his conscience troubled his boots. There, too, had I first seen the funny countryman, but countryman of noble principles in a flowered waistcoat, crunch up his little hat and throw it on the ground, and pull off his coat, saying, 'Dom thee, squire, coom on with thy fistes, then!' At which the lovely young woman who kept company with him (and who went out gleaning, in a narrow white muslin apron, with five beautiful bars of five different coloured ribbons across it) was so frightened for his sake, that she fainted away. Many wondrous secrets of Nature had I come to the knowledge of in that sanctuary: of which not the least terrific were, that the witches in Macbeth bore an awful resemblance to the Thanes and other proper inhabitants of Scotland; and that the good King Duncan couldn't rest in his grave, but was constantly coming out of it, and calling himself somebody else. To the Theatre, therefore, I repaired for consolation. But I found very little, for it was in a bad and declining way. A dealer in wine and bottled beer had already squeezed his trade into the box-office, and the theatrical money was taken – when it came – in a kind of meat-safe in the passage. The dealer in wine and bottled beer must have insinuated himself under the stage too; for he announced that he had various descriptions of alcoholic drinks 'in the wood,' and there was no possible stowage for the wood anywhere else. Evidently, he was by degrees eating the establishment away to the core, and would soon have sole possession of it. It was To Let, and hopelessly so, for its old purposes; and there had been no entertainment within its walls for a long time, except a Panorama; and even that had been announced as 'pleasingly instructive,' and I knew too well the fatal meaning and the leaden import of those terrible expressions. No, there was no comfort in the Theatre. It was mysteriously gone, like my own youth. Unlike my own youth, it might be coming back some day; but there was little promise of it.

As the town was placarded with references to the Dullborough Mechanics' Institution, I thought I would go and look at that establishment next. There had been no such thing in the town, in my young day, and it occurred to me that its extreme prosperity might have brought adversity upon the Drama. I found the Institution with some difficulty, and should scarcely have known that I had found it if I had judged from its external appearance only; but this was attributable to its never having been finished, and having no front: consequently, it led a modest and retired existence up a stable-yard. It was (as I learnt, on inquiry) a most flourishing Institution, and of the highest benefit to the town: two triumphs which I was glad to understand were not at all impaired by the seeming drawbacks that no mechanics belonged to it, and that it was steeped in debt to the chimney-pots. It had a large room, which was approached by an infirm stepladder: the builder having declined to construct the intended staircase, without a present payment in cash, which Dullborough (though profoundly appreciative of the Institution) seemed unaccountably bashful about subscribing. The large room had cost – or would, when paid for – five hundred pounds; and it had more mortar in it and more echoes, than one might have expected to get for the money. It was fitted up with a platform, and the usual lecturing tools, including a large black board of a menacing appearance. On referring to lists of the courses of lectures that had been given in this thriving Hall, I fancied I detected a shyness in admitting that human nature when at leisure has any desire whatever to be relieved and diverted; and a furtive sliding in of any poor make-weight piece of amusement, shamefacedly and edgewise. Thus, I observed that it was necessary for the members to be knocked on the head with Gas, Air, Water, Food, the Solar System, the Geological periods, Criticism on Milton, the Steam-engine, John Bunyan and Arrow-Headed Inscriptions, before they might be tickled by those unaccountable choristers, the negro singers in the court costume of the reign of George the Second. Likewise, that they must be stunned by a weighty inquiry whether there was internal evidence in SHAKESPEARE's works, to prove that his uncle by the mother's side lived for some years at Stoke Newington, before they were brought-to by a Miscellaneous Concert. But indeed the masking of entertainment, and pretending it was something else – as people mask bedsteads when they are obliged to have them in sitting-rooms, and make believe that they are bookcases, sofas, chests of drawers, anything rather than bedsteads – was manifest even in the pretence of dreariness that the unfortunate entertainers themselves felt obliged in decency to put forth when they came here. One very agreeable professional singer who travelled with two pro- fessional ladies, knew better than to introduce either of those ladies to sing the ballad 'Comin' through the Rye' without prefacing it himself, with some general remarks on wheat and clover; and even then, he dared not for his life call the song, a song, but disguised it in the bill as an 'Illustration.' In the library, also – fitted with shelves for three thousand books, and containing upwards of one hundred and seventy (presented copies mostly) seething their edges in damp plaster – there was such a painfully apologetic return of 62 offenders who had read Travels, Popular Biography, and mere Fiction descriptive of the aspirations of the hearts and souls of mere human creatures like themselves; and such an elaborate parade of 2 bright examples who had had down Euclid after the day's occupation and confinement; and 3 who had had down Metaphysics after ditto; and 1 who had had down Theology after ditto; and 4 who had worried Grammar, Political Economy, Botany, and Logarithms all at once after ditto; that I suspected the boasted class to be one man, who had been hired to do it.

Emerging from the Mechanics' Institution, and continuing my walk about the town, I still noticed everywhere the prevalence, to an extra- ordinary degree, of this custom of putting the natural demand for amusement out of sight, as some untidy housekeepers put dust, and pretending that it was swept away. And yet it was ministered to, in a dull and abortive manner, by all who made this feint. Looking in at what is called in Dullborough 'the serious bookseller's,' where, in my childhood, I had studied the faces of numbers of gentlemen depicted in rostrums with a gaslight on each side of them, and casting my eyes over the open pages of certain printed discourses there, I found a vast deal of aiming at jocosity and dramatic effect, even in them – yes, verily, even on the part of one very wrathful expounder who bitterly anathematised a poor little Circus. Similarly, in the reading provided for the young people enrolled in the Lasso of Love, and other excellent unions, I found the writers generally under a distressing sense that they must start (at all events) like story-tellers, and delude the young persons into the belief that they were going to be interesting. As I looked in at this window for twenty minutes by the clock, I am in a position to offer a friendly remonstrance – not bearing on this particular point – to the designers and engravers of the pictures in those publications. Have they considered the awful consequences likely to flow from their representations of Virtue? Have they asked themselves the question, whether the terrific prospect of acquiring that fearful chubbiness of head, unwieldiness of arm, feeble dislocation of leg, crispness of hair, and enormity of shirt-collar, which they represent as inseparable from Goodness, may not tend to confirm sensitive waverers, in Evil? A most impressive example (if I had believed it) of what a Dustman and a Sailor may come to, when they mend their ways, was presented to me in this same shop-window. When they were leaning (they were intimate friends) against a post, drunk and reckless, with surpassingly bad hats on, and their hair over their foreheads, they were rather picturesque, and looked as if they might be agreeable men if they would not be beasts. But when they had got over their bad propensities, and when, as a consequence, their heads had swelled alarmingly, their hair had got so curly that it lifted their blown-out cheeks up, their coat-cuffs were so long that they never could do any work, and their eyes were so wide open that they never could do any sleep, they presented a spectacle calculated to plunge a timid nature into the depths of Infamy.

But, the clock that had so degenerated since I saw it last, admonished me that I had stayed here long enough; and I resumed my walk again.

I had not gone fifty paces along the street when I was suddenly brought up by the sight of a man who got out of a little phaeton at the doctor's door, and went into the doctor's house. Immediately, the air was filled with the scent of trodden grass, and the perspective of years opened, and at the end of it was a little likeness of this man keeping a wicket, and I said, 'God bless my soul! Joe Specks!'

Through many changes and much work, I had preserved a tenderness for the memory of Joe, forasmuch as we had made the acquaintance of Roderick Random together, and had believed him to be no ruffian, but an ingenuous and engaging hero. Scorning to ask the boy left in the phaeton whether it was really Joe, and scorning even to read the brass plate on the door – so sure was I – I rang the bell and informed the servant maid that a stranger sought audience of Mr Specks. Into a room, half surgery, half study, I was shown to await his coming, and I found it, by a series of elaborate accidents, bestrewn with testimonies to Joe. Portrait of Mr Specks, bust of Mr Specks, silver cup from grateful patient to Mr Specks, presentation sermon from local clergyman, dedication poem from local poet, dinner-card from local nobleman, tract on balance of power from local refugee, inscribed *Hommage de l'auteur à Specks*.

When my old schoolfellow came in, and I informed him with a smile that I was not a patient, he seemed rather at a loss to perceive any reason for smiling in connexion with that fact, and inquired to what he was to attribute the honour? I asked him, with another smile, could he remember me at all? He had not (he said) that pleasure. I was beginning to have but a poor opinion of Mr Specks, when he said, reflectively, 'And yet there's a something, too.' Upon that, I saw a boyish light in his eyes that looked well, and I asked him if he could inform me, as a stranger who desired to know and had not the means of reference at hand, what the name of the young lady was who married Mr Random? Upon that, he said 'Narcissa,' and, after staring for a moment, called me by my name, shook me by the hand, and melted into a roar of laughter. 'Why, of course you'll remember Lucy Green,' he said, after we had talked a little. 'Of course,' said I. 'Whom do you think she married?' said he. 'You?' I hazarded. 'Me,' said Specks, 'and you shall see her.' So I saw her, and she was fat, and if all the hay in the world had been heaped upon her, it could scarcely have altered her face more than Time had altered it from my remembrance of the face that had once looked down upon me into the fragrant dungeons of Seringapatam. But when her youngest child came in after dinner (for I dined with them, and we had no other company than Specks, Junior, Barrister-at-Law, who went away as soon as the cloth was removed, to look after the young lady to whom he was going to be married next week), I saw again, in that little daughter, the little face of the hayfield, unchanged, and it quite touched my heart. We talked immensely, Specks and Mrs Specks, and I, and we spoke of our old selves as though our old selves were dead and gone, and indeed indeed they were – dead and gone, as the playing-field that had become a wilderness of rusty iron, and the property of S.E.R.

Specks, however, illuminated Dullborough with the rays of interest that I wanted and should otherwise have missed in it, and linked its present to its past, with a highly agreeable chain. And in Specks's society I had new occasion to observe what I had before noticed in similar communications among other men. All the schoolfellows and others of old, whom I inquired about, had either done superlatively well or superlatively ill – had either become uncertificated bankrupts, or been felonious and got themselves transported; or had made great hits in life, and done wonders. And this is so commonly the case, that I never can imagine what becomes of all the mediocre people of people's youth – especially, considering that we find no lack of the species in our maturity. But I did not propound this difficulty to Specks, for no pause in the conversation gave me an occasion. Nor could I discover one single flaw in the good doctor – when he reads this, he will receive in a friendly spirit the pleasantly meant record – except that he had forgotten his Roderick Random, and that he confounded Strap with Lieutenant

Hatchway: who never knew Random, howsoever intimate with Pickle.

When I went alone to the Railway to catch my train at night (Specks had meant to go with me, but was inopportunely called out), I was in a more charitable mood with Dullborough than I had been all day; and yet in my heart I had loved it all day too. Ah! who was I that I should quarrel with the town for being changed to me, when I myself had come back, so changed, to it! All my early readings and early imaginations dated from this place, and I took them away so full of innocent construction and guileless belief, and I brought them back so worn and torn, so much the wiser and so much the worse!

16

The Uncommercial Traveller

All The Year Round, 21 July 1860 (*UT1* as 'Night Walks')

In March of the year 1851 Dickens's father entered a painful last illness, resulting in his death on the final day of the month. He was buried on 4 April, in Highgate cemetery. On the morning of the 3rd, Dickens wrote to W. H. Wills from his bed at Tavistock House, to say that 'I took my threatened walk last night' and that 'I am so worn out by the sad arrangements ... that I cannot take my natural rest' (see *Pilgrim*, Vol. VI, pp. 345–6 & n.). The letter goes on to propose an all-night visit to the Bow-street Station House, described in 'The Metropolitan Protectives' (*HW*, Vol. III [26 April 1851], pp. 97–105; repr. in Stone, Vol. I, pp. 253–73), and remind Wills that the following night 'we go to the gas-works'. The letter thus indicates at least three consecutive night expeditions made by Dickens during a period of insomnia provoked by his father's death, and suggests a possible derivation of the narrator's opening remarks (and the description of Bow-street coffee shops, pp. 155–6 below) in Dickens's personal experience. The narrator locates the 'series of nights' described in the month of March and dates them to before 1857, as on 9 October of that year a dismembered corpse – the 'chopped-up murdered man' referred to (p. 151) – had been discovered in a bag on a pier of Waterloo Bridge. Foreign Office and Scotland Yard evidence suggested that the victim had been an Italian police agent murdered by London-based revolutionists (see

W. Matchett, 'The Chopped-Up Murdered Man', *The Dickensian*, Vol. 14 [1918], pp. 117–19).

Nevertheless, Dickens's experience of night-walking cannot be confined to any particular year or decade. Planning *Dombey and Son* in March 1846, for example, he records 'wandering about at night into the strangest places, according to my usual propensity at such a time – seeking rest, and finding none' (*Pilgrim*, Vol. IV, p. 510 & n.). In an essay of October 1852, 'Lying Awake', he recalls defeating insomnia 'the other night' by resolving 'to lie awake no more, but to get up and go out for a night walk' (see Vol. 3 of this edition, article 13). As with daylight walking, nocturnal rambling was a lifelong habit, and since 'Boz's' celebrated sketch of 'The Streets – Night' (1836; see Vol. 1 of this edition, p. 55ff), the experience had been providing him with inspiration for writing. By 1860, accounts of 'noctambulisme' in London had become the specialty of Dickens's talented protégé, G. A. Sala, by now a rival magazine editor, whose racy and sometimes risqué articles were republished in the popular collections *Gaslight and Daylight* (1859) and *Twice Round the Clock* (1859).

Articles 26 and 42 of this volume reiterate Dickens's serious concern with the state of London's homeless youth. The mention of the Newgate 'lodge' with a 'spiked' wicket-gate manned by the 'turnkeys' (p. 152) forms a group of references Dickens returns to in the twentieth instalment of *Great Expectations*, when describing Pip's visit to the prison (*ATYR*, Vol. 5 [13 April 1861]).

Literary allusions (p. 151) 'Yorick's skull': Shakespeare, *Hamlet* Act 5, Sc. 1; (p.152) 'the peasantry of Naples dancing among the vines': Auber's opera *Masaniello* (1828), Act 5, Sc. 2; (p. 152) 'this degenerate Aceldama': Acts 1:19; (p. 154) 'the great master ... the death of each day's life': Shakespeare, *Macbeth*, Act 2, Sc. 2; (p. 154) '(as the philosopher has suggested)': Bacon has broadly similar things to say about the movement of sound in *Sylva Sylvarum: or, a Natural History* ([1627] 1826, ed. Montagu), Vol. 4, Century II, pp. 88, 110; (p. 155) 'young man in the New Testament': Mark 14:51–2; (p. 157) 'houseless wanderer': 'poor houseless wanderers', Thomas De Quincey, *Works*, Vol. 5, *Confessions of an English Opium-Eater* (1856), p. 170; (p. 157) 'have its own solitary way': echoes the last line of Milton's *Paradise Lost* (1674) (Book XII, l. 641).

Textual note (p. 150) copy-text has 'another drunken object would probably stagger up': *UTI* has '... would stagger up'; (p. 154) copy-text has 'God knows how far: seemingly to the confines of the earth': *UTI* has 'God knows how far.'

Some years ago, a temporary inability to sleep, referable to a distressing impression, caused me to walk about the streets all night, for a series of several nights. The disorder might have taken a long time to conquer, if it had been faintly experimented on in bed; but it was soon defeated by the brisk treatment of getting up directly after lying down, and going out, and coming home tired at sunrise.

In the course of those nights, I finished my education in a fair amateur experience of houselessness. My principal object being to get through the night, the pursuit of it brought me into sympathetic relations with people who have no other object every night in the year.

The month was March, and the weather damp, cloudy, and cold. The sun not rising before half-past five, the night perspective looked sufficiently long at half-past twelve: which was about my time for confronting it.

The restlessness of a great city, and the way in which it tumbles and tosses before it can get to sleep, formed one of the first entertainments offered to the contemplation of us houseless people. It lasted about two hours. We lost a great deal of companionship when the late public-houses turned their lamps out, and when the potmen thrust the last brawling drunkards into the street; but stray vehicles and stray people were left us, after that. If we were very lucky, a policeman's rattle sprang, and a fray turned up; but, in general, surprisingly little of this diversion was provided. Except in the Haymarket, which is the worst kept part of London, and about Kent-street in the Borough, and along a portion of the line of the Old Kent-road, the peace was seldom violently broken. But it was always the case that London, as if in imitation of individual citizens belonging to it, had expiring fits and starts of restlessness. After all seemed quiet, if one cab rattled by, half a dozen would surely follow; and Houselessness even observed that intoxicated people appeared to be magnetically attracted towards each other, so that we knew, when we saw one drunken object staggering against the shutters of a shop, that another drunken object would probably stagger up before five minutes were out, to fraternise or fight with it. When we made a divergence from the regular species of drunkard, the thin-armed puff-faced, leaden-lipped gin-drinker, and encountered a rarer specimen of a more decent appearance, fifty to one but that specimen was dressed in soiled mourning. As the street experience in the night, so the street experience in the day; the common folk who come unexpectedly into a little property, come unexpectedly into a deal of liquor.

At length these flickering sparks would die away, worn out – the last veritable sparks of waking life trailed from some late pieman or hot potato man – and London would sink to rest. And then the yearning of the houseless mind would be for any sign of company, any lighted place, any movement, anything suggestive of anyone being up – nay, even so much as awake, for the houseless eye looked out for lights in windows.

Walking the streets under the pattering rain, Houselessness would walk and walk and walk, seeing nothing but the interminable tangle of streets, save at a corner, here and there, two policemen in conversation, or the sergeant or inspector looking after his men. Now and then in the night – but rarely – Houselessness would become aware of a furtive head peering out of a doorway a few yards before him, and, coming up with the head, would find a man standing bolt upright to keep within the doorway's shadow, and evidently intent upon no particular service to society. Under a kind of fascination, and in a ghostly silence suitable to the time, Houselessness and this gentleman would eye one another from head to foot, and so, without exchange of speech, part, mutually suspicious. Drip, drip, drip, from ledge and coping, splash from pipes and water-spouts, and by-and-by the houseless shadow would fall upon the stones that pave the way to Waterloo-bridge; it being in the houseless mind to have a halfpennyworth of excuse for saying 'Good night' to the toll-keeper, and catching a glimpse of his fire. A good fire, and a good great-coat and a good woollen neck-shawl, were comfortable things to see in conjunction with the toll-keeper; also his brisk wakefulness was excellent company when he rattled the change of halfpence down upon that metal table of his, like a man who defied the night, with all its sorrowful thoughts, and didn't care for the coming of dawn. There was need of encouragement on the threshold of the bridge, for the bridge was dreary. The chopped up murdered man, had not been lowered with a rope over the parapet when those nights were; he was alive, and slept then quietly enough most likely, and undisturbed by any dream of where he was to come. But the river had an awful look, the buildings on the banks were muffled in black shrouds, and the reflected lights seemed to originate deep in the water, as if the spectres of suicides were holding them to show where they went down. The wild moon and clouds were as restless as an evil conscience in a tumbled bed, and the very shadow of the immensity of London seemed to lie oppressively upon the river.

Between the bridge and the two great theatres, there was but the distance of a few hundred paces, so the theatres came next. Grim and black within, at night, those great dry Wells, and lonesome to imagine, with the rows of faces faded out, the lights extinguished, and the seats all empty. One would think that nothing in them knew itself at such a time but Yorick's skull. In one of my night walks, as the church steeples were shaking the March wind and rain with the strokes of Four, I passed the outer boundary of one of these great deserts, and entered it. With a dim lantern in my hand, I groped my well-known way to the stage and looked over the orchestra – which was like a great grave dug for a time of pestilence – into the void beyond. A dismal cavern of an immense aspect, with the chandelier gone dead like everything else, and nothing visible through mist and fog and space, but tiers of winding-sheets. The ground at my feet where, when last there, I had seen the peasantry of Naples dancing among the vines, reckless of the burning mountain which threatened to overwhelm them, was now in possession of a strong serpent of engine-hose, watchfully lying in wait for the serpent Fire, and ready to fly at it if it showed its forked tongue. A ghost of a watchman carrying a faint corpse-candle, haunted the distant upper gallery and flitted away. Retiring within the proscenium, and holding my light above my head towards the rolled-up curtain – green no more, but black as ebony – my sight lost itself in a gloomy vault, showing faint indications in it of a shipwreck of canvas and cordage. Methought I felt much as a diver might, at the bottom of the sea.

In those small hours when there was no movement in the streets, it afforded matter for reflection to take Newgate in the way, and, touching its rough stone, to think of the prisoners in their sleep, and then to glance in at the lodge over the spiked wicket, and see the fire and light of the watching turnkeys, on the white wall. Not an inappropriate time either to linger by that wicked little Debtor's Door – shutting tighter than any other door one ever saw – which has been Death's Door to so many. In the days of the uttering of forged one-pound notes by people tempted up from the country, how many hundreds of wretched creatures of both sexes – many quite innocent – swung out of a pitiless and inconsistent world, with the tower of yonder Christian church of Saint Sepulchre monstrously before their eyes! Is there any haunting of the Bank Parlour by the remorseful souls of old directors, in the nights of these later days, I wonder, or is it as quiet as this degenerate Aceldama of an Old Bailey?

To walk on to the Bank, lamenting the good old times and bemoaning the present evil period, would be an easy next step, so I would take it, and would make my houseless circuit of the Bank, and give a thought to the treasure within; likewise to the guard of soldiers passing the night there, and nodding over the fire. Next, I went to Billingsgate, in some hope of market-people, but, it proving as yet too early, crossed London-bridge and got down by the water-side on the Surrey shore, among the buildings of the great brewery. There was plenty going on at the brewery; and the reek, and the smell of grains, and the rattling of the plump dray horses at their mangers, were capital company. Quite refreshed by having mingled with this good society, I made a new start with a new heart, setting the old King's Bench prison before me for my next object, and resolving, when I should come to the wall, to think of poor Horace Kinch, and the Dry Rot in men.

A very curious disease the Dry Rot in men, and difficult to detect the beginning of. It had carried Horace Kinch inside the wall of the old King's Bench prison, and it had carried him out with his feet foremost.

He was a likely man to look at, in the prime of life, well to do, as clever as he needed to be, and popular among many friends. He was suitably married, and had healthy and pretty children. But, like some fair-looking houses or fair-looking ships, he took the Dry Rot. The first strong external revelation of the Dry Rot in men, is a tendency to lurk and lounge; to be at street-corners without intelligible reason; to be going anywhere when met; to be about many places rather than at any; to do nothing tangible, but to have an intention of performing a variety of intangible duties tomorrow or the day after. When this manifestation of the disease is observed, the observer will usually connect it with a vague impression once formed or received, that the patient was living a little too hard. He will scarcely have had leisure to turn it over in his mind and form the terrible suspicion 'Dry Rot,' when he will notice a change for the worse in the patient's appearance: a certain slovenliness and deterioration which is not poverty, nor dirt, nor intoxication, nor ill-health, but simply Dry Rot. To this, succeeds a smell as of strong waters, in the morning; to that, a looseness respecting money; to that, a stronger smell as of strong waters, at all times; to that, a looseness respecting everything; to that, a trembling of the limbs, somnolency, misery, and crumbling to pieces. As it is in wood, so it is in men. Dry Rot advances at a compound usury quite incalculable. A plank is found infected with it, and the whole structure is devoted. Thus it had been with the unhappy Horace Kinch, lately buried by a small subscription. Those who knew him had not nigh done saying, 'So well off, so comfortably established, with such hope before him – and yet, it is feared, with a slight touch of Dry Rot!' when lo! the man was all Dry Rot and dust.

From the dead wall associated on those houseless nights with this too common story, I chose next to wander by Bethlehem Hospital; partly because it lay on my road round to Westminster; partly, because I had a night-fancy in my head which could be best pursued within sight of its walls and dome. And the fancy was this: Are not the sane and insane equal at night as the sane lie a dreaming? Are not all of us outside this hospital, who dream, more or less in the condition of those inside it, every night of our lives? Are we not nightly persuaded, as they daily are, that we associate preposterously with kings and queens, emperors and empresses, and notabilities of all sorts? Do we not nightly jumble events and personages, and times and places, as these do daily? Are we not sometimes troubled by our own sleeping inconsistencies, and do we not vexedly try to account for them or excuse them, just as these do sometimes in respect of their waking delusions? Said an afflicted man to me, when I was last in a hospital like this, 'Sir, I can frequently fly.' I was half ashamed to reflect that so could I – by night. Said a woman to me on the same occasion, 'Queen Victoria frequently comes to dine with me, and her Majesty and I dine off peaches and maccaroni in our night-gowns, and his Royal Highness the Prince Consort does us the honour to make a third on horseback in a Field-Marshal's uniform.' Could I refrain from reddening with consciousness when I remembered the amazing royal parties I myself had given (at night), the unaccountable viands I had put on table, and my extraordinary manner of conducting myself on those distinguished occasions? I wonder that the great master who knew everything, when he called Sleep the death of each day's life, did not call Dreams the insanity of each day's sanity.

By this time I had left the Hospital behind me, and was again setting towards the river; and in a short breathing space I was on Westminster-bridge, regaling my houseless eyes with the external walls of the British Parliament – the perfection of a stupendous institution, I know, and the admiration of all surrounding nations and succeeding ages, I do not doubt, but perhaps a little the better now and then for being pricked up to its work. Turning off into Old Palace-yard, the Courts of Law kept me company for a quarter of an hour; hinting in low whispers what numbers of people they were keeping awake, and how intensely wretched and horrible they were rendering the small hours to unfortunate suitors. Westminster Abbey was fine gloomy society for another quarter of an hour; suggesting a wonderful procession of its dead among the dark arches and pillars, each century more amazed by the century following it than by all the centuries going before. And indeed in those houseless night walks – which even included cemeteries where watchmen went round among the graves at stated times, and moved the tell-tale handle of an index which recorded that they had touched it at such an hour – it was a solemn consideration what enormous hosts of dead belong to one old great city, and how, if they were raised while the living slept, there would not be the space of a pin's point in all the streets and ways for the living to come out into. Not only that, but the vast armies of dead would overflow the hills and valleys beyond the city, and would stretch away all round it, God knows how far: seemingly to the confines of the earth.

When a church clock strikes, on houseless ears in the dead of the night, it may be at first mistaken for company and hailed as such. But, as the spreading circles of vibration, which you may perceive at such a time with great clearness, go opening out, for ever and ever afterwards widening perhaps (as the philosopher has suggested) in eternal space, the mistake is rectified, and the sense of loneliness is profounder. Once – it was after leaving the Abbey and turning my face north – I came to the great steps of Saint Martin's church as the clock was striking Three. Suddenly, a thing that in a moment more I should have trodden upon without seeing, rose up at my feet with a cry of loneliness and houselessness, struck out of it by the bell, the like of which I never heard. We then stood face to face looking at one another, frightened by one another. The creature was like a beetle-browed hare-lipped youth of twenty, and it had a loose bundle of rags on, which it held together with one of its hands. It shivered from head to foot, and its teeth chattered, and as it stared at me – persecutor, devil, ghost, whatever it thought me – it made with its whining mouth as if it were snapping at me, like a worried dog. Intending to give this ugly object, money, I put out my hand to stay it – for it recoiled as it whined and snapped – and laid my hand upon its shoulder. Instantly, it twisted out of its garment, like the young man in the New Testament, and left me standing alone with its rags in my hand.

Covent-garden Market, when it was market morning, was wonderful company. The great waggons of cabbages, with growers' men and boys lying asleep under them, and with sharp dogs from market-garden neighbourhoods looking after the whole, were as good as a party. But one of the worst night sights I know in London, is to be found in the children who prowl about this place; who sleep in the baskets, fight for the offal, dart at any object they think they can lay their thieving hands on, dive under the carts and barrows, dodge the constables, and are perpetually making a blunt pattering on the pavement of the Piazza with the rain of their naked feet. A painful and unnatural result comes of the comparison one is forced to institute between the growth of corruption as displayed in the so much improved and cared for fruits of the earth, and the growth of corruption as displayed in these all uncared for (except inasmuch as ever-hunted) savages.

There was early coffee to be got about Covent-garden Market, and that was more company – warm company, too, which was better. Toast of a very substantial quality, was likewise procurable: though the towzled-headed man who made it, in an inner chamber within the coffee-room, hadn't got his coat on yet, and was so heavy with sleep that in every interval of toast and coffee he went off anew behind the partition into complicated crossroads of choke and snore, and lost his way directly. Into one of these establishments (among the earliest) near Bow-street, there came, one morning as I sat over my houseless cup, pondering where to go next, a man in a high and long snuff-coloured coat, and shoes, and, to the best of my belief, nothing else but a hat, who took out of his hat a large cold meat pudding; a meat pudding so large that it was a very tight fit, and brought the lining of the hat out with it. This mysterious man was known by his pudding, for, on his entering, the man of sleep brought him a pint of hot tea, a small loaf, and a large knife and fork and plate. Left to himself in his box, he stood the pudding on the bare table, and, instead of cutting it, stabbed it, over-hand, with the knife, like a mortal enemy; then took the knife out, wiped it on his sleeve, tore the pudding asunder with his fingers, and ate it all up. The remembrance of this man with the pudding remains with me as the remembrance of the most spectral person my houselessness encountered. Twice only was I in that establishment, and twice I saw him stalk in (as I should say, just out of bed, and presently going back to bed), take out his pudding, stab his pudding, wipe the dagger, and eat his pudding all up. He was a man whose figure promised cadaverousness, but who had an excessively red face, though shaped like a horse's. On the second occasion of my seeing him, he said, huskily, to the man of sleep, 'Am I red tonight?' 'You are,' he uncompromisingly answered. 'My mother,' said the spectre, 'was a red-faced woman that liked drink, and I looked at her hard when she laid in her coffin, and I took the complexion.' Somehow, the pudding seemed an unwholesome pudding after that, and I put myself in its way no more.

When there was no market, or when I wanted variety, a railway terminus with the morning mails coming in, was remunerative company. But like most of the company to be had in this world, it lasted only a very short time. The station lamps would burst out ablaze, the porters would emerge from places of concealment, the cabs and trucks would rattle to their places (the post-office carts were already in theirs), and, finally, the bell would strike up, and the train would come banging in. But there were few passengers and little luggage, and everything scuttled away with the greatest expedition. The locomotive post-offices, with their great nets – as if they had been dragging the country for bodies – would fly open as to their doors, and would disgorge a smell of lamp, an exhausted clerk, a guard in a red coat, and their bags of letters; the engine would blow and heave and perspire, like an engine wiping its forehead, and saying what a run it had had; and within ten minutes the lamps were out, and I was houseless and alone again.

But now, there were driven cattle on the high road near, wanting (as cattle always do) to turn into the midst of stone walls, and squeeze themselves through six inches' width of iron railing, and getting their heads down (also as cattle always do) for tossing-purchase at quite imaginary dogs, and giving themselves and every devoted creature associated with them a most extraordinary amount of unnecessary trouble. Now, too, the conscious gas began to grow pale with the knowledge that daylight was coming, and straggling workpeople were already in the streets, and, as waking life had become extinguished with the last pieman's sparks, so it began to be rekindled with the fires of the first street corner breakfast-sellers. And so by faster and faster degrees, until the last degrees were very fast, the day came, and I was tired and could sleep. And it is not, as I used to think, going home at such times, the least wonderful thing in London, that in the real desert region of the night, the houseless wanderer is alone there. I knew well enough where to find Vice and Misfortune of all kinds, if I had chosen; but they were put out of sight, and my houselessness had many miles upon miles of streets in which it could, and did, have its own solitary way.

17

The Uncommercial Traveller

All The Year Round, 18 August 1860 (*UT1* as 'Chambers')

Dickens's interest in London's Inns of Court goes back to his vivid experiences of renting chambers and entertaining friends there in the early 1830s. From May 1827 to November 1828, he had worked in Gray's Inn as a clerk in Edward Blackmore's attorney's office, and then from December 1834 to March 1837 he was in chambers at 13 and 15 Furnival's Inn, where latterly he lived with his new wife, first child and sister-in-law, Mary Hogarth, as semi-permanent guest (see Vol. 1 of this edition, pp. xxxii–xxxiii). Some of Dickens's earliest fiction tells of tenants in similar circumstances to himself, professional visits to lawyers in chambers (see Vol. 1 of this edition, 'The Steam Excursion', p. 369; *Pickwick Papers*, Ch. 31), or 'queer' stories relating to them (see Jack Bamber's tales, *Pickwick*, Ch. 21). Writing to Forster in 1839 with 'rough notes of proposals for the New Work' to be undertaken with Chapman & Hall (*Master Humphrey's Clock*), Dickens commented that 'the Chapters on Chambers which I have long thought and spoken of, might be very well incorporated with it' (*Pilgrim*, Vol. I [14 July 1839], p. 564). Although these were never published, the idea mooted in 1839 seems eventually to find an outlet in the present article.

The chambers Dickens has in mind are those belonging to the four ancient Inns of Court: the Inner and Middle Temple, Lincoln's Inn and, particularly, Gray's Inn; and the lesser Inns of Chancery: Furnival's, Lyon's, Clement's, Barnard's, the New and Staple Inn. In 1688 Gray's Inn was still divided into three courts: Holborn, Coney and Middle (later Chapel), but by 1793 Chapel and Coney had been replaced by what is now Gray's Inn Square. South Square has likewise replaced Holborn Court, which in turn 'must have included Field Court', mentioned below on p. 163 (see W. R. Douthwaite, *Gray's Inn, its History and Associations* [1886], pp. 101–2). The preamble to a *HW* essay of 1850, 'The Ghost of Art' (see Vol. 2 of this edition, article 49), gives a brief portrait of 'a dreary set of chambers in the Temple', and Dickens returns to the theme again in *Great Expectations*, by putting Pip and Herbert Pocket in a 'top set' at Barnard's Inn. As Scott Foll has noted in *The Dickensian* (Vol. 81 [1985], pp. 109–16), even the phrasing of the present article (see below p. 160) is repeated in Ch. 21 (*ATYR*, 23 February 1861), where Pip recalls his first impressions of the Inn:

> I thought it had the most dismal trees in it ... and the most dismal houses ... that I had ever seen. I thought the windows of the sets of chambers into which these houses were divided, were in every stage of dilapidated blind and curtain, crippled flower-pot, cracked glass, dusty decay, and miserable makeshift; while To Let To Let To Let, glared at me from empty rooms, as if no new wretches ever came there....

Dickens's own experience of the Inns of Court was renewed in 1849 when he began eating dinners in the Middle Temple, a decade after first registering his name there as a student. The description on p. 165 of the narrator 'uncommercially preparing for the Bar' would appear to be a direct reference to this.

The grim story of the 'great judge and lover of port wine' elaborates on the macabre death of Rowland Durrant, a stockbroker, bon-viveur and fellow-member of the Garrick Club '... who came to a sad end, poor fellow, dying alone in his Temple chambers, on a Christmas Eve, of loss of blood from an accident, while men in the rooms below heard him staggering about and groaning, but took no notice, imagining their neighbour to be only in his normal condition' (*Edmund Yates: His Recollections and Experiences* [1884], Vol. 2, p. 4). The kneeling statue of a negro in Clement's Inn, referred to on p. 169, was brought from Italy in 1700, but removed to the Inner Temple Gardens on the construction of Aldwych in 1905; it now faces the King's Bench Walk.

Literary allusions (p. 160) 'the last old prolix bencher all of the olden time ...': puns on the title of C.H. Purday's popular song 'The Fine Old English Gentleman, All of the Olden Time'; (p. 162) 'lumbering Marius among the ruins of Carthage ...': 'go tell him that you have seen C. Marius sitting upon the rubbish of Carthage', an image from Plutarch's *Life* of Caius Marius (c. 75 AD) memorably rendered in Stapleton's translation of 1684 (ed. Dryden, Vol. III, p. 145), which became a commonplace; (p. 163) 'Prometheus Bound': allusion to the tragedy by Aeschylus (5th century BC); (p. 166) 'Macbeth's Amen sticking in their throats': '"Amen"/ Stuck in my throat', *Macbeth*, Act 2, Sc. 2; (p. 166) 'in furniture stepped so far': 'I am in blood/ Stepp'd in so far, that ... / Returning were as tedious as go o'er', Shakespeare, *ibid.*, Act 3, Sc. 4; (p. 168) 'Robinson Crusoe': eponymous hero of Daniel Defoe's narrative (1719).

Textual note (below) copy-text has 'a very mysterious bunk': *UT1* has 'a mysterious bunk'; (p. 160) copy-text has 'a lady, in figure extremely like an old family umbrella, named Sweeney': *UT1* has 'a lady named Sweeney, in figure extremely like an old family umbrella'; (p. 164) copy-text has 'having lain buried': *UT1* has 'having remained buried.'

Having occasion to transact some business with a solicitor who occupies a highly suicidal set of chambers in Gray's Inn, I afterwards took a turn in the large square of that stronghold of Melancholy, reviewing, with congenial surroundings, my experiences of Chambers.

I began, as was natural, with the Chambers I had just left. They were an upper set on a rotten staircase, with a very mysterious bunk or bulkhead on the landing outside them, of a rather nautical and Screw Collier-like appearance than otherwise, and painted an intense black. Many dusty years have passed since the appropriation of this Davy Jones's locker to any purpose, and during the whole period within the memory of living man, it has been hasped and padlocked. I cannot quite satisfy my mind whether it was originally meant for the reception of coals, or bodies, or as a place of temporary security for the plunder 'looted' by laundresses; but I incline to the last opinion. It is about breast-high, and usually serves as a bulk for defendants in reduced circumstances to lean against and ponder at, when they come on the hopeful errand of trying to make an arrangement without money – under which auspicious circumstances it mostly happens that the legal gentleman they want to see, is much engaged, and they pervade the staircase for a considerable period. Against this opposing bulk, in the absurdest manner, the tomb-like outer door of the solicitor's chambers (which is also of an intense black) stands in dark ambush, half open and half shut, all day. The solicitor's apartments are three in number; consisting of a slice, a cell, and a wedge. The slice is assigned to the two clerks, the cell is occupied by the principal, and the wedge is devoted to stray papers, old game baskets from the country, a washing-stand, and a model of a patent Ship's Caboose which was exhibited in Chancery at the commencement of the present century on an application for an injunction to restrain infringement. At about half-past nine on every week-day morning, the younger of the two clerks (who, I have reason to believe, leads the fashion at Pentonville in the articles of pipes and shirts) may be found knocking the dust out of his official door-key on the bunk or locker before mentioned; and so exceedingly subject to dust is his key, and so very retentive of that superfluity, that in exceptional summer weather when a ray of sunlight has fallen on the locker in my presence, I have noticed its inexpressive countenance to be deeply marked by a kind of Bramah erysipelas or small-pox.

This set of chambers (as I have gradually discovered, when I have had restless occasion to make inquiries or leave messages, after office hours) is under the charge of a lady, in figure extremely like an old family-umbrella, named Sweeney: whose dwelling confronts a dead wall in a court off Gray's Inn-lane, and who is usually fetched into the passage of that bower, when wanted, from some neighbouring home of industry which has the curious property of imparting an inflammatory appearance to her visage. Mrs Sweeney is one of the race of professed laundresses, and is the compiler of a remarkable manuscript volume entitled 'Mrs Sweeney's Book,' from which much curious statistical information may be gathered respecting the high prices and small uses of soda, soap, sand, firewood, and other such articles. I have created a legend in my mind – and consequently I believe it with the utmost pertinacity – that the late Mr Sweeney was a ticket-porter under the Honourable Society of Gray's Inn, and that, in consideration of his long and valuable services, Mrs Sweeney was appointed to her present post. For, though devoid of personal charms, I have observed this lady to exercise a fascination over the elderly ticket-porter mind (particularly under the gateway, and in corners and entries), which I can only refer to her being one of the fraternity, yet not competing with it. All that need be said concerning this set of chambers, is said, when I have added that it is in a large double house in Gray's Inn-square, very much out of repair, and that the outer portal is ornamented in a hideous manner with certain stone remains, which have the appearance of the dismembered bust, torso, and limbs, of a petrified bencher.

Indeed, I look upon Gray's Inn generally as one of the most depressing institutions in brick and mortar known to the children of men. Can anything be more dreary than its arid Square, Sahara Desert of the law, with the ugly old tile-topped tenements, the dirty windows, the bills To Let To Let, the door-posts inscribed like gravestones, the crazy gateway giving upon the filthy Lane, the scowling iron-barred prison-like passage into Verulam-buildings, the mouldy red-nosed ticket-porters with little coffin plates, and why with aprons, the dry hard atomy-like appearance of the whole dust-heap? When my uncommercial travels tend to this dismal spot, my comfort is, its rickety state. Imagination gloats over the fulness of time, when the staircases shall have quite tumbled down – they are daily wearing into an ill-savoured powder, but have not quite tumbled down yet – when the last old prolix bencher all of the olden time, shall have been got out of an upper window by means of a Fire-Ladder, and carried off to the Holborn Union; when the last clerk shall have engrossed the last parchment behind the last splash on the last of

Laundresses

the mud-stained windows which, all through the miry year, are pilloried
out of recognition in Gray's Inn-lane. Then shall a squalid little trench,
with rank grass and a pump in it, lying between the coffee-house and
South-square, be wholly given up to cats and rats, and not, as now, have
its empire divided between those animals and a few briefless bipeds –
surely called to the Bar by the voices of deceiving spirits, seeing that they

are wanted there by no mortal – who glance down, with eyes better glazed than their casements, from their dreary and lacklustre rooms. Then shall the way Nor' Westward, now lying under a short grim colonnade where in summer time pounce flies from law-stationering windows into the eyes of laymen, be choked with rubbish and happily become impassable. Then shall the gardens where turf, trees, and gravel wear a legal livery of black, run rank, and pilgrims go to Gorhambury to see Bacon's effigy as he sat, and not come here (which in truth they seldom do) to see where he walked. Then, in a word, shall the old-established vendor of periodicals sit alone in his little crib of a shop behind the Holborn Gate, like that lumbering Marius among the ruins of Carthage, who has sat heavy on a thousand million of similes.

At one period of my uncommercial career I much frequented another set of chambers in Gray's Inn-square. They were what is familiarly called 'a top set,' and all the eatables and drinkables introduced into them acquired a flavour of Cockloft. I have known an unopened Strasbourg pâté, fresh from Fortnum and Mason's, to draw in this cockloft tone through its crockery dish, and become penetrated with cockloft to the core of its inmost truffle in three-quarters of an hour. This, however, was not the most curious feature of those chambers; that, consisted in the profound conviction entertained by my esteemed friend Parkle (their tenant) that they were clean. Whether it was an inborn hallucination, or whether it was imparted to him by Mrs Miggot the laundress, I never could ascertain. But I believe he would have gone to the stake upon the question. Now, they were so dirty that I could take off the distinctest impression of my figure on any article of furniture by merely lounging upon it for a few moments; and it used to be a private amusement of mine to print myself off – if I may use the expression – all over the rooms. It was the first large circulation I had. At other times I have accidentally shaken a window-curtain while in animated conversation with Parkle, and struggling insects which were certainly red, and were certainly not ladybirds, have dropped on the back of my hand. Yet Parkle lived in that top set years, bound body and soul to the superstition that they were clean. He used to say, when congratulated upon them, 'Well, they are not like chambers in one respect, you know; they are clean.' Concurrently, he had an idea which he could never explain, that Mrs Miggot was in some way connected with the Church. When he was in particularly good spirits, he used to believe that a deceased uncle of hers had been a Dean; when he was poorly and low, he believed that her brother had been a Curate. I and Mrs Miggot (she was a genteel woman) were on confidential terms, but I never knew her to commit herself to any distinct assertion on the subject; she merely claimed a proprietorship in the Church, by looking when it was mentioned, as if the reference awakened the slumbering Past, and were personal. It may have been his amiable confidence in Mrs Miggot's better days that inspired my friend with his delusion respecting the chambers, but he never wavered in his fidelity to it for a moment, though he wallowed in dirt seven years.

Two of the windows of these chambers looked down into the garden; and we have sat up there together many a summer evening, saying how pleasant it was, and talking of many things. To my intimacy with that top set, I am indebted for three of my liveliest personal impressions of the loneliness of life in chambers. They shall follow here, in order; first, second, and third.

First. My Gray's Inn friend, on a time, hurt one of his legs, and it became seriously inflamed. Not knowing of his indisposition, I was on my way to visit him as usual, one summer evening, when I was much surprised by meeting a lively leech in Field-court, Gray's Inn, seemingly on his way to the West End of London. As the leech was alone, and was of course unable to explain his position, even if he had been inclined to do so (which he had not the appearance of being), I passed him and went on. Turning the corner of Gray's Inn-square, I was beyond expression amazed by meeting another leech − also entirely alone, and also proceeding in a westerly direction, though with less decision of purpose. Ruminating on this extraordinary circumstance, and endeavouring to remember whether I had ever read, in the Philosophical Transactions or any work on Natural History, of a migration of Leeches, I ascended to the top set, past the dreary series of closed outer doors of offices, and an empty set or two which intervened between that lofty region and the surface. Entering my friend's rooms, I found him stretched upon his back, like Prometheus Bound, with a perfectly demented ticket-porter in attendance on him instead of the Vulture: which helpless individual, who was feeble and frightened, had (my friend explained to me, in great choler) been endeavouring for some hours to apply leeches to his leg, and as yet had only got on two out of twenty. To this Unfortunate's distraction between a damp cloth on which he had placed the leeches to freshen them, and the wrathful adjurations of my friend to 'Stick 'em on, sir!' I referred the phenomenon I had encountered: the rather as two fine specimens were at that moment going out at the door, while a general insurrection of the rest was in progress on the table. After a while our united efforts prevailed, and, when the leeches came off and had recovered their spirits, we carefully tied them up in a decanter. But I never heard more of them than that they were all gone next morning, and that the Out-of-door young man of Bickle Bush and Bodger, on the ground floor, had been bitten and blooded by some creature not identified. They never 'took' on Mrs Miggot, the laundress; but I have always preserved fresh, the belief that she unconsciously carried several about her, until they gradually found openings in life.

Second. On the same staircase with my friend Parkle, and on the same floor, there lived a man of law who pursued his business elsewhere, and used those chambers as his place of residence. For three or four years, Parkle rather knew of him than knew him, but after that – for Englishmen – short pause of consideration, they began to speak. Parkle exchanged words with him in his private character only, and knew nothing of his business ways, or means. He was a man a good deal about town, but always alone. We used to remark to one another, that although we often encountered him in theatres, concert-rooms, and similar public places, he was always alone. Yet he was not a gloomy man, and was of a decidedly conversational turn; insomuch that he would sometimes of an evening lounge with a cigar in his mouth, half in and half out of Parkle's rooms, and discuss the topics of the day by the hour. He used to hint on these occasions that he had four faults to find with life: firstly, that it obliged a man to be always winding up his watch; secondly, that London was too small; thirdly, that it therefore wanted variety; fourthly, that there was too much dust in it. There was so much dust in his own faded chambers, certainly, that they reminded me of a sepulchre, furnished in prophetic anticipation of the present time, which had newly been brought to light, after having lain buried a few thousand years. One dry hot autumn evening at twilight, this man, being then five years turned of fifty, looked in upon Parkle in his usual lounging way, with his cigar in his mouth as usual, and said, 'I am going out of town.' As he never went out of town, Parkle said, 'Oh, indeed! At last?' 'Yes,' says he, 'at last. For what is a man to do? London is so small! If you go West, you come to Hounslow. If you go East, you come to Bow. If you go South, there's Brixton or Norwood. If you go North, you can't get rid of Barnet. Then, the monotony of all the streets, streets, streets – and of all the roads, roads, roads – and the dust, dust, dust!' When he had said this, he wished Parkle a good evening, but came back again and said, with his watch in his hand, 'Oh, I really cannot go on winding up this watch over and over again; I wish you would take care of it.' So Parkle laughed and consented, and the man went out of town. The man remained out of town so long, that his letter-box became choked, and no more letters could be got into it, and they began to be left at the lodge and to accumulate there. At last the head-porter decided, on conference with the steward, to use his master-key and look into the chambers, and give them the benefit of a whiff of air. Then, it was found that he had hanged himself to his bedstead, and had left this written memorandum: 'I should prefer to be cut down by my neighbour and friend (if he will allow me to call him so), H. Parkle, Esq.' This was the end of Parkle's occupancy of chambers. He went into lodgings immediately.

Third. While Parkle lived in Gray's Inn, and I myself was uncommercially preparing for the Bar – which is done, as everybody knows, by having a frayed old gown put on in a pantry by an old woman in a chronic state of Saint Anthony's fire and dropsy, and, so decorated, bolting a bad dinner in a party of four, whereof each individual mistrusts the other three – I say, while these things were, there was a certain elderly gentleman who lived in a court of the Temple, and was a great judge and lover of port wine. Every day, he dined at his club and drank his bottle or two of port wine, and every night came home to the Temple and went to bed in his lonely chambers. This had gone on many years without variation, when one night he had a fit on coming home, and fell and cut his head deep, but partly recovered and groped about in the dark to find the door. When he was afterwards discovered, dead, it was clearly established by the marks of his hands about the room that he must have done so. Now, this chanced on the night of Christmas Eve, and over him lived a young fellow who had sisters and young country-friends, and who gave them a little party that night, in the course of which they played at Blindman's Buff. They played that game, for their greater sport, by the light of the fire only; and once when they were all quietly rustling and stealing about, and the blindman was trying to pick out the prettiest sister (for which I am far from blaming him), somebody cried, Hark! The man below must be playing Blindman's Buff by himself tonight! They listened, and they heard sounds of someone falling about and stumbling against furniture, and they all laughed at the conceit, and went on with their play, more light-hearted and merry than ever. Thus, those two so different games of life and death were played out together, blindfold, in the two sets of chambers.

Such are the occurrences which, coming to my knowledge, imbued me long ago with a strong sense of the loneliness of chambers. There was a fantastic illustration to much the same purpose, implicitly believed by a strange sort of man now dead, whom I knew when I had not quite arrived at legal years of discretion, though I was already in the uncommercial line.

This was a man who, though not more than thirty, had seen the world in divers irreconcilable capacities – had been an officer in a South American regiment among other odd things – but had not achieved much in any way of life, and was in debt, and in hiding. He occupied chambers of the dreariest nature in Lyons Inn; his name, however, was not upon the door, or door-post, but in lieu of it stood the name of a friend who had died in the chambers, and had given him the furniture. The story arose out of the furniture, and was to this effect: – Let the former holder of the chambers, whose name was still upon the door and door-post, be Mr Testator.

Mr Testator took a set of chambers in Lyons Inn when he had but very scanty furniture for his bedroom, and none for his sitting-room. He had lived some wintry months in this condition, and had found it very bare and cold. One night, past midnight, when he sat writing, and still had writing to do that must be done before he went to bed, he found himself out of coals. He had coals downstairs, but had never been to his cellar; however, the cellar-key was on his mantelshelf, and if he went down and opened the cellar it fitted, he might fairly assume the coals in that cellar to be his. As to his laundress, she lived among the coal-waggons and Thames watermen – for there were Thames watermen at that time – in some unknown rat-hole by the river, down lanes and alleys on the other side of the Strand. As to any other person to meet him or obstruct him, Lyons Inn was dreaming, drunk, maudlin, moody, betting, brooding over bill-discounting or renewing – asleep or awake, minding its own affairs. Mr Testator took his coalscuttle in one hand, his candle and key in the other, and descended to the dismallest underground dens of Lyons Inn, where the late vehicles in the streets became thunderous and all the water-pipes in the neighbourhood seemed to have Macbeth's Amen sticking in their throats, and to be trying to get it out. After groping here and there among low doors to no purpose, Mr Testator at length came to a door with a rusty padlock which his key fitted. Getting the door open with much trouble, and looking in, he found, no coals, but a confused pile of furniture. Alarmed by this intrusion on another man's property, he locked the door again, found his own cellar, filled his scuttle, and returned upstairs.

But the furniture he had seen, ran on castors across and across Mr Testator's mind incessantly, when, in the chill hour of five in the morning he got to bed. He particularly wanted a table to write at, and a table expressly made to be written at had been the piece of furniture in the foreground of the heap. When his laundress emerged from her burrow in the morning to make his kettle boil, he artfully led up to the subject of cellars and furniture; but the two ideas had evidently no connexion in her mind. When she left him, and he sat at his breakfast, thinking about the furniture, he recalled the rusty state of the padlock, and inferred that the furniture must have been stored in the cellars for a long time – was perhaps forgotten – owner dead, perhaps? After thinking it over, a few days, in the course of which he could pump nothing out of Lyons Inn about the furniture, he became desperate, and resolved to borrow that table. He did so, that night. He had not had the table long, when he determined to borrow an easy-chair; he had not had that long, when he made up his mind to borrow a bookcase; then, a couch; then, a carpet and rug. By that time, he felt he was 'in furniture stepped in so far,' as that it could be no worse to borrow it all. Consequently, he borrowed it all, and locked up the cellar for good. He had always locked it, after every visit. He had carried up every separate article in the dead of the night, and, at the best, had felt as wicked as a Resurrection Man. Every article was blue and furry when brought into his rooms, and he had had, in a murderous and guilty sort of way, to polish it up while London slept.

Mr Testator lived in his furnished chambers two or three years, or more, and gradually lulled himself into the opinion that the furniture was his own. This was his convenient state of mind when, late one night, a step came up the stairs, and a hand passed over his door feeling for his knocker, and then one deep and solemn rap was rapped that might have been a spring in Mr Testator's easy-chair to shoot him out of it: so promptly was it attended with that effect.

With a candle in his hand, Mr Testator went to the door, and found there, a very pale and very tall man; a man who stooped; a man with very high shoulders, a very narrow chest, and a very red nose; a shabby genteel man. He was wrapped in a long threadbare black coat, fastened up the front with more pins than buttons, and under his arm he squeezed an umbrella without a handle, as if he were playing bagpipes. He said, 'I ask your pardon, but can you tell me —' and stopped; his eyes resting on some object within the chambers.

'Can I tell you what?' asked Mr Testator, noting this stoppage with quick alarm.

'I ask your pardon,' said the stranger, 'but — this is not the inquiry I was going to make — *do* I see in there any small article of property belonging to *me?*'

Mr Testator was beginning to stammer that he was not aware — when the visitor slipped past him, into the chambers. There, in a goblin way which froze Mr Testator to the marrow, he examined, first, the writing-table, and said, 'Mine;' then, the easy-chair, and said, 'Mine;' then, the bookcase, and said, 'Mine;' then, turned up a corner of the carpet, and said, 'Mine;' in a word, inspected every item of furniture from the cellar in succession, and said, 'Mine!' Towards the end of this investigation, Mr Testator perceived that he was sodden with liquor, and that the liquor was gin. He was not unsteady with gin, either in his speech or carriage; but he was stiff with gin in both particulars.

Mr Testator was in a dreadful state, for (according to his making out of the story) the possible consequences of what he had done in recklessness and hardihood flashed upon him in their fulness for the first time. When they had stood gazing at one another for a little while, he tremulously began:

'Sir, I am conscious that the fullest explanation, compensation, and restitution, are your due. They shall be yours. Allow me to entreat that, without temper, without even natural irritation on your part, we may have a little —'

'Drop of something to drink,' interposed the stranger. 'I am agreeable.'

Mr Testator had intended to say, 'a little quiet conversation,' but with great relief of mind adopted the amendment. He produced a decanter of gin, and was bustling about for hot water and sugar, when he found that his visitor had already drunk half of the decanter's contents. With hot water and sugar the visitor drank the remainder before he had been an hour in the chambers by the chimes of the church of Saint Mary in the Strand; and during the process he frequently whispered to himself, 'Mine!'

The gin gone, and Mr Testator wondering what was to follow it, the visitor rose and said, with increased stiffness, 'At what hour of the morning, sir, will it be convenient?' Mr Testator hazarded, 'At ten?' 'Sir,' said the visitor, 'at ten, to the moment, I shall be here.' He then contemplated Mr Testator somewhat at leisure, and said, 'God bless you! How is your wife?' Mr Testator (who never had a wife) replied with much feeling, 'Deeply anxious, poor soul, but otherwise well.' The visitor thereupon turned and went away, and fell twice in going downstairs. From that hour he was never heard of. Whether he was a ghost, or a spectral illusion of conscience, or a drunken man who had no business there, or the drunken rightful owner of the furniture, with a transitory gleam of memory; whether he got safe home, or had no home to get to; whether he died of liquor on the way, or lived in liquor ever afterwards; he never was heard of more. This was the story, received with the furniture and held to be as substantial, by its second possessor in an upper set of chambers in grim Lyons Inn.

It is to be remarked of chambers in general, that they must have been built for chambers, to have the right kind of loneliness. You may make a great dwelling-house very lonely by isolating suites of rooms and calling them chambers, but you cannot make the true kind of loneliness. In dwelling-houses, there have been family festivals; children have grown in them, girls have bloomed into women in them, courtships and marriages have taken place in them. True chambers never were young, childish, maidenly; never had dolls in them, or rocking-horses, or christenings, or betrothals, or little coffins. Let Gray's Inn identify the child who first touched hands and hearts with Robinson Crusoe, in any one of its many 'sets,' and that child's little statue, in white marble with a golden inscription, shall be at its service, at my cost and charge, as a drinking fountain for the spirit to freshen its thirsty square. Let Lincoln's produce from all its houses, a twentieth of the procession derivable from any dwelling-house one-twentieth of its age, of fair young brides who married for love and hope, not settlements, and all the Vice-Chancellors shall thenceforward be kept in nosegays for nothing, on application at this office. It is not denied that on the terrace of the Adelphi, or in any of the streets of that subterranean-stable-haunted spot, or about Bedford-row, or James-street of that ilk (a grewsome place), or anywhere among the neighbourhoods that have done flowering and have run to seed, you may find Chambers replete with the accommodations of Solitude, Closeness, and Darkness, where you may be as low spirited as in the genuine article, and might be as easily murdered, with the placid reputation of having merely gone down to the seaside. But the many waters of life did run musical in those dry channels once; – among the Inns, never. The only popular legend known in relation to any one of the dull family of Inns is a dark Old Bailey whisper concerning Clement's, and importing how the black creature who holds the sun-dial there, was a negro who slew his master and built the dismal pile out of the contents of his strong-box – for which architectural offence alone he ought to have been condemned to live in it. But what populace would waste fancy upon such a place, or on New Inn, Staple Inn, Barnard's Inn, or any of the shabby crew?

The genuine laundress, too, is an institution not to be had in its entirety out of and away from the genuine Chambers. Again, it is not denied that you may be robbed elsewhere. Elsewhere you may have – for money – dishonesty, drunkenness, dirt, laziness, and profound incapacity. But the veritable shining-red-faced, shameless laundress; the true Mrs Sweeney – in figure, colour, texture, and smell, like the old damp family umbrella; the tiptop complicated abomination of stockings, spirits, bonnet, limpness, looseness, and larceny, is only to be drawn at the fountain-head. Mrs Sweeney is beyond the reach of individual art. It requires the united efforts of several men to insure that great result, and it is only developed in perfection under an Honourable Society and in an Inn of Court.

18

The Uncommercial Traveller

All The Year Round, 8 September 1860 (*UT1* as 'Nurse's Stories')

The present article appears to hark back to Dickens's remarks on the psychology of young children in article 10 of this volume (p. 91, but it also acts as a companion piece to article 15, 'Dullborough Town': both pieces were indexed in Vol. III of *ATYR* under 'Childhood Associations', and in para. 5 below the narrator refers to 'revisiting the associations of my childhood as recorded in previous pages of these notes.' In the preceding paragraphs, however, 'revisiting' is taken by analogy to mean the process of re-reading books of voyage and travel, of which Dickens was passionately fond (see Introduction, pp. xv–xvi & n.), and in general of re-reading children's classics such as *Robinson Crusoe*. He had already celebrated his ability to go back to an almost identical selection of details from this text – Will Atkins, the 'grave and gentlemanly Spaniard', Crusoe's 'parrot, or his dog ... or the horrible old staring goat he came upon in the cave', the cannibals' dinner, and the blowing up of the wolves – in a *HW* essay of 1853, 'Where We Stopped Growing' (see article 15 of Vol. 3 of this edition). Mention is made there too of Le Sage's *The Adventures of Gil Blas of Santillane* and of Cervantes's *Don Quixote*. The present article also recalls his grand tribute to horror stories and winter's tales in 'A Christmas Tree' (*HW*, 21 December 1850; repr. in *Reprinted Pieces*, 1858), which illustrates Dickens's point here about the 'authentication' of ghost stories by their tellers (p. 179), by making the tales told happen to 'a friend of somebody's whom most of us know', or to 'the uncle of my brother's wife', or 'a connexion of our family'.

The 'identity' of the nurse described here has been the subject of some debate. Charles Dickens Jr suggests (*UT4*, p. xxiii) that the character figures also in 'The Guest', one of Dickens's contributions to the *HW* Christmas Number for 1855 (repr. in *Christmas Stories* [1874], in 'The Holly Tree: Three Branches'), in which she is depicted as 'a sallow woman with a fishy eye, an aquiline nose, and a green gown, whose speciality was a dismal narrative of a landlord by the roadside, whose visitors unaccountably disappeared for many a year, until it was discovered that the pursuit of his life had been to convert them into pies'. The narrator of 'The Guest' also recalls that '[t]his same narrator, ... had a Ghoulish pleasure, I have long been persuaded, in terrifying me to the utmost confines of my reason' (*ibid.*). It should be noted that both the speaker of this account and 'The Uncommercial Traveller' are personae whose nurses may be supposed similarly fictitious, but this has not discouraged biographers from taking Dickens's references to be, as Peter Ackroyd puts it, 'true transcripts from memory, considerably enlivening Dickens's childhood as a result' (*Dickens* [1990], p. 30). The most popular identification for the nurse is Mary Weller, a young nursemaid employed in the Dickens household at Chatham from 1817 to 1822. Michael Slater provides a full summary of such biographical interpretations in 'How Many Nurses Had Charles Dickens? *The Uncommercial Traveller* and Dickensian Biography', and cautions against the 'tendency to read *The Uncommercial Traveller* as though it contained straightforward chunks of autobiography' (*Prose Studies*, Vol. 10 [1987], pp. 250–8).

It is similarly difficult to find printed sources for the ghoulish stories which Dickens links to the nursery, but Harry Stone explores the possible impact of such material, and of 'tales … heard from Mary Weller's lips', in 'Dark Corners of the Mind: Dickens's Childhood Reading' (*The Horn Book Magazine*, June 1963, p. 310f.) and in *The Night Side of Dickens* [1994], pp. 15–18.

Literary allusions (pp. 171–2) 'the little creek which Friday swam across', 'Mr Atkins's … track on the memorable evening' 'the flaring eyes of the old goat …', 'belated among wolves … makes me tremble': episodes from the later stages of the narrative in Defoe's *Robinson Crusoe* (1719); (p. 172) 'the robber's cave, where Gil Blas lived': Le Sage, *Adventures of Gil Blas of Santillane* (1715) Chs 4–10; (p. 172); 'Don Quixote's study' is described in Cervantes's *Don Quixote*, Part I (1605), Chs 1 and 5; (p. 173) 'the little old woman … the Talisman of Oromanes': events in the Rev. J. Ridley's *Tales of the Genii* (1764), Vol. I, Tale the First 'History of the Merchant Abudah; or, the Talisman of Oromanes'; (p. 173) 'the boy Horatio Nelson … with a sheet': Southey's *Life of Nelson* (1813), Ch. 1; (p. 173) 'Damascus, and Bagdad': general allusions to the settings of *The Arabian Nights' Entertainments*; (p. 173) 'Brobdingnag … and Lilliput, and Laputa': places visited by Gulliver in Swift's *Gulliver's Travels* (1726); (p. 173) 'the Blue Beard family': allusion to Charles Perrault's telling of the fairy-tale 'Blue Beard' in *Histoires ou Contes du temps passé* (1697); (p. 175) 'commended the awful chalice to my lips': Shakespeare, *Macbeth*, Act 1, Sc. 7.

Textual note (p. 173) copy-text has 'Brobdingnag (which has the curious fate of being usually misspelt when written)': *UT1* and some subsequent editions have 'Brobingnag (which…)' &c. The former is the correct spelling.

There are not many places that I find it more agreeable to revisit when I am in an idle mood, than some places to which I have never been. For, my acquaintance with those spots is of such long standing, and has ripened into an intimacy of so affectionate a nature, that I take a particular interest in assuring myself that they are unchanged.

I never was in Robinson Crusoe's Island, yet I frequently return there. The colony he established on it soon faded away, and it is uninhabited by any descendants of the grave and courteous Spaniards, or of Will Atkins and the other mutineers, and has relapsed into its original condition. Not a twig of its wicker houses remains, its goats have long run wild again, its screaming parrots would darken the sun with a cloud of many flaming colours if a gun were fired there, no face is ever reflected in the waters of the little creek which Friday swam across when pursued by his two brother cannibals with sharpened stomachs. After comparing notes with other travellers who have similarly revisited the Island and conscientiously inspected it, I have satisfied myself that it contains no vestige of Mr Atkins's domesticity or theology, though his track on the memorable evening of his landing to set his captain ashore, when he was decoyed about and round about until it was dark, and his boat was stove, and his strength and spirits failed him, is yet plainly to be traced. So is the hilltop on which Robinson was struck dumb with joy when the reinstated captain pointed to the ship, riding within half a mile of the shore, that was to bear him away, in the nine-and-twentieth year of his seclusion in that lonely place. So is the sandy beach on which the memorable footstep was impressed, and where the savages hauled up their canoes when they came ashore for those dreadful public dinners, which led to a dancing worse than speech-making. So is the cave where the flaring eyes of the old goat made such a goblin appearance in the dark. So is the site of the hut where Robinson lived with the dog and the parrot and the cat, and where he endured those first agonies of solitude, which – strange to say – never involved any ghostly fancies; a circumstance so very remarkable, that perhaps he left out something in writing his record? Round hundreds of such objects, hidden in the dense tropical foliage, the tropical sea breaks evermore; and over them the tropical sky, saving in the short rainy season, shines bright and cloudless.

Neither, was I ever belated among wolves, on the borders of France and Spain; nor, did I ever, when night was closing in and the ground was covered with snow, draw up my little company among some felled trees which served as a breastwork, and there fire a train of gunpowder so dexterously that suddenly we had three or four score blazing wolves illuminating the darkness around us. Nevertheless, I occasionally go back to that dismal region and perform the feat again; when indeed to smell the singeing and the frying of the wolves afire, and to see them setting one another alight as they rush and tumble, and to behold them rolling in the snow vainly attempting to put themselves out, and to hear their howlings taken up by all the echoes as well as by all the unseen wolves within the woods, makes me tremble.

I was never in the robbers' cave, where Gil Blas lived, but I often go back there, and find the trap-door just as heavy to raise as it used to be, while that wicked old disabled Black lies everlastingly cursing in bed. I was never in Don Quixote's study where he read his books of chivalry until he rose and hacked at imaginary giants, and then refreshed himself with great draughts of water, yet you couldn't move a book in it without my knowledge, or with my consent. I was never (thank Heaven) in company with the little old woman who hobbled out of the chest and told the merchant Abudah to go in search of the Talisman of Oromanes, yet I make it my business to know that she is well preserved and as intolerable as ever. I was never at the school where the boy Horatio Nelson got out of bed to steal the pears: not because he wanted any, but because every other boy was afraid: yet I have several times been back to this Academy, to see him let down out of window with a sheet. So with Damascus, and Bagdad, and Brobdingnag (which has the curious fate of being usually misspelt when written), and Lilliput, and Laputa, and the Nile, and Abyssinia, and the Ganges, and the North Pole, and many hundreds of places – I was never at them, yet it is an affair of my life to keep them intact, and I am always going back to them.

But when I was in Dullborough one day, revisiting the associations of my childhood as recorded in previous pages of these notes, my experience in this wise was made quite inconsiderable and of no account, by the quantity of places and people – utterly impossible places and people, but none the less alarmingly real – that I found I had been introduced to by my nurse before I was six years old, and used to be forced to go back to at night without at all wanting to go. If we all knew our own minds (in a more enlarged sense than the popular acceptation of that phrase), I suspect we should find our nurses responsible for most of the dark corners we are forced to go back to, against our wills.

The first diabolical character who intruded himself on my peaceful youth (as I called to mind that day at Dullborough), was a certain Captain Murderer. This wretch must have been an offshoot of the Blue Beard family, but I had no suspicion of the consanguinity in those times. His warning name would seem to have awakened no general prejudice against him, for he was admitted into the best society and possessed immense wealth. Captain Murderer's mission was matrimony, and the gratification of a cannibal appetite with tender brides. On his marriage morning, he always caused both sides of the way to church to be planted with curious flowers; and when his bride said, 'Dear Captain Murderer, I never saw flowers like these before: what are they called?' he answered, 'They are called Garnish for house-lamb,' and laughed at his ferocious practical joke in a horrid manner, disquieting the minds of the noble bridal company, with a very sharp show of teeth, then displayed for the first time. He made love in a coach and six, and married in a coach and twelve, and all his horses were milk-white horses with one red spot on the back which he caused to be hidden by the harness. For, the spot *would* come there, though every horse was milk-white when Captain Murderer bought him. And the spot was young bride's blood. (To this terrific point I am indebted for my first personal experience of a shudder and cold beads on the forehead.) When Captain Murderer had made an end of feasting and revelry, and had dismissed the noble guests, and was alone with his wife on the day month after their marriage, it was his whimsical custom to produce a golden rolling-pin and a silver pie-board. Now, there was this special feature in the Captain's courtships, that he always asked if the young lady could make pie-crust; and if she couldn't by nature or education, she was taught. Well. When the bride saw Captain Murderer produce the golden rolling-pin and silver pie-board, she remembered this, and turned up her laced-silk sleeves to make a pie. The Captain brought out a silver pie-dish of immense capacity, and the Captain brought out flour and butter and eggs and all things needful, except the inside of the pie; of materials for the staple of the pie itself, the Captain brought out none. Then said the lovely bride, 'Dear Captain Murderer, what pie is this to be?' He replied, 'A meat pie.' Then said the lovely bride, 'Dear Captain Murderer, I see no meat.' The Captain humorously retorted, 'Look in the glass.' She looked in the glass, but still she saw no meat, and then the Captain roared with laughter, and, suddenly frowning and drawing his sword, bade her roll out the crust. So she rolled out the crust, dropping large tears upon it all the time because he was so cross, and when she had lined the dish with crust and had cut the crust all ready to fit the top, the Captain called out, '*I see the meat in the glass!*' And the bride looked up at the glass, just in time to see the Captain cutting her head off; and he chopped her in pieces, and peppered her, and salted her, and put her in the pie, and sent it to the baker's, and ate it all, and picked the bones.

Captain Murderer went on in this way, prospering exceedingly, until he came to choose a bride from two twin sisters, and at first didn't know which to choose. For, though one was fair and the other dark, they were both equally beautiful. But the fair twin loved him, and the dark twin hated him, so he chose the fair one. The dark twin would have prevented the marriage if she could, but she couldn't; however, on the night before it, much suspecting Captain Murderer, she stole out and climbed his garden wall, and looked in at his window through a chink in the shutter, and saw him having his teeth filed sharp. Next day she listened all day, and heard him make his joke about the house-lamb. And that day month, he had the paste rolled out, and cut the fair twin's head off, and chopped her in pieces, and peppered her, and salted her, and put her in the pie, and sent it to the baker's, and ate it all, and picked the bones.

Now, the dark twin had had her suspicions much increased by the filing of the Captain's teeth, and again by the house-lamb joke. Putting all things together when he gave out that her sister was dead, she divined the truth, and determined to be revenged. So she went up to Captain Murderer's house, and knocked at the knocker and pulled at the bell, and when the Captain came to the door, said: 'Dear Captain Murderer, marry me next, for I always loved you and was jealous of my sister.' The Captain took it as a compliment, and made a polite answer, and the marriage was quickly arranged. On the night before it, the bride again climbed to his window, and again saw him having his teeth filed sharp. At this sight, she laughed such a terrible laugh, at the chink in the shutter, that the Captain's blood curdled, and he said: 'I hope nothing has disagreed with me!' At that, she laughed again, a still more terrible laugh, and the shutter was opened and search made, but she was nimbly gone and there was no one. Next day they went to church in the coach and twelve, and were married. And that day month she rolled the pie-crust out, and Captain Murderer cut her head off, and chopped her in pieces, and peppered her, and salted her, and put her in the pie, and sent it to the baker's, and ate it all, and picked the bones.

But before she began to roll out the paste she had taken a deadly poison of a most awful character, distilled from toads' eyes and spiders' knees; and Captain Murderer had hardly picked her last bone, when he began to swell, and to turn blue, and to be all over spots, and to scream. And he went on swelling and turning bluer and being more all over spots and screaming, until he reached from floor to ceiling, and from wall to wall; and then, at one o'clock in the morning, he blew up with a loud explosion. At the sound of it, all the milk-white horses in the stables broke their halters and went mad, and then they galloped over everybody in Captain Murderer's house (beginning with the family blacksmith who had filed his teeth) until the whole were dead, and then they galloped away.

Hundreds of times did I hear this legend of Captain Murderer, in my early youth, and added hundreds of times was there a mental compulsion upon me in bed, to peep in at his window as the dark twin peeped, and to revisit his horrible house, and look at him in his blue and spotty and screaming stage, as he reached from floor to ceiling and from wall to wall. The young woman who brought me acquainted with Captain Murderer, had a fiendish enjoyment of my terrors, and used to begin, I remember – as a sort of introductory overture – by clawing the air with both hands, and uttering a long low hollow groan. So acutely did I suffer from this ceremony in combination with this infernal Captain, that I sometimes used to plead I thought I was hardly strong enough and old enough to hear the story again just yet. But she never spared me one word of it, and indeed commended the awful chalice to my lips as the only preservative known to science against 'The Black Cat' – a weird and glaring-eyed supernatural Tom, who was reputed to prowl about the world by night, sucking the breath of infancy, and who was endowed with a special thirst (as I was given to understand) for mine.

This female bard – may she have been repaid my debt of obligation to her in the matter of nightmares and perspirations! – reappears in my memory as the daughter of a shipwright. Her name was Mercy, although she had none on me. There was something of a ship-building flavour in the following story. As it always recurs to me in a vague association with calomel pills, I believe it to have been reserved for dull nights when I was low with medicine.

There was once a shipwright, and he wrought in a Government Yard, and his name was Chips. And *his* father's name before *him* was Chips, and his father's name before him was Chips, and they were all Chipses. And Chips the father had sold himself to the Devil for an iron pot and a bushel of tenpenny nails and half a ton of copper and a rat that could speak; and Chips the grandfather had sold himself to the Devil for an iron pot and a bushel of tenpenny nails and half a ton of copper and a rat that could speak; and Chips the great-grandfather had disposed of himself in the same direction on the same terms; and the bargain had run in the family for a long long time. So one day, when young Chips was at work in the Dock Slip all alone, down in the dark hold of an old Seventy-four that was hauled up for repairs, the Devil presented himself, and remarked:

> 'A Lemon has pips,
> And a Yard has ships,
> And *I'*ll have Chips!'

(I don't know why, but this fact of the Devil's expressing himself in rhyme was peculiarly trying to me.) Chips looked up when he heard the words, and there he saw the Devil with saucer eyes that squinted on a terrible great scale, and that struck out sparks of blue fire continually. And whenever he winked his eyes, showers of blue sparks came out, and his eyelashes made a clattering like flints and steels striking lights. And hanging over one of his arms by the handle was an iron pot, and under that arm was a bushel of tenpenny nails, and under his other arm was half a ton of copper, and sitting on one of his shoulders was a rat that could speak. So the Devil said again:

> 'A Lemon has pips,
> And a Yard has ships,
> And *I'*ll have Chips!'

(The invariable effect of this alarming tautology on the part of the Evil Spirit was to deprive me of my senses for some moments.) So Chips answered never a word, but went on with his work. 'What are you doing, Chips?' said the rat that could speak. 'I am putting in new planks where you and your gang have eaten old away,' said Chips. 'But we'll eat them too,' said the rat that could speak; 'and we'll let in the water and drown the crew, and we'll eat them too.' Chips, being only a shipwright, and not a Man-of-war's man, said, 'You are welcome to it.' But he couldn't keep his eyes off the half a ton of copper, or the bushel of tenpenny nails; for nails and copper are a shipwright's sweethearts, and shipwrights will run away with them whenever they can. So the Devil said, 'I see what you are looking at, Chips. You had better strike the bargain. You know the terms. Your father before you was well acquainted with them, and so were your grandfather and great-grandfather before him.' Says Chips, 'I like the copper, and I like the nails, and I don't mind the pot, but I don't like the rat.' Says the Devil, fiercely, 'You can't have the metal without him – and *he's* a curiosity. I'm going.' Chips, afraid of losing the half a ton of copper and the bushel of nails, then said, 'Give us hold!' So he got the copper and the nails and the pot and the rat that could speak, and the Devil vanished.

Chips sold the copper, and he sold the nails, and he would have sold the pot; but whenever he offered it for sale, the rat was in it, and the dealers dropped it, and would have nothing to say to the bargain. So Chips resolved to kill the rat, and, being at work in the Yard one day with a great kettle of hot pitch on one side of him and the iron pot with the rat in it on the other, he turned the scalding pitch into the pot, and filled it full. Then he kept his eye upon it till it cooled and hardened, and then he let it stand for twenty days, and then he heated the pitch again and turned it back into the kettle, and then he sank the pot in water for twenty days more, and then he got the smelters to put it in the furnace for twenty days more, and then they gave it him out, red hot, and looking like red-hot glass instead of iron – yet there was the rat in it, just the same as ever! And the moment it caught his eye, it said with a jeer:

> 'A Lemon has pips,
> And a Yard has ships,
> And *I*'ll have Chips!'

(For this Refrain I had waited since its last appearance, with inexpressible horror, which now culminated.) Chips now felt certain in his own mind that the rat would stick to him; the rat, answering his thought, said, 'I will – like pitch!'

Now, as the rat leaped out of the pot when it had spoken, and made off, Chips began to hope that it wouldn't keep its word. But a terrible thing happened next day. For, when dinner-time came and the Dock-bell rang to strike work, he put his rule into the long pocket at the side of his trousers, and there he found a rat – not that rat, but another rat. And in his hat he found another; and in his pocket-handkerchief, another; and in the sleeves of his coat, when he pulled it on to go to dinner, two more. And from that time he found himself so frightfully intimate with all the rats in the Yard, that they climbed up his legs when he was at work, and sat on his tools while he used them. And they could all speak to one another, and he understood what they said. And they got into his lodging, and into his bed, and into his teapot, and into his beer, and into his boots. And he was going to be married to a corn-chandler's daughter; and when he gave her a workbox he had himself made for her, a rat jumped out of it; and when he put his arm round her waist, a rat clung about her; so the marriage was broken off, though the banns were already twice put up – which the parish clerk well remembers, for, as he handed the book to the clergyman for the second time of asking, a large fat rat ran over the leaf. (By this time a special cascade of rats was rolling down my back, and the whole of my small listening person was overrun with them. At intervals ever since, I have been morbidly afraid of my own pocket, lest my exploring hand should find a specimen or two of those vermin in it.)

You may believe that all this was very terrible to Chips; but even all this was not the worst. He knew besides, what the rats were doing, wherever they were. So sometimes he would cry aloud, when he was at his club at night, 'Oh! Keep the rats out of the convicts' burying-ground! Don't let them do that!' Or, 'There's one of them at the cheese downstairs!' Or, 'There's two of them smelling at the baby in the garret!' Or, other things of that sort. At last, he was voted mad, and lost his work in the Yard, and could get no other work. But, King George wanted men, so before very long he got pressed for a sailor. And so he was taken off in a boat one evening to his ship, lying at Spithead, ready to sail. And so the first thing he made out in her as he got near her, was the figure-head of the old Seventy-four, where he had seen the Devil. She was called the Argonaut, and they rowed right under the bowsprit, where the figure-head of the Argonaut, with a sheepskin in his hand and a blue gown on, was looking out to sea; and sitting staring on his forehead was the rat who could speak, and his exact words were these: 'Chips ahoy! Old boy! We've pretty well eat them too, and will drown the crew, and will eat them too!' (Here I always became exceedingly faint, and would have asked for water, but that I was speechless.)

The ship was bound for the Indies; and if you don't know where that is, you ought to it, and angels will never love you. (Here I felt myself an outcast from a future state.) The ship set sail that very night, and she sailed, and sailed, and sailed. Chips's feelings were dreadful. Nothing ever equalled his terrors. No wonder. At last, one day, he asked leave to speak to the Admiral. The Admiral giv' leave. Chips went down on his knees in the Great State Cabin. 'Your Honour, unless your Honour, without a moment's loss of time, makes sail for the nearest shore, this is a doomed ship, and her name is the Coffin!' 'Young man, your words are a madman's words.' 'Your Honour no; they are nibbling us away.' 'They?' 'Your Honour, them dreadful rats. Dust and hollowness where solid oak ought to be! Rats nibbling a grave for every man on board! Oh! Does your Honour love your Lady and your pretty children?' 'Yes, my man, to be sure.' 'Then, for God's sake, make for the nearest shore, for at this present moment the rats are all stopping in their work, and are all looking straight towards you with bare teeth, and are all saying to one another that you shall never, never, never, never, see your Lady and your children more.' 'My poor fellow, you are a case for the doctor. Sentry, take care of this man!'

So he was bled and he was blistered, and he was this and that, for six whole days and nights. So then he again asked leave to speak to the Admiral. The Admiral giv' leave. He went down on his knees in the Great State Cabin. 'Now, Admiral, you must die! You took no warning; you must die! The rats are never wrong in their calculations, and they make out that they'll be through, at twelve tonight. So, you must die! – With me and all the rest!' And so at twelve o'clock there was a great leak reported in the ship, and a torrent of water rushed in and nothing could stop it, and they all went down, every living soul. And what the rats – being water-rats – left of Chips, at last floated to shore, and sitting on him was an immense overgrown rat, laughing, that dived when the corpse touched the beach and never came up. And there was a deal of seaweed on the remains. And if you get thirteen bits of seaweed, and dry them and burn them in the fire, they will go – off – like in these thirteen words as plain as plain can be:

'A Lemon has pips,
And a Yard has ships,
And *I*'ve got Chips!'

The same female bard – descended, possibly, from those terrible old Scalds who seem to have existed for the express purpose of addling the brains of mankind when they begin to investigate languages – made a standing pretence which greatly assisted in forcing me back to a number of hideous places that I would by all means have avoided. This pretence was, that all her ghost stories had occurred to her own relations. Politeness towards a meritorious family, therefore forbade my doubting them, and they acquired an air of authentication that impaired my digestive powers for life. There was a narrative concerning an unearthly animal foreboding death, which appeared in the open street to a parlour-maid who 'went to fetch the beer' for supper: first (as I now recal it) assuming the likeness of a black dog, and gradually rising on its hind-legs and swelling into the semblance of some quadruped greatly surpassing a hippopotamus: which apparition – not because I deemed it in the least improbable, but because I felt it to be really too large to bear – I feebly endeavoured to explain away. But on Mercy's retorting with wounded dignity that the parlour-maid was her own sister-in-law, I perceived there was no hope, and resigned myself to this zoological phenomenon as one of my many pursuers. There was another narrative describing the apparition of a young woman who came out of a glass-case and haunted another young woman until the other young woman questioned it and elicited that its bones (Lord! To think of its being so particular about its bones!) were buried under the glass-case, whereas she required them to be interred, with every Undertaking solemnity up to twenty-four pound ten, in another particular place. This narrative I considered I had a personal interest in disproving, because we had glass-cases at home, and how, otherwise, was I to be guaranteed from the intrusion of young women requiring *me* to bury them up to twenty-four pound ten, when I had only twopence a week? But my remorseless nurse cut the ground from under my tender feet, by informing me that She was the other young woman; and I couldn't say 'I don't believe you;' it was not possible.

Such are a few of the uncommercial journeys that I was forced to make, against my will, when I was very young and unreasoning. And really, as to the latter part of them, it is not so very long ago – now I come to think of it – that I was asked to undertake them once again, with a steady countenance.

19

The Uncommercial Traveller

All The Year Round, 29 September 1860 (*UT1* as 'Arcadian London')

The theme of the present article – London during the autumn recess of Parliament – was something of a set piece for Victorian sketch-writers: three essays all entitled 'Out of Town' by Dickens, Thackeray and Edmund Yates make interesting parallel reading (see Vol. 3 of this edition, article 42; *Punch*, Vol. 17 [11, 18 August 1849], pp. 53, 66–9, repr. in *Sketches and Travels*, Vol. 6 of the Biographical Edn of Thackeray's works, 1899; *After Office Hours* [1861], Ch. 8). The title and subsequent development of this paper play on the word Arcadia, as the traveller's autumn lodgings are in

London's fashionable West End, close to the Burlington Arcade, a permanent covered shopping mall of a kind becoming common in London and other European capitals. In a literary context, however, 'Arcadia' was celebrated in the pastoral tradition as the home of the most primitive of the Ancient Greek peoples, those least corrupted by civilisation.

Between August and September 1860, Dickens was waiting for his rooms above the *ATYR* office to be fitted out (see Introduction, pp. xvi–xvii), and had not yet fully moved into Gad's Hill Place, and although his published correspondence is not revealing, it is possible that in this period he was indeed in temporary lodgings in London. Bond Street had been divided into 'Old' and 'New' since 1721, so Dickens's narrator is deliberately unspecific, but Gwen Major has suggested that Hood's, formerly the hatter's at 2 New Bond Street, is the most 'likely' site ('Arcadian London', *The Dickensian*, Vol. 45 [1949], pp. 208–12). Various letters to family and friends written in Autumn 1853, however, show that the topic had been in Dickens's mind for some considerable time, and need not have required any fresh personal experience as an inspiration:

> The West End of London is entirely deserted, and no business . . . is being carried on. I went to three shops this morning, for some things I want to wear. Blackmore the tailor was at Brighton. Butler the Tailor was playing the piano among some mignionette boxes, in the bosom of his family. Only two subordinates were in attendance at Beale's the hosier's, and they were playing at draughts. . . . [*Pilgrim*, Vol. VII (7 September 1853), p. 138]
>
> I suppose that part of London never was so empty.... This is really the experience of a solitary traveller in those regions at eleven o'Clock yesterday forenoon. [*Ibid.* ([9] September 1853), p. 141; see also (21 September 1853), p. 154]

The description of the volunteering activities of the hatter's young man (p. 181) is both topical and accurate: the headquarters of the 11th Middlesex Volunteers (formed 1792; re-established 1859) were in Hanover Square, close to New Bond Street, and their rifle-green uniform included a shako hat with a dark green cock's feather plume, and knickerbocker shorts for field days and manoeuvres (Hill). But for a flâneur of Dickens's perceptiveness, such observation could easily be the product of a short stroll.

Literary allusions (p. 186) 'they drowsily bide or recal their turn for chasing the ebbing Neptune on the ribbed sea-sand': Shakespeare, *The Tempest*, Act 5, Sc. 1; (p. 186) 'where all the lights are not fled ... but I have not departed': paraphrases Thomas Moore's ballad 'Oft in the stilly night', *National Airs* (1815); (p. 187) 'the New Zealander of the grand English History ... gloat upon the ruins of Talk': Dickens refers to an image not from

Macaulay's *History of England* (1849–61) but from his *Edinburgh Review* article on Leopold von Ranke's *History of the Popes* (1834–6), repr. in Vol. 1 of *Essays Critical and Historical* (1843 etc.); the controversy over 'this unfortunate man' refers either to debate over whether Macaulay had himself derived the image from Horace Walpole's letter to Sir Horace Mann of 24 November 1774 (*Correspondence* [1967], Vol. 24, p. 62; see also *Notes and Queries*, Vol. 9 [28 January 1854], p.74, col. b et seq.) or to the fact that reference to 'the New Zealander' had become a popular journalistic device for speculating about futurity (see, for example, *Blackwood's Edinburgh Magazine*, Vol. 85 [January 1859], p. 73, col. a; Vol. 86 [December 1859], p. 683, col. b); (p. 187) 'rookery of mares' nests': John Fletcher, *Bonduca* (acted c. 1614; printed 1647), Act 5, Sc. 2; (p. 187) 'tomorrow, and tomorrow, and tomorrow': Shakespeare, *Macbeth*, Act 5, Sc. 5; (p. 189) 'my hatter hermitage will then know them no more': Job 7:10.

Textual note: (p. 184) copy-text has 'It's on'y Mr Klem': *UT1* has 'It's only Mr Klem'; (p. 184) copy-text has 'another 'ouse in Serjameses Street': *UT1* has 'a 'ouse in Serjameses street'; (p. 187) copy-text has 'If I get up': *UT1* has 'If I rise from my bed'.

Being in a humour for complete solitude and uninterrupted meditation this autumn, I have taken a lodging for six weeks in the most unfrequented part of England – in a word, in London.

The retreat into which I have withdrawn myself is Bond-street. From this lonely spot I make pilgrimages into the surrounding wilderness, and traverse extensive tracts of the Great Desert. The first solemn feeling of isolation overcome, the first oppressive consciousness of profound retirement conquered, I enjoy that sense of freedom, and feel reviving within me that latent wildness of the original savage, which has been (upon the whole somewhat frequently) noticed by Travellers.

My lodgings are at a hatter's – my own hatter's. After exhibiting no articles in his window for some weeks, but sea-side wide-awakes, shooting-caps, and a choice of rough waterproof head-gear for the moors and mountains, he has put upon the heads of his family as much of this stock as they could carry, and has taken them off to the Isle of Thanet. His young man alone remains – and remains alone – in the shop. The young man has let out the fire at which the irons are heated, and, saving his strong sense of duty, I see no reason why he should take the shutters down.

Happily for himself and for his country, the young man is a Volunteer; most happily for himself, or I think he would become the prey of a settled melancholy. For, to live surrounded by human hats, and alienated from human heads to fit them on, is surely a great endurance. But, the young man, sustained by practising his exercise, and by constantly furbishing up his regulation plume (it is unnecessary to observe that, as a hatter, he is in a cock's-feather corps), is resigned, and uncomplaining. On a Saturday, when he closes early and gets his knickerbockers on, he is even cheerful. I am gratefully particular in this reference to him, because he is my companion through many peaceful hours. My hatter has a desk up certain steps behind his counter, enclosed like the clerk's desk at Church. I shut myself into this place of seclusion, after breakfast, and meditate. At such times, I observe the young man loading an imaginary rifle with the greatest precision, and maintaining a most galling and destructive fire upon the national enemy. I thank him publicly for his companionship and his patriotism.

The simple character of my life, and the calm nature of the scenes by which I am surrounded, occasion me to rise early. I go forth in my slippers, and promenade the pavement. It is pastoral to feel the freshness of the air in the uninhabited town, and to appreciate the shepherdess character of the few milkwomen who purvey so little milk that it would be worth nobody's while to adulterate it, if anybody were left to undertake the task. On the crowded sea-shore, the great demand for milk, combined with the strong local temptation of chalk, would betray itself in the lowered quality of the article. In Arcadian London, I derive it from the cow.

The Arcadian simplicity of the metropolis altogether, and the primitive ways into which it has fallen in this autumnal Golden Age, make it entirely new to me. Within a few hundred yards of my retreat, is the house of a friend who maintains a most sumptuous butler. I never, until yesterday, saw that butler out of superfine black broadcloth. Until yesterday, I never saw him off duty, never saw him (he is the best of butlers) with the appearance of having any mind for anything but the glory of his master and his master's friends. Yesterday morning, walking in my slippers near the house of which he is the prop and ornament – a house now a waste of shutters – I encountered that butler, also in his slippers, and in a shooting suit of one colour, and in a low-crowned straw hat, smoking an early cigar. He felt that we had formerly met in another state of existence, and that we were translated into a new sphere. Wisely and well, he passed me without recognition. Under his arm he carried the morning paper, and shortly afterwards I saw him sitting on a rail in the pleasant open landscape of Regent-street, perusing it at his ease under the ripening sun.

My landlord having taken his whole establishment to be salted down, I am waited on by an elderly woman labouring under a chronic sniff, who, at the shadowy hour of half-past nine o'clock of every evening, gives admittance at the street door to a meagre and mouldy old man whom I have never yet seen detached from a flat pint of beer in a pewter pot. The meagre and mouldy old man is her husband, and the pair have a dejected consciousness that they are not justified in appearing on the surface of the earth. They come out of some hole when London empties itself, and go in again when it fills. I saw them arrive on the evening when I myself took possession, and they arrived with the flat pint of beer, and their bed in a bundle. The old man is a weak old man, and appeared to me to get the bed down the kitchen stairs by tumbling down with and upon it. They make their bed in the lowest and remotest corner of the basement, and they smell of bed, and have no possession but bed: unless it be (which I rather infer from an under-current of flavour in them) cheese. I know their name, through the chance of having called the wife's attention, at half-past nine on the second evening of our acquaintance, to the circumstance of there being someone at the house door; when she apologetically explained, 'It's on'y Mister Klem.' What becomes of Mr Klem all day, or when he goes out, or why, is a mystery I cannot penetrate; but at half-past nine he never fails to turn up on the door-step with the flat pint of beer. And the pint of beer, flat as it is, is so much more important than himself, that it always seems to my fancy as if it had found him drivelling in the street and had humanely brought him home. In making his way below, Mr Klem never goes down the middle of the passage, like another Christian, but shuffles against the wall as if entreating me to take notice that he is occupying as little space as possible in the house; and whenever I come upon him face to face, he backs from me in fascinated confusion. The most extraordinary circumstance I have traced in connexion with this aged couple, is, that there is a Miss Klem, their daughter, apparently ten years older than either of them, who has also a bed and smells of it, and carries it about the earth at dusk and hides it in deserted houses. I came into this piece of knowledge through Mrs Klem's beseeching me to sanction the sheltering of Miss Klem under that roof for a single night, 'between her takin' care of the upper part of a 'ouse in Pall Mall which the family of his back, and another 'ouse in Serjameses-street, which the family of leaves towng termorrer.' I gave my gracious consent (having nothing that I know of to do with it), and in the shadowy hours Miss Klem became perceptible on the door-step, wrestling with a bed in a bundle. Where she made it up for the night I cannot positively state, but, I think, in a sink. I know that with the instinct of a reptile or an insect, she stowed it and herself away in deep obscurity. In the Klem family, I have noticed another remarkable gift of nature, and that is a power they possess of converting everything into flue. Such broken victuals as they take by stealth, appear (whatever the nature of the viands) invariably to generate flue; and even the nightly pint of beer, instead of assimilating naturally, strikes me as breaking out in that form, equally on the shabby gown of Mrs Klem, and the threadbare coat of her husband.

Mrs Klem has no idea of my name – as to Mr Klem, he has no idea of anything – and only knows me as her good gentleman. Thus, if doubtful whether I am in my room or no, Mrs Klem taps at the door and says, 'Is my good gentleman here?' Or, if a messenger desiring to see me were consistent with my solitude, she would show him in with 'Here is my good gentleman.' I find this to be a generic custom. For, I meant to have observed before now, that in its Arcadian time all my part of London is indistinctly pervaded by the Klem species. They creep about with beds, and go to bed in miles of deserted houses. They hold no companionship, except that sometimes, after dark, two of them will emerge from opposite houses, and meet in the middle of the road as on neutral ground, or will peep from adjoining houses over an interposing barrier of area railings, and compare a few reserved mistrustful notes respecting their good ladies or good gentlemen. This I have discovered in the course of various solitary rambles I have taken Northward from my retirement, along the awful perspectives of Wimpole-street, Harley-street, and similar frowning regions. Their effect would be scarcely distinguishable from that of the primeval forests, but for the Klem stragglers; these may be dimly observed, when the heavy shadows fall, flitting to and fro, putting up the door-chain, taking in the pint of beer, lowering like phantoms at the dark parlour windows, or secretly consorting underground with the dust-bin and the water cistern.

In the Burlington Arcade, I observe, with peculiar pleasure, a primitive state of manners to have superseded the baneful influences of ultra civilisation. Nothing can surpass the innocence of the ladies' shoe-shops, the artificial flower repositories, and the head-dress depôts. They are in strange hands at this time of the year – hands of unaccustomed persons, who are imperfectly acquainted with the prices of the goods, and contemplate them with unsophisticated delight and wonder. The children of these virtuous people exchange familiarities in the Arcade, and temper the asperity of the two tall beadles. Their youthful prattle blends in an unwonted manner with the harmonious shade of the scene, and the general effect is, as of the voices of birds in a grove. In this happy restoration of the golden time, it has been my privilege even to see the bigger beadle's wife. She brought him his dinner in a basin, and he ate it in his arm-chair, and afterwards fell asleep like a satiated child. At Mr Truefitt's , the excellent hairdresser's, they are learning French to beguile the time; and even the few solitaries left on guard at Mr Atkinson's, the perfumer's round the corner (generally the most inexorable gentleman in London, and the most scornful of three-and-sixpence), condescend a

little as they drowsily bide or recal their turn for chasing the ebbing
Neptune on the ribbed sea-sand. From Messrs Hunt and Roskell's, the
jewellers, all things are absent but the precious stones, and the gold and
silver, and the soldierly pensioner at the door with his decorated breast.
I might stand night and day, for a month to come, in Saville-row, with
my tongue out, yet not find a doctor to look at it for love or money. The
dentists' instruments are rusting in their drawers, and their horrible cool
parlours, where people pretend to read the Every-Day Book and not to
be afraid, are doing penance for their grimness in white sheets. The
light-weight of shrewd appearance, with one eye always shut up, as if he
were eating a sharp gooseberry in all seasons, who usually stands at the
gateway of the livery stables on very little legs under a very large
waistcoat, has gone to Doncaster. Of such undesigning aspect is his
guileless Yard now, with its gravel and scarlet beans, and the yellow
Break housed under a glass roof in a corner, that I almost believe I could
not be taken in there, if I tried. In the places of business of the great
tailors, the cheval-glasses are dim and dusty for lack of being looked into.
Ranges of brown paper coat and waistcoat bodies look as funereal as if
they were the hatchments of the customers with whose names they are
inscribed; the measuring tapes hang idle on the wall; the order-taker, left
on the hopeless chance of someone looking in, yawns in the last extremity
over the books of patterns, as if he were trying to read that entertaining
library. The hotels in Brook-street have no one in them, and the staffs
of servants stare disconsolately for next season out of all the windows.
The very man who goes about like an erect Turtle, between two boards
recommendatory of the Sixteen Shilling Trousers, is aware of himself as
a hollow mockery, and eats filberts while he leans his hinder shell against
a wall.

Among these tranquillising objects, it is my delight to walk and
meditate. Soothed by the repose around me, I wander insensibly to
considerable distances, and guide myself back by the stars. Thus, I enjoy
the contrast of a few still partially inhabited and busy spots where all the
lights are not fled, where all the garlands are not dead, whence all but I
have not departed. Then, does it appear to me that in this age
three things are clamorously required of Man in the miscellaneous
thoroughfares of the metropolis. Firstly, that he have his boots cleaned.
Secondly, that he eat a penny ice. Thirdly, that he get himself photographed. Then do I speculate, What have those seam-worn artists been
who stand at the photograph doors in Greek caps, sample in hand, and
mysteriously salute the public – the female public with a pressing
tenderness – to come in and be 'took'? What did they do with their
greasy blandishments, before the era of cheap photography? Of what
class were their previous victims, and how victimised? And how did they

get, and how did they pay for, that large collection of likenesses, all purporting to have been taken inside, with the taking of none of which had that establishment any more to do than with the taking of Delhi?

But these are small oases, and I am soon back again in metropolitan Arcadia. It is my impression that much of its serene and peaceful character is attributable to the absence of customary Talk. How do I know but there may be subtle influences in Talk, to vex the souls of men who don't hear it? How do I know but that Talk, five, ten, twenty miles off, may get into the air and disagree with me? If I get up, vaguely troubled and wearied and sick of my life, in the session of Parliament, who shall say that my noble friend, my right reverend friend, my right honourable friend, my honourable friend, my honourable and learned friend, or my honourable and gallant friend, may not be responsible for that effect upon my nervous system? Too much Ozone in the air, I am informed and fully believe (though I have no idea what it is), would affect me in a marvellously disagreeable way; why may not too much Talk? I don't see or hear the Ozone; I don't see or hear the Talk. And there is so much Talk; so much too much; such loud cry, and such scant supply of wool; such a deal of fleecing, and so little fleece! Hence, in the Arcadian season, I find it a delicious triumph to walk down to deserted Westminster, and see the Courts shut up; to walk a little further, and see the Two Houses shut up; to stand in the Abbey Yard, like the New Zealander of the grand English History (concerning which unfortunate man a whole rookery of mares' nests is generally being discovered), and gloat upon the ruins of Talk. Returning to my primitive solitude and lying down to sleep, my grateful heart expands with the consciousness that there is no adjourned Debate, no ministerial explanation, nobody to give notice of intention to ask the noble Lord at the head of her Majesty's Government five-and-twenty bootless questions in one, no term time with legal argument, no Nisi Prius with eloquent appeal to British Jury; that the air will tomorrow, and tomorrow, and tomorrow, remain untroubled by this superabundant generating of Talk. In a minor degree it is a delicious triumph to me to go into the club, and see the carpets up, and the Bores and the other dust dispersed to the four winds. Again New Zealander-like, I stand on the cold hearth, and say in the solitude, 'Here I watched Bore A 1, with voice always mysteriously low and head always mysteriously drooped, whispering political secrets into the ears of Adam's confiding children. Accursed be his memory for ever and a day!'

But I have all this time been coming to the point, that the happy nature of my retirement is most sweetly expressed in its being the abode of Love. It is, as it were, an inexpensive Agapemone: nobody's speculation: everybody's profit. The one great result of the resumption of primitive habits, and (convertible terms) the not having much to do, is, the abounding of Love.

The Klem species are incapable of the softer emotions; probably, in that low nomadic race, the softer emotions have all degenerated into flue. But with this exception, all the sharers of my retreat make love.

I have mentioned Saville-row. We all know the Doctor's servant. We all know what a respectable man he is, what a hard dry man, what a firm man, what a confidential man: how he lets us into the waiting-room, like a man who knows minutely what is the matter with us, but from whom the rack should not wring the secret. In the prosaic 'season,' he has distinctly the appearance of a man conscious of money in the savings bank, and taking his stand on his respectability with both feet. At that time it is as impossible to associate him with relaxation, or any human weakness, as it is to meet his eye without feeling guilty of indisposition. In the blest Arcadian time, how changed! I have seen him in a pepper-and-salt jacket − jacket − and drab trousers, with his arm round the waist of a bootmaker's housemaid, smiling in open day. I have seen him at the pump by the Albany, unsolicitedly pumping for two fair young creatures, whose figures as they bent over their cans, were − if I may be allowed an original expression − a model for a sculptor. I have seen him trying the piano in the Doctor's drawing-room with his forefinger, and have heard him humming tunes in praise of lovely woman. I have seen him seated on a fire-engine, and going (obviously in search of excitement) to a fire. I saw him, one moonlight evening when the peace and purity of our Arcadian west were at their height, polk with the lovely daughter of a cleaner of gloves, from the door-steps of his own residence, across Saville-row, round by Clifford-street and Old Burlington-street, back to Burlington-gardens. Is this the Golden Age revived, or Iron London?

The Dentist's servant. Is that man no mystery to us, no type of invisible power? The tremendous individual knows (who else does?) what is done with the extracted teeth; he knows what goes on in the little room where something is always being washed or filed; he knows what warm spicy infusion is put into the comfortable tumbler from which we rinse our wounded mouth, with a gap in it that feels a foot wide; he knows whether the thing we spit into is a fixture communicating with the Thames, or could be cleared away for a dance; he sees the horrible parlour when there are no patients in it, and he could reveal, if he would, what becomes of the Every-Day Book then. The conviction of my coward conscience when I see that man in a professional light, is, that he knows all the statistics of my teeth and gums, my double teeth, my single teeth, my stopped teeth, and my sound. In this Arcadian rest, I am fearless of him as of a harmless powerless creature in a Scotch cap, who adores a young lady in a voluminous crinoline, at a neighbouring billiard-room, and whose passion would be uninfluenced if every one of her teeth were false. They may be. He takes them all on trust.

In secluded corners of the place of my seclusion, there are little shops withdrawn from public curiosity, and never two together, where servants' perquisites are bought. The cook may dispose of grease at these modest and convenient marts; the butler, of bottles; the valet and lady's maid, of clothes; most servants, indeed, of most things they may happen to lay hold of. I have been told that in sterner times loving correspondence otherwise interdicted may be maintained by letter through the agency of some of these useful establishments. In the Arcadian autumn, no such device is necessary. Everybody loves, and openly and blamelessly loves. My landlord's young man loves the whole of one side of the way of old Bond-street, and is beloved several doors up new Bond-street besides. I never look out of window but I see kissing of hands going on all around me. It is the morning custom to glide from shop to shop, and exchange tender sentiments; it is the evening custom for couples to stand hand in hand at house doors, or roam, linked in that flowery manner, through the unpeopled streets. There is nothing else to do but love; and what there is to do, is done.

In unison with this pursuit, a chaste simplicity obtains in the domestic habits of Arcadia. Its few scattered people dine early, live moderately, sup socially, and sleep soundly. It is rumoured that the Beadles of the Arcade, from being the mortal enemies of boys, have signed with tears an address to Lord Shaftesbury, and subscribed to a ragged school. No wonder! For they might turn their heavy maces into crooks and tend sheep in the Arcade, to the purling of the water-carts as they give the thirsty streets much more to drink than they can carry.

A happy Golden Age, and a serene tranquillity. Charming picture, but it will fade. The iron age will return; London will come back to town. If I show my tongue then in Saville-row for half a minute, I shall be prescribed for, the Doctor's man and the Dentist's man will then pretend that these days of unprofessional innocence never existed. Where Mr and Mrs Klem and their bed will be, at that time, passes human knowledge; but my hatter hermitage will then know them no more, nor will it then know me. The desk at which I have written these meditations will retributively assist at the making out of my account, and the wheels of gorgeous carriages and the hoofs of high-stepping horses will crush the silence out of Bond-street – will grind Arcadia away, and give it to the elements in granite powder.

20

The Uncommercial Traveller

All The Year Round, 13 October 1860 (*UT1* as 'The Italian Prisoner')

Giuseppe Mazzini, the radical leader of the Young Italy movement and joint leader of the short-lived 'Roman Republic' in 1849, spent much of his life in exile, including many years in London where he ran a school for the sons of Italian exiles in the Tottenham Court Road district (see William Roberts, *Prophet in Exile: Joseph Mazzini in England, 1837–1868* [1989], pp. 6–7). Dickens, as Forster records, was 'brought into contact with the great Italian by having given money to a begging impostor who made unauthorised use of his name' (*Forster*, Book 6, Ch. 6), and their subsequent friendship strengthened Dickens's support for the Italians in their struggle for freedom from what he saw as the twin evils of tyranny and priestcraft. In August 1849, on learning of Mazzini's safe escape after the re-taking of Rome, Dickens drafted an 'Appeal to the English People on Behalf of the Italian Refugees' for the national Italian Appeal Committee, which was published in various newspapers and *The Examiner* of 8 September (see *The Dickensian*, Vol. 10 [1914], p. 320ff.). Following the founding of *HW*, Dickens used the platform of his own journals to support Mazzini's cause: between June 1859 and the date of the present article, for example, he published over thirty papers in *ATYR* concerning the latest stages of the fight for Unification, or illustrating aspects of Italian and Piedmontese national life and character (see Oppenlander, under Gallenga, A., and Fitzgerald, P.). In the present article Dickens writes with strong feelings and seems to abandon the 'Uncommercial' persona in order to relate what is said to be 'strictly a true story' from the period of his Italian travels and residence in 1844–5. The 'gentle English nobleman' is Lord Dudley Coutts Stuart, MP, a cousin of Angela Burdett Coutts, whose wife, Christine Bonaparte, had grown up in the papal principate of Canino. The couple therefore had extensive connections in Italy. 'Giovanni Carlavero' is a certain Sanvanero, about whom little is known, but whose story generally resembles that of Carlo Poerio, another political prisoner famously helped to freedom in 1859 through Gladstone's intercession. Dickens's correspondence shows that he did indeed carry a bottle of wine as a memento from Sanvanero to Lord Dudley, but reveals a certain amount of artistic licence taken with its dimensions in the present item: 'My Dear Lord Dudley. Behold Sanvanero's little Bottle of Wine! His whole heart is in it, I am certain' (*Pilgrim*, Vol. IV [24 July 1845], p. 335 & n.). Dickens seems to have completed this paper in late September 1860, writing to Wills on the 26th that '[t]he No. is made up, and the Uncommercial is in, and all is right' (*Pilgrim*, Vol. IX, p. 319; the *Pilgrim* editors take this to refer to the composition of article 19, but this had already been printed on the day Dickens wrote).

Fuller summaries of Dickens's engagement with, and public support for, the Italian uprisings can be found in Michael Hollington's 'Dickens and Italy,' *Journal of Anglo-Italian Studies*, Vol. 1 (1991), pp. 126–36, and M. Gabriella Caponi-Doherty's 'Charles Dickens and the Italian Risorgimento', *Dickens Quarterly*, Vol. 13 (September 1996), pp. 151–63.

Literary allusions (p. 194) 'English Circumlocution': allusion to Dickens's satire on the Civil Service, the 'Circumlocution Office' in *Little Dorrit*; (p. 197) 'the Imp of the same name' (i.e. Bottle Imp): probably Asmodeus in Le Sage's *The Devil on Two Sticks* (1726), Ch. 1, described as enclosed in 'a plain glass bottle'; (p. 197) 'I might have served Mr Cruikshank as a subject for a new illustration of the miseries of the Bottle': George Cruikshank's book of cautionary engravings *The Bottle* (1847; see Vol. 2 of this edition, article 26); (p. 197) 'the apple pie in the child's book': alphabetical nursery rhyme of uncertain origin, beginning 'A was an Apple-pie' (current in the reign of Charles II, according to the editors of the *Oxford Dictionary of Nursery Rhymes*, 1951); (p. 198) 'fine old English gentleman, all of the olden time': C. H. Purday's popular song 'The Fine Old English Gentleman, All of the Olden Time'.

Textual note (p. 193) copy-text has 'and I mention the name of': *UT1* has '. . . and I mentioned the name of';' (p. 194) copy-text has 'If it continues to be neglected': *UT1* has 'If he continues to be neglected'; (p. 195) copy-text has 'Giovanni Carlavero leaped into his room': *UT1* has 'Giovanni Carlavero leaped into the room'.

The rising of the Italian people from under their unutterable wrongs, and the tardy burst of day upon them after the long long night of oppression that has darkened their beautiful country, have naturally caused my mind to dwell often of late on my own small wanderings in Italy. Connected with them, is a curious little drama, in which the character I myself sustained was so very subordinate, that I may relate its story without any fear of being suspected of self-display. It is strictly a true story.

I am newly arrived one summer evening, in a certain small town on the Mediterranean. I have had my dinner at the inn, and I and the mosquitoes are coming out into the streets together. It is far from Naples; but a bright brown plump little woman-servant at the inn, is a Neapolitan, and is so vivaciously expert in pantomimic action, that in the single moment of answering my request to have a pair of shoes cleaned which I have left upstairs, she plies imaginary brushes, and goes completely through the motions of polishing the shoes up, and laying them at my feet. I smile at the brisk little woman in perfect satisfaction with her briskness; and the brisk little woman, amiably pleased with me because I am pleased with her, claps her hands and laughs delightfully. We are in the inn yard. As the little woman's bright eyes sparkle on the cigarette I am smoking, I make bold to offer her one; she accepts it none the less merrily, because I touch a most charming little dimple in her fat cheek, with its light paper end. Glancing up at the many green lattices to assure herself that the mistress is not looking on, the little woman then puts her two little dimpled arms a-kimbo, and stands on tiptoe to light her cigarette at mine. 'And now, dear little sir,' says she, puffing out smoke in a most innocent and Cherubic manner, 'keep quite straight on, take the first to the right, and probably you will see him standing at his door.'

I have a commission to 'him,' and I have been inquiring about him. I have carried the commission about Italy, several months. Before I left England, there came to me one night a certain generous and gentle English nobleman (he is dead in these days when I relate the story, and exiles have lost their best British friend), with this request: 'Whenever you come to such a town, will you seek out one Giovanni Carlavero, who keeps a little wine-shop there, mention my name to him suddenly, and observe how it affects him?' I accepted the trust, and am on my way to discharge it.

The sirocco has been blowing all day, and it is a hot unwholesome evening with no cool sea-breeze. Mosquitoes and fire-flies are lively enough, but most other creatures are faint. The coquettish airs of pretty young women in the tiniest and wickedest of dolls' straw hats, who lean out at opened lattice blinds, are almost the only airs stirring. Very ugly and haggard old women with distaffs, and with a grey tow upon them that looks as if they were spinning out their own hair (I suppose they were once pretty, too, but it is very difficult to believe so), sit on the footway leaning against house walls. Everybody who has come for water to the fountain, stays there, and seems incapable of any such energetic idea as going home. Vespers are over, though not so long but that I can smell the heavy resinous incense as I pass the church. No man seems to be at work, save the coppersmith. In an Italian town he is always at work, and always thumping in the deadliest manner.

I keep straight on, and come in due time to the first on the right: a narrow dull street, where I see a well-favoured man of good stature and military bearing, in a great cloak, standing at a door. Drawing nearer to this threshold, I see it is the threshold of a small wine-shop; and I can just make out, in the dim light, the inscription that it is kept by Giovanni Carlavero.

I touch my hat to the figure in the cloak, and pass in, and draw a stool to a little table. The lamp (just such another as they dig out of Pompeii) is lighted, but the place is empty. The figure in the cloak has followed me in, and stands before me.

'The master?'

'At your service, sir.'

'Please to give me a glass of the wine of the country.'

He turns to a little counter, to get it. As his striking face is pale, and his action is evidently that of an enfeebled man, I remark that I fear he has been ill. It is not much, he courteously and gravely answers, though bad while it lasts: the fever.

As he sets the wine on the little table, to his manifest surprise I lay my hand on the back of his, look him in the face, and say in a low voice: 'I am an Englishman, and you are acquainted with a friend of mine. Do you recollect—?' and I mention the name of my generous countryman.

Instantly, he utters a loud cry, bursts into tears, and falls on his knees at my feet, clasping my legs in both his arms and bowing his head to the ground.

Some years ago, this man at my feet, whose overfraught heart is heaving as if it would burst from his breast, and whose tears are wet upon the dress I wear, was a galley-slave in the North of Italy. He was a political offender, having been concerned in the then last rising, and was sentenced to imprisonment for life. That he would have died in his chains is certain, but for the circumstance that the Englishman happened to visit his prison.

It was one of the vile old prisons of Italy, and a part of it was below the waters of the harbour. The place of his confinement was an arched underground and under-water gallery, with a grill-gate at the entrance, through which it received such light and air as it got. Its condition was insufferably foul, and a stranger could hardly breathe in it, or see in it with the aid of a torch. At the upper end of this dungeon, and consequently in the worst position, as being the furthest removed from light and air, the Englishman first beheld him, sitting on an iron bedstead to which he was chained by a heavy chain. His countenance impressed the Englishman as having nothing in common with the faces of the malefactors with whom he was associated, and he talked with him, and learnt how he came to be there.

When the Englishman emerged from the dreadful den into the light of day, he asked his conductor, the governor of the gaol, why Giovanni Carlavero was put into the worst place?

'Because he is particularly recommended,' was the stringent answer.

'Recommended, that is to say, for death?'

'Excuse me; particularly recommended,' was again the answer.

'He has a bad tumour in his neck, no doubt occasioned by the hardship of his miserable life. If it continues to be neglected, and he remains where he is, it will kill him.'

'Excuse me, I can do nothing. He is particularly recommended.'

The Englishman was staying in that town, and he went to his home there; but the figure of this man chained to the bedstead made it no home, and destroyed his rest and peace. He was an Englishman of an extraordinarily tender heart, and he could not bear the picture. He went back to the prison grate: went back again and again, and talked to the man and cheered him. He used his utmost influence to get the man unchained from the bedstead, were it only for ever so short a time in the day, and permitted to come to the grate. It took a long time, but the Englishman's station, personal character, and steadiness of purpose, wore out opposition so far, and that grace was at last accorded. Through the bars, when he could thus get light upon the tumour, the Englishman lanced it, and it did well, and healed. His strong interest in the prisoner had greatly increased by this time, and he formed the desperate resolution that he would exert his utmost self-devotion and use his utmost efforts, to get Carlavero pardoned.

If the prisoner had been a brigand and a murderer, if he had committed every non-political crime in the Newgate Calendar and out of it, nothing would have been easier than for a man of any court or priestly influence to obtain his release. As it was, nothing could have been more difficult. Italian authorities, and English authorities who had interest with them, alike assured the Englishman that his object was hopeless. He met with nothing but evasion, refusal, and ridicule. His political prisoner became a joke in the place. It was especially observable that English Circumlocution, and English Society on its travels, were as humorous on the subject as Circumlocution and Society may be on any subject without loss of caste. But, the Englishman possessed (and proved it well in his life) a courage very uncommon among us: he had not the least fear of being considered a bore, in a good humane cause. So he went on persistently trying, and trying, and trying, to get Giovanni Carlavero out. That prisoner had been rigorously re-chained, after the tumour operation, and it was not likely that his miserable life could last very long.

One day, when all the town knew about the Englishman and his political prisoner, there came to the Englishman, a certain sprightly Italian Advocate of whom he had some knowledge; and he made this strange proposal. 'Give me a hundred pounds to obtain Carlavero's release. I think I can get him a pardon, with that money. But I cannot tell you what I am going to do with the money, nor must you ever ask me the question if I succeed, nor must you ever ask me for an account of the money if I fail.' The Englishman decided to hazard the hundred pounds. He did so, and heard not another word of the matter. For half a year and more, the Advocate made no sign, and never once 'took on' in any way, to have the subject on his mind. The Englishman was then obliged to change his residence to another and more famous town in the North of Italy. He parted from the poor prisoner with a sorrowful heart, as from a doomed man for whom there was no release but Death.

The Englishman lived in his new place of abode another half-year and more, and had no tidings of the wretched prisoner. At length, one day, he received from the Advocate a cool concise mysterious note, to this effect. 'If you still wish to bestow that benefit upon the man in whom you were once interested, send me fifty pounds more, and I think it can be ensured.' Now, the Englishman had long settled in his mind that the Advocate was a heartless sharper, who had preyed upon his credulity and his interest in an unfortunate sufferer. So, he sat down and wrote a dry answer, giving the Advocate to understand that he was wiser now than he had been formerly, and that no more money was extractable from his pocket.

He lived outside the city gates, some mile or two from the post-office, and was accustomed to walk into the city with his letters and post them himself. On a lovely spring day, when the sky was exquisitely blue, and the sea Divinely beautiful, he took his usual walk, carrying this letter to the Advocate in his pocket. As he went along, his gentle heart was much moved by the loveliness of the prospect, and by the thought of the slowly-dying prisoner chained to the bedstead, for whom the universe had no delights. As he drew nearer and nearer to the city where he was to post the letter, he became very uneasy in his mind. He debated with himself, was it remotely possible, after all, that this sum of fifty pounds could restore the fellow-creature whom he pitied so much, and for whom he had striven so hard, to liberty? He was not a conventionally rich Englishman – very far from that – but he had a spare fifty pounds at the banker's. He resolved to risk it. Without doubt, GOD has re-compensed him for the resolution.

He went to the banker's, and got a bill for the amount, and enclosed it in a letter to the Advocate that I wish I could have seen. He simply told the Advocate that he was quite a poor man, and that he was sensible it might be a great weakness in him to part with so much money on the faith of so vague a communication; but that there it was, and that he prayed the Advocate to make good use of it. If he did otherwise no good could ever come of it, and it would lie heavy on his soul one day.

Within a week, the Englishman was sitting at his breakfast, when he heard some suppressed sounds of agitation on the staircase, and Giovanni Carlavero leaped into his room and fell upon his breast, a free man!

Conscious of having wronged the Advocate in his own thoughts, the Englishman wrote him an earnest and grateful letter, avowing the fact, and entreating him to confide by what means and through what agency he had succeeded so well. The Advocate returned for answer through the post, 'There are many things, as you know, in this Italy of ours, that are safest and best not even spoken of – far less written of. We may meet some day, and then I may tell you what you want to know; not here, and now.' But, the two never did meet again. The Advocate was dead when the Englishman gave me my trust; and how the man had been set free, remained as great a mystery to the Englishman, and to the man himself, as it was to me.

But, I knew this: – here was the man, this sultry night, on his knees at my feet, because I was the Englishman's friend; here were his tears upon my dress; here were his sobs choking his utterance; here were his kisses on my hands, because they had touched the hands that had worked out his release. He had no need to tell me it would be happiness to him to die for his benefactor; I doubt if I ever saw real, sterling, fervent gratitude of soul, before or since.

He was much watched and suspected, he said, and had had enough to do to keep himself out of trouble. This, and his not having prospered in his worldly affairs, had led to his having failed in his usual communications to the Englishman for – as I now remember the period – some two or three years. But, his prospects were brighter, and his wife, who had been very ill had recovered, and his fever had left him, and he had bought a little vineyard, and would I carry to his benefactor the first of its wine? Ay, that I would (I told him with enthusiasm), and not a drop of it should be spilled or lost!

He had cautiously closed the door before speaking of himself, and had talked with such excess of emotion, and in a provincial Italian so difficult to understand, that I had more than once been obliged to stop him, and beg him to have compassion on me and be slower and calmer. By degrees he became so, and tranquilly walked back with me to the hotel. There, I sat down before I went to bed, and wrote a faithful account of him to the Englishman: which I concluded by saying that I would bring the wine home, against any difficulties, every drop.

Early next morning when I came out at the hotel door to pursue my journey, I found my friend waiting with one of those immense bottles in which the Italian peasants store their wine – a bottle holding some half-dozen gallons – bound round with basket-work for greater safety on the journey. I see him now, in the bright sunlight, tears of gratitude in his eyes, proudly inviting my attention to this corpulent bottle. (At the street corner hard by, two high-flavoured able-bodied monks – pretending to talk together, but keeping their four evil eyes upon us.)

How the bottle had been got there, did not appear; but the difficulty of getting it into the ramshackle vetturino carriage in which I was departing, was so great, and it took up so much room when it was got in, that I elected to sit outside. The last I saw of Giovanni Carlavero was his running through the town by the side of the jingling wheels, clasping my hand as I stretched it down from the box, charging me with a thousand last loving and dutiful messages to his dear patron, and finally looking in at the bottle as it reposed inside, with an admiration of its honourable way of travelling that was beyond measure delightful.

And now, what disquiet of mind this dearly-beloved and highly-treasured Bottle began to cost me, no man knows. It was my precious charge through a long tour, and, for hundreds of miles, I never had it off my mind by day or by night. Over bad roads – and they were many – I clung to it with affectionate desperation. Up mountains, I looked in at it and saw it helplessly tilting over on its back, with terror. At innumerable inn doors when the weather was bad, I was obliged to be put into my vehicle before the Bottle could be got in, and was obliged to have the Bottle lifted out before human aid could come near me. The Imp of the same name, except that his associations were all evil and these associations were all good, would have been a less troublesome travelling companion. I might have served Mr Cruikshank as a subject for a new illustration of the miseries of the Bottle. The National Temperance Society might have made a powerful Tract of me.

The suspicions that attached to this innocent Bottle, greatly aggravated my difficulties. It was like the apple-pie in the child's book. Parma pouted at it, Modena mocked it, Tuscany tackled it, Naples nibbled it, Rome refused it, Austria accused it, Soldiers suspected it, Jesuits jobbed it. I composed a neat Oration, developing my inoffensive intentions in connexion with this Bottle, and delivered it in an infinity of guard-houses, at a multitude of town gates, and on every drawbridge, angle, and rampart, of a complete system of fortifications. Fifty times a day, I got down to harangue an infuriated soldiery about the Bottle. Through the filthy degradation of the abject and vile Roman States, I had as much difficulty in working my way with the Bottle, as if it had bottled up a complete system of heretical theology. In the Neapolitan country, where everybody was a spy, a soldier, a priest, or a lazzarone, the shameless beggars of all four denominations incessantly pounced on the Bottle and made it a pretext for extorting money from me. Quires – quires do I say? Reams – of forms illegibly printed on whity-brown paper were filled up about the Bottle, and it was the subject of more stamping and sanding than I had ever seen before. In consequence of which haze of sand, perhaps, it was always irregular, and always latent with dismal penalties of going back, or not going forward, which were only to be abated by the silver crossing of a base hand, poked shirtless out of a ragged uniform sleeve. Under all discouragements, however, I stuck to my Bottle, and held firm to my resolution that every drop of its contents should reach the Bottle's destination.

The latter refinement cost me a separate heap of troubles on its own separate account. What corkscrews did I see the military power bring out against that Bottle: what gimlets, spikes, divining rods, gauges, and unknown tests and instruments! At some places, they persisted in declaring that the wine must not be passed, without being opened and tasted; I, pleading to the contrary, used then to argue the question seated on the Bottle lest they should open it in spite of me. In the southern parts of Italy, more violent shrieking, face-making, and gesticulating, greater vehemence of speech and countenance and action, went on about that Bottle than would attend fifty murders in a northern latitude. It raised important functionaries out of their beds, in the dead of night. I have known half a dozen military lanterns to disperse themselves at all points of a great sleeping Piazza, each lantern summoning some official creature to get up, put on his cocked-hat instantly, and come and stop the Bottle. It was characteristic that while this innocent Bottle had such immense difficulty in getting from little town to town, Signor Mazzini and the fiery cross were traversing Italy from end to end.

Still, I stuck to my Bottle, like any fine old English gentleman all of the olden time. The more the Bottle was interfered with, the stauncher I became (if possible) in my first determination that my countryman should have it delivered to him intact, as the man whom he had so nobly restored to life and liberty had delivered it to me. If ever I had been obstinate in my days – and I may have been, say, once or twice – I was obstinate about the Bottle. But, I made it a rule always to keep a pocket full of small coin at its service, and never to be out of temper in its cause. Thus I and the Bottle made our way. Once, we had a break-down; rather a bad break-down, on a steep high place with the sea below us, on a tempestuous evening when it blew great guns. We were driving four wild horses abreast, Southern fashion, and there was some little difficulty in stopping them. I was outside, and not thrown off; but no words can describe my feelings when I saw the Bottle – travelling inside, as usual – burst the door open, and roll obesely out into the road. A blessed Bottle with a charmed existence, he took no hurt, and we repaired damage, and went on triumphant.

A thousand representations were made to me that the Bottle must be left at this place, or that, and called for again. I never yielded to one of them, and never parted from the Bottle, on any pretence, consideration, threat, or entreaty. I had no faith in any official receipt for the Bottle, and nothing would induce me to accept one. These unmanageable politics at last brought me and the Bottle, still triumphant, to Genoa. There, I took a tender and reluctant leave of him for a few weeks, and consigned him to a trusty English captain, to be conveyed to the Port of London by sea.

While the Bottle was on his voyage to England, I read the Shipping Intelligence as anxiously as if I had been an underwriter. There was some stormy weather after I myself had got to England by way of Switzerland and France, and my mind greatly misgave me that the Bottle might be wrecked. At last to my great joy, I received notice of his safe arrival, and immediately went down to Saint Katharine's Docks, and found him in a state of honourable captivity in the Custom House.

The wine was mere vinegar when I set it down before the generous Englishman — probably it had been something like vinegar when I took it up from Giovanni Carlavero — but not a drop of it was spilled or gone. And the Englishman told me, with much emotion in his face and voice, that he had never tasted wine that seemed to him so sweet and sound. And long afterwards, the Bottle graced his table. And the last time I saw him in this world that misses him, he took me aside in a crowd, to say, with his amiable smile: 'We were talking of you only today at dinner, and I wished you had been there, for I had some claret up in Carlavero's Bottle.'

Following the publication of the above article, Dickens temporarily stopped contributing 'Uncommercial Traveller' papers in order to concentrate on writing the weekly instalments of *Great Expectations*, which commenced publication in *ATYR* on 1 December (see To Forster, *Pilgrim*, Vol. IX, pp. 319–20 & n.). The sixteen essays and the introductory profile which had already appeared were quickly collected up for publication, and the first volume editions appeared in Leipzig (published by Tauchnitz) on 13 December and London (Chapman & Hall) on 15 December. Dickens commented in his short Preface that '... the Series is, for the time, complete ... [but] it is the Uncommercial Traveller's intention to take to the road again before another winter sets in'. The demands of his new novel, long series of public readings in the provinces and in London, and a multitude of other pressing commitments, meant that it would be over two and a half years before his 'uncommercial' travels were resumed. See article 23.

21

An Enlightened Clergyman

All The Year Round, 8 March 1862

The Rev. Coles's pompously sanctimonious letter, reproduced below, was, like the literary snobbery of the gentility of Eye, symptomatic of attitudes towards both literature and religion that Dickens had always detested, and we can feel the relish behind his promise to the correspondent who sent him the Vicar's letter when he says that he will 'give the reverend gentleman a large audience for his composition' (*Pilgrim*, Vol. X, p.36).

Literary allusions (below) 'a tale ... from the last Christmas Number': the 1861 Christmas Number of *ATYR* followed a similar format to that of its predecessors, i.e., a framework story provided by Dickens ('Tom Tiddler's Ground') for the introduction of subsidiary stories by various hands; (below) 'the taste and musical glasses of that important town': Ch. 9 of Goldsmith's *The Vicar of Wakefield* (1766) introduces into the Vicar's circle two fashionable young ladies who 'would talk of nothing but high life ... with other fashionable topics, such as pictures, taste, Shakespeare and the musical glasses'; (below) 'he covered his face with his robe, previous to dying decently ...': alludes to the death of Julius Caesar as represented in Shakespeare's play.

At various places in Suffolk (as elsewhere) penny readings take place 'for the instruction and amusement of the lower classes.' There is a little town in Suffolk called Eye, where the subject of one of these readings was a tale (by Mr Wilkie Collins) from the last Christmas Number of this Journal, entitled 'Picking up Waifs at Sea.' It appears that the Eye gentility was shocked by the introduction of this rude piece among the taste and musical glasses of that important town, on which the eyes of Europe are notoriously always fixed. In particular, the feelings of the vicar's family were outraged; and a Local Organ (say, the Tattlesnivel Bleater) consequently doomed the said piece to everlasting oblivion, as being of an 'injurious tendency'!

When this fearful fact came to the knowledge of the unhappy writer of the doomed tale in question, he covered his face with his robe, previous to dying decently under the sharp steel of the ecclesiastical gentility of the terrible town of Eye. But the discovery that he was not alone in his gloomy glory, revived him, and he still lives.

For, at Stowmarket, in the aforesaid county of Suffolk, at another of those penny readings, it was announced that a certain juvenile sketch, culled from a volume of sketches (by Boz) and entitled THE BLOOMSBURY CHRISTENING, would be read. Hereupon, the clergyman of that place took heart and pen, and addressed the following terrific epistle to a gentleman bearing the very appropriate name of Gudgeon:

Stowmarket Vicarage, Feb. 25, 1861.

SIR,—My attention has been directed to a piece called the Bloomsbury Christening which you propose to read this evening. Without presuming to claim any interference in the arrangement of the readings, I would suggest to you whether you have on this occasion sufficiently considered the character of the composition you have selected. I quite appreciate the laudable motive of the promoters of the readings to raise the moral tone amongst the working class of the town and to direct this taste in a familiar and pleasant manner. The Bloomsbury Christening cannot possibly do this. It trifles with a sacred ordinance, and the language and style, instead of improving the taste, has a direct tendency to lower it.

I appeal to your right feeling whether it is desirable to give publicity to that which must shock several of your audience, and create a smile amongst others, to be indulged in only by violating the conscientious scruples of their neighbours.

The ordinance which is here exposed to ridicule is one which is much misunderstood and neglected amongst many families belonging to the Church of England, and the mode in which it is treated in this chapter cannot fail to appear as giving a sanction to, or at least excusing, such neglect.

Although you are pledged to the public to give this subject, yet I cannot but believe that they would fully justify your substitution of it for another did they know the circumstances. An abridgment would only lessen the evil in a degree, as it is not only the style of the writing but the subject itself which is objectionable.

Excuse me for troubling you, but I felt that, in common with yourself, I have a grave responsibility in the matter, and I am most truly yours,

T. S. COLES.

To Mr J. Gudgeon.

It is really necessary to explain that this is not a bad joke. It is simply a bad fact.

22

Rather a Strong Dose

All The Year Round, 21 March 1863

Dickens had more than once publicly ridiculed the Spiritualist movement and the craze for seances and table-rapping that was exported from America to Britain in the early 1850s (see article 62, 'Well-authenticated Rappings' [*HW*, 20 February 1858], in Vol. 3 of this edition). In 1859 the miscellaneous writer and former contributor to *HW*, William Howitt, a Quaker who had become a fervent Spiritualist, 'rapper' and believer in ghosts, tried to embroil Dickens in controversy about the existence or otherwise of genuinely haunted houses. Dickens, accompanied by Wilkie Collins, W. H. Wills and John Hollingshead, actually went to investigate one supposedly haunted house (an episode referred to in this article) and could find no local corroboration of its having any reputation for being haunted. Meanwhile, he had further annoyed Howitt by his comic use of the idea of a supposedly haunted house to construct the framework for the 1859 Christmas Number of *ATYR* in which he heaped further ridicule on the Spiritualists. Despite all this, *The Spiritual Magazine* continued to pursue Dickens, hoping to convert him, and even had the hardihood to claim that he was turning *ATYR* into 'a deputy Spiritual Magazine' by publishing a series of ghost stories as well as Bulwer Lytton's tale of the supernatural, *A Strange Story* (see p. 82 of Noel C. Peyrouton's splendidly informative two-part article 'Rapping the Rappers: More Grist for the Biographers' Mill', *The Dickensian*, Vol. 55 [1959], pp. 19–33, 75–89). With the 1863 publication of Howitt's two-volume *History of the Supernatural*, Dickens seems to have decided that he would take the opportunity to make crystal-clear, yet once more, his complete and unwavering hostility towards Spiritualism, 'rappers' and the like, hence the following article.

For details of the various individuals referred to below, see the Glossary/Index.

Literary allusions (p. 204) re Johnson, Boswell and the Cock Lane Ghost: for the passages Dickens quotes, see G. B. Hill's edition of Boswell's *Life of Dr Johnson*, revised by L. F. Powell (1934), Vol. 1, pp. 406–7 (25 June 1763), and Vol. 3, p. 268 (10 April 1778); (p. 204) 'in the words of Captain Bobadil ...': see Ben Jonson, *Every Man in His Humour* (1598), Act 4, Sc. 5; (p. 206) '(not Mrs) Harris': joking allusion to Mrs Gamp's never-visible friend in *Martin Chuzzlewit*; (p. 207) 'gnats ... camels': Matthew 23:24.

'DOCTOR JOHN CAMPBELL, the minister of the Tabernacle Chapel,

Finsbury, and editor of the British Banner, &c., with that massive vigour which distinguishes his style,' did, we are informed by Mr HOWITT, 'deliver a verdict in the Banner, for November, 1852,' of great importance and favour to the Table-rapping cause. We are not informed whether the Public, sitting in judgment on the question, reserved any point in this great verdict for subsequent consideration; but the verdict would seem to have been regarded by a perverse generation as not quite final, inasmuch as Mr Howitt finds it necessary to re-open the case, a round ten years afterwards, in nine hundred and sixty-two stiff octavo pages, published by Messrs Longman and Company.

Mr Howitt is in such a bristling temper on the Supernatural subject, that we will not take the great liberty of arguing any point with him. But – with the view of assisting him to make converts – we will inform our readers, on his conclusive authority, what they are required to believe; premising what may rather astonish them in connexion with their views of a certain historical trifle, called The Reformation, that their present state of unbelief is all the fault of Protestantism, and that 'it is high time, therefore, to protest against Protestantism.'

They will please to believe, by way of an easy beginning, all the stories of good and evil demons, ghosts, prophecies, communication with spirits, and practice of magic, that ever obtained, or are said to have ever obtained, in the North, in the South, in the East, in the West, from the earliest and darkest ages, as to which we have any hazy intelligence, real or supposititious, down to the yet unfinished displacement of the red men in North America. They will please to believe that nothing in this wise was changed by the fulfilment of Our Saviour's mission upon earth; and further, that what Saint Paul did, can be done again, and has been done again. As this is not much to begin with, they will throw in at this point rejection of FARADAY and BREWSTER, and 'poor PALEY,' and implicit acceptance of those shining lights, the Reverend CHARLES BEECHER, and the Reverend HENRY WARD BEECHER ('one of the most vigorous and eloquent preachers of America'), and the Reverend ADIN BALLOU.

Having thus cleared the way for a healthy exercise of faith, our advancing readers will next proceed especially to believe in the old story of the Drummer of Tedworth, in the inspiration of George Fox, in 'the spiritualism, prophecies, and prevision' of Huntington the coalporter (him who prayed for the leather breeches which miraculously fitted him), and even in the Cock-lane Ghost. They will please wind up, before fetching their breath, with believing that there is a close analogy between rejection of any such plain and proved facts as those contained in the whole foregoing catalogue, and the opposition encountered by the inventors of railways, lighting by gas, microscopes and telescopes, and vaccination. This stinging consideration they will always carry rankling in their remorseful hearts as they advance.

As touching the Cock-lane ghost, our conscience-stricken readers will please particularly to reproach themselves for having ever supposed that important spiritual manifestation to have been a gross imposture which was thoroughly detected. They will please to believe that Dr JOHNSON believed in it, and that, in Mr Howitt's words, he 'appears to have had excellent reasons for his belief.' With a view to this end, the faithful will be so good as to obliterate from their BOSWELLS the following passage: 'Many of my readers, I am convinced, are to this hour under an impression that Johnson was thus foolishly deceived. It will therefore surprise them a good deal when they are informed upon undoubted authority that Johnson was one of those by whom the imposture was detected. The story had become so popular, that he thought it should be investigated, and in this research he was assisted by the Rev. Dr Douglas, now Bishop of Salisbury, the great detector of impostures' – and therefore tremendously obnoxious to Mr Howitt – 'who informs me that after the gentlemen who went and examined into the evidence were satisfied of its falsity, Johnson wrote in their presence an account of it, which was published in the newspapers and Gentleman's Magazine, and undeceived the world.' But as there will still remain another highly inconvenient passage in the Boswells of the true believers, they must likewise be at the trouble of cancelling the following also, referring to a later time: 'He (Johnson) expressed great indignation at the imposture of the Cock-lane Ghost, and related with much satisfaction how he had assisted in detecting the cheat, and had published an account of it in the newspapers.'

They will next believe (if they be, in the words of Captain Bobadil, 'so generously minded') in the transatlantic trance-speakers 'who professed to speak from direct inspiration,' Mrs CORA HATCH, Mrs HENDERSON, and Miss EMMA HARDINGE; and they will believe in those eminent ladies having 'spoken on Sundays to five hundred thousand hearers' – small audiences, by the way, compared with the intelligent concourse recently assembled in the city of New York, to do honour to the Nuptials of General the Honourable T. BARNUM THUMB. At about this stage of their spiritual education, they may take the opportunity of believing in 'letters from a distinguished gentleman of New York, in which the frequent appearance of the gentleman's deceased wife and of Dr Franklin, to him and other well-known friends, are unquestionably unequalled in the annals of the marvellous.' Why these modest appearances should seem at all out of the common way to Mr Howitt (who would be in a state of flaming indignation if we thought them so), we could not imagine, until we found on reading further, 'it is solemnly stated that the witnesses have not only seen but touched these spirits, and handled the clothes and hair of Franklin.' Without presuming to go Mr Howitt's length of considering this by any means a marvellous experience, we yet venture to confess that it has awakened in our mind many interesting speculations touching the present whereabout in space, of the spirits of Mr Howitt's own departed boots and hats.

The next articles of belief are Belief in the moderate figures of 'thirty thousand media in the United States in 1853;' and in two million five hundred thousand spiritualists in the same country of composed minds, in 1855, 'professing to have arrived at their convictions of spiritual communication from personal experience;' and in 'an average rate of increase of three hundred thousand per annum,' still in the same country of calm philosophers. Belief in spiritual knockings, in all manner of American places, and, among others, in the house of 'a Doctor Phelps at Stratford, Connecticut, a man of the highest character for intelligence,' says Mr Howitt, and to whom we willingly concede the possession of far higher intelligence than was displayed by his spiritual knocker, in 'frequently cutting to pieces the clothes of one of his boys,' and in breaking 'seventy-one panes of glass' – unless, indeed, the knocker, when in the body, was connected with the tailoring and glazing interests. Belief in immaterial performers playing (in the dark though: they are obstinate about its being in the dark) on material instruments of wood, catgut, brass, tin, and parchment. Your belief is further requested in 'the Kentucky Jerks.' The spiritual achievements thus euphoniously denominated 'appear,' says Mr Howitt, 'to have been of a very disorderly kind.' It appears that a certain Mr Doke, a Presbyterian clergyman, 'was first seized by the jerks,' and the jerks laid hold of Mr Doke in that unclerical way and with that scant respect for his cloth, that they 'twitched him about in a most extraordinary manner, often when in the pulpit, and caused him to shout aloud, and run out of the pulpit into the woods, screaming like a madman. When the fit was over, he returned calmly to his pulpit and finished the service.' The congregation having waited, we presume, and edified themselves with the distant bellowings of Doke in the woods, until he came back again, a little warm and hoarse, but otherwise in fine condition, 'People were often seized at hotels, and at table would, on lifting a glass to drink, jerk the liquor to the ceiling; ladies would at the breakfast-table suddenly be compelled to throw aloft their coffee, and frequently break the cup and saucer.' A certain venturesome clergyman vowed that he would preach down the Jerks, 'but he was seized in the midst of his attempt, and made so ridiculous that he withdrew himself from further notice' – an example much to be commended. That same favoured land of America has been particularly favoured in the development of 'innumerable mediums' and Mr Howitt orders you to believe in DANIEL DUNGLAS HOME, ANDREW DAVIS JACKSON, and THOMAS L. HARRIS, as 'the three most remarkable, or most familiar, on this side of the Atlantic.' Concerning Mr Home, the articles of belief (besides removal of furniture) are, That through him raps have been given and communications made from deceased friends. That 'his hand has been seized by spiritual influence, and rapid communications written out, of a surprising character to those to whom they were addressed.' That at his bidding, 'spirit hands have appeared which have been seen, felt, and recognised frequently, by persons present, as those of deceased friends.' That he has been frequently lifted up and carried, floating 'as it were' through a room, near the ceiling. That in America, 'all these phenomena have displayed themselves in greater force than here' – which we have not the slightest doubt of. That he is 'the planter of spiritualism all over Europe.' That 'by circumstances that no man could have devised, he became the guest of the Emperor of the French, of the King of Holland, of the Czar of Russia, and of many lesser princes.' That he returned from 'this unpremeditated missionary tour,' 'endowed with competence;' but not before, 'at the Tuileries, on one occasion when the emperor, empress, a distinguished lady, and himself only were sitting at table, a hand appeared, took up a pen, and wrote, in a strong and well-known character, the word NAPOLEON. The hand was then successively presented to the several personages of the party to kiss.' The stout believer, having disposed of Mr Home, and rested a little, will then proceed to believe in ANDREW DAVIS JACKSON, or ANDREW JACKSON DAVIS (Mr Howitt, having no Medium at hand to settle this difference and reveal the right name of the seer, calls him by both names), who merely 'beheld all the essential natures of things, saw the interior of men and animals, as perfectly as their exterior; and described them in language so correct, that the most able technologists could not surpass them. He pointed out the proper remedies for all the complaints, and the shops where they were to be obtained;' – in the latter respect appearing to hail from an advertising circle, as we conceive. It was also in this gentleman's limited department to 'see the metals in the earth,' and to have 'the most distant regions and their various productions present before him.' Having despatched this tough case, the believer will pass on to Thomas L. Harris, and will swallow *him* easily, together with 'whole epics' of his composition; a certain work 'of scarcely less than Miltonic grandeur,' called The Lyric of the Golden Age – a lyric pretty nigh as long as one of Mr Howitt's volumes – dictated by Mr (not Mrs) Harris to the publisher in ninety four hours; and several extempore sermons, possessing the remarkably lucid property of being 'full, unforced, out-gushing, unstinted, and absorbing.' The candidate for examination in pure belief, will then pass on to the spirit-photography department; this, again, will be found in so-favoured America, under the superintendence of Medium MUMLER, a photographer of Boston: who was 'astonished' (though, on Mr Howitt's showing, he surely ought not to have been) 'on taking a photograph of himself, to find also by his side the figure of a young girl, which he immediately recognised as that of a deceased relative. The circumstance made a great excitement. Numbers of persons rushed to his rooms, and many have found deceased friends photographed with themselves.' (Perhaps Mr Mumler, too, may become 'endowed with competence' in time. Who knows?) Finally, the true believers in the gospel according to Howitt, have, besides, but to pin their faith on 'ladies who see spirits habitually,' on ladies who *know* they have a tendency to soar in the air on sufficient provocation, and on a few other gnats to be taken after their camels, and they shall be pronounced by Mr Howitt not of 'the stereotyped class of minds,' and not partakers of 'the astonishing ignorance of the press,' and shall receive a first-class certificate of merit.

But before they pass through this portal into the Temple of Serene Wisdom, we, halting blind and helpless on the steps, beg to suggest to them what they must at once and for ever disbelieve. They must disbelieve that in the dark times, when very few were versed in what are now the mere recreations of Science, and when those few formed a priesthood-class apart, any marvels were wrought by the aid of concave mirrors and a knowledge of the properties of certain odours and gases, although the self-same marvels could be reproduced before their eyes at the Polytechnic Institution, Regent-street, London, any day in the year. They must by no means believe that Conjuring and Ventriloquism are old trades. They must disbelieve all Philosophical Transactions containing the records of painful and careful inquiry into now familiar disorders of the senses of seeing and hearing, and into the wonders of somnambulism, epilepsy, hysteria, miasmatic influence, vegetable poisons derived by whole communities from corrupted air, diseased imitation, and moral infection. They must disbelieve all such awkward leading cases as the case of the Woodstock Commissioners and their man, and the case of the identity of the Stockwell Ghost with the maid-servant. They must disbelieve the vanishing of champion haunted houses (except, indeed, out of Mr Howitt's book), represented to have been closed and ruined for years, before one day's inquiry by four gentlemen associated with this Journal, and one hour's reference to the local Rate-books. They must disbelieve all possibility of a human creature on the last verge of the dark bridge from Life to Death, being mysteriously able, in occasional cases, so to influence the mind of one very near and dear, as vividly to impress that mind with some disturbed sense of the solemn change impending. They must disbelieve the possibility of the lawful existence of a class of intellects which, humbly conscious of the illimitable power of GOD and of their own weakness and ignorance, never deny that He can cause the souls of the dead to revisit the earth, or that He may have caused the souls of the dead to revisit the earth, or that He can cause any awful or wondrous thing to be; but do deny the likelihood of apparitions or spirits coming here upon the stupidest of bootless errands, and producing credentials tantamount to a solicitation of our vote and interest and next proxy, to get them into the Asylum for Idiots. They must disbelieve the right of Christian people who do *not* protest against Protestantism, but who hold it to be a barrier against the darkest superstitions that can enslave the soul, to guard with jealousy all approaches tending down to Cock-lane Ghosts and such-like infamous swindles, widely degrading when widely believed in; and they must disbelieve that such people have the right to know, and that it is their duty to know, wonder-workers by their fruits, and to test miracle-mongers by the tests of probability, analogy, and common sense. They must disbelieve all rational explanations of thoroughly proved experiences (only) which appear supernatural, derived from the average experience and study of the visible world. They must disbelieve the speciality of the Master and the Disciples, and that it is a monstrosity to test the wonders of show-folk by the same touchstone. Lastly, they must disbelieve that one of the best accredited chapters in the history of mankind is the chapter that records the astonishing deceits continually practised, with no object or purpose but the distorted pleasure of deceiving.

We have summed up a few – not nearly all – of the articles of belief and disbelief to which Mr Howitt most arrogantly demands an implicit adherence. To uphold these, he uses a book as a Clown in a Pantomime does, and knocks everybody on the head with it who comes in his way. Moreover, he is an angrier personage than the Clown, and does not experimentally try the effect of his red-hot poker on your shins, but straightway runs you through the body and soul with it. He is always raging to tell you that if you are not Howitt, you are Atheist and Anti-Christ. He is the sans-culotte of the Spiritual Revolution, and will not hear of your accepting this point and rejecting that; – down your throat with them all, one and indivisible, at the point of the pike; No Liberty, Totality, Fraternity, or Death!

Without presuming to question that 'it is high time to protest against Protestantism' on such very substantial grounds as Mr Howitt sets forth, we do presume to think that it is high time to protest against Mr Howitt's spiritualism, as being a little in excess of the peculiar merit of Thomas L. Harris's sermons, and somewhat *too* 'full, out-gushing, unstinted, and absorbing.'

Dickens followed up 'Rather a Strong Dose' with another broadside against the Spiritualists when he published 'The Martyr Medium' (*ATYR*, 4 April 1863;

collected in *MP*), in which he quoted extracts from *Incidents in My Life*, the autobiography of the celebrated medium Daniel Dunglas Home, supplying ludicrous titles for the extracts ('The Testimony of Mr Home's Boots', etc.) and adding a withering commentary on what he calls 'this odious book'. He wrote to Wilkie Collins on 22 April 1863:

> Howitt has gone mad (madder, I mean) about an article I wrote on his Spirit book, and sends me a printed advertisement of it with notices appended 'with Mr Howitt's compliments to Mr Dickens, and many thanks for the impulse given to his work by All the Year Round, and the other Infidel Journals.' ...
>
> The stupendous absurdity of Howitt's book is inconceivable. Home's is clearly (to me) the book of a scoundrel without shame. [*Pilgrim*, Vol. X, p. 238f.]

Browning clearly shared Dickens's view of Home and portrayed him in his *Dramatis Personae* (1864) as 'Mr Sludge the Medium', a shameless hypocrite.

23

The Uncommercial Traveller

All The Year Round, 2 May 1863 (*UT1* as 'The Calais Night Mail')

Dickens had already recorded his impressions of travelling on the South Eastern Railway's 'Special Express Train and Steam Ship' service between London and Paris, in a *HW* article of August 1851 (see Vol. 3 of this edition, article 4). In the present article, he draws on memories of cross-Channel trips going back to his first journey abroad in July 1837, when he had written to Forster of his sea-sickness as 'that dismal extremity of qualmishness into which I am accustomed to sink whenever I have "the blue above and the blue below". I have always thought that "the silence where'er I go" is a beautiful touch of Barry Cornwall's ... descriptive of the depression produced by sea voyaging' (*Pilgrim*, Vol. I, p. 280). The allusion then was to 'Cornwall's' [Procter's] song 'The Sea' (*English Songs*, 1832); in the present article, poetry again distracts him, this time a ballad by Thomas Moore (see literary allusions, below). Dominic Rainsford explores Dickens's representation of such voyages in 'Crossing the Channel with Dickens', the opening essay in *Dickens, Europe and the New Worlds*, ed. Anny Sadrin (1999).

Descriptions of both Dover and Calais, modern and historical, had featured in Dickens's fiction of the late 1850s. Dickens offers a depressing portrait of the latter through the eyes of Arthur Clennam in *Little Dorrit*, Book 2, Ch. 20 (1857), as he approaches at low tide, while an affectionate description of 'The Ship Hotel', Dover, where Dickens overnighted on cross-Channel trips prior to the building of the Lord Warden Hotel (see p. 212), is given in *A Tale of Two Cities* (1859) under the name of the 'Royal George Hotel' (Ch. 4 et seq.). Dickens's knowledge of northern France and the towns of French Flanders dates from a similar period in the 1850s. He had celebrated Boulogne as 'Our French Watering-Place' in *HW* in 1854 and holidayed there in 1853, 1854 and 1856 (see Vol. 3 of this edition, article 30). He increased his familiarity with the interior of what are now the Départements du Nord and Pas de Calais during trips in 1862 and 1863, probably in the course, as various biographers have surmised, of making clandestine visits to or with Ellen Ternan, centring around the village of Condette (see Introduction, pp. xvii–xviii & n., and headnote to article 32 below). During one such trip in February 1863, he wrote to Forster from Arras on his birthday (the 7th) mentioning a version of the incident described on p. 218 below:

> An odd birthday, but I am as little out of heart as you would have me be. . . . I wanted to see this town ... and I find a Grande Place so very remarkable and picturesque that it is astonishing how people miss it. Here too I found, in a by-country place just near, a Fair going on, with a Religious Richardson's in it – THÉÂTRE RELIGIEUX – 'donnant six fois par jour, l'histoire de la Croix en tableaux vivants, depuis la naissance de notre Seigneur jusqu'à son sépulture ...' [presenting six performances daily of the Story of the Cross given in dramatic tableaux from the birth of Our Lord until his Burial. . .]. It was just before nightfall when I came upon it; and one of the three wise men was up to his eyes in lamp oil, hanging the moderators. A woman in blue and fleshings (whether an angel or Joseph's wife I don't know) was addressing a crowd through an enormous speaking-trumpet; and a very small boy with a property lamb (I leave you to judge who *he* was) was standing on his head on a barrel-organ. [*Pilgrim*, Vol. X, p. 212]

Literary allusions (p. 212) 'the distant dogs of Dover ... Richard the Third': Shakespeare, *Richard III*, Act 1, Sc. 1; (p. 213) 'commit us to the deep': 'At the Burial of their Dead at Sea', Forms of Prayer to be Used at Sea, *The Book of Common Prayer* (1662); (pp. 214–15) 'Rich and rare were the gems she wore': one of Thomas Moore's *Irish Melodies* (1807), of which the relevant stanzas run

Rich and rare were the gems she wore,
And a bright gold ring on her wand she bore;
But oh! her beauty was far beyond
Her sparkling gems, or snow-white wand.

'Lady! dost thou not fear to stray,
So lone and lovely, through this bleak way?
Are ERIN's sons so good or so cold,
As not to be tempted by woman or gold?'

'Sir Knight! I fear not the least alarm,
No son of ERIN will offer me harm:–
For though they love woman and golden store,
Sir Knight! they love honour and virtue more!'

On she went, and her maiden smile
In safety lighted her round the green isle.
And blest for ever is she who relied
Upon ERIN's honour and ERIN's pride!

(p. 215) 'Robinson Crusoe ... was near foundering': Defoe's *Robinson Crusoe* (1719); (p. 216) 'Calais will be found written on my heart': adaptation of phrase attributed to Mary I of England following the loss of the city in 1558, and recorded in Holinshed's *Chronicles* (1808, Vol. IV, p. 107); (p.216) 'an ancient and fish-like smell': words used by Trinculo with reference to Caliban in Shakespeare's *The Tempest*, Act 2, Sc. 2; (p. 217) 'such corporals ... and many a blue-eyed Bebelle': Corporal Théophile and 'Bebelle' (Gabrielle), characters in Dickens's story, 'His Boots', contributed to *Somebody's Luggage*, the Christmas Number of *ATYR* for 1862.

It is an unsettled question with me whether I shall leave Calais something handsome in my will, or whether I shall leave it my malediction. I hate it so much, and yet I am always so very glad to see it, that I am in a state of constant indecision on this subject.

When I first made acquaintance with Calais, it was as a maundering young wretch in a clammy perspiration and dripping saline particles, who was conscious of no extremities but the one great extremity, seasickness – who was a mere bilious torso, with a mislaid headache somewhere in its stomach – who had been put into a horrible swing in Dover Harbour, and had tumbled giddily out of it on the French coast, or the Isle of Man, or anywhere. Times have changed, and now I enter Calais self-reliant and rational. I know where it is beforehand, I keep a look out for it, I recognise its landmarks when I see any of them, I am

acquainted with its ways, and I know – and I can bear – its worst
behaviour.

Malignant Calais! Low-lying alligator, evading the eyesight and dis-
couraging hope! Dodging flat streak, now on this bow, now on that, now
anywhere, now everywhere, now nowhere! In vain Cape Grinez, coming
frankly forth into the sea, exhorts the failing to be stout of heart and
stomach; sneaking Calais, prone behind its bar, invites emetically to
despair. Even when it can no longer quite conceal itself in its muddy
dock, it has an evil way of falling off, has Calais, which is more hopeless
than its invisibility. The pier is all but on the bowsprit, and you think
you are there – roll, roar, wash! – Calais has retired miles inland, and
Dover has burst out to look for it. It has a last dip and a slide in its
character, has Calais, to be especially commended to the infernal gods.
Thrice accursed be that garrison-town, when it dives under the boat's
keel, and comes up a league or two to the right, with the packet shivering
and spluttering and staring about for it!

Not but what I have my animosities towards Dover. I particularly
detest Dover for the self-complacency with which it goes to bed. It always
goes to bed (when I am going to Calais) with a more brilliant display of
lamp and candle than any other town. Mr and Mrs Birmingham, host
and hostess of the Lord Warden Hotel, are my much-esteemed friends,
but they are too conceited about the comforts of that establishment when
the Night Mail is starting. I know it is a good house to stay at, and I
don't want the fact insisted upon in all its warm bright windows at such
an hour. I know the Warden is a stationary edifice that never rolls or
pitches, and I object to its big outline seeming to insist upon that
circumstance, and, as it were, to come over me with it, when I am
reeling on the deck of the boat. Beshrew the Warden likewise, for
obstructing that corner, and making the wind so angry as it rushes round.
Shall I not know that it blows, quite soon enough, without the officious
Warden's interference?

As I wait here on board the night packet, for the South Eastern Train
to come down with the Mail, Dover appears to me to be illuminated for
some intensely aggravating festivity in my personal dishonour. All its
noises smack of taunting praises of the land, and dispraises of the gloomy
sea, and of me for going on it. The drums upon the heights have gone
to bed, or I know they would rattle taunts against me for having my
unsteady footing on this slippery deck. The many gas eyes of the Marine
Parade twinkle in an offensive manner, as if with derision. The distant
dogs of Dover bark at me in my misshapen wrappers, as if I were
Richard the Third.

A screech, a bell, and two red eyes come gliding down the Admiralty
Pier with a smoothness of motion rendered more smooth by the heaving

of the boat. The sea makes noises against the pier, as if several hippopotami were lapping at it, and were prevented by circumstances over which they had no control from drinking peaceably. We, the boat, become violently agitated – rumble, hum, scream, roar, and establish an immense family washing-day at each paddle-box. Bright patches break out in the train as the doors of the post-office vans are opened, and instantly stooping figures with sacks upon their backs begin to be beheld among the piles, descending, as it would seem in ghostly procession to Davy Jones's Locker. The passengers come on board; a few shadowy Frenchmen, with hatboxes shaped like the stoppers of gigantic case-bottles; a few shadowy Germans in immense fur coats and boots; a few shadowy Englishmen prepared for the worst and pretending not to expect it. I cannot disguise from my uncommercial mind the miserable fact that we are a body of outcasts; that the attendants on us are as scant in number as may serve to get rid of us with the least possible delay; that there are no night-loungers interested in us; that the unwilling lamps shiver and shudder at us; that the sole object is to commit us to the deep and abandon us. Lo, the two red eyes glaring in increasing distance, and then the very train itself has gone to bed before we are off!

What is the moral support derived by some sea-going amateurs from an umbrella? Why do certain voyagers across the Channel always put up that article, and hold it up with a grim and fierce tenacity? A fellow-creature near me – whom I only know to be a fellow-creature because of his umbrella: without which he might be a dark bit of cliff, pier, or bulkhead – clutches that instrument with a desperate grasp, that will not relax until he lands at Calais. Is there any analogy, in certain constitutions, between keeping an umbrella up, and keeping the spirits up? A hawser thrown on board with a flop replies, 'Stand by!' 'Stand by, below!' 'Half a turn ahead!' 'Half a turn ahead!' 'Half speed!' 'Half speed!' 'Port!' 'Port!' 'Steady!' 'Steady!' 'Go on!' 'Go on!'

A stout wooden wedge driven in at my right temple and out at my left, a floating deposit of lukewarm oil in my throat, and a compression of the bridge of my nose in a blunt pair of pincers, – these are the personal sensations by which I know we are off, and by which I shall continue to know it until I am on the soil of France. My symptoms have scarcely established themselves comfortably, when two or three skating shadows that have been trying to walk or stand, get flung together, and other two or three shadows in tarpaulin slide with them into corners, and cover them up. Then the South Foreland lights begin to hiccup at us in a way that bodes no good.

It is about this period that my detestation of Calais knows no bounds. Inwardly I resolve afresh that I never will forgive that hated town. I have done so before, many times, but that is past. Let me register a vow.

Implacable animosity to Calais everm – that was an awkward sea, and the funnel seems of my opinion, for it gives a complaining roar.

The wind blows stiffly from the Nor'-East, the sea runs high, we ship a deal of water, the night is dark and cold, and the shapeless passengers lie about in melancholy bundles, as if they were sorted out for the laundress; but for my own uncommercial part I cannot pretend that I am much inconvenienced by any of these things. A general howling whistling flopping gurgling and scooping, I am aware of, and a general knocking about of Nature; but the impressions I receive are very vague. In a sweet faint temper, something like the smell of damaged oranges, I think I should feel languidly benevolent if I had time. I have not time, because I am under a curious compulsion to occupy myself with the Irish melodies. 'Rich and rare were the gems she wore,' is the particular melody to which I find myself devoted. I sing it to myself in the most charming manner and with the greatest expression. Now and then, I raise my head (I am sitting on the hardest of wet seats, in the most uncomfortable of wet attitudes, but I don't mind it,) and notice that I am a whirling shuttlecock between a fiery battledore of a lighthouse on the French coast and a fiery battledore of a lighthouse on the English coast; but I don't notice it particularly, except to feel envenomed in my hatred of Calais. Then I go on again, 'Rich and rare were the ge-ems she-e-e-e wore, And a bright gold ring on her wa-and she bo-ore, But O her beauty was fa-a-a-a-r beyond' – I am particularly proud of my execution here, when I become aware of another awkward shock from the sea, and another protest from the funnel, and a fellow-creature at the paddle-box more audibly indisposed than I think he need be – 'Her sparkling gems, or snow white wand, But O her beauty was fa-a-a-a-r be-yond' – another awkward one here, and the fellow-creature with the umbrella down and picked up, 'Her spa-a-rkling ge-ems, or her Port! port! steady! steady! Snow white fellow-creature at the paddle-box very selfishly audible, bump roar wash white wand.'

As my execution of the Irish melodies partakes of my imperfect perceptions of what is going on around me, so what is going on around me becomes something else than what it is. The stokers open the furnace doors below, to feed the fires, and I am again on the box of the old Exeter Telegraph fast coach, and that is the light of the for ever extinguished coach-lamps, and the gleam on the hatches and paddle-boxes is *their* gleam on cottages and haystacks, and the monotonous noise of the engines is the steady jingle of the splendid team. Anon, the intermittent funnel roar of protest at every violent roll, becomes the regular blast of a high pressure engine, and I recognise the exceedingly explosive steamer in which I ascended the Mississippi when the American civil war was not and when only its causes were. A fragment of mast on which the light of a lantern falls, an end of rope, and a jerking block or so, become suggestive of Franconi's Circus at Paris where I shall be this very night mayhap (for it must be morning now), and they dance to the self-same time and tune as the trained steed, Black Raven. What may be the speciality of these waves as they come rushing on, I cannot desert the pressing demands made upon me by the gems she wore, to inquire, but they are charged with something about Robinson Crusoe, and I think it was in Yarmouth Roads that he first went a seafaring and was near foundering (what a terrific sound that word had for me when I was a boy!) in his first gale of wind. Still, through all this, I must ask her (who *was* she I wonder!) for the fiftieth time, and without ever stopping, Does she not fear to stray, So lone and lovely through this bleak way, And are Erin's sons so good or so cold, As not to be tempted by more fellow-creatures at the paddle-box or gold? Sir knight I feel not the least alarm, No son of Erin will offer me harm, For though they love fellow-creature with umbrella down again and golden store, Sir Knight they what a tremendous one love honour and virtue more: For though they love Stewards with a bull's-eye bright, they'll trouble you for your ticket, sir – rough passage tonight!

I freely admit it to be a miserable piece of human weakness and inconsistency, but I no sooner become conscious of those last words from the steward than I begin to soften towards Calais. Whereas I have been vindictively wishing that those Calais burghers who came out of their town by a short cut into the History of England, with those fatal ropes round their necks by which they have since been towed into so many cartoons, had all been hanged on the spot, I now begin to regard them as highly respectable and virtuous tradesmen. Looking about me, I see the light of Cape Grinez well astern of the boat on the davits to leeward, and the light of Calais Harbour, undeniably at its old tricks, but still ahead and shining. Sentiments of forgiveness of Calais, not to say of attachment to Calais, begin to expand my bosom. I have weak notions that I will stay there a day or two on my way back. A faded and recumbent stranger pausing in a profound reverie over the rim of a basin, asks me what kind of place Calais is? I tell him (Heaven forgive me!) a very agreeable place indeed – rather hilly than otherwise.

So strangely goes the time, and, on the whole, so quickly – though still I seem to have been on board a week – that I am bumped rolled gurgled washed and pitched into Calais Harbour before her maiden smile has finally lighted her through the Green Isle, When blest for ever is she who relied, On entering Calais at the top of the tide. For we have not to land tonight down among those slimy timbers – covered with green hair as if it were the mermaids' favourite combing-place – where one crawls to the surface of the jetty like a stranded shrimp, but we go steaming up the harbour to the Railway Station Quay. And as we go, the sea washes in and out among piles and planks, with dead heavy beats and in quite a furious manner (whereof we are proud), and the lamps shake in the wind, and the bells of Calais striking One seem to send their vibrations struggling against troubled air, as we have come struggling against troubled water. And now, in the sudden relief and wiping of faces, everybody on board seems to have had a prodigious double-tooth out, and to be this very instant free of the Dentists' hands. And now we all know for the first time how wet and cold we are, and how salt we are; and now I love Calais with my heart of hearts!

'Hôtel Dessin!' (but in this one case it is not a vocal cry; it is but a bright lustre in the eyes of the cheery representative of that best of inns). 'Hôtel Meurice!' 'Hôtel de France!' 'Hôtel de Calais!' 'The Royal Hôtel, Sir, Angaishe ouse!' 'You going to Parry, Sir?' 'Your baggage, registair froo, Sir?' Bless ye, my Touters, bless ye, my commissionaires, bless ye, my hungry-eyed mysteries in caps of a military form, who are always here, day or night, fair weather or foul, seeking inscrutable jobs which I never see you get! Bless ye, my Custom House officers in green and grey; permit me to grasp the welcome hands that descend into my travelling-bag, one on each side, and meet at the bottom to give my change of linen a peculiar shake up, as if it were a measure of chaff or grain! I have nothing to declare, Monsieur le Douanier, except that when I cease to breathe, Calais will be found written on my heart. No article liable to local duty have I with me, Monsieur l'Officier de l'Octroi, unless the overflowing of a breast devoted to your charming town should be in that wise chargeable. Ah! see at the gangway by the twinkling lantern, my dearest brother and friend, he once of the Passport Office, he who collects the names! May he be for ever changeless in his buttoned black surtout, with his notebook in his hand, and his tall black hat, surmounting his round smiling patient face! Let us embrace, my dearest brother. I am yours à tout jamais – for the whole of ever.

Calais up and doing at the railway station, and Calais down and dreaming in its bed; Calais with something of 'an ancient and fish-like smell' about it, and Calais blown and sea-washed pure; Calais represented at the Buffet by savoury roast fowls, hot coffee, cognac, and Bordeaux; and Calais represented everywhere by flitting persons with a monomania for changing money – though I never shall be able to understand in my present state of existence how they live by it, but I suppose I should, if I understood the currency question – Calais *en gros*, and Calais *en détail*, forgive one who has deeply wronged you. – I was not fully aware of it on the other side, but I meant Dover.

Ding, ding! To the carriages, gentlemen the travellers. Ascend then, gentlemen the travellers, for Hazebroucke, Lille, Douai, Bruxelles, Arras,

Amiens, and Paris! I, humble representative of the Uncommercial interest, ascend with the rest. The train is light tonight, and I share my compartment with but two fellow-travellers; one, a compatriot in an obsolete cravat, who thinks it a quite unaccountable thing that they don't keep 'London time' on a French railway, and who is made angry by my modestly suggesting the possibility of Paris time being more in their way; the other, a young priest, with a very small bird in a very small cage, who feeds the small bird with a quill, and then puts him up in the network above his head, where he advances twittering, to his front wires, and seems to address me in an electioneering manner. The compatriot (who crossed in the boat, and whom I judge to be some person of distinction, as he was shut up, like a stately species of rabbit, in a private hutch on deck) and the young priest (who joined us at Calais) are soon asleep, and then the bird and I have it all to ourselves.

A stormy night still; a night that sweeps the wires of the electric telegraph with a wild and fitful hand; a night so very stormy, with the added storm of the train-progress through it, that when the Guard comes clambering round to mark the tickets while we are at full speed (a really horrible performance in an Express train, though he holds on to the open window by his elbows in the most deliberate manner), he stands in such a whirlwind that I grip him fast by the collar, and feel it next to manslaughter to let him go. Still, when he is gone, the small small bird remains at his front wires feebly twittering to me – twittering and twittering, until, leaning back in my place, and looking at him in drowsy fascination, I find that he seems to jog my memory as we rush along.

Uncommercial travels (thus the small small bird) have lain in their idle thriftless way through all this range of swamp and dyke, as through many other odd places; and about here, as you very well know, are the queer old stone farmhouses approached by drawbridges, and the windmills that you get at by boats. Here, are the lands where the women hoe and dig, paddling canoe-wise from field to field, and here are the cabarets and other peasant-houses where the stone dovecotes in the littered yards are as strong as warders' towers in old castles. Here, are the long monotonous miles of canal, with the great Dutch-built barges garishly painted, and the towing girls, sometimes harnessed by the forehead, sometimes by the girdle and the shoulders, not a pleasant sight to see. Scattered through this country are mighty works of VAUBAN, whom you know about, and regiments of such corporals as you heard of once upon a time, and many a blue-eyed Bebelle. Through these flat districts, in the shining summer days, walk those long grotesque files of young novices in enormous shovel hats, whom you remember blackening the ground checkered by the avenues of leafy trees. And now that Hazebroucke slumbers certain kilometres ahead, recal the summer evening when your dusty feet strolling

up from the station tended hap-hazard to a Fair there, where the oldest
inhabitants were circling round and round a barrel-organ on hobby-
horses, with the greatest gravity, and where the principal show in the
fair was a Religious Richardson's – literally, on its own announcement
in great letters, THEATRE RELIGIEUX. In which improving Temple, the
dramatic representation was of 'all the interesting events in the life of
Our Lord, from the Manger to the Tomb;' the principal female character,
without any reservation or exception, being at the moment of your
arrival, engaged in trimming the external Moderators (as it was growing
dusk), while the next principal female character took the money, and the
Young St John disported himself upside down on the platform.

Looking up at this point to confirm the small small bird in every
particular he has mentioned, I find he has ceased to twitter, and has put
his head under his wing. Therefore, in my different way I follow the
good example.

24

The Uncommercial Traveller

All The Year Round, 16 May 1863 (*UT1* as 'Some Recollections of
Mortality')

Georges Haussmann, later Baron, had been appointed prefect of the
Seine under Napoleon III in 1853, and was responsible for many of the
improvements in the layout and appearance of Paris which Dickens notes
in the present article. Dickens had been lodging in the Rue du Faubourg
St Honoré in the last few months of 1862; letters of 24 October and 4
November comment on the 'vast changes ... and the vast works doing and
done' in the city, and the way 'the Genius of the Lamp is always building
Palaces in the night' (see *Pilgrim*, Vol. X, pp. 149, 154). He returned to Paris
in the early months of 1863, staying intermittently at the Hôtel du Helder.

Dickens's fascination with the Morgue – also apparent in article 10 (pp.
88–91 above) and article 49 of Vol. 3 of this edition – was by no means
unusual amongst Victorian visitors. Guidebooks had included descriptions
of it for many years (see, for example, A. and W. Galignani's *Galignani's
New Paris Guide for 1851* [1851], pp. 84, 325). Although much of the Île de
la Cité where the Morgue stood had already been cleared by Haussmann

in 1863, the Morgue itself was not to be demolished until 1923.

In January 1840, shortly after taking up residence at 1 Devonshire Terrace in the parish of Marylebone, Dickens did jury service at the inquest into the death of the infant child of a young housemaid, Eliza Burgess, employed by Mrs Mary Symmons of 65 Edgware Road. Burgess's presence at the inquest on 14 January and subsequent trial at the Old Bailey on the charge of concealing birth was reported by *The Times* on 15 January and 10 March (p. 7, col. a; p. 7, col. d). Forster records a letter sent to him by Dickens on [15?] January –

> Whether it was the poor baby, or its poor mother, or the coffin, or my fellow-jurymen, or what not, I can't say, but last night I had a most violent attack of sickness and indigestion which not only prevented me from sleeping, but even from lying down. Accordingly Kate and I sat up through the dreary watches. [*Pilgrim*, Vol. II, p. 10 & n.]

– and describes the episode as an illustration of 'the practical turn of [Dickens's] kindness and humanity' (*Forster*, Book 2, Ch. 7). Eliza Burgess was defended at her trial on 9 March by barrister Richard Doane of the Inner Temple, and the jury, while finding her guilty of concealment, made a strong recommendation to mercy. She was taken back into service by a sympathetic previous employer and seems to have been eventually admitted to the Magdalen Asylum (see W. J. Carlton, 'Dickens in the Jury Box', *The Dickensian*, Vol. 52 [1956], pp. 65–9). Dickens had already paid public tribute to Thomas Wakley's performance of his duties as coroner for West Middlesex, in his *Examiner* article 'The Paradise at Tooting' in 1849 (see headnote and text of article 33 in Vol. 2 of this edition).

Literary allusions (p. 218) Dickens's later title for this paper, 'Some Recollections of Mortality', plays on the title 'Ode: Intimations of Immortality from Recollections of Early Childhood' chosen by Wordsworth in 1815 for his ode 'There was a time …' (1807); (p. 220) 'as if he had been Cassim Baba': brother of Ali, cut up into quarters in the *Arabian Nights'* tale of the forty thieves; (p. 220) 'a Masaniello look': Auber's opera *Masaniello* (1828), featuring colourful scenes among the fishermen of Naples; (p. 224) 'our dear sister here departed': Burial Service from *The Book of Common Prayer*; (p. 225) 'the youth in Gray's Elegy … for his own': Thomas Gray's 'Elegy Written in a Country Churchyard' (1751), ll. 118–20; (p. 225) ' "for safety and for succour" … believing in him': Home's tragedy *Douglas* (1756), Act 2, Sc. 1; (p. 226) 'what race of Patagonians': Goldsmith's *The Citizen of the World* (1762 [1761]), Letter 114.

Textual note (p. 223) copy-text has '… old man, so quiet for evermore': *UT1* has '… old man, quiet for evermore'.

I had parted from the small bird at somewhere about four o'clock in the morning, when he had got out at Arras, and had been received by two shovel-hats in waiting at the station, who presented an appropriately orni-thological and crow-like appearance. My compatriot and I had gone on to Paris; my compatriot enlightening me occasionally with a long list of the enormous grievances of French railway travelling: every one of which, as I am a sinner, was perfectly new to me, though I have as much experience of French railways as most uncommercials. I had left him at the terminus (through his conviction, against all explanation and remonstrance, that his baggage-ticket was his passenger-ticket), insisting in a very high temper to the functionary on duty, that in his own personal identity he was four packages weighing so many kilogrammes – as if he had been Cassim Baba! I had bathed and breakfasted, and was strolling on the bright quays. The subject of my meditations was the question whether it is positively in the essence and nature of things, as a certain school of Britons would seem to think it, that a Capital must be ensnared and enslaved before it can be made beautiful: when I lifted up my eyes, and found that my feet, straying like my mind, had brought me to Notre-Dame.

That is to say, Notre-Dame was before me, but there was a large open space between us. A very little while gone, I had left that space covered with buildings densely crowded; and now it was cleared for some new wonder in the way of public Street, Place, Garden, Fountain, or all four. Only the obscene little Morgue, slinking on the brink of the river and soon to come down, was left there, looking mortally ashamed of itself, and supremely wicked. I had but glanced at this old acquaintance, when I beheld an airy procession coming round in front of Notre-Dame, past the great hospital. It had something of a Masaniello look, with fluttering striped curtains in the midst of it, and it came dancing round the cathedral in the liveliest manner.

I was speculating on a marriage in Blouse-life, or a Christening, or some other domestic festivity which I would see out, when I found, from the talk of a quick rush of Blouses past me, that it was a Body coming to the Morgue. Having never before chanced upon this initiation, I constituted myself a Blouse likewise, and ran into the Morgue with the rest. It was a very muddy day, and we took in a quantity of mire with us, and the procession coming in upon our heels brought a quantity more. The procession was in the highest spirits, and consisted of idlers who had come with the curtained litter from its starting-place, and of all the reinforcements it had picked up by the way. It set the litter down in the midst of the Morgue, and then two Custodians proclaimed aloud that we were all 'invited' to go out. This invitation was rendered the more pressing, if not the more flattering, by our being shoved out, and the folding-gates being barred upon us.

Those who have never seen the Morgue, may see it perfectly, by presenting to themselves an indifferently paved coach-house accessible from the street by a pair of folding-gates; on the left of the coach-house, occupying its width, any large London tailor's or linendraper's plate-glass window reaching to the ground; within the window, on two rows of inclined planes, what the coach-house has to show; hanging above, like irregular stalactites from the roof of a cave, a quantity of clothes – the clothes of the dead and buried shows of the coach-house.

We had been excited in the highest degree by seeing the Custodians pull off their coats and tuck up their shirt-sleeves as the procession came along. It looked so interestingly like business. Shut out in the muddy street, we now became quite ravenous to know all about it. Was it river, pistol, knife, love, gambling, robbery, hatred, how many stabs, how many bullets, fresh or decomposed, suicide or murder? All wedged together, and all staring at one another with our heads thrust forward, we propounded these inquiries and a hundred more such. Imperceptibly, it came to be known that Monsieur the tall and sallow mason yonder, was acquainted with the facts. Would Monsieur the tall and sallow mason, surged at by a new wave of us, have the goodness to impart? It was but a poor old man, passing along the street under one of the new buildings, on whom a stone had fallen, and who had tumbled dead. His age? Another wave surged up against the tall and sallow mason, and our wave swept on and broke, and he was any age from sixty-five to ninety.

An old man was not much: moreover, we could have wished he had been killed by human agency – his own, or somebody else's: the latter, preferable – but our comfort was, that he had nothing about him to lead to his identification, and that his people must seek him here. Perhaps they were waiting dinner for him even now? We liked that. Such of us as had pocket-handkerchiefs took a slow intense protracted wipe at our noses, and then crammed our handkerchiefs into the breast of our blouses. Others of us who had no handkerchiefs administered a similar relief to our overwrought minds, by means of prolonged smears or wipes of our mouths on our sleeves. One man with a gloomy malformation of brow – a homicidal worker in white-lead, to judge from his blue tone of colour, and a certain flavour of paralysis pervading him – got his coat-collar between his teeth, and bit at it with an appetite. Several decent women arrived upon the outskirts of the crowd, and prepared to launch themselves into the dismal coach-house when opportunity should come; among them, a pretty young mother, pretending to bite the forefinger of her baby-boy, kept it between her rosy lips that it might be handy for guiding to point at the show. Meantime, all faces were turned towards the building, and we men waited with a fixed and stern resolution: – for the most part with folded arms. Surely, it was the only public French sight these uncommercial eyes had seen, at which the expectant people did not form *en queue*. But there was no such order of arrangement here; nothing but a general determination to make a rush for it, and a disposition to object to some boys who had mounted on the two stone posts by the hinges of the gates, with the design of swooping in when the hinges should turn.

Now, they turned, and we rushed! Great pressure, and a scream or two from the front. Then a laugh or two, some expressions of disappointment, and a slackening of the pressure and subsidence of the struggle. – Old man not there.

'But what would you have?' the Custodian reasonably argues, as he looks out at his little door. 'Patience, patience! We make his toilette, gentlemen. He will be exposed presently. It is necessary to proceed according to rule. His toilette is not made all at a blow. He will be exposed in good time, gentlemen, in good time.' And so retires, smoking, with a wave of his sleeveless arm towards the window, importing, 'Entertain yourselves in the meanwhile with the other curiosities. Fortunately the Museum is not empty today.'

Who would have thought of public fickleness even at the Morgue? But there it was, on that occasion. Three lately popular articles that had been attracting greatly when the litter was first descried coming dancing round the corner by the great cathedral, were so completely deposed now, that nobody save two little girls (one showing them to a doll) would look at them. Yet the chief of the three, the article in the front row, had received jagged injury of the left temple; and the other two in the back row, the drowned two lying side by side with their heads very slightly turned towards each other, seemed to be comparing notes about it. Indeed, those two of the back row were so furtive of appearance, and so (in their puffed way) assassinatingly knowing as to the one of the front, that it was hard to think the three had never come together in their lives, and were only chance companions after death. Whether or no this was the general, as it was the uncommercial, fancy, it is not to be disputed that the group had drawn exceedingly within ten minutes. Yet now, the inconstant public turned its back upon them, and even leaned its elbows carelessly against the bar outside the window, and shook off the mud from its shoes, and also lent and borrowed fire for pipes.

Custodian re-enters from his door, 'Again once, gentlemen, you are invited –' No further invitation necessary. Ready dash into the street. Toilette finished. Old man coming out.

This time, the interest was grown too hot to admit of toleration of the boys on the stone posts. The homicidal white-lead worker made a pounce upon one boy who was hoisting himself up, and brought him to earth amidst general commendation. Closely stowed as we were, we yet formed into groups – groups of conversation, without separation from the mass – to discuss the old man. Rivals of the tall and sallow mason sprang into being, and here again was popular inconstancy. These rivals attracted audiences, and were greedily listened to; and whereas they had derived their information solely from the tall and sallow one, officious members of the crowd now sought to enlighten *him* on their authority. Changed by this social experience into an iron-visaged and inveterate misanthrope, the mason glared at mankind, and evidently cherished in his breast the wish that the whole of the present company could change places with the deceased old man. And now listeners became inattentive, and people made a start forward at a slight sound, and an unholy fire kindled in the public eye, and those next the gates beat at them impatiently, as if they were of the cannibal species and hungry.

Again the hinges creaked, and we rushed. Disorderly pressure for some time ensued before the uncommercial unit got figured into the front row of the sum. It was strange to see so much heat and uproar seething about one poor spare white-haired old man, so quiet for evermore. He was calm of feature and undisfigured, as he lay on his back – having been struck upon the hinder part of the head, and thrown forward – and something like a tear or two had started from the closed eyes, and lay wet upon the face. The uncommercial interest, sated at a glance, directed itself upon the striving crowd on either side and behind: wondering whether one might have guessed, from the expression of those faces merely, what kind of sight they were looking at. The differences of expression were not many. There was a little pity, but not much, and that mostly with a selfish touch in it – as who would say, 'Shall I, poor I, look like that, when the time comes!' There was more of a secretly brooding contemplation and curiosity, as, 'That man I don't like, and have the grudge against; would such be his appearance, if some one – not to mention names – by any chance gave him an ugly knock?' There was a wolfish stare at the object, in which the homicidal white-lead worker shone conspicuous. And there was a much more general, purposeless, vacant staring at it – like looking at waxwork, without a catalogue, and not knowing what to make of it. But all these expressions concurred in possessing the one under-lying expression of *looking at something that could not return a look.* The uncommercial notice had established this as very remarkable, when a new pressure all at once coming up from the street pinioned him ignominiously, and hurried him into the arms (now sleeved again) of the Custodian smoking at his door, and answering questions, between-puffs, with a certain placid meritorious air of not being proud, though high in office. And mentioning pride, it may be observed, by the way, that one could not well help investing the original sole occupant of the front row with an air depreciatory of the legitimate attraction of the poor old man: while the two in the second row seemed to exult at his superseded popularity.

Pacing presently round the garden of the Tower of St Jacques de la Boucherie, and presently again in front of the Hôtel de Ville, I called to mind a certain desolate open-air Morgue that I happened to light upon in London, one day in the hard winter of 1861, and which seemed as strange to me, at the time of seeing it, as if I had found it in China. Towards that hour of a winter's afternoon when the lamplighters are beginning to light the lamps in the streets a little before they are wanted, because the darkness thickens fast and soon, I was walking in from the country on the northern side of the Regent's Park – hard frozen and deserted – when I saw an empty Hansom cab drive up to the lodge at Gloucester-gate, and the driver with great agitation call to the man there: who quickly reached a long pole from a tree, and, deftly collared by the driver, jumped to the step of his little seat, and so the Hansom rattled out at the gate, galloping over the iron-bound road. I followed running, though not so fast but that when I came to the right-hand Canal Bridge, near the cross-path to Chalk Farm, the Hansom was stationary, the horse was smoking hot, the long pole was idle on the ground, and the driver and the park-keeper were looking over the bridge parapet. Looking over too, I saw, lying on the towing-path, with her face turned up towards us, a woman, dead a day or two, and under thirty, as I guessed, poorly dressed in black. The feet were lightly crossed at the ankles, and the dark hair, all pushed back from the face, as though that had been the last action of her desperate hands, streamed over the ground. Dabbled all about her, was the water and the broken ice that had dropped from her dress, and had splashed as she was got out. The policeman who had just got her out, and the passing costermonger who had helped him, were standing near the body; the latter, with that stare at it which I have likened to being at a waxwork exhibition without a catalogue; the former, looking over his stock, with professional stiffness and coolness, in the direction in which the bearers he had sent for, were expected. So dreadfully forlorn, so dreadfully sad, so dreadfully mysterious, this spectacle of our dear sister here departed! A barge came up, breaking the floating ice and the silence, and a woman steered it. The man with the horse that towed it, cared so little for the body, that the stumbling hoofs had been among the hair, and the tow-rope had caught and turned the head, before our cry of horror took him to the bridle. At which sound the steering woman looked up at us on the bridge, with contempt unutterable, and then looking down at the body with a similar expression – as if it were made in another likeness from herself, had been informed with other passions, had been lost by other chances, had had another nature dragged down to perdition – steered a spurning streak of mud at it, and passed on.

A better experience, but also of the Morgue kind, in which chance happily made me useful in a slight degree, arose to my remembrance as I took my way by the Boulevard de Sébastopol to the brighter scenes of Paris.

The thing happened, say, five-and-twenty years ago. I was a modest young uncommercial then, and timid and inexperienced. Many suns and winds have browned me in the line, but those were my pale days. Having newly taken the lease of a house in a certain distinguished metropolitan parish – a house which then appeared to me to be a frightfully first-class Family Mansion, involving awful responsibilities – I became the prey of a Beadle. I think the Beadle must have seen me going in or coming out, and must have observed that I tottered under the weight of my grandeur. Or, he may have been hiding under straw when I bought my first horse (in the desirable stable-yard attached to the first-class Family Mansion), and when the vendor remarked to me, in an original manner, on bringing him for approval, taking his cloth off, and smacking him, 'There, sir! *There's* a Orse!' And when I said gallantly, 'How much do you want for him?' and when the vendor said, 'No more than sixty guineas, from you,' and when I said smartly, 'Why not more than sixty from *me*?' And when he said crushingly, 'Because upon my soul and body, he'd be considered cheap at seventy, by one who understood the subject – but you don't.' I say, the Beadle may have been in hiding under straw, when this disgrace befell me, or he may have noted that I was too raw and young an Atlas to carry the first-class Family Mansion in a knowing manner. Be this as it may, the Beadle did what Melancholy did to the youth in Gray's Elegy – he marked me for his own. And the way in which the Beadle did it, was this: he summoned me as a Juryman on his Coroner's Inquests.

In my first feverish alarm I repaired 'for safety and for succour' – like those sagacious Northern shepherds who, having had no previous reason whatever to believe in young Norval, very prudently did not originate the hazardous idea of believing in him – to a deep householder. This profound man informed me that the Beadle counted on my buying him off; on my bribing him not to summon me; and that if I would attend an Inquest with a cheerful countenance, and profess alacrity in that branch of my country's service, the Beadle would be disheartened, and would give up the game.

I roused my energies, and the next time the wily Beadle summoned me, I went. The Beadle was the blankest Beadle I have ever looked on when I answered to my name; and his discomfiture gave me courage to go through with it.

We were impannelled to inquire concerning the death of a very little mite of a child. It was the old miserable story. Whether the mother had committed the minor offence of concealing the birth, or whether she had committed the major offence of killing the child, was the question on which we were wanted. We must commit her on one of the two issues.

The Inquest came off in the parish workhouse, and I have yet a lively impression that I was unanimously received by my brother Jurymen as a brother of the utmost conceivable insignificance. Also, that before we began, a broker who had lately cheated me fearfully in the matter of a pair of card-tables, was for the utmost rigour of the law. I remember that we sat in a sort of board-room, on such very large square horsehair chairs that I wondered what race of Patagonians they were made for; and further, that an undertaker gave me his card when we were in the full moral freshness of having just been sworn, as 'an inhabitant that was newly come into the parish, and was likely to have a young family.' The case was then stated to us by the coroner, and then we went downstairs – led by the plotting Beadle – to view the body. From that day to this, the poor little figure, on which that sounding legal appellation was bestowed, has lain in the same place, and with the same surroundings, to my thinking. In a kind of crypt devoted to the warehousing of the parochial coffins, and in the midst of a perfect Panorama of coffins of all sizes, it was stretched on a box; the mother had put it in her box – this box – almost as soon as it was born, and it had been presently found there. It had been opened, and neatly sewn up, and regarded from that point of view, it looked like a stuffed creature. It rested on a clean white cloth, with a surgical instrument or so at hand, and regarded from that point of view, it looked as if the cloth were 'laid,' and the Giant were coming to dinner. There was nothing repellant about the poor piece of innocence, and it demanded a mere form of looking at. So, we looked at an old pauper who was going about among the coffins with a foot-rule, as if he were a case of Self-Measurement; and we looked at one another; and we said the place was well white-washed anyhow; and then our conversational powers as a British Jury flagged, and the fore-man said, 'All right, gentlemen? Back again, Mr Beadle!'

The miserable young creature who had given birth to this child within a very few days, and who had cleaned the cold wet doorsteps immediately afterwards, was brought before us when we resumed our horse-hair chairs, and was present during the proceedings. She had a horse-hair chair herself, being very weak and ill; and I remember how she turned to the unsympathetic nurse who attended her, and who might have been the figure-head of a pauper-ship, and how she hid her face and sobs and tears upon that wooden shoulder. I remember, too, how hard her mistress was upon her (she was a servant-of-all-work), and with what a cruel pertinacity that piece of Virtue spun her thread of evidence double, by intertwisting it with the sternest thread of construction. Smitten hard by the terrible low wail from the utterly friendless orphan girl, which never ceased during the whole inquiry, I took heart to ask this witness a question or two, which hopefully admitted of an answer that might give a favourable turn to the case. She made the turn as little favourable as it could be, but it did some good, and the Coroner, who was nobly patient and humane (he was the late Mr Wakley), cast a look of strong encouragement in my direction. Then, we had the doctor who had made the examination, and the usual tests as to whether the child was born alive; but he was a timid muddle-headed doctor, and got confused and contradictory, and wouldn't say this, and couldn't answer for that, and the immaculate broker was too much for him, and our side slid back again. However, I tried again, and the Coroner backed me again, for which I ever afterwards felt grateful to him as I do now to his memory; and we got another favourable turn out of some other witness, some member of the family with a strong prepossession against the sinner; and I think we had the doctor back again; and I know that the Coroner summed up for our side, and that I and my British brothers turned round to discuss our verdict, and get ourselves into great difficulties with our large chairs and the broker. At that stage of the case I tried hard again, being convinced that I had cause for it; and at last we found for the minor offence of only concealing the birth; and the poor desolate creature, who had been taken out during our deliberation, being brought in again to be told of the verdict, then dropped upon her knees before us, with protestations that we were right – protestations among the most affecting that I have ever heard in my life – and was carried away insensible.

(In private conversation after this was all over, the Coroner showed me his reasons as a trained surgeon, for perceiving it to be impossible that the child could, under the most favourable circumstances, have drawn many breaths, in the very doubtful case of its having ever breathed at all; this, owing to the discovery of some foreign matter in the windpipe, quite irreconcilable with many moments of life.)

When the agonised girl had made those final protestations, I had seen her face, and it was in unison with her distracted heartbroken voice, and it was very moving. It certainly did not impress me by any beauty that it had, and if I ever see it again in another world I shall only know it by the help of some new sense or intelligence. But it came to me in my sleep that night, and I selfishly dismissed it in the most efficient way I could think of. I caused some extra care to be taken of her in the prison, and counsel to be retained for her defence when she was tried at the Old Bailey; and her sentence was lenient, and her history and conduct proved that it was right. In doing the little I did for her, I remember to have had the kind help of some gentle-hearted functionary to whom I addressed myself – but what functionary I have long forgotten – who I suppose was officially present at the Inquest.

I regard this as a very notable uncommercial experience, because this good came of a Beadle. And to the best of my knowledge, information, and belief, it is the only good that ever did come of a Beadle since the first Beadle put on his cocked-hat.

25

The Uncommercial Traveller

All The Year Round, 6 June 1863 (*UT1* as 'Birthday Celebrations')

The 'accidental circumstance' described in paragraph 1 below sounds attractively like a reference to a birthday in the Dickens family at the time of the paper's composition, but the only Dickens child with a birthday near was Sydney Smith Dickens ('The Admiral'), sixteen on 18 April and already enlisted as a naval cadet – hardly a likely candidate. As so often with the 'Uncommercial Papers', the reliability of the present article as autobiography is suspect, however intimate and allusive its manner. Dickens's reason for not writing recollections of 'hostelries' and 'Inns' may have been the more pragmatic one that he had already done so at length in the opening section ('The Guest') he contributed to the Christmas Number of *HW* for 1855, *The Holly-tree Inn*.

The same caveat applies to much of the narrator's reminiscences about birthdays. The 'peach-faced creature' (p. 230) is unlikely to be a representation of Dickens's childhood friend Lucy Stroughill, and the entire passage about birthday hampers is purely fictive, as Dickens never boarded at school (see Michael Slater, *Dickens and Women* [1983], pp. 40–1, and 'How Many Nurses Had Charles Dickens? *The Uncommercial Traveller* and Dickensian Biography', *Prose Studies*, Vol. 10 [1987], p. 255). Similar recollections of a childhood sweetheart are given to the young David in *David Copperfield*, who 'adored' Miss Shepherd of the 'round face and curly flaxen hair': 'in my own room, I am sometimes moved to cry out, "Oh, Miss Shepherd!" in a transport of love' (Ch. 18). Nevertheless, it is hard not to associate the narrator's wry memories of being thwarted in love at his coming-of-age party with what is known of Dickens's love for Maria

Beadnell in the early 1830s, or to sense that Dickens is working around a distinct autobiographical matrix. Dickens first met Maria Beadnell in May 1830, and, commenting upon his infatuation with her in 1855, recalled how 'it excluded every other idea from my mind for four years' (*Pilgrim*, Vol. VII, pp. 556–7 & n.). An evening party was held to celebrate Dickens's twenty-first birthday on 11 February 1833, and letters to Maria of 18 March and 14 May confirm that her painful rejection of his suit did occur at this time – as well as touch the same note of earnest self-importance which Dickens parodies in the imaginary letters to 'Mrs Onowenever' (pp. 232–3). Again in *David Copperfield*, a similar set of relationships is depicted: in Ch. 18 David is a youth of seventeen who 'shall be one-and-twenty in no time almost' and is hopelessly in love with the flirtatious but cruel 'eldest Miss Larkins', before meeting and setting his heart on Dora Spenlow (Ch. 26 et seq.).

Dickens's dislike of over-didactic and 'improving' entertainments for children, such as the 'Orrery' described (an early form of planetarium), was lifelong and forms the basis for a later 'Uncommercial' paper in 1869 (see article 41 below). The speaker who praises the entertainment as 'devoid of anything that could call a blush into the cheek of youth' (p. 231) looks forward to the creation of Podsnap in *Our Mutual Friend*, and his anxiety about anything that might 'bring a blush into the cheek of the young person' (see Book 1, Ch. 11). The meaning of the allusion to the South Kensington Museum is unclear. Gordon Spence has noted that sage green was in fact a prevalent colour in displays at the Museum's opening in 1857 (*Charles Dickens as a Familiar Essayist* [1977], p. 130), but as the Museum and its first General Superintendent, Henry Cole, made much of its educational and didactic aims, the remark may simply reflect the same dislike of pedagogy and pedagogues noted earlier.

Literary allusions (p. 231) 'the coming hamper cast its shadow before': Thomas Campbell, 'Lochiel's Warning' (1803), l. 56; (p. 232) 'volumes of Imaginary Conversations': Walter Savage Landor's *Imaginary Conversations* (1824–9); (p. 232) 'letters more in number than Horace Walpole's': Dickens had recently acquired Peter Cunningham's edition of Walpole's *Letters* in 9 vols (1857–9; Stonehouse); (p. 234) 'made a vacuum in Nature': '... the air, which but for vacancy/Had gone to gaze on Cleopatra too,/And made a gap in nature', Shakespeare, *Antony and Cleopatra*, Act 2, Sc. 5; (p. 237) 'Was there sufficient ground for supposing that the Immortal Shakespeare ever stole deer': allusion to Walter Savage Landor's *Citation and examination of William Shakspeare ... before ... Sir Thomas Lucy, Knight, touching Deer-stealing* (1834).

It came into my mind that I would recal in these notes a few of the many hostelries I have rested at in the course of my journeys; and, indeed, I had taken up my pen for the purpose, when I was baffled by an accidental circumstance. It was the having to leave off, to wish the owner of a certain bright face that looked in at my door, 'many happy returns of the day.' Thereupon a new thought came into my mind, driving its predecessor out, and I began to recal – instead of Inns – the birthdays that I have put up at, on my way to this present sheet of paper.

I can very well remember being taken out to visit some peach-faced creature in a blue sash, and shoes to correspond, whose life I supposed to consist entirely of birthdays. Upon seed-cake, sweet wine, and shining presents, that glorified young person seemed to me to be exclusively reared. At so early a stage of my travels did I assist at the anniversary of her nativity (and become enamoured of her), that I had not yet acquired the recondite knowledge that a birthday is the common property of all who are born, but supposed it to be a special gift bestowed by the favouring Heavens on that one distinguished infant. There was no other company, and we sat in a shady bower – under a table, as my better (or worse) knowledge leads me to believe – and were regaled with saccharine substances and liquids, until it was time to part. A bitter powder was administered to me next morning, and I was wretched. On the whole, a pretty accurate foreshadowing of my more mature experiences in such wise!

Then came the time when, inseparable from one's own birthday, was a certain sense of merit, a consciousness of well-earned distinction. When I regarded my birthday as a graceful achievement of my own, a monument of my perseverance, independence, and good sense, redounding greatly to my honour. This was at about the period when Olympia Squires became involved in the anniversary. Olympia was most beautiful (of course), and I loved her to that degree, that I used to be obliged to get out of my little bed in the night, expressly to exclaim to Solitude, 'O, Olympia Squires!' Visions of Olympia, clothed entirely in sage-green, from which I infer a defectively educated taste on the part of her respected parents, who were necessarily unacquainted with the South Kensington Museum, still arise before me. Truth is sacred, and the visions are crowned by a shining white beaver bonnet, impossibly suggestive of a little feminine postboy. My memory presents a birthday when Olympia and I were taken by an unfeeling relative – some cruel uncle, or the like – to a slow torture called an Orrery. The terrible instrument was set up at the local Theatre, and I had expressed a profane wish in the morning that it was a Play: for which a serious aunt had probed my conscience deep, and my pocket deeper, by reclaiming a bestowed half-crown. It was a venerable and a shabby Orrery, at least one thousand stars and twenty-five comets behind the age. Nevertheless, it was awful. When the low-spirited gentleman with a wand said, 'Ladies and gentlemen' (meaning particularly Olympia and me), 'the lights are about to be put out, but there is not the slightest cause for alarm,' it was very alarming. Then the planets and stars began. Sometimes they wouldn't come on, sometimes they wouldn't go off, sometimes they had holes in them, and mostly they didn't seem to be good likenesses. All this time the gentleman with the wand was going on in the dark (tapping away at the Heavenly bodies between whiles, like a wearisome woodpecker), about a sphere revolving on its own axis eight hundred and ninety-seven thousand millions of times – or miles – in two hundred and sixty-three thousand five hundred and twenty-four millions of something elses, until I thought, if this was a birthday it were better never to have been born. Olympia, also, became much depressed, and we both slumbered and woke cross, and still the gentleman was going on in the dark – whether up in the stars, or down on the stage, it would have been hard to make out, if it had been worth trying – cyphering away about planes of orbits, to such an infamous extent that Olympia, stung to madness, actually kicked me. A pretty birthday spectacle when the lights were turned up again, and all the schools in the town (including the National, who had come in for nothing, and serve them right, for they were always throwing stones) were discovered with exhausted countenances, screwing their knuckles into their eyes, or clutching their heads of hair. A pretty birthday speech when Doctor Sleek of the City-Free bobbed up his powdered head in the stage-box, and said that before this assembly dispersed he really must beg to express his entire approval of a lecture as improving, as informing, as devoid of anything that could call a blush into the cheek of youth, as any it had ever been his lot to hear delivered. A pretty birthday altogether, when Astronomy couldn't leave poor small Olympia Squires and me alone, but must put an end to our loves! For, we never got over it; the threadbare Orrery outwore our mutual tenderness; the man with the wand was too much for the boy with the bow.

When shall I disconnect the combined smells of oranges, brown paper, and straw, from those other birthdays at school, when the coming hamper cast its shadow before, and when a week of social harmony – shall I add of admiring and affectionate popularity – led up to that Institution? What noble sentiments were expressed to me in the days before the hamper, what vows of friendship were sworn to me, what exceedingly old knives were given me, what generous avowals of having been in the wrong emanated from else obstinate spirits once enrolled among my enemies! The birthday of the potted game and guava jelly, is still made special to me by the noble conduct of Bully Globson. Letters from home had mysteriously inquired whether I should be much surprised and disappointed if among the treasures in the coming hamper I discovered potted game, and guava jelly from the Western Indies. I had mentioned those hints in confidence to a few friends, and had promised to give away, as I now see reason to believe, a handsome covey of partridges potted, and about a hundred-weight of guava jelly. It was now that Globson, Bully no more, sought me out in the playground. He was a big fat boy, with a big fat head and a big fat fist, and at the beginning of that Half had raised such a bump on my forehead that I couldn't get my hat of state on, to go to church. He said that after an interval of cool reflection (four months) he now felt this blow to have been an error of judgment, and that he wished to apologise for the same. Not only that, but, holding down his big head between his two big hands in order that I might reach it conveniently, he requested me, as an act of justice which would appease his awakened conscience, to raise a retributive bump upon it, in the presence of witnesses. This handsome proposal I modestly declined, and he then embraced me, and we walked away conversing. We conversed respecting the West India islands, and in the pursuit of knowledge he asked me with much interest whether in the course of my reading I had met with any reliable description of the mode of manu-facturing guava jelly; or whether I had ever happened to taste that conserve, which he had been given to understand was of rare excellence.

Seventeen, eighteen, nineteen, twenty; and then with the waning months came an ever-augmenting sense of the dignity of twenty-one. Heaven knows I had nothing to 'come into,' save the bare birthday, and yet I esteemed it as a great possession. I now and then paved the way to my state of dignity, by beginning a proposition with the casual words, 'say that a man of twenty-one,' or by the incidental assumption of a fact that could not sanely be disputed, as, 'for when a fellow comes to be a man of twenty-one.' I gave a party on the occasion. She was there. It is unnecessary to name Her, more particularly; She was older than I, and had pervaded every chink and crevice of my mind for three or four years. I had held volumes of Imaginary Conversations with her mother on the subject of our union, and I had written letters more in number than Horace Walpole's, to that discreet woman, soliciting her daughter's hand in marriage. I had never had the remotest intention of sending any of those letters; but to write them, and after a few days tear them up, had been a sublime occupation. Sometimes, I had begun 'Honoured Madam. I think that a lady gifted with those powers of observation which I know you to possess, and endowed with those womanly sympathies with the young and ardent which it were more than heresy to doubt, can scarcely have failed to discover that I love your adorable daughter deeply, devotedly.' In less buoyant states of mind I had begun, 'Bear with me, Dear Madam, bear with a daring wretch who is about to make a surprising confession to you, wholly unanticipated by yourself, and which he beseeches you to commit to the flames as soon as you have become aware to what a towering height his mad ambition soars.' At other times – periods of profound mental depression, when She had gone out to balls where I was not – the draft took the affecting form of a paper to be left on my table after my departure to the confines of the globe. As thus: 'For Mrs Onowenever, these lines when the hand that traces them shall be far away. I could not bear the daily torture of hopelessly loving the dear one whom I will not name. Broiling on the Coast of Africa, or congealing on the shores of Greenland, I am far far better there than here.' (In this sentiment my cooler judgment perceives that the family of the beloved object would have most completely concurred.) 'If I ever emerge from obscurity, and my name is ever heralded by Fame, it will be for her dear sake. If I ever amass Gold, it will be to pour it at her feet. Should I, on the other hand, become the prey of Ravens –' I doubt if I ever quite made up my mind what was to be done in that affecting case; I tried, 'then it is better so;' but not feeling convinced that it would be better so, I vacillated between leaving all else blank, which looked expressive and bleak, or winding up with 'Farewell!'

This fictitious correspondence of mine is to blame for the foregoing digression. I was about to pursue the statement that on my twenty-first birthday I gave a party, and She was there. It was a beautiful party. There was not a single animate or inanimate object connected with it (except the company and myself) that I had ever seen before. Everything was hired, and the mercenaries in attendance were profound strangers to me. Behind a door, in the crumby part of the night when wine-glasses were to be found in unexpected spots, I spoke to Her – spoke out to Her. What passed, I cannot as a man of honour reveal. She was all angelical gentleness, but a word was mentioned – a short and dreadful word of three letters, beginning with a B – which, as I remarked at the moment, 'scorched my brain.' She went away soon afterwards, and when the hollow throng (though to be sure it was no fault of theirs) dispersed, I issued forth, with a dissipated scorner, and, as I mentioned expressly to him, 'sought oblivion.' It was found, with a dreadful headache in it, but it didn't last; for, in the shaming light of next day's noon, I raised my heavy head in bed, looking back to the birthdays behind me, and tracking the circle by which I had got round, after all, to the bitter powder and the wretchedness again.

This reactionary powder (taken so largely by the human race that I am inclined to regard it as the Universal Medicine once sought for in Laboratories) is capable of being made up in another form for birthday use. Anybody's long-lost brother will do ill to turn up on a birthday. If I had a long-lost brother, I should know beforehand that he would prove a tremendous fraternal failure if he appointed to rush into my arms on my birthday. The first Magic Lantern I ever saw, was secretly and elaborately planned to be the great effect of a very juvenile birthday; but it wouldn't act, and its images were dim. My experience of adult birthday Magic Lanterns may possibly have been unfortunate, but has certainly been similar. I have an illustrative birthday in my eye: a birthday of my friend Flipfield, whose birthdays had long been remarkable as social successes. There had been nothing set or formal about them; Flipfield having been accustomed merely to say, two or three days before, 'Don't forget to come and dine, old boy, according to custom;' – I don't know what he said to the ladies he invited, but I may safely assume it *not* to have been 'old girl.' Those were delightful gatherings, and were enjoyed by all participators. In an evil hour, a long-lost brother of Flipfield's came to light in foreign parts. Where he had been hidden, or what he had been doing, I don't know, for Flipfield vaguely informed me that he had turned up 'on the banks of the Ganges' – speaking of him as if he had been washed ashore. The Long-lost was coming home, and Flipfield made an unfortunate calculation, based on the well-known regularity of the P. and O. Steamers, that matters might be so contrived as that the Long-lost should appear in the nick of time on his (Flipfield's) birthday. Delicacy commanded that I should repress the gloomy anticipations with which my soul became fraught when I heard of this plan. The fatal day arrived, and we assembled in force. Mrs Flipfield senior formed an interesting feature in the group, with a blue-veined miniature of the late Mr Flipfield round her neck, in an oval, resembling a tart from the pastrycook's: his hair powdered, and the bright buttons on his coat evidently very like. She was accompanied by Miss Flipfield, the eldest of her numerous family, who held her pocket-handkerchief to her bosom in a majestic manner, and spoke to all of us (none of us had ever seen her before), in pious and condoning tones, of all the quarrels that had taken place in the family, from her infancy – which must have been a long time ago – down to that hour. The Long-lost did not appear. Dinner, half an hour later than usual, was announced, and still no Long-lost. We sat down to table. The knife and fork of the Long-lost made a vacuum in Nature, and when the champagne came round for the first time, Flipfield gave him up for the day, and had them removed. It was then that the Long-lost gained the height of his popularity with the company; for my own part, I felt convinced that I loved him dearly. Flipfield's dinners are perfect, and he is the easiest and best of entertainers. Dinner went on brilliantly, and the more the Long-lost didn't come, the more comfortable we grew, and the more highly we thought of him. Flipfield's own man (who has a regard for me) was in the act of struggling with an ignorant stipendiary, to wrest from him the wooden leg of a Guinea-fowl which he was pressing on my acceptance, and to substitute a slice of the breast, when a ringing at the door-bell suspended the strife. I looked round me, and perceived the sudden pallor which I knew my own visage revealed, reflected on the faces of the company. Flipfield hurriedly excused himself, went out, was absent for about a minute or two, and then re-entered with the Long-lost.

I beg to say distinctly that if the stranger had brought Mont Blanc with him, or had come attended by a retinue of eternal snows, he could not have chilled the circle to the marrow in a more efficient manner. Embodied Failure sat enthroned upon the Long-lost's brow, and pervaded him to his Long-lost boots. In vain Mrs Flipfield senior, opening her arms, exclaimed, 'My Tom!' and pressed his nose against the counterfeit presentment of his other parent. In vain Miss Flipfield, in the first transports of this reunion, showed him a dint upon her maidenly cheek, and asked him if he remembered when he did that with the bellows? We, the bystanders, were overcome, but overcome by the palpable, undisguisable, utter, and total breakdown of the Long-lost. Nothing he could have done would have set him right with us but his instant return to the Ganges. In the very same moments it became established that the feeling was reciprocal, and that the Long-lost detested us. When a friend of the family (not myself, upon my honour), wishing to set things going again, asked him, while he partook of soup – asked him with an amiability of intention beyond all praise, but with a weakness of execution open to defeat – what kind of river he considered the Ganges, the Long-lost, scowling at the friend of the family over his spoon, as one of an abhorrent race, replied, 'Why a river of water, I suppose,' and spooned his soup into himself with a malignancy of hand and eye that blighted the amiable questioner. Not an opinion could be elicited from the Long-lost, in unison with the sentiments of any individual present. He contradicted Flipfield dead, before he had eaten his salmon. He had no idea – or affected to have no idea – that it was his brother's birthday, and on the communication of that interesting fact to him, merely wanted to make him out four years older than he was. He was an antipathetical being, with a peculiar power and gift of treading on everybody's tenderest place. They talk in America of a man's 'Platform.' I should describe the Platform of the Long-lost as a Platform composed of other people's corns, on which he had stumped his way, with all his might and main, to his present position. It is needless to add that Flipfield's great birthday went by the board, and that he was a wreck when I pretended at parting to wish him many happy returns of it.

There is another class of birthdays at which I have so frequently assisted, that I may assume such birthdays to be pretty well known to the human race. My friend Mayday's birthday is an example. The guests have no knowledge of one another except on that one day in the year, and are annually terrified for a week by the prospect of meeting one another again. There is a fiction among us that we have uncommon reasons for being particularly lively and spirited on the occasion, whereas deep despondency is no phrase for the expression of our feelings. But the wonderful feature of the case is, that we are in tacit accordance to avoid the subject – to keep it as far off as possible, as long as possible – and to talk about anything else, rather than the joyful event. I may even go so far as to assert that there is a dumb compact among us that we will pretend that it is NOT Mayday's birthday. A mysterious and gloomy Being, who is said to have gone to school with Mayday, and who is so lank and lean that he seriously impugns the Dietary of the establishment at which they were jointly educated, always leads us, as I may say, to the block, by laying his grisly hand on a decanter and begging us to fill our glasses. The devices and pretences that I have seen put in practice to defer the fatal moment, and to interpose between this man and his purpose, are innumerable. I have known desperate guests, when they saw the grisly hand approaching the decanter, wildly to begin, without any antecedent whatsoever, 'That reminds me –' and to plunge into long stories. When at last the hand and the decanter come together, a shudder, a palpable perceptible shudder, goes round the table. We receive the reminder that it is Mayday's birthday, as if it were the anniversary of some profound disgrace he had undergone, and we sought to comfort him. And when we have drunk Mayday's health, and wished him many happy returns, we are seized for some moments with a ghastly blitheness, an unnatural levity, as if we were in the first flushed reaction of having undergone a surgical operation.

Birthdays of this species have a public as well as a private phase. My 'boyhood's home,' Dullborough, presents a case in point. An Immortal Somebody was wanted in Dullborough, to dimple for a day the stagnant face of the waters; he was rather wanted by Dullborough generally, and much wanted by the principal hotel-keeper. The County history was looked up for a locally Immortal Somebody, but the registered Dullborough worthies were all Nobodies. In this state of things, it is hardly necessary to record that Dullborough did what every man does when he wants to write a book or deliver a lecture, and is provided with all the materials except a subject. It fell back upon Shakespeare.

No sooner was it resolved to celebrate Shakespeare's birthday in Dullborough, than the popularity of the immortal bard became surprising. You might have supposed the first edition of his works to have been published last week, and enthusiastic Dullborough to have got half through them. (I doubt, by the way, whether it had ever done half that, but this is a private opinion.) A young gentleman with a sonnet, the retention of which for two years had enfeebled his mind and undermined his knees, got the sonnet into the Dullborough Warden, and gained flesh. Portraits of Shakespeare broke out in the book-shop windows, and our principal artist painted a large original portrait in oils for the decoration of the dining-room. It was not in the least like any of the other portraits, and was exceedingly admired, the head being much swollen. At the Institution, the Debating Society discussed the new question, Was there sufficient ground for supposing that the Immortal Shakespeare ever stole deer? This was indignantly decided by an overwhelming majority in the negative; indeed, there was but one vote on the Poaching side, and that was the vote of the orator who had undertaken to advocate it, and who became quite an obnoxious character – particularly to the Dullborough 'roughs,' who were about as well informed on the matter as most other people. Distinguished speakers were invited down, and very nearly came (but not quite). Subscriptions were opened, and committees sat, and it would have been far from a popular measure in the height of the excitement, to have told Dullborough that it wasn't Stratford-upon-Avon. Yet, after all these preparations, when the great festivity took place, and the portrait, elevated aloft, surveyed the company as if it were in danger of springing a mine of intellect and blowing itself up, it did undoubtedly happen, according to the inscrutable mysteries of things, that nobody could be induced, not to say to touch upon Shakespeare, but to come within a mile of him, until the crack speaker of Dullborough rose to propose the immortal memory. Which he did with the perplexing and astonishing result that before he had repeated the great name half a dozen times, or had been upon his legs as many minutes, he was assailed with a general shout of 'Question!'

26

The Uncommercial Traveller

All The Year Round, 20 June 1863 (*UT2* as 'The Short-Timers')

The Uncommercial's recollection of being 'one of seventy boys' at a school is closer to the circumstances of Dickens's life than the depiction of schooldays in the previous article: Wellington House Academy, Hampstead Road, which Dickens attended between 1825 and 1827, was a day school of about this size (see Vol. 1 of this edition, pp. xxx–xxxi). Dickens's interest in the schools of London's East End went back at least to [?18] February 1846, when he was conducted round the pauper schools of the Stepney Parish Union by the then Chairman of the Board, George F. Young (see *Pilgrim*, Vol. IV, p. 552 & n.). The present paper describes a return visit to the Stepney Union schools, located on the south side of Northey Street, and the trip was made in the company of Edwin Chadwick, the veteran sanitary reformer and commissioner, on 27 May 1863 (see *Pilgrim*, Vol. X, p. 251).

In 1860 Chadwick had written and publicised at least one short paper on the benefits of combining 'the military or the naval drill ... with half-time book instruction' (title page missing; [November 1860], p. xxvii), and praising the research into the half-time system conducted by Scottish educationalist and philosopher Horace Grant (see also *The Examiner's* report on a paper read by Chadwick earlier in the year, 'Military Drill in Public Schools', 31 March 1860, p. 195, cols a, b). In his *Biographical Notice of Mr Horace Grant* prefaced to Grant's *Geography for Young Children* (1861), Chadwick noted his own role in promoting the latter's research:

[A]s one of the commissioners for inquiring into the labor of young persons in factories, I proposed with my colleagues, that compulsory school attendance should be limited to three hours daily. ... At my instance, the same limit of half-time school attendance was adopted for district and other schools under control of the Poor-Law Board. [p. xxviii]

On leaving the Stepney schools, Dickens signed the Visitors' Book, commenting: 'I have never visited any similar establishment with so much pleasure. I have never seen any so well administered, and I have never seen children more reasonably, humanely, and intelligently treated' (see *The Dickensian*, Vol. 15 [1919], p. 146f.).

Three other articles in *ATYR* in the early 1860s had previously demonstrated the journal's commitment to promoting the Half-Time system: 'Stomach for Study' (20 October 1860), 'Children of all Work (8 June 1861), and 'In and Out of School' (19 October 1861).

Literary allusions (p.243) 'Cheer boys, Cheer': song popular during the US Civil War (1850; words by Charles Mackay, music by Henry Russell); (p. 243) 'Yankee Doodle': popular partisan song (anon.; 1755 or earlier); (p. 243) 'God Save the Queen': version of the British National Anthem, attributed to various authors (1745, or earlier); (p. 243) 'God bless the Prince of Wales': patriotic song by Henry Richards (1862); (p. 244) 'wise as the serpent', 'wisdom of the serpent' etc.: St Matthew 10:16; (p. 244) '... the cymbals to dash at a sounding answer': 1 Corinthians 13:1; (p. 247) 'little children ... Kingdom of Heaven': Matthew 18:3; (p. 247) 'the child's jingle ... bells of Step-ney': the old English nursery rhyme 'Oranges and lemons'.

'Within so many yards of this Covent Garden lodging of mine, as within so many yards of Westminster Abbey, Saint Paul's Cathedral, the Houses of Parliament, the Prisons, the Courts of Justice, all the Institutions that govern the land, I can find – *must* find, whether I will or no – in the open streets, shameful instances of neglect of children, intolerable toleration of the engenderment of paupers, idlers, thieves, races of wretched and destructive cripples both in body and mind, a misery to themselves, a misery to the community, a disgrace to civilisation, and an outrage on Christianity. I know it to be a fact as easy of demonstration as any sum in any of the elementary rules of arithmetic, that if the State would begin its work and duty at the beginning, and would with the strong hand take those children out of the streets, while they are yet children, and wisely train them, it would make them a part of England's glory, not its shame – of England's strength, not its weakness – would raise good soldiers and sailors, and good citizens, and many great men, out of the seeds of its criminal population. Yet I go on bearing with the enormity as if it were nothing, and I go on reading the Parliamentary Debates as if they were something, and I concern myself far more about one railway-bridge across a public thoroughfare, than about a dozen generations of scrofula, ignorance, wickedness, prostitution, poverty, and felony. I can slip out at my door, in the small hours after any midnight, and, in one circuit of the purlieus of Covent Garden Market, can behold a state of infancy and youth, as vile as if a Bourbon sat upon the English throne; a great police force looking on with authority to do no more than worry and hunt the dreadful vermin into corners, and there leave them. Within the length of a few streets I can find a workhouse, mismanaged with that dull short-sighted obstinacy that its greatest opportunities as to the children it receives are lost, and yet not a farthing saved to anyone. But the wheel goes round, and round, and round; and because it goes round – so I am told by the politest authorities – it goes well.'

Thus I reflected, one day in the Whitsun week last past, as I floated down the Thames among the bridges, looking – not inappropriately – at the drags that were hanging up at certain dirty stairs to hook the drowned out, and at the numerous conveniences provided to facilitate their tumbling in. My object in that uncommercial journey called up another train of thought, and it ran as follows:

'When I was at school, one of seventy boys, I wonder by what secret understanding our attention began to wander when we had pored over our books for some hours. I wonder by what ingenuity we brought on that confused state of mind when sense became nonsense, when figures wouldn't work, when dead languages wouldn't construe, when live languages wouldn't be spoken, when memory wouldn't come, when dulness and vacancy wouldn't go. I cannot remember that we ever conspired to be sleepy after dinner, or that we ever particularly wanted to be stupid, and to have flushed faces and hot beating heads, or to find blank hopelessness and obscurity this afternoon in what would become perfectly clear and bright in the freshness of tomorrow morning. We suffered for these things, and they made us miserable enough. Neither do I remember that we ever bound ourselves by any secret oath or other solemn obligation, to find the seats getting too hard to be sat upon after a certain time; or to have intolerable twitches in our legs, rendering us aggressive and malicious with those members; or to be troubled with a similar uneasiness in our elbows, attended with fistic consequences to our neighbours; or to carry two pounds of lead in the chest, four pounds in the head, and several active blue-bottles in each ear. Yet, for certain, we suffered under those distresses, and were always charged at for labouring under them, as if we had brought them on of our own deliberate act and deed. As to the mental portion of them being my own fault in my own case – I should like to ask any well-trained and experienced teacher, not to say psychologist. And as to the physical portion – I should like to ask Professor Owen.'

It happened that I had a small bundle of papers with me, on what is called 'The Half-Time System' in schools. Referring to one of those papers, I found that the indefatigable Mr Chadwick had been beforehand with me, and had already asked Professor Owen: who had handsomely replied that I was not to blame, but that, being troubled with a skeleton, and having been constituted according to certain natural laws, I and my skeleton were unfortunately bound by those laws – even in school – and had comported ourselves accordingly. Much comforted by the good Professor's being on my side, I read on to discover whether the indefatigable Mr Chadwick had taken up the mental part of my afflictions. I found that he had, and that he had gained on my behalf Sir Benjamin Brodie, Sir David Wilkie, Sir Walter Scott, and the common sense of mankind. For which I beg Mr Chadwick, if this should meet his eye, to accept my warm acknowledgments.

Up to that time I had retained a misgiving that the seventy unfortunates of whom I was one, must have been, without knowing it, leagued together by the spirit of evil in a sort of perpetual Guy Fawkes Plot, to grope about in vaults with dark lanterns after a certain period of continuous study. But now the misgiving vanished, and I floated on with a quieted mind to see the Half-Time System in action. For that was the purpose of my journey, both by steamboat on the Thames, and by very dirty railway on the shore. To which last institution, I beg to recommend the legal use of coke as engine-fuel, rather than the illegal use of coal; the recommendation is quite disinterested, for I was most liberally supplied with small coal on the journey, for which no charge was made. I had not only my eyes, nose, and ears filled, but my hat, and all my pockets, and my pocket-book, and my watch.

The V.D.S.C.R.C. (or Very Dirty and Small Coal Railway Company) delivered me close to my destination, and I soon found the Half-Time System established in spacious premises, and freely placed at my convenience and disposal.

What would I see first, of the Half-Time System? I chose Military Drill. 'Atten–tion!' Instantly, a hundred boys stood forth in the paved yard as one boy; bright, quick, eager, steady, watchful for the look of command, instant and ready for the word. Not only was there complete precision – complete accord to the eye and to the ear – but an alertness in the doing of the thing which deprived it, curiously, of its monotonous or mechanical character. There was perfect uniformity, and yet an individual spirit and emulation. No spectator could doubt that the boys liked it. With non-commissioned officers varying from a yard to a yard and a half high, the result could not possibly have been attained otherwise. They marched, and counter-marched, and formed in line and square, and company, and single file and double file, and performed a variety of evolutions; all most admirably. In respect of an air of enjoyable under-standing of what they were about, which seems to be forbidden to English soldiers, the boys might have been small French troops. When they were dismissed, and the broadsword exercise, limited to a much smaller number, succeeded, the boys who had no part in that new drill either looked on attentively, or disported themselves in a gymnasium hard by. The steadiness of the broadsword boys on their short legs, and the firmness with which they sustained the different positions, was truly remarkable.

The broadsword exercise over, suddenly there was great excitement and a rush. Naval Drill!

In a corner of the ground stood a decked mimic ship, with real masts, yards, and sails – mainmast seventy feet high. At the word of command from the Skipper of this ship – a mahogany-faced Old Salt, with the indispensable quid in his cheek, the true nautical roll, and all wonderfully complete – the rigging was covered with a swarm of boys: one, the first to spring into the shrouds, outstripping all the others, and resting on the truck of the main-topmast in no time.

And now we stood out to sea, in a most amazing manner; the Skipper himself, the whole crew, the Uncommercial, and all hands present, implicitly believing that there was not a moment to lose, that the wind had that instant chopped round and sprung up fair, and that we were away on a voyage round the world. Get all sail upon her! With a will my lads! Lay out upon the main-yard there! Look alive at the weather earring! Cheery, my boys! Let go the sheet now! Stand by at the braces, you! With a will, aloft there! Belay, starboard watch! Fifer! Come aft, fifer, and give 'em a tune! Forthwith, springs up fifer, fife in hand – smallest boy ever seen – big lump on temple, having lately fallen down on a paving-stone – gives 'em a tune with all his might and main. Hooroar, fifer! With a will, my lads! Tip 'em a livelier one, fifer! Fifer tips 'em a livelier one, and excitement increases. Shake 'em out, my lads! Well done! There you have her! Pretty, pretty! Every rag upon her she can carry, wind right astern, and ship cutting through the water fifteen knots an hour!

At this favourable moment of our voyage, I gave the alarm 'A man overboard!' (on the gravel), but he was immediately recovered, none the worse. Presently, I observed the Skipper overboard, but forebore to mention it, as he seemed in no wise disconcerted by the accident. Indeed, I soon came to regard the Skipper as an amphibious creature, for he was so perpetually plunging overboard to look up at the hands aloft, that he was oftener in the bosom of the ocean than on deck. His pride in his crew on those occasions was delightful, and the conventional unintelligibility of his orders in the ears of uncommercial land-lubbers and loblolly boys, though they were always intelligible to the crew, was hardly less pleasant. But we couldn't expect to go on in this way for ever; dirty weather came on, and then worse weather, and when we least expected it we got into tremendous difficulties. Screw loose in the chart, perhaps – something certainly wrong somewhere – but here we were with breakers ahead, my lads, driving head on, slap on a lee shore! The Skipper broached this terrific announcement in such great agitation, that the small fifer, not fifeing now, but standing looking on near the wheel with his fife under his arm, seemed for the moment quite unboyed, though he speedily recovered his presence of mind. In the trying circumstances that ensued, the Skipper and the crew proved worthy of one another. The Skipper got dreadfully hoarse, but otherwise was master of the situation. The man at the wheel did wonders; all hands (except the fifer) were turned up to wear ship; and I observed the fifer, when we were at our greatest extremity, to refer to some document in his waistcoat-pocket, which I conceived to be his will. I think she struck. I was not myself conscious of any collision, but I saw the Skipper so very often washed overboard and back again, that I could only impute it to the beating of the ship. I am not enough of a seaman to describe the manoeuvres by which we were saved, but they made the Skipper very hot (French polishing his mahogany face) and the crew very nimble, and succeeded to a marvel; for, within a few minutes of the first alarm, we had wore ship and got her off, and were all a-tauto – which I felt very grateful for: not that I knew what it was, but that I perceived that we had not been all a-tauto lately. Land now appeared on our weather-bow, and we shaped our course for it, having the wind abeam, and frequently changing the man at the helm, in order that every man might have his spell. We worked into harbour under prosperous circumstances, and furled our sails, and squared our yards, and made all ship-shape and handsome, and so our voyage ended. When I complimented the Skipper at parting on his exertions and those of his gallant crew, he informed me that the latter were provided for the worst, all hands being taught to swim and dive; and he added that the able seaman at the main-topmast truck especially, could dive as deep as he could go high.

The next adventure that befel me in my visit to the Short-Timers, was the sudden apparition of a military band. I had been inspecting the hammocks of the crew of the good ship, when I saw with astonishment that several musical instruments, brazen and of great size, appeared to have suddenly developed two legs each, and to be trotting about a yard. And my astonishment was heightened when I observed a large drum, that had previously been leaning helpless against a wall, taking up a stout position on four legs. Approaching this drum and looking over it, I found two boys behind it (it was too much for one), and then I found that each of the brazen instruments had brought out a boy, and was going to discourse sweet sounds. The boys – not omitting the fifer, now playing a new instrument – were dressed in neat uniform, and stood up in a circle at their music-stands, like any other Military Band. They played a march or two, and then we had Cheer boys, Cheer, and then we had Yankee Doodle, and we finished, as in loyal duty bound, with God Save the Queen. The band's proficiency was perfectly wonderful, and it was not at all wonderful that the whole body corporate of Short-Timers listened with faces of the liveliest interest and pleasure.

What happened next among the Short-Timers? As if the band had blown me into a great class-room out of their brazen tubes, *in* a great class-room I found myself now, with the whole choral force of Short-Timers singing the praises of a summer's day to the harmonium, and my small but highly-respected friend the fifer blazing away vocally, as if he had been saving up his wind for the last twelvemonth; also the whole crew of the good ship Nameless swarming up and down the scale as if they had never swarmed up and down the rigging. This done, we threw our whole power into God bless the Prince of Wales, and blessed his Royal Highness to such an extent that, for my own uncommercial part, I gasped again when it was over. The moment this was done, we formed, with surpassing freshness, into hollow squares, and fell to work at oral lessons, as if we never did, and had never thought of doing, anything else.

Let a veil be drawn over the self-committals into which the Uncommercial Traveller would have been betrayed but for a discreet reticence, coupled with an air of absolute wisdom on the part of that artful personage. Take the square of five, multiply it by fifteen, divide it by three, deduct eight from it, add four dozen to it, give me the result in pence, and tell me how many eggs I could get for it at three farthings apiece. The problem is hardly stated, when a dozen small boys pour out answers. Some wide, some very nearly right, some worked as far as they go with such accuracy, as at once to show what link of the chain has been dropped in the hurry. For the moment, none are quite right; but behold a labouring spirit beating the buttons on its corporeal waistcoat, in a process of internal calculation, and knitting an accidental bump on its corporeal forehead in a concentration of mental arithmetic! It is my honourable friend (if he will allow me to call him so) the fifer. With right arm eagerly extended in token of being inspired with an answer, and with right leg foremost, the fifer solves the mystery: then recals both arm and leg, and with bump in ambush awaits the next poser. Take the square of three, multiply it by seven, divide it by four, add fifty to it, take thirteen from it, multiply it by two, double it, give me the result in pence, and say how many halfpence. Wise as the serpent is the four feet of performer on the nearest approach to that instrument, whose right arm instantly appears, and quenches this arithmetical fire. Tell me something about Great Britain, tell me something about its principal productions, tell me something about its ports, tell me something about its seas and rivers, tell me something about coal, iron, cotton, timber, tin, and turpentine. The hollow square bristles with extended right arms; but ever faithful to fact is the fifer, ever wise as the serpent is the performer on that instrument, ever prominently buoyant and brilliant are all members of the band. I observe the player of the cymbals to dash at a sounding answer now and then rather than not cut in at all; but I take that to be in the way of his instrument. All these questions, and many such, are put on the spur of the moment, and by one who has never examined these boys. The Uncommercial, invited to add another, falteringly demands how many birthdays a man born on the twenty-ninth of February will have had on completing his fiftieth year? A general perception of trap and pitfal instantly arises, and the fifer is seen to retire behind the corduroys of his next neighbours, as perceiving special necessity for collecting himself and communing with his mind. Mean-while, the wisdom of the serpent suggests that the man will have had only one birthday in all that time, for how can any man have more than one, seeing that he is born once and dies once? The blushing Uncommercial stands corrected, and amends the formula. Pondering ensues, two or three wrong answers are offered, and Cymbals strikes up 'Six!' but doesn't know why. Then modestly emerging from his Academic Grove of corduroys appears the fifer, right arm extended, right leg foremost, bump irradiated. 'Twelve, and two over!'

The feminine Short-Timers passed a similar examination, and very creditably too. Would have done better perhaps, with a little more geniality on the part of their pupil-teacher; for a cold eye, my young friend, and a hard abrupt manner, are not by any means the powerful engines that your innocence supposes them to be. Both girls and boys wrote excellently, from copy and dictation; both could cook; both could mend their own clothes; both could clean up everything about them in an orderly and skilful way, the girls having womanly household knowledge superadded. Order and method began in the songs of the Infant School which I visited likewise, and they were even in their dwarf degree to be found in the Nursery, where the Uncommercial walking-stick was carried off with acclamations, and where 'the Doctor' – a medical gentleman of two, who took his degree on the night when he was found at an apothecary's door – did the honours of the establishment with great urbanity and gaiety.

These have long been excellent schools; long before the days of the Short-Time. I first saw them, twelve or fifteen years ago. But since the introduction of the Short-Time system it has been proved here that eighteen hours a week of book-learning are more profitable than thirty-six, and that the pupils are far quicker and brighter than of yore. The good influences of music on the whole body of children have likewise been surprisingly proved. Obviously another of the immense advantages of the Short-Time System to the cause of good education is the great diminution of its cost, and of the period of time over which it extends. The last is a most important consideration, as poor parents are always impatient to profit by their children's labour.

It will be objected: Firstly, that this is all very well, but special local advantages and special selection of children must be necessary to such success. Secondly, that this is all very well, but must be very expensive. Thirdly, that this is all very well, but we have no proof of the results, sir, no proof.

On the first head of local advantages and special selection. Would Limehouse Hole be picked out for the site of a Children's Paradise? Or would the legitimate and illegitimate pauper children of the long-shore population of such a river-side district, be regarded as unusually favourable specimens to work with? Yet these schools are at Limehouse, and are the Pauper Schools of the Stepney Pauper Union.

On the second head of expense. Would sixpence a week be considered a very large cost for the education of each pupil, including all salaries of teachers and rations of teachers? But supposing the cost were not sixpence a week, not fivepence? It is FOURPENCE-HALFPENNY.

On the third head of no proof, sir, no proof. Is there any proof in the facts that Pupil Teachers more in number, and more highly qualified, have been produced here under the Short-Time system than under the Long-Time system? That the Short-Timers, in a writing competition, beat the Long-Timers of a first-class National School? That the sailor-boys are in such demand for merchant ships, that whereas, before they were trained, £10 premium used to be given with each boy – too often to some greedy brute of a drunken skipper, who disappeared before the term of apprenticeship was out, if the ill-used boy didn't – captains of the best character now take these boys more than willingly, with no premium at all? That they are also much esteemed in the Royal Navy, which they prefer, 'because everything is so neat and clean and orderly'? Or, is there any proof in Naval captains writing, 'Your little fellows are all that I can desire'? Or, is there any proof in such testimony as this: 'The owner of a vessel called at the school, and said that as his ship was going down Channel on her last voyage, with one of the boys from the school on board, the pilot said, "It would be as well if the royal were lowered; I wish it were down." Without waiting for any orders, and unobserved by the pilot, the lad, whom they had taken on board from the school, instantly mounted the mast and lowered the royal, and at the next glance of the pilot to the masthead, he perceived that the sail had been let down. He exclaimed, "Who's done that job?" The owner, who was on board, said, "That was the little fellow whom I put on board two days ago." The pilot immediately said, "Why, where could he have been brought up?" That boy had never seen the sea or been on a real ship before'? Or, is there any proof in these boys being in greater demand for Regimental Bands than the Union can meet? Or, in ninety-eight of them having gone into Regimental Bands in three years? Or, in twelve of them being in the band of one regiment? Or, in the colonel of that regiment writing, 'We want six more boys; they are excellent lads'? Or, in one of the boys having risen to be band-corporal in the same regiment? Or, in employers of all kinds chorusing, 'Give us drilled boys, for they are prompt, obedient, and punctual?' Other proofs I have myself beheld with these Uncommercial eyes, though I do not regard myself as having a right to relate in what social positions they have seen respected men and women who were once pauper children of the Stepney Union.

Into what admirable soldiers others of these boys have the capabilities for being turned, I need not point out. Many of them are always ambitious of military service; and once upon a time when an old boy came back to see the old place, a cavalry soldier all complete, *with his spurs on,* such a yearning broke out to get into cavalry regiments and wear those sublime appendages, that it was one of the greatest excitements ever known in the school. The girls make excellent domestic servants, and at certain periods come back, a score or two at a time, to see the old building, and to take tea with the old teachers, and to hear the old band, and see the old ship with her masts towering up above the neighbouring roofs and chimneys. As to the physical health of these schools, it is so exceptionally remarkable (simply because the sanitary regulations are as good as the other educational arrangements), that when MR TUFNELL, the Inspector, first stated it in a report, he was supposed, in spite of his high character, to have been betrayed into some extraordinary mistake or exaggeration. In the moral health of these schools – where corporal punishment is unknown – Truthfulness stands high. When the ship was first erected, the boys were forbidden to go aloft, until the nets, which are now always there, were stretched as a precaution against accidents. Certain boys, in their eagerness, disobeyed the injunction, got out of window in the early daylight, and climbed to the masthead. One boy unfortunately fell, and was killed. There was no clue to the others; but all the boys were assembled, and the chairman of the Board addressed them. 'I promise nothing; you see what a dreadful thing has happened; you know what a grave offence it is that has led to such a consequence; I cannot say what will be done with the offenders; but, boys, you have been trained here, above all things, to respect the truth. I want the Truth. Who are the delinquents?' Instantly, the whole number of boys concerned, separated from the rest and stood out.

Now, the head and heart of that gentleman (it is needless to say, a good head and a good heart) have been deeply interested in these schools for many years, and are so still; and the establishment is very fortunate in a most admirable master, and moreover the schools of the Stepney Union cannot have got to be what they are, without the Stepney Board of Guardians having been earnest and humane men, strongly imbued with a sense of their responsibility. But what one set of men can do in this wise, another set of men can do; and this is a noble example to all other Bodies and Unions, and a noble example to the State. Followed, and enlarged upon by its enforcement on bad parents, it would clear London streets of the most terrible objects they smite the sight with – myriads of little children who awfully reverse Our Saviour's words, and are not of the Kingdom of Heaven, but of the Kingdom of Hell.

Clear the public streets of such shame, and the public conscience of such reproach? Ah! Almost prophetic, surely, the child's jingle:

> When will that be,
> Say the bells of Step-ney?

27

The Uncommercial Traveller

All The Year Round, 4 July 1863 (*UT1* as 'Bound for the Great Salt Lake')

The first thirty years of Victoria's reign saw the emigration of over five million British and Irish subjects, and while the British North American territories of what is now Canada were an increasingly popular destination for pioneers, the majority – over three and a half million – were bound for the United States, already an industrialised society. Conditions on board emigrant ships were frequently appalling and disease rife, as Lord Durham's controversial *Report on the Affairs of British North America* had made clear (Parliamentary Papers, House of Commons, Session 1839. Vol. 17, no. 3 &c., repr. J. W. Southgate: London [1839]). Despite various legislative attempts to regulate conditions under sail, and the establishment of a supervisory Colonial Land and Emigration Commission, with offices at the chief ports of departure, regulations were frequently flouted, and emigrants remained prey to exploitation and trickery on land, both before and after embarkation (see Douglas Woodruff's 'Expansion and Emigration', *Early Victorian England*, ed. G. M. Young [1935], Vol. 2, pp. 351–75). Dickens had depicted the perils and discomforts of the transatlantic journey for steerage passengers emigrating from Britain in the sixth number of *Martin Chuzzlewit* (June 1843).

The first Mormon mission to Britain began operating in 1837, and between 1839 and 1841, some 70,000 converts emigrated to settlements in the United States. A second Mormon mission was undertaken in 1863 and had chartered the *Amazon* for the voyage of which Dickens writes. On 20 June 1863, a fortnight before the publication of the present article, an account of the same event was published in the Mormon paper *Millennial Star*, quoted at length by R. J. Dunn in 'The Unnoticed Uncommercial Traveller', *The Dickensian*, Vol. 60 (1964), pp. 103–4. The report noted that the '*Amazon*, Captain H. K. Hovey, ... sailed from London on the 4th instant [i.e. June], with a company of 895 souls of the Saints on board ...', and that the 'company passed the Government Emigration Officers on the 3rd, who eulogized their order, harmony, and general appearance'. Also noted was the presence of various visitors witnessing the departure, and the 'deep impression' evidently made on them by the 'unanimity of feeling manifested by the Saints, and the deep interest with which they listened to the instructions given and took part in the proceedings ... displaying, as it did, a something so different from all their [i.e. the visitors'] conceptions of us as a people'.

The recollections of the artist George Dunlop Leslie confirm that Dickens was among a party of visitors who gathered to see the ship on Wednesday, 3 June, before it embarked from 'London New Dock' basin, to the south of Shadwell Church. The party 'drove in an open carriage from the office of [*ATYR*] ... Dickens talked and laughed the whole way, and was in great form as we passed through Ratcliffe Highway' (*Charles Dickens by Pen and Pencil*, ed. F. G. Kitton [1890], pp. 164–5). On 4 June, he attended a dinner in Westbourne Terrace organised by his German friend, Frederick Lehmann, and according to a fellow guest, the musicologist Sir George Grove, Dickens 'was full of a ship of Mormon emigrants which he had been seeing; 1200 of the cleanest, best conducted, most excellent looking people he ever saw. No doubt there will be an account of it in *All the Year Round*' ([6 June 1863]; *Life and Letters of Sir George Grove* [1903], p. 978).

Dickens's footnote to his own article refers to Richard Monckton Milnes's review of Sir Richard F. Burton's *The City of the Saints* (1859), which had appeared in the *Edinburgh Review* for January 1862 (pp. 185–210). Among other things, the review confirms Dickens's observation that many Mormon emigrants were Welsh: '... the persons abducted are almost invariably Dissenters, and Wales supplies a larger proportion than any other part of Great Britain' (p. 198).

Literary allusions (p. 250) 'the daughters of wave-ruling Britannia': alluding to Thomson's 'Rule Britannia!' in *Alfred, A Masque* (1740), Act 2, Scene the Last; (p. 250) 'Standard of England': popular title for patriotic songs of the period; (p. 251) 'a flattering carver ... not as they were': adapts Goldsmith's couplet from *Retaliation* (1774), 'A flattering painter, who made it his care/To draw men as they ought to be, not as they are'; (p. 254) 'Geese, Villain?': Shakespeare, *Macbeth*, Act 5, Sc. 3; (p. 256) 'Circumlocution Office': Dickens's satirical name for the Civil Service in *Little Dorrit*.

Textual note (p. 260) copy-text has 'the experience it describes to MR MONCKTON MILNES, M.P.': *UTI* has '... to Lord Houghton'. (Milnes was raised to the peerage in 1863.)

Behold me on my way to an Emigrant Ship, on a hot morning early in June. My road lies through that part of London generally known to the initiated as 'Down by the Docks.' Down by the Docks, is Home to a good many people – to too many, if I may judge from the overflow of local population in the streets – but my nose insinuates that the number to whom it is Sweet Home might be easily counted. Down by the Docks, is a region I would choose as my point of embarkation aboard ship if I were an emigrant. It would present my intention to me in such a sensible light; it would show me so many things to be run away from.

Down by the Docks, they eat the largest oysters, and scatter the roughest oyster-shells, known to the descendants of Saint George and the Dragon. Down by the Docks, they consume the slimiest of shell-fish, which seem to have been scraped off the copper bottoms of ships. Down by the Docks, the vegetables at greengrocers' doors acquire a saline and a scaly look, as if they had been crossed with fish and seaweed. Down by the Docks, they 'board seamen' at the eating-houses, the public-houses, the slop-shops, the coffee-shops, the tally shops, all kinds of shops mentionable and unmentionable – board them, as it were, in the piratical sense, making them bleed terribly, and giving no quarter. Down by the Docks, the seamen roam in mid-street and mid-day, their pockets inside-out, and their heads no better. Down by the Docks, the daughters of wave-ruling Britannia also rove, clad in silken attire, with uncovered tresses streaming in the breeze, bandanna kerchiefs floating from their shoulders, and crinoline not wanting. Down by the Docks, you may hear the Incomparable Joe Jackson sing the Standard of England, with a hornpipe, any night; or any day may see at the waxwork, for a penny and no waiting, him as killed the policeman at Acton and suffered for it. Down by the Docks, you may buy polonies, saveloys, and sausage preparations various, if you are not particular what they are made of besides seasoning. Down by the Docks, the children of Israel creep into any gloomy cribs and entries they can hire, and hang slops there – pewter watches, sou'-wester hats, waterproof overalls – 'firtht-rate art-icleth, Thjack.' Down by the Docks, such dealers exhibiting on a frame a complete nautical suit without the refinement of a waxen visage in the hat, present the imaginary wearer as drooping at the yard-arm, with his seafaring and earthfaring troubles over. Down by the Docks, the placards in the shops apostrophise the customer, knowing him familiarly before-hand, as, 'Look here, Jack!' 'Here's your sort, my lad!' 'Try our sea-going mixed, at two and nine!' 'The right kit for the British Tar!' 'Ship ahoy!' 'Splice the main-brace, brother!' 'Come, cheer up, my lads! We've the best liquors here, And you'll find something new In our wonderful Beer!' Down by the Docks, the pawnbroker lends money on Union-Jack pocket-handkerchiefs, on watches with little ships pitching fore and aft on the dial, on telescopes, nautical instruments in cases, and such-like. Down by the Docks, the apothecary sets up in business on the wretchedest scale – chiefly on lint and plaster for the strapping of wounds – and with no bright bottles, and with no little drawers. Down by the Docks, the shabby undertaker's shop will bury you for next to nothing, after the Malay or Chinaman has stabbed you for nothing at all: so you can hardly hope to make a cheaper end. Down by the Docks, anybody drunk will quarrel with anybody drunk or sober, and everybody else will have a hand in it, and on the shortest notice you may revolve in a whirlpool of red shirts, shaggy beards, wild heads of hair, bare tattooed arms, Britannia's daughters, malice, mud, maundering, and madness. Down by the Docks, scraping fiddles go in the public-houses all day long, and, shrill above their din and all the din, rises the screeching of innumerable parrots brought from foreign parts, who appear to be very much astonished by what they find on these native shores of ours. Possibly the parrots don't know, possibly they do, that Down by the Docks is the road to the Pacific Ocean, with its lovely islands, where the savage girls plait flowers, and the savage boys carve cocoa-nut shells, and the grim blind idols muse in their shady groves to exactly the same purpose as the priests and chiefs. And possibly the parrots don't know, possibly they do, that the noble savage is a wearisome impostor wherever he is, and has five hundred thousand volumes of indifferent rhyme, and no reason, to answer for.

Shadwell church! Pleasant whispers of there being a fresher air down the river than down by the Docks, go pursuing one another, playfully, in and out of the openings in its spire. Gigantic in the basin just beyond the church, looms my Emigrant Ship: her name, the Amazon. Her figurehead is not *dis*figured as those beauteous founders of the race of strong-minded women are fabled to have been, for the convenience of drawing the bow; but I sympathise with the carver:

> A flattering carver who made it his care
> To carve busts as they ought to be – not as they were.

My Emigrant Ship lies broadside-on to the wharf. Two great gangways made of spars and planks connect her with the wharf; and up and down these gangways, perpetually crowding to and fro and in and out, like ants, are the Emigrants who are going to sail in my Emigrant Ship. Some with cabbages, some with loaves of bread, some with cheese and butter, some with milk and beer, some with boxes beds and bundles, some with babies – nearly all with children – nearly all with bran-new tin cans for their daily allowance of water, uncomfortably suggestive of a tin flavour in the drink. To and fro, up and down, aboard and ashore, swarming here and there and everywhere, my Emigrants. And still as the Dock-Gate swings upon its hinges, cabs appear, and carts appear, and vans appear, bringing more of my Emigrants, with more cabbages, more loaves, more cheese and butter, more milk and beer, more boxes beds and bundles, more tin cans, and on those shipping investments accumulated compound interest of children.

I go aboard my Emigrant Ship. I go first to the great cabin, and find it in the usual condition of a Cabin at that pass. Perspiring lands-men, with loose papers, and with pens and inkstands, pervade it; and the general appearance of things is as if the late Mr Amazon's funeral had just come home from the cemetery, and the disconsolate Mrs Amazon's trustees found the affairs in great disorder, and were looking high and low for the will. I go out on the poop-deck for air, and surveying the emigrants on the deck below (indeed they are crowded all about me, up there too), find more pens and inkstands in action, and more papers, and interminable complication respecting accounts with individuals for tin cans and what not. But nobody is in an ill temper, nobody is the worse for drink, nobody swears an oath or uses a coarse word, nobody appears depressed, nobody is weeping, and down upon the deck in every corner where it is possible to find a few square feet to kneel, crouch, or lie in, people, in every unsuitable attitude for writing, are writing letters.

Now, I have seen emigrant ships before this day in June. And these people are so strikingly different from all other people in like circumstances whom I have ever seen, that I wonder aloud, 'What *would* a stranger suppose these emigrants to be!'

The vigilant bright face of the weather-browned captain of the Amazon is at my shoulder, and he says, 'What, indeed! The most of these came aboard yesterday evening. They came from various parts of England, in small parties that had never seen one another before. Yet they had not been a couple of hours on board, when they established their own police, made their own regulations, and set their own watches at all the hatchways. Before nine o'clock, the ship was as orderly and as quiet as a man-of-war.'

I looked about me again, and saw the letter-writing going on with the most curious composure. Perfectly abstracted in the midst of the crowd; while great casks were swinging aloft, and being lowered into the hold; while hot agents were hurrying up and down, adjusting the interminable accounts; while two hundred strangers were searching everywhere for two hundred other strangers, and were asking questions about them of two hundred more; while the children played up and down all the steps, and in and out among all the people's legs, and were beheld, to the general dismay, toppling over all the dangerous places; the letter-writers wrote on calmly. On the starboard side of the ship, a grizzled man dictated a long letter to another grizzled man in an immense fur cap: which letter was of so profound a quality, that it became necessary for the amanuensis at intervals to take off his fur cap in both his hands, for the ventilation of his brain, and stare at him who dictated, as a man of many mysteries who was worth looking at. On the larboard side, a woman had covered a belaying-pin with a white cloth, to make a neat desk of it, and was sitting on a little box, writing with the deliberation of a bookkeeper. Down upon her breast on the planks of the deck at this woman's feet, with her head diving in under a beam of the bulwarks on that side, as an eligible place of refuge for her sheet of paper, a neat and pretty girl wrote for a good hour (she fainted at last), only rising to the surface occasionally for a dip of ink. Alongside the boat, close to me on the poop-deck, another girl, a fresh well-grown country girl, was writing another letter on the bare deck. Later in the day, when this selfsame boat was filled with a choir who sang glees and catches for a long time, one of the singers, a girl, sang her part mechanically all the while, and wrote a letter in the bottom of the boat while doing so.

'A stranger would be puzzled to guess the right name for these people, Mr Uncommercial,' says the captain.

'Indeed he would.'

'If you hadn't known, could you ever have supposed –?'

'How could I! I should have said they were in their degree, the pick and flower of England.'

'So should I,' says the captain.

'How many are they?'

'Eight hundred in round numbers.'

I went between-decks, where the families with children swarmed in the dark, where unavoidable confusion had been caused by the last arrivals, and where the confusion was increased by the little preparations for dinner that were going on in each group. A few women here and there, had got lost, and were laughing at it, and asking their way to their own people, or out on deck again. A few of the poor children were crying; but otherwise the universal cheerfulness was amazing. 'We shall shake down by tomorrow.' 'We shall come all right in a day or so.' 'We shall have more light at sea.' Such phrases I heard everywhere, as I groped my way among chests and barrels and beams and unstowed cargo and ring-bolts and Emigrants, down to the lower deck, and thence up to the light of day again and to my former station.

Surely, an extraordinary people in their power of self-abstraction! All the former letter-writers were still writing calmly, and many more letter-writers had broken out in my absence. A boy with a bag of books in his hand, and a slate under his arm, emerged from below, concentrated himself in my neighbourhood (espying a convenient skylight for his purpose), and went to work at a sum as if he were stone deaf. A father and mother and several young children, on the main deck below me, had formed a family circle close to the foot of the crowded restless gangway, where the children made a nest for themselves in a coil of rope, and the father and mother, she suckling the youngest, discussed family affairs as peaceably as if they were in perfect retirement. I think the most noticeable characteristic in the eight hundred as a mass, was their exemption from hurry.

Eight hundred what? 'Geese, villain?' EIGHT HUNDRED MORMONS. I, Uncommercial Traveller for the firm of Human Interest Brothers, had come aboard this Emigrant Ship to see what Eight Hundred Latter-Day Saints were like, and I found them (to the rout and overthrow of all my expectations) like what I now describe with scrupulous exactness.

The Mormon Agent who had been active in getting them together, and in making the contract with my friends the owners of the ship to take them as far as New York on their way to the Great Salt Lake, was pointed out to me. A compactly-made handsome man in black, rather short, with rich-brown hair and beard, and clear bright eyes. From his speech, I should set him down as American. Probably, a man who had 'knocked about the world' pretty much. A man with a frank open manner, and unshrinking look; withal a man of great quickness. I believe he was wholly ignorant of my Uncommercial individuality, and consequently of my immense Uncommercial importance.

UNCOMMERCIAL. These are a very fine set of people you have brought together here.

MORMON AGENT. Yes, sir, they are a *very* fine set of people.

UNCOMMERCIAL (looking about). Indeed, I think it would be difficult to find Eight hundred people together anywhere else, and find so much beauty and so much strength and capacity for work among them.

MORMON AGENT (not looking about, but looking steadily at Uncommercial). I think so. – We sent out about a thousand more, yes'day, from Liverpool.

UNCOMMERCIAL. You are not going with these emigrants?

MORMON AGENT. No, sir. I remain.

UNCOMMERCIAL. But you have been in the Mormon Territory?

MORMON AGENT. Yes; I left Utah about three years ago.

UNCOMMERCIAL. It is surprising to me that these people are all so cheery, and make so little of the immense distance before them.

MORMON AGENT. Well, you see; many of 'em have friends out at Utah, and many of 'em look forward to meeting friends on the way.

UNCOMMERCIAL. On the way?

MORMON AGENT. This way 'tis. This ship lands 'em in New York City. Then they go on by rail right away beyond St Louis, to that part of the Banks of the Missouri where they strike the Plains. There, waggons from the settlement meet 'em to bear 'em company on their journey 'cross – twelve hundred miles about. Industrious people who come out to the settlement soon get waggons of their own, and so the friends of some of these will come down in their own waggons to meet 'em. They look forward to that, greatly.

UNCOMMERCIAL. On their long journey across the Desert, do you arm them?

MORMON AGENT. Mostly you would find they have arms of some kind or another already with them. Such as had not arms we should arm across the Plains, for the general protection and defence.

UNCOMMERCIAL. Will these waggons bring down any produce to the Missouri?

MORMON AGENT. Well, since the war broke out, we've taken to growing cotton, and they'll likely bring down cotton to be exchanged for machinery. We want machinery. Also we have taken to growing indigo, which is a fine commodity for profit. It has been found that the climate on the further side of the Great Salt Lake suits well for raising indigo.

UNCOMMERCIAL. I am told that these people now on board are principally from the South of England?

MORMON AGENT. And from Wales. That's true.

UNCOMMERCIAL. Do you get many Scotch?

MORMON AGENT. Not many.

UNCOMMERCIAL. Highlanders, for instance?

MORMON AGENT. No, not Highlanders. They ain't interested enough in universal brotherhood and peace and good will.

UNCOMMERCIAL. The old fighting blood is strong in them?

MORMON AGENT. Well, yes. And, besides; they've no faith.

UNCOMMERCIAL (who has been burning to get at the Prophet Joe Smith, and seems to discover an opening). Faith in –!

MORMON AGENT (far too many for Uncommercial). Well. – In anything!

Similarly on this same head, the Uncommercial underwent discomfiture from a Wiltshire labourer: a simple fresh-coloured farm-labourer of eight-and-thirty, who at one time stood beside him looking on at new arrivals, and with whom he held this dialogue:

UNCOMMERCIAL. Would you mind my asking you what part of the country you come from?

WILTSHIRE. Not a bit. Theer! (exultingly) I've worked all my life o' Salisbury Plain, right under the shadder o' Stonehenge. You mightn't think it, but I haive.

UNCOMMERCIAL. And a pleasant country too.

WILTSHIRE. Ah! 'Tis a pleasant country.

UNCOMMERCIAL. Have you any family on board?

WILTSHIRE. Two children, boy and gal. I am a widderer, *I* am, and I'm going out alonger my boy and gal. That's my gal, and she's a fine gal o' sixteen (pointing out the girl who is writing by the boat). I'll go and fetch my boy. I'd like to show you my boy. (Here Wiltshire disappears, and presently comes back with a big shy boy of twelve, in a superabundance of boots, who is not at all glad to be presented.) He is a fine boy too, and a boy fur to work! (Boy having undutifully bolted, Wiltshire drops him.)

UNCOMMERCIAL. It must cost you a great deal of money to go so far, three strong.

WILTSHIRE. A power of money. Theer! Eight shillen a week, eight shillen a week, eight shillen a week, put by out of the week's wages for ever so long.

UNCOMMERCIAL. I wonder how you did it.

WILTSHIRE (recognising in this a kindred spirit). See theer now! I wonder how I done it! But what with a bit o' subscription heer, and what with a bit o' help theer, it were done at last, though I don't hardly know how. Then it were unfort'net for us, you see, as we got kep' in Bristol so long – nigh a fortnight, it were – on accounts of a mistake wi' Brother Halliday. Swaller'd up money, it did, when we might have come straight on.

UNCOMMERCIAL (delicately approaching Joe Smith). You are of the Mormon religion, of course?

WILTSHIRE (confidently). Oh yes, *I'm* a Mormon. (Then reflectively.) I'm a Mormon. (Then, looking round the ship, feigns to descry a particular friend in an empty spot, and evades the Uncommercial for evermore.)

After a noontide pause for dinner, during which my Emigrants were nearly all between-decks, and the Amazon looked deserted, a general muster took place. The muster was for the ceremony of passing the Government Inspector and the Doctor. Those authorities held their temporary state amidships, by a cask or two; and, knowing that the whole Eight hundred emigrants must come face to face with them, I took my station behind the two. They knew nothing whatever of me, I believe, and my testimony to the unpretending gentleness and good nature with which they discharged their duty, may be of the greater worth. There was not the slightest flavour of the Circumlocution Office about their proceedings.

The emigrants were now all on deck. They were densely crowded aft, and swarmed upon the poop-deck like bees. Two or three Mormon agents stood ready to hand them on to the Inspector, and to hand them forward when they had passed. By what successful means, a special aptitude for organisation had been infused into these people, I am, of course, unable to report. But I know that, even now, there was no disorder, hurry, or difficulty.

All being ready, the first group are handed on. That member of the party who is entrusted with the passenger-ticket for the whole, has been warned by one of the agents to have it ready, and here it is in his hand. In every instance through the whole eight hundred, without an exception, this paper is always ready.

INSPECTOR (reading the ticket). Jessie Jobson, Sophronia Jobson, Jessie Jobson again, Matilda Jobson, William Jobson, Jane Jobson, Matilda Jobson again, Brigham Jobson, Leonardo Jobson, and Orson Jobson. Are you all here? (glancing at the party, over his spectacles).

JESSIE JOBSON NUMBER TWO. All here, sir.

This group is composed of an old grandfather and grandmother, their married son and his wife, and *their* family of children. Orson Jobson is a little child asleep in his mother's arms. The Doctor, with a kind word or so, lifts up the corner of the mother's shawl, looks at the child's face, and touches the little clenched hand. If we were all as well as Orson Jobson, doctoring would be a poor profession.

INSPECTOR. Quite right, Jessie Jobson. Take your ticket, Jessie, and pass on.

And away they go. Mormon agent, skilful and quiet, hands them on. Mormon agent, skilful and quiet, hands next party up.

INSPECTOR (reading ticket again). Susannah Cleverly and William Cleverly. Brother and sister, eh?

SISTER (young woman of business, hustling slow brother). Yes, sir.

INSPECTOR. Very good, Susannah Cleverly. Take your ticket, Susannah, and take care of it.

And away they go.

INSPECTOR (taking ticket again). Sampson Dibble and Dorothy Dibble (surveying a very old couple over his spectacles with some surprise). Your husband quite blind, Mrs Dibble?

MRS DIBBLE. Yes, sir, he be stone-blind.

MR DIBBLE (addressing the mast). Yes, sir, I be stone-blind.

INSPECTOR. That's a bad job. Take your ticket, Mrs Dibble, and don't lose it, and pass on.

Doctor taps Mr Dibble on the eyebrow with his forefinger, and away they go.

INSPECTOR (taking ticket again). Anastatia Weedle.

Anastatia (a pretty girl, in a bright Garibaldi, this morning elected by universal suffrage the Beauty of the Ship). That is me, sir.

INSPECTOR. Going alone, Anastatia?

ANASTATIA (shaking her curls). I am with Mrs Jobson, sir, but I've got separated for the moment.

INSPECTOR. Oh! You are with the Jobsons? Quite right. That'll do, Miss Weedle. Don't lose your ticket.

Away she goes, and joins the Jobsons who are waiting for her, and stoops and kisses Brigham Jobson – who appears to be considered too young for the purpose by several Mormons rising twenty, who are looking on. Before her extensive skirts have departed from the casks, a decent widow stands there with four children, and so the roll goes.

The faces of some of the Welsh people, among whom there were many old persons, were certainly the least intelligent. Some of these emigrants would have bungled sorely, but for the directing hand that was always ready. The intelligence here was unquestionably of a low order, and the heads were of a poor type. Generally the case was the reverse. There were many worn faces bearing traces of patient poverty and hard work, and there was great steadiness of purpose and much undemonstrative self-respect among this class. A few young men were going singly. Several girls were going two or three together. These latter I found it very difficult to refer back, in my mind, to their relinquished homes and pursuits. Perhaps they were more like country milliners, and pupil teachers rather tawdrily dressed, than any other classes of young women. I noticed, among many little ornaments worn, more than one photograph-brooch of the Princess of Wales, and also of the late Prince Consort. Some single women of from thirty to forty, whom one might suppose to be embroiderers, or straw-bonnet-makers, were obviously going out in quest of husbands, as finer ladies go to India. That they had any distinct notions of a plurality of husbands or wives, I do not believe. To suppose the family groups of whom the majority of emigrants were composed, polygamically possessed, would be to suppose an absurdity, manifest to anyone who saw the fathers and mothers.

I should say (I had no means of ascertaining the fact) that most familiar kinds of handicraft trades were represented here. Farm-labourers, shepherds, and the like, had their full share of representation, but I doubt if they preponderated. It was interesting to see how the leading spirit in the family circle never failed to show itself, even in the simple process of answering to the names as they were called, and checking off the owners of the names. Sometimes it was the father, much oftener the mother, sometimes a quick little girl second or third in order of seniority. It seemed to occur for the first time to some heavy fathers, what large families they had; and their eyes rolled about, during the calling of the list, as if they half misdoubted some other family to have been smuggled into their own. Among all the fine handsome children, I observed but two with marks upon their necks that were probably scrofulous. Out of the whole number of emigrants, but one old woman was temporarily set aside by the doctor, on suspicion of fever; but even she afterwards obtained a clean bill of health.

When all had 'passed,' and the afternoon began to wear on, a black box became visible on deck, which box was in charge of certain personages also in black, of whom only one had the conventional air of an itinerant preacher. This box contained a supply of hymn-books, neatly printed and got up, published at Liverpool, and also in London at the 'Latter-Day Saints' Book Depôt, 30, Florence-street.' Some copies were handsomely bound; the plainer were the more in request, and many were bought. The title ran: 'Sacred Hymns and Spiritual Songs for the Church of Jesus Christ of Latter-Day Saints.' The Preface, dated Manchester, 1840, ran thus: – 'The Saints in this country have been very desirous for a Hymn Book adapted to their faith and worship, that they might sing the truth with an understanding heart, and express their praise joy and gratitude in songs adapted to the New and Everlasting Covenant. In accordance with their wishes, we have selected the following volume, which we hope will prove acceptable until a greater variety can be added. With sentiments of high consideration and esteem, we subscribe ourselves your brethren in the New and Everlasting Covenant, BRIGHAM YOUNG, PARLEY P. PRATT, JOHN TAYLOR.' From this book – by no means explanatory to myself of the New and Everlasting Covenant, and not at all making my heart an understanding one on the subject of that mystery – a hymn was sung, which did not attract any great amount of attention, and was supported by a rather select circle. But the choir in the boat was very popular and pleasant; and there was to have been a Band, only the Cornet was late in coming on board. In the course of the afternoon, a mother appeared from shore, in search of her daughter, 'who had run away with the Mormons.' She received every assistance from the Inspector, but her daughter was not found to be on board. The saints did not seem to me, particularly interested in finding her.

Towards five o'clock, the galley became full of tea-kettles, and an agreeable fragrance of tea pervaded the ship. There was no scrambling or jostling for the hot water, no ill humour, no quarrelling. As the Amazon was to sail with the next tide, and as it would not be high water before two o'clock in the morning, I left her with her tea in full action, and her idle Steam Tug lying by, deputing steam and smoke for the time being to the Tea-kettles.

I afterwards learned that a Despatch was sent home by the captain before he struck out into the wide Atlantic, highly extolling the behaviour of these Emigrants, and the perfect order and propriety of all their social arrangements. What is in store for the poor people on the shores of the Great Salt Lake, what happy delusions they are labouring under now, on what miserable blindness their eyes may be opened then, I do not pretend to say. But I went on board their ship to bear testimony against them if they deserved it, as I fully believed they would; to my great astonishment, they did not deserve it; and my predispositions and tendencies must not affect me as an honest witness. I went over the Amazon's side, feeling it impossible to deny that, so far, some remarkable influence had produced a remarkable result, which better known influences have often missed.[*]

28

The Uncommercial Traveller

All The Year Round, 18 July 1863 (*UT1* as 'The City of the Absent')

Between 1841 and 1901, the population of the City shrank from 123,000 to 27,000. In the present article Dickens offers a companion piece to his paper of 5 May 1860 on deserted churches in the City of London (see article 12): both explore the phenomenon now known to social scientists as depopulation of the urban core.

Dickens's interest in City churchyards – many of which belonged to churches that were not rebuilt after the ravages of the Great Fire of 1666 – went well beyond the aesthetic. Amongst pamphlets in his library at Gad's Hill were George A. Walker's four series of *Lectures ... on the actual condition of the Metropolitan Graveyards &c.* (1846–9), J. D. Parry's essay *Urban Burial: The London Churchyards &c.* (1847), and a copy of the General Board of Health's influential *Report on a General Scheme for Extramural Sepulture* (Parliamentary Papers. Session 1850. Vol. 21.), forwarded by Dickens's brother-in-law Henry Austin who was Secretary to the Board. Dickens found the Report 'extraordinarily interesting', beginning it 'in bed' one night and 'dream[ing] of putrefaction generally' (*Pilgrim*, Vol. VI, p. 47 & n.). The major problem with the City churchyards, as these sources clearly document, was that not only did they lack the future capacity for the proper interment of London's mush-

---

[*] After this Uncommercial Journey was printed, I happened to mention the experience it describes to MR MONCKTON MILNES, M.P. That gentleman then showed me an article of his writing, in *The Edinburgh Review* for January, 1862, which is highly remarkable for its philosophical and literary research concerning these Latter-Day Saints. I find in it the following sentences: 'The Select Committee of the House of Commons on emigrant ships for 1854 summoned the Mormon agent and passenger-broker before it, and came to the conclusion that no ships under the provisions of the "Passengers Act" could be depended upon for comfort and security in the same degree as those under his administration. The Mormon ship is a Family under strong and accepted discipline, with every provision for comfort, decorum, and internal peace.'

rooming population, but that existing overcrowding presented a serious risk to health that government needed to act upon. Dickens wrote frequently in *HW* in support of the Board of Health and its mission to improve sanitation (see Vol. 2 of this edition, endnote to article 41, and article 57; Vol. 3 of this edition, articles 14 and 27). He also commissioned an article for *HW*, 'Heathen and Christian Burial' (attributed to George Hogarth and W. H. Wills), specifically dealing with the Board's 'admirable report on Burials', and supporting its recommendations to remedy the problem of 'closely-packed burial-grounds in crowded cities' (6 April 1850; see also *Pilgrim*, Vol. VI, pp. 55–6 & n.). Agitation of this nature contributed in the mid-1850s to the City's establishing its own cemetery at a greenfields site in Little Ilford, then in Essex. This did nothing to improve the condition of existing City burial grounds, however.

The churchyard dubbed 'Saint Ghastly Grim' by the Uncommercial Traveller is that belonging to St Olave's on Hart Street, within sight of Fenchurch Street Station, which Dickens used for many of his East End expeditions ('O. Sack', 'Saint Ghastly Grim', *The Dickensian*, Vol. 9 [1913], pp. 323–4). The ghoulish churchyard gateway described (p. 263) dates from 1658 and follows a design by Dutch architect Hendrik de Keyser. Gwen Major has supplied probable 'originals' for a number of the other churchyards described in the paper: that with the 'Lombardy Poplar' (p. 262) belonging to St Swithin's on St Swithin's Lane; that between 'Gracechurch-street and the Tower' (p. 263) belonging to St Mary-at-Hill on the street of the same name; and that where the two 'charity children' make love (p. 265) belonging to St Michael Paternoster Royal on College Hill ('Into the Shadowy Past', *The Dickensian*, Vol. 64 [1968], pp. 28–33).

Observations about the elderly men 'let out of workhouses by the hour', according to the Poor Law regulations of the time, recall the essay-like opening to Ch. 31 of *Little Dorrit* (1857) and the circumstances of the character 'Old Nandy'. Likewise, Dickens's description of 'Nadgett' in Ch. 27 of *Martin Chuzzlewit* (1844) – 'always keeping appointments in the City and the other man never seemed to come' – is generalised here in meditations on the 'men who wait at Garraway's' (p. 268). The original Garraway's coffee house stood in Exchange Alley, Cornhill No. 3, and, though celebrated for being the first coffee house to sell tea, was more famous in the 1860s for its sherry and sandwiches. John Timbs notes in *Curiosities of London* (1855) the existence of a fourteenth-or fifteenth-century crypt below Garraway's (see p. 268 below), described as 'ecclesiastical in character [with a] … piscine … now used as the coffee-house wine cellar' (quoted in Bryant Lillywhite, *Reference Book of the Coffee Houses of the Seventeenth, Eighteenth and Nineteenth Centuries* [1963], Item no. 433).

Literary allusions (p. 266) 'their song is Willow, Willow': 'Sing willow, willow, willow' &c., Desdemona's song in Shakespeare, *Othello*, Act 4,

Sc. 3, adapted from John Heywood's lyric 'The Green Willow'; (p. 267) 'regions of the Wonderful Lamp': the story of 'Aladdin and the Wonderful Lamp' from the *Arabian Nights*; (p. 269) 'the Last Man': playful allusion to Thomas Campbell's poem 'The Last Man' (1823), or to Mary Shelley's novel with this title (1826).

Textual note (p. 265) copy-text has 'It was so freshening': *UT1* has 'It was so refreshing'.

When I think I deserve particularly well of myself, and have earned the right to enjoy a little treat, I stroll from Covent-garden into the City of London, after business-hours there, on a Saturday, or − better yet − on a Sunday, and roam about its deserted nooks and corners. It is necessary to the full enjoyment of these journeys that they should be made in summer-time, for then the retired spots that I love to haunt are at their idlest and dullest. A gentle fall of rain is not objectionable, and a warm mist sets off my favourite retreats to decided advantage.

Among these, City Churchyards hold a high place. Such strange churchyards hide in the City of London; churchyards sometimes so entirely detached from churches, always so pressed upon by houses; so small, so rank, so silent, so forgotten, except by the few people who ever look down into them from their smoky windows. As I stand peeping in through the iron gates and rails, I can peel the rusty metal off, like bark from an old tree. The illegible tombstones are all lop-sided, the grave-mounds lost their shape in the rains of a hundred years ago, the Lombardy Poplar or Plane-Tree that was once a drysalter's daughter and several common councilmen, has withered like those worthies, and its departed leaves are dust beneath it. Contagion of slow ruin overhangs the place. The discoloured tiled roofs of the environing buildings stand so awry, that they can hardly be proof against any stress of weather. Old crazy stacks of chimneys seem to look down as they overhang, dubiously calculating how far they will have to fall. In an angle of the walls, what was once the tool-house of the grave-digger rots away, encrusted with toadstools. Pipes and spouts for carrying off the rain from the encompassing gables, broken or feloniously cut for old lead long ago, now let the rain drip and splash as it lists upon the weedy earth. Sometimes there is a rusty pump somewhere near, and, as I look in at the rails and meditate, I hear it working under an unknown hand with a creaking protest: as though the departed in the churchyard urged, 'Let us lie here in peace; don't suck us up and drink us!'

One of my best beloved churchyards, I call the churchyard of Saint Ghastly Grim; touching what men in general call it, I have no information.

It lies at the heart of the City, and the Blackwall Railway shrieks at it daily. It is a small small churchyard, with a ferocious strong spiked iron gate, like a jail. This gate is ornamented with skulls and cross-bones, larger than the life, wrought in stone; but it likewise came into the mind of Saint Ghastly Grim, that to stick iron spikes a-top of the stone skulls, as though they were impaled, would be a pleasant device. Therefore the skulls grin aloft horribly, thrust through and through with iron spears. Hence, there is attraction of repulsion for me in Saint Ghastly Grim, and, having often contemplated it in the daylight and the dark, I once felt drawn towards it in a thunderstorm at midnight. 'Why not?' I said, in self excuse. 'I have been to see the Colosseum by the light of the moon; is it worse to go to see Saint Ghastly Grim by the light of the lightning?' I repaired to the Saint in a hackney cab, and found the skulls most effective, having the air of a public execution, and seeming, as the lightning flashed, to wink and grin with the pain of the spikes. Having no other person to whom to impart my satisfaction, I communicated it to the driver. So far from being responsive, he surveyed me – he was naturally a bottle-nosed red-faced man – with a blanched countenance. And as he drove me back, he ever and again glanced in over his shoulder through the little front window of his carriage, as mistrusting that I was a fare originally from a grave in the churchyard of Saint Ghastly Grim, who might have flitted home again without paying.

Sometimes, the queer Hall of some queer Company gives upon a churchyard such as this, and, when the Livery dine, you may hear them (if you are looking in through the iron rails, which you never are when I am) toasting their own Worshipful prosperity. Sometimes, a wholesale house of business, requiring much room for stowage, will occupy one or two or even all three sides of the enclosing space, and the backs of bales of goods will lumber up the windows, as if they were holding some crowded trade-meeting of themselves within. Sometimes, the commanding windows are all blank, and show no more sign of life than the graves below – not so much, for *they* tell of what once upon a time was life undoubtedly. Such was the surrounding of one City churchyard that I saw last summer, on a Volunteering Saturday evening towards eight of the clock, when with astonishment I beheld an old old man and an old old woman in it, making hay. Yes, of all occupations in this world, making hay! It was a very confined patch of churchyard lying between Gracechurch-street and the Tower, capable of yielding, say an apronful of hay. By what means the old old man and woman had got into it, with an almost toothless hay-making rake, I could not fathom. No open window was within view; no window at all was within view, sufficiently near the ground to have enabled their old legs to descend from it; the rusty churchyard-gate was locked, the mouldy church was locked. Gravely

Time and His Wife

among the graves, they made hay, all alone by themselves. They looked like Time and his wife. There was but the one rake between them, and they both had hold of it in a pastorally-loving manner, and there was hay on the old woman's black bonnet, as if the old man had recently been playful. The old man was quite an obsolete old man, in knee-breeches and coarse grey stockings, and the old woman wore mittens like unto his stockings in texture and in colour. They took no heed of me as I looked on, unable to account for them. The old woman was much too bright for a pew-opener, the old man much too meek for a beadle. On an old tombstone in the foreground between me and them, were two cherubim; but for those celestial embellishments being represented as having no possible use for knee-breeches, stockings, or mittens, I should have compared them with the haymakers, and sought a likeness. I coughed and awoke the echoes, but the haymakers never looked at me. They used the rake with a measured action, drawing the scanty crop towards them; and so I was fain to leave them under three yards and a half of darkening sky, gravely making hay among the graves, all alone by themselves. Perhaps they were Spectres, and I wanted a Medium?

In another City churchyard of similar cramped dimensions, I saw, that self-same summer, two comfortable charity children. They were making love – tremendous proof of the vigour of that immortal article, for they were in the graceful uniform under which English Charity delights to hide herself – and they were overgrown, and their legs (his legs at least, for I am modestly incompetent to speak of hers) were as much in the wrong as mere passive weakness of character can render legs. O it was a leaden churchyard, but no doubt a golden ground to those young persons! I first saw them on a Saturday evening, and, perceiving from their occupation that Saturday evening was their trysting-time, I returned that evening se'nnight, and renewed the contemplation of them. They came there to shake the bits of matting which were spread in the church aisles, and they afterwards rolled them up, he rolling his end, she rolling hers, until they met, and over the two once divided now united rolls – sweet emblem! – gave and received a chaste salute. It was so freshening to find one of my faded churchyards blooming into flower thus, that I returned a second time, and a third, and ultimately this befel: – They had left the church door open, in their dusting and arranging. Walking in to look at the church, I became aware, by the dim light, of him in the pulpit, of her in the reading-desk, of him looking down, of her looking up, exchanging tender discourse. Immediately both dived, and became as it were non-existent on this sphere. With an assumption of innocence I turned to leave the sacred edifice, when an obese form stood in the portal, puffily demanding Joseph, or, in default of Joseph, Celia. Taking this monster by the sleeve, and luring him forth on pretence of showing him whom he sought, I gave time for the emergence of Joseph and Celia, who presently came towards us in the churchyard, bending under dusty matting, a picture of thriving and unconscious industry. It would be superfluous to hint that I have ever since deemed this the proudest passage in my life.

But such instances, or any tokens of vitality, are rare indeed in my

City churchyards. A few sparrows occasionally try to raise a lively chirrup in their solitary tree — perhaps, as taking a different view of worms from that entertained by humanity — but they are flat and hoarse of voice, like the clerk, the organ, the bell, the clergyman, and all the rest of the Church-works when they are wound up for Sunday. Caged larks, thrushes, or blackbirds, hanging in neighbouring courts, pour forth their strains passionately, as scenting the tree, trying to break out, and see leaves again before they die, but their song is Willow, Willow — of a churchyard cast. So little light lives inside the churches of my churchyards, when the two are co-existent, that it is often only by an accident and after long acquaintance that I discover their having stained glass in some odd window. The westering sun slants into the churchyard by some unwonted entry, a few prismatic tears drop on an old tombstone, and a window that I thought was only dirty, is for the moment all bejewelled. Then the light passes and the colours die. Though even then, if there be room enough for me to fall back so far as that I can gaze up to the top of the Church Tower, I see the rusty vane new burnished, and seeming to look out with a joyful flash over the sea of smoke at the distant shore of country.

Blinking old men who are let out of workhouses by the hour, have a tendency to sit on bits of coping-stone in these churchyards, leaning with both hands on their sticks and asthmatically gasping. The more depressed class of beggars too, bring hither broken meats, and munch. I am on nodding terms with a meditative turncock who lingers in one of them, and whom I suspect of a turn for poetry: the rather, as he looks out of temper when he gives the fire-plug a disparaging wrench with that large tuning-fork of his which would wear out the shoulder of his coat, but for a precautionary piece of inlaid leather. Fire-ladders, which I am satisfied nobody knows anything about, and the keys of which were lost in ancient times, moulder away in the larger churchyards, under eaves like wooden eyebrows; and so removed are those corners from the haunts of men and boys, that once on a fifth of November I found a 'Guy' trusted to take care of himself there, while his proprietors had gone to dinner. Of the expression of his face I cannot report, because it was turned to the wall; but his shrugged shoulders and his ten extended fingers, appeared to denote that he had moralised in his little straw chair on the mystery of mortality until he gave it up as a bad job.

You do not come upon these churchyards violently; there are shades of transition in the neighbourhood. An antiquated news shop, or barber's shop, apparently bereft of customers in the earlier days of George the Third, would warn me to look out for one, if any discoveries in this respect were left for me to make. A very quiet court, in combination with an unaccountable dyer's and scourer's, would prepare me for a churchyard. An exceedingly retiring public-house, with a bagatelle-board shadily visible in a sawdusty parlour shaped like an omnibus, and with a shelf of punch-bowls in the bar, would apprise me that I stood near consecrated ground. A 'Dairy,' exhibiting in its modest window one very little milk can and three eggs, would suggest to me the certainty of finding the poultry hard by, pecking at my forefathers. I first inferred the vicinity of Saint Ghastly Grim, from a certain air of extra repose and gloom pervading a vast stack of warehouses.

From the hush of these places, it is congenial to pass into the hushed resorts of business. Down the lanes I like to see the carts and waggons huddled together in repose, the cranes idle, and the warehouses shut. Pausing in the alleys behind the closed Banks of mighty Lombard-street, it gives one as good as a rich feeling to think of the broad counters with a rim along the edge, made for telling money out on, the scales for weighing precious metals, the ponderous ledgers, and, above all, the bright copper shovels for shovelling gold. When I draw money, it never seems so much money as when it is shovelled at me out of a bright copper shovel. I like to say 'In gold,' and to see seven pounds musically pouring out of the shovel, like seventy; the Bank appearing to remark to me – I italicise *appearing* – 'If you want more of this yellow earth, we keep it in barrows at your service.' To think of the banker's clerk with his deft finger turning the crisp edges of the Hundred-Pound Notes he has taken in a fat roll out of a drawer, is again to hear the rustling of that delicious south-cash wind. 'How will you have it?' I once heard this usual question asked at a Bank Counter of an elderly female, habited in mourning and steeped in simplicity, who answered, open-eyed, crook-fingered, laughing with expectation, 'Anyhow!' Calling these things to mind as I stroll among the Banks, I wonder whether the other solitary Sunday man I pass, has designs upon the Banks. For the interest and mystery of the matter, I almost hope he may have, and that his confederate may be at this moment taking impressions of the keys of the iron closets in wax, and that a delightful robbery may be in course of transaction. About College-hill, Mark-lane, and so on towards the Tower, and Dockward, the deserted wine-merchants' cellars are fine subjects for consideration; but the deserted money-cellars of the Bankers, and their plate-cellars, and their jewel-cellars, what subterranean regions of the Wonderful Lamp are these! And again: possibly some shoeless boy in rags passed through this street yesterday, for whom it is reserved to be a Banker in the fulness of time, and to be surpassing rich. Such reverses have been, since the days of Whittington; and were, long before. I want to know whether the boy has any foreglittering of that glittering fortune now, when he treads these stones, hungry. Much as I also want to know whether the next man to be hanged at Newgate yonder, had any suspicion upon him that he was moving steadily towards that fate, when he talked so much about the last man who paid the same great debt at the same small Debtors' Door.

Where are all the people who on busy working-days pervade these scenes? The locomotive banker's clerk, who carries a black portfolio chained to him by a chain of steel, where is he? Does he go to bed with his chain on – to church with his chain on – or does he lay it by? And if he lays it by, what becomes of his portfolio when he is unchained for a holiday? The wastepaper baskets of these closed counting-houses would let me into many hints of business matters if I had the exploration of them; and what secrets of the heart should I discover on the 'pads' of the young clerks – the sheets of cartridge-paper and blotting-paper interposed between their writing and their desks! Pads are taken into confidence on the tenderest occasions, and oftentimes when I have made a business visit, and have sent in my name from the outer office, have I had it forced on my discursive notice that the officiating young gentleman has over and over again inscribed AMELIA, in ink of various dates, on corners of his pad. Indeed, the pad may be regarded as the legitimate modern successor of the old forest-tree: whereon these young knights (having no attainable forest nearer than Epping) engrave the names of their mistresses. After all, it is a more satisfactory process than carving, and can be oftener repeated. So these courts in their Sunday rest are courts of Love Omnipotent (I rejoice to bethink myself), dry as they look. And here is Garraway's, bolted and shuttered hard and fast! It is possible to imagine the man who cuts the sandwiches, on his back in a hayfield; it is possible to imagine his desk, like the desk of a clerk at church, without him; but imagination is unable to pursue the men who wait at Garraway's all the week for the men who never come. When they are forcibly put out of Garraway's on Saturday night – which they must be, for they never would go out of their own accord – where do they vanish until Monday morning? On the first Sunday that I ever strayed here, I expected to find them hovering about these lanes, like restless ghosts, and trying to peep into Garraway's through chinks in the shutters, if not endeavouring to turn the lock of the door with false keys, picks, and screw-drivers. But the wonder is, that they go clean away! And now I think of it, the wonder is, that every working-day pervader of these scenes goes clean away. The man who sells the dogs' collars and the little toy coal-scuttles, feels under as great an obligation to go afar off, as Glyn and Co., or Smith, Payne, and Smith. There is an old monastery-crypt under Garraway's (I have been in it among the port wine), and perhaps Garraway's, taking pity on the mouldy men who wait in its public-room all their lives, gives them cool house-room down there over Sundays; but the catacombs of Paris would not be large enough to hold the rest of the missing. This characteristic of London City greatly helps its being the quaint place it is in the weekly pause of business, and greatly helps my Sunday sensation in it of being the Last Man. In my solitude, the ticket-porters being all gone with the rest, I venture to breathe to the quiet bricks and stones my confidential wonderment why a ticket-porter, who never does any work with his hands, is bound to wear a white apron, and why a great Ecclesiastical Dignitary, who never does any work with his hands either, is equally bound to wear a black one.

29

The Uncommercial Traveller

All The Year Round, 1 August 1863 (*UT1* as 'An Old Stage-Coaching House')

Dickens touches on the national decline in coaching activity in the face of railway competition in 'Dullborough Town' (see p. 140), but had first publicly predicted it in 1837, in his final editorial contribution to *Bentley's Miscellany* (see Vol. 1 of this edition, p. 553). Likewise, in the third number of *Master Humphrey's Clock*, Tony Weller had blasted the railway as 'unconstitootional and an inwaser o' priwileges ... a outrage and a insult ... to sich coachmen and guards as is sometimes forced to go by it' (18 April 1840).

Dickens's narrator avoids specifically naming or otherwise identifying the town on which the essay focuses; the 'Dolphin's Head' is likewise an invented name. The first editor of Dickens's journalism, B. W. Matz, concluded that 'there is nothing by which we can ... identify the Dolphin's Head' (*Dickensian Inns and Taverns* [1922], p. 251). However, W. J. Carlton and Alan S. Watts have since argued in detail that the town is based on Newbury, in Berkshire, and that the coaching-house is based on the 'George and Pelican', overriding objections from Pansy Pakenham that Beaconsfield or Aylesbury are better qualified candidates (see Carlton, 'Dickens's "Old Stage-Coaching House"', *The Dickensian*, Vol. 54 [1958], pp. 13–20; Watts, 'Charles Dickens – A Visitor to Newbury', *Newbury Weekly News*, 21 August 1980, p. 4; Pakenham, Letter to the Editor, *The Dickensian*, Vol. 54 [1958], pp. 121–2).

The George and Pelican stood at the busy crossing of the Great Western Road between London and Bath and the road from Oxford to Winchester, in the parish of Speenhamland, and later became a popular choice for literary reflections on the departed glories of the coaching era, featuring in this capacity in Lord William Pitt Lennox's novel *Percy Hamilton* (1851) and in John Hollingshead's fine essay 'The Last Stage-Coach' – strikingly similar to Dickens's treatment – collected in *Odd Journeys In and Out of London* (1860). Dickens had stayed at the George and Pelican in its heyday, putting up there on 7 November 1835 en route to report for the *Morning Chronicle* on a speech given by Lord John Russell in Bristol. He wrote to his fiancée Catherine Hogarth of 'a chaotic state of confusion just now' at the inn, being 'surrounded by maps, road-books, ostlers, and post-boys', before finishing with the postscript, 'I hear the Coach at this moment' (*Pilgrim*, Vol. I, p. 90). Between this and the composition of the present paper, there is no instance in which he is known to have been in Newbury (thus Carlton's assertion that Dickens is writing about a return visit to Newbury 'made in the summer or Autumn of 1845' cannot be confirmed), but his frequent trips to the West Country to see his parents, or tours of public readings and amateur theatricals, are likely to have taken him there on several occasions.

Literary allusions (below) 'Dolphin ... showed no bright colours': Byron, *Childe Harold* (1818), Canto 4, Stanza 29 ('Parting day/ Dies like the dolphin, whom each parting pang imbues/ With a new colour as it gasps away'); (p. 273) 'Valley of the Shadow': *The Book of Common Prayer* (1662), Psalm 23:4; (p. 273) 'a world too wide': Shakespeare, *As You Like It*, Act 2, Sc. 7.

Before the waitress had shut the door, I had forgotten how many stage-coaches she said used to change horses in the town every day. But it was of little moment; any high number would do as well as another. It had been a great stage-coaching town in the great stage-coaching times, and the ruthless railways had killed and buried it.

The sign of the house was the Dolphin's Head. Why only head, I don't know; for the Dolphin's effigy at full length, and upside down – as a Dolphin is always bound to be when artistically treated, though I suppose he is sometimes right side upward in his natural condition – graced the sign-board. The sign-board chafed its rusty hooks outside the bow-window of my room, and was a shabby work. No visitor could have denied that the Dolphin was dying by inches, but he showed no bright colours. He had once served another master; there was a newer streak of paint below him, displaying with inconsistent freshness the legend, By J. MELLOWS.

My door opened again, and J. Mellows's representative came back. I had asked her what I could have for dinner, and she now returned with the counter-question, what would I like? As the Dolphin stood possessed of nothing that I do like, I was fain to yield to the suggestion of a duck, which I don't like. J. Mellows's representative was a mournful young woman, with one eye susceptible of guidance, and one uncontrollable eye; which latter, seeming to wander in quest of stage-coaches, deepened the melancholy in which the Dolphin was steeped.

This young woman had but shut the door on retiring again when I bethought me of adding to my order, the words, 'with nice vegetables.' Looking out at the door to give them emphatic utterance, I found her already in a state of pensive catalepsy in the deserted gallery, picking her teeth with a pin.

At the Railway Station seven miles off, I had been the subject of wonder when I ordered a fly in which to come here. And when I gave the direction 'To the Dolphin's Head,' I had observed an ominous stare on the countenance of the strong young man in velveteen, who was the platform servant of the Company. He had also called to my driver at parting, 'All ri-ight! Don't hang yourself when you get there, Geo-o-rge!' in a sarcastic tone, for which I had entertained some transitory thoughts of reporting him to the General Manager.

I had no business in the town – I never have any business in any town – but I had been caught by the fancy that I would come and look at it in its degeneracy. My purpose was fitly inaugurated by the Dolphin's Head, which everywhere expressed past coachfulness and present coach-lessness. Coloured prints of coaches, starting, arriving, changing horses, coaches in the sunshine, coaches in the snow, coaches in the wind, coaches in the mist and rain, coaches on the King's birthday, coaches in all circumstances compatible with their triumph and victory, but never in the act of breaking down or overturning, pervaded the house. Of these works of art, some, framed and not glazed, had holes in them; the varnish of others had become so brown and cracked, that they looked like overdone pie-crust; the designs of others were almost obliterated by the flies of many summers. Broken glasses, damaged frames, lop-sided hanging, and consignment of incurable cripples to places of refuge in dark corners, attested the desolation of the rest. The old room on the ground floor where the passengers of the Highflyer used to dine, had nothing in it but a wretched show of twigs and flower-pots in the broad window to hide the nakedness of the land, and in a corner little Mellows's perambulator, with even its parasol-head turned despondently to the wall. The other room, where post-horse company used to wait while relays were getting ready down the yard, still held its ground, but was as airless as I conceive a hearse to be: insomuch that Mr Pitt, hanging high against the partition (with spots on him like port wine, though it is mysterious how port wine ever got squirted up there), had good reason for perking his nose and sniffing. The stopperless cruets on the spindle-shanked sideboard were in a miserably dejected state: the anchovy sauce having turned blue some years ago, and the cayenne pepper (with a scoop in it like a small model of a wooden leg) having turned solid. The old fraudulent candles which were always being paid for and never used, were burnt out at last; but their tall stilts of candlesticks still lingered, and still outraged the human intellect by pretending to be silver. The mouldy old unreformed Borough Member, with his right hand buttoned up in the breast of his coat, and his back characteristically turned on bales of petitions from his constituents, was there too; and the poker which never had been among the fire-irons, lest post-horse company should overstir the fire, was *not* there, as of old.

Pursuing my researches in the Dolphin's Head, I found it sorely shrunken. When J. Mellows came into possession, he had walled off half the bar, which was now a tobacco-shop with its own entrance in the yard – the once glorious yard where the postboys, whip in hand and always buttoning their waistcoats at the last moment, used to come running forth to mount and away. A 'Scientific Shoeing-Smith and Veterinary Surgeon,' had further encroached upon the yard; and a grimly satirical Jobber, who announced himself as having to Let 'A neat one-horse fly, and a one-horse cart,' had established his business, himself, and his family, in a part of the extensive stables. Another part was lopped clean off from the Dolphin's Head, and now comprised a chapel, a wheelwright's, and a Young Men's Mutual Improvement and Discussion Society (in a loft): the whole forming a back lane. No audacious hand had plucked down the vane from the central cupola of the stables, but it had grown rusty and stuck at N–Nil: while the score or two of pigeons that remained true to their ancestral traditions and the place, had collected in a row on the roof-ridge of the only outhouse retained by the Dolphin, where all the inside pigeons tried to push the outside pigeon off. This I accepted as emblematical of the struggle for post and place in railway times.

Sauntering forth into the town, by way of the covered and pillared entrance to the Dolphin's Yard, once redolent of soup and stable-litter, now redolent of musty disuse, I paced the street. It was a hot day, and the little sun-blinds of the shops were all drawn down, and the more enterprising tradesmen had caused their 'Prentices to trickle water on the pavement appertaining to their frontage. It looked as if they had been shedding tears for the stage-coaches, and drying their ineffectual pocket-handkerchiefs. Such weakness would have been excusable; for business was – as one dejected porkman who kept a shop which refused to reciprocate the compliment by keeping him, informed me – 'bitter bad.' Most of the harness-makers and corn-dealers were gone the way of the coaches, but it was a pleasant recognition of the eternal procession of Children down that old original steep Incline, the Valley of the Shadow, that those tradesmen were mostly succeeded by vendors of sweetmeats and cheap toys. The opposition house to the Dolphin, once famous as the New White Hart, had long collapsed. In a fit of abject depression, it had cast whitewash on its windows, and boarded up its front door, and reduced itself to a side entrance; but even that had proved a world too wide for the Literary Institution which had been its last phase; for the Institution had collapsed too, and of the ambitious letters of its inscription on the White Hart's front, all had fallen off but these:

L   Y   INS   T

– suggestive of Lamentably Insolvent. As to the neighbouring market-place, it seemed to have wholly relinquished marketing, to the dealer in crockery whose pots and pans straggled half across it, and to the Cheap Jack who sat with folded arms on the shafts of his cart, superciliously gazing around: his velveteen waistcoat, evidently harbouring grave doubts whether it was worth his while to stay a night in such a place.

The church bells began to ring as I left this spot, but they by no means improved the case, for they said, in a petulant way, and speaking with some difficulty in their irritation, 'WHAT's-be-come-of-THE-coach-ES!' Nor would they (I found on listening) ever vary their emphasis, save in respect of growing more sharp and vexed, but invariably went on, 'WHAT's-be-come-of-THE-coach-ES! – always beginning the inquiry with an unpolite abruptness. Perhaps from their elevation they saw the railway, and it aggravated them.

Coming upon a coachmaker's workshop, I began to look about me with a revived spirit, thinking that perchance I might behold there some remains of the old times of the town's greatness. There was only one man at work – a dry man, grizzled, and far advanced in years, but tall and upright, who, becoming aware of me looking on, straightened his back, pushed up his spectacles against his brown paper cap, and appeared inclined to defy me. To whom I pacifically said:

'Good day, sir!'

'What?' said he.

'Good day, sir.'

He seemed to consider about that, and not to agree with me. – 'Was you a looking for anything?' he then asked, in a pointed manner.

'I was wondering whether there happened to be any fragment of an old stage-coach here.'

'Is that all?'

'That's all.'

'No, there ain't.'

It was now my turn to say 'Oh!' and I said it. Not another word did the dry and grizzled man say, but bent to his work again. In the coachmaking days, the coach-painters had tried their brushes on a post beside him; and quite a Calendar of departed glories was to be read upon it, in blue and yellow and red and green, some inches thick. Presently he looked up again.

'You seem to have a deal of time on your hands,' was his querulous remark.

I admitted the fact.

'I think it's a pity you was not brought up to something,' said he.

I said I thought so too.

Appearing to be informed with an idea, he laid down his plane (for it was a plane he was at work with), pushed up his spectacles again, and came to the door.

'Would a po-shay do for you?' he asked.

'I am not sure that I understand what you mean.'

'Would a po-shay,' said the coachmaker, standing close before me, and folding his arms in the manner of a cross-examining counsel – 'would a po-shay meet the views you have expressed? Yes, or no?'

'Yes.'

'Then you keep straight along down there till you see one. *You'll* see one if you go fur enough.'

With that, he turned me by the shoulder in the direction I was to take, and went in and resumed his work against a background of leaves and grapes. For, although he was a soured man and a discontented, his workshop was that agreeable mixture of town and country, street and garden, which is often to be seen in a small English town.

I went the way he had turned me, and I came to the Beer-shop with the sign of The First and Last, and was out of the town on the old London road. I came to the Turnpike, and I found it, in its silent way, eloquent respecting the change that had fallen on the road. The Turnpike-house was all overgrown with ivy; and the Turnpike-keeper, unable to get a living out of the tolls, plied the trade of a cobbler. Not only that, but his wife sold ginger-beer, and, in the very window of espial through which the Toll-takers of old times used with awe to behold the grand London coaches coming on at a gallop, exhibited for sale little barbers'-poles of sweet-stuff in a sticky lantern.

The political economy of the master of the turnpike thus expressed itself.

'How goes turnpike business, master?' said I to him, as he sat in his little porch, repairing a shoe.

'It don't go at all, master,' said he to me. 'It's stopped.'

'That's bad,' said I.

'Bad?' he repeated. And he pointed to one of his sunburnt dusty children who was climbing the turnpike-gate, and said, extending his open right hand in remonstrance with Universal Nature. 'Five on 'em!'

'But how to improve Turnpike business?' said I.

'There's a way, master,' said he, with the air of one who had thought deeply on the subject.

'I should like to know it.'

'Lay a toll on everything as comes through; lay a toll on walkers. Lay another toll on everything as don't come through; lay a toll on them as stops at home.'

'Would the last remedy be fair?'

'Fair? Them as stops at home, could come through if they liked; couldn't they?'

'Say they could.'

'Toll 'em. If they don't come through, it's *their* look out. Anyways, – Toll 'em!'

Finding it was as impossible to argue with this financial genius as if he had been Chancellor of the Exchequer, and consequently the right man in the right place, I passed on meekly.

My mind now began to misgive me that the disappointed coachmaker had sent me on a wild-goose errand, and that there was no post-chaise in those parts. But coming within view of certain allotment-gardens by the roadside, I retracted the suspicion, and confessed that I had done him an injustice. For, there I saw, surely, the poorest superannuated post-chaise left on earth.

It was a post-chaise taken off its axletree and wheels, and plumped down on the clayey soil among a ragged growth of vegetables. It was a post-chaise not even set straight upon the ground, but tilted over, as if it had fallen out of a balloon. It was a post-chaise that had been a long time in those decayed circumstances, and against which scarlet beans were trained. It was a post-chaise patched and mended with old tea-trays, or with scraps of iron that looked like them, and boarded up as to the windows, but having A KNOCKER on the off-side door. Whether it was a post-chaise used as tool-house, summer-house, or dwelling-house, I could not discover, for there was nobody at home at the post-chaise when I knocked; but it was certainly used for something, and locked up. In the wonder of this discovery, I walked round and round the post-chaise many times, and sat down by the post-chaise, waiting for further elucidation. None came. At last, I made my way back to the old London road by the further end of the allotment-gardens, and consequently at a point beyond that from which I had diverged. I had to scramble through a hedge and down a steep bank, and I nearly came down atop of a little spare man who sat breaking stones by the roadside.

He stayed his hammer, and said, regarding me mysteriously through his dark goggles of wire:

'Are you aware, sir, that you've been trespassing?'

'I turned out of the way,' said I, in explanation, 'to look at that odd post-chaise. Do you happen to know anything about it?'

'I know it was many a year upon the road,' said he.

'So I supposed. Do you know to whom it belongs?'

The stone-breaker bent his brows and goggles over his heap of stones, as if he were considering whether he should answer the question or not. Then, raising his barred eyes to my features as before, he said:

'To me.'

Being quite unprepared for the reply, I received it with a sufficiently awkward 'Indeed! Dear me!' Presently I added, 'Do you–' I was going to say 'live there,' but it seemed so absurd a question, that I substituted, 'live near here?'

The stone-breaker, who had not broken a fragment since we began to converse, then did as follows. He raised himself by poising his figure on his hammer, and took his coat, on which he had been seated, over his arm. He then backed to an easier part of the bank than that by which I had come down, keeping his dark goggles silently upon me all the time, and then shouldered his hammer, suddenly turned, ascended, and was gone. His face was so small, and his goggles were so large, that he left me wholly uninformed as to his countenance; but he left me a profound impression that the curved legs I had seen from behind, as he vanished, were the legs of an old postboy. It was not until then that I noticed he had been working by a grass-grown milestone, which looked like a tombstone erected over the grave of the London road.

My dinner-hour being close at hand, I had no leisure to pursue the goggles or the subject then, but made my way back to the Dolphin's Head. In the gateway I found J. Mellows, looking at nothing, and apparently experiencing that it failed to raise his spirits.

'*I* don't care for the town,' said J. Mellows, when I complimented him on the sanitary advantages it may or may not possess; 'I wish I had never seen the town!'

'You don't belong to it, Mr Mellows?'

'Belong to it!' repeated Mellows. 'If I didn't belong to a better style of town than this, I'd take and drown myself in a pail.' It then occurred to me that Mellows, having so little to do, was habitually thrown back on his internal resources – by which I mean the Dolphin's cellar.

'What we want,' said Mellows, pulling off his hat, and making as if he emptied it of the last load of Disgust that had exuded from his brain, before he put it on again for another load; 'what we want, is a Branch.

The Petition for the Branch Bill is in the coffee-room. Would you put your name to it? Every little helps.'

I found the document in question stretched out flat on the coffee-room table by the aid of certain weights from the kitchen, and I gave it the additional weight of my uncommercial signature. To the best of my belief, I bound myself to the modest statement that universal traffic, happiness, prosperity, and civilisation, together with unbounded national triumph in competition with the foreigner, would infallibly flow from the Branch.

Having achieved this constitutional feat, I asked Mr Mellows if he could grace my dinner with a pint of good wine? Mr Mellows thus replied:

'If I couldn't give you a pint of good wine, I'd–there!–I'd take and drown myself in a pail. But I was deceived when I bought this business, and the stock was higgledy-piggledy, and I haven't yet tasted my way quite through it with a view to sorting it. Therefore, if you order one kind and get another, change till it comes right. For what,' said Mellows, unloading his hat as before, 'what would you or any gentleman do, if you ordered one kind of wine and was required to drink another? Why, you'd (and naturally and properly, having the feelings of a gentleman), you'd take and drown yourself in a pail!'

30

The Uncommercial Traveller

All The Year Round, 15 August 1863 (*UT1* as 'The Boiled Beef of New England')

In 'The Great Baby' (see Vol. 3 of this edition, article 40) and 'The Poor Man and His Beer' (see article 1 of this volume), Dickens had attacked the combination of patronage and mistrust of the working man evinced by many charity workers and social reformers. Similar ideas are rehearsed in both the present article and an *ATYR* article of 26 March 1864, 'Working Men's Clubs', co-written by Dickens and Edmund Ollier. Writing to Ollier about the project, Dickens insists on a similar series of principles to those stressed in the present article, namely: that '... to trust a man, as one of a body of men, is to place him under a wholesome restraint of social opinion, and is a very much better thing than to make a baby of him' (see p. 286 below); that 'the rejection of beer in this club, tobacco in that club ... are instances that such clubs are founded on mere whims, and therefore cannot successfully address human nature in the general ...' (see p. 286 below); and, finally, that 'Patronage is the curse and blight of all such endeavours, and to impress upon the working men that they must originate and manage for themselves' (see p. 281 below; letter given in *Pilgrim*, Vol. X, pp. 369–70).

The idea of cheap dining-halls run for the benefit of working men had been mooted in Dickens's journals as early as 1855, in the penultimate instalment of Elizabeth Gaskell's *North and South* (*HW*, 20 January 1855), but had been given a new impetus by the high unemployment in manufacturing towns caused by the American Civil War in the early 1860s. More than a dozen dining-halls, or 'Depôts' as they were commonly known, had been opened in Glasgow and Manchester, following models proposed by Scottish merchant Thomas Corbett, and by John Pender and Hugh Birley, stimulating some argument over whether such institutions should ideally be charitable or independent (see *The Times*, 20 April 1863, p. 7, col. d). By the time Dickens came to research and write his views on the issue, there was something of a race between rival associations in London to set up 'dining-halls for the million'.

The initiative which attracted Dickens's attention was the 'Association for Providing the Establishment in London of Self-Supporting Cooking Depôts for the Working Classes', whose Hon. Secretary, Alexander Burrell, wrote to *The Times* on 7 April to inform readers that 'an eligible site in Whitechapel' had been secured, and that 'the leading feature of Mr Corbett's scheme, that the depôts should ... be ... self-supporting' would be strictly preserved (p. 7, col. d). Burrell also wrote to Dickens in May/June 1863 publicising the new depot and mentioning Edwin Chadwick's name in their connection. Dickens wrote to Chadwick on 24 July that he had inspected the Whitechapel dining-hall – which stood on the corner of Flower & Dean Street and Commercial Street – 'some ten days ago', and was considering his proposals for establishing a dining-hall or 'early breakfast room' specifically for the newsboys of the metropolis (see *Pilgrim*, Vol. X, pp. 274, 474 [Appendix B]).

The 'appalling accident' referred to (p. 280 below) was the death on 20 July 1863 of Selina Powell, alias Madame Genevieve, 'The Female Blondin', from a 30-foot fall on to gravel during a high-wire performance at a fête organised by the Order of Foresters at Aston Park, Birmingham. Only a few weeks before, on 25 June, artist Carlo Valerio had met his death falling from a high-wire at Cremorne Gardens. A lengthy editorial in *The Times* of 23 July condemned the members of the Foresters Committee, who, notwithstanding the accident, 'determined "to go on with the programme, omitting the dangerous parts" ', but considered it 'even more revolting ... that the spectators ... continued to enjoy themselves as if nothing had happened'. Such heartlessness was not characteristic of the English in general, the editorial opined, 'and we should be sorry to think it could have been shown thus offensively anywhere but in the "Black Country" ' ('The Female Blondin at Aston Park', p. 10, col. e). Dickens clearly responds to *The Times* in the present article and comes to the defence of the spectators. He did not blame the public for wanting to see successful spectacles of daring, but objected strongly when commercial exploitation and lax safety precautions were involved (see Vol. 3 of this edition, article 13, p. 92).

Literary allusions (p. 277) The title chosen by Dickens for the volume publication of this paper plays on that of 'The Roast Beef of Old England' (words and music by Richard Leveridge); (p. 281) 'called by Providence to walk all his days in a station in life ...': '... keep God's holy will and commandments, and walk in the same all the days of my life', 'A Catechism', *The Book of Common Prayer*; (p. 281) 'impotent conclusions': Shakespeare, *Othello*, Act 2, Sc. 1.

Textual note (p. 280) copy-text has 'This is the text ... fashions': *UT1* has 'This is a text ... fashions'.

The shabbiness of our English capital, as compared with Paris, Bordeaux, Frankfurt, Milan, Geneva – almost any important town on the continent of Europe – I find very striking after absence of any duration in foreign parts. London is shabby in contrast with Edinburgh, with Aberdeen, with Exeter, with Liverpool, with a bright little town like Bury St Edmunds. London is shabby in contrast with New York, with Boston, with Philadelphia. In detail, one would say it can rarely fail to be a disappointing piece of shabbiness, to a stranger from any of those places. There is nothing shabbier than Drury-lane, in Rome itself. The meanness of Regent-street, set against the great line of Boulevards in Paris, is as striking as the abortive ugliness of Trafalgar-square, set against the gallant beauty of the Place de la Concorde. London is shabby by daylight, and shabbier by gaslight. No Englishman knows what gaslight is, until he sees the Rue de Rivoli and the Palais Royal after dark.

The mass of London people are shabby. The absence of distinctive dress has, no doubt, something to do with it. The porters of the Vintners' Company, the draymen, and the butchers, are about the only people who wear distinctive dresses; and even these do not wear them on holidays. We have nothing which for cheapness, cleanliness, convenience, or picturesqueness, can compare with the belted blouse. As to our women; – next Easter or Whitsuntide, look at the bonnets at the British Museum or the National Gallery, and think of the pretty white French cap, the Spanish mantilla, or the Genoese mezzero.

Probably there are not more second-hand clothes sold in London than in Paris, and yet the mass of the London population have a second-hand look which is not to be detected on the mass of the Parisian population. I think this is mainly because a Parisian workman does not in the least trouble himself about what is worn by a Parisian idler, but dresses in the way of his own class, and for his own comfort. In London, on the contrary, the fashions descend; and you never fully know how inconvenient or ridiculous a fashion is until you see it in its last descent. It was but the other day, on a race-course, that I observed four people in a barouche deriving great entertainment from the contemplation of four people on foot. The four people on foot were two young men and two young women; the four people in the barouche were two young men and two young women. The four young women were dressed in exactly the same style; the four young men were dressed in exactly the same style. Yet the two couples on wheels were as much amused by the two couples on foot, as if they were quite unconscious of having themselves set those fashions, or of being at that very moment engaged in the display of them.

Is it only in the matter of clothes that fashion descends here in London – and consequently in England – and thence shabbiness arises? Let us think a little, and be just. The 'Black Country' round about Birmingham, is a very black country; but is it quite as black as it has been lately painted? An appalling accident happened at the People's Park, near Birmingham, this last July, when it was crowded with people from the Black Country – an appalling accident consequent on a shamefully dangerous exhibition. Did the shamefully dangerous exhibition originate in the moral blackness of the Black Country, and in the Black People's peculiar love of the excitement attendant on great personal hazard, which they looked on at, but in which they did not participate? Light is much wanted in the Black Country. O we are all agreed on that. But, we must not quite forget the crowds of gentlefolks who set the shamefully dangerous fashion, either. We must not quite forget the enterprising Directors of an Institution vaunting mighty educational pretences, who made the low sensation as strong as they possibly could make it, by hanging the Blondin rope as high as they possibly could hang it. All this must not be eclipsed in the Blackness of the Black Country. The reserved seats high up by the rope, the cleared space below it, so that no one should be smashed but the performer, the pretence of slipping and falling off, the baskets for the feet and the sack for the head, the photographs everywhere, and the virtuous indignation nowhere – all this must not be wholly swallowed up in the blackness of the jet-black country.

Whatsoever fashion is set in England, is certain to descend. This is the text for a perpetual sermon on care in setting fashions. When you find a fashion low down, look back for the time (it will never be far off) when it was the fashion high up. This is the text for a perpetual sermon on social justice. From imitations of Ethiopian Serenaders, to imitations of Prince's coats and waistcoats, you will find the original model in St James's Parish. When the Serenaders become tiresome, trace them beyond the Black Country; when the coats and waistcoats become insupportable, refer them to their source in the Upper Toady Regions.

Gentlemen's clubs were once maintained for purposes of savage party warfare; working men's clubs of the same day assumed the same character. Gentlemen's clubs became places of quiet inoffensive recreation; working men's clubs began to follow suit. If working men have seemed rather slow to appreciate advantages of combination which have saved the pockets of gentlemen, and enhanced their comforts, it is because working men could scarcely, for want of capital, originate such combinations without help; and because help has not been separable from that great impertinence, Patronage. The instinctive revolt of his spirit against patronage, is a quality much to be respected in the English working man. It is the base of the base of his best qualities. Nor is it surprising that he should be unduly suspicious of patronage, and sometimes resentful of it even where it is not, seeing what a flood of washy talk has been let loose on his devoted head, or with what complacent condescension the same devoted head has been smoothed and patted. It is a proof to me of his self-control that he never strikes out pugilistically, right and left, when addressed as one of 'My friends,' or 'My assembled friends'; that he does not become inappeasable, and run amuck like a Malay, whenever he sees a biped in broadcloth getting on a platform to talk to him; that any pretence of improving his mind, does not instantly drive him out of his mind, and cause him to toss his obliging patron like a mad bull.

For, how often have I heard the unfortunate working man lectured as if he were a little charity-child, humid as to his nasal development, strictly literal as to his Catechism, and called by Providence to walk all his days in a station in life represented on festive occasions by a mug of warm milk-and-water and a bun! What popguns of jokes have these ears tingled to hear let off at him, what asinine sentiments, what impotent conclusions, what spelling-book moralities, what adaptations of the orator's insufferable tediousness to the assumed level of his understanding! If his sledge-hammers, his spades and pickaxes, his saws and chisels, his paint-pots and brushes, his forges furnaces and engines, the horses that he drove at his work, and the machines that drove him at his work, were all toys in one little paper box, and he the baby who played with them, he could not have been discoursed to, more impertinently and absurdly than I have heard him discoursed to, times innumerable. Consequently, not being a fool or a fawner, he has come to acknowledge his patronage by virtually saying: 'Let me alone. If you understand me no better than *that*, sir and madam, let me alone. You mean very well, I dare say, but I don't like it, and I won't come here again to have any more of it.'

Whatever is done for the comfort and advancement of the working man must be so far done by himself as that it is maintained by himself. And there must be in it no touch of condescension, no shadow of patronage. In the great working districts, this truth is studied and understood. When the American civil war rendered it necessary, first in Glasgow, and afterwards in Manchester, that the working people should be shown how to avail themselves of the advantages derivable from system, and from the combination of numbers, in the purchase and the cooking of their food, this truth was above all things borne in mind. The quick consequence was, that suspicion and reluctance were vanquished, and that the effort resulted in an astonishing and a complete success.

Such thoughts passed through my mind on a July morning of this summer, as I walked towards Commercial-street (not Uncommercial-street), Whitechapel. The Glasgow and Manchester system had been lately set a-going there, by certain gentlemen who felt an interest in its diffusion, and I had been attracted by the following hand-bill, printed on rose-coloured paper:

SELF-SUPPORTING
COOKING DEPOT
FOR THE WORKING CLASSES,
Commercial-street, Whitechapel,
Where Accommodation is provided for Dining comfortably 300 Persons at
a time.
Open from 7 A.M. till 7 P.M.
PRICES.
All Articles of the BEST QUALITY.

Cup of Tea or Coffee...One Penny
Bread and Butter...One Penny
Bread and Cheese ....One Penny
Slice of Bread ....One halfpenny or One Penny
Boiled Egg ....One Penny
Ginger Beer ....One Penny

The above Articles always ready.
Besides the above may be had, from 12 to 3 o'clock,

Bowl of Scotch Broth..One Penny
Bowl of Soup...One Penny
Plate of Potatoes...One Penny

Plate of Minced Beef...Twopence
Plate of Cold Beef...Twopence
Plate of Cold Ham...Twopence
Plate of Plum Pudding, or Rice..............................One Penny

As the Economy of Cooking depends greatly upon the simplicity of the arrangements with which a great number of persons can be served at one time, the Upper Room of this Establishment will be especially set apart for a

PUBLIC DINNER EVERY DAY
From 12 till 3 o'clock,
Consisting of the following Dishes:
Bowl of Broth, or Soup,
Plate of Cold Beef or Ham,
Plate of Potatoes,
Plum Pudding, or Rice.
FIXED CHARGE $4\frac{1}{2}$ d.
THE DAILY PAPERS PROVIDED.

N.B.–This Establishment is conducted on the strictest business principles, with the full intention of making it self-supporting, so that every one may frequent it with a feeling of perfect independence.

The assistance of all frequenting the Depôt is confidently expected in checking anything interfering with the comfort, quiet, and regularity of the establishment.

Please do not destroy this Hand Bill, but hand it to some other person whom it may interest.

This Self-Supporting Cooking Depôt (not a very good name, and one would rather give it an English one) had hired a newly-built warehouse that it found to let; therefore it was not established in premises especially designed for the purpose. But, at a small cost they were exceedingly well adapted to the purpose: being light, well ventilated, clean, and cheerful. They consisted of three large rooms. That on the basement story was the kitchen; that on the ground floor was the general dining-room; that on the floor above, was the Upper Room referred to in the hand-bill, where the Public Dinner at fourpence-halfpenny a head was provided every day. The cooking was done, with much economy of space and fuel, by American cooking-stoves, and by young women not previously brought up as cooks; the walls and pillars of the two dining-rooms were agreeably brightened with ornamental colours; the tables were capable of accommodating six or eight persons each; the attendants were all young women, becomingly and neatly dressed, and dressed alike. I think the whole staff was female, with the exception of the steward or manager.

My first inquiries were directed to the wages of this staff; because, if any establishment claiming to be self-supporting live upon the spoliation of anybody or anything, or eke out a feeble existence by poor mouths and beggarly resources (as too many so-called Mechanics' Institutions do), I make bold to express my Uncommercial opinion that it has no business to live, and had better die. It was made clear to me, by the account-books, that every person employed was properly paid. My next inquiries were directed to the quality of the provisions purchased, and to the terms on which they were bought. It was made equally clear to me that the quality was the very best, and that all bills were paid weekly. My next inquiries were directed to the balance-sheet for the last two weeks – only the third and fourth of the establishment's career. It was made equally clear to me, that after everything bought was paid for, and after each week was charged with its full share of wages, rent and taxes, depreciation of plant in use, and interest on capital at the rate of four per cent per annum, the last week had yielded a profit of (in round numbers) one pound ten; and the previous week a profit of six pounds ten. By this time I felt that I had a healthy appetite for the dinners.

It had just struck twelve, and a quick succession of faces had already begun to appear at a little window in the wall of the partitioned space where I sat looking over the books. Within this little window, like a pay-box at a theatre, a neat and brisk young woman presided to take money and issue tickets. Everyone coming in must take a ticket. Either the fourpence-halfpenny ticket for the upper room (the most popular ticket, I think), or a penny ticket for a bowl of soup, or as many penny tickets as he or she chose to buy. For three penny tickets one had quite a wide range of choice. A plate of cold boiled beef and potatoes; or a plate of cold ham and potatoes; or a plate of hot minced beef and potatoes; or a bowl of soup, bread and cheese, and a plate of plum-pudding. Touching what they should have, some customers on taking their seats fell into a reverie – became mildly distracted – postponed decision, and said in bewilderment, they would think of it. One old man I noticed when I sat among the tables in the lower room, who was startled by the bill of fare, and sat contemplating it as if it were something of a ghostly nature. The decision of the boys was as rapid as their execution, and always included pudding.

There were several women among the diners, and several clerks and shopmen. There were carpenters and painters from the neighbouring buildings under repair, and there were nautical men, and there were, as one diner observed to me, 'some of most sorts.' Some were solitary, some came two together, some dined in parties of three or four, or six. The latter talked together, but assuredly no one was louder than at my club in Pall-Mall. One young fellow whistled in rather a shrill manner while he waited for his dinner, but I was gratified to observe that he did so in evident defiance of my Uncommercial individuality. Quite agreeing with him, on consideration, that I had no business to be there, unless I dined like the rest, I 'went in,' as the phrase is, for fourpence-halfpenny.

The room of the fourpence-halfpenny banquet had, like the lower room, a counter in it, on which were ranged a great number of cold portions ready for distribution. Behind this counter, the fragrant soup was steaming in deep cans, and the best-cooked of potatoes were fished out of similar receptacles. Nothing to eat was touched with the hand. Every waitress had her own tables to attend to. As soon as she saw a new customer seat himself at one of her tables, she took from the counter all his dinner – his soup, potatoes, meat, and pudding – piled it up dexterously in her two hands, set it before him, and took his ticket. This serving of the whole dinner at once had been found greatly to simplify the business of attendance, and was also popular with the customers: who were thus enabled to vary the meal by varying the routine of dishes: beginning with soup today, putting soup in the middle tomorrow, putting soup at the end the day after tomorrow, and ringing similar changes on meat and pudding. The rapidity with which every new comer got served was remarkable: and the dexterity with which the waitresses (quite new to the art a month before) discharged their duty, was as agreeable to see, as the neat smartness with which they wore their dress and had dressed their hair.

If I seldom saw better waiting, so I certainly never ate better meat, potatoes, or pudding. And the soup was an honest and stout soup, with rice and barley in it, and 'little matters for the teeth to touch,' as had been observed to me by my friend below stairs already quoted. The dinner-service, too, was neither conspicuously hideous for High Art nor for Low Art, but was of a pleasant and pure appearance. Concerning the viands and their cookery, one last remark. I dined at my club in Pall-Mall aforesaid, a few days afterwards, for exactly twelve times the money, and not half as well.

The company thickened after one o'clock struck, and changed pretty quickly. Although experience of the place had been so recently attainable, and although there was still considerable curiosity out in the street and about the entrance, the general tone was as good as could be, and the customers fell easily into the ways of the place. It was clear to me, however, that they were there to have what they paid for, and to be on an independent footing. To the best of my judgment, they might be patronised out of the building in a month. With judicious visiting, and by dint of being questioned, read to, and talked at, they might even be got rid of (for the next quarter of a century) in half the time.

This disinterested and wise movement is fraught with so many whole-some changes in the lives of the working people, and with so much good in the way of overcoming that suspicion which our own unconscious impertinence has engendered, that it is scarcely gracious to criticise details as yet; the rather, because it is indisputable that the managers of the Whitechapel establishment most thoroughly feel that they are upon their honour with the customers, as to the minutest points of admin-istration. But, although the American stoves cannot roast, they can surely boil one kind of meat as well as another, and need not always circumscribe their boiling talents within the limits of ham and beef. The most enthusiastic admirer of those substantials, would probably not object to occasional inconstancy in respect of pork and mutton: or, especially in cold weather, to a little innocent trifling with Irish stews, meat pies, and toads in holes. Another drawback on the Whitechapel establishment, is the absence of beer. Regarded merely as a question of policy, it is very impolitic, as having a tendency to send the working men to the public-house, where gin is reported to be sold. But, there is a much higher ground on which this absence of beer is objectionable. It expresses distrust of the working man. It is a fragment of that old mantle of patronage in which so many estimable Thugs, so darkly wandering up and down the moral world, are sworn to muffle him. Good beer is a good thing for him, he says, and he likes it; the Depôt could give it him good, and he now gets it bad. Why does the Depôt not give it him good? Because he would get drunk. Why does the Depôt not let him have a pint with his dinner, which would not make him drunk? Because he might have had another pint, or another two pints, before he came. Now, this distrust is an affront, is exceedingly inconsistent with the confidence the managers express in their hand-bills, and is a timid stopping-short upon the straight highway. It is unjust and unreasonable, also. It is unjust, because it punishes the sober man for the vice of the drunken man. It is unreasonable, because anyone at all experienced in such things knows that the drunken workman does not get drunk where he goes to eat and drink, but where he goes to drink – expressly to drink. To suppose that the working man cannot state this question to himself quite as plainly as I state it here, is to suppose that he is a baby, and is again to tell him in the old wearisome condescending patronising way, that he must be goody-poody, and do as he is toldy-poldy, and not be a manny-panny or a voter-poter, but fold his handy-pandys, and be a childy-pildy.

I found, from the accounts of the Whitechapel Self-Supporting Cooking Depôt, that every article sold in it, even at the prices I have quoted, yields a certain small profit! Individual speculators are of course already in the field, and are of course already appropriating the name. The classes for whose benefit the real depôts are designed, will distinguish between the two kinds of enterprise.

31

The Uncommercial Traveller

All The Year Round, 29 August 1863 (*UT1* as 'Chatham Dockyard')

Henry VIII first rented storehouses at Chatham to service his fleet in 1547. From the *Sunne* in 1586, until HM Submarine *Ocelot* in 1962, Chatham Dockyard built and launched vessels of the Royal Fleet, including such famous names as HMS *Victory, Revenge, Temeraire* (see p. 294 below) and *Leviathan,* the so-called 'wooden walls' of England. In its hey-day, the Yard covered eighty acres, and it currently boasts forty-seven Scheduled Ancient Monuments, mainly consisting of Georgian and early Victorian dock buildings: shops, houses, slips, lofts, storehouses, offices and officers' accommodation.

In the early years of *ATYR*, Dickens commissioned several articles describing in detail visits to British and French military and naval installations (see Oppenlander, under Collins, Charles, and Hannay, James). Dickens had himself, moreover, already co-written with R. H. Horne a paper on the Dockyard at Chatham, titled 'One Man in a Dockyard' and published in *HW* on 6 September 1851 (Vol. III; repr. in Stone, Vol. I, pp. 331–42). In a letter of July 1851 proposing the general notion of this article, Dickens had explained to his sub-editor that '[t]he notion I think of trying … is a kind of adaptation of an old idea I once had (when I was making my name) of a fanciful and picturesque "beauties of England and Wales". … Don't you think a series of places, *well* chosen, and described *well*, with their peculiarities and popularities thoroughly seized, would be a very promising series? – And one that people would be particularly likely to identify with me?' (*Pilgrim,* Vol. VI, p. 451). However, all the papers mentioned so far tend to the factual and informative, rather than the 'fanciful and picturesque', which is brought out much more clearly in the present article.

In the summer of 1863 Sydney Smith Haldimand Dickens (Dickens's fifth son) was 'pretty constantly at home', as the ship on which he was serving as a midshipman, HMS *Orlando,* was 'fortunately in Chatham

Dockyard ... while the shipwrights are repairing a leak in her' (*Pilgrim*, Vol. X, p. 253). In his letters, Dickens refers to Sydney with evident pride as 'my Sailor-boy' or 'the Admiral', and recounts how, among his peers, he was referred to as ' "Young Dickens, who can do everything" ' (*ibid.*, Vol. IX, p. 247). It is probable that in the description here of the 'wise boy' with his store of nautical knowledge, Dickens gives an affectionate portrait of Sydney accompanying his father to inspect the repairs to the *Orlando* in July or August 1863.

The HMS *Achilles*, one of ten new iron-clad broadside-armed ships commissioned in the 1860s, was launched on 23–24 December 1863 and was the first iron-hulled boat to be built for a national government in its own yard. The 'Military and Naval Intelligence' column of *The Times* reported in detail on the progress of its construction, noting the following details:

> Advantage has been taken at Chatham of the recent fine weather to lay the main and upper deck planking of the Achilles. ... The mechanics have been employed overtime for about a fortnight in order that the entire deck might be completed before any change of weather sets in. The iron plating of all the decks is 5–16ths of an inch in thickness, with iron ties 5/8[ths of an inch] thick. ... The only remaining portions of the exterior of the Achilles now waiting to receive the armour-plates [are] the stem and stern portions, but in consequence of the difficulty experienced in bending the plates the work proceeds but slowly. [25 August 1863, p. 10, col. f]

Although dated 29 August 1863, the edition of *ATYR* in which Dickens's 'rival' (and much fuller) report on the construction of the *Achilles* appeared, would in fact have become available the previous Wednesday, i.e. on 26 August: the day after the *Times* feature. HMS *Achilles* remained afloat until 1923 (see Philip MacDougall, *The Chatham Dockyard Story* [1987], pp. 111–15).

Literary allusions (p. 291) 'the identical little man who had the little gun ... lead, lead, lead': *Mother Goose* nursery rhyme called 'The Little Man'; (p. 291) 'note of preparation': Shakespeare, *Henry V*, Act 4, 'Chorus'; (p. 295) 'Chinese Enchanter's Car ... country': Dickens is here probably recalling some pantomime seen in his early years (D. Mayer notes in his *Harlequin in his Element* [1969], p. 140f., that there was a strong Chinese element in English pantomime between 1812 and 1823, though makes no mention either of an Enchanter or a Car; 'The Chinese Enchanter' was, however, the name of a spectacular equestrian act devised by Ducrow in 1826, though again no car was involved; see A. H. Saxon's *Life and Art of Andrew Ducrow* [1978], pp. 204–5); (p. 295) 'telling his keys like Blue Beard': allusion to Charles Perrault's tale 'La Barbe Bleue' (1697); (p. 296) 'braggart

Pistol and his brood': group of rogues, companions of Falstaff, who feature in Shakespeare, *2 Henry IV*, *Henry V* and *Merry Wives of Windsor*.

There are some small out-of-the-way landing-places on the Thames and the Medway, where I do much of my summer idling. Running water is favourable to day-dreams, and a strong tidal river is the best of running water for mine. I like to watch the great ships standing out to sea or coming home richly laden, the active little steam-tugs confidently puffing with them to and from the sea-horizon, the fleet of barges that seem to have plucked their brown and russet sails from the ripe trees in the landscape, the heavy old colliers, light in ballast, floundering down before the tide, the light screw barks and schooners imperiously holding a straight course while the others patiently tack and go about, the yachts with their tiny hulls and great white sheets of canvas, the little sailing-boats bobbing to and fro on their errands of pleasure or business, and – as it is the nature of little people to do – making a prodigious fuss about their small affairs. Watching these objects, I still am under no obligation to think about them, or even so much as to see them, unless it perfectly suits my humour. As little am I obliged to hear the plash and flop of the tide, the ripple at my feet, the clinking windlass afar off, or the humming steam-ship paddles further away yet. These, with the creaking little jetty on which I sit, and the gaunt high-water marks and low-water marks in the mud, and the broken causeway, and the broken bank, and the broken stakes and piles leaning forward as if they were vain of their personal appearance and looking for their reflexion in the water, will melt into any train of fancy. Equally adaptable to any purpose or to none, are the pasturing sheep and kine upon the marshes, the gulls that wheel and dip around me, the crows (well out of gunshot) going home from the rich harvest-fields, the heron that has been out a-fishing and looks as melancholy, up there in the sky, as if it hadn't agreed with him. Everything within the range of the senses will, by the aid of the running water, lend itself to everything beyond that range, and work into a drowsy whole, not unlike a kind of tune, but for which there is no exact definition.

One of these landing-places is near an old fort (I can see the Nore Light from it with my pocket-glass), from which fort mysteriously emerges a boy, to whom I am much indebted for additions to my scanty stock of knowledge. He is a young boy, with an intelligent face burnt to a dust colour by the summer sun, and with crisp hair of the same hue. He is a boy in whom I have perceived nothing incompatible with habits of studious inquiry and meditation, unless an evanescent black eye (I was delicate of inquiring how occasioned) should be so considered. To him am I indebted for ability to identify a Custom-house boat at any distance, and for acquaintance with all the forms and ceremonies observed by a homeward-bound Indiaman coming up the river, when the Custom-house officers go aboard her. But for him, I might never have heard of the 'dumb-ague,' respecting which malady I am now learned. Had I never sat at his feet, I might have finished my mortal career and never known that when I see a white horse on a barge's sail, that barge is a lime barge. For precious secrets in reference to beer, am I likewise beholden to him, involving warning against the beer of a certain establishment, by reason of its having turned sour through failure in point of demand: though my young sage is not of opinion that similar deterioration has befallen the ale. He has also enlightened me touching the mushrooms of the marshes, and has gently reproved my ignorance in having supposed them to be impregnated with salt. His manner of imparting information, is thoughtful, and appropriate to the scene. As he reclines beside me, he pitches into the river a little stone or piece of grit, and then delivers himself oracularly, as though he spoke out of the centre of the spreading circle that it makes in the water. He never improves my mind without observing this formula.

With the wise boy – whom I know by no other name than the Spirit of the Fort – I recently consorted on a breezy day, when the river leaped about us and was full of life. I had seen the sheaved corn carrying in the golden fields as I came down to the river; and the rosy farmer, watching his labouring-men in the saddle on his cob, had told me how he had reaped his two hundred and sixty acres of long-strawed corn last week, and how a better week's work he had never done in all his days. Peace and abundance were on the country-side in beautiful forms and beautiful colours, and the harvest seemed even to be sailing out to grace the never-reaped sea in the yellow-laden barges that mellowed the distance.

It was on this occasion that the Spirit of the Fort, directing his remarks to a certain floating iron battery lately lying in that reach of the river, enriched my mind with his opinions on naval architecture, and informed me that he would like to be an engineer. I found him up to everything that is done in the contracting line by Messrs Peto and Brassey – cunning in the article of concrete – mellow in the matter of iron – great on the subject of gunnery. When he spoke of pile-driving and sluice-making, he left me not a leg to stand on, and I can never sufficiently acknowledge his forbearance with me in my disabled state. While he thus discoursed, he several times directed his eyes to one distant quarter of the landscape, and spoke with vague mysterious awe of 'the Yard.' Pondering his lessons after we had parted, I bethought me that the Yard was one of our large public Dockyards, and that it lay hidden among the crops down in the dip behind the windmills, as if it modestly kept itself out of view in peaceful times, and sought to trouble no man. Taken with this modesty on the part of the Yard, I resolved to improve the Yard's acquaintance.

My good opinion of the Yard's retiring character was not dashed by nearer approach. It resounded with the noise of hammers beating upon iron; and the great sheds or slips under which the mighty men-of-war are built, loomed business-like when contemplated from the opposite side of the river. For all that, however, the Yard made no display, but kept itself snug under hill-sides of corn-fields, hop-gardens, and orchards; its great chimneys smoking with a quiet − almost a lazy − air, like giants smoking tobacco; and the great Shears moored off it, looking meekly and inoffensively out of proportion, like the Giraffe of the machinery creation. The store of cannon on the neighbouring gun-wharf, had an innocent toy-like appearance, and the one red-coated sentry on duty over them was a mere toy figure, with a clockwork movement. As the hot sunlight sparkled on him, he might have passed for the identical little man who had the little gun, and whose bullets they were made of lead, lead, lead.

Crossing the river and landing at the Stairs, where a drift of chips and weed had been trying to land before me and had not succeeded, but had got into a corner instead, I found the very street posts to be cannon, and the architectural ornaments to be shells. And so I came to the Yard, which was shut up tight and strong with great folded gates, like an enormous patent safe. These gates devouring me, I became digested into the Yard; and it had, at first, a clean-swept holiday air, as if it had given over work until next war-time. Though indeed a quantity of hemp for rope was tumbling out of storehouses, even there, which would hardly be lying like so much hay on the white stones if the Yard were as placid as it pretended.

Ding, Clash, Dong, Bang, Boom, Rattle, Clash, Bang, Clink, Bang, Dong, Bang, Clatter, bang bang BANG! What on earth is this! This is, or soon will be, the Achilles, iron armour-plated ship. Twelve hundred men are working at her now; twelve hundred men working on stages over her sides, over her bows, over her stern, under her keel, between her decks, down in her hold, within her and without, crawling and creeping into the finest curves of her lines wherever it is possible for men to twist. Twelve hundred hammerers, measurers, caulkers, armourers, forgers, smiths, shipwrights; twelve hundred dingers, clashers, dongers, rattlers, clinkers, bangers bangers bangers! Yet all this stupendous uproar around the rising Achilles is as nothing to the reverberations with which the perfected Achilles shall resound upon the dreadful day when the full work is in hand for which this is but note of preparation − the day when the scuppers that are now fitting like great dry thirsty conduit-pipes, shall run red. All these busy figures between decks, dimly seen bending at their work in smoke and fire, are as nothing to the figures that shall do work here of another kind, in smoke and fire, that day. These steam-worked engines alongside, helping the ship by travelling to and fro, and wafting tons of iron plates about, as though they were so many leaves of trees, would be rent limb from limb if they stood by here for a minute then. To think that this Achilles, monstrous compound of iron tank and oaken chest, can ever swim or roll! To think that any force of wind and wave could ever break her! To think that wherever I see a glowing red-hot iron point thrust out of her side from within – as I do now, there, and there, and there! – and two watching men on a stage without, with bared arms and sledge-hammers, strike at it fiercely, and repeat their blows until it is black and flat, I see a rivet being driven home, of which there are many in every iron plate, and thousands upon thousands in the ship! To think that the difficulty I experience in appreciating the ship's size when I am on board, arises from her being a series of iron tanks and oaken chests, so that internally she is ever finishing and ever beginning, and half of her might be smashed, and yet the remaining half suffice and be sound! Then, to go over the side again and down among the ooze and wet to the bottom of the dock, in the depths of the subterranean forest of dog-shores and stays that hold her up, and to see the immense mass bulging out against the upper light, and tapering down towards me, is, with great pains and much clambering, to arrive at an impossibility of realising that this is a ship at all, and to become possessed by the fancy that it is an enormous immovable edifice set up in an ancient amphitheatre (say, that at Verona), and almost filling it! Yet what would even these things be, without the tributary workshops and their mechanical powers for piercing the iron plates – four inches and a half thick – for rivets, shaping them under hydraulic pressure to the finest tapering turns of the ship's lines, and paring them away, with knives shaped like the beaks of strong and cruel birds, to the nicest requirements of the design! These machines of tremendous force, so easily directed by one attentive face and presiding hand, seem to me to have in them something of the retiring character of the Yard. 'Obedient monster, please to bite this mass of iron through and through, at equal distances, where these regular chalk-marks are, all round.' Monster looks at its work, and lifting its ponderous head, replies, 'I don't particularly want to do it; but if it must be done–!' The solid metal wriggles out, hot from the monster's crunching tooth, and it *is* done. 'Dutiful monster, observe this other mass of iron. It is required to be pared away, according to this delicately lessening and arbitrary line, which please to look at.' Monster (who has been in a reverie) brings down its blunt head, and, much in the manner of Doctor Johnson, closely looks along the line – very closely, being somewhat near-sighted. 'I don't particularly want to do it; but if it must be done–!' Monster takes another near-sighted look, takes aim, and the tortured piece writhes off, and falls, a hot tight-twisted snake, among the ashes. The making of the rivets is merely a pretty round game, played by a man and a boy, who put red-hot barley-sugar in a Pope Joan board, and immediately rivets fall out of window; but the tone of the great machines is the tone of the great Yard and the great country: 'We don't particularly want to do it; but if it must be done—!'

How such a prodigious mass as the Achilles can ever be held by such comparatively little anchors as those intended for her and lying near her here, is a mystery of seamanship which I will refer to the wise boy. For my own part, I should as soon have thought of tethering an elephant to a tent-peg, or the larger hippopotamus in the Zoological Gardens to my shirt-pin. Yonder in the river, alongside a hulk, lie two of this ship's hollow iron masts. *They* are large enough for the eye, I find, and so are all her other appliances. I wonder why only her anchors look small.

I have no present time to think about it, for I am going to see the workshops where they make all the oars used in the British Navy. A pretty large pile of building, I opine, and a pretty long job! As to the building, I am soon disappointed, because the work is all done in one loft. And as to a long job – what is this? Two rather large mangles with a swarm of butterflies hovering over them? What can there be in the mangles that attracts butterflies?

Drawing nearer, I discern that these are not mangles, but intricate machines, set with knives and saws and planes, which cut smooth and straight here, and slantwise there, and now cut such a depth, and now miss cutting altogether, according to the predestined requirements of the pieces of wood that are pushed on below them: each of which pieces is to be an oar, and is roughly adapted to that purpose before it takes its final leave of far-off forests, and sails for England. Likewise I discern that the butterflies are not true butterflies, but wooden shavings, which, being spirted up from the wood by the violence of the machinery, and kept in rapid and not equal movement by the impulse of its rotation on the air, flutter and play, and rise and fall, and conduct themselves as like butterflies as heart could wish. Suddenly the noise and motion cease, and the butterflies drop dead. An oar has been made since I came in, wanting the shaped handle. As quickly as I can follow it with my eye and thought, the same oar is carried to a turning lathe. A whirl and a Nick! Handle made. Oar finished.

The exquisite beauty and efficiency of this machinery need no illustration, but happen to have a pointed illustration today. A pair of oars of unusual size chance to be wanted for a special purpose, and they have to be made by hand. Side by side with the subtle and facile machine, and side by side with the fast-growing pile of oars on the floor, a man shapes out these special oars with an axe. Attended by no butterflies, and chipping and dinting, by comparison as leisurely as if he were a labouring Pagan getting them ready against his decease at threescore and ten, to take with him as a present to Charon for his boat, the man (aged about thirty) plies his task. The machine would make a regulation oar while the man wipes his forehead. The man might be buried in a mound made of the strips of thin broad wooden ribbon torn from the wood whirled into oars as the minutes fall from the clock, before he had done a forenoon's work with his axe.

Passing from this wonderful sight to the Ships again – for my heart, as to the Yard, is where the ships are – I notice certain unfinished wooden walls left seasoning on the stocks, pending the solution of the merits of the wood and iron question, and having an air of biding their time with surly confidence. The names of these worthies are set up beside them, together with their capacity in guns – a custom highly conducive to ease and satisfaction in social intercourse, if it could be adapted to mankind. By a plank more gracefully pendulous than substantial, I make bold to go aboard a transport ship (iron screw) just sent in from the contractor's yard to be inspected and passed. She is a very gratifying experience, in the simplicity and humanity of her arrangements for troops, in her provision for light and air and cleanliness, and in her care for women and children. It occurs to me, as I explore her, that I would require a handsome sum of money to go aboard her, at midnight by the Dockyard bell, and stay aboard alone till morning; for surely she must be haunted by a crowd of ghosts of obstinate old martinets, mournfully flapping their cherubic epaulettes over the changed times. Though still we may learn from the astounding ways and means in our Yards now, more highly than ever to respect the forefathers who got to sea, and fought the sea, and held the sea, without them. This remembrance putting me in the best of tempers with an old hulk, very green as to her copper, and generally dim and patched, I pull off my hat to her. Which salutation a callow and downy-faced young officer of Engineers, going by at the moment, perceiving, appropriates – and to which he is most heartily welcome, I am sure.

Having been torn to pieces (in imagination) by the steam circular saws, perpendicular saws, horizontal saws, and saws of eccentric action, I come to the sauntering part of my expedition, and consequently to the core of my Uncommercial pursuits.

Everywhere, as I saunter up and down the Yard, I meet with tokens of its quiet and retiring character. There is a gravity upon its red brick offices and houses, a staid pretence of having nothing worth mentioning to do, an avoidance of display, which I never saw out of England. The white stones of the pavement present no other trace of Achilles and his twelve hundred banging men (not one of whom strikes an attitude) than a few occasional echoes. But for a whisper in the air suggestive of sawdust and shavings, the oar-making and the saws of many movements might be miles away. Down below here, is the great reservoir of water where timber is steeped in various temperatures, as a part of its seasoning process. Above it, on a tramroad supported by pillars, is a Chinese Enchanter's Car, which fishes the logs up, when sufficiently steeped, and rolls smoothly away with them to stack them. When I was a child (the Yard being then familiar to me) I used to think that I should like to play at Chinese Enchanter, and to have that apparatus placed at my disposal for the purpose by a beneficent country. I still think that I should rather like to try the effect of writing a book in it. Its retirement is complete, and to go gliding to and fro among the stacks of timber would be a convenient kind of travelling in foreign countries – among the forests of North America, the sodden Honduras swamps, the dark pine woods, the Norwegian frosts, and the tropical heats, rainy seasons, and thunderstorms. The costly store of timber is stacked and stowed away in sequestered places, with the pervading avoidance of flourish or effect. It makes as little of itself as possible, and calls to no one 'Come and look at me!' And yet it is picked out from the trees of the world; picked out for length, picked out for breadth, picked out for straightness, picked out for crookedness, chosen with an eye to every need of ship and boat. Strangely twisted pieces lie about, precious in the sight of shipwrights. Sauntering through these groves, I come upon an open glade where workmen are examining some timber recently delivered. Quite a pastoral scene, with a background of river and windmill! and no more like War than the American States are like an Union.

Sauntering among the ropemaking, I am spun into a state of blissful indolence, wherein my rope of life seems to be so untwisted by the process as that I can see back to very early days indeed, when my bad dreams – they were frightful, though my more mature understanding has never made out why – were of an interminable sort of ropemaking, with long minute filaments for strands, which, when they were spun home together close to my eyes, occasioned screaming. Next, I walk among the quiet lofts of stores – of sails, spars, rigging, ships' boats – determined to believe that somebody in authority wears a girdle and bends beneath the weight of a massive bunch of keys, and that, when such a thing is wanted, he comes telling his keys like Blue Beard, and opens such a door. Impassive as the long lofts look, let the electric battery send down the word, and the shutters and doors shall fly open, and such a fleet of armed ships, under steam and under sail, shall burst forth as will charge the old Medway – where the merry Stuart let the Dutch come, while his not so merry sailors starved in the streets – with something worth looking at to carry to the sea. Thus I idle round to the Medway again, where it is now flood tide; and I find the river evincing a strong solicitude to force a way into the dry dock where Achilles is waited on by the twelve hundred bangers, with the intent to bear the whole away before they are ready.

To the last, the Yard puts a quiet face upon it; for, I make my way to the gates through a little quiet grove of trees, shading the quaintest of Dutch landing-places, where the leaf-speckled shadow of a shipwright just passing away at the further end might be the shadow of Russian Peter himself. So, the doors of the great patent safe at last close upon me, and I take boat again: somehow, thinking as the oars dip, of braggart Pistol and his brood, and of the quiet monsters of the Yard, with their 'We don't particularly want to do it; but if it must be done–!' Scrunch.

32

The Uncommercial Traveller

All The Year Round, 12 September 1863 (*UT1* as 'In the French-Flemish Country')

The 'French-Flemish Country' depicted here was a former province of France known as Flandre Française, now comprising the Département du Nord, the most northerly of the French departments, bordering Belgium. Then, as now, it was divided into seven arrondissements, each named after its principal town: Lille (the administrative centre or 'préfecture'), Avesnes, Cambrai, Douai, Dunkerque, Hazebroucke and Valenciennes (all sous-préfectures). Along with Amiens and Arras in the neighbouring department of Pas de Calais, these are all towns mentioned in article 23, 'The Calais Night Mail'. Dickens was in northern France during the last two weeks of August 1863, writing to Wilkie Collins that 'I have not been anywhere for ever and ever so long, but am thinking of evaporating for a fortnight on the 18th [of August]', and noting on the last day of the month that he had recently 'com[e] back from a fortnight's Uncommercial Travelling abroad' (*Pilgrim*, Vol. X, pp. 281, 283). As suggested in the Introduction to this volume (pp. xvii–xviii & n.), Dickens's references in his letters to trips made 'in the Uncommercial interest' at this time may well have been a handy smokescreen for visits with or to Ellen Ternan centring on Condette, near

Boulogne. If so, it is even less likely that Dickens would allow the 'Uncommercial Traveller' to give away clues about his movements in an article such as the present.

As the Count de Suzannet observes, the 'famille P. Salcy', of whom Dickens writes at length, must have been artists of 'the most humble and local reputation, now quite unknown; the town, possibly Gravelines or Dunkerque could not possibly be identified' from the descriptions given (Hill, 27.1). Hazebroucke would be an equally possible candidate, however, as Dickens had already identified it as the location of 'a Fair ... where the oldest inhabitants were circling round and round a barrel-organ on hobby-horses' (p. 218; compare p. 301 below). The remark concerning a stout lady who is 'irrepressible' and thus 'a parallel case to the American Negro' (p. 300) refers to the catchphrase 'irrepressible nigger' current at the time of the Civil War. The earliest example traced comes in George Strong's *Diary of the Civil War, 1860–65* (1962 [1952]), where he notes (10 January 1860) that during recent electioneering, politicians had been spending their time 'speech-making about ... fugitive slaves ... and the irrepressible nigger generally' (p. 3).

Mention of the 'Mexican victories' on display at peep-shows at the Fair (p. 304) refers to recent victories of the French army in Mexico, of which the most celebrated was the triumphal entry into a deserted Mexico City of General Foley and Imperial troops on 7 June 1863.

Textual note (p. 298) copy-text has 'like the toast out of a Giant's toast-and-water': *UT1* has 'like the toast of a Giant's toast-and-water'.

'It is neither a bold nor a diversified country,' said I to myself, 'this country which is three-quarters Flemish, and a quarter French; yet it has its attractions too. Though great lines of railway traverse it, the trains leave it behind, and go puffing off to Paris and the South, to Belgium and Germany, to the Northern Sea-Coast of France, and to England, and merely smoke it a little in passing. Then I don't know it, and that is a good reason for being here; and I can't pronounce half the long queer names I see inscribed over the shops, and that is another good reason for being here, since I surely ought to learn how.' In short, I was 'here,' and I wanted an excuse for not going away from here, and I made it to my satisfaction, and stayed here.

What part in my decision was borne by Monsieur P. Salcy, is of no moment, though I own to encountering that gentleman's name on a red bill on the wall, before I made up my mind. Monsieur P. Salcy, 'par permission de M. le Maire,' had established his theatre in the whitewashed Hôtel de Ville, on the steps of which illustrious edifice I stood. And

Monsieur P. Salcy, privileged director of such theatre, situate in 'the first theatrical arrondissement of the department of the North,' invited French-Flemish mankind to come and partake of the intellectual banquet provided by his family of dramatic artists, fifteen subjects in number. 'La Famille P. SALCY, composée d'artistes dramatiques, au nombre de 15 sujets.'

Neither a bold nor a diversified country, I say again, and withal an untidy country, but pleasant enough to ride in, when the paved roads over the flats and through the hollows, are not too deep in black mud. A country so sparely inhabited, that I wonder where the peasants who till and sow and reap the ground, can possibly dwell, and also by what invisible balloons they are conveyed from their distant homes into the fields at sunrise and back again at sunset. The occasional few poor cottages and farms in this region, surely cannot afford shelter to the numbers necessary to the cultivation, albeit the work is done so very deliberately, that on one long harvest day I have seen, in twelve miles, about twice as many men and women (all told) reaping and binding. Yet have I seen more cattle, more sheep, more pigs, and all in better case, than where there is purer French spoken, and also better ricks – round swelling peg-top ricks, well thatched: not a shapeless brown heap, like the toast out of a Giant's toast-and-water, pinned to the earth with one of the skewers out of his kitchen. A good custom they have about here, likewise, of prolonging the sloping tiled roof of farm or cottage, so that it overhangs three or four feet, carrying off the wet, and making a good drying place wherein to hang up herbs, or implements, or what not. A better custom than the popular one of keeping the refuse-heap and puddle close before the house door: which, although I paint my dwelling never so brightly blue (and it cannot be too blue for me, hereabouts), will bring fever inside my door. Wonderful poultry of the French-Flemish country, why take the trouble to *be* poultry? Why not stop short at eggs in the rising generation, and die out and have done with it? Parents of chickens have I seen this day, followed by their wretched young families, scratching nothing out of the mud with an air – tottering about on legs so scraggy and weak, that the valiant word drumsticks becomes a mockery when applied to them, and the crow of the lord and master has been a mere dejected case of croup. Carts have I seen, and other agricultural instruments, unwieldy, dislocated, monstrous. Poplar-trees by the thousand fringe the fields and fringe the end of the flat landscape, so that I feel, looking straight on before me, as if, when I pass the extremest fringe on the low horizon, I shall tumble over into space. Little whitewashed black holes of chapels, with barred doors and Flemish inscriptions, abound at roadside corners, and often they are garnished with a sheaf of wooden crosses, like children's swords: or, in their default, some hollow old tree with a saint roosting in it, is similarly decorated, or a pole with a very diminutive saint enshrined aloft in a sort of sacred pigeon-house. Not that we are deficient in such decoration in the town here, for, over at the church yonder, outside the building, is a scenic representation of the Crucifixion, built up with old bricks and stones, and made out with painted canvas and wooden figures: the whole surmounting the dusty skull of some holy personage (perhaps), shut up behind a little ashy iron grate, as if it were originally put there to be cooked, and the fire had long gone out. A windmilly country this, though the windmills are so damp and rickety, that they nearly knock themselves off their legs at every turn of their sails, and creak in loud complaint. A weaving country, too, for in the wayside cottages the loom goes wearily – rattle and click, rattle and click – and, looking in, I see the poor weaving peasant, man or woman, bending at the work, while the child, working too, turns a little hand-wheel put upon the ground to suit its height. An unconscionable monster, the loom in a small dwelling, asserting himself ungenerously as the bread-winner, straddling over the children's straw beds, cramping the family in space and air, and making himself generally objectionable and tyrannical. He is tributary, too, to ugly mills and factories and bleaching-grounds, rising out of the sluiced fields in an abrupt bare way, disdaining, like himself, to be ornamental or accommodating. Surrounded by these things, here I stood on the steps of the Hôtel de Ville, persuaded to remain by the P. Salcy family, fifteen dramatic subjects strong.

There was a Fair besides. The double persuasion being irresistible, and my sponge being left behind at the last Hotel, I made the tour of the little town to buy another. In the small sunny shops – mercers, opticians, and druggist-grocers, with here and there an emporium of religious images – the gravest of old spectacled Flemish husbands and wives sat contemplating one another across bare counters, while the wasps, who seemed to have taken military possession of the town, and to have placed it under wasp-martial law, executed warlike manœuvres in the windows. Other shops the wasps had entirely to themselves, and nobody cared and nobody came when I beat with a five-franc piece upon the board of custom. What I sought, was no more to be found than if I had sought a nugget of Californian gold: so I went, spongeless, to pass the evening with the Family P. Salcy.

The members of the Family P. Salcy were so fat and so like one another – fathers, mothers, sisters, brothers, uncles, and aunts – that I think the local audience were much confused about the plot of the piece under representation, and to the last expected that everybody must turn out to be the long-lost relative of everybody else. The Theatre was established on the top story of the Hôtel de Ville, and was approached by a long bare staircase, whereon, in an airy situation, one of the P. Salcy Family – a stout gentleman, imperfectly repressed by a belt – took the money. This occasioned the greatest excitement of the evening; for, no sooner did the curtain rise on the introductory Vaudeville, and reveal in the person of the young lover (singing a very short song with his eyebrows) apparently the very same identical stout gentleman imperfectly repressed by a belt, than everybody rushed out to the paying-place, to ascertain whether he could possibly have put on that dress-coat, that clear complexion, and those arched black vocal eyebrows, in so short a space of time. It then became manifest that this was another stout gentleman imperfectly repressed by a belt: to whom, before the spectators had recovered their presence of mind, entered a third stout gentleman imperfectly repressed by a belt, exactly like him. These two 'subjects,' making with the money-taker three of the announced fifteen, fell into conversation touching a charming young widow: who, presently appearing, proved to be a stout lady altogether irrepressible by any means – quite a parallel case to the American Negro – fourth of the fifteen subjects, and sister of the fifth who presided over the check department. In good time the whole of the fifteen subjects were dramatically presented, and we had the inevitable Ma Mère, Ma Mère! and also the inevitable malédiction d'un père, and likewise the inevitable Marquis, and also the inevitable provincial young man, weak-minded but faithful, who followed Julie to Paris, and cried and laughed and choked all at once. The story was wrought out with the help of a virtuous spinning-wheel in the beginning, a vicious set of diamonds in the middle, and a rheumatic blessing (which arrived by post) from Ma Mère towards the end; the whole resulting in a small sword in the body of one of the stout gentlemen imperfectly repressed by a belt, fifty thousand francs per annum and a decoration to the other stout gentleman imperfectly repressed by a belt, and an assurance from everybody to the provincial young man that if he were not supremely happy – which he seemed to have no reason whatever for being – he ought to be. This afforded him a final opportunity of crying and laughing and choking all at once, and sent the audience home sentimentally delighted. Audience more attentive or better behaved there could not possibly be, though the places of second rank in the Theatre of the Family P. Salcy were sixpence each in English money, and the places of first rank a shilling. How the fifteen subjects ever got so fat upon it, the kind Heavens know.

What gorgeous china figures of knights and ladies, gilded till they gleamed again, I might have bought at the Fair for the garniture of my home, if I had been a French-Flemish peasant, and had had the money! What shining coffee-cups and saucers, I might have won at the turntables, if I had had the luck! Ravishing perfumery also, and sweetmeats, I might have speculated in, or I might have fired for prizes at a multitude of little dolls in niches, and might have hit the doll of dolls, and won francs and fame. Or, being a French-Flemish youth, I might have been drawn in a hand-cart by my compeers, to tilt for municipal rewards at the water-quintain: which, unless I sent my lance clean through the ring, emptied a full bucket over me; to fend off which, the competitors wore grotesque old scarecrow hats. Or, being French-Flemish man or woman, boy or girl, I might have circled all night on my hobby-horse, in a stately cavalcade of hobby-horses four abreast, interspersed with triumphal cars, going round and round and round and round, we the goodly company singing a ceaseless chorus to the music of the barrel-organ, drum, and cymbals. On the whole, not more monotonous than the Ring in Hyde Park, London, and much merrier; for when do the circling company sing chorus, *there*, to the barrel-organ, when do the ladies embrace their horses round the neck with both arms, when do the gentlemen fan the ladies with the tails of their gallant steeds? On all these revolving delights, and on their own especial lamps and Chinese lanterns revolving with them, the thoughtful weaver-face brightens, and the Hôtel de Ville sheds an illuminated line of gas-light: while above it, the Eagle of France, gas-outlined and apparently afflicted with the prevailing infirmities that have lighted on the poultry, is in a very undecided state of policy, and as a bird moulting. Flags flutter all around. Such is the prevailing gaiety that the keeper of the prison sits on the stone steps outside the prison-door, to have a look at the world that is not locked up; while that agreeable retreat, the wine-shop opposite to the prison in the prison-alley (its sign La Tranquillité, because of its charming situation), resounds with the voices of the shepherds and shepherdesses who resort there this festive night. And it reminds me that only this afternoon, I saw a shepherd in trouble, tending this way, over the jagged stones of a neighbouring street. A magnificent sight it was, to behold him in his blouse, a feeble little jog-trot rustic, swept along by the wind of two immense gendarmes, in cocked-hats for which the street was hardly wide enough, each carrying a bundle of stolen property that would not have held his shoulder-knot, and clanking a sabre that dwarfed the prisoner.

'Messieurs et Mesdames, I present to you at this Fair, as a mark of my confidence in the people of this so-renowned town, and as an act of homage to their good sense and fine taste, the Ventriloquist, the Ventriloquist! Further, Messieurs et Mesdames, I present to you the Face-Maker, the Physiognomist, the great Changer of countenances, who transforms the features that Heaven has bestowed upon him into an endless succession of surprising and extraordinary visages, comprehending, Messieurs et Mesdames, all the contortions, energetic and expressive, of which the human face is capable, and all the passions of the human heart, as Love, Jealousy, Revenge, Hatred, Avarice, Despair! Hi hi! Ho ho! Lu lu! Come in!' To this effect, with an occasional smite upon a sonorous kind of tambourine – bestowed with a will, as if it represented the people who won't come in – holds forth a man of lofty and severe demeanour; a man in stately uniform, gloomy with the knowledge he possesses of the inner secrets of the booth. 'Come in, come in! Your opportunity presents itself tonight; tomorrow it will be gone for ever. Tomorrow morning by the Express Train the railroad will reclaim the Ventriloquist and the Face-Maker! Algeria will reclaim the Ventriloquist and the Face-Maker! Yes! For the honour of their country they have accepted propositions of a magnitude incredible, to appear in Algeria. See them for the last time before their departure! We go to commence on the instant. Hi hi! Ho ho! Lu Lu! Come in! Take the money that now ascends, Madame; but after that, no more, for we commence! Come in!'

Nevertheless, the eyes both of the gloomy speaker and of Madame receiving sous in a muslin bower, survey the crowd pretty sharply after the ascending money has ascended, to detect any lingering sous at the turning-point. 'Come in, come in! Is there any more money, Madame, on the point of ascending? If so, we wait for it. If not, we commence!' The orator looks back over his shoulder to say it, lashing the spectators with the conviction that he beholds through the folds of the drapery into which he is about to plunge, the Ventriloquist and the Face-Maker. Several sous burst out of pockets, and ascend. 'Come up, then, Messieurs!' exclaims Madame in a shrill voice, and beckoning with a bejewelled finger. 'Come up! This presses. Monsieur has commanded that they commence!' Monsieur dives into his Interior, and the last half-dozen of us follow. His Interior is comparatively severe; his Exterior also. A true Temple of Art needs nothing but seats, drapery, a small table with two moderator lamps hanging over it, and an ornamental looking-glass let into the wall. Monsieur in uniform gets behind the table and surveys us with disdain, his forehead becoming diabolically intellectual under the moderators. 'Messieurs et Mesdames, I present to you the Ventriloquist. He will commence with the celebrated Experience of the bee in the window. The bee, apparently the veritable bee of Nature, will hover in the window, and about the room. He will be with difficulty caught in the hand of Monsieur the Ventriloquist – he will escape – he will again hover – at length he will be recaptured by Monsieur the Ventriloquist, and will be with difficulty put into a bottle. Achieve then, Monsieur!' Here the Proprietor is replaced behind the table by the Ventriloquist, who is thin and sallow, and of a weakly aspect. While the bee is in progress, Monsieur the Proprietor sits apart on a stool, immersed in dark and remote thought. The moment the bee is bottled, he stalks forward, eyes us gloomily as we applaud, and then announces, sternly waving his hand: 'The magnificent Experience of the child with the whooping-cough!' The child disposed of, he starts up as before. 'The superb and extraordinary Experience of the dialogue between Monsieur Tatambour in his dining-room, and his domestic, Jerome, in the cellar; concluding with the songsters of the grove, and the Concert of domestic Farmyard animals.' All this done, and well done, Monsieur the Ventriloquist withdraws, and Monsieur the Face-Maker bursts in, as if his retiring-room were a mile long instead of a yard. A corpulent little man in a large white waistcoat, with a comic countenance, and with a wig in his hand. Irreverent disposition to laugh, instantly checked by the tremendous gravity of the Face-Maker, who intimates in his bow that if we expect that sort of thing we are mistaken. A very little shaving-glass with a leg behind it is handed in, and placed on the table before the Face-Maker. 'Messieurs et Mesdames, with no other assistance than this mirror and this wig, I shall have the honour of showing you a thousand characters.' As a preparation, the Face-Maker with both hands gouges himself, and turns his mouth inside out. He then becomes frightfully grave again, and says to the Proprietor, 'I am ready!' Proprietor stalks forth from baleful reverie, and announces 'The Young Conscript!' Face-Maker claps his wig on, hind side before, looks in the glass, and appears above it as a conscript so very imbecile, and squinting so extremely hard, that I should think the State would never get any good of him. Thunders of applause. Face-Maker dips behind the looking-glass, brings his own hair forward, is himself again, is awfully grave. 'A distinguished inhabitant of the Faubourg St Germain.' Face-Maker dips, rises, is supposed to be aged, blear-eyed, toothless, slightly palsied, supernaturally polite, evidently of noble birth. 'The oldest member of the Corps of Invalides on the fête-day of his master.' Face-Maker dips, rises, wears the wig on one side, has become the feeblest military bore in existence, and (it is clear) would lie frightfully about his past achievements, if he were not confined to pantomime. 'The Miser!' Face-Maker dips, rises, clutches a bag, and every hair of the wig is on end to express that he lives in continual dread of thieves. 'The Genius of France!' Face-Maker dips, rises, wig pushed back and smoothed flat, little cocked-hat (artfully concealed till now) put a-top of it, Face-Maker's white waistcoat much advanced, Face-Maker's left hand in bosom of white waistcoat, Face-Maker's right hand behind his back. Thunders. This is the first of three positions of the Genius of France. In the second position, the Face-Maker takes snuff; in the third, rolls up his right hand, and surveys illimitable armies through that pocket-glass. The Face-Maker then, by putting out his tongue, and wearing the wig nohow in particular, becomes the Village Idiot. The most remarkable feature in the whole of his ingenious performance, is, that whatever he does to disguise himself, has the effect of rendering him rather more like himself than he was at first.

There were peep-shows in this Fair, and I had the pleasure of recognising several fields of glory with which I became well acquainted a year or two ago as Crimean battles, now doing duty as Mexican victories. The change was neatly effected by some extra smoking of the Russians, and by permitting the camp followers free range in the foreground to despoil the enemy of their uniforms. As no British troops had ever happened to be within sight when the artist took his original sketches, it followed fortunately that none were in the way now.

The Fair wound up with a ball. Respecting the particular night of the week on which the ball took place, I decline to commit myself; merely mentioning that it was held in a stable-yard so very close to the railway, that it is a mercy the locomotive did not set fire to it. (In Scotland, I suppose it would have done so.) There, in a tent prettily decorated with looking-glasses and a myriad of toy flags, the people danced all night. It was not an expensive recreation, the price of a double ticket for a cavalier and lady being one-and-threepence in English money, and even of that small sum fivepence was reclaimable for 'consommation': which word I venture to translate into refreshments of no greater strength, at the strongest, than ordinary wine made hot, with sugar and lemon in it. It was a ball of great good humour and of great enjoyment, though very many of the dancers must have been as poor as the fifteen subjects of the P. Salcy Family.

In short, not having taken my own pet national pint pot with me to this Fair, I was very well satisfied with the measure of simple enjoyment that it poured into the dull French-Flemish country life. How dull that is, I had an opportunity of considering when the Fair was over – when the tri-colored flags were withdrawn from the windows of the houses on the Place where the Fair was held – when the windows were close shut, apparently until next Fair-time – when the Hôtel de Ville had cut off its gas and put away its eagle – when the two paviours, whom I take to form the entire paving population of the town, were ramming down the stones which had been pulled up for the erection of decorative poles – when the jailer had slammed his gate, and sulkily locked himself in with his charges. But then, as I paced the ring which marked the track of the departed hobby-horses on the market-place, pondering in my mind how long some hobby-horses do leave their tracks in public ways, and how difficult they are to erase, my eyes were greeted with a goodly sight. I beheld four male personages thoughtfully pacing the Place together in the sunlight, evidently not belonging to the town, and having upon them a certain loose cosmopolitan air of not belonging to any town. One was clad in a suit of white canvas, another in a cap and blouse, the third in an old military frock, the fourth in a shapeless dress that looked as if it had been made out of old umbrellas. All wore dust-coloured shoes. My heart beat high; for, in those four male personages, although complexionless and eyebrowless, I beheld four subjects of the Family P. Salcy. Blue-bearded though they were, and bereft of the youthful smoothness of cheek which is imparted by what is termed in Albion a 'Whitechapel shave' (and which is, in fact, whitening, judiciously applied to the jaws with the palm of the hand), I recognised them. As I stood admiring, there emerged from the yard of a lowly Cabaret, the excellent Ma Mère, Ma Mère, with the words, 'The soup is served;' words which so elated the subject in the canvas suit, that when they all ran in to partake, he went last, dancing with his hands stuck angularly into the pockets of his canvas trousers, after the Pierrot manner. Glancing down the Yard, the last I saw of him was, that he looked in through a window (at the soup, no doubt) on one leg.

Full of this pleasure, I shortly afterwards departed from the town, little dreaming of an addition to my good fortune. But more was in reserve. I went by a train which was heavy with third-class carriages, full of young fellows (well guarded) who had drawn unlucky numbers in the last conscription, and were on their way to a famous French garrison town where much of the raw military material is worked up into soldiery. At the station they had been sitting about, in their threadbare homespun blue garments, with their poor little bundles under their arms, covered with dust and clay, and the various soils of France; sad enough at heart, most of them, but putting a good face upon it, and slapping their breasts and singing choruses on the smallest provocation; the gayer spirits shouldering half loaves of black bread speared upon their walking-sticks. As we went along, they were audible at every station, chorusing wildly out of tune, and feigning the highest hilarity. After a while, however, they began to leave off singing, and to laugh naturally, while at intervals there mingled with their laughter the barking of a dog. Now, I had to alight short of their destination, and, as that stoppage of the train was attended with a quantity of horn blowing, bell ringing, and proclamation of what Messieurs les Voyageurs were to do, and were not to do, in order to reach their respective destinations, I had ample leisure to go forward on the platform to take a parting look at my recruits, whose heads were all out at window, and who were laughing like delighted children. Then, I perceived that a large poodle with a pink nose, who had been their travelling companion and the cause of their mirth, stood on his hind-legs presenting arms on the extreme verge of the platform, ready to salute them as the train went off. This poodle wore a military shako (it is unnecessary to add, very much on one side over one eye), a little military coat, and the regulation white gaiters. He was armed with a little musket and a little sword-bayonet, and he stood presenting arms in perfect attitude, with his unobscured eye on his master or superior officer, who stood by him. So admirable was his discipline, that, when the train moved, and he was greeted with the parting cheers of the recruits, and also with a shower of centimes, several of which struck his shako, and had a tendency to discompose him, he remained staunch on his post until the train was gone. He then resigned his arms to his officer, took off his shako by rubbing his paw over it, dropped on four legs, bringing his uniform-coat into the absurdest relations with the overarching skies, and ran about the platform in his white gaiters, wagging his tail to an exceeding great extent. It struck me that there was more waggery than this in the poodle, and that he knew that the recruits would neither get through their exercises, nor get rid of their uniforms, as easily as he; revolving which in my thoughts, and seeking in my pockets some small money to bestow upon him, I casually directed my eyes to the face of his superior officer, and in him beheld the Face-Maker! Though it was not the way to Algeria, but quite the reverse, the military poodle's Colonel was the Face-Maker in a dark blouse, with a small bundle dangling over his shoulder at the end of an umbrella, and taking a pipe from his breast to smoke as he and the poodle went their mysterious way.

33

The Uncommercial Traveller

All The Year Round, 26 September 1863 (*UT1* as 'Medicine Men of Civilisation')

Dickens had expressed exasperation with the resurgence of popular support for the concept of 'the noble savage' in an article in *HW* of the same name (see Vol. 3 of this edition, article 19), but the present article, and others, display a considerable interest in the customs and rituals of aboriginal peoples in Asia, Australasia, Africa and the Americas, together with a tendency – central to the present paper – to instigate comparisons with the forms and ceremonies of so-called 'civilised' societies (i.e. the European) that are flattering to neither category (see, for example, Vol. 2 of this edition, article 25). In particular, Dickens uses the opportunity to criticise yet again the hypocrisy and 'jobbery' involved in English funerals, most recently attacked by him in Ch. 35 of *Great Expectations* (*ATYR*, 20 April 1861; see also Vol. 3 of this edition, article 14). It seems likely that the death of Dickens's mother on 12 September 1863 and his 'hav[ing] to look after the funeral' influenced the writing of the article. On 14 September he was writing to Wills that he had 'jobbed up an Uncommercial and sent *Revise* to Birtles [of Whitings, the printers of *ATYR*] to day per messenger' (see *Pilgrim*, Vol. X, pp. 288–9 & n.). For Dickens's extensive reading of colonial literature of voyages and travels – glossed here as 'voyages (in paper boats) among savages' – see Part I of John M. L. Drew's essay 'Voyages Extraordinaires – Dickens's "Travelling Essays and *The Uncommercial Traveller*"' (see Select Bibliography).

The episode concerning 'Mr Kindheart' is a version of events concerning the eccentric sculptor Angus Fletcher, who was living in Genoa in 1844 and who was probably instrumental in persuading Dickens to select the city as his place of residence in 1844–5 (see *Pilgrim*, Vol. IV, p. 123n.). Fletcher arranged the lease of the Villa di Bagnerello on the Dickenses' behalf, and seems to have occupied a room there for the initial period of their stay. Forster quotes a sentence from a letter of Dickens's of (?12–17) May, describing how the locals employed by Fletcher to conduct the funeral of his unknown acquaintance 'were obliged to leave one of the coach-doors open for the accommodation even of the coffin; the widower walked beside the carriage to the protestant ceremony; and Fletcher followed on a big grey horse' (*Forster*, Book 4, Ch. 7; *Pilgrim*, Vol. IV, pp. 310–11 & n.).

Literary allusions (p. 308) 'In the Tonga Islands ... buried with him': Dickens recalls details incorrectly from John Martin's *Account of the Tonga Islands* ... &c. ([1817] 3rd ed. 1827, Stonehouse), Vol. II, Ch. 5, where this belief is attributed, not to the Tongans, but to 'the Fiji people' (pp. 122–3); (p. 313) 'Tala Mungongo': Livingstone's *Missionary Travels and Researches in South Africa* (1857), Ch. 22 *passim*; (p. 313) 'at least one tribe of blacks with a very strong sense of the ridiculous ... irrepressible laughter': *ibid.*, Ch. 8 ('The Bakalahari'); (p. 313) 'Mataboos – or some such name – who are the Masters of all the public ceremonies': 'Matabooles ... have the management of all ceremonies', John Martin's *Account of the Tonga Islands* ... &c. (1827, Stonehouse), Vol. II, pp. 89–90 et seq.

My voyages (in paper boats) among savages often yield me matter for reflection at home. It is curious to trace the savage in the civilised man, and to detect the hold of some savage customs on conditions of society rather boastful of being high above them.

I wonder, is the Medicine Man of the North American Indians never to be got rid of, out of the North American country? He comes into my Wigwam on all manner of occasions, and with the absurdest 'Medicine.' I always find it extremely difficult, and I often find it simply impossible, to keep him out of my Wigwam. For his legal 'Medicine' he sticks upon his head the hair of quadrupeds, and plasters the same with fat, and dirty white powder, and talks a gibberish quite unknown to the men and squaws of his tribe. For his religious 'Medicine' he puts on puffy white sleeves, little black aprons, large black waistcoats of a peculiar cut, collarless coats with Medicine button-holes, Medicine stockings and gaiters and shoes, and tops the whole with a highly grotesque Medicinal hat. In one respect, to be sure, I am quite free from him. On occasions when the Medicine Men in general, together with a large number of the miscellaneous inhabitants of his village, both male and female, are presented to the principal Chief, his native 'Medicine' is a comical mixture of old odds and ends (hired of traders) and new things in antiquated shapes, and pieces of red cloth (of which he is particularly fond), and white and red and blue paint for the face. The irrationality of this particular Medicine culminates in a mock battle-rush, from which many of the squaws are borne out much dilapidated. I need not observe how unlike this is to a Drawing Room at St James's Palace.

The African magician I find it very difficult to exclude from my Wigwam too. This creature takes cases of death and mourning under his supervision, and will frequently impoverish a whole family by his preposterous enchantments. He is a great eater and drinker, and always conceals a rejoicing stomach under a grieving exterior. His charms consist of an infinite quantity of worthless scraps, for which he charges very high. He impresses on the poor bereaved natives, that the more of his followers they pay to exhibit such scraps on their persons for an hour or two (though they never saw the deceased in their lives, and are put in high spirits by his decease), the more honourably and piously they grieve for the dead. The poor people submitting themselves to this conjurer, an expensive procession is formed, in which bits of sticks, feathers of birds, and a quantity of other unmeaning objects besmeared with black paint, are carried in a certain ghastly order of which no one understands the meaning, if it ever had any, to the brink of the grave, and are then brought back again.

In the Tonga Islands, everything is supposed to have a soul, so that when a hatchet is irreparably broken, they say, 'His immortal part has departed; he is gone to the happy hunting-plains.' This belief leads to the logical sequence that when a man is buried, some of his eating and drinking vessels, and some of his warlike implements, must be broken and buried with him. Superstitious and wrong, but surely a more respectable superstition than the hire of antic scraps for a show that has no meaning based on any sincere belief.

Let me halt on my Uncommercial road, to throw a passing glance on some funeral solemnities that I have seen where North American Indians, African Magicians, and Tonga Islanders, are supposed not to be.

Once, I dwelt in an Italian city, where there dwelt with me for a while, an Englishman of an amiable nature, great enthusiasm, and no discretion. This friend discovered a desolate stranger, mourning over the unexpected death of one very dear to him, in a solitary cottage among the vineyards of an outlying village. The circumstances of the bereavement were unusually distressing; and the survivor, new to the peasants and the country, sorely needed help, being alone with the remains. With some difficulty, but with the strong influence of a purpose at once gentle, disinterested, and determined, my friend – Mr Kindheart – obtained access to the mourner, and undertook to arrange the burial.

There was a small Protestant cemetery near the city walls, and as Mr Kindheart came back to me, he turned into it and chose the spot. He was always highly flushed when rendering a service unaided, and I knew that to make him happy I must keep aloof from his ministration. But when at dinner he warmed with the good action of the day, and conceived the brilliant idea of comforting the mourner with 'an English funeral,' I ventured to intimate that I thought that institution, which was not absolutely sublime at home, might prove a failure in Italian hands. However, Mr Kindheart was so enraptured with his conception, that he presently wrote down into the town requesting the attendance with tomorrow's earliest light of a certain little upholsterer. This upholsterer was famous for speaking the unintelligible local dialect (his own) in a far more unintelligible manner than any other man alive.

When from my bath next morning I overheard Mr Kindheart and the upholsterer in conference on the top of an echoing staircase; and when I overheard Mr Kindheart rendering English Undertaking phrases into very choice Italian, and the upholsterer replying in the unknown Tongues; and when I furthermore remembered that the local funerals had no resemblance to English funerals; I became in my secret bosom apprehensive. But Mr Kindheart informed me at breakfast that measures had been taken to ensure a signal success.

As the funeral was to take place at sunset, and as I knew to which of the city gates it must tend, I went out at that gate as the sun descended, and walked along the dusty, dusty road. I had not walked far when I encountered this procession:

1. Mr Kindheart, much abashed, on an immense grey horse.

2. A bright yellow coach and pair, driven by a coachman in bright red velvet knee-breeches and waistcoat. (This was the established local idea of State.) Both coach doors kept open by the coffin, which was on its side within, and sticking out at each.

3. Behind the coach, the mourner, for whom the coach was intended, in the dust.

4. Concealed behind a roadside well for the irrigation of a garden, the unintelligible Upholsterer, admiring.

It matters little now. Coaches of all colours are alike to poor Kindheart, and he rests far North of the little cemetery with the cypress-trees, by the city walls where the Mediterranean is so beautiful.

My first funeral, a fair representative funeral after its kind, was that of the husband of a married servant, once my nurse. She married for money. Sally Flanders, after a year or two of matrimony, became the relict of Flanders, a small master-builder; and either she or Flanders had done me the honour to express a desire that I should 'follow.' I may have been seven or eight years old; – young enough, certainly, to feel rather alarmed by the expression, as not knowing where the invitation was held to terminate, and how far I was expected to follow the deceased Flanders. Consent being given by the heads of houses, I was jobbed up into what was pronounced at home decent mourning (comprehending somebody else's shirt, unless my memory deceives me), and was admonished that if, when the funeral was in action, I put my hands in my pockets, or took my eyes out of my pocket-handkerchief, I was personally lost, and my family disgraced. On the eventful day, having tried to get myself into a disastrous frame of mind, and having formed a very poor opinion of myself because I couldn't cry, I repaired to Sally's. Sally was an excellent creature, and had been a good wife to old Flanders, but the moment I saw her I knew that she was not in her own real natural state. She formed a sort of Coat of Arms, grouped with a smelling-bottle, a handkerchief, an orange, a bottle of vinegar, Flanders's sister, her own sister, Flanders's brother's wife, and two neighbouring gossips – all in mourning, and all ready to hold her whenever she fainted. At sight of poor little me she became much agitated (agitating me much more), and having exclaimed, 'O here's dear Master Uncommercial!' became hysterical, and swooned as if I had been the death of her. An affecting scene followed, during which I was handed about and poked at her by various people, as if I were the bottle of salts. Reviving a little, she embraced me, said, 'You knew him well, dear Master Uncommercial, and he knew you!' and fainted again: which, as the rest of the Coat of Arms soothingly said, 'done her credit.' Now, I knew that she needn't have fainted unless she liked, and that she wouldn't have fainted unless it had been expected of her, quite as well as I know it at this day. It made me feel uncomfortable, and hypocritical besides. I was not sure but that it might be manners in *me* to faint next, and I resolved to keep my eye on Flanders's uncle, and if I saw any signs of his going in that direction, to go too, politely. But Flanders's uncle (who was a weak little old retail grocer) had only one idea, which was that we all wanted tea; and he handed us cups of tea all round, incessantly, whether we refused or not. There was a young nephew of Flanders's present, to whom Flanders, it was rumoured, had left nineteen guineas. He drank all the tea that was offered him, this nephew – amounting, I should say, to several quarts – and ate as much plum-cake as he could possibly come by; but he felt it to be decent mourning that he should now and then stop in the midst of a lump of cake, and appear to forget that his mouth was full, in the contemplation of his uncle's memory. I felt all this to be the fault of the undertaker, who was handing us gloves on a tea-tray as if they were muffins, and tying us into cloaks (mine had to be pinned up all round, it was so long for me), because I knew that he was making game. So, when we got out into the streets, and I constantly disarranged the procession by tumbling on the people before me because my handkerchief blinded my eyes, and tripping up the people behind me because my cloak was so long, I felt that we were all making game. I was truly sorry for Flanders, but I knew that it was no reason why we should be trying (the women with their heads in hoods like coal-scuttles with the black side outward) to keep step with a man in a scarf, carrying a thing like a mourning spy-glass, which he was going to open presently and sweep the horizon with. I knew that we should not all have been speaking in one particular key-note struck by the undertaker, if we had not been making game. Even in our faces we were every one of us as like the undertaker as if we had been his own family, and I perceived that this could not have happened unless we had been making game. When we returned to Sally's, it was all of a piece. The continued impossibility of getting on without plum-cake; the ceremonious apparition of a pair of decanters containing port and sherry and cork; Sally's sister at the tea-table, clinking the best crockery and shaking her head mournfully every time she looked down into the teapot, as if it were the tomb; the Coat of Arms again, and Sally as before; lastly, the words of consolation administered to Sally when it was considered right that she should 'come round nicely:' which were, that the deceased had had 'as com-for-ta-ble a fu-ne-ral as comfortable could be!'

Other funerals have I seen with grown-up eyes, since that day, of which the burden has been the same childish burden. Making game. Real affliction, real grief and solemnity, have been outraged, and the funeral has been 'performed.' The waste for which the funeral customs of many tribes of savages are conspicuous, has attended these civilised obsequies; and once, and twice, have I wished in my soul that if the waste must be, they would let the undertaker bury the money, and let me bury the friend.

In France, upon the whole, these ceremonies are more sensibly regulated, because they are upon the whole less expensively regulated. I cannot say that I have ever been much edified by the custom of tying a bib and apron on the front of the house of mourning, or that I would myself particularly care to be driven to my grave in a nodding and bobbing car, like an infirm four-post bedstead, by an inky fellow creature in a cocked-hat. But it may be that I am constitutionally insensible to the virtues of a cocked-hat. In provincial France, the solemnities are sufficiently hideous, but are few and cheap. The friends and townsmen of the departed, in their own dresses and not masquerading under the auspices of the African Conjuror, surround the hand-bier, and often carry it. It is not considered indispensable to stifle the bearers, or even to elevate the burden on their shoulders; consequently it is easily taken up, and easily set down, and is carried through the streets without the distressing floundering and shuffling that we see at home. A dirty priest or two, and a dirtier acolyte or two, do not lend any especial grace to the proceedings; and I regard with personal animosity the bassoon, which is blown at intervals by the big legged priest (it is always a big legged priest who blows the bassoon), when his fellows combine in a lugubrious stalwart drawl. But there is far less of the Conjuror and the Medicine Man in the business than under like circumstances here. The grim coaches that we reserve expressly for such shows, are non-existent; if the cemetery be far out of the town, the coaches that are hired for other purposes of life are hired for this purpose; and although the honest vehicles make no pretence of being overcome, I have never noticed that the people in them were the worse for it. In Italy, the hooded Members of Confraternities who attend on funerals, are dismal and ugly to look upon; but the services they render are at least voluntarily rendered, and impoverish no one, and cost nothing. Why should high civilisation and low savagery ever come together on the point of making them a wantonly wasteful and contemptible set of forms?

Once I lost a friend by death, who had been troubled in his time by the Medicine Man and the Conjuror, and upon whose limited resources there were abundant claims. The Conjuror assured me that I must positively 'follow,' and both he and the Medicine Man entertained no doubt that I must go in a black carriage, and must wear 'fittings.' I objected to fittings as having nothing to do with my friendship, and I objected to the black carriage as being in more senses than one a job.

So, it came into my mind to try what would happen if I quietly walked, in my own way, from my own house to my friend's burial-place, and stood beside his open grave in my own dress and person, reverently listening to the best of Services. It satisfied my mind, I found, quite as well as if I had been disguised in a hired hatband and scarf both trailing to my very heels, and as if I had cost the orphan children, in their greatest need, ten guineas.

Can anyone who ever beheld the stupendous absurdities attendant on 'A message from the Lords' in the House of Commons, turn upon the Medicine Man of the poor Indians? Has he any 'Medicine' in that dried skin pouch of his, so supremely ludicrous as the two Masters in Chancery holding up their black petticoats and butting their ridiculous wigs at Mr Speaker? Yet there are authorities innumerable to tell me – as there are authorities innumerable among the Indians to tell them – that the nonsense is indispensable, and that its abrogation would involve most awful consequences. What would any rational creature who had never heard of judicial and forensic 'fittings,' think of the Court of Common Pleas on the first day of Term? Or with what an awakened sense of humour would LIVINGSTONE's account of a similar scene be perused, if the fur and red cloth and goats' hair and horse hair and powdered chalk and black patches on the top of the head, were all at Tala Mungongo instead of Westminster? That model missionary and good brave man found at least one tribe of blacks with a very strong sense of the ridiculous, insomuch that although an amiable and docile people, they never could see the missionaries dispose of their legs in the attitude of kneeling, or hear them begin a hymn in chorus, without bursting into roars of irrepressible laughter. It is much to be hoped that no member of this facetious tribe may ever find his way to England and get committed for contempt of Court.

In the Tonga Island already mentioned, there are a set of personages called Mataboos – or some such name – who are the Masters of all the public ceremonies, and who know the exact place in which every chief must sit down when a solemn public meeting takes place: a meeting which bears a family resemblance to our own Public Dinner, in respect of its being a main part of the proceedings that every gentleman present is required to drink something nasty. These Mataboos are a privileged order, so important is their avocation, and they make the most of their high functions. A long way out of the Tonga Islands, indeed, rather near the British Islands, was there no calling in of the Mataboos the other day to settle an earth-convulsing question of precedence; and was there no weighty opinion delivered on the part of the Mataboos which, being interpreted to that unlucky tribe of blacks with the sense of the ridiculous, would infallibly set the whole population screaming with laughter?

My sense of justice demands the admission, however, that this is not quite a one-sided question. If we submit ourselves meekly to the Medicine Man and the Conjuror, and are not exalted by it, the savages may retort upon us that we act more unwisely than they, in other matters wherein we fail to imitate them. It is a widely diffused custom among savage tribes, when they meet to discuss any affair of public importance, to sit up all night making a horrible noise, dancing, blowing shells, and (in cases where they are familiar with fire-arms), flying out into open places and letting off guns. It is questionable whether our legislative assemblies might not take a hint from this. A shell is not a melodious wind-instrument, and it is monotonous; but it is as musical as, and not more monotonous than, my Honourable friend's own trumpet, or the trumpet that he blows so hard for the Minister. The uselessness of arguing with any supporter of a Government or of an Opposition, is well known. Try dancing. It is a better exercise, and has the unspeakable recommendation that it couldn't be reported. The honourable and savage member who has a loaded gun, and has grown impatient of debate, plunges out of doors, fires in the air, and returns calm and silent to the Palaver. Let the honourable and civilised member similarly charged with a speech, dart into the cloisters of Westminster Abbey in the silence of night, let his speech off, and come back harmless. It is not at first sight a very rational custom to paint a broad blue stripe across one's nose and both cheeks, and a broad red stripe from the forehead to the chin, to attach a few pounds of wood to one's under lip, to stick fish-bones in one's ears and a brass curtain-ring in one's nose, and to rub one's body all over with rancid oil, as a preliminary to entering on business. But this is a question of taste and ceremony, and so is the Windsor Uniform. The manner of entering on the business itself is another question. A council of six hundred savage gentlemen entirely independent of tailors, sitting on their hams in a ring, smoking, and occasionally grunting, seem to me, according to the experience I have gathered in my voyages and travels, somehow to do what they come together for; whereas that is not at all the general experience of a council of six hundred civilised gentlemen very dependent on tailors and sitting on mechanical contrivances. It is better that an Assembly should do its utmost to envelop itself in smoke, than that it should direct its endeavours to enveloping the public in smoke; and I would rather it buried half a hundred hatchets than buried one subject demanding attention.

34

The Uncommercial Traveller

All The Year Round, 24 October 1863 (*UT2* as 'Titbull's Alms-Houses')

Dickens clearly signals that a composite sketch of east London almshouses is intended in the present paper. There were numerous such establishments, most of which have now disappeared (a Post Office map of 1860 shows at least five almshouses on or near the Mile End Road: the Vintners', Trinity, Bancroft's, Drapers' & Merchant Seamen's, and Maritime). However, B. W. Matz has argued in *The Dickensian* that significant details of 'Titbull's Alms-Houses' 'appl[y] to the Vintners' Almshouses as they are today' ('Through Whitechapel with Dickens', Vol. 1 [1905], p. 238).

Dickens began work on the paper rather late, some time after the 7th of October, and the manuscript found its way into the hands of *ATYR* compositor, Daniel F. Bastie, of the printer Charles Whiting & Co. Bastie saved the MS at the request of Samuel Clapp, who passed it on to his daughter (see MS Note below; report from the Dickens Fellowship Vancouver Branch in *The Dickensian*, Vol. 43 [1947], pp. 61–2).

Literary allusions (p. 316) 'Jack's bean-stalk': alludes to the traditional German fairy story of Jack and the Beanstalk; (p. 319) 'disparaged Titbull and all his works': 'renounce the devil and all his works', 'A Catechism', *The Book of Common Prayer* (1662); (p. 322) 'Titbull's was to Titbull's true': 'If England to itself do rest but true', Shakespeare, *King John*, Act V, Sc. 7.

MS Robert H. Taylor Collection, Princeton University Library. The MS is unusual amongst the nine which survive of the 'Uncommercial Traveller' papers in its relative freedom from heavy correction. The cleanest of the twelve slips, the seventh, has only thirty-six words altered or inserted from a total of 418. Few changes seem to have occurred at proof stage. The suppression of the adjective 'benevolent' qualifying 'visitor' (p. 316) may point to a visit made by Dickens in company with Angela Burdett Coutts, in his capacity as her almoner; Dickens was always careful to avoid public references which might begin to identify her. MS 'My earliest journies have been among' altered to 'They refer back to journeys made among' in copy-text (p. 316).

By the side of most railways out of London, one may see Alms-Houses and Retreats (generally with a Wing or a Centre wanting, and ambitious of being much bigger than they are), some of which are newly-founded Institutions, and some old establishments transplanted. There is a tendency in these pieces of architecture to shoot upward unexpectedly, like Jack's bean-stalk, and to be ornate in spires of Chapels and lanterns of Halls, which might lead to the embellishment of the air with many castles of questionable beauty but for the restraining consideration of expense. However, the managers, being always of a sanguine temperament, comfort themselves with plans and elevations of Loomings in the future, and are influenced in the present by philanthropy towards the railway passengers. For, the question how prosperous and promising the buildings can be made to look in their eyes, usually supersedes the lesser question how they can be turned to the best account for the inmates.

Why none of the people who reside in these places ever look out of window, or take an airing in the piece of ground which is going to be a garden by-and-by, is one of the wonders I have added to my always-lengthening list of the wonders of the world. I have got it into my mind that they live in a state of chronic injury and resentment, and on that account refuse to decorate the building with a human interest. As I have known legatees deeply injured by a bequest of five hundred pounds because it was not five thousand, and as I was once acquainted with a pensioner on the Public to the extent of two hundred a year, who perpetually anathematised his Country because he was not in the receipt of four, having no claim whatever to sixpence: so perhaps it usually happens, within certain limits, that to get a little help is to get a notion of being defrauded of more. 'How do they pass their lives in this beautiful and peaceful place!' was the subject of my speculation with a visitor who once accompanied me to a charming rustic retreat for old men and women: a quaint ancient foundation in a pleasant English county, behind a picturesque church and among rich old convent gardens. There were but some dozen or so of houses, and we agreed that we would talk with the inhabitants, as they sat in their groined rooms between the light of their fires and the light shining in at their latticed windows, and would find out. They passed their lives in considering themselves mulcted of certain ounces of tea by a deaf old steward who lived among them in the quadrangle. There was no reason to suppose that any such ounces of tea had ever been in existence, or that the old steward so much as knew what was the matter; – he passed *his* life in considering himself periodically defrauded of a birch-broom by the beadle.

But it is neither to old Alms-Houses in the country, nor to new Alms-Houses by the railroad, that these present Uncommercial notes relate. They refer back to journeys made among those common-place smoky-fronted London Alms-Houses, with a little paved court-yard in front enclosed by iron railings, which have got snowed up, as it were, by bricks and mortar; which were once in a suburb, but are now in the densely populated town; gaps in the busy life around them, parentheses in the close and blotted texts of the streets.

Sometimes, these Alms-Houses belong to a Company or Society. Sometimes, they were established by individuals, and are maintained out of private funds bequeathed in perpetuity long ago. My favourite among them is Titbull's, which establishment is a picture of many. Of Titbull I know no more than that he deceased in 1723, that his christian name was Sampson, and his social designation Esquire, and that he founded these Alms-Houses as Dwellings for Nine Poor Women and Six Poor Men by his Will and Testament. I should not know even this much, but for its being inscribed on a grim stone very difficult to read, let into the front of the centre house of Titbull's Alms-Houses, and which stone is ornamented atop with a piece of sculptured drapery resembling the effigy of Titbull's bath-towel.

Titbull's Alms-Houses are in the east of London, in a great highway, in a poor busy and thronged neighbourhood. Old iron and fried fish, cough drops and artificial flowers, boiled pigs'-feet and household furniture that looks as if it were polished up with lip-salve, umbrellas full of vocal literature and saucers full of shellfish in a green juice which I hope is natural to them when their health is good, garnish the paved sideways as you go to Titbull's. I take the ground to have risen in those parts since Titbull's time, and you drop into his domain by three stone steps. So did I first drop into it, very nearly striking my brows against Titbull's pump, which stands with its back to the thoroughfare just inside the gate, and has a conceited air of reviewing Titbull's pensioners.

'And a worse one,' said a virulent old man with a pitcher, 'there isn't nowhere. A harder one to work, nor grudginer one to yield, there isn't nowhere!' This old man wore a long coat, such as we see Hogarth's Chairmen represented with, and it was of that peculiar green-pea hue without the green, which seems to come of poverty. It had also that peculiar smell of cupboard which seems to come of poverty.

'The pump is rusty, perhaps,' said I.

'Not *it*,' said the old man, regarding it with undiluted virulence in his watery eye. 'It never were fit to be termed a pump. That's what's the matter with *it*.'

'Whose fault is that?' said I.

The old man, who had a working mouth which seemed to be trying to masticate his anger and to find that it was too hard and there was too much of it, replied, 'Them gentlemen.'

'What gentlemen?'

'Maybe you're one of 'em?' said the old man, suspiciously.

'The trustees?'

'I wouldn't trust 'em myself,' said the virulent old man.

'If you mean the gentlemen who administer this place, no, I am not one of them; nor have I ever so much as heard of them.'

'I wish *I* never heard of them,' gasped the old man: 'at my time of life – with the rheumatics – drawing water – from that thing!' Not to be deluded into calling it a Pump, the old man gave it another virulent look, took up his pitcher, and carried it into a corner dwelling-house, shutting the door after him.

Looking around and seeing that each little house was a house of two little rooms; and seeing that the little oblong court-yard in front was like a graveyard for the inhabitants, saving that no word was engraven on its flat dry stones; and seeing that the currents of life and noise ran to and fro outside, having no more to do with the place than if it were a sort of low-water mark on a lively beach; I say, seeing this and nothing else, I was going out at the gate when one of the doors opened.

'Was you looking for anything, sir?' asked a tidy well-favoured woman.

Really, no; I couldn't say I was.

'Not wanting anyone, sir?'

'No – at least I – pray what is the name of the elderly gentleman who lives in the corner there?'

The tidy woman stepped out to be sure of the door I indicated, and she and the pump and I stood all three in a row, with our backs to the thoroughfare.

'Oh! *His* name is Mr Battens,' said the tidy woman, dropping her voice.

'I have just been talking with him.'

'Indeed?' said the tidy woman. 'Ho! I wonder Mr Battens talked!'

'Is he usually so silent?'

'Well, Mr Battens is the oldest here – that is to say, the oldest of the old gentlemen – in point of residence.'

She had a way of passing her hands over and under one another as she spoke, that was not only tidy, but propitiatory; so I asked her if I might look at her little sitting-room? She willingly replied Yes, and we went into it together: she leaving the door open, with an eye as I understood to the social proprieties. The door opening at once into the room without any intervening entry, even scandal must have been silenced by the precaution.

It was a gloomy little chamber, but clean, and with a mug of wallflower in the window. On the chimney-piece were two peacock's feathers, a carved ship, a few shells, and a black profile with one eyelash; whether this portrait purported to be male or female passed my comprehension, until my hostess informed me that it was her only son, and 'quite a speaking one.'

'He is alive, I hope?'

'No, sir,' said the widow, 'he were cast away in China.' This was said with a modest sense of its reflecting a certain geographical distinction on his mother.

'If the old gentlemen here are not given to talking,' said I, 'I hope the old ladies are? – Not that you are one.'

She shook her head. 'You see they get so cross.'

'How is that?'

'Well, whether the gentlemen really do deprive us of any little matters which ought to be ours by rights, I cannot say for certain; but the opinion of the old ones is they do. And Mr Battens he do even go so far as to doubt whether credit is due to the Founder. For Mr Battens he do say, anyhow he got his name up by it and he done it cheap.'

'I am afraid the pump has soured Mr Battens.'

'It may be so,' returned the tidy widow, 'but the handle does go very hard. Still, what I say to myself is, the gentlemen *may* not pocket the difference between a good pump and a bad one and I would wish to think well of them. And the dwellings,' said my hostess, glancing round her room; 'perhaps they were convenient dwellings in the Founder's time, considered *as* his time, and therefore he should not be blamed. But Mrs Saggers is very hard upon them.'

'Mrs Saggers is the oldest here?'

'The oldest but one. Mrs Quinch being the oldest, and have totally lost her head.'

'And you?'

'I am the youngest in residence, and consequently am not looked up to. But when Mrs Quinch makes a happy release, there will be one below me. Nor is it to be expected that Mrs Saggers will prove herself immortal.'

'True. Nor Mr Battens.'

'Regarding the old gentlemen,' said my widow, slightingly, 'they count among themselves. They do not count among us. Mr Battens is that exceptional that he have written to the gentlemen many times and have worked the case against them. Therefore he have took a higher ground. But we do not, as a rule, greatly reckon the old gentlemen.'

Pursuing the subject, I found it to be traditionally settled among the poor ladies, that the poor gentlemen, whatever their ages, were all very old indeed, and in a state of dotage. I also discovered that the juniors and newcomers preserved, for a time, a waning disposition to believe in Titbull and his trustees, but that as they gained social standing, they lost this faith, and disparaged Titbull and all his works.

Improving my acquaintance subsequently with this respected lady, whose name was Mrs Mitts, and occasionally dropping in upon her with a little offering of sound Family Hyson in my pocket, I gradually became familiar with the inner politics and ways of Titbull's Alms-Houses. But I never could find out who the trustees were, or where they were: it being one of the fixed ideas of the place that those authorities must be vaguely and mysteriously mentioned as 'the gentlemen' only. The secretary of 'the gentlemen' was once pointed out to me, evidently engaged in championing the obnoxious pump against the attacks of the discontented Mr Battens; but I am not in a condition to report further of him than that he had the sprightly bearing of a lawyer's clerk. I had it from Mrs Mitts's lips in a very confidential moment, that Mr Battens was once 'had up before the gentlemen' to stand or fall by his accusations, and that an old shoe was thrown after him on his departure from the building on this dread errand; – not ineffectually, for, the interview resulting in a plumber, was considered to have encircled the temples of Mr Battens with the wreath of victory.

In Titbull's Alms-Houses, the local society is not regarded as good society. A gentleman or lady receiving visitors from without, or going out to tea, counts, as it were, accordingly; but visitings or tea-drinkings interchanged among Titbullians do not score. Such interchanges, however, are rare, in consequence of internal dissensions occasioned by Mrs Saggers's pail: which household article has split Titbull's into almost as many parties as there are dwellings in that precinct. The extremely complicated nature of the conflicting articles of belief on the subject prevents my stating them here with my usual perspicuity, but I think they have all branched off from the root-and-trunk question, Has Mrs Saggers any right to stand her pail outside her dwelling? The question has been much refined upon, but roughly stated may be stated in those terms.

There are two old men in Titbull's Alms-Houses who, I have been given to understand, knew each other in the world beyond its pump and iron railings, when they were both 'in trade.' They make the best of their reverses, and are looked upon with great contempt. They are little stooping blear-eyed old men of cheerful countenance, and they hobble up and down the court-yard wagging their chins and talking together quite gaily. This has given offence, and has, moreover, raised the question whether they are justified in passing any other windows than their own. Mr Battens, however, permitting them to pass *his* windows, on the disdainful ground that their imbecility almost amounts to irresponsibility, they are allowed to take their walk in peace. They live next door to one another, and take it by turns to read the newspaper aloud (that is to say, the newest newspaper they can get), and they play cribbage at night. On warm and sunny days they have been known to go so far as to bring out two chairs and sit by the iron railings, looking forth; but this low conduct being much remarked upon throughout Titbull's, they were deterred by an outraged public opinion from repeating it. There is a rumour – but it may be malicious – that they hold the memory of Titbull in some weak sort of veneration, and that they once set off together on a pilgrimage to the parish churchyard to find his tomb. To this, perhaps, might be traced a general suspicion that they are spies of 'the gentlemen:' to which they were supposed to have given colour in my own presence on the occasion of the weak attempt at justification of the pump by the gentlemen's clerk; when they emerged bare-headed from the doors of their dwellings, as if their dwellings and themselves constituted an old-fashioned weather-glass of double action with two figures of old ladies inside, and deferentially bowed to him at intervals until he took his departure. They are understood to be perfectly friendless and relationless. Unquestionably the two poor fellows make the very best of their lives in Titbull's Alms-Houses, and unquestionably they are (as before mentioned) the subjects of unmitigated contempt there.

On Saturday nights, when there is a greater stir than usual outside, and when itinerant vendors of miscellaneous wares even take their stations and light up their smoky lamps before the iron railings, Titbull's becomes flurried. Mrs Saggers has her celebrated palpitations of the heart, for the most part on Saturday nights. But Titbull's is unfit to strive with the uproar of the streets in any of its phases. It is religiously believed at Titbull's that people push more than they used, and likewise that the foremost object of the population of England and Wales is to get you down and trample on you. Even of railroads they know, at Titbull's, little more than the shriek (which Mrs Saggers says goes through her, and ought to be taken up by Government); and the penny postage may even yet be unknown there, for I have never seen a letter delivered to any inhabitant. But there is a tall straight sallow lady resident in Number Seven, Titbull's, who never speaks to anybody, who is surrounded by a superstitious halo of lost wealth, who does her household work in housemaid's gloves, and who is secretly much deferred to, though openly cavilled at; and it has obscurely leaked out that this old lady has a son, grandson, nephew, or other relative, who is 'a Contractor,' and who would think it nothing of a job to knock down Titbull's, pack it off into Cornwall, and knock it together again. An immense sensation was made by a gipsy-party calling in a spring van, to take this old lady up to go for a day's pleasure into Epping Forest, and notes were compared as to which of the company was the son, grandson, nephew, or other relative, the Contractor. A thick-set personage with a white hat and a cigar in his mouth, was the favourite: though as Titbull's had no other reason to believe that the Contractor was there at all, than that this man was supposed to eye the chimney-stacks as if he would like to knock them down and cart them off, the general mind was much unsettled in arriving at a conclusion. As a way out of this difficulty, it concentrated itself on the acknowledged Beauty of the party, every stitch in whose dress was verbally unripped by the old ladies then and there, and whose 'goings on' with another and a thinner personage in a white hat might have suffused the pump (where they were principally discussed) with blushes, for months afterwards. Herein Titbull's was to Titbull's true, for it has a constitutional dislike of all strangers. As concerning innovations and improvements, it is always of opinion that what it doesn't want itself, nobody ought to want. But I think I have met with this opinion outside Titbull's.

Of the humble treasures of furniture brought into Titbull's by the inmates when they establish themselves in that place of contemplation for the rest of their days, by far the greater and more valuable part belongs to the ladies. I may claim the honour of having either crossed the threshold, or looked in at the door, of every one of the nine ladies, and I have noticed that they are all particular in the article of bedsteads, and maintain favourite and long-established bedsteads and bedding, as a regular part of their rest. Generally an antiquated chest of drawers is among their cherished possessions; a tea-tray always is. I know of at least two rooms in which a little tea-kettle of genuine burnished copper, vies with the cat in winking at the fire; and one old lady has a tea-urn set forth in state on the top of her chest of drawers, which urn is used as her library, and contains four duodecimo volumes, and a black-bordered newspaper giving an account of the funeral of her Royal Highness the Princess Charlotte. Among the poor old gentlemen there are no such niceties. Their furniture has the air of being contributed, like some obsolete Literary Miscellany, 'by several hands;' their few chairs never match; old patchwork coverlets linger among them; and they have an untidy habit of keeping their wardrobes in hat-boxes. When I recal one old gentleman who is rather choice in his shoe-brushes and blacking-bottle, I have summed up the domestic elegancies of that side of the building.

On the occurrence of a death in Titbull's, it is invariably agreed among the survivors – and it is the only subject on which they do agree – that the departed did something 'to bring it on.' Judging by Titbull's, I should say the human race need never die, if they took care. But they don't take care, and they do die, and when they die in Titbull's they are buried at the cost of the Foundation. Some provision has been made for the purpose, in virtue of which (I record this on the strength of having seen the funeral of Mrs Quinch), a lively neighbouring undertaker dresses up four of the old men, and four of the old women, hustles them into a procession of four couples, and leads off with a large black bow at the back of his hat, looking over his shoulder at them airily from time to time, to see that no member of the party has got lost, or has tumbled down; as if they were a company of dim old dolls.

Resignation of a dwelling is of very rare occurrence in Titbull's. A story does obtain there, how an old lady's son once drew a prize of Thirty Thousand Pounds in the Lottery, and presently drove to the gate in his own carriage, with French Horns playing up behind, and whisked his mother away, and left ten guineas for a Feast. But I have been unable to substantiate it by any evidence, and regard it as an Alms-House Fairy Tale. It is curious that the only proved case of resignation happened within my knowledge.

It happened on this wise. There is a sharp competition among the ladies respecting the gentility of their visitors, and I have so often observed visitors to be dressed as for a holiday occasion, that I suppose the ladies to have besought them to make all possible display when they come. In these circumstances much excitement was one day occasioned by Mrs Mitts receiving a visit from a Greenwich Pensioner. He was a Pensioner of a bluff and warlike appearance, with an empty coat-sleeve, and he was got up with unusual care; his coat-buttons were extremely bright, he wore his empty coat-sleeve in a graceful festoon, and he had a walking-stick in his hand that must have cost money. When, with the head of his walking-stick, he knocked at Mrs Mitts's door – there are no knockers in Titbull's – Mrs Mitts was overheard by a next-door neighbour to utter a cry of surprise expressing much agitation; and the same neighbour did afterwards solemnly affirm that when he was admitted into Mrs Mitts's room, she heard a smack. Heard a smack which was not a blow.

There was an air about this Greenwich Pensioner when he took his departure, which imbued all Titbull's with the conviction that he was coming again. He was eagerly looked for, and Mrs Mitts was closely watched. In the meantime, if anything could have placed the unfortunate six old gentlemen at a greater disadvantage than that at which they chronically stood, it would have been the apparition of this Greenwich Pensioner. They were well shrunken already, but they shrunk to nothing in comparison with the Pensioner. Even the poor old gentlemen themselves seemed conscious of their inferiority, and to know submissively that they could never hope to hold their own against the Pensioner with his warlike and maritime experience in the past, and his tobacco-money in the present: his chequered career of blue water, black gunpowder, and red bloodshed for England home and beauty.

Before three weeks were out, the Pensioner reappeared. Again he knocked at Mrs Mitts's door with the handle of his stick, and again was he admitted. But not again did he depart alone; for, Mrs Mitts, in a

A Phenomenon at Titbull's

bonnet identified as having been re-embellished, went out walking with him, and stayed out till the ten o'clock beer, Greenwich time.

There was now a truce, even as to the troubled waters of Mrs Saggers's pail; nothing was spoken of among the ladies but the conduct of Mrs Mitts and its blighting influence on the reputation of Titbull's. It was agreed that Mr Battens 'ought to take it up,' and Mr Battens was communicated with on the subject. That unsatisfactory individual replied 'that he didn't see his way yet,' and it was unanimously voted by the ladies that aggravation was in his nature.

How it came to pass, with some appearance of inconsistency, that Mrs Mitts was cut by all the ladies and the Pensioner admired by all the ladies, matters not. Before another week was out, Titbull's was startled by another phenomenon. At ten o'clock in the forenoon appeared a cab, containing not only the Greenwich Pensioner with one arm, but, to boot, a Chelsea Pensioner with one leg. Both dismounting to assist Mrs Mitts into the cab, the Greenwich Pensioner bore her company inside, and the Chelsea Pensioner mounted the box by the driver: his wooden leg sticking out after the manner of a bowsprit, as if in jocular homage to his friend's sea-going career. Thus the equipage drove away. No Mrs Mitts returned that night.

What Mr Battens might have done in the matter of taking it up, goaded by the infuriated state of public feeling next morning, was anticipated by another phenomenon. A Truck, propelled by the Greenwich Pensioner and the Chelsea Pensioner, each placidly smoking a pipe, and pushing his warrior-breast against the handle.

The display on the part of the Greenwich Pensioner of his 'marriage-lines,' and his announcement that himself and friend had looked in for the furniture of Mrs G. Pensioner, late Mitts, by no means reconciled the ladies to the conduct of their sister; on the contrary, it is said that they appeared more than ever exasperated. Nevertheless, my stray visits to Titbull's since the date of this occurrence, have confirmed me in an impression that it was a wholesome fillip. The nine ladies are smarter, both in mind and dress, than they used to be, though it must be admitted that they despise the six gentlemen to the last extent. They have a much greater interest in the external thoroughfare too, than they had when I first knew Titbull's. And whenever I chance to be leaning my back against the pump or the iron railings, and to be talking to one of the junior ladies, and to see that a flush has passed over her face, I immediately know without looking round that a Greenwich Pensioner has gone past.

35

In Memoriam. W. M. Thackeray

The Cornhill, February 1864

Dickens and Thackeray had known each other since 1836 when Thackeray unsuccessfully proposed himself as a replacement for the original illustrator of *Pickwick Papers*, Robert Seymour, after Seymour's suicide. For many years they were on friendly and sociable, but not intimate, terms. For an illuminating recent discussion of the tensions underlying their relationship, see D. J. Taylor's *Thackeray* (1999), pp. 400–5 (Taylor highlights Thackeray's obsession with Dickens, 'simultaneously admiring, emulative and envious'). These tensions were exacerbated by their disagreement in the so-called 'Dignity of Literature' debate (Thackeray's letter to the *Morning Chronicle*, 12 January 1850; see p. 629 of Vol. 13, *Ballads and Miscellanies*, of the Biographical Edn of Thackeray's works [1900]) and by the great success of Thackeray's *Vanity Fair* (1847–8), which, together with his later novels, was seen by many as challenging Dickens's pre-eminence in the field. In 1858 came a complete rupture as a result of the so-called 'Garrick Club Affair' (for details of this see Taylor, pp. 405–14) and, though the warm friendship between their daughters continued unimpaired, the two men did not speak again until they were reconciled at a chance meeting at the Athenaeum less than a fortnight before Thackeray's death.

Dickens felt that he could not refuse the invitation to write an obituary for *The Cornhill* of which Thackeray had been the first editor. Although Thackeray had been a close student of Dickens's books and had often warmly praised them in public, Dickens seems to have paid little attention to Thackeray's work. Here he bestows high praise on *Denis Duval*, the story Thackeray was serialising in *The Cornhill* at the time of his death, and expresses the belief that it was 'the best of all his works'. In his magisterial biography Gordon N. Ray comments (*Thackeray: The Age of Wisdom* [1958], p. 411), 'so excessive a claim is interesting chiefly as an illustration of how blind Dickens was to Thackeray's true genius'. The 'picture' drawn by Thackeray in *Duval* that Dickens says must have caused Thackeray 'extreme distress' is the portrayal of the madness of one of the leading characters, Madame de Saverne, a young mother who, in her unhinged state, leaves her baby to be drowned on the seashore. Thackeray's own wife had gradually descended into incurable insanity after the birth of her second child, and at one point, walking on the seashore with her three-year-old daughter, she had tried to drag the little girl into the sea but recovered her sanity just in time. Dickens was unlikely to have known this harrowing detail but he would, of course, have known the general sad situation.

The reference to one of Thackeray's daughters having a literary career marked out for her concerns his elder daughter, Annie, later Lady Ritchie, who had published essays in *The Cornhill* under Thackeray's editorship and whose first novel, *The Story of Elizabeth*, was published in 1863.

Literary allusions (p.328) 'his very best contribution to *Punch*': 'The Curate's Walk' in *Travels in London* serialised in *Punch* 1847 – this particular paper appeared on 27 November (Vol. 13, p. 201); (p. 329) 'I've writ the foolish fancy of his brain ...': from one of Thackeray's ballads, 'The Pen and the Album' (1853); (p. 330) 'And when, its force expended ...': from the mainly comic poem, 'The White Squall', which forms Ch. 9 of Thackeray's *Notes of a Journey from Cornhill to Grand Cairo* (1846).

Proofs A corrected proof of Dickens's obituary was sold at Christie's in May 1986, together with a covering letter from him. Extracts were published in Christie's catalogue and the *Pilgrim* Editors note that these reveal 'a number of small differences in order of sentences and choice of words' (*Pilgrim*, Vol. X, p. 341). In particular, they note that the original conclusion to the piece was deleted by Dickens. Following the words '... bowed around his tomb' in the proof is the sentence: 'His funeral will always be as memorable to me in that wise, as for its shabby representation of the order usually called "the Great": upon which he, as a man of genius, perhaps had sometimes condescended to bestow too much of his attention'.

It has been desired by some of the personal friends of the great English writer who established this magazine, that its brief record of his having been stricken from among men should be written by the old comrade and brother in arms who pens these lines, and of whom he often wrote himself, and always with the warmest generosity.

I saw him first, nearly twenty-eight years ago, when he proposed to become the illustrator of my earliest book. I saw him last, shortly before Christmas, at the Athenæum Club, when he told me that he had been in bed three days – that, after these attacks, he was troubled with cold shiverings, 'which quite took the power of work out of him' – and that he had it in his mind to try a new remedy which he laughingly described. He was very cheerful, and looked very bright. In the night of that day week, he died.

The long interval between those two periods is marked in my remembrance of him by many occasions when he was supremely humourous, when he was irresistibly extravagant, when he was softened and serious, when he was charming with children. But, by none do I recall him more tenderly than by two or three that start out of the crowd, when he unexpectedly presented himself in my room, announcing how that some passage in a certain book had made him cry yesterday, and how that he had come to dinner, 'because he couldn't help it,' and must talk such passage over. No one can ever have seen him more genial, natural, cordial, fresh, and honestly impulsive, than I have seen him at those times. No one can be surer than I, of the greatness and the goodness of the heart that then disclosed itself.

We had our differences of opinion. I thought that he too much feigned a want of earnestness, and that he made a pretence of under-valuing his art, which was not good for the art that he held in trust. But, when we fell upon these topics, it was never very gravely, and I have a lively image of him in my mind, twisting both his hands in his hair, and stamping about, laughing, to make an end of the discussion.

When we were associated in remembrance of the late Mr Douglas Jerrold, he delivered a public lecture in London, in the course of which, he read his very best contribution to PUNCH, describing the grown-up cares of a poor family of young children. No one hearing him could have doubted his natural gentleness, or his thoroughly unaffected manly sympathy with the weak and lowly. He read the paper most pathetically, and with a simplicity of tenderness that certainly moved one of his audience to tears. This was presently after his standing for Oxford, from which place he had dispatched his agent to me, with a droll note (to which he afterwards added a verbal postscript), urging me to 'come down and make a speech, and tell them who he was, for he doubted whether more than two of the electors had ever heard of him, and he thought there might be as many as six or eight who had heard of me.' He introduced the lecture just mentioned, with a reference to his late electioneering failure, which was full of good sense, good spirits, and good humour.

He had a particular delight in boys, and an excellent way with them. I remember his once asking me with fantastic gravity, when he had been to Eton where my eldest son then was, whether I felt as he did in regard of never seeing a boy without wanting instantly to give him a sovereign? I thought of this when I looked down into his grave, after he was laid there, for I looked down into it over the shoulder of a boy to whom he had been kind.

These are slight remembrances; but it is to little familiar things suggestive of the voice, look, manner, never, never more to be encountered on this earth, that the mind first turns in a bereavement. And greater things that are known of him, in the way of his warm affections, his quiet endurance, his unselfish thoughtfulness for others, and his munificent hand, may not be told.

If, in the reckless vivacity of his youth, his satirical pen had ever gone astray or done amiss, he had caused it to prefer its own petition for forgiveness, long before:

> I've writ the foolish fancy of his brain;
> The aimless jest that, striking, hath caused pain;
> The idle word that he'd wish back again.

In no pages should I take it upon myself at this time to discourse of his books, of his refined knowledge of character, of his subtle acquaintance with the weaknesses of human nature, of his delightful playfulness as an essayist, of his quaint and touching ballads, of his mastery over the English language. Least of all, in these pages, enriched by his brilliant qualities from the first of the series, and beforehand accepted by the Public through the strength of his great name.

But, on the table before me, there lies all that he had written of his latest and last story. That it would be very sad to anyone – that it is inexpressibly so to a writer – in its evidences of matured designs never to be accomplished, of intentions begun to be executed and destined never to be completed, of careful preparation for long roads of thought that he was never to traverse, and for shining goals that he was never to reach, will be readily believed. The pain, however, that I have felt in perusing it, has not been deeper than the conviction that he was in the healthiest vigour of his powers when he wrought on this last labour. In respect of earnest feeling, far-seeing purpose, character, incident, and a certain loving picturesqueness blending the whole, I believe it to be much the best of all his works. That he fully meant it to be so, that he had become strongly attached to it, and that he bestowed great pains upon it, I trace in almost every page. It contains one picture which must have cost him extreme distress, and which is a masterpiece. There are two children in it, touched with a hand as loving and tender as ever a father caressed his little child with. There is some young love, as pure and innocent and pretty as the truth. And it is very remarkable that, by reason of the singular construction of the story, more than one main incident usually belonging to the end of such a fiction is anticipated in the beginning, and thus there is an approach to completeness in the fragment, as to the satisfaction of the reader's mind concerning the most interesting persons, which could hardly have been better attained if the writer's breaking-off had been foreseen.

The last line he wrote, and the last proof he corrected, are among these papers through which I have so sorrowfully made my way. The condition of the little pages of manuscript where Death stopped his hand, shows that he had carried them about, and often taken them out of his pocket here and there, for patient revision and interlineation. The last words he corrected in print, were, 'And my heart throbbed with an exquisite bliss.' GOD grant that on that Christmas Eve when he laid his head back on his pillow and threw up his arms as he had been wont to do when very weary, some consciousness of duty done and Christian hope throughout life humbly cherished, may have caused his own heart so to throb, when he passed away to his Redeemer's rest!

He was found peacefully lying as above described, composed, undisturbed, and to all appearance asleep, on the twenty-fourth of December, 1863. He was only in his fifty-third year; so young a man, that the mother who blessed him in his first sleep, blessed him in his last. Twenty years before, he had written, after being in a white squall:

> And when, its force expended,
> The harmless storm was ended,
> And, as the sunrise splendid
>   Came blushing o'er the sea;
> I thought, as day was breaking,
> My little girls were waking,
> And smiling, and making
>   A prayer at home for me.

Those little girls had grown to be women when the mournful day broke that saw their father lying dead. In those twenty years of companionship with him, they had learned much from him; and one of them has a literary course before her, worthy of her famous name.

On the bright wintry day, the last but one of the old year, he was laid in his grave at Kensal Green, there to mingle the dust to which the mortal part of him had returned, with that of a third child, lost in her infancy, years ago. The heads of a great concourse of his fellow-workers in the Arts, were bowed around his tomb.

36

The Late Mr Stanfield

All The Year Round, 1 June 1867

The painter Clarkson Stanfield, a former sailor who became a celebrated scene-painter and marine artist (he became a Royal Academician in 1835), was one of Dickens's best-loved friends, his 'dear Stanny', to whom he wrote a letter in 1844 which began, 'I love you so truly and have such pride and joy of heart in your friendship, that I don't know how to begin writing to you' (*Pilgrim*, Vol. IV, p. 182). Stanfield supplied a number of delightful illustrations for the last four Christmas Books, as well as a frontispiece for *American Notes*. His withdrawal from the commission to illustrate *Pictures from Italy* because of the book's pronounced anti-Catholic bias caused no estrangement between Dickens and himself. He painted the scenery, and greatly assisted in stage-managing, Dickens's amateur theatricals during the 1840s and 1850s (the backdrop he painted in 1855 for the production of Collins's *The Lighthouse* at Dickens's home, Tavistock House, is now at the Dickens House Museum), and Dickens dedicated *Little Dorrit* to him as 'a little record ... that we loved one another' (*Pilgrim*, Vol. VIII, p. 328). For a detailed account of his friendship with Dickens, see Jane R. Cohen, *Dickens and His Original Illustrators* (1980), pp. 179–89. Cohen comments that 'the proliferation of nicknames over the years testifies to the affection between Dickens ... and the former seaman, variously referred to as "Stanfell", "Old Salt", "Old Tarpaulin", "the lad with the tarry legs" and "Messmet" '.

With Dickens's scornful reference to the failure of his country to honour Stanfield with a knighthood, compare the words he puts into Esther Summerson's mouth in *Bleak House*, Ch. 35: 'I said it was not the custom in England to confer titles on men distinguished by peaceful services, however good and great; unless occasionally, when they consisted of the accumulation of some very large amount of money.'

Literary allusions (p. 333) 'Mrs Inchbald's story, Nature and Art': the dramatist Elizabeth Inchbald's second novel *Nature and Art* was published in 1796.

Every Artist, be he writer, painter, musician, or actor, must bear his private sorrows as he best can, and must separate them from the exercise of his public pursuit. But it sometimes happens, in compensation, that his private loss of a dear friend represents a loss on the part of the whole community. Then he may, without obtrusion of his individuality, step forth to lay his little wreath upon that dear friend's grave.

On Saturday, the eighteenth of this present month, CLARKSON STANFIELD died. On the afternoon of that day, England lost the great marine painter of whom she will be boastful ages hence; the National Historian of her speciality, the Sea; the man famous in all countries for his marvellous rendering of the waves that break upon her shores, of her ships and seamen, of her coasts and skies, of her storms and sunshine, of the many marvels of the deep. He who holds the oceans in the hollow of His hand had given, associated with them, wonderful gifts into his keeping; he had used them well through threescore and fourteen years; and, on the afternoon of that spring day, relinquished them for ever.

It is superfluous to record that the painter of 'The Battle of Trafalgar,' of the 'Victory being towed into Gibraltar with the body of Nelson on Board,' of 'The Morning after the Wreck,' of 'The Abandoned,' of fifty more such works, died in his seventy-fourth year, 'Mr' Stanfield. – He was an Englishman.

Those grand pictures will proclaim his powers while paint and canvas last. But the writer of these words had been his friend for thirty years; and when, a short week or two before his death, he laid that once so skilful hand upon the writer's breast and told him they would meet again, 'but not here,' the thoughts of the latter turned, for the time, so little to his noble genius, and so much to his noble nature!

He was the soul of frankness, generosity, and simplicity. The most genial, the most affectionate, the most loving, and the most lovable of men. Success had never for an instant spoiled him. His interest in the Theatre as an Institution – the best picturesqueness of which may be said to be wholly due to him – was faithful to the last. His belief in a Play, his delight in one, the ease with which it moved him to tears or to laughter, were most remarkable evidences of the heart he must have put into his old theatrical work, and of the thorough purpose and sincerity with which it must have been done. The writer was very intimately associated with him in some amateur plays; and day after day, and night after night, there were the same unquenchable freshness, enthusiasm, and impressibility in him, though broken in health, even then.

No Artist can ever have stood by his art with a quieter dignity than he always did. Nothing would have induced him to lay it at the feet of any human creature. To fawn, or to toady, or to do undeserved homage to anyone, was an absolute impossibility with him. And yet his character was so nicely balanced that he was the last man in the world to be suspected of self-assertion, and his modesty was one of his most special qualities.

He was a charitable, religious, gentle, truly good man. A genuine man, incapable of pretence or of concealment. He had been a sailor once; and all the best characteristics that are popularly attributed to sailors, being his, and being in him refined by the influences of his Art, formed a whole not likely to be often seen. There is no smile that the writer can recall, like his; no manner so naturally confiding and so cheerfully engaging. When the writer saw him for the last time on earth, the smile and the manner shone out once through the weakness, still: the bright unchanging Soul within the altered face and form.

No man was ever held in higher respect by his friends, and yet his intimate friends invariably addressed him and spoke of him by a pet name. It may need, perhaps, the writer's memory and associations to find in this a touching expression of his winning character, his playful smile, and pleasant ways. 'You know Mrs Inchbald's story, Nature and Art?' wrote THOMAS HOOD, once, in a letter: 'What a fine Edition of Nature and Art is STANFIELD!'

Gone! And many and many a dear old day gone with him! But their memories remain. And his memory will not soon fade out, for he has set his mark upon the restless waters, and his fame will long be sounded in the roar of the sea.

37

The Ruffian. By The Uncommercial Traveller

All The Year Round, 10 October 1868 (*UT3* as 'The Ruffian')

Matthew Arnold uses the word 'rough' in the euphemistic, softening sense Dickens objects to, throughout Ch. 2 ('Doing as One Likes') of *Culture and Anarchy* (1869), where he argues that 'the difference between an Irish Fenian and an English rough is ... immense', and that 'the Hyde Park rough' 'has not yet quite found his groove and settled down to his work, and so he is just asserting his personal liberty a little, going where he likes, assembling where he likes, bawling as he likes, hustling as he likes' (pp. 63–5). Dickens uses the term himself in article 25 (p. 237).

As the present paper belongs to neither of the previous 'Series' of 'Uncommercial Traveller' papers, and awkwardly pre-empts the return of the column which Dickens planned to coincide with the commencement of a complete New Series of *ATYR* on 5 December 1868 (see article 38), it is clear that Dickens felt provoked into publishing it by reading of particular offences. On 3 September 1868, a 'Police Report' in *The Times* noted that the cases had been heard at Southwark magistrates' court 'of desperate highway robbery committed within the past few weeks by an organised gang known as the Waterloo highwaymen'; four members of the 'gang' had been captured, though not all were detained (p. 9, col. f). Several other *Times* reports later in the month illustrate further offences of which Dickens complains here. But the general penological question of the treatment of habitual criminals was one in which Dickens shows an abiding interest. The Habitual Criminals Bill was on the Commons agenda for 1868 and became law the following year. On 3 April 1869, an article called 'Injured Innocents' appeared in *ATYR*, containing the following passage which complements Dickens's views in the present article:

> It may be the case (we do not say it is) that the efficiency of the force is not what it was; but how that can affect the question of making professional crime as difficult and dangerous a pursuit as it can be made, or what argument can be found in it against a measure eminently preventive and not detective, is more than we can understand. Habitual criminals exist and carry on their trade ... for no other reason than because the police have no preventive power whatever over them, unless detected in some offence. It is illogical in the last degree to punish severely detected crime, so long as, undetected, it is thus tacitly encouraged.... [N.S. Vol. I, p. 415]

The 'Society for the protection of remonstrant Ruffians' mentioned below seems to be Dickens's satirical version of the 'Discharged Prisoners Society', which shared with the police responsibility for monitoring prisoners released on tickets-of-leave.

The prosecution of a teenage girl, apparently a prostitute, narrated in the second part of the paper is an episode also recalled by Dickens in the *HW* article 'Stores for the First of April', in which he attacks a mixed range of contemporary abuses, including police toleration of thieves' gatherings and the use of foul language in places of public resort:

> The writer has himself obtained a conviction by a police magistrate ... for this shameful and demoralising offence – which is as common as the mud in the streets. He obtained it with difficulty, the charge not being within the experience of anyone concerned; but, he insisted on the law, and it was clear (wonderful to relate!) and it was enforced.... [Vol. XV, 7 March 1857; repr. in *MP*]

In bringing this action, Dickens appears to have made use of the clause in the *Act for Further Improving the Police in and near the Metropolis* (2 and 3 Vict., cap. 47) which states that '[e]very person who shall use any threatening, abusive, or insulting words or behaviour with intent to provoke a breach of the peace, or whereby a breach of the peace shall be occasioned' should be liable to 'a penalty of not more than 40 shillings' (54.13). Assuming the internal evidence of the present item to be reliable, K. J. Fielding has argued that the episode Dickens describes 'certainly took place some twenty-five years before he wrote the [present] article' in *ATYR*, when the 'newest Police Act' (1839) was still relatively new, and Dickens and his young family were living at 1 Devonshire Terrace, near Regent's Park ('Charles Dickens and "The Ruffian" ', *English*, Vol. X [1954], pp. 88–92). This conclusion is employed to counter the tendency of critics and biographers to confuse the date of the episode with the date of the article, and thus to read it as evidence of Dickens's increasingly authoritarian attitudes in later years. With greater justice, Philip Collins has called attention to the aggression apparent in Dickens's call for assaults on women to be punished by flogging (p. 337; *Dickens and Crime* [1963], pp. 17–18). This too, however, should be set in context of an overall hardening of attitudes in public debates on penology in 1868. During the reading of the Bill to carry out 'Capital Punishment within Prisons' in the Commons, for example, the celebrated humanitarian J. S. Mill had, in supporting the continuation of the death penalty, spoken in defence of whipping as 'a most objectionable punishment in ordinary cases, but a particularly appropriate one for crimes of brutality, especially against women' (*Hansard*, 3rd Series, 21 April 1868, Vol. CXCI, p. 1054).

Literary allusions (p. 337) 'hewing wood and drawing water': Joshua

9:27; (p. 339) 'Mr Carlyle, some time since, awakened a little pleasantry by writing of his own experience of the Ruffian of the streets': Carlyle's essay 'Model Prisons' (*Latter Day Pamphlets* [1850], No. II), with its insistence that 'scoundrel is scoundrel' and attack on 'universal Sluggard-and-Scoundrel Protection Societies' contains many passages similar in style and substance to 'The Ruffian' and was heavily criticised in the edition of *Punch* for 16 March 1850 (Vol. 18, p. 107); (p. 341) 'Red Riding Hood ... the Wolf': the popular fairy tale; (p. 342) 'all his evils deeds upon his head': version of Shylock's 'My deeds upon my head! I crave the law' in Shakespeare, *The Merchant of Venice*, Act 4, Sc. 1.

I entertain so strong an objection to the euphonious softening of Ruffian into Rough, which has lately become popular, that I restore the right word to the heading of this paper; the rather, as my object is to dwell upon the fact that the Ruffian is tolerated among us to an extent that goes beyond all unruffianly endurance. I take the liberty to believe that if the Ruffian besets my life, a professional Ruffian at large in the open streets of a great city, notoriously having no other calling than that of Ruffian, and of disquieting and despoiling me as I go peacefully about my lawful business, interfering with no one, then the Government under which I have the great constitutional privilege, supreme honour and happiness, and all the rest of it, to exist, breaks down in the discharge of any Government's most simple elementary duty.

What did I read in the London daily papers in the early days of this last September? That the Police had 'At length succeeded in capturing Two of the notorious gang that have so long infested the Waterloo-road.' Is it possible? What a wonderful Police! Here is a straight, broad, public thoroughfare of immense resort; half a mile long; gas-lighted by night; with a great gas-lighted railway station in it, extra the street lamps; full of shops; traversed by two popular cross thoroughfares of considerable traffic; itself the main road to the South of London; and the admirable Police have, after long infestment of this dark and lonely spot by a gang of Ruffians, actually got hold of two of them. Why, can it be doubted that any man of fair London knowledge and common resolution, armed with the powers of the Law, could have captured the whole confederacy in a week?

It is to the saving up of the Ruffian class by the Magistracy and Police – to the conventional preserving of them, as if they were Partridges – that their number and audacity must be in great part referred. Why is a notorious Thief and Ruffian ever left at large? He never turns his liberty to any account but violence and plunder, he never did a day's work out of jail, he never will do a day's work out of jail. As a proved notorious

Thief he is always consignable to prison for three months. When he comes out, he is surely as notorious a Thief as he was when he went in. Then send him back again. 'Just Heaven!' cries the Society for the protection of remonstrant Ruffians, 'This is equivalent to a sentence of perpetual imprisonment!' Precisely for that reason it has my advocacy. I demand to have the Ruffian kept out of my way, and out of the way of all decent people. I demand to have the Ruffian employed, perforce, in hewing wood and drawing water somewhere for the general service, instead of hewing at her Majesty's subjects and drawing their watches out of their pockets. If this be termed an unreasonable demand, then the tax-gatherer's demand on me must be far more unreasonable, and cannot be otherwise than extortionate and unjust.

It will be seen that I treat of the Thief and Ruffian as one. I do so, because I know the two characters to be one, in the vast majority of cases, just as well as the Police know it. (As to the Magistracy, with a few exceptions, they know nothing about it but what the Police choose to tell them.) There are disorderly classes of men who are not thieves; as railway-navigators, brickmakers, wood-sawyers, costermongers. These classes are often disorderly and troublesome; but it is mostly among themselves, and at any rate they have their industrious avocations, they work early and late, and work hard. The generic Ruffian – honourable member for what is tenderly called the Rough Element – is either a Thief, or the companion of Thieves. When he infamously molests women coming out of chapel on Sunday evenings (for which I would have his back scarified often and deep) it is not only for the gratification of his pleasant instincts, but that there may be a confusion raised by which either he or his friends may profit, in the commission of highway robberies or in picking pockets. When he gets a police-constable down and kicks him helpless for life, it is because that constable once did his duty in bringing him to justice. When he rushes into the bar of a public-house and scoops an eye out of one of the company there, or bites his ear off, it is because the man he maims gave evidence against him. When he and a line of comrades extending across the footway – say of that solitary mountain-spur of the Abruzzi, the Waterloo Road – advance towards me, 'skylarking' among themselves, my purse or shirt pin is in predestined peril from his playfulness. Always a Ruffian, always a Thief. Always a Thief, always a Ruffian.

Now, when I, who am not paid to know these things, know them daily on the evidence of my senses and experience; when I know that the Ruffian never jostles a lady in the street, or knocks a hat off, but in order that the Thief may profit, is it surprising that I should require from those who *are* paid to know these things, prevention of them?

Look at this group at a street corner. Number one is a shirking fellow of five-and-twenty, in an ill-favoured and ill-savoured suit, his trousers of corduroy, his coat of some indiscernible ground-work for the deposition of grease, his neckerchief like an eel, his complexion like dirty dough, his mangy fur cap pulled low upon his beetle brows to hide the prison cut of his hair. His hands are in his pockets. He puts them there when they are idle, as naturally as in other people's pockets when they are busy, for he knows that they are not roughened by work, and that they tell a tale. Hence, whenever he takes one out to draw a sleeve across his nose – which is often, for he has weak eyes and a constitutional cold in his head – he restores it to its pocket immediately afterwards. Number two is a burly brute of five-and-thirty, in a tall stiff hat; is a composite as to his clothes of betting man and fighting-man; is whiskered; has a staring pin in his breast, along with his right hand; has insolent and cruel eyes; large shoulders; strong legs, booted and tipped for kicking. Number three is forty years of age; is short, thickset, strong, and bow-legged; wears knee cords and white stockings, a very long-sleeved waistcoat, a very large neckerchief doubled or trebled round his throat, and a crumpled white hat crowns his ghastly parchment face. This fellow looks like an executed postboy of other days, cut down from the gallows too soon, and restored and preserved by express diabolical agency. Numbers five, six, and seven, are hulking, idle, slouching young men, patched and shabby, too short in the sleeves and too tight in the legs, slimily clothed, foul-spoken, repulsive wretches inside and out. In all the party there obtains a certain twitching character of mouth and furtiveness of eye, that hints how the coward is lurking under the bully. The hint is quite correct, for they are a slinking, sneaking set, far more prone to lie down on their backs and kick out, when in difficulty, than to make a stand for it. (This may account for the street mud on the backs of Numbers five, six, and seven, being much fresher than the stale splashes on their legs.)

These engaging gentry a Police-constable stands contemplating. His Station, with a Reserve of assistance, is very near at hand. They cannot pretend to any trade, not even to be porters or messengers. It would be idle if they did, for he knows them, and they know that he knows them, to be nothing but professed Thieves and Ruffians. He knows where they resort, knows by what slang names they call one another, knows how often they have been in prison, and how long, and for what. All this is known at his Station, too, and is (or ought to be) known at Scotland Yard, too. But does he know, or does his Station know, or does Scotland Yard know, or does anybody know, why these fellows should be here at liberty, when, as reputed Thieves to whom a whole Division of Police could swear, they might all be under lock and key at hard labour? Not he; truly he would be a wise man if he did! He only knows that these are members of the 'notorious gang,' which, according to the newspaper

Police-office reports of this past September, 'have so long infested' the awful solitudes of the Waterloo Road, and out of which almost impregnable fastnesses the Police have at length dragged Two, to the unspeakable admiration of all good civilians.

The consequences of this contemplative habit on the part of the Executive – a habit to be looked for in a hermit, but not in a Police System – are familiar to us all. The Ruffian becomes one of the established orders of the body politic. Under the playful name of Rough (as if he were merely a practical joker) his movements and successes are recorded on public occasions. Whether he mustered in large numbers or small; whether he was in good spirits, or depressed; whether he turned his generous exertions to very prosperous account, or Fortune was against him; whether he was in a sanguinary mood, or robbed with amiable horse-play and a gracious consideration for life and limb; all this is chronicled as if he were an Institution. Is there any city in Europe, out of England, in which these terms are held with the pests of Society? Or in which, at this day, such violent robberies from the person are constantly committed as in London?

The Preparatory Schools of Ruffianism are similarly borne with. The young Ruffians of London – not Thieves yet, but training for scholarships and fellowships in the Criminal Court Universities – molest quiet people and their property, to an extent that is hardly credible. The throwing of stones in the streets has become a dangerous and destructive offence, which surely could have got to no greater height though we had had no Police but our own riding-whips and walking-sticks – the Police to which I myself appeal on these occasions. The throwing of stones at the windows of railway carriages in motion – an act of wanton wickedness with the very Arch-Fiend's hand in it – had become a crying evil when the railway companies forced it on Police notice. Constabular contemplation had until then been the order of the day.

Within these twelve months, there arose among the young gentlemen of London aspiring to Ruffianism, and cultivating that much encouraged social art, a facetious cry of 'I'll have this!' accompanied with a clutch at some article of a passing lady's dress. I have known a lady's veil to be thus humourously torn from her face and carried off in the open streets at noon; and I have had the honour of myself giving chase, on Westminster Bridge, to another young Ruffian, who, in full daylight early on a summer evening, had nearly thrown a modest young woman into a swoon of indignation and confusion, by his shameful manner of attacking her with this cry as she harmlessly passed along before me. MR CARLYLE, some time since, awakened a little pleasantry by writing of his own experience of the Ruffian of the streets. I have seen the Ruffian act, in exact accordance with Mr Carlyle's description, innumerable times, and I never saw him checked.

The blaring use of the very worst language possible, in our public thoroughfares – especially in those set apart for recreation – is another disgrace to us, and another result of constabular contemplation, the like of which I have never heard in any other country to which my uncommercial travels have extended. Years ago, when I had a near interest in certain children who were sent with their nurses, for air and exercise, into the Regent's Park, I found this evil to be so abhorrent and horrible there, that I called public attention to it, and also to its contemplative reception by the Police. Looking afterwards into the newest Police Act, and finding that the offence was punishable under it, I resolved, when striking occasion should arise, to try my hand as prosecutor. The occasion arose soon enough, and I ran the following gauntlet.

The utterer of the base coin in question, was a girl of seventeen or eighteen, who, with a suitable attendance of blackguards, youths and boys, was flaunting along the streets, returning from an Irish funeral, in a Progress interspersed with singing and dancing. She had turned round to me and expressed herself in the most audible manner, to the great delight of that select circle. I attended the party, on the opposite side of the way, for a mile further, and then encountered a Police constable. The party had made themselves merry at my expense until now, but seeing me speak to the constable, its male members instantly took to their heels, leaving the girl alone. I asked the constable did he know my name? Yes, he did. 'Take that girl into custody, on my charge, for using bad language in the streets.' He had never heard of such a charge. I had. Would he take my word that he should get into no trouble? Yes, sir, he would do that. So he took the girl, and I went home for my Police Act.

With this potent instrument in my pocket, I literally as well as figuratively, 'returned to the charge,' and presented myself at the Police Station of the district. There, I found on duty a very intelligent Inspector (they are all intelligent men), who, likewise, had never heard of such a charge. I showed him my clause, and we went over it together twice or thrice. It was plain, and I engaged to wait upon the suburban Magistrate tomorrow morning at ten o'clock.

In the morning, I put my Police Act in my pocket again, and waited on the suburban Magistrate. I was not quite so courteously received by him as I should have been by The Lord Chancellor or The Lord Chief Justice, but that was a question of good breeding on the suburban Magistrate's part, and I had my clause ready with its leaf turned down. Which was enough for *me*.

Conference took place between the Magistrate and clerk, respecting the charge. During conference I was evidently regarded as a much more objectionable person than the prisoner; – one giving trouble by coming there voluntarily, which the prisoner could not be accused of doing. The prisoner had been got up, since I last had the pleasure of seeing her, with a great effect of white apron and straw bonnet. She reminded me of an elder sister of Red Riding Hood, and I seemed to remind the sympathising Chimney Sweep by whom she was attended, of the Wolf.

The Magistrate was doubtful, Mr Uncommercial Traveller, whether this charge could be entertained. It was not known. Mr Uncommercial Traveller replied that he wished it were better known, and that, if he could afford the leisure, he would use his endeavours to make it so. There was no question about it, however, he contended. Here was the clause.

The clause was handed in, and more conference resulted. After which I was asked the extraordinary question: 'Mr Uncommercial, do you really wish this girl to be sent to prison?' To which I grimly answered, staring: 'If I didn't, why should I take the trouble to come here?' Finally, I was sworn, and gave my agreeable evidence in detail, and White Riding Hood was fined ten shillings, under the clause, or sent to prison for so many days. 'Why, Lord bless you, Sir,' said the Police-officer who showed me out, with a great enjoyment of the jest of her having been got up so effectively, and caused so much hesitation: 'If she goes to prison, that will be nothing new to *her*. She comes from Charles-street, Drury-lane!'

The Police, all things considered, are an excellent force, and I have borne my small testimony to their merits. Constabular contemplation is the result of a bad system; a system which is administered, not invented, by the man in constable's uniform, employed at twenty shillings a week. He has his orders, and would be marked for discouragement if he overstepped them. That the system is bad, there needs no lengthened argument to prove, because the fact is self-evident. If it were anything else, the results that have attended it, could not possibly have come to pass. Who will say that under a good system, our streets could have got into their present state?

The objection to the whole Police system, as concerning the Ruffian, may be stated, and its failure exemplified, as follows. It is well known that on all great occasions, when they come together in numbers, the mass of the English people are their own trustworthy Police. It is well known that wheresoever there is collected together any fair general representation of the people, a respect for law and order, and a determination to discountenance lawlessness and disorder, may be relied upon. As to one another, the people are a very good Police, and yet are quite willing in their good nature that the stipendiary Police should have the credit of the people's moderation. But we are all of us powerless against the Ruffian, because we submit to the law, and it is his only trade, by superior force and by violence, to defy it. Moreover, we are constantly admonished from high places (like so many Sunday-school children out for a holiday of buns and milk-and-water) that we are not to take the law into our own hands, but are to hand our defence over to it. It is clear that the common enemy to be punished and exterminated first of all, is the Ruffian. It is clear that he is, of all others, *the* offender for whose repressal we maintain a costly system of Police. Him, therefore, we expressly present to the Police to deal with, conscious that, on the whole, we can, and do, deal reasonably well with one another. Him the Police deal with so inefficiently and absurdly that he flourishes, and multiplies, and, with all his evil deeds upon his head as notoriously as his hat is, pervades the streets with no more let or hindrance than ourselves.

38

New Uncommercial Samples. By Charles Dickens. Aboard Ship

All The Year Round, 5 December 1868 (*UT2* as 'Aboard Ship')

The present article and the six which follow it comprise the final series of Uncommercial Traveller papers. Their general title, 'New Uncommercial Samples', indicates (as do Dickens's opening words below) that they are designed to complement the 'New Series' of *ATYR* which began publication on 5 December 1868 (see Introduction, p. xviii & n.).

Dickens left New York at the end of his exhausting final tour of public readings in America on 22 April, aboard the Cunard liner *Russia* and impressions of the voyage clearly provide material for the present item. A letter to W. H. Wills written on his return indicates that during the journey he began work on a piece of writing intended to form an introduction to the 'Christmas Number' of *ATYR* for 1868: 'I have begun something ... (aboard the American mail steamer) but I don't like it, because the stories must come limping in after the old fashion – though of course, what I *have* done will be good for A.Y.R.' (31 July 1868; *Nonesuch*, Vol. III, p. 661). In the event, there was no 'Christmas Number' in 1868, and assuming Dickens did make use of the fragment described above for *ATYR*, then the present article constitutes the most likely place (see note on MS below).

Before embarking, Dickens had taken an emotional farewell of many American friends, and his parody of Sterne (see literary allusions below) also involves a private joke shared with two of the closest: James T. Fields – here addressed as 'Eugenius' – and his wife, Annie. Following publication, Dickens wrote to Annie Fields, addressing her husband during the letter as '... my dear Eugenius', and trusting 'that you have recognised yourself in a certain Uncommercial, and also some small reference to a name rather dear to you?' (16 December 1868; *Nonesuch*, Vol. III, p. 687). Dickens suppresses all reference to his own ill-health and partial lameness on board the *Russia* in his account here, but, as his travelling companion George Dolby recalled, he was in fact obliged to 'keep his room' for the first three days of the voyage, and it was only 'on the fourth day [that] he was enabled to get a boot on his right foot' (*Charles Dickens as I Knew Him* [1885], p. 328).

Throughout November 1867 (the period of Dickens's 'passage out' to America, see p. 345 below), British troops under Sir Robert Napier were being prepared to march on Abyssinia (Ethiopia), where the British consul had been imprisoned, prompting Dickens's reference to the turn of British 'public events' on p. 346. The ensuing references to a 'savage boy' prince inspecting British Volunteers, and to an 'old screw' of a horse at the Crystal Palace, are not easy to trace to news stories, but may be connected with the state visit of the Turkish Sultan and family during July and August 1867. The Sultan's young son, Prince Youssouf Izzedin Effendi, had indeed become popular with the British public and had visited the Crystal Palace, while his father had inspected British Volunteers at Wimbledon, mounted on one of Queen Victoria's splendid Arab horses, though it seems unlikely that Dickens, even as satire, would refer to a Turkish prince as 'a poor young savage boy' (see *The Times* reports of 14 August, p. 9, col. f; 19 July, p. 12, col. d; 22 July, p. 5, col. c). The deliberately vague presentation of memories in the essay, and the distance of these events from the writing of the article, might account for the inconsistencies.

Literary allusions (p. 344) 'My salad-days, when I was green of visage and sea-sick': 'my salad days/When I was green in judgement,' Shakespeare, *Antony and Cleopatra*, Act 1, Scene 5; (p. 344) 'no coming event cast its shadow before': Thomas Campbell, 'Lochiel's Warning' (1803), l. 56; (p. 344) 'have imitated Sterne ... Eugenius was gone': parallels Parson Yorick's phrasing in Laurence Sterne's *Life and Adventures of Tristram Shandy* (1760–7) Vol. I, Ch. 12, Vol. VII, Ch. 1; (p. 346) 'grown-up brood of Giant Despair': John Bunyan, *The Pilgrim's Progress* (1678), Part 1; (p. 347) 'poisoned chalice': Shakespeare, *Macbeth*, Act 1, Sc. 7; (p. 347) 'as I lay, part of that day, in the Bay of New York, O': adapts the chorus of Andrew Cherry's song 'The Bay of Biscay O!' from John Davy's opera *Spanish Dollars* (1805);

(p. 348) 'had ceased from troubling': Job 3:17; (p. 351) 'the Miller and his Men': Isaac Pocock's melodrama (often adapted for toy theatre performance), *The Miller and His Men* (1813).

MS Draft fragment, British Library MS Add 56082. 1 page, numbered '11' ('... relief from a long strain' to '... in the theatre of our boyhood, and comporting'). Written in the present tense, and in an unsteady hand (105 deletions and 16 interpolations in circa 433 words), this section of MS was possibly drafted on board the *Russia* (see above). The only alteration between MS and copy-text is the substitution of 'Light' for the more technical 'Calf Light' to refer to the beacon of the port authorities at Queenstown.

My journeys as Uncommercial Traveller for the firm of Human Interest Brothers, have not slackened since I last reported of them, but have kept me continually on the move. I remain in the same idle employment. I never solicit an order, I never get any commission, I am the rolling stone that gathers no moss – unless any should by chance be found among these Samples.

Some half a year ago, I found myself in my idlest, dreamiest, and least accountable condition altogether, on board ship, in the harbour of the City of New York, in the United States of America. Of all the good ships afloat, mine was the good steam-ship RUSSIA, CAPTAIN COOK, Cunard Line, bound for Liverpool. What more could I wish for?

I had nothing to wish for, but a prosperous passage. My salad-days, when I was green of visage and sea-sick, being gone with better things (and no worse), no coming event cast its shadow before. I might, but a few moments previously, have imitated Sterne, and said, ' "And yet, methinks, Eugenius," – laying my forefinger wistfully on his coat-sleeve thus, – "and yet, methinks, Eugenius, 'tis but sorry work to part with thee, for what fresh fields * * * my dear Eugenius * * * can be fresher than thou art, and in what pastures new shall I find Eliza – or call her, Eugenius, if thou wilt, Annie" ' – I say I might have done this, but Eugenius was gone, and I hadn't done it.

I was resting on a skylight on the hurricane-deck, watching the working of the ship very slowly about, that she might head for England. It was high noon on a most brilliant day in April, and the beautiful bay was glorious and glowing. Full many a time, on shore there, had I seen the snow come down, down, down (itself like down), until it lay deep in all the ways of men, and particularly, as it seemed, in my way, for I had not gone dry-shod many hours for months. Within two or three days last past, had I watched the feathery fall setting in with the ardour of a new idea, instead of dragging at the skirts of a worn out winter, and permitting glimpses of a fresh young spring. But a bright sun and a clear sky had melted the snow in the great crucible of nature, and it had been poured out again that morning over sea and land, transformed into myriads of gold and silver sparkles.

The ship was fragrant with flowers. Something of the old Mexican passion for flowers may have gradually passed into North America, where flowers are luxuriously grown and tastefully combined in the richest profusion; but be that as it may, such gorgeous farewells in flowers had come on board, that the small Officer's Cabin on deck, which I tenanted, bloomed over into the adjacent scuppers, and banks of other flowers that it couldn't hold, made a garden of the unoccupied tables in the passengers' saloon. These delicious scents of the shore, mingling with the fresh airs of the sea, made the atmosphere a dreamy, an enchanting one. And so, with the watch aloft setting all the sails, and with the screw below revolving at a mighty rate, and occasionally giving the ship an angry shake for resisting, I fell into my idlest ways and lost myself.

As, for instance, whether it was I lying there, or some other entity even more mysterious, was a matter I was far too lazy to look into. What did it signify to me if it were I – or to the more mysterious entity – if it were he? Equally as to the remembrances that drowsily floated by me – or by him – why ask when, or where, the things happened? Was it not enough that they befel at some time, somewhere?

There was that assisting at the Church Service on board another steam-ship, one Sunday, in a stiff breeze. Perhaps on the passage out. No matter. Pleasant to hear the ship's bells go, as like church-bells as they could; pleasant to see the watch off duty mustered, and come in; best hats, best Guernseys, washed hands and faces, smoothed heads. But then arose a set of circumstances so rampantly comical, that no check which the gravest intentions could put upon them would hold them in hand. Thus the scene. Some seventy passengers assembled at the saloon tables. Prayerbooks on tables. Ship rolling heavily. Pause. No minister. Rumour has related that a modest young clergyman on board has responded to the captain's request that he will officiate. Pause again, and very heavy rolling. Closed double doors suddenly burst open, and two strong stewards skate in, supporting minister between them. General appearance as of somebody picked up, drunk and incapable, and under conveyance to station-house. Stoppage, pause, and particularly heavy rolling. Stewards watch their opportunity, and balance themselves, but cannot balance minister: who, struggling with a drooping head and a backward tendency, seems determined to return below, while they are as determined that he shall be got to the reading-desk in mid-saloon. Desk portable, sliding away down a long table, and aiming itself at the breasts of various members of the congregation. Here the double doors, which have been carefully closed by other stewards, fly open again, and worldly passenger tumbles in, seemingly with Pale Ale designs: who, seeking friend, says 'Joe!' Perceiving incongruity, says 'Hullo! Beg yer pardon!' and tumbles out again. All this time the congregation have been breaking up into sects – as the manner of congregations often is – each sect sliding away by itself, and all pounding the weakest sect which slid first into the corner. Utmost point of dissent soon attained in every corner, and violent rolling. Stewards at length make a dash; conduct minister to the mast in the centre of the saloon, which he embraces with both arms; skate out; and leave him in that condition to arrange affairs with flock.

There was another Sunday, when an officer of the ship read the Service. It was quiet and impressive, until we fell upon the dangerous and perfectly unnecessary experiment of striking up a hymn. After it was given out, we all rose, but everybody left it to somebody else to begin. Silence resulting, the officer (no singer himself) rather reproachfully gave us the first line again, upon which a rosy pippin of an old gentleman, remarkable throughout the passage for his cheerful politeness, gave a little stamp with his boot (as if he were leading off a country dance), and blithely warbled us into a show of joining. At the end of the first verse we became, through these tactics, so much refreshed and encouraged, that none of us, howsoever unmelodious, would submit to be left out of the second verse; while as to the third we lifted up our voices in a sacred howl that left it doubtful whether we were the more boastful of the sentiments we united in professing, or of professing them with a most discordant defiance of time, and tune.

'Lord bless us,' thought I, when the fresh remembrance of these things made me laugh heartily, alone in the dead water-gurgling waste of the night, what time I was wedged into my berth by a wooden bar, or I must have rolled out of it, 'what errand was I then upon, and to what Abyssinian point had public events then marched? No matter as to me. And as to them, if the wonderful popular rage for a plaything (utterly confounding in its inscrutable unreason) had not then lighted on a poor young savage boy, and a poor old screw of a horse, and hauled the first off by the hair of his princely head to "inspect" British volunteers, and hauled the second off by the hair of his equine tail to the Crystal Palace, why so much the better for all of us outside Bedlam!'

So, sticking to the ship, I was at the trouble of asking myself would I like to show the grog distribution in 'the fiddle' at noon to the Grand United Amalgamated Total Abstinence Society. Yes, I think I should. I think it would do them good to smell the rum, under the circumstances. Over the grog, mixed in a bucket, presides the boatswain's mate, small tin can in hand. Enter the crew, the guilty consumers, the grown up Brood of Giant Despair, in contradistinction to the Band of youthful angel Hope. Some in boots, some in leggings, some in tarpaulin overalls, some in frocks, some in pea-coats, a very few in jackets, most with sou' wester hats, all with something rough and rugged round the throat; all, dripping salt water where they stand; all pelted by weather, besmeared with grease, and blackened by the sooty rigging. Each man's knife in its sheath in his girdle, loosened for dinner. As the first man, with a knowingly-kindled eye, watches the filling of the poisoned chalice (truly but a very small tin mug, to be prosaic), and tossing back his head, tosses the contents into himself, and passes the empty chalice and passes on, so the second man with an anticipatory wipe of his mouth on sleeve or neck-kerchief, bides his turn, and drinks and hands, and passes on. In whom, and in each as his turn approaches, beams a knowingly-kindled eye, a brighter temper and a suddenly awakened tendency to be jocose with some shipmate. Nor do I even observe that the man in charge of the ship's lamps, who in right of his office has a double allowance of poisoned chalices, seems thereby vastly degraded, even though he empties the chalices into himself, one after the other, much as if he were delivering their contents at some absorbent establishment in which he had no personal interest. But vastly comforted I note them all to be, on deck presently, even to the circulation of redder blood in their cold blue knuckles; and when I look up at them lying out on the yards and holding on for life among the beating sails, I cannot for *my* life see the justice of visiting on them – or on me – the drunken crimes of any number of criminals arraigned at the heaviest of Assizes.

Abetting myself in my idle humour, I closed my eyes and recalled life on board of one of those mail packets, as I lay, part of that day, in the bay of New York O! The regular life began – mine always did, for I never got to sleep afterwards – with the rigging of the pump while it was yet dark, and washing down of decks. Any enormous giant at a prodigious hydropathic establishment, conscientiously undergoing the Water Cure in all its departments, and extremely particular about cleaning his teeth, would make those noises. Swash, splash, scrub, rub, toothbrush, bubble, swash, splash, bubble, toothbrush, splash, splash, bubble, rub. Then the day would break, and descending from my berth by a graceful ladder composed of half-opened drawers beneath it, I would reopen my outer deadlight and my inner sliding window (closed by a watchman during the Water Cure), and would look out at the long-rolling lead-coloured white-topped waves, over which the dawn, on a cold winter morning, cast a level lonely glance, and through which the ship fought her melancholy way at a terrific rate. And now, lying down again, awaiting the season for broiled ham and tea, I would be compelled to listen to the voice of conscience – the Screw.

It might be, in some cases, no more than the voice of Stomach, but I called it in my fancy by the higher name. Because, it seemed to me that we were all of us, all day long, endeavouring to stifle the Voice. Because, it was under everybody's pillow, everybody's plate, everybody's camp-stool, everybody's book, everybody's occupation. Because, we pretended not to hear it, especially at meal times, evening whist, and morning conversation on deck; but it was always among us in an under monotone, not to be drowned in pea soup, not to be shuffled with cards, not to be diverted by books, not to be knitted into any pattern, not to be walked away from. It was smoked in the weediest cigar, and drunk in the strongest cocktail; it was conveyed on deck at noon with limp ladies, who lay there in their wrappers until the stars shone; it waited at table with the stewards; nobody could put it out with the lights. It was considered (as on shore) ill bred to acknowledge the Voice of Conscience. It was not polite to mention it. One squally day an amiable gentleman in love gave much offence to a surrounding circle, including the object of his attachment, by saying of it, after it had goaded him over two easy chairs and a skylight: – 'Screw!'

Sometimes it would appear subdued. In fleeting moments when bubbles of champagne pervaded the nose, or when there was 'hot pot' in the bill of fare, or when an old dish we had had regularly every day was described in that official document by a new name. Under such excitements, one would almost believe it hushed. The ceremony of washing plates on deck, performed after every meal by a circle as of ringers of crockery triple-bob majors for a prize, would keep it down. Hauling the reel, taking the sun at noon, posting the twenty-four hours' run, altering the ship's time by the meridian, casting the waste food overboard, and attracting the eager gulls that followed in our wake; these events would suppress it for a while. But the instant any break or pause took place in any such diversion, the Voice would be at it again, importuning us to the last extent. A newly married young pair, who walked the deck affectionately some twenty miles per day, would, in the full flush of their exercise, suddenly become stricken by it, and stand trembling, but otherwise immovable, under its reproaches.

When this terrible monitor was most severe with us, was when the time approached for our retiring to our dens for the night. When the lighted candles in the saloon grew fewer and fewer. When the deserted glasses with spoons in them, grew more and more numerous. When waifs of toasted cheese, and strays of sardines fried in batter, slid languidly to and fro in the table-racks. When the man who always read had shut up his book, and blown out his candle. When the man who always talked, had ceased from troubling. When the man who was always medically reported as going to have delirium tremens, had put it off till tomorrow. When the man who every night devoted himself to a midnight smoke on deck, two hours in length, and who every night was in bed within ten minutes afterwards, was buttoning himself up in his third coat for his hardy vigil. For then, as we fell off one by one, and, entering our several hutches, came into a peculiar atmosphere of bilge water and Windsor soap, the Voice would shake us to the centre. Woe to us when we sat down on our sofa, watching the swinging candle for ever trying and retrying to stand upon his head, or our coat upon its peg imitating us as we appeared in our gymnastic days, by sustaining itself horizontally from the wall, in emulation of the lighter and more facile towels. Then would the Voice especially claim us for its prey and rend us all to pieces.

Lights out, we in our berths, and the wind rising, the Voice grows angrier and deeper. Under the mattress and under the pillow, under the sofa and under the washing stand, under the ship and under the sea, seeming to rise from the foundations under the earth with every scoop of the great Atlantic (and O why scoop so!), always the Voice. Vain to deny its existence in the night season; impossible to be hard of hearing; Screw, Screw, Screw. Sometimes it lifts out of the water, and revolves with a whirr, like a ferocious firework – except that it never expends itself, but is always ready to go off again; sometimes it seems to be anguish and shivers; sometimes it seems to be terrified by its last plunge, and has a fit which causes it to struggle, quiver, and for an instant stop. And now the ship sets in rolling, as only ships so fiercely screwed through time and space, day and night, fair weather and foul, *can* roll. Did she ever take a roll before, like that last? Did she ever take a roll before, like this worse one that is coming now? Here is the partition at my ear, down in the deep on the lee side. Are we ever coming up again together? I think not; the partition and I are so long about it that I really do believe we have overdone it this time. Heavens, what a scoop! What a deep scoop, what a hollow scoop, what a long scoop! Will it ever end, and can we bear the heavy mass of water we have taken on board, and which has let loose all the table furniture in the officers' mess, and has beaten open the door of the little passage between the purser and me, and is swashing about even there and even here? The purser snores reassuringly, and the ship's bells striking, I hear the cheerful 'All's well!' of the watch musically given back the length of the deck as the lately diving partition, now high in air, tries (unsoftened by what we have gone through together) to force me out of bed and berth.

'All's well!' Comforting to know, though surely all might be better. Put aside the rolling, and the rush of water, and think of darting through such darkness with such velocity. Think of any other similar object coming in the opposite direction! Whether there may be an attraction in two such moving bodies out at sea, which may help accident to bring them into collision? Thoughts too arise (the Voice never silent all the while, but marvellously suggestive) of the gulf below; of the strange unfruitful mountain ranges and deep valleys over which we are passing; of monstrous fish, midway; of the ship's suddenly altering her course on her own account, and with a wild plunge settling down, and making *that* voyage with a crew of dead discoverers. Now, too, one recalls an almost universal tendency on the part of passengers to stumble, at some time or other in the day, on the topic of a certain large steamer making this same run, which was lost at sea and never heard of more. Everybody has seemed under a spell, compelling approach to the threshold of the grim subject, stoppage, discomfiture, and pretence of never having been near it. The boatswain's whistle sounds! A change in the wind, hoarse orders issuing, and the watch very busy. Sails come crashing home overhead, ropes (that seem all knot) ditto; every man engaged appears to have twenty feet, with twenty times the average amount of stamping power in each. Gradually the noise slackens, the hoarse cries die away, the boatswain's whistle softens into the soothing and contented notes, which rather reluctantly admit that the job is done for the time, and the Voice sets in again. Thus come unintelligible dreams of up hill and down hill, and swinging and swaying, until consciousness revives of atmospherical Windsor soap and bilge water, and the Voice announces that the giant has come for the Water Cure again.

Such were my fanciful reminiscences as I lay, part of that day, in the Bay, of New York O! Also, as we passed clear of the Narrows and got out to sea; also, in many an idle hour at sea in sunny weather. At length the observations and computations showed that we should make the coast of Ireland tonight. So I stood watch on deck all night tonight, to see how we made the coast of Ireland.

Very dark, and the sea most brilliantly phosphorescent. Great way on the ship, and double look-out kept. Vigilant captain on the bridge, vigilant first officer looking over the port side, vigilant second officer standing by the quarter-master at the compass, vigilant third officer posted at the stern-rail with a lantern. No passengers on the quiet decks, but expectation everywhere nevertheless. The two men at the wheel, very steady, very serious, and very prompt to answer orders. An order issued sharply now and then, and echoed back; otherwise the night drags slowly, silently, and with no change. All of a sudden, at the blank hour of two in the morning, a vague movement of relief from a long strain expresses itself in all hands; the third officer's lantern twinkles, and he fires a rocket, and another rocket. A sullen solitary light is pointed out to me in the black sky yonder. A change is expected in the Light, but none takes place. 'Give them two more rockets, Mr Vigilant.' Two more, and a blue light burnt. All eyes watch the light again. At last a little toy sky-rocket is flashed up from it, and even as that small streak in the darkness dies away, we are telegraphed to Queenstown, Liverpool, and London, and back again under the Ocean to America.

Then, up come the half-dozen passengers who are going ashore at Queenstown, and up comes the Mail-Agent in charge of the bags, and up come the men who are to carry the bags into the Mail Tender that will come off for them out of the harbour. Lamps and lanterns gleam here and there about the decks, and impeding bulks are knocked away with handspikes, and the port-side bulwark, barren but a moment ago, bursts into a crop of heads of seamen, stewards, and engineers. The light begins to be gained upon, begins to be alongside, begins to be left astern. More rockets, and, between us and the land, steams beautifully the Inman steam-ship City of Paris, for New York, outward bound. We observe with complacency that the wind is dead against her (it being *with* us), and that she rolls and pitches. (The sickest passenger on board is the most delighted by this circumstance.) Time rushes by, as we rush on, and now we see the light in Queenstown Harbour, and now the lights of the Mail Tender coming out to us. What vagaries the Mail Tender performs on the way, in every point of the compass, especially in those where she has no business, and why she performs them, Heaven only knows! At length she is seen plunging within a cable's length of our port broadside, and is being roared at through our speaking trumpets to do this thing, and not to do that, and to stand by the other, as if she were a very demented Tender indeed. Then, we slackening amidst a deafening roar of steam, this much-abused Tender is made fast to us by hawsers, and the men in readiness carry the bags aboard, and return for more, bending under their burdens, and looking just like the pasteboard figures of the Miller and his Men in the Theatre of our boyhood, and comporting themselves almost as unsteadily. All the while, the unfortunate Tender plunges high and low, and is roared at. Then the Queenstown passengers are put on board of her, with infinite plunging and roaring, and the Tender gets heaved up on the sea to that surprising extent, that she looks within an ace of washing aboard of us, high and dry. Roared at with contumely to the last, this wretched Tender is at length let go, with a final plunge of great ignominy, and falls spinning into our wake.

The Voice of conscience resumed its dominion, as the day climbed up the sky, and kept by all of us passengers into port. Kept by us as we passed other lighthouses, and dangerous islands off the coast, where some of the officers, with whom I stood my watch, had gone ashore in sailing ships in fogs (and of which by that token they seem to have quite an affectionate remembrance), and past the Welsh coast, and past the Cheshire coast, and past everything and everywhere lying between our ship and her own special dock in the Mersey. Off which, at last, at nine of the clock, on a fair evening early in May, we stopped, and the Voice ceased. A very curious sensation, not unlike having my own ears stopped, ensued upon that silence, and it was with a no less curious sensation that I went over the side of the good Cunard ship Russia (whom Prosperity attend through all her voyages!), and surveyed the outer hull of the gracious monster that the Voice had inhabited. So, perhaps, shall we all, in the spirit, one day survey the frame that held the busier Voice, from which my vagrant fancy derived this similitude.

39

New Uncommercial Samples. By Charles Dickens. A Small Star in the East

All The Year Round, 19 December 1868 (*UT2* as 'A Small Star in the East')

The electioneering described in the present item relates to the campaign which led to the resounding Liberal victory in the general election of November 1868, following which Disraeli resigned as Prime Minister on 2 December and Gladstone formed his first ministry, with Lord Clarendon as Foreign Secretary and Robert Lowe as Chancellor. In 1841 Dickens had acquired Douce and Pickering's edition of *The Dance of Death* containing reproductions of famous wood engravings by Hans Holbein first published in 1538, and an essay on the different treatments the subject had received (Stonehouse; *Pilgrim*, Vol. II, p. 229n.). The images, showing men of every condition being led in a dance to the grave by Death in a variety of disguises, had always impressed Dickens greatly and he makes many references to the idea in his writings.

In the same letter to Annie and James Fields cited in the headnote to article 38, Dickens observed:

> As an instance of how strangely something comic springs up in the midst of the direst misery, look to a succeeding Uncommercial, called A Small Star in the East, published today, by-the-bye. I have described, *with exactness*, the poor places into which I went, and how the people behaved, and what they said. I was wretched, looking on; and yet the boiler-maker and the poor man with the legs filled me with a sense of drollery not to be kept down by any pressure.
> [16 December 1868; *Nonesuch*, Vol. III, p. 687]

As George F. Young has reported, these visits were not made at random, but under the direction of Nathaniel Heckford, the doctor in charge of the hospital which is described later in the essay (see Young's 'A Small Star in the East in Three Twinkles', *The Dickensian*, Vol. 30 [1934], pp. 286–91). After showing Dickens over the site, Heckford took him to inspect the houses of certain out-patients of the hospital, including that of the sufferer from white lead poisoning described below (p. 355). An employer's record, preserved by the successors of the firm of white lead manufacturers mentioned, identifies the nameless Irish family: 'Mrs Crawford, 1 Ratcliff Cross, living with her mother, Mary Hurley – has four children. Sister, Mary Hurley, has been here 3 years on and off at 10/- a week. Was ill 6 weeks with lead poisoning and was attended by Dr Rogers, M.O., and Dr Heckford.'

Heckford had married Sarah Goff on 28 January 1867 and, using her capital, had bought premises at Old Ratcliff Cross (now Narrow Street, E14) for £2,000, which were opened exactly a year later as 'The East London Hospital for Children and Dispensary for Women'. On Heckford's premature death of consumption in 1871, his widow left England for a new life among the Boers in the Transvaal, and the hospital was carried on by a Committee of Management until 1875, when it moved to Glamis Road, Shadwell (renamed the Princess Elizabeth of York Hospital in the 1930s, it merged with the Queen's Hospital, Hackney Road, in 1942, and moved to that site).

In an account of the early years of the hospital, Heckford's widow recalled that by the last post on the day Dickens's essay was published in *ATYR*, her husband received a letter stating that 'Mamma has just read to me the story of your hospital. I am only a little girl of six, but I would like to give the contents of my money-box for your little children.' This was 'the poetical beginning of an influx of money and other help. ... The next day, and for long after, letters flowed in' (Sarah Heckford, 'Story of the East London Hospital for Children', intro. to *Voluntaries for an East London Children's Hospital* by the Earl of Lytton et al. [1887], pp. xxvii–xxviii). Over nine months later, Dickens was still re-directing enquiries from prospective donors (see *Nonesuch*, Vol. III, p. 740), and his interest in the hospital remained lively. When James and Annie Fields visited him at Gad's Hill the following year, he took them to see it, as Annie recorded in a book of memoranda published under her late husband's name:

Friday [14 May 1869], he came at half-past ten A.M. to go to the hospital, bringing with him some small alleviations for colds, with recipes. Started promptly. ... Dickens was perfectly at home in this part of London. He was full of interest in the young physician and his wife ... who looked upon him as one of their best friends. It was evidently always [their] gala day when he arrived. He could not say enough to express his admiration for the simple reverent earnestness of their lives. 'How they bear it,' he said, 'I cannot imagine. I wish you could have seen,' he continued, 'the little child I wrote of, who died afterward, so exquisite in beauty and so patient.... Certainly there is nothing more touching than the suffering of a child, nothing more overwhelming.' The doctor carried us, before our return, into one of the poor-houses in the neighborhood. A mother, father, & seven children in one room! [J. T. Fields, *Biographical Notes and Personal Sketches &c.* (1881), pp. 173–4]

Literary allusions (below) 'hewers of wood and drawers of water': Joshua 9:21; (p. 359) 'when Mrs Fitzwilliam was the friend of Victorine': J. B. Buckstone's highly popular melodrama *Victorine; or 'I'll Sleep on it'* was first performed at the Adelphi Theatre in December 1831 with Mrs Fitzwilliam starring; (p. 364) 'An affecting play ... acted in Paris years ago, called The Children's Doctor ... the Paris artist's ideal': Messrs Anicet-Bourgeois and A. Dennery's *Le Médecin Des Enfants* (1855), seen by Dickens in Paris in April 1856, with M. Laferrière as the doctor, Lucien Lemonier, and Eugène Bignon as M. Delormel (repr. in *Le Théâtre Contemporain*, 1856).

I had been looking, yesternight, through the famous Dance of Death, and today the grim old woodcuts arose in my mind with the new significance of a ghastly monotony not to be found in the original. The weird skeleton rattled along the streets before me, and struck fiercely, but it was never at the pains of assuming a disguise. It played on no dulcimer here, was crowned with no flowers, waved no plume, minced in no flowing robe or train, lifted no wine-cup, sat at no feast, cast no dice, counted no gold. It was simply a bare, gaunt, famished skeleton, slaying his way along.

The borders of Ratcliffe and Stepney, Eastward of London, and giving on the impure river, were the scene of this uncompromising Dance of Death, upon a drizzling November day. A squalid maze of streets, courts, and alleys of miserable houses let out in single rooms. A wilderness of dirt, rags, and hunger. A mud-desert chiefly inhabited by a tribe from whom employment has departed, or to whom it comes but fitfully and rarely. They are not skilled mechanics in any wise. They are but labourers. Dock labourers, waterside labourers, coal porters, ballast heavers, such like hewers of wood and drawers of water. But they have come into existence, and they propagate their wretched race.

One grisly joke alone, methought, the skeleton seemed to play off here. It had stuck Election Bills on the walls, which the wind and rain had deteriorated into suitable rags. It had even summed up the state of the poll, in chalk, on the shutters of one ruined house. It adjured the free and independent starvers to vote for Thisman and vote for Thatman; not to plump, as they valued the state of parties and the national prosperity (both of great importance to them, I think!), but, by returning Thisman and Thatman, each nought without the other, to compound a glorious and immortal whole. Surely the skeleton is nowhere more cruelly ironical in the original monkish idea!

Pondering in my mind the far-seeing schemes of Thisman and Thatman, and of the public blessing called Party, for staying the degeneracy, physical and moral, of many thousands (who shall say how many?) of the English race; for devising employment useful to the community, for those who want but to work and live; for equalising rates, cultivating waste lands, facilitating emigration, and above all things, saving and utilising the oncoming generations, and thereby changing ever-growing national weakness into strength; pondering in my mind, I say, these hopeful exertions, I turned down a narrow street to look into a house or two.

It was a dark street with a dead wall on one side. Nearly all the outer doors of the houses stood open. I took the first entry, and knocked at a parlour door. Might I come in? I might, if I plased, Sur.

The woman of the room (Irish) had picked up some long strips of wood, about some wharf or barge, and they had just now been thrust into the otherwise empty grate, to make two iron pots boil. There was some fish in one, and there were some potatoes in the other. The flare of the burning wood enabled me to see a table and a broken chair or so, and some old cheap crockery ornaments about the chimneypiece. It was not until I had spoken with the woman a few minutes that I saw a horrible brown heap on the floor in a corner, which, but for previous experience in this dismal wise, I might not have suspected to be 'the bed.' There was something thrown upon it; and I asked what that was?

' 'Tis the poor craythur that stays here, Sur; and 'tis very bad she is, and 'tis very bad she's been this long time, and 'tis better she'll never be, and 'tis slape she doos all day, and 'tis wake she doos all night, and 'tis the lead, Sur.'

'The what?'

'The lead, Sur. Sure 'tis the lead-mills, where the women gets took on at eighteen-pence a day, Sur, when they makes applicaytion early enough and is lucky and wanted, and 'tis lead-pisoned she is, Sur, and some of them gits lead-pisoned soon and some of them gets lead-pisoned later, and some but not many niver, and 'tis all according to the constitooshun, Sur, and some constitooshuns is strong and some is weak; and her constitooshun is lead-pisoned, bad as can be, Sur; and her brain is coming out at her ear, and it hurts her dreadful, and that's what it is and niver no more and niver no less, Sur.'

The sick young woman moaning here, the speaker bent over her, took a bandage from her head, and threw open a back door to let in the daylight upon it, from the smallest and most miserable backyard I ever saw.

'That's what cooms from her, Sur, being lead-pisoned, and it cooms from her night and day the poor sick craythur, and the pain of it is dreadful, and God he knows that my husband has walked the sthreets these four days being a labourer and is walking them now and is ready to work and no work for him and no fire and no food but the bit in the pot, and no more than ten shillings in a fortnight, God be good to us, and it is poor we are and dark it is and could it is indeed!'

Knowing that I could compensate myself thereafter for my self-denial, if I saw fit, I had resolved that I would give nothing in the course of these visits. I did this to try the people. I may state at once that my closest observation could not detect any indication whatever of an expectation that I would give money; they were grateful to be talked to about their miserable affairs, and sympathy was plainly a comfort to them; but they neither asked for money in any case, nor showed the least trace of surprise or disappointment or resentment at my giving none.

The woman's married daughter had by this time come down from her room on the floor above, to join in the conversation. She herself had been to the lead-mills very early that morning to be 'took on,' but had not succeeded. She had four children, and her husband, also a water-side labourer and then out seeking work, seemed in no better case as to finding it, than her father. She was English, and by nature of a buxom figure and cheerful. Both in her poor dress, and in her mother's, there was an effort to keep up some appearance of neatness. She knew all about the sufferings of the unfortunate invalid, and all about the lead-poisoning, and how the symptoms came on, and how they grew: having often seen them. The very smell, when you stood inside the door of the works, was enough to knock you down, she said, yet she was going back again to get 'took on.' What could she do? Better be ulcerated and paralysed for eighteenpence a day, while it lasted, than see the children starve.

A dark and squalid cupboard in this room, touching the back door and all manner of offence, had been for some time the sleeping-place of the sick young woman. But the nights being now wintry, and the blankets and coverlets 'gone to the leaving shop,' she lay all night where she lay all day, and was lying then. The woman of the room, her husband, this most miserable patient, and two others, lay on the one brown heap together for warmth.

'God bless you, sir, and thank you!' were the parting words from these people – gratefully spoken too – with which I left this place.

Some streets away, I tapped at another parlour door on another ground floor. Looking in, I found a man, his wife, and four children, sitting at a washing stool by way of table, at their dinner of bread and infused tea-leaves. There was a very scanty cinderous fire in the grate by which they sat, and there was a tent bedstead in the room with a bed upon it and a coverlet. The man did not rise when I went in, nor during my stay, but civilly inclined his head on my pulling off my hat, and, in answer to my inquiry whether I might ask him a question or two, said, 'Certainly.' There being a window at each end of this room, back and front, it might have been ventilated; but it was shut up tight, to keep the cold out, and was very sickening.

The wife, an intelligent quick woman, rose and stood at her husband's elbow, and he glanced up at her as if for help. It soon appeared that he was rather deaf. He was a slow simple fellow of about thirty.

'What was he by trade?'

'Gentleman asks what are you by trade, John?'

'I am a boiler-maker;' looking about him with an exceedingly perplexed air, as if for a boiler that had unaccountably vanished.

'He ain't a mechanic, you understand, sir,' the wife put in, 'he's only a labourer.'

'Are you in work?'

He looked up at his wife again. 'Gentleman says are you in work, John?'

'In work!' cried this forlorn boiler-maker, staring aghast at his wife, and then working his vision's way very slowly round to me; 'Lord, no!'

'Ah! He ain't indeed!' said the poor woman, shaking her head, as she looked at the four children in succession, and then at him.

'Work!' said the boiler-maker, still seeking that evaporated boiler, first in my countenance, then in the air, and then in the features of his second son at his knee: 'I wish I *was* in work! I haven't had more than a day's work to do, this three weeks.'

'How have you lived?'

A faint gleam of admiration lighted up the face of the would-be boiler-maker, as he stretched out the short sleeve of his threadbare canvas jacket, and replied, pointing her out, 'On the work of the wife.'

I forget where boiler-making had gone to, or where he supposed it had gone to; but he added some resigned information on that head, coupled with an expression of his belief that it was never coming back.

The cheery helpfulness of the wife was very remarkable. She did slop-work; made pea-jackets. She produced the pea-jacket then in hand, and spread it out upon the bed: the only piece of furniture in the room on which to spread it. She showed how much of it she made, and how much was afterwards finished off by the machine. According to her calculation at the moment, deducting what her trimming cost her, she got for making a pea-jacket tenpence halfpenny, and she could make one in something less than two days. But, you see, it come to her through two hands, and of course it didn't come through the second hand for nothing. Why did it come through the second hand at all? Why, this way. The second hand took the risk of the given-out work, you see. If she had money enough to pay the security deposit – call it two pound – she could get the work from the first hand, and so the second would not have to be deducted for. But having no money at all, the second hand come in and took its profit, and so the whole worked down to tenpence halfpenny. Having explained all this with great intelligence, even with some little pride, and without a whine or murmur, she folded her work again, sat down by her husband's side at the washing stool, and resumed her dinner of dry bread. Mean as the meal was, on the bare board, with its old gallipots for cups, and what not other sordid makeshifts; shabby as the woman was in dress, and toning down towards the Bosjesman colour, with want of nutriment and washing; there was positively a dignity in her, as the family anchor just holding the poor shipwrecked boiler-maker's bark. When I left the room, the boiler-maker's eyes were slowly turned towards her, as if his last hope of ever again seeing that vanished boiler lay in her direction.

These people had never applied for parish relief but once; and that was when the husband met with a disabling accident at his work.

Not many doors from here, I went into a room on the first floor. The woman apologised for its being in 'an untidy mess.' The day was Saturday, and she was boiling the children's clothes in a saucepan on the hearth. There was nothing else into which she could have put them. There was no crockery, or tinware, or tub, or bucket. There was an old gallipot or two, and there was a broken bottle or so, and there were some broken boxes for seats. The last small scraping of coals left, was raked together in a corner of the floor. There were some rags in an open cupboard, also on the floor. In a corner of the room was a crazy old French bedstead, with a man lying on his back upon it in a ragged pilot jacket, and rough oilskin fantail hat. The room was perfectly black. It was difficult to believe, at first, that it was not purposely coloured black: the walls were so begrimed.

As I stood opposite the woman boiling the children's clothes, – she had not even a piece of soap to wash them with – and apologising for her occupation, I could take in all these things without appearing to notice them, and could even correct my inventory. I had missed, at the first glance, some half a pound of bread in the otherwise empty safe, an old red ragged crinoline hanging on the handle of the door by which I had entered, and certain fragments of rusty iron scattered on the floor, which looked like broken tools and a piece of stove-pipe. A child stood looking on. On the box nearest to the fire sat two younger children; one, a delicate and pretty little creature whom the other sometimes kissed.

This woman, like the last, was woefully shabby, and was degenerating to the Bosjesman complexion. But her figure, and the ghost of a certain vivacity about her, and the spectre of a dimple in her cheek, carried my memory strangely back to the old days of the Adelphi Theatre, London, when Mrs Fitzwilliam was the friend of Victorine.

'May I ask you what your husband is?'

'He's a coal porter, sir.' With a glance and a sigh towards the bed.

'Is he out of work?'

'Oh yes, sir, and work's at all times very very scanty with him, and now he's laid up.'

'It's my legs,' said the man upon the bed, 'I'll unroll 'em.' And immediately began.

'Have you any older children?'

'I have a daughter that does the needlework, and I have a son that does what he can. She's at her work now, and he's trying for work.'

'Do they live here?'

'They sleep here. They can't afford to pay more rent, and so they come here at night. The rent is very hard upon us. It's rose upon us, too, now – sixpence a week – on account of these new changes in the law, about the rates. We are a week behind; the landlord's been shaking and rattling at that door, frightful; he says he'll turn us out. I don't know what's to come of it.'

The man upon the bed ruefully interposed: 'Here's my legs. The skin's broke, besides the swelling. I have had a many kicks, working, one way and another.'

He looked at his legs (which were much discoloured and misshapen) for a while, and then appearing to remember that they were not popular with his family, rolled them up again, as if they were something in the nature of maps or plans that were not wanted to be referred to, lay hopelessly down on his back once more with his fantail hat over his face, and stirred not.

'Do your eldest son and daughter sleep in that cupboard?'

'Yes,' replied the woman.

'With the children?'

'Yes. We have to get together for warmth. We have little to cover us.'

'Have you nothing by you to eat but the piece of bread I see there?'

'Nothing. And we had the rest of the loaf for our breakfast, with water. I don't know what's to come of it.'

'Have you no prospect of improvement?'

'If my eldest son earns anything today, he'll bring it home. Then we shall have something to eat tonight, and may be able to do something towards the rent. If not, I don't know what's to come of it.'

'This is a sad state of things.'

'Yes, sir; it's a hard, hard life. Take care of the stairs as you go sir – they're broken – and good day, sir!'

These people had a mortal dread of entering the workhouse, and received no out-of-door relief.

In another room in still another tenement, I found a very decent woman with five children – the last, a baby, and she herself a patient of the parish doctor – to whom, her husband being in the Hospital, the Union allowed for the support of herself and family, four shillings a week and five loaves. I suppose when Thisman, M.P., and Thatman, M.P., and the public blessing Party, lay their heads together in course of time, and come to an Equalisation of Rating, she may go down the Dance of Death to the tune of sixpence more.

I could enter no other houses for that one while, for I could not bear the contemplation of the children. Such heart as I had summoned to sustain me against the miseries of the adults, failed me when I looked at the children. I saw how young they were, how hungry, how serious and still. I thought of them, sick and dying in those lairs. I could think of them dead, without anguish; but to think of them, so suffering and so dying, quite unmanned me.

Down by the river's bank in Ratcliffe, I was turning upward by a side street, therefore, to regain the railway, when my eyes rested on the inscription across the road, 'East London Children's Hospital.' I could scarcely have seen an inscription better suited to my frame of mind; and I went across and went straight in.

I found the Children's Hospital established in an old sail-loft or storehouse, of the roughest nature, and on the simplest means. There were trap-doors in the floors where goods had been hoisted up and down; heavy feet and heavy weights had started every knot in the well-trodden planking; inconvenient bulks and beams and awkward staircases perplexed my passage through the wards. But I found it airy, sweet, and clean. In its seven-and-thirty beds I saw but little beauty, for starvation in the second or third generation takes a pinched look; but I saw the sufferings both of infancy and childhood tenderly assuaged, I heard the little patients answering to pet playful names, the light touch of a delicate lady laid bare the wasted sticks of arms for me to pity; and the claw-like little hands, as she did so, twined themselves lovingly around her wedding-ring.

One baby mite there was, as pretty as any of Raphael's angels. The tiny head was bandaged, for water on the brain, and it was suffering with acute bronchitis too, and made from time to time a plaintive, though not impatient or complaining little sound. The smooth curve of the cheeks and of the chin was faultless in its condensation of infantine beauty, and the large bright eyes were most lovely. It happened, as I stopped at the foot of the bed, that these eyes rested upon mine, with that wistful expression of wondering thoughtfulness which we all know sometimes in very little children. They remained fixed on mine, and never turned from me while I stood there. When the utterance of that plaintive sound shook the little form, the gaze still remained unchanged. I felt as though the child implored me to tell the story of the little hospital in which it was sheltered, to any gentle heart I could address. Laying my world-worn hand upon the little unmarked clasped hand at the chin, I gave it a silent promise that I would do so.

A gentleman and lady, a young husband and wife, have bought and fitted up this building for its present noble use, and have quietly settled themselves in it as its medical officers and directors. Both have had considerable practical experience of medicine and surgery; he, as house-surgeon of a great London Hospital; she, as a very earnest student, tested by severe examination, and also as a nurse of the sick poor, during the prevalence of cholera. With every qualification to lure them away, with youth and accomplishments and tastes and habits that can have no response in any breast near them, close begirt by every repulsive circumstance inseparable from such a neighbourhood, there they dwell. They live in the Hospital itself, and their rooms are on its first floor. Sitting at their dinner table, they could hear the cry of one of the children in pain. The lady's piano, drawing materials, books, and other such evidences of refinement, are as much a part of the rough place as the iron bedsteads of the little patients. They are put to shifts for room, like passengers on board ship. The dispenser of medicines (attracted to them, not by self-interest, but by their own magnetism and that of their cause) sleeps in a recess in the dining-room, and has his washing apparatus in the sideboard.

Their contented manner of making the best of the things around them, I found so pleasantly inseparable from their usefulness! Their pride in this partition that we put up ourselves, or in that partition that we took down, or in that other partition that we moved, or in the stove that was given us for the waiting-room, or in our nightly conversion of the little consulting-room into a smoking-room! Their admiration of the situation, if we could only get rid of its one objectionable incident, the coal-yard at the back! 'Our hospital carriage, presented by a friend, and very useful.' That was my presentation to a perambulator, for which a coach-house had been discovered in a corner downstairs, just large enough to hold it. Coloured prints in all stages of preparation for being added to those already decorating the wards, were plentiful; a charming wooden phenomenon of a bird, with an impossible top-knot, who ducked his head when you set a counter weight going, had been inaugurated as a public statue that very morning; and trotting about among the beds, on familiar terms with all the patients, was a comical mongrel dog, called Poodles. This comical dog (quite a tonic in himself) was found characteristically starving at the door of the Institution, and was taken in and fed, and has lived here ever since. An admirer of his mental endowments has presented him with a collar bearing the legend, 'Judge not Poodles by external appearances.' He was merrily wagging his tail on a boy's pillow when he made this modest appeal to me.

When this Hospital was first opened in January of the present year, the people could not possibly conceive but that somebody paid for the services rendered there; and were disposed to claim them as a right, and to find fault if out of temper. They soon came to understand the case better, and have much increased in gratitude. The mothers of the patients avail themselves very freely of the visiting rules; the fathers, often on Sundays. There is an unreasonable (but still, I think, touching and intelligible) tendency in the parents to take a child away to its wretched home, if on the point of death. One boy who had been thus carried off on a rainy night, when in a violent state of inflammation, and who had been afterwards brought back, had been recovered with exceeding difficulty; but he was a jolly boy, with a specially strong interest in his dinner, when I saw him.

Insufficient food and unwholesome living are the main causes of disease among these small patients. So, nourishment, cleanliness, and ventilation, are the main remedies. Discharged patients are looked after, and invited to come and dine now and then; so are certain famishing creatures who were never patients. Both the lady and the gentleman are well acquainted, not only with the histories of the patients and their families, but with the characters and circumstances of great numbers of their neighbours: of these they keep a register. It is their common experience that people sinking down by inches into deeper and deeper poverty, will conceal it, even from them, if possible, unto the very last extremity.

The nurses of this Hospital are all young; ranging, say, from nineteen to four-and-twenty. They have, even within these narrow limits, what many well-endowed Hospitals would not give them: a comfortable room of their own in which to take their meals. It is a beautiful truth that interest in the children and sympathy with their sorrows, bind these young women to their places far more strongly than any other con-sideration could. The best skilled of the nurses came originally from a kindred neighbourhood, almost as poor, and she knew how much the

Poodles Going the Round

work was needed. She is a fair dressmaker. The Hospital cannot pay her as many pounds in the year as there are months in it, and one day the lady regarded it as a duty to speak to her about her improving her prospects and following her trade. No, she said; she could never be so useful, or so happy, elsewhere, any more; she must stay among the children. And she stays. One of the nurses, as I passed her, was washing a baby-boy. Liking her pleasant face, I stopped to speak to her charge: a common, bullet-headed, frowning charge enough, laying hold of his own nose with a slippery grasp, and staring very solemnly out of a blanket. The melting of the pleasant face into delighted smiles as this young gentleman gave an unexpected kick and laughed at me, was almost worth my previous pain.

An affecting play was acted in Paris years ago, called The Children's Doctor. As I parted from my Children's Doctor now in question, I saw in his easy black necktie, in his loose buttoned black frock coat, in his pensive face, in the flow of his dark hair, in his eyelashes, in the very turn of his moustache, the exact realisation of the Paris artist's ideal as it was presented on the stage. But no romancer that I know of, has had the boldness to prefigure the life and home of this young husband and young wife, in the Children's Hospital in the East of London.

I came away from Ratcliffe by the Stepney railway station to the Terminus at Fenchurch-street. Anyone who will reverse that route, may retrace my steps.

40

New Uncommercial Samples. By Charles Dickens. A Little Dinner in an Hour

All The Year Round, 2 January 1869 (*UT2* as 'A Little Dinner in an Hour')

Dickens had been in Paris in early June 1868, staying at the Hôtel du Helder prior to the opening night at the Vaudeville of his play *No Thoroughfare*, co-written with Wilkie Collins. There is no record of his visiting Paris during the autumn, however; nor is there strong reason to suppose that the present article is based on any particular episode of Dickens's experience. T. W. Hill suggests that Namelesston, with its 'ancient dandies ... from the time of George the Fourth', may be a depiction of Brighton (originally, 'Brighthelmstone'), which owed its fashionable reputation to the patronage of George IV, when Prince Regent (Hill, 32.6). In earlier essays, Dickens had attacked the poor standards of service and cuisine in British refreshment houses and contrasted them unfavourably with the excellence of French provision (see article 9 above, and article 4 of Vol. 3 of this edition). Here, he chooses for the name of the shabby hotel that has lost its former glory that of the elderly 'First Rate' warship HMS *Temeraire*, one of the 'wooden walls' of England which had seen service at Trafalgar in 1805.

Literary allusions (p. 366) 'began to babble of green geese': Falstaff 'babbled of green fields' on his deathbed in Shakespeare, *King Henry V*, Act 2, Sc. 3; (p. 367) 'set our own stomachs on a cast ... hazard of the die': 'I have set my life upon a cast,/And I will stand the hazard of the die', Shakespeare, *Richard III*, Act 5, Sc. 4; (p. 368) 'out at the portal': Shakespeare, *Hamlet*, Act 3, Sc. 4; (p. 369 et seq.) 'Mr Indignation Cocker': the surname ironically recalling that of Edward Cocker, arithmetician and author of a much-reprinted textbook (1664).

MS Draft fragment, Robert H. Taylor Collection, Princeton University Library. 1 page, numbered six, showing c. 56 deletions and 34 interpolations in a text of some 360 words.

It fell out on a day in this last autumn that I had to go down from London to a place of sea-side resort, on an hour's business, accompanied by my esteemed friend Bullfinch. Let the place of sea-side resort be, for the nonce, called Namelesston.

I had been loitering about Paris in very hot weather, pleasantly breakfasting in the open air in the garden of the Palais Royal or the Tuileries, pleasantly dining in the open air in the Elysian Fields, pleasantly taking my cigar and lemonade in the open air on the Italian Boulevard towards the small hours after midnight. Bullfinch – an excellent man of business – had summoned me back across the Channel, to transact this said hour's business at Namelesston, and thus it fell out that Bullfinch and I were in a railway carriage together on our way to Namelesston, each with his return ticket in his waistcoat pocket.

Says Bullfinch: 'I have a proposal to make. Let us dine at the Temeraire.'

I asked Bullfinch, did he recommend the Temeraire? Inasmuch as I had not been rated on the books of the Temeraire for many years.

Bullfinch declined to accept the responsibility of recommending the Temeraire, but on the whole was rather sanguine about it. He 'seemed to remember,' Bullfinch said, that he had dined well there. A plain dinner but good. Certainly not like a Parisian dinner (here Bullfinch obviously became the prey of want of confidence), but of its kind very fair.

I appealed to Bullfinch's intimate knowledge of my wants and ways, to decide whether I was usually ready to be pleased with any dinner, or – for the matter of that – with anything, that was fair of its kind and really what it claimed to be. Bullfinch doing me the honour to respond in the affirmative, I agreed to ship myself as an Able Trencherman on board the Temeraire.

'Now, our plan shall be this,' says Bullfinch, with his forefinger at his nose. 'As soon as we get to Namelesston, we'll drive straight to the Temeraire, and order a little dinner in an hour. And as we shall not have more than enough time in which to dispose of it comfortably, what do you say to giving the house the best opportunities of serving it hot and quickly, by dining in the coffee-room?'

What I had to say was, Certainly. Bullfinch (who is by nature of a hopeful constitution) then began to babble of green geese. But I checked him in that Falstaffian vein, urging considerations of time and cookery.

In due sequence of events, we drove up to the Temeraire and alighted. A youth in livery received us on the doorstep. 'Looks well,' said Bullfinch, confidentially. And then aloud, 'Coffee-room!'

The youth in livery (now perceived to be mouldy) conducted us to the desired haven, and was enjoined by Bullfinch to send the waiter at once, as we wished to order a little dinner in an hour. Then Bullfinch and I waited for the waiter until, the waiter continuing to wait in some unknown and invisible sphere of action, we rang for the waiter: which ring produced the waiter, who announced himself as not the waiter who ought to wait upon us, and who didn't wait a moment longer.

So Bullfinch approached the coffee-room door, and melodiously pitching his voice into a bar where two young ladies were keeping the books of the Temeraire, apologetically explained that we wished to order a little dinner in an hour, and that we were debarred from the execution of our inoffensive purpose, by consignment to solitude.

Hereupon one of the young ladies rang a bell which reproduced – at the bar this time – the waiter who was not the waiter who ought to wait upon us; that extraordinary man, whose life seemed consumed in waiting upon people to say that he wouldn't wait upon them, repeated his former protest with great indignation, and retired.

Bullfinch with a fallen countenance was about to say to me 'This won't do,' when the waiter who ought to wait upon us, left off keeping us waiting at last. 'Waiter,' said Bullfinch piteously, 'we have been a long time waiting.' The waiter who ought to wait upon us, laid the blame upon the waiter who ought not to wait upon us, and said it was all that waiter's fault.

'We wish,' said Bullfinch, much depressed, 'to order a little dinner in an hour. What can we have?'

'What would you like to have, gentlemen?'

Bullfinch, with extreme mournfulness of speech and action, and with a forlorn old fly-blown bill of fare in his hand which the waiter had given him, and which was a sort of general manuscript Index to any Cookery-Book you please, moved the previous question.

We could have mock-turtle soup, a sole, curry, and roast duck. Agreed. At this table by this window. Punctually in an hour.

I had been feigning to look out of this window; but I had been taking note of the crumbs on all the tables, the dirty tablecloths, the stuffy soupy airless atmosphere, the stale leavings everywhere about, the deep gloom of the waiter who ought to wait upon us, and the stomach-ache with which a lonely traveller at a distant table in a corner was too evidently afflicted. I now pointed out to Bullfinch the alarming circumstance that this traveller had *dined*. We hurriedly debated whether, without infringement of good breeding, we could ask him to disclose if he had partaken of mock-turtle, sole, curry, or roast duck? We decided that the thing could not be politely done, and we had set our own stomachs on a cast, and they must stand the hazard of the die.

I hold phrenology, within certain limits, to be true; I am much of the same mind as to the subtler expressions of the hand; I hold physiognomy to be infallible; though all these sciences demand rare qualities in the student. But I also hold that there is no more certain index to personal character, than the condition of a set of casters is to the character of any hotel. Knowing and having often tested this theory of mine, Bullfinch resigned himself to the worst, when, laying aside any remaining veil of disguise, I held up before him in succession the cloudy oil and furry vinegar, the clogged cayenne, the dirty salt, the obscene dregs of soy, and the anchovy sauce in a flannel waistcoat of decomposition.

We went out to transact our business. So inspiriting was the relief of passing into the clean and windy streets of Namelesston from the heavy and vapid closeness of the coffee-room of the Temeraire, that hope began to revive within us. We began to consider that perhaps the lonely traveller had taken physic, or done something injudicious to bring his complaint on. Bullfinch remarked that he thought the waiter who ought to wait upon us had brightened a little when suggesting curry; and although I knew him to have been at that moment the express image of despair, I allowed myself to become elevated in spirits. As we walked by the softly lapping sea, all the notabilities of Namelesston, who are for ever going up and down with the changelessness of the tides, passed to and fro in procession. Pretty girls on horseback, and with detested riding-masters; pretty girls on foot; mature ladies in hats – spectacled, strongminded, and glaring at the opposite or weaker sex. The Stock Exchange was strongly represented, Jerusalem was strongly represented, the bores of the prosier London clubs were strongly represented. Fortune hunters of all denominations were there, from hirsute insolvency in a curricle, to closely buttoned-up swindlery in doubtful boots, on the sharp lookout for any likely young gentleman disposed to play a game at billiards round the corner. Masters of languages, their lessons finished for the day, were going to their homes out of sight of the sea; mistresses of accomplishments, carrying small portfolios, likewise tripped homeward; pairs of scholastic pupils, two and two, went languidly along the beach, surveying the face of the waters as if waiting for some Ark to come and take them off. Spectres of the George the Fourth days flitted unsteadily among the crowd, bearing the outward semblance of ancient dandies, of every one of whom it might be said, not that he had one leg in the grave, or both legs, but that he was steeped in grave to the summit of his high shirt-collar, and had nothing real about him but his bones. Alone stationary in the midst of all the movement the Namelesston boatmen leaned against the railings and yawned, and looked out to sea, or looked at the moored fishing-boats and at nothing. Such is the unchanging manner of life with this nursery of our hardy seamen, and very dry nurses they are, and always wanting something to drink. The only two nautical personages detached from the railing, were the two fortunate possessors of the celebrated monstrous unknown barking fish, just caught (frequently just caught off Namelesston), who carried him about in a hamper, and pressed the scientific to look in at the lid.

The sands of the hour had all run out when we got back to the Temeraire. Says Bullfinch then to the youth in livery, with boldness: 'Lavatory!'

When we arrived at the family vault with a sky-light, which the youth in livery presented as the Institution sought, we had already whisked off our cravats and coats; but finding ourselves in the presence of an evil smell, and no linen but two crumpled towels newly damp from the countenances of two somebody elses, we put on our cravats and coats again, and fled unwashed to the coffee-room.

There, the waiter who ought to wait upon us had set forth our knives and forks and glasses, on the cloth whose dirty acquaintance we had already had the pleasure of making, and which we were pleased to recognise by the familiar expression of its stains. And now there occurred the truly surprising phenomenon that the waiter who ought not to wait upon us, swooped down upon us, clutched our loaf of bread, and vanished with the same.

Bullfinch with distracted eyes was following this unaccountable figure 'out at the portal,' like the Ghost in Hamlet, when the waiter who ought to wait upon us jostled against it, carrying a tureen.

'Waiter!' said a severe diner, lately finished, perusing his bill fiercely through his eye-glass.

The waiter put down our tureen on a remote side table, and went to see what was amiss in this new direction.

'This is not right, you know, waiter. Look here. Here's yesterday's sherry, one and eightpence, and here we are again, two shillings. And what does Sixpence mean?'

So far from knowing what sixpence meant, the waiter protested that he didn't know what anything meant. He wiped the perspiration from his clammy brow, and said it was impossible to do it – not particularising what – and the kitchen was so far off.

'Take the bill to the bar, and get it altered,' said Mr Indignation Cocker: so to call him.

The waiter took it, looked intensely at it, didn't seem to like the idea of taking it to the bar, and submitted as a new light upon the case, that perhaps sixpence meant sixpence.

'I tell you again,' said Mr Indignation Cocker, 'here's yesterday's sherry – can't you see it? – one and eightpence, and here we are again, two shillings. What do you make of one and eightpence and two shillings?'

Totally unable to make anything of one and eightpence and two shillings, the waiter went out to try if anybody else could; merely casting a helpless backward glance at Bullfinch, in acknowledgment of his pathetic entreaties for our soup tureen. After a pause, during which Mr Indignation Cocker read a newspaper, and coughed defiant coughs, Bullfinch rose to get the tureen, when the waiter reappeared and brought it: dropping Mr Indignation Cocker's altered bill on Mr Indignation Cocker's table as he came along.

'It's quite impossible to do it, gentlemen,' murmured the waiter; 'and the kitchen is so far off.'

'Well. You don't keep the house; it's not your fault, we suppose. Bring some sherry.'

'Waiter!' From Mr Indignation Cocker, with a new and burning sense of injury upon him.

The waiter, arrested on his way to our sherry, stopped short, and came back to see what was wrong now.

'Will you look here? This is worse than before. *Do* you understand? Here's yesterday's sherry one and eightpence, and here we are again two shillings. And what the devil does Ninepence mean?'

This new portent utterly confounded the waiter. He wrung his napkin, and mutely appealed to the ceiling.

'Waiter, fetch that sherry,' says Bullfinch, in open wrath and revolt.

'I want to know,' persisted Mr Indignation Cocker, 'the meaning of Ninepence. I want to know the meaning of sherry one and eightpence yesterday, and of here we are again two shillings. Send somebody.'

The distracted waiter got out of the room, under pretext of sending somebody, and by that means got our wine. But the instant he appeared with our decanter, Mr Indignation Cocker descended on him again.

'Waiter!'

'You will now have the goodness to attend to our dinner, waiter,' says Bullfinch, sternly.

'I am very sorry, but it's quite impossible to do it, gentlemen,' pleaded the waiter; 'and the kitchen –'

'Waiter!' said Mr Indignation Cocker.

– 'Is,' resumed the waiter, 'so far off, that –'

'Waiter!' persisted Mr Indignation Cocker, 'send somebody.'

We were not without our fears that the waiter rushed out to hang himself, and we were much relieved by his fetching somebody – in gracefully flowing skirts and with a waist – who very soon settled Mr Indignation Cocker's business.

'Oh!' said Mr Cocker, with his fire surprisingly quenched by this apparition. 'I wished to ask about this bill of mine, because it appears to me that there's a little mistake here. Let me show you. Here's yesterday's sherry one and eightpence, and here we are again two shillings. And how do you explain Ninepence?'

However it was explained in tones too soft to be overheard, Mr Cocker was heard to say nothing more than 'Ah-h-h! Indeed! Thank you! Yes,' and shortly afterwards went out, a milder man.

The lonely traveller with the stomach-ache had all this time suffered severely; drawing up a leg now and then, and sipping hot brandy and water with grated ginger in it. When we tasted our (very) mock turtle soup, and were instantly seized with symptoms of some disorder simulating apoplexy, and occasioned by the surcharge of the nose and brain with lukewarm dish-water holding in solution sour flour, poisonous condiments, and (say) seventy-five per cent of miscellaneous kitchen stuff rolled into balls, we were inclined to trace his disorder to that source. On the other hand, there was a silent anguish upon him too strongly resembling the results established within ourselves by the sherry, to be discarded from alarmed consideration. Again: we observed him, with terror, to be much overcome by our sole's being aired in a temporary retreat close to him, while the waiter went out (as we conceived) to see his friends. And when the curry made its appearance he suddenly retired in great disorder.

In fine, for the uneatable part of this little dinner (as contradistinguished from the undrinkable) we paid only seven shillings and sixpence each. And Bullfinch and I agreed unanimously that no such ill-served, ill-appointed, ill-cooked, nasty little dinner could be got for the money anywhere else under the sun. With that comfort to our backs, we turned them on the dear old Temeraire, the charging Temeraire, and resolved (in the Scottish dialect) to gang nae mair to the flabby Temeraire.

41

New Uncommercial Samples. By Charles Dickens. Mr Barlow

All The Year Round, 16 January 1869 (*UT2* as 'Mr Barlow')

In a letter to Forster of September 1847, Dickens refers to 'the great British novelists' – Fielding, Smollett and Sterne – suggesting that many people would be interested in an essay 'recalling how one read them as a child (no one read them younger than I, I think), and how one gradually grew up into a different knowledge of them, and so forth' (*Pilgrim*, Vol. V, p. 158). In different ways, the *HW* essay 'Where We Stopped Growing' (see Vol. 3 of this edition, article 15), and Ch. 4 of *David Copperfield*, work around this original idea.

The present article, however, while referring yet again to Dickens's cherished *Arabian Nights* (see literary allusions, below), shows how Dickens 'grew up' with a work he claimed to have disliked intensely as a child. This was Thomas Day's *History of Sandford and Merton*, a ruthlessly improving fiction for children first published in three volumes between 1783 and 1789, but which had gone through twenty-three editions by the year of Dickens's article. Its author was noticeably influenced by Rousseau, and was involved in the 1780s with schemes to improve the social and moral welfare of the poor. 'Mr Barlow' features in Day's text as the story-telling tutor of two pupils from contrasting backgrounds: the plebeian Harry (who is unbearably hard-working and honest) and the aristocratic Tommy (who is unbearably spoilt and conceited). Dickens clearly remembered the book vividly and supposed that others did. Writing to his friend Richard H. Horne in 1848 about the latter's proposals for a series of lectures on literature, he recommended *Sandford and Merton* as one which ought to be included in the section dealing with children's books: 'I should say that the story had had great influence on many boys' (and consequently many men's) minds' (*Pilgrim*, Vol. V, p. 373).

In 'A Christmas Tree', a grand retrospect of childhood memories which opened the Christmas Number of *HW* for 1850 (21 December), Dickens had recalled the figures of 'Sandford and Merton with Mr Barlow' grouped with others from books read at the same period. By the 1860s, Dickens's denunciation of 'Mr Barlow' as the epitome of a killjoy had become a feature of his table-talk, and something he entertained friends with, as James T. Fields's anecdote attests:

There were certain books particularly hateful to [Dickens], of which he never spoke except in terms of most ludicrous raillery. Mr Barlow in 'Sandford and Merton', he said, was the favourite enemy of his boyhood, and his first experience of a bore. . . .

Dickens, rattling his mental cane over the head of Mr Barlow was as much better than any play as can be imagined. [*In and Out of Doors with Charles Dickens* (1876), pp. 154–5]

An intense dislike of 'monomanias', and especially of didacticism intruding into popular entertainments, is frequently detectable in Dickens's journalism.

Literary allusions (below) 'the consumption of a plate of cherries to the contemplation of a starlight night': *Sandford and Merton* (6th edn, 1791), Vol. II, pp. 54, 61; (below) 'the example of a certain awful Master Mash . . . at the theatre . . . facing a mad bull single-handed': *Sandford and Merton (ibid.)*, pp. 246, 305–8; (p. 373) 'Sindbad the Sailor': Sinbad, the sailor-hero of a sequence of stories full of wonders collected in *The Arabian Nights*; (p. 373) 'the Wonderful Lamp': from the story of 'Aladdin and the Wonderful Lamp' in *The Arabian Nights*; (p. 373) 'the peg in the neck of the Enchanted Horse': from the story of 'The Enchanted Horse' in *The Arabian Nights*; (p. 373) 'Casgar, on the frontiers of Tartary . . . you couldn't let a Hunchback down an eastern chimney with a cord': from the story of 'The Little Hunchback' in *The Arabian Nights* ('Kashgar' is the more common form in English); (p. 375) 'a piece of Mr Carlyle's own Dead-Sea Fruit': the so-called 'Apples of Sodom' which, though of fair appearance, turn to ashes when picked or tasted, are mentioned by Carlyle in 'Stump-Orator' (*Latter Day Pamphlets* No. V, May 1850); (p. 376) 'every schoolboy knows that': 'Every schoolboy knows who imprisoned Montezuma, and who strangled Atahualpa', Thomas Babington Macaulay's essay 'Lord Clive', *Essays Critical and Historical* (1843 etc.), Vol. III; (p. 377) 'A Promethean Tommy, bound; and he is the vulture that gorges itself upon the liver . . .' alludes to the title of Aeschylus's tragedy *Prometheus Bound* (date uncertain) and the myth concerning Prometheus's punishment by Zeus.

A great reader of good fiction at an unusually early age, it seems to me as though I had been born under the superintendence of the estimable but terrific gentleman whose name stands at the head of my present reflections. The instructive monomaniac, Mr Barlow, will be remembered as the tutor of Master Harry Sandford and Master Tommy Merton. He knew everything, and didactically improved all sorts of occasions, from the consumption of a plate of cherries to the contemplation of a starlight night. What youth came to without Mr Barlow, was displayed in the history of Sandford and Merton, by the example of a certain awful

Master Mash. This young wretch wore buckles and powder, conducted himself with insupportable levity at the theatre, had no idea of facing a mad bull single-handed (in which I think him less reprehensible, as remotely reflecting my own character), and was a frightful instance of the enervating effects of luxury upon the human race.

Strange destiny on the part of Mr Barlow, to go down to posterity as childhood's experience of a Bore! Immortal Mr Barlow, boring his way through the verdant freshness of ages!

My personal indictment against Mr Barlow is one of many counts. I will proceed to set forth a few of the injuries he has done me.

In the first place, he never made, or took, a joke. This insensibility on Mr Barlow's part not only cast its own gloom over my boyhood, but blighted even the sixpenny jest books of the time. For, groaning under a moral spell constraining me to refer all things to Mr Barlow, I could not choose but ask myself in a whisper when tickled by a printed jest, 'What would *he* think of it? What would *he* see in it?' The point of the jest immediately became a sting, and stung my conscience. For, my mind's eye saw him stolid, frigid, perchance taking from its shelf some dreary Greek book and translating at full length what some dismal sage said (and touched up afterwards, perhaps, for publication), when he banished some unlucky joker from Athens.

The incompatibility of Mr Barlow with all other portions of my young life but himself, the adamantine inadaptability of the man to my favourite fancies and amusements, is the thing for which I hate him most. What right had he to bore his way into my Arabian Nights? Yet he did. He was always hinting doubts of the veracity of Sindbad the Sailor. If he could have got hold of the Wonderful Lamp, I knew he would have trimmed it, and lighted it, and delivered a lecture over it on the qualities of sperm oil, with a glance at the whale fisheries. He would so soon have found out – on mechanical principles – the peg in the neck of the Enchanted Horse, and would have turned it the right way in so workmanlike a manner, that the horse could never have got any height into the air, and the story couldn't have been. He would have proved, by map and compass, that there was no such kingdom as the delightful kingdom of Casgar, on the frontiers of Tartary. He would have caused that hypocritical young prig, Harry, to make an experiment – with the aid of a temporary building in the garden and a dummy – demonstrating that you couldn't let a choked Hunchback down an eastern chimney with a cord, and leave him upright on the hearth to terrify the Sultan's purveyor.

The golden sounds of the overture to the first metropolitan pantomime I remember, were alloyed by Mr Barlow. Click click, ting ting, bang bang, weedle weedle weedle, Bang! I recall the chilling air that ran across my frame and cooled my hot delight, as the thought occurred to me: 'This would never do for Mr Barlow!' After the curtain drew up, dreadful doubts of Mr Barlow's considering the costumes of the Nymphs of the Nebula as being sufficiently opaque, obtruded themselves on my enjoyment. In the Clown I perceived two persons; one, a fascinating unaccountable creature of a hectic complexion, joyous in spirits though feeble in intellect with flashes of brilliancy: the other, a pupil for Mr Barlow. I thought how Mr Barlow would secretly rise early in the morning, and butter the pavement for *him*, and, when he had brought him down, would look severely out of his study window, and ask him how he enjoyed the fun. I thought how Mr Barlow would heat all the pokers in the house and singe him with the whole collection, to bring him better acquainted with the properties of incandescent iron, on which he (Barlow) would fully expatiate. I pictured Mr Barlow's instituting a comparison between the clown's conduct at his studies – drinking up the ink, licking his copybook, and using his head for blotting-paper – and that of the already mentioned young Prig of Prigs, Harry, sitting at the Barlovian feet, sneakingly pretending to be in a rapture of useful knowledge. I thought how soon Mr Barlow would smooth the clown's hair down, instead of letting it stand erect in three tall tufts; and how, after a couple of years or so with Mr Barlow, he would keep his legs close together when he walked, and would take his hands out of his big loose pockets, and wouldn't have a jump left in him.

That I am particularly ignorant what most things in the universe are made of, and how they are made, is another of my charges against Mr Barlow. With the dread upon me of developing into a Harry, and with a further dread upon me of being Barlowed if I made inquiries, by bringing down upon myself a cold shower-bath of explanations and experiments, I forbore enlightenment in my youth, and became, as they say in melodramas, 'the wreck you now behold.' That I consorted with idlers and dunces is another of the melancholy facts for which I hold Mr Barlow responsible. That Pragmatical Prig, Harry, became so detestable in my sight, that, he being reported studious in the South, I would have fled idle to the extremest North. Better to learn misconduct from a Master Mash than science and statistics from a Sandford! So I took the path which, but for Mr Barlow, I might never have trodden. Thought I with a shudder, 'Mr Barlow is a bore, with an immense constructive power of making bores. His prize specimen is a bore. He seeks to make a bore of me. That Knowledge is Power I am not prepared to gainsay; but, with Mr Barlow, Knowledge is Power to bore.' Therefore I took refuge in the Caves of Ignorance, wherein I have resided ever since, and which are still my private address.

But the weightiest charge of all my charges against Mr Barlow is, that he still walks the earth in various disguises, seeking to make a Tommy of me, even in my maturity. Irrepressible instructive monomaniac, Mr Barlow fills my life with pitfalls, and lies hiding at the bottom to burst out upon me when I least expect him.

A few of these dismal experiences of mine shall suffice.

Knowing Mr Barlow to have invested largely in the Moving Panorama trade, and having on various occasions identified him in the dark, with a long wand in his hand, holding forth in his old way (made more appalling in this connection by his sometimes cracking a piece of Mr Carlyle's own Dead-Sea Fruit in mistake for a joke), I systematically shun pictorial entertainment on rollers. Similarly I should demand responsible bail and guarantee against the appearance of Mr Barlow, before committing myself to attendance at any assemblage of my fellow-creatures where a bottle of water and a note-book were conspicuous objects. For, in either of those associations, I should expressly expect him. But such is the designing nature of the man, that he steals in where no reasonable precaution or provision could expect him. As in the following case:

Adjoining the Caves of Ignorance is a country town. In this country town, the Mississippi Momuses, nine in number, were announced to appear in the Town Hall, for the general delectation, this last Christmas week. Knowing Mr Barlow to be unconnected with the Mississippi, though holding republican opinions, and deeming myself secure, I took a stall. My object was to hear and see the Mississippi Momuses in what the bills described as their 'National Ballads, Plantation Break-Downs, Nigger Part-Songs, Choice Conundrums, Sparkling Repartees, &c.' I found the nine dressed alike, in the black coat and trousers, white waistcoat, very large shirt-front, very large shirt-collar, and very large white tie and wristbands, which constitute the dress of the mass of the African race, and which has been observed by travellers to prevail over a vast number of degrees of latitude. All the nine rolled their eyes exceedingly, and had very red lips. At the extremities of the curve they formed seated in their chairs, were the performers on the Tambourine and Bones. The centre Momus, a black of melancholy aspect (who inspired me with a vague uneasiness for which I could not then account), performed on a Mississippi instrument closely resembling what was once called in this Island a hurdy-gurdy. The Momuses on either side of him had each another instrument peculiar to the Father of Waters, which may be likened to a stringed weather-glass held upside down. There were likewise a little flute, and a violin. All went well for a while, and we had had several sparkling repartees exchanged between the performers on the tambourine and bones, when the black of melancholy aspect, turning to the latter, and addressing him in a deep and improving voice as 'Bones, sir,' delivered certain grave remarks to him concerning the juveniles present, and the season of the year; whereon I perceived that I was in the presence of Mr Barlow – corked!

Another night – and this was in London – I attended the representation of a little comedy. As the characters were life-like (and consequently not improving), and as they went upon their several ways and designs without personally addressing themselves to me, I felt rather confident of coming through it without being regarded as Tommy; the more so, as we were clearly getting close to the end. But I deceived myself. All of a sudden, and apropos of nothing, everybody concerned came to a check and halt, advanced to the footlights in a general rally to take dead aim at me, and brought me down with a moral homily, in which I detected the dread hand of Barlow.

Nay, so intricate and subtle are the toils of this hunter, that on the very next night after that, I was again entrapped, where no vestige of a springe could have been apprehended by the timidest. It was a burlesque that I saw performed; an uncompromising burlesque, where everybody concerned, but especially the ladies, carried on at a very considerable rate indeed. Most prominent and active among the corps of performers was what I took to be (and she really gave me very fair opportunities of coming to a right conclusion) a young lady, of a pretty figure. She was dressed as a picturesque young gentleman, whose pantaloons had been cut off in their infancy; and she had very neat knees, and very neat satin boots. Immediately after singing a slang song and dancing a slang dance, this engaging figure approached the fatal lamps, and, bending over them, delivered in a thrilling voice a random Eulogium on, and Exhortation to pursue, the Virtues. 'Great Heaven!' was my exclamation. 'Barlow!'

There is still another aspect in which Mr Barlow perpetually insists on my sustaining the character of Tommy, which is more unendurable yet, on account of its extreme aggressiveness. For the purposes of a Review or newspaper, he will get up an abstruse subject with infinite pains, will Barlow, utterly regardless of the price of midnight oil, and indeed of everything else, save cramming himself to the eyes. But mark. When Mr Barlow blows his information off, he is not contented with having rammed it home and discharged it upon me, Tommy, his target, but he pretends that he was always in possession of it, and made nothing of it – that he imbibed it with his mother's milk – and that I, the wretched Tommy, am most abjectly behind-hand in not having done the same. I ask why is Tommy to be always the foil of Mr Barlow to this extent? What Mr Barlow had not the slightest notion of, himself, a week ago, it surely cannot be any very heavy backsliding in me not to have at my fingers' ends today! And yet Mr Barlow systematically carries it over me with a high hand, and will tauntingly ask me in his articles whether it is possible that I am not aware that every schoolboy knows that the fourteenth turning on the left in the steppes of Russia will conduct to such-and-such a wandering tribe? With other disparaging questions of like nature. So, when Mr Barlow addresses a letter to any journal as a volunteer correspondent (which I frequently find him doing), he will previously have gotten somebody to tell him some tremendous technicality, and will write in the coolest manner: 'Now, Sir, I may assume that every reader of your columns, possessing average information and intelligence, knows as well as I do that' – say that the draught from the touch-hole of a cannon of such a calibre, bears such a proportion in the nicest fractions to the draught from the muzzle; or some equally familiar little fact. But whatever it is, be certain that it always tends to the exaltation of Mr Barlow, and the depression of his enforced and enslaved pupil.

Mr Barlow's knowledge of my own pursuits, I find to be so profound, that my own knowledge of them becomes as nothing. Mr Barlow (disguised and bearing a feigned name, but detected by me) has occasionally taught me, in a sonorous voice, from end to end of a long dinner table, trifles that I took the liberty of teaching him five-and-twenty years ago. My closing article of impeachment against Mr Barlow, is, that he goes out to breakfast, goes out to dinner, goes out everywhere, high and low, and that he WILL preach to me, and that I CAN'T get rid of him. He makes of me a Promethean Tommy, bound; and he is the vulture that gorges itself upon the liver of my uninstructed mind.

42

New Uncommercial Samples. By Charles Dickens. On an Amateur Beat

All The Year Round, 27 February 1869 (*UT2* as 'On an Amateur Beat')

Between 1866 and 1868, some eight acres of narrow streets and courts were cleared 'hard by Temple Bar' (see p. 381) in preparation for the building of the Royal Courts of Justice, to ambitious designs by George E. Street; construction work continued until 1882 (Hill, 35.5). The motivation for the return to Limehouse in the present article was a letter of complaint following the publication of references to lead poisoning in the essay 'A Small Star in the East' (see article 39). Robert A. Johnson of Johnson & Sons, one of two sons running the firm of white lead manufacturers to which Dickens had alluded, wrote on 24 December 1868 to inform Dickens of thirteen distinct health and safety precautions taken to protect workers in their dangerous occupation, and to object to the bad impression given by Dickens's article of the condition of the sick employee whose brain was described 'coming out at her ear' (see p. 355):

> The girl who was ill was at work yesterday and appeared quite well. Our medical man saw her and tells us the discharge from the ears would not arise from the Lead, but probably from some pressure on the head; the girl having been used to carrying great weights in connection with her work at sack making, which employment she also follows. [Quoted in George F. Young, 'Limehouse Luck or the Lead Mills Located', *The Dickensian*, Vol. 30 (1934), pp. 174–5]

Johnson concluded the letter by inviting Dickens, '[k]nowing the great interest you take in the welfare and improvement of the poorer classes', to visit the firm's offices at 4 Waterloo Place and their factory in Burdett Road, to test 'the accuracy of our statements' and to interview employees:

> We also venture to add that we think ourselves ... entitled to a little sympathy in the matter and that it is somewhat hard after all we have done, to be held up, though certainly not by name, to the public as employing those who have no choice between starvation and being ulcerated and paralysed for 1/6 a day' [*Ibid.*, p. 175]

The letter was accompanied by a note from a Mr J. S. Cummings, the firm's 'Medical Man'. Dickens replied on 29 December, assuring the owners that he had 'not the slightest doubt of the strict accuracy of every word of your communication' but reminding them that

> The Lead Mills were a mere abstraction to me when I wrote the paper ... and that I did not then know where they were, or the name of your firm. But I was so anxious to be just, that although I was attended ... by a physician, and although we saw other clear indications of Lead Poisoning besides the one instance named (and that only in the words of the Irishwoman; not in mine or with remark of mine), I forebore to state them. [*Nonesuch*, Vol. III, p. 692]

Dickens went on to accept the invitation, stating that he would arrive in about three weeks time, giving a 'few hours notice of my coming', but then returned to the defence of his journalistic method, pointing out that Cummings's note was less reasonable than the Johnsons' because he does not sufficiently discriminate between the Irishwoman and her visitor, and surely cannot in reason suppose that the caller, in graphically presenting her exact words, endorses them! If they were presented otherwise than as a piece of character, can he possibly suppose that a writer at all accustomed to read or observe, would record that a young woman's brains were coming out at her ear. [*Ibid.*, p. 693]

In the following decades some improvement in safety standards came about through the replacement of the old Dutch process of manufacture by the American 'MacIvor' process, but cases of lead-poisoning persisted until the 1890s, when publicity surrounding R. H. Sherard's exposés in *White Slaves of England* (1897) attracted the attention of a Parliamentary Commission (see Ch. 5, 'The White-Lead Workers of Newcastle'). In the Preface to the second edition of his book, Sherard was able to rejoice that, following the passing of the Workmen's Compensation Act of 1897, 'it will be illegal to employ women in the white lead factories' (1898; p. 23).

Dickens's revisions to the article as it passed from manuscript through to publication show signs of an effort to make the advice being offered to the newly appointed Chief Commissioner of the Metropolitan Police, Lieutenant-Colonel Edmund Henderson, seem less critical and presumptuous (see p. 380 and MS and textual note, below).

Literary allusions (p. 382) 'to cross the kennel at the bottom of the Canongate ... as Scott relates': in Walter Scott's *Chronicles of the Canongate* (1827 [1826]), Chrystal Croftangry relates that while being pursued for debt he remained within the confines of the palace of Holyrood, while 'all Elysium seemed opening on the other side of the kennel ... I was so childish as even to make an occasional excursion across, were it only for a few yards' (Preface).

MS and textual note Draft (?January-February 1869), Robert H. Taylor Collection, Princeton University Library. Ff. 1–10; Corrected proof (9 May 1869), Huntington Library, San Marino, Los Angeles, MS RB 114202. All ten slips of MS are heavily corrected, and a final paragraph of twelve lines deleted by seven vertical pen strokes and one horizontal. The paragraph is further obscured by a superimposed cutting from the *ATYR* of 19 December 1868, excerpting from 'A Small Star in the East' (see page 355 [from 'some of them gits lead-pisoned soon' ... to 'niver no less, Sur']) those remarks of the Irish mother concerning lead-poisoning which Dickens wanted repeated in the present article. Around and below the cutting, some of the text can be deciphered, showing that the essay originally reverted to the topic with which it opens: the problem of how best to police the streets. On the return leg of his journey, the narrator sees 'assembled a crowd of well known thieves and violent characters' and adds: 'I have observed this daily on many days of my life. Might I take the liberty of suggesting to the authorities that it strikes me with some astonishment, and that for my own part I would lay these gentry by the heels, or know the reason why? Which I certainly don't know at present.' Referring to the recent appointment of a new police Chief Commissioner for London, MS has '... I can tell him, if I reigned in Scotland Yard,' while the corrected proof and copy-text (see below) have '... I can tell him, if I could deal with him physically.' At proof stage, Dickens added the phrase 'in whom I thoroughly believe as a tried and efficient public servant' to the end of the MS sentence '... which I respectfully offer to the new Chief Commissioner'; copy-text later amends MS 'believe' to 'confide' (below). At proof stage, Dickens also altered the MS phrase 'Now, suppose that a Chief Commissioner, *on coming into office*, sent round a circular ...' (my italics) by deleting the italicised section (see p. 381). MS has '... and give him a guinea, as if he didn't expect it': proof alters to '... a guinea, wrapped in paper' (see p. 384); MS has '... conversion of Pig-Lead into White Lead, *for the use of Painters, Gas-Fitters, and so forth*' (my italics): italicised phrase deleted at proof stage (p. 384).

It is one of my fancies that even my idlest walk must always have its appointed destination. I set myself a task before I leave my lodging in Covent Garden on a street expedition, and should no more think of altering my route by the way, or turning back and leaving a part of it unachieved, than I should think of fraudulently violating an agreement entered into with somebody else. The other day, finding myself under this kind of obligation to proceed to Limehouse, I started punctually at noon, in compliance with the terms of the contract with myself to which my good faith was pledged.

On such an occasion, it is my habit to regard my walk as my Beat, and myself as a higher sort of Police Constable doing duty on the same. There is many a Ruffian in the streets whom I mentally collar and clear out of them, who would see mighty little of London, I can tell him, if I could deal with him physically.

Issuing forth upon this very Beat, and following with my eyes three hulking garotters on their way home: which home I could confidently swear to be within so many yards of Drury Lane, in such a narrowed and restricted direction (though they live in their lodging quite as undisturbed as I in mine), I went on duty with a consideration which I respectfully offer to the new Chief Commissioner – in whom I thoroughly confide as a tried and efficient public servant. How often (thought I) have I been forced to swallow in Police reports, the intolerable stereotyped pill of nonsense how that the Police Constable informed the worthy magistrate how that the associates of the Prisoner did at that present speaking dwell in a Street or Court which no man dared go down, and how that the worthy magistrate had heard of the dark reputation of such Street or Court, and how that our readers would doubtless remember that it was always the same Street or Court which was thus edifyingly discoursed about, say once a fortnight. Now, suppose that a Chief Commissioner sent round a circular to every Division of Police employed in London, requiring instantly the names in all districts of all such much-puffed Streets or Courts which no man durst go down; and suppose that in such circular he gave plain warning: 'If those places really exist, they are a proof of Police inefficiency which I mean to punish; and if they do not exist, but are a conventional fiction, then they are a proof of lazy tacit Police connivance with professional crime, which I also mean to punish' – what then? Fictions or realities, could they survive the touch-stone of this atom of common sense? To tell us in open court, until it has become as trite a feature of news as the great gooseberry, that a costly Police system such as was never before heard of, has left in London, in the days of steam and gas and photographs of thieves and electric telegraphs, the sanctuaries and stews of the Stuarts! Why, a parity of practice, in all departments, would bring back the Plague in two summers, and the Druids in a century!

Walking faster under my share of this public injury, I overturned a wretched little creature who, clutching at the rags of a pair of trousers with one of its claws, and at its ragged hair with the other, pattered with bare feet over the muddy stones. I stopped to raise and succour this poor weeping wretch, and fifty like it, but of both sexes, were about me in a moment: begging, tumbling, fighting, clamouring, yelling, shivering in their nakedness and hunger. The piece of money I had put into the claw of the child I had overturned, was clawed out of it, and was again clawed out of that wolfish gripe, and again out of that, and soon I had no notion in what part of the obscene scuffle in the mud, of rags and legs and arms and dirt, the money might be. In raising the child, I had drawn it aside out of the main thoroughfare, and this took place among some wooden hoardings and barriers and ruins of demolished buildings, hard by Temple Bar. Unexpectedly from among them emerged a genuine Police Constable, before whom the dreadful brood dispersed in various dir-ections: he making feints and darts in this direction and in that, and catching nothing. When all were frightened away, he took off his hat, pulled out a handkerchief from it, wiped his heated brow, and restored the handkerchief and hat to their places, with the air of a man who had discharged a great moral duty – as indeed he had, in doing what was set down for him. I looked at him, and I looked about at the disorderly traces in the mud, and I thought of the drops of rain and the footprints of an extinct creature, hoary ages upon ages old, that geologists have identified on the face of a cliff; and this speculation came over me: – If this mud could petrify at this moment, and could lie concealed here for ten thousand years, I wonder whether the race of men then to be our successors on the earth could, from these or any marks, by the utmost force of the human intellect, unassisted by tradition, deduce such an astounding inference as the existence of a polished state of society that bore with the public savagery of neglected children in the streets of its capital city, and was proud of its power by sea and land, and never used its power to seize and save them!

After this, when I came to the Old Bailey and glanced up it towards Newgate, I found that the prison had an inconsistent look. There seemed to be some unlucky inconsistency in the atmosphere, that day, for though the proportions of Saint Paul's Cathedral are very beautiful, it had an air of being somewhat out of drawing, in my eyes. I felt as though the cross were too high up, and perched upon the intervening golden ball too far away.

Facing eastward, I left behind me Smithfield and Old Bailey – fire and fagot, condemned Hold, public hanging, whipping through the city at the cart-tail, pillory, branding-iron, and other beautiful ancestral landmarks, which rude hands have rooted up, without bringing the stars quite down upon us as yet – and went my way upon my Beat, noting how oddly characteristic neighbourhoods are divided from one another, hereabout, as though by an invisible line across the way. Here, shall cease the bankers and the money-changers; here, shall begin the shipping interest and the nautical instrument shops; here, shall follow a scarcely perceptible flavouring of groceries and drugs; here, shall come a strong infusion of butchers; now, small hosiers shall be in the ascendant; henceforth, everything exposed for sale shall have its ticketed price attached. All this, as if specially ordered and appointed. A single stride at Houndsditch Church, no wider than sufficed to cross the kennel at the bottom of the Canongate, which the Debtors in Holyrood Sanctuary were wont to relieve their minds by skipping over, as Scott relates, and standing in delightful daring of Catchpoles on the free side – a single stride, and everything is entirely changed in grain and character. West of the stride, a table, or a chest of drawers on sale shall be of mahogany and French-polished; East of the stride, it shall be of deal, smeared with a cheap counterfeit resembling lip-salve. West of the stride, a penny loaf or bun shall be compact and self-contained; East of the stride, it shall be of a sprawling and splay-footed character, as seeking to make more of itself for the money. My Beat lying round by Whitechapel Church, and the adjacent Sugar Refineries – great buildings, tier upon tier, that have the appearance of being nearly related to the Dock-Warehouses at

Liverpool – I turned off to my right, and passing round the awkward corner on my left, came suddenly on an apparition familiar to London streets afar off.

What London peripatetic of these times has not seen the woman who has fallen forward, double, through some affection of the spine, and whose head has of late taken a turn to one side, so that it now droops over the back of one of her arms at about the wrist? Who does not know her staff, and her shawl, and her basket, as she gropes her way along, capable of seeing nothing but the pavement, never begging, never stopping, for ever going somewhere on no business? How does she live, whence does she come, whither does she go, and why? I mind the time when her yellow arms were nought but bone and parchment. Slight changes steal over her, for there is a shadowy suggestion of human skin on them now. The Strand may be taken as the central point about which she revolves in a half mile orbit. How comes she so far East as this? And coming back too! Having been how much further? She is a rare spectacle in this neighbourhood. I receive intelligent information to this effect from a dog: a lop-sided mongrel with a foolish tail, plodding along with his tail up, and his ears pricked, and displaying an amiable interest in the ways of his fellow-men – if I may be allowed the expression. After pausing at a porkshop, he is jogging Eastward like myself, with a benevolent countenance and a watery mouth, as though musing on the many excellences of pork, when he beholds this doubled-up bundle approaching. He is not so much astonished at the bundle (though amazed by that), as at the circumstance that it has within itself the means of locomotion. He stops, pricks his ears higher, makes a slight point, stares, utters a short low growl, and glistens at the nose – as I conceive, with terror. The bundle continuing to approach, he barks, turns tail, and is about to fly, when, arguing with himself that flight is not becoming in a dog, he turns and once more faces the advancing heap of clothes. After much hesitation it occurs to him that there may be a face in it somewhere. Desperately resolving to undertake the adventure and pursue the inquiry, he goes slowly up to the bundle, goes slowly round it, and coming at length upon the human countenance down there where never human countenance should be, gives a yelp of horror, and flies for the East India Docks.

Being now in the Commercial-road district of my Beat, and bethinking myself that Stepney Station is near, I quicken my pace that I may turn out of the road at that point, and see how my small Eastern Star is shining.

The Children's Hospital, to which I gave that name, is in full force. All its beds are occupied. There is a new face on the bed where my pretty baby lay, and that sweet little child is now at rest for ever. Much kind sympathy has been here, since my former visit, and it is good to see the walls profusely garnished with dolls. I wonder what Poodles may think of them, as they stretch out their arms above the beds, and stare, and display their splendid dresses. Poodles has a greater interest in the patients. I find him making the rounds of the beds, like a house surgeon, attended by another dog – a friend – who appears to trot about with him in the character of his pupil dresser. Poodles is anxious to make me known to a pretty little girl, looking wonderfully healthy, who has had a leg taken off for cancer of the knee. A difficult operation, Poodles intimates, wagging his tail on the counterpane, but perfectly successful, as you see, dear Sir! The patient, patting Poodles, adds with a smile: 'The leg was so much trouble to me, that I am glad it's gone.' I never saw anything in doggery finer than the deportment of Poodles, when another little girl opens her mouth to show a peculiar enlargement of the tongue. Poodles (at that time on a table, to be on a level with the occasion) looks at the tongue (with his own sympathetically out), so very gravely and knowingly, that I feel inclined to put my hand in my waistcoat pocket, and give him a guinea, wrapped in paper.

On my Beat again, and close to Limehouse Church, its termination, I found myself near to certain 'Lead Mills.' Struck by the name, which was fresh in my memory, and finding on inquiry that these same Lead Mills were identical with those same Lead Mills of which I made mention when I first visited the East London Children's Hospital and its neighbourhood, as Uncommercial Traveller, I resolved to have a look at them.

Received by two very intelligent gentlemen, brothers, and partners with their father in the concern, and who testified every desire to show their works to me freely, I went over the Lead Mills. The purport of such works is the conversion of Pig-Lead into White Lead. This conversion is brought about by the slow and gradual effecting of certain successive chemical changes in the lead itself. The processes are picturesque and interesting; the most so, being the burying of the lead at a certain stage of preparation, in pots; each pot containing a certain quantity of acid besides; and all the pots being buried in vast numbers, in layers, under tan, for some ten weeks.

Hopping up ladders and across planks and on elevated perches until I was uncertain whether to liken myself to a Bird or a Bricklayer, I became conscious of standing on nothing particular, looking down into one of a series of large cocklofts, with the outer day peeping in through the chinks in the tiled roof above. A number of women were ascending to, and descending from, this cockloft, each carrying on the upward journey a pot of prepared lead and acid, for deposition under the smoking tan. When one layer of pots was completely filled, it was carefully covered in with planks, and those were carefully covered with tan again, and then another layer of pots was begun above: sufficient means of ventilation being preserved through wooden tubes. Going down into the cockloft then filling, I found the heat of the tan to be surprisingly great, and also the odour of the lead and acid to be not absolutely exquisite, though I believe not noxious at that stage. In other cocklofts where the pots were being exhumed, the heat of the steaming tan was much greater, and the smell was penetrating and peculiar. There were cocklofts in all stages; full and empty, half filled and half emptied; strong active women were clambering about them busily; and the whole thing had rather the air of the upper part of the house of some immensely rich old Turk, whose faithful Seraglio were hiding his money because the Sultan or the Pasha was coming.

As is the case with most pulps or pigments so in the instance of this White Lead, processes of stirring, separating, washing, grinding, rolling, and pressing, succeed. Some of these are unquestionably inimical to health; the danger arising from inhalation of particles of lead, or from contact between the lead and the touch, or both. Against these dangers, I found good respirators provided (simply made of flannel and muslin, so as to be inexpensively renewed, and in some instances washed with scented soap), and gauntlet gloves, and loose gowns. Everywhere, there was as much fresh air as windows, well placed and opened, could possibly admit. And it was explained, that the precaution of frequently changing the women employed in the worst parts of the work (a precaution originating in their own experience or apprehension of its ill effects) was found salutary. They had a mysterious and singular appearance with the mouth and nose covered, and the loose gown on, and yet bore out the simile of the old Turk and the Seraglio all the better for the disguise.

At last this vexed white lead having been buried and resuscitated, and heated, and cooled, and stirred, and separated, and washed, and ground, and rolled, and pressed, is subjected to the action of intense fiery heat. A row of women, dressed as above described, stood, let us say, in a large stone bake-house, passing on the baking-dishes as they were given out by the cooks, from hand to hand, into the ovens. The oven or stove, cold as yet, looked as high as an ordinary house, and was full of men and women on temporary footholds, briskly passing up and stowing away the dishes. The door of another oven or stove, about to be cooled and emptied, was opened from above, for the Uncommercial countenance to peer down into. The Uncommercial countenance withdrew itself, with expedition and a sense of suffocation from the dull-glowing heat and the overpowering smell. On the whole, perhaps the going into these stoves to work, when they are freshly opened, may be the worst part of the occupation.

But I made it out to be indubitable that the owners of these lead mills honestly and sedulously try to reduce the dangers of the occupation to the lowest point. A washing-place is provided for the women (I thought there might have been more towels), and a room in which they hang their clothes, and take their meals, and where they have a good fire-range and fire, and a female attendant to help them, and to watch that they do not neglect the cleansing of their hands before touching their food. An experienced medical attendant is provided for them, and any premonitory symptoms of lead-poisoning are carefully treated. Their tea-pots and such things were set out on tables ready for their afternoon-meal, when I saw their room, and it had a homely look. It is found that they bear the work much better than men; some few of them have been at it for years, and the great majority of those I observed were strong and active. On the other hand it should be remembered that most of them are very capricious and irregular in their attendance.

American inventiveness would seem to indicate that before very long White Lead may be made entirely by machinery. The sooner, the better. In the meantime, I parted from my two frank conductors over the mills, by telling them that they had nothing there to be concealed, and nothing to be blamed for. As to the rest, the philosophy of the matter of lead poisoning and workpeople, seems to me to have been pretty fairly summed up by the Irishwoman whom I quoted in my former paper: 'Some of them gets lead-pisoned soon, and some of them gets lead-pisoned later, and some but not many niver, and 'tis all according to the constitooshun, Sur, and some constitooshuns is strong and some is weak.'

Retracing my footsteps over my Beat, I went off duty.

43

New Uncommercial Samples. By Charles Dickens. A Fly-Leaf in a Life

All The Year Round, 22 May 1869 (*UT3* as 'A Fly-Leaf in a Life')

Dickens's 'Farewell Tour' of public readings in the provinces had come to an abrupt end at Preston on 22 April, when medical advisers agreed with him that 'the readings must be *stopped*' in view of 'symptoms that must not be disregarded' (*Nonesuch*, Vol. III, p. 722). That night's reading, and twenty-five subsequent dates, were cancelled, causing considerable disruption, and during his convalescence Dickens found himself having to write to friends as far afield as Australia to scotch rumours that his health had failed him (see *To* Mr Rusden, 18 May 1869; *Nonesuch*, Vol. III, p. 725). Friends feared, however, that the recovery was not so complete as Dickens wished to suggest, and his death just over a year later from a related condition seems to have influenced Chapman & Hall's decision in 1874 to omit the present article – which so clearly yet uncharacteristically takes this private matter as its subject – from their enlarged edition of *The Uncommercial Traveller* (*UT2*). It was collected later by B. W. Matz for the 'Gadshill Edition' of Dickens's works for Chapman & Hall in 1897–8, and Charles Dickens Jr subsequently noted the paper's 'pathetic interest in connection with its author's premature death. It is always the saddest of reflections to me that, if he could have been induced to take warning of the temporary breakdown to which it alludes, the end might have been long postponed' (*UT4*, p. xxi).

Dickens's reference to 'My old acquaintances the begging-letter writers' is expanded on in article 45 of Vol. 2 of this edition, pp. 227–34.

Literary allusions (p. 388) 'At first, he was dead ... for many years': Charles Dickens, *Little Dorrit* (1857), Book 2, Ch. 25; (p. 389) 'playing sick lion': the lovesick lion in the fable 'Le Lion amoureux' allows his teeth and claws to be removed and dogs to be set on him, Jean de la Fontaine, *Fables Choisies Mises en Vers* (1668), Book 4, Fable 1; (p. 390) 'Mrs Trollope's book on America': Frances Trollope's *Domestic Manners of the Americans* (1832), which Dickens read in 1841 and owned in an edition of 1832 'with many humorous illustrations' (Stonehouse).

MS Draft (?May 1869), Houghton Library, University of Harvard, MS Eng. 58.4. Folio 3 of ff. 1–6 consists of p. 448 torn from the 'Cheap Edition' of *Little Dorrit* (Bradbury & Evans, 1861), with two of the three text paragraphs enclosed in MS quotation marks, and the third cancelled with four vertical strokes. MS ff. 1–2 and 4–6 are heavily amended, with rare vertical interpolations on f. 1. The title and all subsequent references to 'the fly-leaf' until f. 6 are later insertions.

Once upon a time (no matter when), I was engaged in a pursuit (no matter what), which could be transacted by myself alone; in which I could have no help; which imposed a constant strain on the attention, memory, observation, and physical powers; and which involved an almost fabulous amount of change of place and rapid railway travelling. I had followed this pursuit through an exceptionally trying winter in an always trying climate, and had resumed it in England after but a brief repose. Thus it came to be prolonged until, at length – and, as it seemed, all of a sudden – it so wore me out that I could not rely, with my usual cheerful confidence, upon myself to achieve the constantly recurring task, and began to feel (for the first time in my life) giddy, jarred, shaken, faint, uncertain of voice and sight and tread and touch, and dull of spirit. The medical advice I sought within a few hours, was given in two words: 'Instant rest.' Being accustomed to observe myself as curiously as if I were another man, and knowing the advice to meet my only need, I instantly halted in the pursuit of which I speak, and rested.

My intention was, to interpose, as it were, a fly-leaf in the book of my life, in which nothing should be written from without for a brief season of a few weeks. But some very singular experiences recorded themselves on this same fly-leaf, and I am going to relate them literally. I repeat the word: literally.

My first odd experience was of the remarkable coincidence between my case, in the general mind, and one MR MERDLE'S as I find it recorded in a work of fiction called LITTLE DORRIT. To be sure, Mr Merdle was a swindler, forger, and thief, and my calling had been of a less harmful (and less remunerative) nature; but it was all one for that.

Here is Mr Merdle's case:

'At first, he was dead of all the diseases that ever were known, and of several bran-new maladies invented with the speed of Light to meet the demand of the occasion. He had concealed a dropsy from infancy, he had inherited a large estate of water on the chest from his grandfather, he had had an operation performed upon him every morning of his life for eighteen years, he had been subject to the explosion of important veins in his body after the manner of fireworks, he had had something the matter with his lungs, he had had something the matter with his heart, he had had something the matter with his brain. Five hundred people who sat down to breakfast entirely uninformed on the whole subject, believed before they had done breakfast, that they privately and personally knew Physician to have said to Mr Merdle, "You must expect to go out, some day, like the snuff of a candle;" and that they knew Mr Merdle to have said to Physician, "A man can die but once." By about eleven o'clock in the forenoon, something the matter with the brain, became the favourite theory against the field; and by twelve the something had been distinctly ascertained to be "Pressure."

'Pressure was so entirely satisfactory to the public mind, and seemed to make every one so comfortable, that it might have lasted all day but for Bar's having taken the real state of the case into Court at half-past nine. Pressure, however, so far from being overthrown by the discovery, became a greater favourite than ever. There was a general moralising upon Pressure, in every street. All the people who had tried to make money and had not been able to do it, said, There you were! You no sooner began to devote yourself to the pursuit of wealth, than you got Pressure. The idle people improved the occasion in a similar manner. See, said they, what you brought yourself to by work, work, work! You persisted in working, you overdid it, Pressure came on, and you were done for! This consideration was very potent in many quarters, but nowhere more so than among the young clerks and partners who had never been in the slightest danger of overdoing it. These, one and all declared, quite piously, that they hoped they would never forget the warning as long as they lived, and that their conduct might be so regulated as to keep off Pressure, and preserve them, a comfort to their friends, for many years.'

Just my case – if I had only known it – when I was quietly basking in the sunshine in my Kentish meadow!

But while I so rested, thankfully recovering every hour, I had experiences more odd than this. I had experiences of spiritual conceit, for which, as giving me a new warning against that curse of mankind, I shall always feel grateful to the supposition that I was too far gone to protest against playing sick lion to any stray donkey with an itching hoof. All sorts of people seemed to become vicariously religious at my expense. I received the most uncompromising warning that I was a Heathen: on the conclusive authority of a field preacher, who, like the most of his ignorant and vain and daring class, could not construct a tolerable sentence in his native tongue or pen a fair letter. This inspired individual called me to order roundly, and knew in the freest and easiest way where I was going to, and what would become of me if I failed to fashion myself on his bright example, and was on terms of blasphemous confidence with the Heavenly Host. He was in the secrets of my heart, and in the lowest soundings of my soul – he! – and could read the depths of my nature better than his A B C, and could turn me inside out, like his own clammy glove. But what is far more extraordinary than this – for such dirty water as this could alone be drawn from such a shallow and muddy source – I found from the information of a beneficed clergyman, of whom I never heard and whom I never saw, that I had not, as I rather supposed I had, lived a life of some reading, contemplation, and inquiry; that I had not studied, as I rather supposed I had, to inculcate some Christian lessons in books; that I had never tried, as I rather supposed I had, to turn a child or two tenderly towards the knowledge and love of our Saviour; that I had never had, as I rather supposed I had had, departed friends, or stood beside open graves; but that I had lived a life of 'uninterrupted prosperity,' and that I needed this 'check, overmuch,' and that the way to turn it to account was to read these sermons and these poems, enclosed, and written and issued by my correspondent! I beg it may be understood that I relate facts of my own uncommercial experience, and no vain imaginings. The documents in proof lie near my hand.

Another odd entry on the fly-leaf, of a more entertaining character, was the wonderful persistency with which kind sympathisers assumed that I had injuriously coupled with the so suddenly relinquished pursuit, those personal habits of mine most obviously incompatible with it, and most plainly impossible of being maintained, along with it. As, all that exercise, all that cold bathing, all that wind and weather, all that uphill training – all that everything else, say, which is usually carried about by express trains in a portmanteau and hat-box, and partaken of under a flaming row of gaslights in the company of two thousand people. This assuming of a whole case against all fact and likelihood, struck me as particularly droll, and was an oddity of which I certainly had had no adequate experience in life until I turned that curious fly-leaf.

My old acquaintances the begging-letter writers came out on the fly-leaf, very piously indeed. They were glad, at such a serious crisis, to afford me another opportunity of sending that Post-office order. I needn't make it a pound, as previously insisted on; ten shillings might ease my mind. And Heaven forbid that they should refuse, at such an insignificant figure, to take a weight off the memory of an erring fellow-creature! One gentleman, of an artistic turn (and copiously illustrating the books of the Mendicity Society), thought it might soothe my conscience, in the tender respect of gifts misused, if I would immediately cash up in aid of his lowly talent for original design – as a specimen of which he enclosed me a work of art which I recognised as a tracing from a woodcut originally published in the late Mrs Trollope's book on America, forty or fifty years ago. The number of people who were prepared to live long years after me, untiring benefactors to their species, for fifty pounds a piece down, was astonishing. Also, of those who wanted bank notes for stiff penitential amounts, to give away: – not to keep, on any account.

Divers wonderful medicines and machines insinuated recommendations of themselves into the fly-leaf that was to have been so blank. It was specially observable that every prescriber, whether in a moral or physical direction, knew me thoroughly – knew me from head to heel, in and out, through and through, upside down. I was a glass piece of general property, and everybody was on the most surprisingly intimate terms with me. A few public institutions had complimentary perceptions of corners in my mind, of which, after considerable self-examination, I have not discovered any indication. Neat little printed forms were addressed to those corners, beginning with the words: 'I give and bequeath.'

Will it seem exaggerative to state my belief that the most honest, the most modest, and the least vain-glorious of all the records upon this strange fly-leaf, was a letter from the self-deceived discoverer of the recondite secret 'how to live four or five hundred years'? Doubtless it will seem so, yet the statement is not exaggerative by any means, but is made in my serious and sincere conviction. With this, and with a laugh at the rest that shall not be cynical, I turn the Fly-leaf, and go on again.

44

New Uncommercial Samples. By Charles Dickens. A Plea for Total Abstinence

All The Year Round, 5 June 1869 (*UT2* as 'A Plea for Total Abstinence')

In the first of his 'Sketches of London' for the *Evening Chronicle* (31 January 1835; see Vol. 1 of this edition, p. 83), Dickens as 'Boz' had declared that 'we are as great friends to horses ... as the renowned Mr Martin'. Richard Martin, an Irish MP, was a founder in 1824 of the Society for the Prevention of Cruelty to Animals (see p. 395 below), and had been instrumental in the passing of the Act for Protecting the Rights of Animals in 1822. Dickens demonstrated the sincerity of this declaration in 1838 by appearing as a leading prosecution witness in the trial of Richard Davis, a London omnibus driver accused of mistreating his horse near Lincoln's Inn Fields on 16 October. The charge was filed by the Secretary of the Society for the Prevention of Cruelty to Animals, and Dickens's testimony, to judge by a report in *The Times* of 20 October, was felt to have weighed heavily against the driver, who was fined twenty shillings by the Bow Street magistrate (see Nils Erik Enkvist, 'Charles Dickens in the Witness Box', *The Dickensian*, Vol. 47 [1951], p. 201). Thus, in spite of proposing the pledge for 'Total Abstinence from Horseflesh' in the present article as something of a *reductio ad absurdum*, Dickens's concern about mistreatment of animals was genuine. His article for *HW* about the poor living conditions for animals exhibited at Regent's Park suggests a continuing interest (see Vol. 3 of this edition, article 46).

In 1849 Dickens had used the platform provided by Forster's *Examiner* to voice his objections to the principles of the movement for 'Total Abstinence' from alcoholic beverages, complaining of the 'large class of minds apparently unable to distinguish between use and abuse'. The same charge is made in the present article, in which more than a whiff of Carlylism is detectable (see headnote to article 35 in Vol. 2 of this edition; also literary allusions below). For other essays in which Dickens attacks Temperance societies and principles, see Vol. 2 of this edition, article 26, and Vol. 3, articles 3, 6, 22 and 40. The title of the essay is clearly designed to shock or intrigue readers by suggesting a sharp divergence from a position Dickens felt he was known to maintain.

Literary allusions (below) 'whether "the husk or shell of him," as the esteemed Herr Teufelsdroch might put it': 'The gladder am I ... to do reverence to those Shells and outer Husks of the Body', Thomas Carlyle *Sartor Resartus, The Life and Opinions of Herr Teufelsdrockh* (1835), Ch. 6; (p. 393) 'this Gilpinian triumvirate': William Cowper's comic poem 'John Gilpin' (1785) recounts the mishaps of an incompetent rider whose horse bolts from Cheapside to Ware and back again; (p. 393) 'Up guards and at 'em': order attributed to the Duke of Wellington at Waterloo in Sir E. Creasy's *Fifteen Decisive Battles of the World* (1851), Vol. II, p. 329; (p. 394) 'I never will desert Mr Micawber': Mrs Micawber's repeated cry in Dickens's *David Copperfield* (1850), Ch. 12 et seq.; (p. 394) 'a gallant, gallant crew': *untraced*; (p. 394) 'if patriotic Peckham picked a peck of pickled poetry ...': adaptation of the traditional child's tongue-twister, 'Peter Piper picked a peck of pickled pepper'; (p. 395) 'the less includes the greater': reversal of Euclid's axiom from *The Elements* (n.d.), 'the greater includes the lesser'.

MS Draft (?May 1869), Houghton Library, Harvard University, MS Eng. 58.4. ff. 1–6, heavily amended, with rare vertical interpolation on f. 1.

One day this last Whitsuntide, at precisely eleven o'clock in the forenoon, there suddenly rode into the field of view commanded by the windows of my lodging, an equestrian phenomenon. It was a fellow-creature on horseback, dressed in the absurdest manner. The fellow-creature wore high boots, some other (and much larger) fellow-creature's breeches, of a slack-baked doughy colour and a baggy form, a blue shirt whereof the skirt or tail was puffily tucked into the waistband of the said breeches, no coat, a red shoulder-belt; and a demi-semi-military scarlet hat with a feathered ornament in front, which to the uninstructed human vision had the appearance of a moulting shuttlecock. I laid down the newspaper with which I had been occupied, and surveyed the fellow-man in question, with astonishment. Whether he had been sitting to any painter as a frontispiece for a new edition of Sartor Resartus; whether 'the husk or shell of him,' as the esteemed Herr Teufelsdroch might put it, were founded on a jockey, on a circus, on General Garibaldi, on cheap porcelain, on a toy-shop, on Guy Fawkes, on Wax-Work, on Gold Digging, on Bedlam, or on all, were doubts that greatly exercised my mind. Meanwhile my fellow-man stumbled and slided, excessively against his will, on the slippery stones of my Covent Garden street, and elicited shrieks from several sympathetic females, by convulsively restraining himself from pitching over his horse's head. In the very crisis of these evolutions, and indeed at the trying moment when his charger's tail was in a tobacconist's shop, and his head anywhere about town, this cavalier was joined by two similar portents, who, likewise stumbling and sliding, caused him to stumble and slide the more distressingly. At length this Gilpinian triumvirate effected a halt, and, looking northward, waved their three right hands as commanding unseen troops to Up guards and at 'em. Hereupon a brazen band burst forth, which caused them to be instantly bolted with to some remote spot of earth in the direction of the Surrey Hills.

Judging from these appearances that a procession was under way, I threw up my window, and, craning out, had the satisfaction of beholding it advancing along the streets. It was a Tee-Total procession, as I learnt from its banners, and was long enough to consume twenty minutes in passing. There were a great number of children in it, some of them so very young in their mothers' arms as to be in the act of practically exemplifying their abstinence from fermented liquors, and attachment to an unintoxicating drink, while the procession defiled. The display was, on the whole, pleasant to see, as any good-humoured holiday assemblage of clean, cheerful, and well-conducted people should be. It was bright with ribbons, tinsel, and shoulder-belts, and abounded in flowers, as if those latter trophies had come up in profusion under much watering. The day being breezy, the insubordination of the large banners was very reprehensible. Each of these, being borne aloft on two poles and stayed with some half dozen lines, was carried, as polite books in the last century used to be written, by 'various hands,' and the anxiety expressed in the upturned faces of those officers – something between the anxiety attendant on the balancing art, and that inseparable from the pastime of kite flying, with a touch of the angler's quality in landing his scaly prey – much impressed me. Suddenly, too, a banner would shiver in the wind, and go about in the most inconvenient manner. This always happened oftenest with such gorgeous standards as those representing a gentleman in black, corpulent with tea and water, in the laudable act of summarily reforming a family feeble and pinched with beer. The gentleman in black distended by wind would then conduct himself with the most unbecoming levity, while the beery family, growing beerier, would frantically try to tear themselves away from his ministration. Some of the inscriptions accompanying the banners were of a highly determined character, as 'We never, never, will give up the temperance cause:' with similar sound resolutions, rather suggestive to the profane mind of Mrs Micawber's 'I never will desert Mr Micawber,' and of Mr Micawber's retort, 'Really, my dear, I am not aware that you were ever required by any human being to do anything of the sort.'

At intervals a gloom would fall on the passing members of the procession, for which I was at first unable to account. But this I discovered, after a little observation, to be occasioned by the coming-on of the Executioners – the terrible official Beings who were to make the speeches bye-and-bye – who were distributed in open carriages at various points of the cavalcade. A dark cloud and a sensation of dampness, as from many wet blankets, invariably preceded the rolling on of the dreadful cars containing these Headsmen, and I noticed that the wretched people who closely followed them, and who were in a manner forced to contemplate their folded arms, complacent countenances, and threatening lips, were more overshadowed by the cloud and damp than those in front. Indeed, I perceived in some of these so moody an implacability towards the magnates of the scaffold, and so plain a desire to tear them limb from limb, that I would respectfully suggest to the managers the expediency of conveying the Executioners to the scene of their dismal labours by unfrequented ways, and in closely tilted carts, next Whitsuntide.

The Procession was composed of a series of smaller processions which had come together, each from its own metropolitan district. An infusion of Allegory became perceptible when patriotic Peckham advanced. So I judged, from the circumstance of Peckham's unfurling a silken banner that fanned Heaven and Earth with the words 'The Peckham Life Boat.' No Boat being in attendance, though Life, in the likeness of 'a gallant, gallant crew,' in nautical uniform followed the flag, I was led to meditate on the fact that Peckham is described by Geographers as an inland settlement with no larger or nearer shore-line than the towing-path of the Surrey Canal, on which stormy station I had been given to understand no Life Boat exists. Thus I deduced an allegorical meaning, and came to the conclusion that if patriotic Peckham picked a peck of pickled poetry, this *was* the peck of pickled poetry which patriotic Peckham picked.

I have observed that the aggregate Procession was on the whole pleasant to see. I made use of that qualified expression with a direct meaning which I will now explain. It involves the title of this paper, and a little fair trying of Tee-Totalism by its own tests.

There were many people on foot, and many people in vehicles of various kinds. The former were pleasant to see, and the latter were not pleasant to see: for the reason that I never, on any occasion or under any circumstances, have beheld heavier overloading of horses than in this public show. Unless the imposition of a great van laden with from ten to twenty people on a single horse be a moderate tasking of the poor creature, then the Temperate use of horses was immoderate and cruel. From the smallest and lightest horse to the largest and heaviest, there were many instances in which the beast of burden was so shamefully overladen, that the Society for the Prevention of Cruelty to Animals has frequently interposed in less gross cases.

Now, I have always held that there may be, and that there unquestionably is, such a thing as Use without Abuse, and that therefore the Total Abolitionists are irrational and wrong-headed. But the Procession completely converted me. For, so large a number of the people using draught-horses in it were so clearly unable to Use them without Abusing them, that I perceived Total Abstinence from Horseflesh to be the only remedy of which the case admitted. As it is all one to Tee-Totallers whether you take half a pint of beer or half a gallon, so it was all one here whether the beast of burden were a pony or a cart-horse. Indeed, my case had the special strength that the half-pint quadruped underwent as much suffering as the half-gallon quadruped. Moral: Total Abstinence from Horseflesh through the whole length and breadth of the scale. This Pledge will be in course of administration to all Tee-Total processionists, not pedestrians, at the publishing office of ALL THE YEAR ROUND, on the first day of April, One Thousand Eight Hundred and Seventy.

Observe a point for consideration. This Procession comprised many persons in their gigs, broughams, tax-carts, barouches, chaises, and what not, who were merciful to the dumb beasts that drew them, and did not overcharge their strength. What is to be done with those unoffending persons? I will not run amuck and vilify and defame them, as Tee-Total tracts and platforms would most assuredly do, if the question were one of drinking instead of driving; I merely ask what is to be done with them? The reply admits of no dispute whatever. Manifestly, in strict accordance with Tee-Total doctrines, THEY must come in too, and take the Total Abstinence from Horseflesh Pledge. It is not pretended that those members of the Procession misused certain auxiliaries which in most countries and all ages have been bestowed upon man for his use, but it is undeniable that other members of the Procession did. Tee-Total mathematics demonstrate that the less includes the greater; that the guilty include the innocent, the blind the seeing, the deaf the hearing, the dumb the speaking, the drunken the sober. If any of the moderate users of draught-cattle in question should deem that there is any gentle violence done to their reason by these elements of logic, they are invited to come out of the Procession next Whitsuntide, and look at it from my window.

45

Landor's Life

All The Year Round, 24 July 1869

Dickens first met Walter Savage Landor, the poet and author of *Imaginary Conversations*, at Gore House in 1840 when Landor was already in his sixty-sixth year. Together with Forster, who had known the older man a few years longer, he shortly afterwards visited Landor, who was an ardent admirer of his writings, at his lodgings in Bath. There Dickens first conceived the idea of Little Nell, and Forster relates in the biography Dickens is here reviewing that when the old man was reminded of this in later years, he would with characteristic comic vehemence declare his regret at not having bought the house and burned it down so that 'no meaner association should ever desecrate the birthplace of Little Nell'. Dickens soon numbered Landor among his dearest friends and invited him to be godfather to his second son, named Walter Landor; the boy's early death is touchingly referred to at the end of this review. Dickens painted an affectionate and what he called (*Pilgrim*, Vol. VI, p. 666) 'a most exact' portrait of Landor as Lawrence Boythorn in *Bleak House*.

In 1808 Landor, who had a large personal fortune, went to Spain and raised a troop to fight under his command for Spanish independence against the invading French and was narrowly saved from capture by the action of Juan Santos de Maria, a poor man of Castro, near Bilbao. In 1811 he made a somewhat hasty marriage with Julia Thuillier, nineteen years his junior and the portionless daughter of a Banbury banker. The marriage proved unhappy and, after many years of marital strain, Landor left the family home in Florence in 1835 and settled again in Bath. The embarrassing near-encounter with Mrs Landor that Dickens describes himself below as having experienced occurred in 1853; he reported it to Georgina Hogarth in a letter from Italy (*Pilgrim*, Vol. VII, p. 209).

Literary allusions (p.397) 'like Hamlet ... would speak daggers but use none': Shakespeare, *Hamlet*, Act 3, Sc. 3; (p. 397) 'the fictitious Mr Boythorn': see *Bleak House* (1853), Ch. 9 et seq.; (p. 397) 'the same masterly writer's *Life and Times of Oliver Goldsmith*': Forster's biography of 1854; (p. 400) 'as Mr Pepys would observe ...': the phrase Dickens quotes occurs frequently in Pepys's famous *Diary* (1660–9).

Prefixed to the second volume of Mr Forster's admirable biography of WALTER SAVAGE LANDOR,* is an engraving from a portrait of that remarkable man when seventy-seven years of age, by BOXALL. The writer of these lines can testify that the original picture is a singularly good likeness, the result of close and subtle observation on the part of the painter; but, for this very reason, the engraving gives a most inadequate idea of the merit of the picture and the character of the man.

From the engraving, the arms and hands are omitted. In the picture, they are, as they were in nature, indispensable to a correct reading of the vigorous face. The arms were very peculiar. They were rather short, and were curiously restrained and checked in their action at the elbows; in the action of the hands, even when separately clenched, there was the same kind of pause, and a noticeable tendency to relaxation on the part of the thumb. Let the face be never so intense or fierce, there was a commentary of gentleness in the hands, essential to be taken along with it. Like Hamlet, Landor would speak daggers but use none. In the expression of his hands, though angrily closed, there was always gentleness and tenderness; just as when they were open, and the handsome old gentleman would wave them with a little courtly flourish that sat well upon him, as he recalled some classic compliment that he had rendered to some reigning Beauty, there was a chivalrous grace about them such as pervades his softer verses. Thus, the fictitious Mr Boythorn (to whom we may refer without impropriety in this connexion, as Mr Forster does) declaims 'with unimaginable energy' the while his bird is 'perched upon his thumb,' and he 'softly smooths its feathers and his forefinger.'

From the spirit of Mr Forster's Biography these characteristic hands are never omitted, and hence (apart from its literary merits) its great value. As the same masterly writer's *Life and Times of Oliver Goldsmith* is a generous and yet conscientious picture of a period, so this is a not less generous and yet conscientious picture of one life; of a life, with all its aspirations, achievements, and disappointments; all its capabilities, opportunities, and irretrievable mistakes. It is essentially a sad book, and herein lies proof of its truth and worth. The life of almost any man possessing great gifts, would be a sad book to himself; and this book enables us not only to see its subject, but to be its subject, if we will.

Mr Forster is of opinion that 'Landor's fame very surely awaits him.' This point admitted or doubted, the value of the book remains the same. It needs not to know his works (otherwise than through his biographer's exposition), it needs not to have known himself, to find a deep interest in these pages. More or less of their warning is in every conscience; and some admiration of a fine genius, and of a great, wild, generous nature, incapable of mean self-extenuation or dissimulation − if unhappily

* Walter Savage Landor, a Biography by John Forster, 2 vols. Chapman and Hall.

incapable of self-repression too – should be in every breast. 'There may be still living many persons,' Walter Landor's brother, Robert, writes to Mr Forster of this book, 'who would contradict any narrative of yours in which the best qualities were remembered, the worst forgotten.' Mr Forster's comment is: 'I had not waited for this appeal to resolve, that, if this memoir were written at all, it should contain, as far as might lie within my power, a fair statement of the truth.' And this eloquent passage of truth immediately follows: 'Few of his infirmities are without something kindly or generous about them; and we are not long in discovering there is nothing so wildly incredible that he will not himself in perfect good faith believe. When he published his first book of poems on quitting Oxford, the profits were to be reserved for a distressed clergyman. When he published his Latin poems, the poor of Leipzig were to have the sum they realised. When his comedy was ready to be acted, a Spaniard who had sheltered him at Castro was to be made richer by it. When he competed for the prize of the Academy of Stockholm, it was to go to the poor of Sweden. If nobody got anything from any one of these enterprises, the fault at all events was not his. With his extraordinary power of forgetting disappointments, he was prepared at each successive failure to start afresh, as if each had been a triumph. I shall have to delineate this peculiarity as strongly in the last half as in the first half of his life, and it was certainly an amiable one. He was ready at all times to set aside, out of his own possessions, something for somebody who might please him for the time; and when frailties of temper and tongue are noted, this other eccentricity should not be omitted. He desired eagerly the love as well as the good opinion of those whom for the time he esteemed, and no one was more affectionate while under such influences. It is not a small virtue to feel such genuine pleasure, as he always did in giving and receiving pleasure. His generosity, too, was bestowed chiefly on those who could make small acknowledgement in thanks and no return in kind.'

Some of his earlier contemporaries may have thought him a vain man. Most assuredly he was not, in the common acceptation of the term. A vain man has little or no admiration to bestow upon competitors. Landor had an inexhaustible fund. He thought well of his writings, or he would not have preserved them. He said and wrote that he thought well of them, because that was his mind. He was one of the few men of whom you might always know the whole: of whom you might always know the worst, as well as the best. He had no reservations or duplicities. 'No, by Heaven!' he would say ('with unimaginable energy'), if any good adjective were coupled with him which he did not deserve: 'I am nothing of the kind. I wish I were; but I don't deserve the attribute, and I never did, and I never shall!' His intense consciousness of himself never led to his poorly excusing himself, and seldom to his violently asserting himself. When he told some little story of his bygone social experiences, in Florence, or where not, as he was fond of doing, it took the innocent form of making all the interlocutors, Landors. It was observable, too, that they always called him 'Mr Landor' – rather ceremoniously and submissively. There was a certain 'Cara Pádre Abáte Marina' – invariably so addressed in these anecdotes – who figured through a great many of them, and who always expressed himself in this deferential tone.

Mr Forster writes of Landor's character thus:

'A man must be judged, at first, by what he says and does. But with him such extravagance as I have referred to was little more than the habitual indulgence (on such themes) of passionate feelings and language, indecent indeed but utterly purposeless; the mere explosion of wrath provoked by tyranny or cruelty; the irregularities of an overheated steam-engine too weak for its own vapour. It is very certain that no one could detest oppression more truly than Landor did in all seasons and times; and if no one expressed that scorn, that abhorrence of tyranny and fraud, more hastily or more intemperately, all his fire and fury signified really little else than ill-temper too easily provoked. Not to justify or excuse such language, but to explain it, this consideration is urged. If not uniformly placable, Landor was always compassionate. He was tender-hearted rather than bloody-minded at all times, and upon only the most partial acquaintance with his writings could other opinion be formed. A completer knowledge of them would satisfy anyone that he had as little real disposition to kill a king as to kill a mouse. In fact there is not a more marked peculiarity in his genius than the union with its strength of a most uncommon gentleness, and in the personal ways of the man this was equally manifest.' – *Vol. I. p. 496.*

Of his works, thus:

'Though his mind was cast in the antique mould, it had opened itself to every kind of impression through a long and varied life; he has written with equal excellence in both poetry and prose, which can hardly be said of any of his contemporaries; and perhaps the single epithet by which his books would be best described is that reserved exclusively for books not characterised only by genius, but also by special individuality. They are unique. Having possessed them, we should miss them. Their place would be supplied by no others. They have that about them, moreover, which renders it almost certain that they will frequently be resorted to in future time. There are none in the language more quotable. Even where impulsiveness and want of patience have left them most fragmentary, this rich compensation is offered to the reader. There is hardly a conceivable subject in life or literature, which they do not illustrate by striking aphorisms, by concise and profound observations, by wisdom ever applicable to the needs of men, and by wit as available for their enjoyment. Nor, above all, will there anywhere be found a more pervading passion for liberty, a fiercer hatred of the base, a wider sympathy with the wronged and the oppressed, or help more ready at all times for those who fight at odds and disadvantage against the powerful and the fortunate, than in the writings of Walter Savage Landor.' – *Last page of second volume.*

The impression was strong upon the present writer's mind, as on Mr Forster's, during years of close friendship with the subject of this biography, that his animosities were chiefly referable to the singular inability in him to dissociate other people's ways of thinking from his own. He had, to the last, a ludicrous grievance (both Mr Forster and the writer have often amused themselves with it), against a good-natured nobleman, doubtless perfectly unconscious of having ever given him offence. The offence was, that on the occasion of some dinner party in another nobleman's house, many years before, this innocent lord (then a commoner) had passed in to dinner, through some door, before him, as he himself was about to pass in through that same door with a lady on his arm. Now, Landor was a gentleman of most scrupulous politeness, and in his carriage of himself towards ladies there was a certain mixture of stateliness and deference, belonging to quite another time and, as Mr Pepys would observe, 'mighty pretty to see.' If he could by any effort imagine himself committing such a high crime and misdemeanour as that in question, he could only imagine himself as doing it of a set purpose, under the sting of some vast injury, to inflict a great affront. A deliberately designed affront on the part of another man, it therefore remained to the end of his days. The manner in which, as time went on, he permeated the unfortunate lord's ancestry with this offence, was whimsically characteristic of Landor. The writer remembers very well, when only the individual himself was held responsible in the story for the breach of good breeding; but in another ten years or so, it began to appear that his father had always been remarkable for ill manners; and in yet another ten years or so, his grandfather developed into quite a prodigy of coarse behaviour.

Mr Boythorn – if he may again be quoted – said of his adversary, Sir Leicester Dedlock: 'That fellow is, *and his father was, and his grandfather was,* the most stiff-necked, arrogant, imbecile, pig-headed numskull, ever, by some inexplicable mistake of Nature, born in any station of life but a walking-stick's!'

The strength of some of Mr Landor's most captivating kind qualities was traceable to the same source. Knowing how keenly he himself would feel the being at any small social disadvantage, or the being unconsciously placed in any ridiculous light, he was wonderfully considerate of shy people, or of such as might be below the level of his usual conversation, or otherwise out of their element. The writer once observed him in the keenest distress of mind in behalf of a modest young stranger who came into a drawing-room with a glove on his head. An expressive commentary on this sympathetic condition, and on the delicacy with which he advanced to the younger stranger's rescue, was afterwards furnished by himself at a friendly dinner at Gore House, when it was the most delightful of houses. His dress – say, his cravat or shirt-collar – had become slightly disarranged on a hot evening, and Count D'Orsay laughingly called his attention to the circumstance as we rose from table. Landor became flushed, and greatly agitated: 'My dear Count D'Orsay, I thank you! My dear Count D'Orsay, I thank you from my soul for pointing out to me the abominable condition to which I am reduced! If I had entered the Drawing-room, and presented myself before Lady Blessington in so absurd a light, I would have instantly gone home, put a pistol to my head, and blown my brains out!'

Mr Forster tells a similar story of his keeping a company waiting dinner, through losing his way; and of his seeing no remedy for that breach of politeness but cutting his throat, or drowning himself, unless a countryman whom he met could direct him by a short road to the house where the party were assembled. Surely these are expressive notes on the gravity and reality of his explosive inclinations to kill kings!

His manner towards boys was charming, and the earnestness of his wish to be on equal terms with them and to win their confidence was quite touching. Few, reading Mr Forster's book, can fail to see in this, his pensive remembrance of that 'studious wilful boy at once shy and impetuous,' who had not many intimacies at Rugby, but who was 'generally popular and respected, and used his influence often to save the younger boys from undue harshness or violence.' The impulsive yearnings of his passionate heart towards his own boy, on their meeting at Bath, after years of separation, likewise burn through this phase of his character.

But a more spiritual, softened, and unselfish aspect of it, was to be derived from his respectful belief in happiness which he himself had missed. His marriage had not been a felicitous one – it may be fairly assumed for either side – but no trace of bitterness or distrust concerning other marriages was in his mind. He was never more serene than in the midst of a domestic circle, and was invariably remarkable for a perfectly benignant interest in young couples and young lovers. That, in his ever-fresh fancy, he conceived in this association innumerable histories of himself involving far more unlikely events that never happened than Isaac D'Israeli ever imagined, is hardly to be doubted; but as to this part of his real history he was mute, or revealed his nobleness in an impulse to be generously just. We verge on delicate ground, but a slight remembrance rises in the writer which can grate nowhere. Mr Forster relates how a certain friend, being in Florence, sent him home a leaf from the garden of his old house at Fiesole. That friend had first asked him what he should send him home, and he had stipulated for this gift – found by Mr Forster among his papers after his death. The friend, on coming back to England, related to Landor that he had been much embarrassed, on going in search of the leaf, by his driver's suddenly stopping his horses in a narrow lane, and presenting him (the friend) to 'La Signora Landora.' The lady was walking alone on a bright Italian-winter-day; and the man, having been told to drive to the Villa Landora, inferred that he must be conveying a guest or visitor. 'I pulled off my hat,' said the friend, 'apologised for the coachman's mistake, and drove on. The lady was walking with a rapid and firm step, had bright eyes, a fine fresh colour, and looked animated and agreeable.' Landor checked off each clause of the description, with a stately nod of more than ready assent, and replied, with all his tremendous energy concentrated into the sentence: 'And the Lord forbid that I should do otherwise than declare that she always WAS agreeable – to every one but *me!*'

Mr Forster step by step builds up the evidence on which he writes this life and states this character. In like manner, he gives the evidence for his high estimation of Landor's works, and – it may be added – for their recompense against some neglect, in finding so sympathetic, acute, and devoted a champion. Nothing in the book is more remarkable than his examination of each of Landor's successive pieces of writing, his delicate discernment of their beauties, and his strong desire to impart his own perceptions in this wise to the great audience that is yet to come. It rarely befals an author to have such a commentator: to become the subject of so much artistic skill and knowledge, combined with such infinite and loving pains. Alike as a piece of Biography, and as a commentary upon the beauties of a great writer, the book is a massive book; as the man and the writer were massive too. Sometimes, when the balance held by Mr Forster has seemed for a moment to turn a little heavily against the infirmities of temperament of a grand old friend, we have felt something of a shock; but we have not once been able to gainsay the justice of the scales. This feeling, too, has only fluttered out of the detail, here or there, and has vanished before the whole. We fully agree with Mr Forster that 'Judgment has been passed' – as it should be – 'with an equal desire to be only just on all the qualities of his temperament which affected necessarily not his own life only. But, now that the story is told, no one will have difficulty in striking the balance between its good and ill; and what was really imperishable in Landor's genius will not be treasured less, or less understood, for the more perfect knowledge of his character.'

Mr Forster's second volume gives a facsimile of Landor's writing at seventy-five. It may be interesting to those who are curious in caligraphy, to know that its resemblance to the recent handwriting of that great genius, M. VICTOR HUGO, is singularly strong.

In a military burial-ground in India, the name of WALTER LANDOR is associated with the present writer's, over the grave of a young officer. No name could stand there, more inseparably associated in the writer's mind with the dignity of generosity: with a noble scorn of all littleness, all cruelty, oppression, fraud, and false pretence.

46

On Mr Fechter's Acting

The Atlantic Monthly, August 1869 (Vol. 23, pp. 242–4)

Charles Albert Fechter made his début as an actor at the Comédie Française in Paris in 1844 when he was twenty years old. His big success, however, did not come until he created the role of the romantic lover Armand in *La Dame aux Camélias* at the Vaudeville in 1852. He first appeared in London (acting in English) in 1860 and was much praised for his performance in the title role of Hugo's *Ruy Blas*. This success was strongly consolidated by his original interpretation of Hamlet (1861) and by his Iago (he did not succeed in the title role in *Othello*). Dickens had, it seems, fervently admired his acting for some years before he wrote him a fan letter in March 1862 ('In Paris, your delicate and subtle knowledge both of nature and of art, and your wonderful hold upon the picturesque and romantic had strongly attracted me' [*Pilgrim*, Vol. X, p. 52]). A close friendship soon developed between the two with Dickens interesting himself strongly in all aspects of Fechter's professional career, particularly during the actor's management of the Lyceum Theatre (1863–7), and often expressing the warmest regard for him both as a friend and as an artist. Fechter was a frequent visitor to Gad's Hill and in 1865 presented his friend with a Swiss chalet that was erected in the grounds and became the novelist's favourite writing-place (the chalet may be seen today at the Charles Dickens Centre in Rochester). In 1867 Fechter scored another triumph playing the villainous Obenreizer in a dramatisation by Dickens, Wilkie Collins and himself of the *ATYR* Christmas story for that year, 'No Thoroughfare', written jointly by Dickens and Wilkie Collins (see Malcolm Morley, 'No Thoroughfare Back Stage', *The Dickensian*, Vol. 50 [1954], pp.37–42, for this and also for details of Fechter's later career).

In the same issue of the *Atlantic Monthly* (the journal was published by Fields, Osgood & Co., Dickens's American publishers) in which Dickens's puff for Fechter appears is the second part of the two-part survey of 'Hamlets of the Stage' by A. Sage. It concludes with a survey of contemporary actors who have distinguished themselves in the role, giving the palm to Edwin Booth; Fechter is mentioned simply to note that he is the only actor ever to have worn 'the yellow locks of the Dane' in the part. In the issue for November 1870 Kate Field eulogised his 'wondrously picturesque' Hamlet at some length (Vol. 26, pp. 558–70), referring to Dickens as 'that best of dramatic critics'.

Literary allusions *(for dramas referred to in the text see the Glossary/Index)* (p. 408) 'going about seeking whom to stab': 'your adversary, the devil, as a roaring lion, walketh about, seeking whom he may devour', l. Peter 5:8; (p. 408) 'glass of fashion ... form': Shakespeare, *Hamlet*, Act 3, Sc. 1; (p. 408) 'fluttered the ... doves': Shakespeare, *Coriolanus*, Act 5, Sc. 6; (p. 409) 'Dr Johnson's celebrated friend': see Boswell's *Life of Dr Johnson*, ed. G. B. Hill, rev. L. F. Powell (1934), Vol. 2, p. 126 (1770), 'Speaking of a dull tiresome fellow, whom he chanced to meet, he said "That fellow seems to me to possess but one idea, and that is a wrong one".'

MS This is in the Houghton Library, Harvard University, and shows a few minor variants from the *Atlantic Monthly* text, also that the phrase 'and on the old student fellowship between Hamlet and Horatio' in the penultimate paragraph must have been added in proof. The most notable difference is the consistent reduction to lower case in the *Monthly* text of Dickens's characteristic capitalising of the first letter of certain key words ('Romance', 'Picture', 'Headsman' and 'Executioner' in paragraph 4; 'Romance', 'Picturesqueness' and 'Artist' in the final paragraph); his italicisation of the word 'her' in the phrase 'and raises her' in the second paragraph is also disregarded.

The distinguished artist whose name is prefixed to these remarks purposes to leave England for a professional tour in the United States. A few words from me, in reference to his merits as an actor, I hope may not be uninteresting to some readers, in advance of his publicly proving them before an American audience, and I know will not be unacceptable to my intimate friend. I state at once that Mr Fechter holds that relation towards me; not only because it is the fact, but also because our friendship originated in my public appreciation of him. I had studied his acting closely, and had admired it highly, both in Paris and in London, years before we exchanged

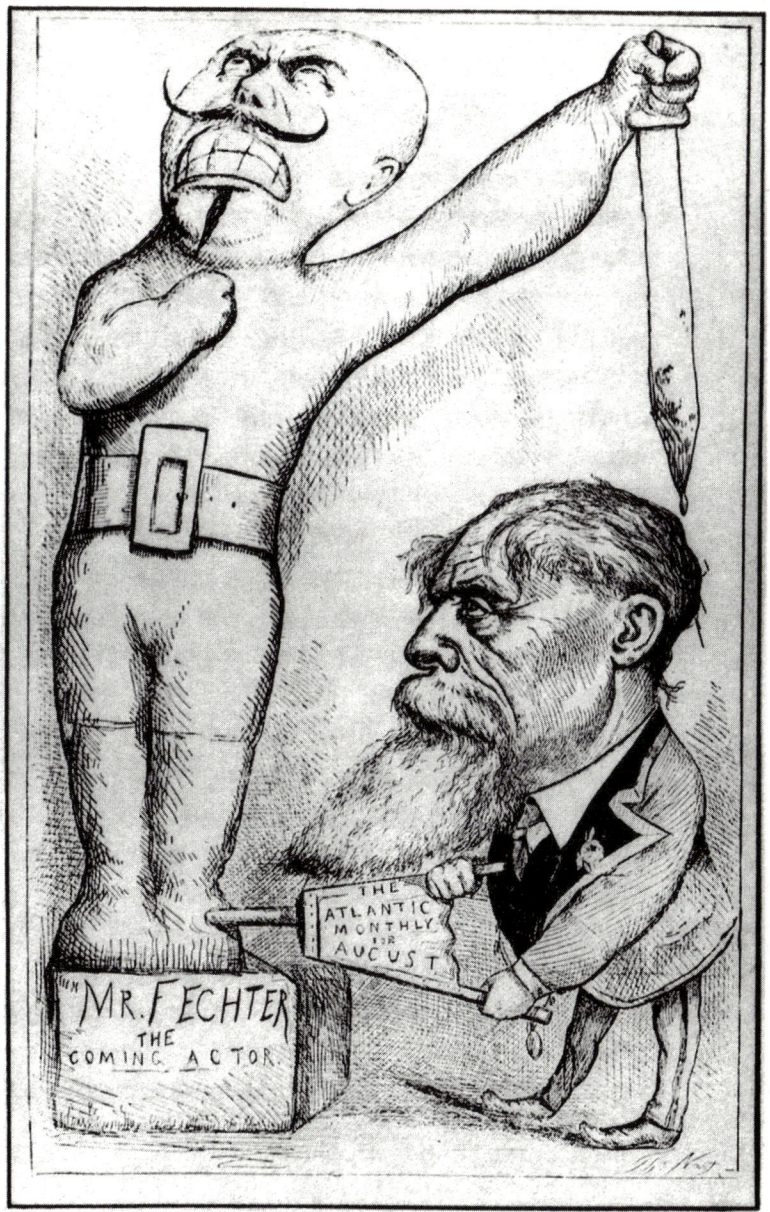

Charles Dickens Raising Great Expectations: 'You just keep still and I'll do all the blowing for you. I know 'ow to 'umbug these blasted Yankees, as I've done it before.' (Cartoon drawn by Thomas Nast, New York Evening Telegraph, 1869.)

a word. Consequently my appreciation is not the result of personal regard, but personal regard has sprung out of my appreciation.

The first quality observable in Mr Fechter's acting is, that it is in the highest degree romantic. However elaborated in minute details, there is always a peculiar dash and vigour in it, like the fresh atmosphere of the story whereof it is a part. When he is on the stage, it seems to me as though the story were transpiring before me for the first and last time. Thus there is a fervour in his love-making – a suffusion of his whole being with the rapture of his passion – that sheds a glory on its object, and raises her, before the eyes of the audience, into the light in which he sees her. It was this remarkable power that took Paris by storm when he became famous in the lover's part in the *Dame aux Camélias*. It is a short part, really comprised in two scenes, but, as he acted it (he was its original representative), it left its poetic and exalting influence on the heroine throughout the play. A woman who could be so loved – who could be so devotedly and romantically adored – had a hold upon the general sympathy with which nothing less absorbing and complete could have invested her. When I first saw this play and this actor, I could not in forming my lenient judgment of the heroine, forget that she had been the inspiration of a passion of which I had beheld such profound and affecting marks. I said to myself, as a child might have said: 'A bad woman could not have been the object of that wonderful tenderness, could not have so subdued that worshipping heart, could not have drawn such tears from such a lover.' I am persuaded that the same effect was wrought upon the Parisian audiences, both consciously and unconsciously, to a very great extent, and that what was morally disagreeable in the *Dame aux Camélias* first got lost in this brilliant halo of romance. I have seen the same play with the same part otherwise acted, and in exact degree as the love became dull and earthy, the heroine descended from her pedestal.

In Ruy Blas, in the Master of Ravenswood, and in the Lady of Lyons – three dramas in which Mr Fechter especially shines as a lover, but notably in the first – this remarkable power of surrounding the beloved creature, in the eyes of the audience, with the fascination that she has for him, is strikingly displayed. That observer must be cold indeed who does not feel, when Ruy Blas stands in the presence of the young unwedded Queen of Spain, that the air is enchanted; or, when she bends over him, laying her tender touch upon his bloody breast, that it is better so to die than to live apart from her, and that she is worthy to be so died for. When the Master of Ravenswood declares his love to Lucy Ashton, and she hers to him, and when in a burst of rapture, he kisses the skirt of her dress, we feel as though we touched it with our lips to stay our goddess from soaring away into the very heavens. And when they plight their troth and break the piece of gold, it is we – not Edgar – who quickly exchange our half for the half she was about to hang about her neck, solely because the latter has for an instant touched the bosom we so dearly love. Again, in the Lady of Lyons: the picture on the easel in the poor cottage studio is not the unfinished portrait of a vain and arrogant girl, but becomes the sketch of a Soul's high ambition and aspiration here and hereafter.

Picturesqueness is a quality above all others pervading Mr Fechter's assumptions. Himself a skilled painter and sculptor, learned in the history of costume, and informing those accomplishments and that knowledge with a similar infusion of romance (for romance is inseparable from the man), he is always a picture, – always a picture in its right place in the group, always in true composition with the background of the scene. For picturesqueness of manner, note so trivial a thing as the turn of the hand in beckoning from a window, in Ruy Blas, to a personage down in an outer courtyard to come up; or his assumption of the Duke's livery in the same scene; or his writing a letter from dictation. In the last scene of Victor Hugo's noble drama, his bearing becomes positively inspired; and his sudden assumption of the attitude of the headsman, in his denunciation of the Duke and threat to be his executioner, is, so far as I know, one of the most ferociously picturesque things conceivable on the stage.

The foregoing use of the word 'ferociously' reminds me to remark that this artist is a master of passionate vehemence; in which aspect he appears to me to represent, perhaps more than in any other, an interesting union of characteristics of two great nations, – the French and the Anglo-Saxon. Born in London of a French mother, by a German father, but reared entirely in England and in France, there is, in his fury, a combination of French suddenness and impressibility with our more slowly demonstrative Anglo-Saxon way when we get, as we say, 'our blood up,' that produces an intensely fiery result. The fusion of two races is in it, and one cannot decidedly say that it belongs to either; but one can most decidedly say that it belongs to a powerful concentration of human passion and emotion, and to human nature.

Mr Fechter has been in the main more accustomed to speak French than to speak English, and therefore he speaks our language with a French accent. But whosoever should suppose that he does not speak English fluently, plainly, distinctly, and with a perfect understanding of the meaning, weight, and value of every word, would be greatly mistaken. Not only is his knowledge of English – extending to the most subtle idiom, or the most recondite cant phrase – more extensive than that of many of us who have English for our mother-tongue, but his delivery of Shakespeare's blank verse is remarkably facile, musical, and intelligent. To be in a sort of pain for him, as one sometimes is for a foreigner speaking English, or to be in any doubt of his having twenty synonymes at his tongue's end if he should want one, is out of the question after having been of his audience.

A few words on two of his Shakespearian impersonations, and I shall have indicated enough, in advance of Mr Fechter's presentation of himself. That quality of picturesqueness, on which I have already laid stress, is strikingly developed in his Iago, and yet it is so judiciously governed that his Iago is not in the least picturesque according to the conventional ways of frowning, sneering, diabolically grinning, and elaborately doing everything else that would induce Othello to run him through the body very early in the play. Mr Fechter's is the Iago who could, and did, make friends; who could dissect his master's soul, without flourishing his scalpel as if it were a walking-stick; who could overpower Emilia by other arts than a sign-of-the-Saracen's-Head grimness; who could be a boon companion without *ipso facto* warning all beholders off by the portentous phenomenon; who could sing a song and clink a can naturally enough, and stab men really in the dark, – not in a transparent notification of himself as going about seeking whom to stab. Mr Fechter's Iago is no more in the conventional psychological mode than in the conventional hussar pantaloons and boots; and you shall see the picturesqueness of his wearing borne out in his bearing all through the tragedy down to the moment when he becomes invincibly and consistently dumb.

Perhaps no innovation in Art was ever accepted with so much favour by so many intellectual persons pre-committed to, and preoccupied by, another system, as Mr Fechter's Hamlet. I take this to have been the case (as it unquestionably was in London), not because of its many scattered beauties, but because of its perfect consistency with itself. As the animal-painter said of his favourite picture of rabbits that there was more nature about those rabbits than you usually found in rabbits, so it may be said of Mr Fechter's Hamlet, that there was more consistency about that Hamlet than you usually found in Hamlets. Its great and satisfying originality was in its possessing the merit of a distinctly conceived and executed idea. From the first appearance of the broken glass of fashion and mould of form, pale and worn with weeping for his father's death, and remotely suspicious of its cause, to his final struggle with Horatio for the fatal cup, there were cohesion and coherence in Mr Fechter's view of the character. Devrient, the German actor, had, some years before in London, fluttered the theatrical doves considerably, by such changes as being seated when instructing the players, and like mild departures from established usage; but he had worn, in the main, the old nondescript dress, and had held forth, in the main, in the old way, hovering between sanity and madness. I do not remember whether he wore his hair crisply curled short, as if he were going to an everlasting dancing-master's party at the Danish court; but I do remember that most other Hamlets since the great Kemble had been bound to do so. Mr

Fechter's Hamlet, a pale, woe-begone Norseman with long flaxen hair, wearing a strange garb never associated with the part upon the English stage (if ever seen there at all) and making a piratical swoop upon the whole fleet of little theatrical prescriptions without meaning, or, like Dr Johnson's celebrated friend, with only one idea in them, and that a wrong one, never could have achieved its extraordinary success but for its animation by one pervading purpose, to which all changes were made intelligently subservient. The bearing of this purpose on the treatment of Ophelia, on the death of Polonius, and on the old student fellowship between Hamlet and Horatio, was exceedingly striking; and the difference between picturesqueness of stage arrangement for mere stage effect, and for the elucidation of a meaning, was well displayed in there having been a gallery of musicians at the Play, and in one of them passing on his way out, with his instrument in his hand, when Hamlet, seeing it, took it from him, to point his talk with Rosencrantz and Guildenstern.

This leads me to the observation with which I have all along desired to conclude: that Mr Fechter's romance and picturesqueness are always united to a true artist's intelligence, and a true artist's training in a true artist's spirit. He became one of the company of the Théâtre Français when he was a very young man, and he has cultivated his natural gifts in the best schools. I cannot wish my friend a better audience than he will have in the American people, and I cannot wish them a better actor than they will have in my friend.

CHARLES DICKENS

APPENDIX A

The Great International Walking-Match of 29 February 1868

Broadsheet printed at Boston for private circulation

During his punishing Reading Tour in America (winter 1867/8), Dickens suffered badly from sleeplessness and a very heavy cold which began over the Christmas period and clung to him for the rest of his time in the country. George Dolby comments frequently in his *Charles Dickens As I Knew Him* (1885) on the astonishing way in which all Dickens's illness and fatigue seemed to vanish when he had to perform. Dolby and the publisher James Osgood, Dickens wrote to Georgina, did 'the most ridiculous things to keep me in spirits' (*Nonesuch*, Vol. III, p. 609) and at one stage they decided, no doubt in tribute to Dickens's well-known passion for pedestrianism, to have a walking-match. Dickens, says Dolby, 'entered heartily into the scheme, volunteering to draw up the articles of agreement, to act as trainer, and to write a "sporting narrative" of the match after it had taken place' (*Charles Dickens As I Knew Him*, p. 220). Dickens told Georgina on 29 January that neither Dolby nor Osgood had 'the least idea what twelve miles at a pace is', and that he had just given them a stiff 'breather' of 'five miles over a bad road in the snow, half the distance uphill', adding, 'I took them at a pace of four miles and a half an hour, and you never beheld such objects as they were when we got back; both smoking like factories ...' (*Nonesuch*, Vol. III, p. 609). He evidently delighted not only in the event itself and the merry feasting afterwards ('the whole thing was a great success, and everybody was delighted' – *Nonesuch*, Vol. III, p. 628), but also in fulfilling his promise to write it up in an exhilarating parody of the style of journalism associated with sporting papers like *Bell's Life in London* (compare his equally spirited parody of provincial journalism in 'The Tattlesnivel Bleater', above pp. 20–6).

Literary allusions (p. 413) 'The Man of Ross (*alias* old Alick Pope, alias Allourpraiseswhyshouldlords&c)': Dickens's nickname for Dolby derives from the fact that he came from Ross in Herefordshire like the charitable John Kyrle (1637–1724), whom Pope calls 'The Man of Ross' when celebrating his admirable use of riches in his *Epistle to Lord Bathurst (Moral*

Essays) – the section on Kyrle begins (l. 249), 'But all our praises why should lords engross?'; (413) 'Izaak Walton ... his book': *The Compleat Angler* (1657); (p. 414) 'as Mrs Cratchit said of Tiny Tim ...': allusion to Dickens's *A Christmas Carol* (1843).

Text from a copy of the broadsheet now in the Suzannet Collection at the Dickens House Museum. The most noticeable difference between it and the version printed in Dolby (pp. 261–9) is at the beginning of the paragraph headed 'THE TRAINING'. For 'Brandy Cocktails' Dolby's text reads 'vigorous attention to diet'.

The origin of this highly exciting and important event cannot be better stated than in the articles of agreement subscribed by the parties.

THE ARTICLES

Articles of Agreement entered into at Baltimore, in the United States of America, this Third day of February in the year of our Lord one thousand eight hundred and sixty-eight, between GEORGE DOLBY, British subject, *alias* the Man of Ross, and JAMES RIPLEY OSGOOD, American Citizen, *alias* the Boston Bantam.

Whereas, some Bounce having arisen between the above men in reference to feats of pedestrianism and agility, they have agreed to settle their differences and prove who is the better man, by means of a walking-match for two hats a side and the glory of their respective countries; and whereas they agree that the said match shall come off, whatsoever the weather, on the Mill Dam Road, outside Boston, on Saturday, the Twenty-ninth day of this present month; and whereas they agree that the personal attendants on themselves during the whole walk, and also the umpires and starters and declarers of victory in the match shall be JAMES T. FIELDS of Boston, known in sporting circles as Massachusetts Jemmy, and CHARLES DICKENS of Falstaff's Gad's Hill, whose surprising performances (without the least variation) on that truly national instrument, the American Catarrh, have won for him the well-merited title of The Gad's Hill Gasper.

Now these are to be the articles of the match: –

1. The men are to be started, on the day appointed, by Massachusetts Jemmy and The Gasper.

2. Jemmy and The Gasper are, on some previous day, to walk out at the rate of not less than four miles an hour by the Gasper's watch, for one hour and a half. At the expiration of that one hour and a half, they are to carefully note the place at which they halt. On the match's coming off, they are to station themselves in the middle of the road, at that

precise point, and the men (keeping clear of them and of each other) are to turn round them, right shoulder inward, and walk back to the starting-point. The man declared by them to pass the starting-point first is to be the victor and the winner of the match.

3. No jostling or fouling allowed.

4. All cautions or orders issued to the men by the umpires, starters, and declarers of victory, to be considered final and admitting of no appeal.

5. A sporting narrative of the match to be written by The Gasper within one week after its coming off, and the same to be duly printed (at the expense of the subscribers to these articles) on a broadside. The said broadside to be framed and glazed, and one copy of the same to be carefully preserved by each of the subscribers to these articles.

6. The men to show on the evening of the day of walking, at six o'clock precisely, at the Parker House, Boston, when and where a dinner will be given them by The Gasper. The Gasper to occupy the chair, faced by Massachusetts Jemmy. The latter promptly and formally to invite, as soon as may be after the date of these presents, the following Guests to honour the said dinner with their presence: that is to say:– Mistress Annie Fields, Mr Charles Eliot Norton and Mrs Norton, Professor James Russell Lowell and Mrs Lowell and Miss Lowell, Dr Oliver Wendell Holmes and Mrs Holmes, Mr Howard Malcolm Ticknor and Mrs Ticknor, Mr Aldrich and Mrs Aldrich, Mr Schlesinger, and an obscure poet named Longfellow (if discoverable) and Miss Longfellow.

Now, Lastly. In token of their accepting the trusts and offices by these articles conferred upon them, these articles are solemnly and formally signed by Massachusetts Jemmy and by the Gad's Hill Gasper, as well as by the men themselves.

Signed by the *Man of Ross*, otherwise George Dolby.

Signed by the *Boston Bantam*, otherwise James R. Osgood.

Signed by *Massachusetts Jemmy*, otherwise James T. Fields.

Signed by *The Gad's Hill Gasper*, otherwise Charles Dickens.

Witness to the signature, William S. Anthony.

THE SPORTING NARRATIVE

THE MEN

The Boston Bantam (*alias* Bright Chanticleer) is a young bird, though too old to be caught with chaff. He comes of a thorough game breed and has a clear thorough modest crow. He pulls down the scale at ten stone and a half and add a pound or two. His previous performances in the Pedestrian line have not been numerous. He once achieved a neat little match against time in two left boots at Philadelphia; but this must be considered as a pedestrian eccentricity, and cannot be accepted by the rigid chronicler as high art. The old mower with the scythe and hour-glass has not yet laid his mawler heavily on the Bantam's frontispiece, but he has had a grip at the Bantam's top feathers, and in plucking out a handful was very near making him like the great Napoleon Bonaparte (with the exception of the victualling-department), when the ancient one found himself too much occupied to carry out the idea, and gave it up. The Man of Ross (*alias* old Alick Pope, *alias* Allourpraiseswhyshouldlords &c) is a thought and a half too fleshy, and, if he accidentally sat down upon his baby, would do it to the tune of fourteen stone. This popular Codger is of the rubicund and jovial sort, and has long been known as a piscatorial pedestrian on the banks of the Wye. But Izaak Walton hadn't Pace, – look at his book and you'll find it slow, – and when that article comes into question, the fishing-rod may prove to some of his disciples a rod in pickle. Howbeit, the Man of Ross is a Lively Ambler, and has a smart stride of his own.

THE TRAINING

If Brandy Cocktails could have brought both men up to the post in tip-top feather, their condition would have left nothing to be desired. But both might have had more daily practice in the poetry of motion. Their breathings were confined to an occasional Baltimore burst under the guidance of the Gasper, and to an amicable toddle between themselves at Washington.

THE COURSE

Six miles and a half, good measure, from the first tree on the Mill Dam road, lies the little village (with no refreshments in it but five oranges and a bottle of blacking) of Newton Centre. Here Massachusetts Jemmy and the Gasper had established the turning-point. The road com-prehended every variety of inconvenience to test the mettle of the men, and nearly the whole of it was covered with snow.

THE START

was effected beautifully. The men, taking their stand in exact line at the starting-post, the first tree aforesaid, received from The Gasper the warning, 'Are you ready?' and then the signal, 'One, two, three, Go!' They got away exactly together, and at a spinning speed, waited on by Massachusetts Jemmy and The Gasper.

THE RACE

In the teeth of an intensely cold and bitter wind before which the snow flew fast and furious across the road from right to left, The Bantam slightly led. But The Man responded to the challenge and soon breasted him. For the first three miles, each led by a yard or so alternately; but the walking was very even. On four miles being called by The Gasper, the men were side by side; and then ensued one of the best periods of the race, the same splitting pace being held by both, through a heavy snow-wreath and up a dragging hill. At this point it was anybody's game, a dollar on Rossius and two half-dollars on the member of the feathery tribe. When five miles were called, the men were still shoulder to shoulder. At about six miles, the Gasper put on a tremendous spirt to leave the men behind and establish himself as the turning-point at the entrance of the village. He afterwards declared that he received a mental knock-downer, on taking his station and facing about, to find Bright Chanticleer close in upon him, and Rossius steaming up like a Locomotive. The Bantam rounded first; Rossius rounded wide; and from that moment the Bantam steadily shot ahead. Though both were breathed at the turn, the Bantam quickly got his bellows into obedient condition, and blew away like an orderly Blacksmith in full work. The forcing-pumps of Rossius likewise proved themselves tough and true, and warranted first-rate, but he fell off in pace; whereas the Bantam pegged away with his little drum-sticks, as if he saw his wives and a peck of barley waiting for him at the family perch. Continually gaining upon him of Ross, Chanticleer gradually drew ahead within a few yards of half a mile, finally doing the whole distance in two hours and forty-eight minutes. Ross had ceased to compete three miles short of the winning-post, but bravely walked it out, and came in seven minutes later.

REMARKS

The difficulties under which this plucky match was walked can only be appreciated by those who were on the ground. To the excessive rigour of the icy blast, and the depth and state of the snow, must be added the constant scattering of the latter into the air and into the eyes of the men, while heads of hair, beards, eyelashes, and eyebrows, were frozen into icicles. To breathe at all, in such a rarefied and disturbed atmosphere, was not easy; but to breathe up to the required mark was genuine, slogging, ding-dong, hard labor. That both competitors were game to the backbone, doing what they did under such conditions, was evident to all; but, to his gameness, the courageous Bantam added unexpected endurance, and (like the sailor's watch that did three hours to the cathedral clock's one) unexpected powers of going when wound up. The knowing eye could not fail to detect considerable disparity between the lads; Chanticleer being, as Mrs Cratchit said of Tiny Tim, 'very light to carry,' and Rossius promising fair to attain the rotundity of the Anonymous Cove in the epigram:

> 'And when he walks the streets the paviors cry,
> God bless you, sir! – and lay their rammers by.'

APPENDIX B

Prefaces

I

Evenings of a Working Man, being the Occupation of his scanty Leisure:
by John Overs. With a Preface relative to the Author by Charles Dickens
Published by T. C. Newby, 1844

John Overs, born a Catholic in Birmingham in 1808, was, according to family tradition, disowned by his father when he married an Anglican in 1828. The young couple came to London where they started a family (eventually there were six children in all) and Overs earned his living as a cabinet-maker. He had strong literary ambitions, however, and towards the end of 1838 submitted some poems to Dickens as editor of *Bentley's Miscellany*. Dickens, as he explains in his Preface, was just then relinquishing the editorship but took a great interest in Overs's work and, during the next five years, acted as his patron, helping him with his writings and getting him work under Macready during the latter's management of Drury Lane Theatre. One of the books he loaned his protégé was Carlyle's *Chartism* (1840), and Overs's long and powerfully argued critique of this work from the viewpoint of a working man has been reprinted with extensive commentary by Sheila Smith in *Victorian Studies* (Vol. 18 [1974–5], pp. 195–217). For information about Overs's family background and comment on his poetry, see Robert Vine and Sheila Smith, 'John Overs: Family Tradition, Poetry and Memorabilia', *The Dickensian*, Vol. 90 (1994), pp. 85–94. Overs died on 28 September 1844.

The papers collected in his *Evenings of a Working Man* consist of three romantic-melodramatic stories from history, a handful of poems and three sketches of trade types (costermonger, baker, carpenter) that show a strong Dickens influence. The Dedication page reads: 'This Little Book/ is affectionately dedicated/ to /DOCTOR ELLIOTSON /by one who has felt his kindness /to those /who have no other claim upon him /(and on such a man can have no higher claim)/ than /sickness and obscure condition'.

The indulgent reader of this little book – not called indulgent, I may hope, by courtesy alone, but with some reference also to its title and pretensions – may very naturally inquire how it comes to have a preface to which my name is attached; nor is the reader's right or inclination to be satisfied on this head, likely to be much diminished, when I state, in the outset, that I do not recommend it as a book of surpassing originality or transcendent merit. That I do not claim to have discovered, in humble life, an extraordinary and brilliant genius. That I cannot charge mankind in general, with having entered into a conspiracy to neglect the author of this volume, or to leave him pining in obscurity. That I have not the smallest intention of comparing him with Burns, the exciseman; or with Bloomfield, the shoemaker; or with Ebenezer Elliott, the worker in iron; or with James Hogg, the shepherd. That I see no reason to be hot, or bitter, or lowering, or sarcastic, or indignant, or fierce, or sour, or sharp, in his behalf. That I have nothing to rail at; nothing to exalt; nothing to flourish in the face of a stony-hearted world; and have but a very short and simple tale to tell.

But, such as it is, it has interested me; and I hope it may interest the reader too, if I state it, unaffectedly and plainly.

John Overs, the writer of the following pages, is, as is set forth on the title-page, a working man. A man who earns his weekly wages (or who did when he was strong enough) by plying of the hammer, plane, and chisel. He became known to me, to the best of my recollection, nearly six years ago, when he sent me some songs, appropriate to the different months of the year, with a letter, stating under what circumstances they had been composed, and in what manner he was occupied from morning until night. I was, just then, relinquishing the conduct of a monthly periodical: or I would gladly have published them. As it was, I returned them to him, with a private expression of the interest I felt in such productions. They were afterwards accepted, with much readiness and consideration, by Mr Tait, of Edinburgh; and were printed in his Magazine.

Finding, after some further correspondence with my new friend, that his authorship had not ceased with these verses, but that he still occupied his leisure moments in writing, I took occasion to remonstrate with him seriously against his pursuing that course. I pointed out to him a few of the uncertainties, anxieties, and difficulties of such a life, at the best. I entreated him to remember the position of heavy disadvantage in which he stood, by reason of his self-education, and imperfect attainments; and I besought him to consider whether, having one or two of his pieces accepted occasionally, here and there, after long suspense and many refusals, it was probable that he would find himself, in the end, a happier or a more contented man. On all these grounds, I told him, his persistence in his new calling made me uneasy; and I advised him to abandon it, as strongly as I could.

In answer to this dissuasion of mine, he wrote me as manly and straightforward, but withal, as modest a letter, as ever I read in my life. He explained to me how limited his ambition was: soaring no higher than the establishment of his wife in some light business, and the better education of his children. He set before me, the difference between his evening and holiday studies, such as they were; and the having no better resource than an alehouse or a skittle-ground. He told me, how every small addition to his stock of knowledge, made his Sunday walks the pleasanter; the hedge-flowers sweeter; every thing more full of interest and meaning to him. He assured me, that his daily work was not neglected for his self-imposed pursuits; but was faithfully and honestly performed; and so, indeed, it was. He hinted to me, that his greater self-respect was some inducement and reward: supposing every other to elude his grasp; and shewed me, how the fancy that he would turn this or that acquisition from his books to account, by-and-by, in writing, made him more fresh and eager to peruse and profit by them, when his long day's work was done.

I would not, if I could, have offered one solitary objection more, to arguments so unpretending and so true.

From that time to the present, I have seen him frequently. It has been a pleasure to me to put a few books in his way; to give him a word or two of counsel in his little projects and difficulties; and to read his compositions with him, when he has had an hour, or so, to spare. I have never altered them, otherwise than by recommending condensation now and then; nor have I, in looking over these sheets, made an emendation in them, beyond the ordinary corrections of the press: desiring them to be his genuine work, as they have been his sober and rational amusement.

The latter observation brings me to the origin of the present volume, and of this my slight share in it. The reader will soon comprehend why I touch the subject lightly, and with a sorrowful and faltering hand.

In all the knowledge I have had of John Overs, and in all the many conversations I have held with him, I have invariably found him, in every essential particular, but one, the same. I have found him from first to last a simple, frugal, steady, upright, honourable man; especially to be noted for the unobtrusive independence of his character, the instinctive propriety of his manner, and the perfect neatness of his appearance. The extent of his information: regard being had to his opportunities of acquiring it: is very remarkable; and the discrimination with which he has risen superior to the mere prejudices of the class with which he is associated, without losing his sympathy for all their real wrongs and grievances – they have a few – impressed me, in the beginning of our acquaintance, strongly in his favour.

The one respect in which he is not what he was, is in his hold on life.

He is very ill; the faintest shadow of the man who came into my little study for the first time half-a-dozen years ago, after the correspondence I have mentioned. He has been very ill for a long, long period; his disease is a severe and wasting affection of the lungs, which has incapacitated him, these many months, for every kind of occupation. 'If I could only do a hard day's work,' he said to me the other day, 'how happy I should be!'

Having these papers by him, amongst others, he bethought himself that if he could get a bookseller to purchase them for publication in a volume, they would enable him to make some temporary provision for his sick wife and very young family. We talked the matter over together; and that it might be easier of accomplishment, I promised him that I would write an introduction to his book.

I would to Heaven that I could do him better service! I would to Heaven it were an introduction to a long, and vigorous, and useful life! But Hope will not trim her lamp the less brightly for him and his, because of this impulse to their struggling fortunes; and trust me, reader, they deserve her light, and need it sorely.

He has inscribed this book to one whose skill will help him, under Providence, in all that human skill can do. To one who never could have recognized in any potentate on earth, a higher claim to constant kindness and attention, than he has recognized in him.

I have little more to say of it. While I do not commend it, on the one hand, as a prodigy, I do sincerely believe it, on the other, to possess some points of real interest, however considered; but which, if considered with reference to its title and origin, are of great interest.

If any delicate readers should approach the perusal of these 'Evenings of a Working Man,' with a genteel distaste to the principle of a working-man turning author at all, I may perhaps be permitted to suggest that the best protection against such an offence will be found in the Universal Education of the people; for the enlightenment of the many will effectually swamp any interest that may now attach in vulgar minds, to the few among them who are enabled, in any degree, to overcome the great difficulties of their position.

And if such readers should deny the immense importance of communicating to this class, at this time, every possible means of knowledge, refinement and recreation; or the cause we have to hail with delight the least token that may arise among them of a desire to be wiser, better, and more gentle; I earnestly entreat them to educate themselves in this neglected branch of their own learning without delay; promising them that it is the easiest in its acquisition of any: requiring only open eyes and ears, and six easy lessons of an hour each in a working town. Which will render them perfect for the rest of their lives.

London, June, 1844.

2

What Shall We Have For Dinner? Satisfactorily Answered by Numerous Bills of Fare for From Two to Eighteen Persons. By Lady Maria Clutterbuck

During 1851 Catherine Dickens was already suffering from some form of nervous disorder when, in April, there came the terrible blow of the sudden death of her eight-month-old daughter Dora. Dickens's letters of the summer and autumn show his concern for her, and it seems likely that the idea that she should compile for publication a collection of her menus and recipes was part of his attempts to distract her and help her to recover some equilibrium. During fourteen years of being hostess for such a highly convivial and hospitable celebrity as Dickens, Catherine would certainly have accumulated quite a store of 'bills of fare'. The pen-name 'Lady Maria Clutterbuck' derives from the role she had played in a little farce, *Used Up* by Boucicault, in some amateur theatricals Dickens had organised at Rockingham Castle at the beginning of the year; and, although there is no external proof that Dickens wrote the following jokey little Preface for the book, his authorship seems, from internal evidence, sufficiently probable to justify its inclusion here. For discussion of the book's contents, the richness and great amount of food in the various menus, etc., see Una Pope-Hennessy, 'Dinner with Mr and Mrs Charles Dickens', *Wine and Food*, No. 44 (Winter 1944), and Margaret Lane, 'Mrs Beeton and Mrs Dickens', in *Purely for Pleasure* (1966). Pope-Hennessy quotes one reviewer of the book as wondering how long any man could survive 'such repeated doses of toasted cheese'.

Text Taken from the British Library copy, which announces itself on its title-page as 'A New Edition' and is dated 1852. According to the *Pilgrim* Editors (Vol. VI, p. ix), the book was first published in October 1851 by Bradbury and Evans, 'with a new edition, "enlarged and improved", the following February'; the phrase cited does not appear on the title-page of the British Library copy, however. A copy seen in the New York Public Library, with the Preface identical to that in the British Library copy, is dated 1851 but calls itself 'Second Edition', while another copy (not seen) was listed in Catalogue no. 83 (Winter 1991–2) of the antiquarian booksellers Jarndyce with a publication date of 1856, the author's name shortened to

'Lady Clutterbuck' and labelled 'A New Edition'. All this would seem to indicate that, although it is a great rarity now, the little book must have sold quite well in its day. The paper cover of the New York Public Library copy announces the price as 'One Shilling'.

The late Sir Jonas Clutterbuck had, in addition to a host of other virtues, a very good appetite and an excellent digestion; to those endowments I was indebted (though some years the junior of my revered husband) for many hours of connubial happiness.

Sir Jonas was not a *gourmand*, although a man of great gastronomical experience. Richmond never saw him more than once a month, and he was as rare a visitor to Blackwall and Greenwich. Of course he attended most of the corporation dinners as a matter of duty (having been elected alderman in 1839), and now and then partook of a turtle feast at some celebrated place in the city; but these were only exceptions, his general practice being to dine at home; and I am consoled in believing that my attention to the requirements of his appetite secured me the possession of his esteem until the last.

My experience in the confidences of many of my female friends tells me, alas! that others are not so happy in their domestic relations as I was. That their daily life is embittered by the consciousness that a delicacy forgotten or misapplied; a surplusage of cold mutton or a redundancy of chops; are gradually making the Club more attractive than the Home, and rendering 'business in the city' of more frequent occurrence than it used to be in the earlier days of their connubial experience; while the over-recurring inquiry of

WHAT SHALL WE HAVE FOR DINNER?

makes the matutinal meal a time to dread, only exceeded in its terrors by the more awful hour of dinner!

It is to rescue many fair friends from such domestic suffering, that I have consented to give to the world

THE BILLS OF FARE

which met with the approval of Sir Jonas Clutterbuck, believing that by a constant reference to them, an easy solution may be obtained to that most difficult of questions, – 'WHAT SHALL WE HAVE FOR DINNER?'

M. C.

3

Legends and Lyrics. By Adelaide Anne Procter. With an Introduction by Charles Dickens

Published by Bell and Daldy, 1866

Enormously popular in her own day, Adelaide Anne Procter has, until the recent revival of interest in her work (see especially Gill Gregory, *The Life and Work of Adelaide Procter: Poetry, Feminism and Fathers* [1998]), been remembered only by one poem, 'A Lost Chord', which mainly owed its survival to its having been magnificently set to music by Sir Arthur Sullivan. Her father, the lawyer-poet Bryan Waller Procter, who wrote under the pen-name of 'Barry Cornwall' (see p. 423), had been a much-loved friend of Dickens since the mid 1830s. Adelaide Procter published her first poetry at the age of eighteen and after 1853 wrote mainly for *HW* and *ATYR*. Her poems were collected under the title *Legends and Lyrics* in 1858 with a second series following under the same title in 1861. Strongly influenced by the Oxford Movement, she converted to Roman Catholicism in 1851. She was also a vigorous campaigner on women's issues, being closely associated with Bessie Rayner Parkes and the 'Langham Place Group'. She wrote poetry for Parkes's *English Woman's Magazine* ('A Lost Chord' appeared here in 1860) and in 1859 became secretary of the Society for Promoting the Employment of Women. She took an active interest, also, in female homelessness and devoted the proceeds of her *Chaplet of Verses* (1862) to support a Catholic night shelter for women. Impressive though her sales figures were, Procter was distinguished by her literary modesty and Parkes quotes her as saying, 'Papa writes poetry. I only write verses' (quoted in Gregory, p. 55). She features as 'Belinda Bates' in the *ATYR* Christmas Number for 1859, where Dickens, whose sympathy with campaigners for women's rights was lamentably restricted, describes her in the following jarringly patronising terms:

... a most intellectual, amiable, and delightful girl [with] a fine genius for poetry, combined with real business earnestness, and 'goes in' ... for Woman's mission, Woman's rights, Woman's wrongs, and everything that is Woman's with a capital W, or is not and ought to be, or is and ought not to be. 'Most praiseworthy, my dear, and Heaven prosper you!' I whispered to her ... 'but don't overdo it. And in respect of the great necessity there is, my darling, for more employments being within the reach of Woman than our civilisation has yet assigned to her, don't fly at the unfortunate men ... as if they were the natural oppressors of your sex; for, trust me, Belinda, they do sometimes spend their wages among wives and daughters, sisters, mothers, aunts and grandmothers; and the play is, really, not all Wolf and Red Riding-Hood, but has other parts in it.' [*Christmas Stories*, 'The Haunted House', Ch. 1]

There is, fortunately, no trace of this tone in the following Introduction in which, Dickens told Mrs Procter, he had 'aimed at perfect simplicity, and an avoidance of all that your beloved Adelaide would have wished avoided' (*Pilgrim*, Vol. XI, p. 97).

Literary allusions (p. 429) 'Why shouldst thou fear ... all to thee': from 'The Angel of Death', pp. 71–2 of *Legends and Lyrics*.

In the spring of the year 1853, I observed, as Conductor of the Weekly Journal HOUSEHOLD WORDS, a short poem among the proffered contributions, very different, as I thought, from the shoal of verses perpetually setting through the office of such a Periodical, and possessing much more merit. Its authoress was quite unknown to me. She was one MISS MARY BERWICK, whom I had never heard of; and she was to be addressed by letter, if addressed at all, at a circulating library in the western district of London. Through this channel, Miss Berwick was informed that her poem was accepted, and was invited to send another. She complied, and became a regular and frequent contributor. Many letters passed between the Journal and Miss Berwick, but Miss Berwick herself was never seen.

How we came gradually to establish, at the office of Household Words, that we knew all about Miss Berwick, I have never discovered. But, we settled somehow, to our complete satisfaction, that she was governess in a family; that she went to Italy in that capacity, and returned; and that she had long been in the same family. We really knew nothing whatever of her, except that she was remarkably business-like, punctual, self-reliant, and reliable: so I suppose we insensibly invented the rest. For myself, my mother was not a more real personage to me, than Miss Berwick the governess became.

This went on until December, 1854, when the Christmas Number, entitled, The Seven Poor Travellers, was sent to press. Happening to be going to dine that day with an old and dear friend, distinguished in literature as BARRY CORNWALL, I took with me an early proof of that Number, and remarked, as I laid it on the drawing-room table, that it contained a very pretty poem, written by a certain Miss Berwick. Next day brought me the disclosure that I had so spoken of the poem to the mother of its writer, in its writer's presence; that I had no such correspondent in existence as Miss Berwick; and that the name had been assumed by Barry Cornwall's eldest daughter, MISS ADELAIDE ANNE PROCTER.

The anecdote I have here noted down, besides serving to explain why the parents of the late Miss Procter have looked to me for these poor words of remembrance of their lamented child, strikingly illustrates the honesty, independence, and quiet dignity, of the lady's character. I had known her when she was very young; I had been honoured with her father's friendship when I was myself a young aspirant; and she had said at home, 'If I send him, in my own name, verses that he does not honestly like, either it will be very painful to him to return them, or he will print them for papa's sake, and not for their own. So I have made up my mind to take my chance fairly with the unknown volunteers.'

Perhaps it requires an Editor's experience of the profoundly unreasonable grounds on which he is often urged to accept unsuitable articles – such as having been to school with the writer's husband's brother-in-law, or having lent an alpenstock in Switzerland to the writer's wife's nephew, when that interesting stranger had broken his own – fully to appreciate the delicacy and the self-respect of this resolution.

Some verses by Miss Procter had been published in the BOOK OF BEAUTY, ten years before she became Miss Berwick. With the exception of two poems in the CORNHILL MAGAZINE, two in GOOD WORDS, and others in a little book called A CHAPLET OF VERSES (issued in 1862 for the benefit of a Night Refuge), her published writings first appeared in HOUSEHOLD WORDS, or ALL THE YEAR ROUND. The present Edition contains the whole of her Legends and Lyrics, and originates in the great favour with which they have been received by the public.

Miss Procter was born in Bedford-square, London, on the 30th of October, 1825. Her love of poetry was conspicuous at so early an age, that I have before me a tiny album made of small note-paper, into which her favourite passages were copied for her by her mother's hand before she herself could write. It looks as if she had carried it about, as another little girl might have carried a doll. She soon displayed a remarkable memory, and a great quickness of apprehension. When she was quite a young child, she learnt with facility several of the problems of Euclid. As she grew older, she acquired the French, Italian, and German, languages; became a clever piano-forte player; and showed a true taste and sentiment in drawing. But, as soon as she had completely vanquished the difficulties of any one branch of study, it was her way to lose interest in it, and pass to another. While her mental resources were being trained, it was not at all suspected in her family that she had any gift of authorship, or any ambition to become a writer. Her father had no idea of her having ever attempted to turn a rhyme, until her first little poem saw the light in print.

When she attained to womanhood, she had read an extraordinary number of books, and throughout her life she was always largely adding to the number. In 1853 she went to Turin and its neighbourhood, on a visit to her aunt, a Roman Catholic lady. As Miss Procter had herself professed the Roman Catholic Faith two years before, she entered with the greater ardour on the study of the Piedmontese dialect, and the observation of the habits and manners of the peasantry. In the former, she soon became a proficient. On the latter head, I extract from her familiar letters written home to England at the time, two pleasant pieces of description.

A BETROTHAL

'We have been to a ball, of which I must give you a description. Last Tuesday we had just done dinner at about seven, and stepped out into the balcony to look at the remains of the sunset behind the mountains, when we heard very distinctly a band of music, which rather excited my astonishment, as a solitary organ is the utmost that toils up here. I went out of the room for a few minutes, and, on my returning, Emily said, 'Oh! That band is playing at the farmer's near here. The daughter is *fiancée* today, and they have a ball.' I said, 'I wish I was going!' 'Well,' replied she, 'the farmer's wife did call to invite us.' 'Then, I shall certainly go,' I exclaimed. I applied to Madame B., who said she would like it very much, and we had better go, children and all. Some of the servants were already gone. We rushed away to put on some shawls, and put off any shred of black we might have about us (as the people would have been quite annoyed if we had appeared on such an occasion with any black), and we started. When we reached the farmer's, which is a stone's throw above our house, we were received with great enthusiasm; the only drawback being, that no one spoke French, and we did not yet speak Piedmontese. We were placed on a bench against the wall, and the people went on dancing. The room was a large whitewashed kitchen (I suppose), with several large pictures in black frames, and very smoky. I distinguished the Martyrdom of Saint Sebastian, and the others appeared equally lively and appropriate subjects. Whether they were Old Masters or not, and if so, by whom, I could not ascertain. The band were seated opposite us. Five men, with wind instruments, part of the band of the National Guard, to which the farmer's sons belong. They played really admirably, and I began to be afraid that some idea of our dignity would prevent my getting a partner; so, by Madame B.'s advice, I went up to the bride, and offered to dance with her. Such a handsome young woman! Like one of Uwins's pictures. Very dark, with a quantity of black hair, and on an immense scale. The children were already dancing, as well as the maids. After we came to an end of our dance, which was what they called a Polka-Mazourka, I saw the bride trying to screw up the courage of her *fiancé* to ask me to dance, which after a little hesitation he did. And admirably he danced, as indeed they all did – in excellent time, and with a little more spirit than one sees in a ball-room. In fact, they were very like one's ordinary partners, except that they wore ear-rings and were in their shirt-sleeves, and truth compels me to state that they decidedly smelt of garlic. Some of them had been smoking, but threw away their cigars when we came in. The only thing that did not look cheerful was, that the room was only lighted by two or three oil-lamps, and that there seemed to be no preparation for refreshments. Madame B., seeing this, whispered to her maid, who disengaged herself from her partner, and ran off to the house; she and the kitchenmaid presently returning with a large tray covered with all kinds of cakes (of which we are great consumers and always have a stock), and a large hamper full of bottles of wine, with coffee and sugar. This seemed all very acceptable. The *fiancée* was requested to distribute the eatables, and a bucket of water being produced to wash the glasses in, the wine disappeared very quickly – as fast as they could open the bottles. But, elated I suppose by this, the floor was sprinkled with water, and the musicians played a Monferrino, which is a Piedmontese dance. Madame B. danced with the farmer's son, and Emily with another distinguished member of the company. It was very fatiguing – something like a Scotch reel. My partner was a little man, like Perrot, and very proud of his dancing. He cut in the air and twisted about, until I was out of breath, though my attempts to imitate him were feeble in the extreme. At last, after seven or eight dances, I was obliged to sit down. We stayed till nine, and I was so dead beat with the heat that I could hardly crawl about the house, and in an agony with the cramp, it is so long since I have danced.'

A MARRIAGE

'The wedding of the farmer's daughter has taken place. We had hoped it would have been in the little chapel of our house, but it seems some special permission was necessary, and they applied for it too late. They all said, 'This is the Constitution. There would have been no difficulty before!' the lower classes making the poor Constitution the scape-goat for everything they don't like. So as it was impossible for us to climb up to the church where the wedding was to be, we contented ourselves with seeing the procession pass. It was not a very large one, for, it requiring some activity to go up, all the old people remained at home. It is not the etiquette for the bride's mother to go, and no unmarried woman can go to a wedding – I suppose for fear of its making her discontented with her own position. The procession stopped at our door, for the bride to receive our congratulations. She was dressed in a shot silk, with a yellow handkerchief, and rows of a large gold chain. In the afternoon they sent to request us to go there. On our arrival we found them dancing out of doors, and a most melancholy affair it was. All the bride's sisters were not to be recognized, they had cried so. The mother sat in the house, and could not appear. And the bride was sobbing so, she could hardly stand! The most melancholy spectacle of all to my mind, was, that the bridegroom was decidedly tipsy. He seemed rather affronted at all the distress. We danced a Monferrino; I with the bridegroom; and the bride crying the whole time. The company did their utmost to enliven her by firing pistols, but without success, and at last they began a series of yells, which reminded me of a set of savages. But even this delicate method of consolation failed, and the wishing good-bye began. It was altogether so melancholy an affair that Madame B. dropped a few tears, and I was very near it, particularly when the poor mother came out to see the last of her daughter, who was finally dragged off between her brother and uncle, with a last explosion of pistols. As she lives quite near, makes an excellent match, and is one of nine children, it really was a most desirable marriage, in spite of all the show of distress. Albert was so discomfited by it, that he forgot to kiss the bride as he had intended to do, and therefore went to call upon her yesterday, and found her very smiling in her new house, and supplied the omission. The cook came home from the wedding, declaring she was cured of any wish to marry – but I would not recommend any man to act upon that threat and make her an offer. In a couple of days we had some rolls of the bride's first baking, which they call Madonna's. The musicians, it seems, were in the same state as the bridegroom, for, in escorting her home, they all fell down in the mud. My wrath against the bridegroom is somewhat calmed by finding that it is considered bad luck if he does not get tipsy at his wedding.'

Those readers of Miss Procter's poems who should suppose from their tone that her mind was of a gloomy or despondent cast, would be curiously mistaken. She was exceedingly humorous, and had a great delight in humour. Cheerfulness was habitual with her, she was very ready at a sally or a reply, and in her laugh (as I remember well) there was an unusual vivacity, enjoyment, and sense of drollery. She was perfectly unconstrained and unaffected: as modestly silent about her productions, as she was generous with their pecuniary results. She was a friend who inspired the strongest attachments; she was a finely sympathetic woman, with a great accordant heart and a sterling noble nature. No claim can be set up for her, thank God, to the possession of any of the conventional poetical qualities. She never by any means held the opinion that she was among the greatest of human beings; she never suspected the existence of a conspiracy on the part of mankind against her; she never recognized in her best friends, her worst enemies; she never cultivated the luxury of being misunderstood and unappreciated; she would far rather have died without seeing a line of her composition in print, than that I should have maundered about her, here, as 'the Poet,' or 'the Poetess.'

With the recollection of Miss Procter as a mere child and as a woman, fresh upon me, it is natural that I should linger on my way to the close of this brief record, avoiding its end. But, even as the close came upon her, so must it come here.

Always impelled by an intense conviction that her life must not be dreamed away, and that her indulgence in her favourite pursuits must be balanced by action in the real world around her, she was indefatigable in her endeavours to do some good. Naturally enthusiastic, and conscientiously impressed with a deep sense of her Christian duty to her neighbour, she devoted herself to a variety of benevolent objects. Now, it was the visitation of the sick, that had possession of her; now, it was the sheltering of the houseless; now, it was the elementary teaching of the densely ignorant; now, it was the raising up of those who had wandered and got trodden under foot; now, it was the wider employment of her own sex in the general business of life; now, it was all these things at once. Perfectly unselfish, swift to sympathize and eager to relieve, she wrought at such designs with a flushed earnestness that disregarded season, weather, time of day or night, food, rest. Under such a hurry of the spirits, and such incessant occupation, the strongest constitution will commonly go down. Hers, neither of the strongest nor the weakest, yielded to the burden, and began to sink.

To have saved her life, then, by taking action on the warning that shone in her eyes and sounded in her voice, would have been impossible, without changing her nature. As long as the power of moving about in the old way was left to her, she must exercise it, or be killed by the restraint. And so the time came when she could move about no longer, and took to her bed.

All the restlessness gone then, and all the sweet patience of her natural disposition purified by the resignation of her soul, she lay upon her bed through the whole round of changes of the seasons. She lay upon her bed through fifteen months. In all that time, her old cheerfulness never quitted her. In all that time, not an impatient or a querulous minute can be remembered.

At length, at midnight on the second of February, 1864, she turned down a leaf of a little book she was reading, and shut it up.

The ministering hand that had copied the verses into the tiny album was soon around her neck, and she quietly asked, as the clock was on the stroke of One:

'Do you think I am dying, mamma?'

'I think you are very, very ill tonight, my dear.'

'Send for my sister. My feet are so cold. Lift me up!'

Her sister entering as they raised her, she said: 'It has come at last!' And with a bright and happy smile, looked upward, and departed.

Well had she written:

> Why shouldst thou fear the beautiful angel, Death,
> Who waits thee at the portals of the skies,
> Ready to kiss away thy struggling breath,
> Ready with gentle hand to close thine eyes?
>
> Oh what were life, if life were all? Thine eyes
> Are blinded by their tears, or thou wouldst see
> Thy treasures wait thee in the far-off skies,
> And Death, thy friend, will give them all to thee.

4

Explanatory Introduction to 'Religious Opinions' by the late Reverend Chauncy Hare Townshend

'Published as directed in his Will, by his Literary Executor', 1869

Dickens had first met Townshend in 1840 as a result of their mutual interest in mesmerism, on which Townshend had written a book. A close friendship developed over the years, Townshend being one of Dickens's most ardent admirers, as he makes clear in some verses addressed to Dickens that appear in his book of poems *Three Gates* (1859; the volume is dedicated to Dickens). After his death Dickens wrote to Georgina Hogarth, 'I truly loved him' and 'I never, never, never was better loved by man than I was by him, I am sure. Poor dear fellow, good affectionate creature' (12 March 1868: *Nonesuch*, Vol. III, p. 631). Townshend, who had taken Holy Orders but whose delicate health apparently debarred him from practising his profession, had substantial private means and was a great collector of pictures, jewels, books and antiques. He lived much of the time in Lausanne, where Dickens visited him in 1853. He left his collections partly to what is now the Victoria and Albert Museum and partly to the Wisbech Museum in Cambridgeshire. Dickens gave striking proof of his great regard and affection for Townshend when he not only dedicated *Great Expectations* to him but also presented him with the manuscript (now in Wisbech). He was, however, as he says below, not at all expecting to be required under Townshend's will (under the terms of which he also received a bequest of £1,000) to edit any 'Religious Opinions' and he found it, as he also makes clear, an almost impossible job. He wrote to their mutual friend in Lausanne, William de Cerjat, that Townshend's 'opinions' were

> distributed in the strangest fragments, through the strangest note-books, pocket-books, slips of paper and what not, and produce a most incoherent and tautological result. I infer that he must have held some always-postponed idea of fitting them together. For these reasons I would certainly publish nothing about them, if I had any discretion in the matter. Having none, I suppose a book must be made. [*Nonesuch*, Vol. III, p. 698]

Percy Fitzgerald believed that Cousin Feenix in *Dombey and Son* and Twemlow in *Our Mutual Friend* were both to some extent inspired by Townshend (*Memories of Charles Dickens* [1913], p. 317; *Life of Charles Dickens*, Vol. 1, p. 259, Vol. 2, p. 135).

MR CHAUNCY HARE TOWNSHEND died in London, on the 25th of February, 1868. His will contained the following passage:

> 'I appoint my friend Charles Dickens, of Gad's-Hill Place, in the county of Kent, Esquire, my literary executor; and beg of him to publish without alteration as much of my notes and reflections as may make known my opinions on religious matters, they being such as I verily believe would be conducive to the happiness of mankind.'

In pursuance of the foregoing injunction, the Literary Executor so appointed (not previously aware that the publication of any Religious Opinions would be enjoined upon him), applied himself to the examination of the numerous papers left by his deceased friend. Some of these were in Lausanne, and some were in London. Considerable delay occurred before they could be got together, arising out of certain claims preferred, and formalities insisted on by the authorities of the Canton de Vaud.

When at length the whole of his late friend's papers passed into the Literary Executor's hands, it was found that 'Religious Opinions' were scattered up and down through a variety of memoranda and note-books, the gradual accumulation of years and years. Many of the following pages were carefully transcribed, numbered, connected, and prepared for the press; but many more were dispersed fragments, originally written in pencil, afterwards inked over, the intended sequence of which in the writer's mind, it was extremely difficult to follow. These again were intermixed with journals of travel, fragments of poems, critical essays, voluminous correspondence, and old school-exercises and college themes, having no kind of connexion with them.

To publish such materials 'without alteration', was simply impossible. But finding everywhere internal evidence that Mr Townshend's 'Religious Opinions' had been constantly meditated and reconsidered with great pains and sincerity throughout his life, the Literary Executor carefully compiled them (always in the writer's exact words), and endeavoured in piecing them together to avoid needless repetition. He does not doubt that Mr Townshend held the clue to a precise plan, which could have greatly simplified the presentation of these views; and he has devoted the first section of this volume to Mr Townshend's own notes of his comprehensive intentions. Proofs of the devout spirit in which they were conceived, and of the sense of responsibility with which he worked at them, abound through the whole mass of papers.

Mr Townshend's varied attainments, delicate tastes, and amiable and gentle nature, caused him to be beloved through life by the variously distinguished men who were his compeers at Cambridge long ago. To his Literary Executor he was always a warmly-attached and sympathetic friend. To the public, he has been a most generous benefactor, both in his munificent bequest of his collection of precious stones to the South Kensington Museum, and in the devotion of the bulk of his property to the education of poor children.

APPENDIX C

Descriptive headlines added by Dickens to articles in this volume which were included in *UT1*

In 1868 the 1st and 2nd Series of 'Uncommercial Traveller' papers were reprinted (omitting one paper from 1863, article 26 of this volume) as *The Uncommercial Traveller* in the Charles Dickens Edition of Dickens's works, the last edition to be published during the author's lifetime. For all volumes in this edition, Dickens added descriptive headlines or running titles at the top of each right-hand page. These are listed below, under the titles by which the papers became known in all volume editions of *UT* (given, in the present volume, in the list of Contents, and after the article number and date of publication), and keyed to the appropriate pages of this volume in *UT1* and various later collections, article 20 ('The Italian Prisoner') is moved out of chronological sequence and printed as the last chapter in the collection.

'His General Line of Business' / *'The Shipwreck'* (article 5)
Driven ashore. (p. 31)
In the Village Church. (p. 33)
Grateful Letters. (p. 36)
Memories of Love and Home. (p. 39)

'Wapping Workhouse' (article 6)
A terrible Trap. (p. 44)
This Young Woman. (p. 46)
Old and bedridden. (p. 49)
A False Freemason. (p. 51)

'Two Views of a Cheap Theatre' (article 7)
Saturday Night's Performance. (p. 55)
Sunday Night's Performance. (p. 58)
What to tell the Sunday Audience. (p. 62)

'Poor Mercantile Jack' (article 8)
Liverpool Police Force. (p. 65)
Mercantile Jack's Diversions. (p. 68)
A stranded Spaniard. (p. 70)

APPENDIX D

Complete listing of Dickens's known journalism, December 1833–August 1869

NOTE: 'Letters to the Editor' and editorial addresses to Dickens's readers have not been included in this listing, with the exception of his 'Preliminary Word' in the first number of *HW* and his 1846 letters to the *Daily News* on Ragged Schools and on Capital Punishment. A parenthetical question-mark following an item means that it cannot be established as Dickens's by external evidence, but that there is circumstantial evidence for the ascription.

The stories and sketches collected in *Sketches by Boz* are indicated by *SB*; they, together with Dickens's contributions to *Bentley's Miscellany*, appear in Vol. 1 of the present edition. An asterisk indicates that an article was a collaboration. In the case of collaborative essays in *HW*, these are indicated by 'Stone', which refers to Harry Stone's edition of *Uncollected Writings*, where these items may be found. Essays included by Dickens in *Reprinted Pieces* (1858) are indicated by *RP*, while those included by Dickens and subsequent editors in editions of *The Uncommercial Traveller* are indicated by *UT*. The latter are listed here under the titles which they were later given in those editions, and by which they have become familiar; they originally appeared in *ATYR* under the headings printed in this volume beneath each respective article number.

Bold type indicates that an item is reprinted in one of the four volumes of this edition; articles reprinted in the present volume are in bold type and (with the exception of two items in Appendix B) fall within the period April 1859–August 1869.

Key to titles of Periodicals:

AM	*Atlantic Monthly*
ATYR	*All The Year Round*
BLL	*Bell's Life in London*
BM	*Bentley's Miscellany*
BWM	*Bell's Weekly Magazine*
C	*Cornhill Magazine*
CC	*Carlton Chronicle*
DJSM	*Douglas Jerrold's Shilling Magazine*
DN	*Daily News*
EC	*Evening Chronicle*

Ex	*Examiner*	
HM	*Hood's Magazine*	
HW	*Household Words*	
LF	*Library of Fiction*	
MM	*Monthly Magazine*	
MC	*Morning Chronicle*	

Date	*Title*	*Periodical*
12/33	**A Dinner at Poplar Walk** *SB*	MM
1/34	**Mrs Joseph Porter 'Over the Way'** *SB*	MM
2/34	**Horatio Sparkins** *SB*	MM
4/34	**The Bloomsbury Christening** *SB*	MM
5/34	**The Boarding House** *SB*	MM
7/6/34	**Sentiment(!)** *SB*	BWM
8/34	**The Boarding House No. 2** *SB*	MM
17/9/34	**Report from Edinburgh on Preparations for the Grey Festival**	MC
18/9/34	**Report of the Edinburgh Dinner to Lord Grey**	MC
26/9/34	**Omnibuses** *SB*	MC
10/34	**The Steam Excursion** *SB*	MM
10/10/34	**Shops and their Tenants** *SB*	MC
14/10/34	**Theatre Review: *The Christening***	MC
23/10/34	**The Old Bailey** *SB*	MC
5/11/34	**Shabby-genteel People** *SB*	MC
1/12/34	Report on meeting of Birmingham Liberals	MC
5/12/34	Report of Southwark parish meeting (?)	MC
15/12/34	**Brokers' and Marine Store Shops** *SB*	MC
18/12/34	**'The Story Without a Beginning'**	MC
1/35	**A Passage in the Life of Mr Watkins Tottle, Chapter the First** *SB*	MM
10/1/35	**Election Report from Colchester**	MC
12/1/35	Election Report from Braintree	MC
13/1/35	Election Report from Chelmsford	MC
14/1/35	Election Report from Sudbury	MC
17/1/35	Election Report from Bury St Edmunds	MC
22/1/35	Theatre Review: *The Maid of Castile*, etc. (?)	MC
31/1/35	**Hackney Coach Stands** *SB*	EC
2/35	**A Passage in the Life of Mr Watkins Tottle, Chapter the Second** *SB*	MM
7/2/35	**Gin Shops** *SB*	EC
19/2/35	**Early Coaches** *SB*	EC

28/2/35	**The Parish (The Beadle – The Parish Engine – The Schoolmaster)** *SB*	EC
7/3/35	**The 'House'** *SB*	EC
17/3/35	**London Recreations** *SB*	EC
7/4/35	**Public Dinners** *SB*	EC
11/4/35	**Bellamy's** *SB*	EC
16/4/35	**Greenwich Fair** *SB*	EC
23/4/35	**Thoughts about People** *SB*	EC
2/5/35	Election Report from Exeter	MC
9/5/35	**Astley's** *SB*	EC
19/5/35	**Our Parish (The Curate – The Old Lady – The Half Pay Captain)** *SB*	EC
6/6/35	**The River** *SB*	EC
18/6/35	**Our Parish (The Four Sisters)** *SB*	EC
30/6/35	**The Pawnbroker's Shop** *SB*	EC
8/7/35	The Colosseum	MC
10/7/35	**Grand Colosseum Fête**	MC
14/7/35	**Our Parish (The Election for Beadle)** *SB*	EC
21/7/35	**The Streets – Morning** *SB*	EC
28/7/35	**Our Parish (The Broker's Man)** *SB*	EC
11/8/35	**Private Theatres** *SB*	EC
20/8/35	**Our Parish (The Ladies' Societies)** *SB*	EC
8/9/35	Theatre Review: *Zarah*, etc. (?)	MC
27/9/35	**Seven Dials** *SB*	BLL
29/9/35	Theatre Review: *Christening*, etc.	MC
4/10/35	**Miss Evans and 'The Eagle'** *SB*	BLL
9/10/35	Theatre Review: *Rival Pages*, etc.	MC
11/10/35	**The Dancing Academy** *SB*	BLL
13/10/35	**The Reopening of the Colosseum**	MC
18/10/35	**Making a Night of It** *SB*	BLL
20/10/35	Theatre Review: *Truth, or a Glass Too Much*, etc. (?)	MC
25/10/35	**Love and Oysters** *SB*	BLL
27/10/35	Theatre Review: *The King's Command* (?)	MC
1/11/35	**Some Account of an Omnibus Cad** *SB*	BLL
4/11/35	Theatre Review: *The Castilian Noble and the Contrabandista*	MC
11/11/35	Report of Speech by Lord John Russell in Bristol (also 12/11)	MC
13/11/35	Report of Political Dinner at Bath	MC
17/11/35	Reopening of the Adelphi under Mrs Nisbett's management	MC
22/11/35	**The Vocal Dressmaker** *SB*	BLL
24/11/35	**Theatre Review: *The Dream at Sea***	MC

29/11/35	**The Prisoners' Van** *SB*	BLL
2/12/35	**Report on the Fire at Hatfield House** (also 3 and 4/12)	MC
13/12/35	**The Parlour** *SB*	BLL
16/12/35	**Report on the Northamptonshire Election** (also 19/12)	MC
27/12/35	**Christmas Festivities** *SB*	BLL
3/1/36	**The New Year** *SB*	BLL
12/1/36	Theatre Review: *One Hour, or a Carnival Ball*	MC
15/1/36	Theatre Review: *The Waterman*, etc.	MC
17/1/36	**The Streets at Night** *SB*	BLL
19/1/36	Theatre Review: *Brown's Horse*	MC
22/1/36	Report of Foundation Stone Laying by Lord Melbourne	MC
4/2/36	Theatre Review: *Rienzi*	MC
18/3/36	**Our Next-door Neighbours** *SB*	MC
4/36	**The Tuggs's at Ramsgate** *SB*	LF
28/5/36	Report of Reform Dinner at Ipswich	MC
6/36	**A Little Talk about Spring and the Sweeps** *SB*	LF
6/36	**Sunday Under Three Heads**	
23/6/36	Report of Norton/Melbourne Trial	MC
6/8/36	**The Hospital Patient** *SB*	CC
17/9/36	**Hackney Cabs, and Their Drivers** *SB*	CC
24/9/36	**Meditations in Monmouth Street** *SB*	MC
4/10/36	**Scotland Yard** *SB*	MC
11/10/36	**Doctors' Commons** *SB*	MC
26/10/36	**Vauxhall – Gardens by Day** *SB*	MC
3/37	**The Pantomime of Life**	BM
5/37	**Some Particulars concerning a Lion**	BM
10/37	**Full Report of the First Meeting of the Mudfog Association for the Advancement of Everything**	BM
3/12/37	Theatre Review: *Joan of Arc*, etc.	Ex
17/12/37	**Theatre Review: *Pierre Bertrand***	Ex
28/1/38	Book Review: *The Ages of Female Beauty*	Ex
28/1/38	Book Review: *Sporting. Edited by Nimrod*	Ex
1/7/38	Report of Coronation Fair in Hyde Park*	Ex
9/38	**Full Report of the Second Meeting of the Mudfog Association for the Advancement of Everything**	BM
2/9/38	**Book Review: Refutations of the Mis-statements . . . in Mr Lockhart's Life of Sir Walter**	Ex

10/3/49	Prison and Convict Discipline (?)*	Ex
7/4/49	Rush's Conviction (?)	Ex
21/4/49	The Verdict for Drouet	Ex
5/5/49	Capital Punishment (?)	Ex
12/5/49	**Theatre Review: *Virginia and Black-eyed Susan***	Ex
2/6/49	False Reliance (re. the Rush murder)	Ex
14/7/49	Drainage and Health of the Metropolis (?)*	Ex
21/7/49	Book Review: *An American in Europe*	Ex
4/8/49	The Sewers' Commission (?)*	Ex
27/10/49	**Demoralisation and Total Abstinence**	Ex
27/10/49	**Theatre Review: Macready as King Lear**	Ex
8/12/49	Central Criminal Court (?)	Ex
15/12/49	**Court Ceremonies**	Ex
30/3/50	**A Preliminary Word**	HW
30/3/50	**The Amusements of the People (I)**	HW
30/3/50	Valentine's Day at the Post Office (Stone)	HW
30/3/50	A Bundle of Emigrants' Letters (Stone)	HW
6/4/50	**A Child's Dream of a Star** *RP*	HW
6/4/50	**Perfect Felicity in a Bird's-Eye View**	HW
13/4/50	**The Amusements of the People (II)**	HW
20/4/50	**Some Account of an Extraordinary Traveller**	HW
20/4/50	Supposing!	HW
27/4/50	**Pet Prisoners**	HW
4/5/50	The Heart of Mid-London (Stone)	HW
11/5/50	From the Raven in the Happy Family	HW
18/5/50	**The Begging-Letter Writer** *RP*	HW
18/5/50	A Card from Mr Booley	HW
27/5/50	**A Walk in the Workhouse** *RP*	HW
1/6/50	A Popular Delusion (Stone)	HW
8/6/50	From the Raven in the Happy Family (ii)	HW
15/6/50	**Old Lamps for New Ones**	HW
22/6/50	**The Sunday Screw**	HW
6/7/50	The Old Lady in Threadneedle Street (Stone)	HW
20/7/50	**The Ghost of Art** *RP*	HW
27/7/50	**A Detective Police Party (I)** *RP*	HW
10/8/50	**A Detective Police Party (II)** *RP*	HW
10/8/50	Supposing (II)	HW
24/8/50	From the Raven in the Happy Family (III)	HW
31/8/50	A Paper-Mill (Stone)	HW
14/9/50	Three 'Detective' Anecdotes *RP*	HW
21/9/50	Foreigners' Portraits of Englishmen (Stone)	HW
21/9/50	**Chips: The Individuality of Locomotives**	HW

11/10/51	**Our School** *RP*	HW
8/11/51	**Sucking Pigs**	HW
15/11/51	Chip: Homeopathy	HW
15/11/51	A Free (and Easy) School (Stone)	HW
22/11/51	A Black Eagle in a Bad Way (Stone)	HW
6/12/51	My Uncle (Stone)	HW
17/1/52	A Curious Dance Round a Curious Tree (Stone)	HW
13/3/52	**A Sleep to Startle Us**	HW
13/3/52	**Chips: The Fine Arts in Australia**	HW
20/3/52	Post-Office Money-Orders (Stone)	HW
3/4/52	Drooping Buds (Stone)	HW
15/5/52	First Fruits (Stone)	HW
26/6/52	**Betting-Shops**	HW
31/7/52	**Our Honorable Friend** *RP*	HW
28/8/52	**Our Vestry** *RP*	HW
11/9/52	Boys to Mend (Stone)	HW
18/9/52	North American Slavery (Stone)	HW
9/10/52	**Our Bore** *RP*	HW
30/10/52	**Lying Awake** *RP*	HW
13/11/52	Discovery of a Treasure Near Cheapside (Stone)	HW
27/11/52	**Trading in Death**	HW
1/1/53	**Where We Stopped Growing**	HW
15/1/53	Chip: The Ghost of The Cock Lane Ghost Wrong Again	HW
5/2/53	**Down with the Tide** *RP*	HW
12/2/53	**Proposals for Amusing Posterity**	HW
19/3/53	Received, a Blank Child (Stone)	HW
16/4/53	H. W. (Stone)	HW
23/4/53	**Home for Homeless Women**	HW
7/5/53	The Spirit Business	HW
14/5/53	In and Out of Jail (Stone)	HW
4/6/53	Idiots (Stone)	HW
11/6/53	**The Noble Savage** *RP*	HW
23/7/53	**A Haunted House**	HW
13/8/53	**Gone Astray**	HW
1/10/53	**Frauds on the Fairies**	HW
8/10/53	**Things that Cannot be Done**	HW
21/12/53	**The Long Voyage** *RP*	HW
7/1/54	On Her Majesty's Service (Stone)	HW
21/1/54	**Fire and Snow**	HW
4/2/54	Chip: Ready Wit	HW
11/2/54	**On Strike**	HW
25/3/54	The Late Mr Justice Talfourd	HW

16/5/57	Chip: The Samaritan Institution	HW
20/6/57	**The Best Authority**	HW
27/6/57	Duelling in France (Stone)	HW
1/8/57	**Curious Misprint in the *Edinburgh Review***	HW
3/10/57	**The Lazy Tour of Two Idle Apprentices. In Five Chapters, Chapter One**	HW
10/10/57	**The Lazy Tour of Two Idle Apprentices. Chapter Two**	HW
17/10/57	**The Lazy Tour of Two Idle Apprentices. Chapter Three**	HW
24/10/57	**The Lazy Tour of Two Idle Apprentices. Chapter Four**	HW
31/10/57	**The Lazy Tour of Two Idle Apprentices. Chapter Five**	HW
20/2/58	**Well-Authenticated Rappings**	HW
13/3/58	An Idea of Mine	HW
1/5/58	**Please to Leave Your Umbrella**	HW
12/6/58	**Personal**	HW
9/10/58	A Clause for the New Reform Bill (Stone)	HW
18/12/58	Doctor Dulcamara, MP (Stone)	HW
1/5/59	**New Year's Day**	HW
30/4/59	**The Poor Man and His Beer**	ATYR
24/9/59	**5 New Points of Criminal Law**	ATYR
24/12/59	**Leigh Hunt: A Remonstrance**	ATYR
31/12/59	**The Tattersnivel Bleater**	ATYR
28/1/60	**His General Line of Business / The Shipwreck *UT***	ATYR
18/2/60	**Wapping Workhouse *UT***	ATYR
25/2/60	**Two Views of a Cheap Theatre *UT***	ATYR
10/3/60	**Poor Mercantile Jack *UT***	ATYR
24/3/60	**Refreshments for Travellers *UT***	ATYR
7/4/60	**Travelling Abroad *UT***	ATYR
21/4/60	**The Great Tasmania's Cargo *UT***	ATYR
5/5/60	**City of London Churches *UT***	ATYR
26/5/60	**Shy Neighbourhoods *UT***	ATYR
16/6/60	**Tramps *UT***	ATYR
30/6/60	**Dullborough Town *UT***	ATYR
21/7/60	**Night Walks *UT***	ATYR
18/8/60	**Chambers *UT***	ATYR
8/9/60	**Nurse's Stories *UT***	ATYR
29/9/60	**Arcadian London *UT***	ATYR
13/10/60	**The Italian Prisoner *UT***	ATYR
1/3/62	The Young Man from The Country	ATYR

8/3/62	**An Enlightened Clergyman**	ATYR
28/2/63	Dress in Paris (?)	ATYR
21/3/63	**Rather a Strong Dose**	ATYR
4/4/63	The Martyr Medium	ATYR
2/5/63	**The Calais Night Mail** *UT*	ATYR
16/5/63	**Some Recollections of Mortality** *UT*	ATYR
6/6/63	**Birthday Celebrations** *UT*	ATYR
20/6/63	**The Short-Timers** *UT*	ATYR
4/7/63	**Bound for The Great Salt Lake** *UT*	ATYR
18/7/63	**City of the Absent** *UT*	ATYR
1/8/63	**An Old Stage-Coaching House** *UT*	ATYR
15/8/63	**The Boiled Beef of New England** *UT*	ATYR
29/8/63	**Chatham Dockyard** *UT*	ATYR
12/9/63	**In the French-Flemish Country** *UT*	ATYR
26/9/63	**Medicine Men of Civilisation** *UT*	ATYR
24/10/63	**Titbull's Alms-Houses** *UT*	ATYR
2/64	**In Memoriam: W.M. Thackeray**	C
26/3/64	Working Men's Clubs (*collab. with Edmund Ollier)	ATYR
27/1/66	A Neat Sample of Translation (?)	ATYR
1/6/67	**The Late Mr Stanfield**	ATYR
29/2/68	**The Great International Walking Match**	ATYR
10/10/68	**The Ruffian** *UT*	ATYR
5/12/68	**Aboard Ship** *UT*	ATYR
19/12/68	**A Small Star in the East** *UT*	ATYR
2/1/69	**A Little Dinner in an Hour** *UT*	ATYR
16/1/69	**Mr. Barlow** *UT*	ATYR
27/2/69	**On an Amateur Beat** *UT*	ATYR
10/4/69	Robert Keeley (*collab. with Herman Merivale)	ATYR
22/5/69	**A Fly-Leaf in a Life** *UT*	ATYR
5/6/69	**A Plea for Total Abstinence** *UT*	ATYR
24/7/69	**Landor's Life**	ATYR
8/69	**On Mr Fechter's Acting**	AM

INDEX AND GLOSSARY

NOTE: This Index and Glossary covers both Dickens's texts and all editorial material. Persons and places are indexed only when there is substantial reference to them, or when places are visited or alluded to by 'The Uncommercial Traveller'. Modern scholars and critics referred to in the editorial material are included, but dates are not supplied for them.

Dickens's writings, whether separately published or not, are indexed under their titles. His many literary quotations and allusions are, wherever possible, identified in the headnotes and are here indexed only as page references to the headnotes under the relevant author's name, and under *ARABIAN NIGHTS*, BIBLE, CLASSICAL MYTH AND LEGEND, FAIRYTALES, LEGENDS AND FOLK-LORE, NURSERY RHYMES, SONGS AND BALLADS.

For some of the information in the Index we are indebted to the incomparable annotation of Dickens's letters contained in the Pilgrim Edition; to the late T. W. Hill's unpublished notes on *The Uncommercial Traveller* (MS Dickens House); to *The London Encyclopaedia*, edited by Ben Weinreb and Christopher Hibbert (1983); and to Mr John Grigg.

The following abbreviations are used: *ATYR* = *All The Year Round*; *b.* = born; *c.* = circa; CD = Charles Dickens; *coll.* = colloquial; *d.* = died; *dem.* = demolished; *est.* = established; *fl.* = flourished; *Fr.* = French; *HW* = *Household Words*; *It.* = Italian; *Lat.* = Latin; *naut.* = nautical; *pseud.* = pseudonym; *sl.* = slang; *Sp.* = Spanish.

ABRUZZI highest and wildest part of the Apennine mountain range in Italy 337

ABYSSINIA former name of Ethiopia 173, 343, 346

ACADEMY MODEL from its foundation in 1768 the Royal Academy had employed models for life-drawing classes 18

ACELDAMA (Aramaic) 'place where blood has been shed', the field south of Jeru-salem purchased by the priests with the blood-money cast down by Judas 149, 152

ACHILLES, HMS ironclad broadside-armed battleship launched at Chatham (December 1863) 288, 291–4, 296

ACKROYD, PETER 15, 170

ACTING 403–9

ADELPHI the New Adelphi (1829–67), theatre in the Strand specialising in melo-dramas 354, 359

ADELPHI, THE the Adelphi Terrace near the Thames in central London, built by the Adam brothers (1772–3) 169

ADDISON, SIR JOSEPH (1672–1719) essayist and Whig statesman, co-author of *The Tatler* (1709–11) and *The Spectator* (1711–12, 1714) xvi

ADULTERATION OF FOODSTUFFS 183, 250

ADVENTITIOUS legal term for collateral rather than direct succession 82

AESCHYLUS (*c.* 525–*c.* 456 BC) Greek tra-gedian; quotations and allusions 372

AFRICA AND AFRICANS 233, 306, 308–9, 312, 375

AGAPEMONE early Christian love feast, later applied to a notorious religious asso-ciation of men and women living pro-miscuously at Charlynch, Somerset (from 1846) 187

ALBERT, PRINCE (1819–61) Prince Consort, husband of Queen Victoria 21, 154, 258

ALDERSGATE STREET City street leading to St Paul's from the north 109

ALDGATE PUMP ancient public source of water at the junction of Leadenhall and Fenchurch Streets in the City of London; now purely ornamental 43

ALDRICH, THOMAS BAILEY (1836–1907) Boston-based author and editor 412

ALEXANDRA, QUEEN (1844–1925) wife of Edward VII (succeeded 1901) 258 ('Princess of Wales')

ALGERIA 302, 306

ALL HALLOWS, LONDON WALL medi-eval church rebuilt (1765–7) by George Dance the Younger 106

sidered exceptional 111; *see also* 'TWENTY PORT

COMMERCIAL ROAD principal East London thoroughfare between Whitechapel and Ratcliffe 43, 383

COMMERCIAL STREET thoroughfare cut through the Spitalfields district of London (1845) 278, 282

COMMERCIAL TRAVELLERS' SCHOOLS founded at Pinner, Middlesex, by J. R. Cuffley (1845); in 1854 and 1859 CD spoke on their behalf at charity dinners xv, 74

CONFRATERNITIES religious brotherhoods and associations 312

CONVERSAZIONE (*It.*) a social gathering for discussion of the arts 77

CORBETT, THOMAS (*fl.* 1860) Glasgow merchant, pioneer of the 'Glasgow system' for feeding working men and the unemployed in cheap dining-halls 278

CORKED with a face blackened by the application of burnt cork 376

CORNHILL MAGAZINE, THE market leader among monthly serials carrying fiction in the latter part of the nineteenth century; founded 1860 and edited by Thackeray until 1862, it offered for one shilling a remarkably high standard of both literature and illustration xiv, xxiii, 326–7, 424

'CORNWALL, BARRY' *see* PROCTER, BRYAN WALLER

CORONER legal officer with local or national powers to hold inquests into violent or accidental deaths 44, 100, 103, 219, 225–7; JURY panel of between 7 and 11 jurors appointed to decide issues at an inquest 97, 103, 105, 219, 225–6; REPORT 96

CORPS DES INVALIDES body of retired or war-disabled soldiers, originally accommodated in the Hôtel des Invalides in Paris 303

CORPSE-CANDLE flickering flame seen in a churchyard or over a grave 152

COSTERMONGER seller of fruit and vegetables from a hand-cart; a barrow boy 56, 120, 224, 337, 416

COURT OF COMMON PLEAS former name of the court in which civil actions were tried such as that of Bardell v. Pickwick in *Pickwick Papers*; in 1881 absorbed into the Queen's Bench division of the High Court 313

COURTS OF JUSTICE *see* COURTS OF LAW

COURTS OF LAW held during term-time in Westminster Hall; also known as the Courts of Justice, i.e. the Royal Courts

of Justice, relocated from Westminster to the Strand in a building designed by Sir John Soane and constructed (1869–82) to house in one place all the higher courts dealing with civil law cases 154, 187, 239, 377

COUTTS, ANGELA BURDETT (1814–1906) philanthropical heiress to an enormous fortune, for whom CD acted as a sort of unofficial almoner 190, 315

COVENT GARDEN xvi–xvii, 28, 43, 53, 107, 122, 239, 262, 380, 393; MARKET 122, 155, 239

COVENT GARDEN THEATRE Bow Street, in London's West End; one of the so-called 'Patent Theatres' (i.e. with exclusive royal licence to present the 'legitimate' drama); originally built in 1731 and rebuilt 1808 and 1858, it is now known as The Royal Opera House 54

COWPER, WILLIAM (1731–1800) poet; quotations and allusions 392

CREASY, SIR EDWARD (1812–78) military historian 392

CREMORNE GARDENS pleasure gardens in Chelsea (*est.* 1832; closed 1877), a venue for spectacular entertainments 278

CRICHTON, JAMES (1560–*c.*1585) scholar, poet, linguist and swordsman, dubbed 'the Admirable' by Thomas Urquhart (1652) 60

CRICKET 140

CRIMEAN WAR (1853–6) war in which British, French and Turkish troops joined forces to resist Russian expansion in the Crimea 304

CRIMP agent or contractor who entrapped men for service in the navy or army, often by trickery and coercion 66

CRIPPLEGATE CHURCH *see* ST GILES, CRIPPLEGATE

CROSS KEYS (*dem.* 1865) large coaching inn at 128–9 Wood Street, Cheapside, the terminus for coaches from Rochester 138, 140

CRUIKSHANK, GEORGE (1792–1878) artist and illustrator 197; quotations and allusions 191

CRYSTAL PALACE, THE glass and iron building designed by Joseph Paxton to house the Great Exhibition (1851), later moved from Hyde Park to Sydenham Hill in South London (1854) 343, 346

CUSTOM HOUSE in Lower Thames Street on the north bank of the Thames between London Bridge and the Tower, originally built as the administrative centre for the collection of customs duty; first erected 1385 and many times rebuilt 199, 289–90

Michael Novosielski (1790–1), enjoyed its heyday 1830–50, for many years the largest theatre in England 54

HERTFORDSHIRE 3–4, 132

HEYWOOD, JOHN (*c.*1497–*c.*1580) dramatist, collector of epigrams and proverbs; quotations and allusions 262

HIGHFLYER fast mail-coach 271

HIGHGATE CEMETERY established in North London by the London Cemetery Company in 1839; with its blend of Gothic architecture and elegant landscaping, it quickly became fashionable 148

'HIS BOOTS' one of CD's contributions to *Somebody's Luggage*, the 1862 Christmas number of *ATYR* 211

HOBBY-HORSE part of a carousel, also an individual's pet topic or obsession 218, 301, 304

HOGARTH, CATHERINE *see* DICKENS, CATHERINE

HOGARTH, GEORGE (1783–1870) CD's father-in-law 261

HOGARTH, GEORGINA (1827–1917) CD's sister-in-law xvii, 27, 396, 410, 429

HOGARTH, MARY 157

HOGARTH, PETER (1819–59) cousin of Mrs Charles Dickens 27

HOGARTH, ROBERT (*d.* 1859) cousin of Mrs Charles Dickens 27

HOGARTH, WILLIAM (1697–1764) painter 72, 317; allusions 106–7

HOGG, JAMES (1770–1835) Scottish poet, known as 'the Ettrick Shepherd'; author of *Confessions of a Justified Sinner* 417

HOLBEIN, HANS (1497–1543) painter, in England from 1526; published illustrations to *The Dance of Death* (1538) 352

HOLBORN London district north of the Strand where Lincoln's Inn and Gray's Inn are located 157, 162; UNION 160

'HOLIDAY ROMANCE' xxi

HOLLINGSHEAD, JOHN (1826–1900) journalist, contributor to *HW* and *ATYR* 52, 117, 202, 270

HOLLINGTON, MICHAEL 191

HOLMES, OLIVER WENDELL (1809–94) Harvard professor of anatomy and author, friend of CD's 412

HOLYROOD HOUSE official residence of the British monarch in Scotland, located at the foot of the Canongate in Edinburgh, formerly an abbey and a medieval palace 379, 382

HOME, DANIEL DUNGLAS (1833–86) Spiritualist medium, born in Scotland but brought up in the United States, who in 1855 returned to England, where many celebrities attended seances 205–6, 209

HOME, JOHN (1722–1808) Scottish playwright; quotations and allusions 219

HOMELESSNESS 149–57

HOOD, THOMAS (1799–1845) poet and humorist 333

HOOD'S hatter's in New Bond Street 181

HORACE Quintus Horatius Flaccus (65–8 BC) Roman poet; quotations and allusions 127

HORNE, RICHARD HENRY or HENGIST (1803–84) poet, journalist, contributor to *HW*; friend of CD's 287, 371

HOTELS 74, 78–83, 88, 90, 186, 196, 210, 212, 216, 218, 299, 364–70; *see also* INNS AND TAVERNS; PUBLIC-HOUSES

HOUNDSDITCH CHURCH St Botolph, Aldgate (rebuilt 1741–4), on the corner of Houndsditch and Aldgate High Street in the City of London 382

HOUNSLOW originally a Middlesex town, now a borough of London 164

HOUSEHOLD WORDS (1850–9) weekly periodical jointly owned by CD and publishers Bradbury and Evans xi–xiv, xvi, xx, 190, 228, 261, 423, 424

HOWITT, WILLIAM (1792–1879) liberal writer of Quaker upbringing who in the 1860s espoused Spiritualism 202–9

HUGHES, REV. HUGH ROBERT (*d.* 1872) curate of Penrhosllugwy, Anglesey (1858–*c.* 1865) 40

HUGHES, REV. STEPHEN ROOSE (?1815–62) Rector of Llaneugrad with Llanallgo, Anglesey 27, 40

HUGO, VICTOR (1802–85) French poet, novelist and dramatist 403, 407; *see also RUY BLAS*

HUNT AND ROSKELL'S, MESSRS Bond Street jewellers (formerly Storr & Mortimer) 186

HUNT, JAMES HENRY LEIGH (1784–1859) poet and essayist; friend of CD's xiv, xx, 14–19

HUNT, THORNTON LEIGH (1810–73) journalist, eldest son of James Henry Leigh Hunt 15–16

'HUNTED DOWN' xxi, 19

HUNTINGTON THE COAL-PORTER William Huntington (1745–1813) became a Calvinist preacher following a vision of Christ assuring him of salvation and at first combined his ministry with other work such as coal-heaving; he ordered that he should be described on his tomb as 'the coalheaver ... beloved of his God but abhorred of men' 203

HYDE PARK the largest of London's royal parks 334; the Ring enclosure created within the park during the reign of Charles II, formerly called the Tour, was a place of rendezvous for the fashionable 301

MORLEY, MALCOLM 404

MORMONS members of the Church of Jesus Christ of Latter-Day Saints, founded in New York by Joseph Smith (1830); they soon moved west, eventually forming a stronghold in Utah, under the guidance of Brigham Young xviii, 248–60

MORNING CHRONICLE London daily paper supportive of the Whigs (*est.* 1769) xx, 27, 270, 326

MULCTED fraudulently deprived of money or goods 316

MUMLER, WILLIAM H. (*fl.* 1870) spirit photographer; published in 1875 *Personal Experiences … in Spirit Photography* 206–7

MUSIC 63, 67–70, 243, 245, 246, 251, 253, 259, 305, 312, 314, 344; CHURCH 112

MYSTERIES cycles of religious plays traditionally performed on Corpus Christi Day by members of town and city trade and craft guilds 115; quotations and allusions 182

NAPLES 152, 191, 197, 219; *see also* SAN CARLO

NAPOLEON BONAPARTE (1769–1821) Emperor of France (1804–15) 141, 303 ('The Genius of France'), 413

NAPOLEON coin of the value of twenty francs 92

NAPOLEON III Louis Napoleon (1808–73), President of the French Republic (1848–52), subsequently proclaimed Emperor of the French 206 ('Emperor of the French'), 218

NATIONAL GALLERY in Trafalgar Square (built 1832–8) 279

NATIONAL (SCHOOL) school run by the National Society for Promoting the Education of the Poor in the Principles of the Established Church; the Society was founded in 1809, and by 1831 there were 13,000 National Schools 231, 246

NAVY, ROYAL 79, 100, 140, 246, 293; MERCHANT 62–4, 246; *see also* SAILORS

NEBULA hazy, luminous area in the night sky, denoting a distant star cluster 374

NEGRO SINGERS *see* ETHIOPIAN SERENADERS

NEW BOND STREET *see* BOND STREET

NEW INN one of the Inns of Chancery (*est.* 1485; *dem. c.* 1890), belonging to the Middle Temple 157

NEW POLICE ACT passed 1839, defining all matters for which the Metropolitan Police were responsible 117, 335, 340

NEW TESTAMENT 32, 61, 155; *see also* BIBLE; BOANERGES

NEW YORK 19, 204, 254, 279, 342, 344, 347, 350, 351

NEWBURY 269

NEWFOUNDLAND 121

NEWGATE CALENDAR, THE title (from 1773) of intermittently published series of biographies of notorious criminals confined in Newgate Prison 194

NEWGATE PRISON in Newgate Street in the City of London, first built in the twelfth century (finally *dem.* 1902) 149, 152, 267, 382

NEWSPAPERS 320, 376; AMERICAN 18; LONDON 336, 338; SPORTING 118, 410; *see also* BATH CHRONICLE; BELL'S LIFE IN LONDON; EXAMINER; ILLUSTRATED LONDON NEWS; LIVERPOOL TIMES, MILLENNIAL STAR; MANCHESTER GUARDIAN; MORNING CHRONICLE; PENNY ILLUSTRATED NEWS; RECORD, THE; TIMES, THE

NICHOLAS NICKLEBY xxii

'NIGHTLY SCENE IN LONDON, A' 41

NILE, RIVER 173

NISI PRIUS (*Lat.*) literally 'unless before'; legal term used for the trial of a civil cause before a judge of assize 187

'NOBLE SAVAGE, THE' 306

NOR' WEST PER RAILWAY the London and North Western Railway was formed in 1846 by amalgamation of a number of lines including one serving Hertfordshire from London 4, 5

NORE LIGHT lighthouse in the Thames estuary 289

NORTH POLE 173

NORTON, CHARLES ELIOT (1827–1908) Harvard professor of fine arts and friend of CD's 412

NORWOOD South London district, originally wooded, between the boroughs of Croydon and Lambeth 164

NORWOOD GYPSY the reputed author of the *Norwood Fortune Teller*, a pamphlet containing notes on fortune-telling and on the significance of days and moles on the body 63, 66

NOTES AND QUERIES weekly paper devoted to correspondence on literary and antiquarian matters, founded 1849 by W. J. Thoms (1803–85) 182

NOTRE DAME Paris cathedral (dating from 1163) 90, 220

NOTTING HILL district with much clay soil, notable for its contrasts of fine housing and slum areas 123

NURSERY RHYMES 43, 85, 191, 238, 288, 392

NURSES 49, 88, 102, 141, 169–80, 226, 310, 340, 362–3

OAKUM loose fibres obtained by untwisting and picking at old rope, used for caulking wooden ships 47–8

YOUNG, GEORGE FREDERICK (1791–1870) ship-owner, merchant and MP; chairman of the Board of Guardians of Stepney Parish Union (1846) 238

ZOOLOGICAL GARDENS (*est.* 1828) in Regent's Park 293, 391 ('animals exhibited')